Law of Employment

Practice and Analysis

Lewis

KOGAN PAGE

First published in 1998

Kogan Page Limited
120 Pentonville Road
London N1 9JN

British Library Cataloguing in Publication Data

A CIP record for this book is available from the British Library.

ISBN 0 7494 1541 X

Typeset by Jean Cussons Typesetting, Diss, Norfolk
Printed and bound in Great Britain by Biddles Ltd, Guildford and King's Lynn

To Lew, Mina, Mary, Sarah and James

Contents

Part III Problems and Perspectives

Figures

Tables

Statutes

Statutory Instruments

Cases

Preface

Employment law is a large, growing and sometimes complex area of law. It is relevant to practising managers, to legal practitioners and others providing advice and/or representation, to those seeking to resolve employment disputes and to law and business students.

Law of Employment: Practice and Analysis aims to be practical and authoritative enough to help managers and legal practitioners deal with employment law problems while being sufficiently analytical for law and business students. Hopefully the keys to this are the integration of a detailed account of substantive law and practical legal problems in Part II of the book and the separate treatment of analysis and wider issues in Part III.

A good knowledge of employment law is an important, perhaps increasingly important, part of a manager's kit. Therefore, *Law of Employment* examines the legal context of the management of employment and the possible legal implications of different types of action in order to provide guidance for managers. It aims to perform a protective function, helping managers to stay within the law, as well as a strategic one, allowing productive use of the law to further organizational objectives.

For legal practitioners, it is hoped that *Law of Employment* is an authoritative account which will inform the processes of advice and representation. For the student, the aim has been to supplement the substantive law with the analytical material found in Part III. This seeks to allow the student to explore the development of employment law, its role and effectiveness and the policy issues that it involves. It identifies problems in employment law and the perspectives which can be brought to bear on them. In doing so, it highlights not only matters of policy and practice but also issues of methodology and theory.

The content of *Law of Employment* is comprehensive but inevitably there are parts of employment law which can be regarded as subjects in themselves, too voluminous and specialist to be fully dealt with in a general text. Pensions law is one such area. No attempt is made to deal with pensions although reference is made at various points to pension arrangements which are discriminatory on the ground of sex. Another such area is the law of health, safety and welfare at work. *Law of Employment* sets out only the general criminal and civil law content of health, safety and welfare at work but does not cover the mass of detailed, specific provisions.

The approach taken in this book is a management one, not in the sense of endorsing managerial interests but by using a management decision-making model as an analytical framework. In this way, the text addresses the central question of employment law, the balance between the interests of employers and workers, without using an analytical framework derived from any perceived desirable social outcome, whether social democracy, free markets or otherwise. The approach has also been to try to write in clear, straightforward language for the non-lawyer while attempting to give an accurate exposition of the law at a standard that satisfies the needs of legal practitioners and law students.

The law is stated as at 1 June 1998. By this date, the Employment Rights (Dispute Resolution) Act 1998 had received the Royal Assent and the government had published a consultative document and draft regulations for implementing the EU Working Time Directive and a white paper outlining a raft of proposals for increasing fairness at work. Other measures, including a Public Interest Disclosure Bill and a National Minimum Wage Bill were making their way through Parliament and in addition certain legislation already adopted by the EU, including that relating to parental leave, was being prepared for implementation in the UK. Where changes in the law seem likely, indication is given at appropriate points in the text.

Section 1 of the Employment Rights (Dispute Resolution) Act 1998 renames industrial tribunals 'employment tribunals' (and substitutes 'employment' for industrial in various statutory sources, such as the Industrial Tribunals Act 1996) but at the time of publication no Order had been made bringing this section into force.

Paul Lewis
Bilbrough
North Yorkshire

Abbreviations

AC	Appeal Cases Reports
ACAS	Advisory, Conciliation and Arbitration Service
ACOP	Approved Code of Practice
AIDS	Acquired Immune Deficiency Syndrome
All ER	All England Reports
anor	another (in the names of legal cases)
APEX	Association of Professional, Executive, Clerical and Computer Staffs
ASLEF	Associated Society of Locomotive Engineers and Firemen
ASRS	Amalgamated Society of Railway Servants
AUT	Association of University Teachers
AVC	Additional voluntary contribution
BS	British Standard
c	Chapter (in relation to statutes)
CA	Court of Appeal
CAB	Citizens' Advice Bureau
CAC	Central Arbitration Committee
CBI	Confederation of British Industry
Ch	Chancery Division Reports
Cm	Command (numbers on official papers)
CMLR	Common Market Law Reports
CO	Certification Officer
COIT	Central Office of Industrial Tribunals
COP	Code of Practice
COSHH	Control of Substances Hazardous to Health
CPAUIA	Commissioner for Protection Against Unlawful Industrial Action
CRE	Commission for Racial Equality
CROTUM	Commissioner for the Rights of Trades Union Members
CS	Court of Session
dB(A)	Decibels (adjusted)
DDA	Disability Discrimination Act 1995
DE	Department of Employment
DfEE	Department for Education and Employment
DHSS	Department of Health and Social Security
DP	Data Protection
DPA	Data Protection Act 1984
DPR	Data Protection Registrar
DSS	Department of Social Security
DTI	Department of Trade and Industry
EA	Employment Act (various)
EAT	Employment Appeal Tribunal
EC	European Communtity
ECHR	European Court of Human Rights
ECJ	European Court of Justice
EDT	Effective date of termination (of employment)
EEC	European Economic Community

EO	Equal opportunities
EOC	Equal Opportunities Commission
EPA	Employment Protection Act 1975
EP(C)A	Employment Protection (Consolidation Act) 1978
EPD	Equal Pay Directive
EqPA	Equal Pay Act 1970
ERA	Employment Rights Act 1996
ER(DR)A	Employment Rights (Dispute Resolution) Act 1998
ETD	Equal Treatment Directive
ETO	Economic, technical or organizational reason (for dismissal arising out of the transfer of an undertaking)
EWC	Expected week of confinement
EU	European Union
FA	Factories Act 1961
FSAVC	Free standing additional voluntary contribution
FTC	Fixed-term contract
FTLR	Financial Times Law Reports
GATT	General Agreement on Tariffs and Trade
GB	Great Britain
GLR	Guardian Law Reports
GOQ	Genuine occupational qualification (RRA and SDA)
GP	General Practitioner
HC	House of Commons
High Ct	High Court
HL	House of Lords
HMSO	Her Majesty's Stationery Office
HRM	Human Resource Management
HSC	Health and Safety Commission
HSE	Health and Safety Executive
HSWA	Health and Safety at Work etc Act 1974
ICR	Industrial Cases Reports
ICTA	Income and Corporation Taxes Act 1988
IDS	Incomes Data Services
ILO	International Labour Organisation
IPD	Institute of Personnel and Development (formerly IPM)
IPM	Institute of Personnel Management (now IPD)
IRLIB	Industrial Relations Legal Information Bulletin
IRLR	Industrial Relations Law Reports
IT	Industrial Tribunals
ITA	Industrial Tribunals Act 1996
ITR	Industrial Tribunal Reports
KB	King's Bench Division Reports
KIR	Knight's Industrial Reports
LJ	Lord Justice
LPC	Low Pay Commission
LSG	Law Society Gazette
LT	Law Times
MATSA	Managerial, Administrative and Technical Staffs Association (part of the General, Municipal, Boilermakers and Allied Trades Union)
MEL	Maximum exposure level

MR	Master of the Rolls
MSF	Manufacturing, Science and Finance Union
NAPO	National Association of Probation Officers
NATFHE	National Association of Teachers in Further and Higher Education
NGA	National Graphical Association (1982)
NHS	National Health Service
NI	National Insurance
NIRC	National Industrial Relations Court
NMW	National Minimum Wage
NRA	Normal retiring age
NUGSAT	National Union of Gold, Silver and Allied Trades
NUM	National Union of Mineworkers
NUR	National Union of Railwaymen
NUS	National Union of Seamen
NUTGW	National Union of Tailors and Garment Workers
OES	Occupational exposure standard
OPAS	Occupational Pensions Advisory Service
OPB	Occupational Pensions Board
ors	Others (in the names of legal cases)
OSRPA	Offices, Shops and Railway Premises Act 1963
PAYE	Pay as you earn (taxation)
PC	Privy Council
PHR	Pre-hearing review (by an industrial tribunal)
POEU	Post Office Engineering Union
PPE	Personal protective equipment
PTE	Part-time Employees (Regulations)
QB	Queen's Bench Division reports
R	Regina (in the names of legal cases)
RIDDOR	Reporting of Injuries, Diseases and Dangerous Occurences Regulations 1996
ROIT	Regional Office of Industrial Tribunals
RP	Redundancy payment
RRA	Race Relations Act 1976
s	Section (of a statute)
SD	Sex Discrimination
SDA	Sex Discrimination Act (1975, 1986)
SEA	Single European Act 1986
Ss	Sections (of a statute)
SERPS	State Earnings-Related Pension Scheme
SI	Statutory instrument
SJ	Solicitors' Journal
SMP	Statutory Maternity Pay
SOGAT	Society of Graphical and Allied Trades (1982)
SOSR	Some other substantial reason (for dismissal)
SR	Safety representative
SSA	Social Security Act (various)
SSAT	Social Security Appeals Tribunal
SSHBA	Social Security and Housing Benefit Act 1982
SSP	Statutory Sick Pay
SSPA	Statutory Sick Pay Act 1991

TGWU	Transport and General Workers' Union
TLR	Times Law Reports
TUA	Trade Union Act (1913, 1984)
TUC	Trades Union Congress
TULR(C)A	Trades Union and Labour Relations (Consolidation) Act 1992
TURETA	Trade Union Reform and Employment Rights Act 1993
UK	United Kingdom
UMA	Union membership agreement ('Closed Shop')
USDAW	Union of Shop, Distributive and Allied Workers
VDU	Visual display unit
WLR	Weekly Law Reports

PART I

THE SYSTEM OF EMPLOYMENT LAW

O N E

Employment Law and the UK Legal System

INTRODUCTION

This chapter is intended primarily for readers who are not lawyers and are not studying for a law degree or other legal qualification. It describes the main sources and types of law and explains some important concepts and doctrines which are part of the UK's legal fabric.[1] It goes on to examine the system of courts and the personnel and procedures of the law.

The general legal context is important because employment law is not a completely separate branch of law. It adopts general legal principles, for example in relation to contracts, and cases may be heard in mainstream legal institutions such as the High Court. However, employment law does have some of its own specialist institutions, notably the industrial tribunals[2] and the Advisory Conciliation and Arbitration Service (ACAS), and these are discussed in chapter 3. The present chapter sets the scene by describing the legal system in general terms; chapter 2 adds the European Union (EU) dimension.

SOURCES AND TYPES OF LAW

Sources of law

The sources of law in the employment field are common law, statute and the law of the European Union.

Common law

The body of common law contains concepts and principles determined by judges through the process of deciding cases. The central legal relationship in the employment field – the contract of employment – is a common law concept. There is no Act of Parliament which says that the relationship between an employee and an employer is governed by a contract of employment, yet it is because this is what the judiciary has determined. Case law, therefore, can be the source of major legal concepts.

It is also very important in the interpretation of the laws passed by Parliament. For example, Parliament has laid down that employee misconduct is a fair reason for dismissal, but the Act – the Employment Rights Act 1996 – does not state in detail how an employer's actions are to be judged if he or she does dismiss for misconduct. Therefore the courts have established the detailed rules through case law, in this instance particularly in *British Homes Stores v Burchell*.

The judges are active, therefore, both in the creation and the interpretation of the law.

Statute law

Statute law is derived from Parliament. It comprises Acts of Parliament, regulations and orders made under such Acts and delegated legislation, for

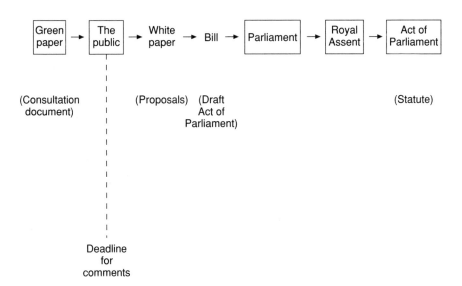

Figure 1.1 The path to statute law

example, bye-laws made by local government under powers given to them by Parliament. The steps involved in the making of statute law are shown in Figure 1.1.

The first step towards the making of statute law is often the issuing of a consultation document by the appropriate government department. In the employment field this is normally the Department for Education and Employment. Consultation documents contain a date by which any interested person or organization can send in their comments. The right to comment is available to individuals as well as to those who hold positions, who may comment on behalf of their organizations. The government may or may not be influenced by these comments.

The next step is likely to be a White Paper, setting out the government's proposals. Later this will be converted into a draft Act of Parliament – a Bill – which will be presented to and debated by, and probably amended by, Parliament. Not only does the whole of each of the Houses of Parliament debate the Bill, but also each establishes a committee to go through it in detail. The amended Bill then comes back to both Houses for voting. Once passed by Parliament, the Bill must receive the Royal Assent before it becomes an Act of Parliament. This does not mean it will become operative immediately. Its operation may be delayed, or different parts of the Act may start to operate at different times.

Many minor and often uncontroversial legal changes need to be made and it would be cumbersome, slow and expensive if all changes required amending legislation which had to follow the full Parliamentary procedure. For example, the government may wish to increase the limits for redundancy pay so that they keep up with inflation. It would be unsatisfactory if this required a Bill to be laid before Parliament, a committee to be established and debate and possibly amendment. Statutory instruments are a way around this problem.

Where law is expected to need extension, or change is anticipated, an Act can give the Minister power to issue orders or regulations to give effect to such changes. For example, the limit on redundancy pay is specified, but alongside it is a right for the Minister to vary it by order. Regulations are another type of statutory instrument. These are often used where an Act lays down only general provisions, but where detailed law is required for particular circumstances. A good example is the Health and Safety at Work etc Act 1974. This lays down very general duties, for example in section 2. Regulations issued under the Act then cover specific circumstances such as the control of substances hazardous to health.

Both orders and regulations have the full force of law and have the same status as the Act under which they are made. Both must have Parliamentary approval using either the negative or the positive procedure. Under the former a statutory instrument will be approved unless a majority of either or both Houses of Parliament vote against it within a specified period. Under the latter, a majority vote in favour will be required if it is to become law. In neither case is there scope for amendment – the instrument is voted upon in its entirety as originally presented to Parliament. However, there may be debate.

Parliament may also delegate legislative power to persons other than the appropriate Minister. In particular, such power may be delegated to local government authorities to be used through the medium of bye-laws. In the employment field this is relevant in respect of the employment of children: bye-laws may control where, when and for how long children are employed.[3] Mention must also be made of what may be called quasi-law which is found in the form of codes of practice. These are discussed in chapter 4 in the context of the role of ACAS.

The law of the European Union

A third source of UK law is statute and case law from the European Union. The relationship between EU and UK law is described in chapter 2 both in general terms and specifically as regards employment.

Types of law

Law may be classified in a number of ways. The principal classifications are: according to source (as discussed above), that is, common law and statute; criminal and civil law (discussed below); and public and private law, that is, public administration and citizenship as distinct from private transactions.

Criminal law

Society has decided that those who do not accept certain rules of conduct shall be punished as a deterrent to others. A crime, therefore, is a breach of society's rules and is punishable by the State. It follows that the criminal law is concerned with preventing breaches of society's rules and with punishing offenders. Those responsible for such breaches commit crimes – such as theft, murder, drunken driving and so on – and an agent of the State will prosecute them if there is sufficient evidence. In most cases that agent is the Crown Prosecution Service, although in very serious cases it may be the Director of Public Prosecutions. In the health and safety at work field the relevant health and safety inspector is responsible for prosecution in the magistrates' courts.[4] The standard of proof in criminal law is that the case is established beyond all reasonable doubt. This is a high standard of proof reflecting the fact that guilt has associated with it a stigma, possible financial penalty (a fine)[5] or loss of liberty (a custodial sentence), although probation, community service and so on are increasingly common forms of punishment. Criminal cases are normally dealt with in the magistrates' courts, although more serious or contested cases may or must (depending upon their nature) then be sent to the Crown Court for trial.

Civil law

The civil law is concerned with settling disputes between private parties, for example, between individuals, between individuals and organizations and between organizations. Thus, a dispute between a householder and his or her neighbour about nuisance created by the neighbour's noise would be a civil matter. So would a dispute between two individuals over a debt; between a worker and an employer over wages due; between a customer and a shop over a faulty product; or between a retail firm and one of its suppliers over late delivery. In the employment field the principal type of civil case is a dispute between an employee and his or her employer. This may be a dispute based on the employee's statutory rights or, for example, over the employer's alleged negligence leading to the employee suffering a personal injury (see chapter 15). A person or organization wishing to pursue a civil claim – the plaintiff – has to establish, on the balance of probabilities, that they have suffered some loss as a result of the defendant's unlawful act, and show the extent of that loss in a claim for damages at common law or compensation under statute. Sometimes an order (or injunction) may be sought to stop the unlawful act (for example, an employer wanting to stop a strike, or a householder wanting to stop a neighbour's noise).

There are three categories of civil law relevant to the employment field – contract, trust and tort. A contract exists where two or more parties agree to make an exchange, but it need not in every case be in writing. There must be consideration – something of value provided by one party in exchange for what is received from the other. In most cases this is money, such as wages for work or money for consumer items. Contracts are entered into after an offer is made by one party and accepted by another. Where there is a contract, a breach by one party may give rise to a legitimate claim for damages for breach of contract by the other. The law of trusts operates in areas where a person is charged with looking after someone else's property. A failure to discharge such a role properly can lead to claims for damages for breach of trust. This would be possible, for instance, in relation to pension fund trustees. A tort is simply a civil wrong (as opposed to a criminal wrong, that is, a crime). There are a variety of different torts, largely the product of judicial creation. Examples are:

- nuisance;
- defamation (libel and slander);
- negligence;
- trespass to the person, land or property;
- inducing a breach of contract; and
- breach of statutory duty.

Whereas a claim for damages for breach of contract can be pursued only where a contract exists, the law of torts applies generally, although different rules apply to different torts. Unions do much work, for example, in assisting members' claims for damages where an employer has been negligent. Here the rules are that there has to be, first, a duty of care; second, a breach of that duty; and, third, a loss suffered as a result. The duty of care can be established by reference to the contract of employment or more generally, and indeed statute law also lays down such a duty (in the HSWA) although the latter cannot be used as a basis for civil actions. By failing in his or her duty of care the employer has committed a tort – the tort of negligence, or possibly the tort of breach of statutory duty (see chapter 15).

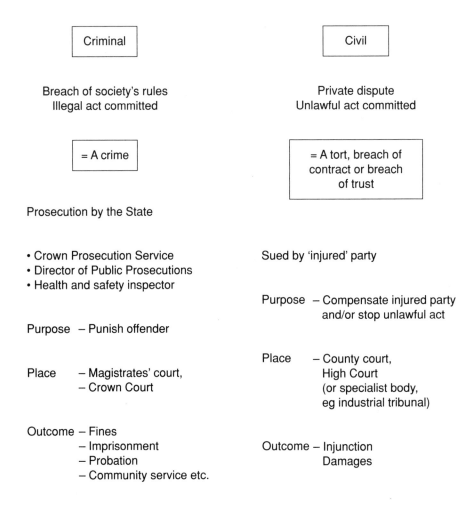

Figure 1.2 Comparison of criminal and civil law cases

Relationship between criminal and civil law

In general there is little commonality between the two systems. As already noted, they have different standards of proof. Moreover, cases take place in different courts and the atmosphere as well as the outcome is different. However, an important factor is that a single event can give rise to both criminal and civil proceedings.

A hole in the floor of the workplace is left uncovered, without being cordoned off and without any warning signs. A worker falls into it, injures his or her back and is absent from work as a result, so suffering financially and otherwise. The worker may pursue a civil case to claim for damages for losses occurring because of the employer's negligence. At the same time the factory inspector may feel that the employer's behaviour constitutes a crime – a failure to perform the duties laid down in HSWA – and may decide to prosecute. The civil case will be heard in the county court or the High Court, the criminal case probably in the magistrates' court. The criminal system tends to be less slow than the civil system so these cases will be heard at different times as well as in different places. The civil court will decide whether there has been negligence, and if so what damages are appropriate. The criminal case will decide if the employer is in breach of the HSWA. Where damages are a relatively minor matter, they may be dealt with in the criminal proceedings. A defendant's conviction in a criminal court can be used as evidence by the plaintiff in civil proceedings.

It is perhaps the civil law which is more likely to be invoked in the employment field, particularly through unfair dismissal and other employment-protection legislation. However, the criminal law plays a significant part in health and safety at work (see chapter 14) and may be relevant to other aspects of employment, such as picketing.

The extent of the law

The word 'extent' refers to the geographical coverage of legislation. For example, Part I of the HSWA, including the various general duties, applies only to Great Britain (ie England, Wales and Scotland, but not Northern Ireland).[6] However, a Ministerial Order (technically an Order in Council by Her Majesty) may extend the legislation to Northern Ireland. This has in fact been done.[7]

CONCEPTS AND DOCTRINES

Torts and crimes

The principal areas of civil law relating to employment were mentioned earlier and the concept of a tort, or civil wrong, was introduced. The law of torts applies generally, the State defining what conduct constitutes a tort and determining the remedies available. A tort may be seen as a breach of a duty – that duty having been created by the general law rather than by agreement (ie, a contract) – for which the injured party may obtain damages. Negligence is one of the principal torts and is of great relevance in the field of health and safety at work.

The criminal law is the concern of the State and covers misconduct – crime – which affects the whole community. The general aim of criminal law is to punish and deter. By contrast, the civil law, encompassing the law of torts, provides individual citizens with the opportunity to enforce their rights against other citizens who owe a duty to them. Usually the aim is to provide damages which compensate the injured person in order to restore them to their former position.

Contracts

It has been seen that a significant difference between a crime and a tort is that the former is a public concern and the latter a private one. But what are the differences between tort and contract? A major difference is the fact that a contract is derived from agreement while a tort is based upon a breach of a duty imposed by the general law. Contractual duties are undertaken by choice, although the respective bargaining power of the parties is rarely considered, and can be enforced only where there is a contract, while duties under the law of torts are imposed and do not require the presence of a contract. In the law of torts the State determines the duties; in contract the parties determine the duties and the courts, historically, will intervene for enforcement purposes (typically to award damages) rather than to pronounce on the fairness or otherwise of what the contracting parties agreed.

Legal personality and liability

In law, the word 'person' may be used to indicate an individual human being or a group of human beings with their own existence in law. The former are 'natural' legal persons, the latter 'artificial' ones. Legal personality involves the acceptance of rights and obligations given effect by the law. Special rules apply to certain categories of natural legal person, such as children, people of insane mind, prisoners, bankrupts and aliens. Artificial legal persons are known as corporations. Those bodies which are not corporations are known as unincorporated associations. It will be seen that trades unions are unincorporated associations, albeit with certain corporate characteristics given them by statute (see chapter 21). Corporations, which include limited liability companies and local authorities, may be established by Royal Charter or by statute. The latter method includes Acts establishing specific corporations as well as the general legislation (the Companies Acts). The achievement of legal personality means a corporation can sue and be sued in its own name, and may be the defendant in criminal proceedings.

The law of employment places duties upon employers and others. Where there is an offence under an Act, eg the HSWA, the employer will be guilty. If the employer is a body corporate, that body will be guilty, although by s 37 of the HSWA an individual 'director, manager, secretary or other similar officer' may also be guilty. Where the employer is unincorporated the individual proprietor will be liable. In a partnership, the partners will be jointly and severally (ie collectively and individually) liable.

If the action is a civil one the employer will be personally liable, if, for example, there is a breach of the duty of care by that employer. If the breach is by an employee of the employer, rather than the employer himself, the doctrine of vicarious liability operates to make the employer liable for acts and omissions during the course of the employee's employment (on vicarious liability see chapter 15). An employer's vicarious liability for the independent contractor is much weaker than his or her liability for employees; therefore the distinction between these two categories of worker is of considerable importance.

It should also be noted that employment legislation places duties upon persons other than employers. For example, the HSWA places obligations upon employees, the self-employed, controllers of premises, designers, manufacturers, importers and suppliers. In addition, the civil law sets out the duties of occupiers towards those who come onto their premises (see chapter 15). Finally, there is a considerable body of legislation imposing duties upon trades unions (chapter 21).

Employment status

As noted, employment status can be an important factor in determining liability. Rights and obligations differ both at common law and under statute. For example, employers' vicarious liability for the acts of contractors is less than it is for employees and only employees may use legislation such as that relating to unfair dismissal. The determination of employment status is considered in chapter 5.

Agency

As noted, a worker may be an employee or an independent contractor. Such a person may, at the same time, be an agent. In essence, a principal acts through an agent, the agent bringing the principal into legal relationships with third parties. In such relationships, the principal is deemed to have acted in person. The duties of the agent will depend upon any contract of agency and the implied terms of agency, which include the duty to exercise care and skill. The principal is under a duty to indemnify his agent against any losses, liabilities and expenses incurred in the performance of his undertaking. The general rule is that the agent is not liable under nor entitled to enforce a contract made on behalf of his principal, although there are exceptions to this rule, such as where the principal is undisclosed. The importance of agency is that it may affect the allocation of liability.

The correct application of the law

The law distinguishes between matters of law and matters of fact, although there can be a mixture of the two. The significance of the distinction is that in many circumstances appeals are permitted only on points of law. That is, the appeal must be on the basis that the courts have applied the law incorrectly – for example, by applying the wrong test, or by applying the right test incorrectly – or have made a finding of fact that is not compatible with the evidence.

An important doctrine, therefore, holds there to be a correct way of applying the law to a given set of facts. This is at its most obvious where the issue to be tried is the correct construction of a written document such as a contract. Here there should be a 'correct' answer, with extraneous material disregarded. Where such a contract is partly written and partly oral, there is less certainty because the courts need to establish facts based on oral evidence before they can decide the issue of interpretation.

THE LEGAL SYSTEM IN ACTION

The system of courts in England and Wales

The system of courts is divided into criminal and civil sections, although in practice there is a degree of overlap. The jurisdiction of the different courts is set out briefly below. Specialist employment law bodies are described in chapter 3.

Magistrates' courts
These deal with the vast majority of criminal cases. Proceedings are either summary – dealt with in the magistrates' court – or committal, where the magistrates conduct a preliminary enquiry before committing the accused for trial in the Crown Court. In practice, there are now very few preliminary

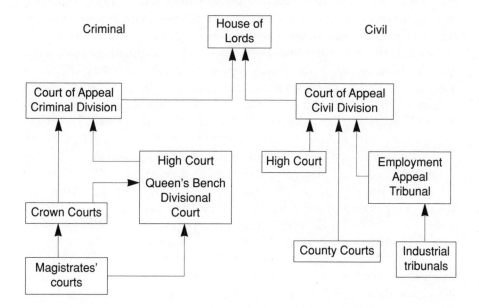

Figure 1.3   The courts system in simplified form

enquiries; in most committals there is no enquiry at all. There is a hearing only if the defence requests it. The summary procedure is used for less serious cases, such as minor theft, drunkenness in a public place and many road traffic offences, while committal is used for more serious offences. The magistrates also have responsibility for some civil matters, for instance, maintenance orders and certain other aspects of family law, and licensing.

Crown Courts
Crown Courts hear appeals on questions of fact from summary cases in the magistrates' courts and deal with indictable offences, that is, where the offence is more serious and the charges are set out in detail. Except on appeal, a jury is present if the defendant pleads not guilty. Magistrates often sit with judges in the Crown Court. Some cases are sent by the magistrates to the Crown Court for sentencing because of the limited sentencing powers in the magistrates' courts.

County courts
These have a wide range of functions and are the main civil court. A large majority of cases start here, although fewer than 5 per cent result in actual trials, the cases usually being settled by the parties. Cases in contract and most types of tort can be dealt with in the county courts, as well as adop-

tion, bankruptcy, divorce, trust disputes and the winding up of companies and the estates of deceased people. Since 1973 the county court has operated a small claims procedure in which individuals can represent themselves. As a result of the Courts and Legal Services Act 1990, there has been a significant extension of the county courts' jurisdiction.[8] Thus, claims for damages in respect of personal injuries must now be commenced in the county courts if the value of the action is less than £50,000 (previously £5,000). Actions with a value of less than £25,000 will normally be tried in the county courts and those valued at £50,000 or more in the High Court. Various criteria (such as the complexity of the case) are set out for determining where actions involving sums between £25,000 and £50,000 should be heard. Many employment cases, including for example claims for damages for breach of the contract of employment and actions in debt for wages owed, as well as claims for damages for personal injuries, are now tried in the county courts rather than in the High Court.

High Court

This comprises three divisions – Queen's Bench, Chancery and Family. The Queen's Bench Division hears all cases in contract and in tort. The Chancery Division's work includes land, financial matters (such as taxation) and company law. The Family Division's remit takes in cases involving children and those involving matrimonial matters. Each of the three divisions has a 'divisional' court. The Queen's Bench Division divisional court hears criminal appeals from Crown Courts and magistrates' courts. It also exercises the supervisory jurisdiction of the High Court over inferior courts, tribunals and public officials, including local authorities. This is known as judicial review. It is done by means of prerogative orders:

- *certiorari* – quashing unlawful decisions;
- *mandamus* – instructing a public body to carry out its statutory duty; and
- *prohibition* – instructing an inferior court to stop hearing a case which is not within its jurisdiction.

In practice, the first of these is the most relevant to employment law because it has been sought to quash dismissal decisions. A decision may be quashed if:

- the body making it had no jurisdiction or was exceeding its jurisdiction;
- the rules of natural justice were not followed, for example, someone was a judge in their own cause, or a person was given no opportunity to state their case (see pages 324–5 below);
- there is an error on the face of the record, that is, a mistake of law in the written reasons for the decision;

- the body making the decision took into account matters that they should not have taken into account, or failed to consider matters that they should have considered; or
- the decision was unreasonable, such that no reasonable authority would have come to it (for instance, the redundancies declared by Liverpool City Council as a result of setting an illegal rate; see page 341).

To obtain a judicial review the person applying must have *locus standi* – that is, be affected by the decision about which they are complaining. This was an issue, resolved in favour of the Equal Opportunities Commission, in *R v Secretary of State for Employment ex parte EOC* (see pages 89 and 120).

In addition, the Divisional Court of the Queen's Bench Division hears appeals against the decisions of industrial tribunals in relation to contested improvement and prohibition notices (see chapter 14).

Appeals

A major feature of the system is the right of appeal. This is granted by the body which has just decided the case or by the appeal body itself. Appeals go to the appropriate division of the Court of Appeal, where they will be heard by three judges, and may go to the House of Lords which constitutes a court comprising five law lords. On matters involving EU law an appeal to the European Court of Justice may be possible.

Precedent

In deciding a case, attention will be paid to whether similar cases have already been decided by the courts. Precedent can be ignored if there is some difference between the cases being considered, that is, one case is distinguished from another. Otherwise precedent will usually apply unless the court has the authority to overturn an earlier decision on the grounds that it was wrong. Courts are normally bound by the precedents set by other courts which are of higher authority, for example, the Court of Appeal is bound by House of Lords decisions and the High Court by Court of Appeal decisions.

The personnel of the law

Solicitors

Solicitors have to pass the examinations of their professional body – the Law Society – and obtain a certificate if they wish to practise. Usually they are self-employed, often in partnerships. They tend to be generalists rather than specialists, although as law firms grow in size specialization is occurring. In general, solicitors are not allowed to act as advocates in the higher courts (for example, the Crown Court, the High Court and above), although recent reforms have started to alter this.[9]

Barristers

Until recently, barristers had a complete monopoly of representation in the higher courts. They tend to be specialists both in the practice of advocacy and in terms of particular areas of law, although the latter is not always true. They need to pass their professional body – the Bar Council – examinations in order to practise. They do not usually deal directly with the client. The client deals with the solicitor, who then hires (and pays) the barrister. Barristers are referred to as Counsel, and senior barristers as Queen's Counsel, entitling them to use the letters QC after their name and to be referred to as 'silks'. Barristers are self-employed and work in chambers, but are not allowed to form partnerships with each other.

Judges

Judges are drawn primarily from the ranks of practising barristers. Most of them are assigned to geographical circuits (hence are known as circuit judges) taking in both county court and Crown Court work. Judges are appointed by the Queen on the advice of the Lord Chancellor. Senior judges, such as those who sit in the Court of Appeal, are appointed by the Queen on the advice of the Prime Minister, but the Lord Chancellor is consulted. Below the level of the circuit judge there are junior judicial posts in the Crown Court and county courts. Immediately senior to the circuit judge (Judge Wisely) is the High Court judge (Mr Justice Wisely, or Wisely J). In the even higher echelons are the judges of the Court of Appeal (Lord Justices, or Wisely LJ) and the Law Lords (simply, Lord Wisely).

Magistrates

Magistrates are one of the most visible examples of 'ordinary' people being involved in the administration of the law. They are appointed by the Lord Chancellor on the advice of local advisory committees. They are often people prominent in local life, for example, in political parties or other voluntary bodies such as charities or trades unions. They are appointed for their soundness of judgement and responsible attitude rather than any legal knowledge. In large cities there is often a full-time, salaried (stipendiary) magistrate.

The burden of proof

As noted, the standard of proof in criminal law is that the case is proven beyond reasonable doubt, while in civil proceedings the less strict test is that the case is established on the balance of probabilities. The general legal rule is that it is for the plaintiff to prove his or her case. However, statute may vary this rule and there are some particularly important variations in the employment field. Under the HSWA, where there is a duty or requirement to do something so far as is practicable or so far as is reasonably practicable, 'it shall be for the accused to prove (as the case may be) that it was not practicable or not reasonably practicable to do more than was in fact done'.[10] In addition, in criminal proceedings, a breach of an approved code of practice will lead to the prosecution case being 'taken as proved' unless the defendant can show that he fulfilled his duty in some way other than by observance of the code.[11] Moreover, in civil cases there is what amounts almost to a presumption of negligence once the plaintiff establishes a *prima facie* case (see chapter 15). Outside health and safety, there is a major reversal of the burden of proof in the law of unfair dismissal: here it is for the employer to establish the reason for the dismissal (see chapter 16). On the burden of proof in discrimination cases, see chapter 6.

Statutory interpretation

The courts are assisted in the matter of statutory interpretation by the Interpretation Act 1978. This states, among other things, that unless the contrary is shown masculine includes feminine (and *vice versa*) and singular includes plural (and *vice versa*). In addition, individual Acts of Parliament (and sometimes parts of Acts) have interpretation sections. For example the Health and Safety at Work etc Act 1974 has four parts, three of which have interpretation sections. The interpretation of Part I is found in section 53 which defines 37 words or phrases (in alphabetical order), including 'employee', 'personal injury', 'plant', 'premises' and 'substance'. In addition, section 52 defines what is meant by 'work' and 'at work'.

There are also rules of statutory interpretation derived from common law.[12] One is the *ejusdem generis* rule. This holds that where specific words are followed by general words, the general words are to be interpreted in the light of the specific words. This rule is particularly significant in employment law because many contracts of employment list the employee's duties but go on to provide that the employee will undertake further duties as may be required (eg, by the head of department) (on contractual duties, see chapter 10).

Hobbs v CG Robertson Ltd

In *Hobbs v CG Robertson Ltd* the Court of Appeal had to construe the Construction (General Provisions) Regulations 1961 in respect of the provision of goggles. These had to be provided where there was 'breaking, cutting, dressing or carving of stone, concrete, slag *or similar materials*' (emphasis added). Was brick, which splintered causing an eye injury, a 'similar material'? No, held the Court of Appeal: thus provision of goggles was not compulsory.

Connected with this is the rule about lists of specific matters which are not followed by general words. Here the interpretation is that only the matters so listed are covered by the legislation in question, although a broader interpretation may occur where the list is preceded by the word 'includes'.

Knowles v Liverpool City Council

Section 1(3) of the Employers' Liability (Defective Equipment) Act 1969 states that 'equipment includes any plant and machinery, vehicle, aircraft and clothing'. But does it include the material with which the employee is working? In *Knowles v Liverpool City Council*, where the material was a paving stone, the Court of Appeal answered this question in the affirmative, saying that the word 'equipment' should be interpreted broadly.

Historically the courts may not use *extrinsic* sources as an aid to the interpretation of statutes. Therefore, sources such as the record of Parliamentary debates and White Papers have not been available. Since 1993, however, following *Pepper v Hart* (a tax case) such sources may be used in certain circumstances.

Intrinsic sources have been used as an aid historically. These include the long title of an Act.

The long title of the Health and Safety at Work etc Act 1974 is 'An Act to make further provision for securing the health, safety and welfare of persons at work, for protecting others against risks to health or safety in connection with the activities of persons at work, for controlling the keeping and use and preventing the unlawful acquisition, possession and use of dangerous substances, and for controlling certain emissions into the atmosphere; to make further provision with respect to the employment medical advisory service; to amend the law relating to building regulations, and the Building (Scotland) Act 1959; and for connected purposes.'

Where the legislation being considered is relevant to any legislation of the European Union, the courts should, where possible, construe the domestic legislation in such a way as to give effect to the European provisions (see chapter 2 for an elaboration of this point).

NOTES

1 Strictly the UK has more than one legal system since the law and legal systems of Northern Ireland and Scotland differ in some respects from those of England and Wales.

2 The Employment Rights (Dispute Resolution) Act 1998 will, if enacted, renames these tribunals 'employment tribunals' and makes other changes (see chapters 3 and 4). This provision, and most other parts of the Act were not yet in force at the time of writing.

3 Children and Young Persons Acts 1933–69. The government is currently reviewing the law relating to children's employment. The review is expected to be complete by the end of 1998.

4 HSWA, s 39.

5 Section 17 of the Criminal Justice Act 1991 provides that the maximum amounts specified in the standard scale of fines shall be as follows: level 1 £200; level 2 £500; level 3 £1,000; level 4 £2,500; and level 5 £5,000. On increased fines under certain sections of the HSWA, see pages 283–4.

6 HSWA, s 84.

7 The Health and Safety at Work (Northern Ireland) Order 1978. Further extensions have been made through the Health and Safety at Work etc Act 1974 (Application Outside Great Britain) Order (SI 1995/263).

8 Courts and Legal Services Act 1990. See the High Court and County Courts Jurisdiction Order (SI 1991/724).

9 Courts and Legal Services Act 1990.

10 HSWA, s 40.

11 HSWA, s 17(2). Approved codes are issued by the Health and Safety Commission under s 16(1).

12 Another example is that where two or more words follow each other, they are taken to be related for the purposes of interpretation. Thus 'health, safety and welfare at work' in s 2(1) of the HSWA clearly means health at work and safety at work, as well as welfare at work.

T W O

The European Union Legal System

This chapter aims to describe the system of European Union law in order to show the relationship between EU and UK law. The substance of EU law is dealt with in the various subject chapters in Part II. However, a brief description of EU social policy is given here. An assessment of the impact of the EU upon UK employment law is attempted in chapter 27.

LEGAL BASIS OF THE EUROPEAN UNION

The legal basis of the European Union lies in the founding treaties. Technically, there are three European Communities: the Coal and Steel Community (set up by the Treaty of Paris, 1951), the Economic Community (Rome, 1957) and the Atomic Energy Community (Rome, 1957). Operationally there is a unified structure combining all three communities, and the term European Community (EC) is commonly used to refer to this.

The name European Union (EU) is now widely used following the Maastricht Treaty on European Union 1991. EU applies principally to the new areas of foreign policy, security and home affairs which are not within the jurisdiction of the EC but are within the jurisdiction of the EU. The original communities exist alongside the wider Union. The term European Union when used here should be taken to include the EC. For consistency the term is used even when describing events prior to the implementation of the Maastricht Treaty.

Each measure enacted by the EU must be based on – that is, justified by reference to – a provision in an EU treaty, otherwise the European Court of Justice (ECJ) may rule it unconstitutional. Proposals from the European Commission thus specify the treaty article on which the proposal rests and this determines aspects of the procedure to be adopted, eg unanimous or majority voting or whether the co-operation procedure involving the European Parliament has to be used (see below). Unless specifically provided for elsewhere in the treaties, article 100 tends to be the base. This involves unanimous voting.

The Single European Act (SEA) of 1986 introduced some fundamental changes. In particular, the Treaty of Rome was amended to include new articles, of which articles 100A and 118A are especially relevant to the field of employment. Both allow qualified majority voting. Article 100A has made possible a quickening of the pace of EU activity in the field of harmonization of technical standards which has implications for health and safety at work through matters such as safety standards for the design and construction of machinery. Article 118A has been the basis for a number of health and safety at work directives and makes a specific commitment to improved health and safety at work on the part of the EU.

SOURCES OF EU LAW

The sources of EU law may usefully be divided into three categories. First are the primary sources, comprising the founding treaties, Community acts (such as the SEA 1986) and further treaties (such as the Maastricht Treaty or accession treaties). These provide the constitutional foundations of the EU as well as establishing fundamental policies (such as the operation of the Single Market) and principles (such as free movement of workers and equal pay). Next come secondary sources – regulations, directives and decisions – by which the EU implements policy in more detail. Finally, there are non-legally binding sources – opinions and other non-treaty acts (memoranda, guidelines, resolutions, communications). In the employment field there is an important recommendation on policies to avoid sexual harassment (see pages 104–6).

By far the most important source of EU law in relation to employment is the directive. The way directives work is discussed below, and shown in diagrammatic form in Figure 2.3.

MAIN INSTITUTIONS OF THE EU

European Council

This is a 'summit' meeting of the heads of government of Member States. It is held two or three times a year in order to discuss major issues and give general direction to the Union.

Council of Ministers

Now formally the Council of the European Union, this is the primary decision-making institution of the EU and takes final decisions on the laws to be applied throughout the Community. It comprises government Ministers from each Member State, although the Ministers actually present will vary according to the subject under discussion. Thus employment Ministers will attend a Council where employment matters are being discussed, finance Ministers for budgetary matters and so on.

European Parliament

The Parliament is elected directly by the voters in each Member State. The elections take place every five years. Parliament is consulted by the Council of Ministers but has increased powers as a result of the Maastricht Treaty.

European Commission

The Commission is the executive of the EU. It comprises full-time, salaried commissioners and their staff. The Commission proposes legislation which is then considered by the Council of Ministers, upholds the treaties and acts to ensure adherence to EU laws. Since Maastricht, the appointment of the Commission is subject to approval by the Parliament, which also has the power to dismiss the Commission by a vote of censure.

The Court of Justice[1]

The European Court of Justice (ECJ) is composed of judges from all Member States. It passes judgment in disputes involving the application and interpretation of EU law, and, since Maastricht, can fine Member States for being in breach of EU legislation. A Court of First Instance now deals with an increasing proportion of EU cases, with the ECJ judging any appeals. A simplified description of the ECJ's role in interpreting and enforcing EU legislation is given in Figure 2.1.

Other institutions

The Court of Auditors is responsible for checking the management of the EU's finances. There are also consultative bodies. The Economic and Social Committee has to be consulted on proposals relating to economic and social matters. It is an advisory body made up of representatives of employers,

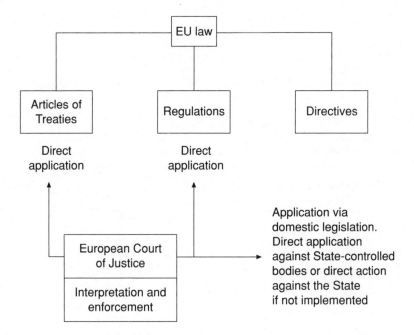

Figure 2.1 Simplified description of the role of the ECJ in interpreting and enforcing EU law

trades unions and consumers. The Maastricht Treaty set up a Committee of the Regions in order to shape and influence EU policy and expenditure in favour of the regions. In the main it comprises representatives of local and/or regional government.

A further committee is the Advisory Committee on Safety, Hygiene and Health Protection at Work. Formed in 1974, and bringing together representatives of governments, employers and trades unions, it discusses, proposes and reviews new health and safety developments. The European Commission consults the Committee before it proposes health and safety measures.

Finally, there is an Ombudsman and a right for citizens of the European Union to petition the European Parliament.

LEGISLATIVE PROCESS OF THE EU

The European law-making process is understandably more distant and complex than that of domestic parliaments. Figure 2.2 sets it out in

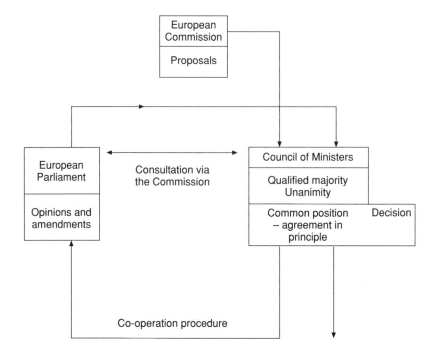

Figure 2.2 Simplified description of the EU legislative process

simplified form. The process starts with a proposal from the European Commission which is discussed in the Council of Ministers. The European Parliament is consulted. The Parliament is in fact consulted a second time (under what is called the co-operation procedure) after the Council has reached a common position, ie an agreement in principle. The Parliament may reject, amend or accept the Council's position. In cases of rejection, the Council will need a unanimous vote in favour if it is to go against the Parliament's expressed wishes. Where the Council's position is amended, the proposal is reviewed by the Commission before being returned to the Council.

Most of the provisions of the Single European Act 1986 use this procedure and are subject to qualified majority voting in the Council. One of the exceptions, however, is the area relating to the rights and interests of employed persons, which includes the Community Charter of Fundamental Social Rights (the Social Charter). Provisions relating to technical standards are not an exception and are resulting in a number of changes in the health and safety field.

Moreover, the general improvement of health and safety at work is emphasised as an EU objective and is subject to qualified majority voting.

The scope and method of EU decision-making has been altered as a result of the Treaty agreed at Maastricht in 1991 and the protocols attached to it (see below). It seems likely that EU influence will increase in areas such as economic and monetary policy and that there will be greater intergovernmental co-operation among Member States over matters such as foreign policy, defence, immigration and crime prevention. Provision is made for the wider use of qualified majority voting and Parliament now has the right to override Council for the first time. This is by means of the new co-decision procedure for certain types of legislation: free movement of workers, the right of establishment, the mutual recognition of diplomas, guidelines for trans-European energy, transport and telecommunications, the framework decisions for the EU's research and development and co-operation in the fields of public health, culture and education.[2]

The new co-decision procedure (which is laid down in article 189B of the revised Treaty) in essence puts the European Parliament on an equal footing with the Member States in the consideration of the relevant proposals for European legislation for the first time. The new procedure permits the European Parliament to enter into direct negotiations with the Council on the content of the legislation, and also gives the Parliament the possibility of rejecting the legislation under certain circumstances.

Moreover, the co-operation procedure, which allows Parliament two readings and the right to table amendments in several areas where Council takes a decision by majority vote, has been extended to some aspects of transport policy, some competition policy, some social policy areas, the social fund, social 'cohesion' decisions, development policy, the implementation of decisions on trans-European networks and to some environment and research areas. In addition the assent procedure, or the requirement of Parliamentary approval by an absolute majority of its members on all foreign treaties, including the accession of new Member States, has been extended to international agreements having important budgetary implications for the EU, such as GATT.

The EU Member States agreed to a Social Policy Protocol being annexed to the Maastricht Treaty. This Protocol allowed the 14 Member States (apart from the UK) to use a procedure for implementing the Social Charter through qualified majority voting. The procedure applies to matters of equal treatment, working conditions and information and consultation of the workforce. The UK would not be bound by decisions made through the use of this procedure and unanimity will still be required in relation to terms and conditions of employment more generally, with the exception of health and safety at work. This procedure has been used to adopt directives on worker consultation and parental leave.

Bodies representing management and labour are being encouraged to negotiate agreements which would meet the EU's requirements as well as taking into account the traditions of each Member State. This development is based upon article 118B of the Treaty of Rome.

An agreement was reached at Maastricht in relation to occupational pensions. Equality will apply only to benefits accruing from and including 17 May 1990 – the date of the *Barber* judgment (see pages 211–220) – unless proceedings had been commenced before that date. The ECJ subsequently confirmed this approach in *Ten Oever.*

The Treaty of Amsterdam 1997 introduced a new article 6A into the Treaty of Rome. This allows the Council of Ministers to take action against a wide range of types of discrimination: sex, race, ethnic origin, religion or belief, disability, age and sexual orientation. The European Commission has already drawn up a framework for proposed action to tackle race discrimination on the basis of article 6A. The UK agreed at Amsterdam to accept the Social Chapter it had opposed at Maastricht. As a result, the Social Chapter became integrated into the body of the Treaty of Rome and became binding on the UK. The UK will now be bound to implement two directives it formerly opposed – on works councils and parental leave – although the dates of implementation will be later than for other Member States to reflect the UK's delayed acceptance of the Social Chapter.

THE RELATIONSHIP BETWEEN EU AND DOMESTIC LAW

The UK's membership of the EU is expressed through the European Communities Act 1972. There are three principal methods by which EU law is effected under the 1972 Act:

- by direct effect;
- by subordinate legislation under the 1972 Act; and
- through interpretation of existing legislation.

In addition, Parliament may enact new statutes or issue regulations under Acts other than the European Communities Act 1972. For example, substantial amounts of EU law have already been given effect through regulations under the HSWA.

Regulations and decisions of the EU have direct effect – that is, no UK legislation is necessary to give effect to them – and so too do articles of EU treaties where they are clear and precise, unconditional and unqualified and do not require further implementing measures by Member States. Article 119 (on equal pay) has been held to be directly enforceable *(Defrenne v SABENA (No 2); Secretary of State for Scotland v Wright).*

Where the EU issues directives, Member States must pass their own legislation in order to comply. The process is illustrated in Figure 2.3. The 'six pack', comprising six sets of health and safety at work regulations, all

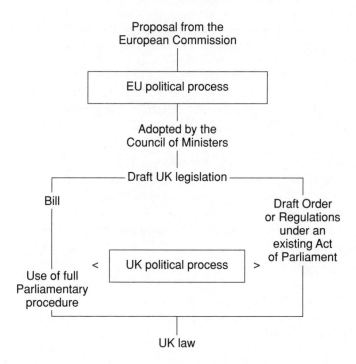

Figure 2.3   The process of implementing EU directives in the UK

operative from 1 January 1993, is an example of the process in action.[3] Other examples include the Sex Discrimination Act 1986, the Equal Pay Amendment Regulations 1983 and the Transfer of Undertakings (Protection of Employment) Regulations 1981. Where a directive is not implemented by a Member State, or not fully implemented, complaints may be taken on the basis of the directive itself against organizations made responsible by the State and given special powers for providing a public service under the control of the State *(Foster v British Gas plc; Griffin v South West Water Services Ltd)*.

Where the organization is not 'an emanation of the State' the proceedings can be taken directly against the State – effectively an action for damages suffered as a result of the State's failure to fully implement the directive *(Francovich v Italian Republic)*. Where there is a conflict between UK and EU law, the latter must prevail *(R v Secretary of State for Transport, ex parte Factortame)* and, in general, UK law is to be interpreted in such a way as to give effect to EU provisions *(Marleasing)*. Even the EU's recommendations (eg, in relation to the prevention of sexual harassment) may be relied on where legislation is insufficiently clear *(Grimaldi)*.

THE EU'S SOCIAL POLICY

The Community Charter of Fundamental Social Rights (the 'Social Charter')

The Social Charter was adopted at the European Council in December 1989 by 11 Member States, excluding the UK. The Social Charter is essentially a declaration; it is not an internationally binding treaty and it has no legal force. The areas covered by the Social Charter are:

- the freedom of movement of workers;
- employment and remuneration;
- improvement of living and working conditions;
- social protection;
- freedom of association and collective bargaining;
- vocational training;
- equal treatment for men and women;
- information, consultation and participation of workers;
- health protection and safety at the workplace;
- the protection of children and adolescents;
- elderly persons; and
- disabled persons.

The European Commission takes the view that responsibility for the initiatives needed to implement the Social Charter lies with the Member States and bodies representing employers and workers as well as with the EU. The principle of 'subsidiarity' is to be applied: the EU will act only where objectives can be reached more effectively by initiatives at the level of the EU as a whole than at the level of the individual Member States. Implementation of the Social Charter can be in the form of legislation or collective agreements.

The Social Action Programme

The Social Charter has been converted into a programme of measures – the 'Social Action Programme' – which was adopted by the European Commission in 1990. This programme is currently going through the EU's legislative process. Neither the individual proposals in the programme nor the various elements of the Social Charter itself are related to particular articles of the Treaty. The Treaty basis of each proposal remains to be determined through the political process.

A major part of the Social Action Programme has been concerned with health and safety at work (see chapter 14). Among the other measures adopted have been:

- a directive on proof of the employment relationship;[4]
- a directive on the protection of pregnant women at work, which is not restricted to matters of health and safety;[5]
- a directive on the limitation of working time;[6]
- a directive on protection of young workers;[7]
- a directive on part-time work;[8]
- a directive on European works councils;[9]
- a directive on the burden of proof in sex discrimination cases;[10] and
- a directive on parental leave.[11]

Because Article 118A, relating to health and safety at work, allows qualified majority voting, it has been found politically expedient to use it as a basis for directives in the employment field even where the health and safety aspects are secondary. For example, the directive on the limitation of working time was adopted under Article 118A. The treaty basis was challenged by the UK at the ECJ, but unsuccessfully.

A principal factor in the non-implementation of part of the programme had been the requirement that matters dealing with terms and conditions of employment be subject to the unanimous voting procedure. However, the Social Policy Protocol agreed at Maastricht now gives social policy a legal status and allows some employment matters to be subject to qualified majority voting. As noted, the UK will now be bound by decisions taken under this procedure.

The Social Action Programme contains proposals under all the Social Charter headings. In some cases, the instrument for realising a proposal is a legally binding one, eg a directive, but in others the instrument proposed may have no legal force, eg a recommendation. In some cases no indication of the type of instrument is given. The main legislative device for implementing the programme is the directive, which requires Member States to enact their own legislation within a given time period. In addition to the Social Action Programme, there is a continuing process of improving existing legislation. For example, in 1992 the Council of Ministers adopted a directive on collective redundancies to strengthen the provisions of an earlier directive.[12] A review of the Acquired Rights Directive is currently being undertaken (see chapter 20).

SOURCES OF INFORMATION

Sources of EU law

The primary source is the *Official Journal of the European Communities* (OJ). The L (legislation) series contains the text of instruments such as directives.

Thus OJ 1975, L48/2–3 means volume 48 of the 1975 OJ, pages 2–3. There is a network of European Information Centres (located, for example, in university libraries) where there should be free access to the OJ and other EU materials.

UK law derived from the EU

This will be available in the same way as any other UK statutory provision, ie from HMSO stockists in the form of orders, regulations or Acts of Parliament. The text will be as originally enacted: it will not contain any amendments which might have been made. To obtain updated legislation it is necessary to make use of one of the encyclopaedias (such as Sweet and Maxwell's *Encyclopaedia of Employment Law* or *Encyclopaedia of Health and Safety at Work*) which are available in libraries or on a subscription basis. Health and Safety Executive publications are a major source of information about the law of health and safety at work.

EU institutions

The European Commission and the European Parliament have their own information offices in the Member States. The European Court of Justice has an information department at its headquarters.

NOTES

1   The ECJ should not be confused with the European Court of Human Rights (ECHR) set up under the European Charter of Human Rights 1950 by the wider Council of Europe. The decisions of the European Court of Human Rights are persuasive, but are not legally binding.

2   The co-decision procedure of Council and Parliament allows Parliament to reject Council decisions in areas of qualified majority voting by absolute majority of the full house. This applies to questions of the internal market, free movement of workers, the environment and new areas of competence such as consumer protection.

3   The 'six pack' comprises:

- the Management of Health and Safety at Work Regulations 1992;
- the Manual Handling Operations Regulations 1992;
- the Workplace (Health, Safety and Welfare) Regulations 1992;
- the Personal Protective Equipment at Work Regulations 1992;
- the Health and Safety (Display Screen Equipment) Regulations 1992; and
- the Provision and Use of Work Equipment Regulations 1992.

For details of where these are dealt with in the text see the list of statutory instruments.

4 91/533/EC, OJ 1991, L288/32. This was implemented in Great Britain through amendments made to Part I of EP(C)A 1978 by the Trade Union Reform and Employment Rights Act (TURERA) 1993. These provisions are now in Part I of ERA.

5 92/85/EC, OJ 1992, L348. The directive also covers maternity leave and maternity pay (see chapter 13).

6 93/104/EC, OJ 1993, L307/18.

7 94/33/EC, OJ 1994, L216/12.

8 Directive on Part-time work, 97/81/EC, OJ 1998, L14/9.

9 This was adopted under the Maastricht Social Policy Protocol, thus originally excluding the UK, but it will now apply to the UK following the government's acceptance of the Social Chapter (94/45/EC, OJ 1994, L254/64).

10 Directive on the Burden of Proof in Sex Discrimination Cases.

11 This was adopted under the Maastricht Social Policy Protocol, thus originally excluding the UK, but will now apply to the UK following the government's acceptance of the Social Chapter (96/34/EC).

12 Directive 75/129/EEC of 17 February 1975 (OJ 1975, L48) and Directive 56/92/EEC of 24 June 1992 (OJ 1992, L245).

The Institutions of Employment Law

The relationship between employment law and the wider legal system was considered in chapters 1 and 2, taking into account both the UK context and that of the European Union. The evolution of employment law is described in chapter 25. The emphasis now switches to the institutions which have evolved as a means of resolving disputes under that law. Like employment law itself, the institutions have some distinctive qualities. The present chapter deals with the constitution and functions of the various bodies, including industrial tribunals. Chapter 4 focuses upon the procedure of industrial tribunals, since these are the central judicial institution of employment law. It should be noted that the Employment Rights (Dispute Resolution) Act 1998 provides for these tribunals to be renamed 'employment tribunals' and for other changes (see chapter 26).

ADVISORY, CONCILIATION AND ARBITRATION SERVICE

The Advisory, Conciliation and Arbitration Service (ACAS) was established under the Employment Protection Act 1975 with a view to continuing and expanding a role performed over many years by the Department of Employment and its predecessors.[1] Although ACAS is financed by government, it is independent in the sense that its activities cannot be directed by any Minister.[2] It prefers to operate through the use of voluntary methods. Like the other statutory bodies of employment law, its functions are regulated by

statute. Its general duty is to 'promote the improvement of industrial relations', in particular through the conciliation and arbitration of trade
disputes.[3] Its brief to extend the subject matter and spread of collective
bargaining was removed in 1993 by TURERA.[4]

A trade dispute, in relation to the functions of ACAS[5] is 'a dispute
between employers and workers, or workers and workers, which is
connected with' one or more of the following:

- terms and conditions of employment or physical conditions of work;
- engagement, non-engagement, suspension or termination of employment;
- work duties or the allocation of work;
- discipline;
- union membership or non-membership;
- facilities for union officials; and
- negotiating, consultative and other procedures relating to any of the
  above including the question of recognition of a union by an employer.

A dispute to which a union or employers' association is a party is to be
treated as a dispute to which the workers or employers are parties.

ACAS is governed by a council comprising employers, trades union
officers and academic industrial relations specialists. In addition, ACAS has
a chairman and staff based at a head office in London and various regional
offices.

Because ACAS has a role to play in the settlement of major disputes and
at such times has a high profile in terms of media attention, there is a danger
of seeing the resolution of major disputes as its main activity. In fact, it has a
number of functions as laid down in TULR(C)A.[6] These are as follows:

- conciliation in trade disputes;
- arbitration;
- conciliation in cases of individual complaints to tribunals;
- advice;
- enquiry; and
- production of codes of practice.

It is important to recognize the difference between processes such as conciliation and arbitration. If the services of ACAS are used, it will be necessary
to establish terms of reference. This will always be the case when a third
party is being used. The minimum involvement of a third party in employment matters is probably when advice is sought and nothing more. ACAS
advisory services are available to individual employees, union officials and
employers.

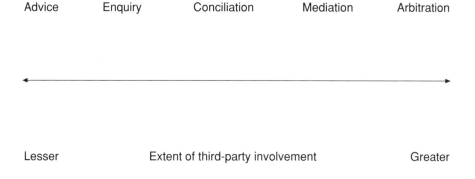

Figure 3.1 Forms of third party assistance

Enquiry is a method by which government seeks to resolve important disputes.[7] An enquiry puts pressure on the parties to settle; but more imporantly it helps clarify points of dispute and identify avenues through which solutions might be reached. Reports of enquiries usually attract media attention.

Conciliation means bringing the sides together. A crucial point here is that the conciliator does not make decisions – the parties themselves do this. Conciliation can be taken a little further by a process known as mediation. Here a third party will suggest solutions – but the parties still make the decision. Finally, arbitration is quite different. Here the parties have decided that it is impossible for them to reach an agreement. The arbitrator is asked to make a decision. He or she, therefore, imposes a solution upon them. None of these are legally enforceable decisions. Their ability to bind depends ultimately on the willingness of the parties to accept them; they are sometimes described as being 'morally binding'.

Conciliation is performed in trade disputes and in cases where individuals complain to industrial tribunals (for example, over unfair dismissal). Most of the ACAS work is performed by its full-time staff. An exception is its arbitration role, where it uses a panel of part-time arbitrators, usually academic industrial relations experts.

ACAS has the power to produce codes of practice in pursuance of its statutory functions. It produced three in the late 1970s – disciplinary procedures, time off for union officials and disclosure of information to unions for bargaining purposes. The time off code was revised to take account of changes brought about by the Employment Act 1989. All three codes were updated in 1998. Also, ACAS has issued detailed advice to supplement its code of practice on discipline. Codes of practice have also been produced by the Department of Employment, reflecting a former government's desire to bypass ACAS because of its consensus approach to employment matters and the involvement of union leaders in its governing body.[8] These have dealt with picketing, closed shop agreements and arrangements and trades union ballots and industrial action. Codes of practice can be important. A breach will not give rise to any legal liability in itself, but in a case before a court or tribunal because of the infringement of an Act or regulation, the breach can be cited and if relevant must be taken into account by the body judging the case. More generally codes of practice are useful in encouraging good employment practices.

INDUSTRIAL TRIBUNALS[9]

Background and constitution

Background

The original jurisdiction of industrial tribunals was set out in the Industrial Training Act 1964. This Act provided for a training board for each industry, with power to levy firms within the industry in order to generate funds for training purposes. Firms carrying out approved training received grants from the board for their industry. Firms had a right to appeal against the amount of the levy and against their industrial classification. Industrial tribunals were established to hear these appeals.[10]

It can be seen that industrial tribunals started life as administrative tribunals. That is, they dealt with public administration disputes rather than private, employer/employee disputes.[11] The earliest employer/employee jurisdictions were disputes over redundancy payments and applications relating to what are now ERA, s 1 statements (ie, written particulars of terms of employment). The major jurisdiction since 1972 has been unfair dismissal,[12] always accounting for over half of the tribunals' caseload and sometimes constituting as much as three-quarters of it. Subsequently equal pay, sex and race discrimination and other types of case were put within the tribunals' jurisdiction (see below).

Constitution

Industrial tribunals continue in existence by virtue of section 1 of the Industrial Tribunals Act 1996. Procedural matters are dealt with in the same Act, which permits the Secretary of State to make regulations.[13] Administratively, industrial tribunals are part of the Department of Trade and Industry.

The composition of industrial tribunals is determined by the Act and the Regulations.[14] A legally qualified chairman (male or female) is appointed by the Lord Chancellor. Legally qualified in this context means a barrister or solicitor of at least seven years' standing. The chairman is accompanied by two lay members, one drawn from a panel nominated by employers' bodies, the other drawn from a panel nominated by employees' organisations. Both are appointed by the Secretary of State for Education and Employment. The lay members are part-time. Chairmen may be full-time or part-time. Subject to the 'chairman-only' provisions dealt with below, a tribunal will be made up of three people constituted in accordance with the IT rules, although with the parties' consent a tribunal can be made up of two people, the chairman having a casting vote.

Throughout the industrial tribunals' history it has been the case that chairmen alone would hear interlocutory matters such as applications for discovery and/or disclosure of documents. A recent development has been the extension of the role of the chairman sitting alone to substantive matters. Under ITA 1996, s 4 a chairman may sit alone in the following types of case:

- interim relief – continuation of employment orders until a full hearing in cases of dismissal on health and safety or trades union grounds or where the employee is an employee representative or an occupational pension scheme trustee;[15]
- insolvency payments – applications by employees for payment of outstanding wages and other sums when the employer is insolvent;[16]
- wages deductions;[17]
- contract cases;[18]
- where the parties consent – ie where the parties have given their written consent to a chairman-only hearing;
- withdrawn applications – where the applicant has withdrawn their application; and
- uncontested cases.

The Secretary of State may amend the above by order subject to Parliamentary approval.

It does not follow automatically that a chairman will sit alone in the above types of case. ITA 1996, s 4(5) provides that these types of case can be heard by a full tribunal if a chairman so decides. The chairman thus has discretion and the criteria governing the exercise of that discretion are:

- whether there is a likelihood of a dispute as to facts – if so, a full tribunal may be preferable;
- whether there is a likelihood of an issue of law arising – if so, a chairman sitting alone may be preferable;
- any views expressed by the parties; and

- whether other concurrent proceedings could be heard which are not within the chairman-only categories laid down in s 4(3).

The chairman has reference to the Industrial Tribunals Practice Direction No 1 which, *inter alia,* provides direction on the detailed operation of the chairman-only provisions.

Finally, in respect of constitutional matters, the Council on Tribunals performs a supervisory role under s 1 of the Tribunals and Inquiries Act 1992 over those tribunals listed in Schedule 1 to that Act. The list includes industrial tribunals in England and Wales.

Jurisdiction

The jurisdiction of industrial tribunals is found in UK statutes but it is now clear that complaints may be pursued directly on the basis of EU law in the absence of a UK statutory right (see *Secretary of State for Scotland v Wright*). There is also a jurisdiction in respect of contractual rights conferred by ITA 1996, s 3 and the Industrial Tribunals Extension of Jurisdiction Order 1994 (see below).

Statutory rights jurisdictions
These are set out in the relevant Acts and are as follows:

- *unfair dismissal:* complaints of unfair dismissal;[19] and refusal to give written reasons for dismissal;
- *health and safety at work:* appeals against improvement and prohibition notices; time off work with pay for union safety representatives; and the right to receive pay on suspension on medical grounds;
- *race relations:* complaints of race discrimination in the employment field;[20] appeals against non-discrimination notices; applications by the Commission for Racial Equality (CRE) relating to discriminatory advertisements, instructions to discriminate and pressure to discriminate; and applications by the CRE prior to county court actions;
- *disability:* applications under the DDA 1995 relating to employment matters;
- *equal pay, sex discrimination and maternity:* complaints of breaches of the Equal Pay Act 1970;[21] complaints of discrimination on grounds of sex or marital status in the employment field;[22] appeals against non-discrimination notices; applications by the EOC relating to discriminatory advertisements, instructions to discriminate and pressure to discriminate; applications by the EOC prior to county court actions; time off work for antenatal care; and decisions on equal access clauses under the Pensions Act 1995 and the Occupational Pension Schemes (Equal Treatment) Regulations 1995[23] (complaints of unfair dismissal for

reasons connected with pregnancy will fall under the SDA or under the unfair dismissal provisions; the same is true of selection for redundancy on grounds of pregnancy; a failure to allow a woman to return to work following absence because of maternity is also within the unfair dismissal provisions);

- *redundancy, reorganization and transfers of undertakings:* complaints that a recognized, independent trades union or employee representative has not been consulted about proposed redundancies; the right to receive payment under a protective award made by an industrial tribunal; the right to receive a redundancy payment and questions relating to the amount of such payments;[24] paid time off in the event of redundancy to look for other work or to make arrangements for training; complaints of failure to inform or consult with trades union or employee representatives in cases of transfers of undertakings; complaints of failure to pay compensation for failure to consult; compensation for loss of office on reorganization under various statutes such as the Local Government (Compensation) Regulations 1974 and the British Transport (Compensation to Employees) Regulations 1970; the right to be paid by the Secretary of State certain debts owed by an insolvent employer; the right to be paid by the Secretary of State occupational pension scheme contributions owing on behalf of employees of insolvent employers; and cases where a redundancy payment is sought from the National Insurance Fund; redundancy payments for civil servants (complaints that a redundancy involved unfair selection or was otherwise unreasonable fall within the unfair dismissal provisions; the same is true of complaints that dismissal occurred because of the transfer of an undertaking);

- *pay and other terms:* failure to give written particulars of the main terms of employment; failure to provide an itemized pay statement; failure to provide guarantee pay during lay-offs; unauthorized deductions from wages (or repayments);[25] wages deductions (or repayments) made outside the 12-month time limit; failure to notify the worker of total liability in cases of repayments for cash shortages or stock deficiencies; and payments or deductions exceeding 10 per cent of gross pay;

- *trades union membership or non-membership:* unjustifiable discipline by a trades union; unreasonable exclusion or expulsion from a union; action short of dismissal taken for union membership or activities, or to compel union membership or payments in lieu of such membership; paid time off for union duties; time off for union activities; interim relief where dismissal is for union membership or activities or non-membership; and unlawful refusal of employment on grounds related to union membership or non-membership; (complaints of dismissal for union membership or activities, or non-membership, fall within the unfair dismissal jurisdiction; the same is true for selection for redundancy on these grounds and for cases involving dismissal for not making payments in lieu of union membership);

- *other matters:* time off for public duties; failure to consult recognized, independent unions over an application for a contracting-out certificate relating to an occupational pension scheme (including determination of questions of independence and recognition); appeals against training levies; appeals formerly heard by referees or boards of referees under certain statutory provisions; and protection of shop and betting workers who do not wish to work on Sundays.[26]

Contractual rights jurisdiction

Industrial tribunal jurisdiction over certain contractual disputes was originally provided for by s131 of EP(C)A 1978 but no order to implement this section was made until 1994.[27]

A number of different types of claim are possible in accordance with ITA 1996, s 3 and article 3 of the Jurisdiction Order:

- a claim for damages for breach of a contract of employment or other contract connected with employment (this is a wide definition of the type of contract to which this jurisdiction applies: it may cover employment agency cases where the worker is not an employee; see chapter 5);
- a claim for a sum due under such a contract;
- a claim for recovery of a sum in pursuance of any enactment relating to the terms of performance of such a contract; and
- a claim by an employer – this is in fact a counter-claim (see below).

In addition, there are other requirements. The claim must be within the existing jurisdiction of the courts. Moreover, it must arise or be outstanding on the termination of the employment (article 3 of the Jurisdiction Order). The maximum payment is £25,000 for each claim or for a number of claims relating to the same contract (article 10).

A number of types of claim are excluded from the jurisdiction by virtue of article 5:

- those for damages or sums due in respect of personal injuries (also excluded by ITA 1996, s 3(3));
- those relating to terms which require the employer to provide living accommodation;
- those relating to terms concerned with intellectual property;
- those relating to terms imposing an obligation of confidence; and
- those relating to covenants in restraint of trade.

Complaints to industrial tribunals under the contract jurisdiction must be made within three months of the effective date of termination (EDT – see chapter 16). An employer may counter-claim within six weeks of receiving from the industrial tribunal a copy of the employee's originating application (article 4). An employer may claim only in response to an employee's claim: an employer has no independent right to claim.

EMPLOYMENT APPEAL TRIBUNAL

The Employment Appeal Tribunal (EAT) is established under ITA 1996, s 20. It comprises a judge of High Court status and two lay members drawn from panels nominated by employers' and employees' organizations respectively. Sometimes there may be four rather than two lay members, for example where the EAT is deciding an issue which has hitherto been the subject of conflicting EAT judgments. Lay members of the EAT tend to be senior employee and employer nominees, holding national rather than local positions.

The EAT hears appeals on points of law (ITA 1996, s 21), which means that it is not generally possible to appeal on the grounds that a tribunal decided the facts incorrectly. An appeal will need to be based on an incorrect legal interpretation (eg, the wrong legal test being applied or the right legal test being applied incorrectly) or upon the tribunal decision being perverse *(British Telecom v Sheridan)*. The role of the industrial tribunal is to find the facts *(Martin v MBS Fastenings (Glynwed) Distribution Ltd)*; the role of the EAT is to correct the industrial tribunal's errors of law *(Lewis v John Adamson Co Ltd)*. It is not the job of the EAT to substitute its own view of the facts for that of the tribunal *(Hereford and Worcester County Council v Neale)*.

The concept of perversity in relation to industrial tribunal decisions appears to have been raised to the status of an error in law. Broadly, it refers to an industrial tribunal decision which is not supported by the evidence. A number of tests have been put forward to assist in determining perversity:

- the 'my goodness' test *(Hereford and Worcester v Neale)*: here the Court of Appeal settled for an intuitive approach: a decision was perverse if the appellate body thought 'my goodness, that must be wrong';
- the 'permissible option' test *(Piggott Bros & Co Ltd v Jackson)*: here the Court of Appeal defined perverse as meaning a tribunal decision which was not a permissible option for the tribunal on the facts before it; that is, there would have to be a finding of fact unsupported by any evidence or a clear self-misdirection in law; and
- the reasonable tribunal test *(East Berkshire Health Authority v Matadeen)*: here the EAT defined perversity to include a tribunal decision which no reasonable tribunal would have reached and generally rejected the narrower definition in *Piggott*.

The procedure of the EAT is governed by ITA 1996 and the EAT Rules 1993.[28]

CENTRAL ARBITRATION COMMITTEE

The Central Arbitration Committee (CAC) was established by the Employment Protection Act 1975.[29] It is a standing arbitral body with members who are experienced in industrial relations, including some with experience as representatives of employers and some with experience as representatives of workers. The members are appointed by the Secretary of State for Education and Employment from persons nominated by ACAS. The CAC is provided with staff and other resources by ACAS, and ACAS reports annually to the Secretary of State on its activities. Like ACAS, the CAC is not subject to direction by any Minister. The chairman and deputy chairmen are appointed by the Secretary of State after consulting ACAS.

There is no appeal from decisions of the CAC but they may be subject to judicial review. The CAC's role is now quite limited: its main work lies in determining complaints by trades unions that employers have not disclosed information for collective bargaining purposes (see chapter 22).[30]

CERTIFICATION OFFICER

The Certification Officer (CO) was established by the EPA 1975[31], commenced operation on 1 February 1976 and replaced the Registrar of Friendly Societies. His office is part of the Department for Education and Employment and he is an independent statutory authority. He is appointed by the Secretary of State after consulting ACAS. The CO is provided with staff and other resources by ACAS and reports annually to ACAS and the Secretary of State.

The CO's role is to exercise the functions laid down by statute and comprises the following:

- *trades union political activities:* ensuring compliance with the statutory requirements for adopting political objects and operating political funds; approving political fund rules, including any changes; approving the ballot rules of unions; dealing with complaints about breaches of political fund rules; and dealing with complaints about political fund ballots;
- *trades union mergers:* ensuring compliance with procedures for amalgamation, transfer of engagements and change of name; and dealing with complaints from members about the conduct of merger ballots;

- *union listing and independence:* maintaining lists of trades unions (and employers' associations); and determining whether trades unions are independent;
- *union financial and administrative matters:* ensuring that trades unions and employers' associations have accounting records, have their accounts audited and submit annual returns; and ensuring that unions' superannuation schemes for members are actuarially examined (the Certification Officer's powers in this area have recently been increased: see chapter 21);
- *membership registers and principal executive committee etc elections:* ensuring that unions keep up-to-date membership registers and that such lists are open for inspection by members; dealing with complaints about union elections to the principal executive committee and related positions; and dealing with complaints about membership registers.

As a result of changes introduced by s 22 of the Employment Act 1988 the CO may now restrict disclosure of the identity of complainants. He or she may also make payments in connection with the expenses of claimants attending hearings (for example, travel, accommodation, loss of earnings). These are payable only to complainants (not to their representatives, nor to representatives of the respondent unions) in cases involving complaints about union elections, mergers, political rules and membership registers. The 1988 Act also offers protection to trades union members making complaints to the CO. Such complaints fall within the definition of matters for which discipline would be unjustifiable (see chapter 21).

The scheme under which the CO reimbursed trades unions for certain expenditure on ballots has now been abolished.[32]

COMMISSIONER FOR THE RIGHTS OF TRADE UNION MEMBERS

The Commissioner for the Rights of Trade Union Members was established under EA 1988 and continues by virtue of s 266 of TULR(C)A.

Scope of the Commissioner's assistance

Court proceedings that can qualify for assistance from the Commissioner are set out in TULR(C)A. Originally, these all related to denials by trades unions of the statutory rights of members.

The Commissioner may grant assistance in connection with applications to the court which arise out of complaints by a union member that his union:

- has, without the support of a properly conducted secret ballot, authorized or endorsed industrial action in which he and other members are likely to be (or have been) induced to take part;
- has not observed statutory requirements in respect of elections to its principal executive committee;
- has applied its funds for party political purposes in breach of statutory requirements;
- has failed to comply with the rules approved by the Certification Officer in any ballot, or proposed ballot, on the use of funds for party political purposes;
- has failed to bring or continue any proceedings to recover union property applied to pay or compensate any individual for any penalty imposed for an offence or for contempt of court;
- trustees have caused or permitted, or propose to cause or permit, any unlawful application of the union's property;
- has denied his statutory right to inspect its accounting records; or
- has not observed statutory requirements in connection with membership registers.

Form of assistance

Assistance provided by the Commissioner may include:

- paying for any legal advice and/or representation; or
- making arrangements for such advice and/or representation to be provided; or
- a combination of both of the above.

Qualifications for assistance

In general, a person will be eligible to bring proceedings if:

- they were a member of the union concerned at the time when the unlawful act was committed; and
- the act complained of was unlawful at the time it took place.

A union member who applies for the Commissioner's assistance is protected against being disciplined by their union because they have done so.

Changes introduced by the Employment Act 1990

The words 'assisted by the Commissioner for the Rights of Trade Union Members' may appear in the title of proceedings after the name of the person being assisted. Presumably this is to hasten the listing of the case.[33]

Furthermore, the Commissioner is now able to assist union members in cases of alleged breaches or threatened breaches of certain union rules, namely those relating to:

- appointment or election to, or removal from office;
- disciplinary proceedings, including expulsion;
- the authorizing or endorsing of industrial action;
- the balloting of members;
- the application of the union's funds or property;
- the imposition, collection or distribution of any levy for the purposes of industrial action; and
- the constitution or proceedings of any committee, conference or other body.

For assistance, the breach must (or may) affect members other than the applicant, or similar breaches have affected (or may affect) other members.[34]

Decision to assist

The Commissioner has discretion, and can assist in cases which may not be successful if they involve a point of principle, are complex, or raise a matter of substantial public interest. The Commissioner must assist if the case follows a CO decision about a union election, membership register or political fund ballot and there is a reasonable prospect of obtaining an order.

Recovery of money

Where an assisted person knowingly made a false statement to the Commissioner, or where they recklessly made a statement which was false, the Commissioner may recover the cost of the assistance. If an assisted person has costs or expenses ordered in their favour, or these are part of an agreed settlement, the Commissioner may recover the cost of assistance from these.

EQUAL OPPORTUNITIES COMMISSION AND COMMISSION FOR RACIAL EQUALITY

In addition, the Equal Opportunities Commission (equal pay and sex discrimination) and the Commission for Racial Equality (race relations) have responsibilities in the employment field as well as in other fields. Each has the aims of working towards the elimination of discrimination and of promoting equality of opportunity in its respective sphere. There is also a responsibility to review the working of the legislation and propose changes if necessary. The role and powers of the two organizations are also the same:

- research and education;
- producing annual reports;
- conducting formal investigations and issuing non-discrimination notices;
- seeking injunctions to stop discrimination which has been declared unlawful by an industrial tribunal;
- applying to industrial tribunals for declarations, for example, in the case of discriminatory advertisements;
- providing assistance to individuals (including representation at industrial tribunal hearings); and
- production of codes of practice; there is a sex discrimination code of practice, an equal pay code and a race relations code.

The EOC and the CRE represent the strategic elements in the public policy of outlawing discrimination. Individuals may complain to industrial tribunals if they feel they have suffered from discrimination, while the EOC and the CRE are charged with monitoring and enforcing the legislation and acting strategically as custodians of public policy. The legislation thus aims to tackle discrimination on two fronts: individual and strategic.

In the context of its strategic role, the EOC successfully sought judicial review of the hours requirement which prevented a large proportion of part-time workers from obtaining employment rights *(R v Secretary of State for Employment ex parte EOC)*. Since most part-timers are women, these requirements amounted to indirect sex discrimination. See chapters 5 and 6.

HEALTH AND SAFETY COMMISSION

The Health and Safety Commission and its operational arm, the Health and Safety Executive, are considered in chapter 14.

COMMISSIONER FOR PROTECTION AGAINST UNLAWFUL INDUSTRIAL ACTION

The Commission for Protection Against Unlawful Industrial Action (CPAUIA) was established under TULR(C)A by means of amendments made through TURERA.[35] Like the Commissioner for the Rights of Trade Union Members, the Commissioner is appointed by the Secretary of State and reports to him.[36] The role of the Commissioner is to assist individuals who are harmed by unlawful industrial action (see chapter 23).

WAGES COUNCILS AND WAGES BOARDS

Wages councils were abolished by TURERA. They were statutory bodies which comprised equal numbers of employers' and workers' representatives and up to five independent members, one of whom was chairman. The function of a wages council was to set minimum wages for workers in a particular industry. The industries covered included clothing manufacture, catering and retail distribution. An employer paying less than the statutorily fixed minimum wage was guilty of a criminal offence and the scheme was enforced by a wages inspectorate. Although wages councils have been abolished, similar bodies covering agriculture – agricultural wages boards – remain.[37] The present government's policy favours a generalized approach to minimum wage legislation and is contained in the National Minimum Wage Bill 1997 (see chapter 11).

NATIONAL DISABILITY COUNCIL

The National Disability Council is established under the Disability Discrimination Act 1995 (DDA). It is not comparable with the EOC and the CRE because it is an advisory rather than an enforcement body. Moreover, it is specifically excluded from advising on the employment aspects of the Act. The government has, however, announced that the Council will be replaced by a commission similar to those operating under the SDA and the RRA.

NOTES

1 ACAS continues in existence by virtue of TULR(C)A 1992, s 247(1).
2 Ibid., s 247(3).
3 Ibid, s 209.
4 ACAS's objectives pre-TURERA specified improving industrial relations, especially by developing and where necessary reforming collective bargaining machinery, and extending collective bargaining. This meant it had a brief to improve the procedures and institutions used by employers and unions to settle employees' terms and conditions, as well as any disputes. It was also charged with extending the range of issues subject to collective bargaining, and the spread of bargaining. The latter would involve workers being unionized and unions being recognized by employers in hitherto non-union workplaces. There was a legal procedure to help achieve this, the *Grunwick* case being the best-known example of its use (see chapter 22). The relevant law was repealed in 1980 after having only a minimal impact. ACAS can still help in recognition

disputes, but will be able to get involved properly only if the employer is willing, there being no legal supports for recognition (see chapter 22).

5 The term 'trade dispute' in relation to the functions of ACAS is defined in TULR(C)A, s 218 and is wider than the definition in s 244 which governs the question of trades union immunity.

6 Sections 210–214. The power to issue codes of practice is conferred by s 199.

7 ACAS's enquiry function is contained in TULR(C)A, s 214. The Secretary of State has separate powers to establish courts of inquiry under s 215.

8 TULR(C)A, s 203. Provision exists for the revision of codes issued by ACAS and the Secretary of State, subject to Parliamentary approval using the negative procedure (ss 201 and 205). Codes can be revoked by the Secretary of State by statutory instrument subject to Parliamentary approval using the positive procedure (ss 202 and 206). In the case of an ACAS code, this must be at the request of ACAS.

9 The procedure of industrial tribunals is dealt with in chapter 4 and a review of the system considered in chapter 26. Further background material can be found in *Resolving Employment Rights Disputes: Options for Reform* (Cm 2707, HMSO, 1994); and in *Trades Unions and Employers' Associations*, report of a Royal Commission 1965–8 (chairman, Lord Donovan) (Cmnd 3623, HMSO, 1968), chapter X.

10 Only two training boards remain and appeals are now made under s 12 of the Industrial Training Act 1982. Classification could be important since individual training boards imposed levies at different rates. Thus being in industry A could result in a higher or lower levy than being in industry B.

11 Another public administration jurisdiction was the appeal against Selective Employment Tax. On administrative tribunals generally, see *Administrative Tribunals*, report of a Committee (chairman, Lord Franks) (Cmnd 218, HMSO, 1957).

12 The original unfair dismissal jurisdiction was contained in ss 22 and 106 of the Industrial Relations Act 1971 and was operative from 28 February 1972.

13 ITA 1996, s 7. Currently the Industrial Tribunals (Constitution and Rules of Procedure) Regulations (SI 1993/2687). See chapter 4. There are separate regulations for Scotland (SI 1993/2688).

14 ITA 1996, s 4 and the IT Regulations, reg 5. See also ER(DR)A ss 3–4.

15 ERA, ss 128–132; TULR(C)A, ss 161, 165 or 166.

16 ERA, s 183.

17 ERA, s 13.

18 Under the jurisdiction conferred by ITA 1996, s 3 and the Industrial Tribunals Extension of Jurisdiction (England and Wales) Order (SI 1994/1623). There is a separate order for Scotland (SI 1994/1624).

19 ERA, s 111.

20 RRA, s 54.

21 EqPA, s 2(1).

22 SDA, s 63.

23 SI 1995/3183.

24 ERA, s 164.

25 ERA, s 13.

26 ERA, Part IV.

27 SI 1994/1623 for England and Wales.

28 EAT Rules (SI 1993/2854). There are also Practice Directions covering appeal procedure, transcripts and estimates of length of hearing.

29 EPA, s 10 and sched 1. Its continued existence is by virtue of TULR(C)A, s 259(1). Details of the CAC are to be found in ss 259–265.

30 Formerly, the CAC's role included making awards where employers refused to recognize trades unions following an ACAS recommendation under the statutory procedure. See note 4 above. The government has announced that it will re-introduce a statutory right of union recognition.

31 EPA, s 7. The CO continues in existence by virtue of TULR(C)A, s 254(1).

32 TURERA, 1993, s 7.

33 TULR(C)A, s 112.

34 TULR(C)A, s 110(4).

35 TULR(C)A, ss 235 B and 235C (inserted by TURERA, s 22).

36 In fact, one person has been appointed to both posts. It is likely that both these offices will be absolved by the present government and their functions integrated with those and the CO.

37 Agricultural Wages Act 1948 and Agricultural Wages (Scotland) Act 1949.

F O U R

Industrial Tribunal Procedure

The aim of this chapter is to describe the procedure involved in pursuing or defending a case at an industrial tribunal. To provide as complete a picture as possible, elements which are not part of the tribunal procedure itself are included, notably, written reasons for dismissal, the questions procedure in sex, race and disability discrimination cases and ACAS conciliation. Since most industrial tribunal cases are complaints of unfair dismissal, this chapter is written as if an unfair dismissal case was being dealt with. Special provisions apply to certain other types of case (such as claims for equal pay for work of equal value and appeals against health and safety notices). The Employment Rights (Dispute Resolution) Act 1998 provides for industrial tribunals to be renamed 'employment tribunals' and for other changes. These changes are discussed in chapter 26.

THE INDUSTRIAL TRIBUNALS

Industrial tribunals are statutory judicial bodies. They were first established under the Industrial Training Act of 1964 to hear employers' appeals against levies made by the various training boards that were set up under the Act. Since then the tribunals have been given the task of deciding many other types of dispute, typically those between individual employees and their employers. Unfair dismissal complaints account for the majority of the tribunals' cases. In addition tribunals deal with disputes about whether an employee is receiving the correct amount of redundancy pay to which they are entitled, claims for equal pay between men and women, time off for union representatives, allegations of race, sex and disability discrimination in the employment field, certain contractual matters and other issues put within their jurisdiction by various statutes (see chapter 3 for a full list of jurisdictions).

Tribunals currently operate as a result of the Industrial Tribunals Act 1996, with most of the procedural detail set out in regulations issued under that Act.[1] Apart from where the chairman sits alone (see pages 36–7) tribunals generally comprise three people – one from a panel nominated by unions, one from a panel nominated by employers and a legally qualified chairman. The chairman is appointed by the Lord Chancellor (Lord President in Scotland) while the two other members are appointed by the Secretary of State for Education and Employment. Many of the chairmen and all of the lay members are part-time. The purpose of having a combination of lay members and a lawyer is to get a blend of legal knowledge and industrial experience. A majority decision suffices, but in all except a handful of cases the decision is unanimous.

From the parties' point of view, industrial tribunals have a number of advantages over the mainstream courts. Firstly, they are cheaper, since legal representation is not compulsory and so legal fees can be avoided. Furthermore, costs are not normally awarded against a losing party. Secondly, tribunals are quicker than the courts. About three months is the average time between application and hearing, and most hearings last only a day. Thirdly, the tribunals are easier to use – the paperwork involved in pursuing or defending a case is relatively straightforward. Finally, although legal procedure is used, and although there is a degree of formality, the setting and proceedings are less formal than would be experienced in a courtroom. There are, for instance, no wigs or gowns, the chairman is not addressed as 'm'lud' or 'your honour' and the parties are not hidden behind bundles tied up with pink ribbons. Nevertheless the parties may find tribunals slow and legalistic when compared with procedures in their own organizations. Moreover, unlike arbitration by ACAS, industrial tribunals' terms of reference do not extend to considering the wider industrial relations aspects of the case.

PROCEDURE PRIOR TO THE MAIN HEARING

Actions prior to a tribunal application

Written statement of reasons for dismissal[2]
An employee has a legal right to request and obtain from their former employer a written statement of the reasons for their dismissal. This right is given to those who had two years' or more continuous employment with their employer prior to termination (but see chapters 5 and 6 on the question of whether this qualifying period is unlawful indirect sex

discrimination). The claim for compensation for refusal to give written reasons is usually put on the same application form as the unfair dismissal claim itself, and the claim must be at the Regional Office of Industrial Tribunals within three months. The respondent employer has 21 days in which to reply to a request for written reasons. Where there is an unreasonable failure to comply, or where the reasons given were stated inadequately or were untrue, a tribunal may make a declaration as to the reasons for the dismissal but must make a penalty award of two weeks' pay. The week's pay is gross, and since the right to have written reasons is separate from the right not to be unfairly dismissed there is no percentage deduction for any contributory fault. The award will usually be made at the end of the hearing of the substantive unfair dismissal claim. If at the time of dismissal the employee is pregnant or the dismissal is after childbirth and terminates her maternity leave period, there is no qualifying period of employment and the requirement to provide written reasons is mandatory, ie the employee does not need to make a request (on maternity leave, see chapter 13).

The questions procedure in race, sex and disability discrimination cases[3]

These procedures are intended to help a person who thinks that they have been discriminated against obtain information in order to:

- decide whether or not to bring legal proceedings; and
- if legal proceedings are brought, to present the complaint in the most effective way.

There are prescribed forms for this purpose, comprising a questionnaire to be completed by the complainant and a form on which the respondent can reply.

The respondent cannot be compelled to reply but a failure to reply within a reasonable period, or an evasive or equivocal reply, allows the tribunal to draw any inference as is just and equitable, including an inference that the person questioned has discriminated unlawfully. An employer would need to have a reasonable excuse if they are to avoid a tribunal drawing adverse inferences.

If the questionnaire is to be admissible in tribunal proceedings it must be served either before an industrial tribunal application is made or within 21 days of one being received by the industrial tribunal. The time limit may be extended by leave of the industrial tribunal.

The questions procedure applies only to race, sex and disability discrimination cases. However, the use of interrogatories – formal questions put by one party to the other before the hearing, in order to obtain evidence – is now provided for in tribunal procedure (see below).[4]

Application to an industrial tribunal and employer defence

The tribunal process is triggered by an individual who thinks they have been unfairly dismissed completing an originating application form – known as an IT1 – and sending it to the Regional Office of the Industrial Tribunals (ROIT) within three months of the effective date of termination. An application may arrive later than this if it was not reasonably practicable to apply within three months but in practice tribunals enforce the three-month time limit quite strictly. For example, an application is unlikely to be accepted if the reason for its lateness was a mistake by a professional advisor such as a solicitor or trades union official (although this is not to be elevated to a rule of law).

Where a tribunal decides that it was not reasonably practicable to present an application in time, it must then satisfy itself that the application was presented within a further period of time which was reasonable. The remedy for an applicant whose application was not admitted because of a failure on the part of their professional advisor would lie against that professional advisor. In race, sex and disability discrimination cases a late application is to be accepted if it is 'just and equitable' to accept it rather than if it was not reasonably practicable to make the application in time (see chapters 6 and 7).

The time is measured from the effective date of termination (see chapter 16) and is expressed in calendar months. Thus, if termination is on 30 November, the three months for unfair dismissal claims expires on 28 February, except in leap years when it would expire on 29 February. The date on which an application is received is the date on which it is delivered to the ROIT, even if this is not a working day. Absence or illness may mean that it is not reasonably practicable to submit an application within three months, but ignorance of the law will not of itself be a sufficient justification. More than one application may be made on a single IT1 form, for instance a complaint of unfair dismissal, a complaint of sex discrimination and so on.

Regardless of whether a request for a written statement of reasons has been made, the respondent employer will need to reply to the originating application. A copy of the IT1 will be sent to them, and a form IT3 on which the reply can be made. The IT3 – known as the notice of appearance – should be returned to the specified regional office within 21 days (previously 14 days[5]). This act secures for the respondent the right to take part in any hearing which might ensue. A copy of the IT3 is sent to the applicant. The regional office of the industrial tribunals then sets in train the arrangements for a hearing. A brief questionnaire is sent to the parties asking about representation at the hearing, and about the number of witnesses they will be bringing. Finally, the regional office will fix a date for a hearing and notify the parties.

The above description constitutes the minimum of what might happen. There may be more. First, the ROIT will notify an applicant if it looks as though the case is not within the tribunals' jurisdiction, and indicate that the case may be struck out unless the applicant confirms in writing that they are determined to go ahead. Secondly, the regional chairman may decide that a full hearing of the case should not go ahead until there has been a pre-hearing review. Thirdly, there may be a preliminary matter to determine. An application may be struck out if it is not pursued and the tribunals can strike out applications and notices of appearance if they are 'scandalous, frivolous or vexatious' or if the proceedings are conducted in a scandalous, frivolous or vexatious manner. Before striking out, a tribunal must give the relevant party an opportunity to show why their case should not be struck out.[6]

ACAS conciliation

The stages of procedure up to the full hearing are summarized in Figure 4.1. It can be seen that there is an important role for ACAS. Copies of the papers – the IT1 and the IT3 – are sent to the regional office of ACAS. The purpose of this is to allow ACAS to perform its statutory duty, which is to conciliate. The duty is 'to endeavour to promote a settlement of the complaint without its being determined by an industrial tribunal'.[7] The duty to conciliate applies if ACAS is requested to do so by the parties, or, in the absence of such a request, if the conciliation officer considers that there is 'a reasonable prospect of success'. Where it is sought by the applicant, and where it is 'practicable', the conciliation officer must try to promote re-employment rather than a monetary settlement. ACAS defines conciliation in the way that the process is commonly understood. The essential features are that the outcome (that is, the agreement) is a joint decision of the two parties, the employee and the employer, and that the conciliator does not impose or even recommend what the particular outcome should be. Nearly all the settlements achieved are in the form of monetary compensation rather than re-employment. Because of this it is useful to have some idea of what a tribunal might award (see pages 70–71 and 330–32). It may be more difficult for the respondent to do this calculation, since only the applicant will know the detail of their own losses, and in any case future loss is something of an imponderable. Nevertheless, a rough estimate will inform the bargaining process. If a hearing looks likely, any party unfamiliar with tribunals should seek advice on how to proceed.

The tribunal may promulgate the agreed decision (that is, publish it and send it to the parties). Any information conveyed to a conciliation officer is privileged – it cannot be admitted in evidence at the hearing without the permission of the person who communicated it. Moreover, it should be noted that, once ACAS has conciliated and an agreed settlement has been

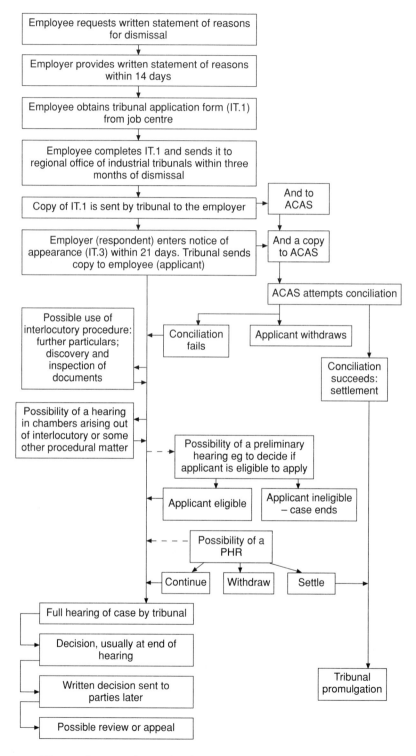

Figure 4.1   Industrial tribunal case: stages of procedure

reached, the right to pursue the case through to a tribunal hearing is lost. The same is not true if the settlement is agreed without ACAS. The ACAS role can continue until all questions of liability and remedy have been decided *(Courage Take Home Trade Ltd v Keys)*. This means that ACAS could be used to conciliate over compensation if the tribunal decides unfair dismissal but leaves it to the parties to settle compensation.

A settlement (as distinct from a tribunal order of compensation) is not subject to the recoupment provisions,[8] so the applicant does not have to repay any social security benefits that they have received. Thus, where social security benefits amount to a substantial sum, the potential for agreeing a settlement is increased. A settlement can be made by withdrawal of the application on the agreed terms or by the tribunal recording the agreement and adjourning the case indefinitely. Reporting the settlement to ACAS for them to record is probably the safest way of guaranteeing no further proceedings on the one hand and the honouring of the terms of the agreement on the other. ACAS may be reluctant to record the settlement (on form COT3) unless they have been involved in settling the case.

An application to a tribunal will be precluded after a settlement only if the conciliation officer has 'taken action' or there has been a 'compromise agreement'.[9] An important question, therefore, is what is meant by the conciliation officer taking action. The facts in *Moore v Duport Furniture Products Ltd* were as follows. The conciliation officer merely reduced to writing, for the signature of the parties, a financial settlement that they had already agreed. The questions at issue were:

- had the conciliation officer fulfilled his statutory duty (now under ITA 1996, s 18) to promote the re-employment of the applicant, or, failing that, to promote a financial settlement?
- should the conciliation officer have addressed the question of the fairness or otherwise of the settlement?
- had the conciliation officer 'taken action' (within the meaning of ERA, s 203(2)(e)) with the effect that the applicant was now prevented from pursuing his case at a tribunal after the settlement?

The House of Lords held that the conciliation officer had fulfilled his duties, that he was not required to address the question of fairness and that he had 'taken action' under what is now s 203 of ERA so no application could be pursued at an industrial tribunal.

Compromise agreements

The rule laid down in ERA, s 203 is that any agreement to exclude or limit the operation of ERA or to prevent a person from pursuing a case to an industrial tribunal is void. As noted, one exception to this rule is where a conciliation officer has 'taken action'. There are others, including contract cases falling within the ITA 1993, s 3 jurisdiction. Another recent development is the exception for compromise agreements. For the exception to apply, the conditions laid down in ERA, s 203(3) must be met:

- the agreement must be in writing and relate to the particular complaint;
- the employee must have received independent legal advice from a qualified lawyer as to the terms and effect of the proposed agreement, especially the effect on his right to apply to an industrial tribunal;
- the advisor must have current insurance covering the risks attached to providing the advice;
- the advisor must be identified; and
- the agreement must state that conditions laid down in the Act are satisfied.

ER(DR)A 1998 substitutes 'independent adviser' for 'qualified lawyer', 'advice' for 'legal advice', and clarifies the insurance position (ss 9–10).

Interlocutory procedure

If there is no pre-hearing review and there is no preliminary matter to decide, the parties will not meet the tribunal until the full hearing. They might, however, meet the chairman if there are any procedural difficulties. Such difficulties might arise if the parties choose to implement the interlocutory procedure. This procedure allows the parties to deal with each other, requesting and providing information, and exchanging documents. Ultimately there may be an agreed bundle of documents. In the event of a refusal to cooperate by one of the parties, a tribunal order may be sought by the other. The tribunal regulations allow orders for discovery and inspection of documents, and for further particulars of the grounds of the case. Discovery means finding out what documents the other side is relying upon, while inspection is the right to see one or more of those documents. If the other party refuses, it will be necessary to make out a case to the regional chairman, and a hearing in chambers (the chairman's room) will be held at which his or her decision will be given. The chairman may order discovery and/or disclosure and it is particularly likely that disclosure will be ordered in sex and race discrimination cases (see chapter 6). The other members of the tribunal are not present. An industrial tribunal may, of its own volition, ask for further particulars. A failure to supply them may result in the IT1 or the IT3 being struck out. Otherwise, it is up to the parties to seek further particulars. It will be justifiable only if the other side's grounds are rather sketchy.

The tribunal may also compel witnesses to attend. An application for witness orders is made to the chairman. If the orders are granted the tribunal will serve them on the witnesses. Failure to abide by tribunal orders is a criminal offence punishable by fine.

The tribunal rules now provide for interrogatories.[10] On the application of a party or of its own motion, a tribunal may require a party to give a written answer to a question if it considers that the answer may help to clarify any issue in the case or may assist the progress of the proceedings. A time limit may be set. Copies of the question(s) and the answer(s) are sent to the other party or parties.

Pre-hearing review

Pre-hearing reviews are a means to prevent meritless cases being pursued. Either party can request a pre-hearing review, or it can be ordered by the chairman of his own volition. The party whose case appears weak is subject to a brief review, lasting perhaps 30 minutes. ITA provides for pre-hearing reviews to be heard by a full tribunal or a chairman sitting alone, but in practice the hearings are usually heard by chairmen sitting alone.[11] The hearing is held in private and consists of argument but no evidence. The rules indicate that the tribunal must consider the IT1, the IT3, any representations in writing and any oral arguments.[12]

The outcome of a pre-hearing review will be either a requirement for a deposit to be paid by the relevant party if they wish to continue, or no such requirement. The requirement will apply if the tribunal considers that the party's case has 'no reasonable prospect of success'. The maximum deposit is £150. The deposit will be offset against any costs awarded against the party or otherwise repaid.

Where a party continues after a pre-hearing review and irrespective of whether a deposit has been required, the tribunal hearing the case will be different from the one hearing the pre-hearing review. Moreover, it will not know of the fact or outcome of the pre-hearing review until after it has determined the case.

Preliminary hearings

Irrespective of whether or not the case involves a pre-hearing review there may be a preliminary matter to settle before a full hearing of the case is considered. Such matters usually concern eligibility:

- is the applicant an employee?
- was the IT1 received in time?
- does the employee have the requisite length of qualifying employment?
- is the applicant under normal retiring age?

A preliminary hearing, therefore, is held to establish whether or not the case can proceed. If the case can proceed, the substantive hearing will then take place, although perhaps on a different date.

PREPARING THE CASE

This section is aimed particularly, but not exclusively, at non-lawyers who may find themselves presenting or defending a case at an industrial tribunal.

General points

Anyone handling an unfair dismissal case at a tribunal will need the following:

- a knowledge of the statutory provisions on unfair dismissal;
- an understanding of the concept of the contract of employment and knowledge of the contract of employment of the applicant;
- a familiarity with industrial tribunal procedure; and
- an awareness of some of the principles established through case law.

Higher courts lay down the rules of approach for the local tribunals through the system of judicial precedent. That may seem a far cry from the original idea of tribunals as a place where the 'ordinary' person could handle their own case. Indeed it is. However, many non-lawyers who present or defend cases at tribunals are not 'ordinary' persons – for example they may be personnel managers, union officials or CAB workers – so they need not be put off by the above requirements. For one thing a degree of familiarity with some or all of the requirements is quite likely, either through day-to-day experience or through training. Moreover, gaps can be quickly filled in as the case begins to loom, either by expert advice or by do-it-yourself means. For example, case law is the subject of a detailed indexing system that directs a person to the issues relevant to the particular type of case, and there are also summaries of established case law on all the important issues.

First, however, the non-lawyer has to make the difficult transition from the world of the workplace to the world of the law. Managers and union officials will not be accustomed to a third party, that is, the tribunal, controlling the proceedings and dictating what can be said and when. More importantly perhaps, they will find it difficult to adjust to the fact that evidence (that is, proof) rather than argument or bargaining power is going to decide the case. In preparation, therefore, a party must ask itself:

- have I got a case? (not on humanitarian or equitable grounds, but in terms of the law).
- have I got the evidence, or can I get the evidence, to establish that case? As noted earlier, the test of proof is the balance of probabilities, not 'beyond all reasonable doubt' as in the criminal courts.

The answer needs to be yes in both cases.

A point to be checked even earlier, however, is whether the case falls within the jurisdiction of the industrial tribunals: is the issue in dispute one which industrial tribunals are empowered to decide? If it is, the next thing to check is whether there is any bar to the applicant pursuing their case, for example, insufficient continuous employment. The onus of proof on preliminary matters of eligibility will lie with the applicant. A case may not proceed, therefore, simply because the applicant cannot prove their eligibility.

It would be unwise for a respondent employer to depend exclusively on the failure of the applicant to establish their eligibility. Thus in a complaint of unfair dismissal an employer should have arguments and evidence to show that any dismissal was fair, even if the preliminary question of eligibility has to be determined first. Indeed, as a generality, it is permissible (and often desirable) to plead in the alternative. Essentially, this means having your cake and eating it. For example: 'Our case is that the applicant was not dismissed – rather, he walked out, thus resigning. However, if it was a dismissal, it was fair because of the applicant's misconduct.'

In pursuing cases, applicants may need to consider the possibility of making more than one application. For example, an alleged dismissal on grounds of sex, race or disability may form the basis of an unfair dismissal application and an application under the respective discrimination Act. The various issues need to be weighed.

Representation

This is the next issue to be decided. The parties may represent themselves or be represented by a person of their own choosing.[13] Because legal representation is not compulsory, legal fees can be avoided. Legal advice is available to applicants under the Legal Aid and Advice Scheme, but Legal Aid (including representation) is not. In a large company there may be clear procedures with the case being handled by in-house solicitors. It may be that outside solicitors are used, or that one of the personnel staff will handle the case. In small firms there will not be an in-house specialist, so it will fall to a proprietor or general manager, unless an outside solicitor is preferred. The applicant has a ready-made advocate if he is a union member because many full-time officers, and some lay officials, are experienced in handling tribunal cases. The non-unionist will perhaps use a law centre, or the local Citizens' Advice Bureau, or may even hire a private solicitor. Free legal advice and assistance in completing the IT1 may be available depending on income, but Legal Aid is not, so representation at the hearing is not covered (but see chapter 6 in relation to race and sex discrimination cases).

The preparation of a case is extremely time-consuming. The advantage of a solicitor is the saving in preparation time and, if that solicitor is familiar with employment law and tribunals, the availability of an experienced representative. On the other hand, the cost is high, especially when compared with the likely level of compensation that the respondent might have to pay. If a representative is named on the IT1 or the IT3 all the documents (including the notice of hearing) will go to the representative, and not to anyone else (that is, not to the applicant or respondent).

Evidence

The filling in of the forms – the IT1 and the IT3 – requires some care, since these are in effect part of the evidence. An employee must set out the grounds of his complaint and an employer has to set out the grounds of his defence. Too vague an answer here might attract a request for further particulars from the other party under the interlocutory procedure mentioned earlier. On the other hand, too much information may help the other party prepare their case. Completion of the forms and the writing of any letters should be handled by the representative, who should also insist on having the ACAS conciliator deal with him rather than with the applicant or respondent in person.

It falls on the representative to consider in detail what evidence can be marshalled. The evidence will comprise witnesses on oath or affirmation, and documents. A witness can read a prepared statement on oath. The written signed statement of a witness not present will count for less because they are not under oath, and cannot be cross-examined. Representatives need to ask themselves:

- what facts do I need to establish?
- which documents and witnesses do I need to establish them?

The representative should be clear as to the role of each witness, including the applicant or respondent, or document. What am I expecting this person to prove? What does this document prove? The fact needs to be considered that when witnesses are under cross-examination they are at the mercy of the other party. Any witness who might not stand up to hostile treatment may be better omitted. So too might any witness who will clearly not come across as credible. The credibility of witnesses is important, especially where there is a conflict of evidence.

Witnesses will need to be interviewed by the representative in advance so that the main lines of their evidence can be agreed. The choice of witnesses and the sequence in which they appear is a matter for each party. However, because reasonableness has to be decided with reference to what was known (or should have been known) at the time of dismissal, the person who carried out the dismissal will be a key witness, and the tribunal may prefer to hear his or her evidence at an early stage. Witness orders may be obtained as described earlier (see page 56). Often they are used by applicants if their witnesses are still in the employment of the respondent. Witnesses may stay throughout the proceedings in England and Wales (but not in Scotland), although a party may ask for a witness to be excluded until they give their evidence.

The best type of evidence is that provided directly by a witness under oath or affirmation. Where documentary evidence is provided, the original (as well as copies) should be available and the author of the document should be there to confirm its legitimacy and his or her authorship. A set of documents should be provided for the other party, for the witness stand and for the tribunal (that is, five copies in total). The best practice is to exchange sets of documents beforehand, or better still to agree a common, properly paginated bundle. In most cases, however, the paperwork is minimal. Where documents are handwritten (for instance, the notes of a meeting) a typed transcript should be provided in addition to the original.

Video and audio tapes are not automatically inadmissible. This is a matter of discretion for the tribunal. There would have to be a transcript for an audio tape and the tribunal might need expert evidence to show that the tape had not been interfered with. Any expert witness fees would have to be paid by the party engaging the witness. The other party would need to hear any tape and have the transcript prior to the hearing.

The flowchart (Figure 4.2) poses the questions that representatives need to ask themselves. It can be seen that a constructive dismissal follows a different route from the normal two-stage process. Here the test is breach of contract. A constructive dismissal is not necessarily unfair, however. There may have been compelling reasons (such as the state of the business) for the employer being in breach. Thus a refusal to be flexible and carry out tasks not within the contract may nevertheless constitute a fair dismissal if the business has its back to the wall.

Sources of information

As already noted, a representative will need knowledge of the law of unfair dismissal, an understanding of the contract of employment and some familiarity with tribunal procedure and the principles established by case law. As far as the legislation is concerned it is probably unnecessary to go to the primary source, the Employment Rights Act 1996, and busy practitioners may find secondary sources both easier and quicker to use. Employment law books have a chapter or more on unfair dismissal. For those who want the statute itself it can be purchased through HMSO or found as chapter 18 in a bound volume of 1996 Acts of Parliament in a central library. It should be noted, however, that the copy purchased, or

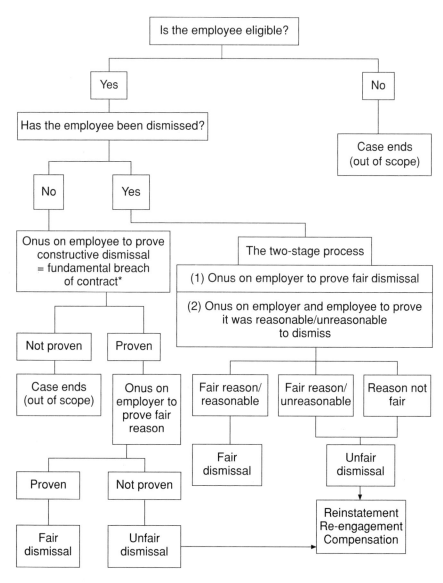

* *Western Excavating (ECC) Ltd v Sharp*

Figure 4.2   Unfair dismissal cases before industrial tribunals

inspected in the library, will be the statute as originally enacted, not including any subsequent amendments. Hence it will be necessary to look at an up-to-date secondary source, or at one of the employment law encyclopaedias containing updated statutes.

The main sources which will help the practitioner understand the concept of the contract of employment will be secondary. Employment law books deal at length with the subject. In preparing the case, however, it is also necessary to look at the primary materials. Representatives should always ask themselves, and try to answer, the question of what were the terms of the dismissed employee's contract. This is especially important if the dismissal was in any way to do with a refusal to obey instructions or accept changes. The following are some of the primary materials which may throw light on the terms of contract:

- any advertisement for the post;
- any particulars sent to would-be applicants on enquiry;
- any letters, for example, appointment and acceptance;
- any conditions laid down on an application form;
- any written particulars issued under section 1 of ERA 1996;
- any works or office rules: these may be issued in the form of handbooks, memos or even notices attached to walls, boards or clocks;
- any job description; and
- collective agreements.

It is important to consider whether the operation of any rules has been overtaken by custom and practice, and what evidence can be adduced on this point.

The busy practitioner might find it difficult to take time off in order to sit in at a tribunal hearing. If they can do this, however, they will be rewarded, since they will get an idea of the procedure, and an indication of the atmosphere. Tribunals, like courts, are open to members of the public, and prior arrangement with the tribunal office is not necessary. In practice, however, a phone call to check that there is a hearing scheduled for that day is sensible. The tribunals are listed under 'Tribunals, Industrial' in local telephone directories. The booklet ITL1 is compulsory if not compulsive reading. Applicants should be given one when they are handed their IT1, and respondents should receive one through the post with their IT3. This is as much detail as is necessary, although employment law books are also a source, and in addition there are books specifically about tribunal procedure. The primary source of procedure is the Industrial Tribunal Regulations, a statutory instrument issued in 1993.[14] This can be purchased from HMSO, or found in the bound volumes of statutory instruments in central libraries.

For case law it is probably best to use either the Industrial Relations Services (IRS) *Legal Bulletin* or the Incomes Data Services (IDS) *Brief.* These are fully indexed by name of case and subject and are available on a subscription basis or in central libraries. Both are issued twice a month. In addition to giving brief reports on major cases, they also cover any changes in the statutes, and provide useful summaries of case law on key issues. Where necessary the fuller law reports may be used. A principal series is the *Industrial Relations Law Reports* (IRLR) which is monthly, and can be subscribed to or found in central libraries. Pages are numbered continuously throughout each calendar year, and references are written as [1986] IRLR 148 to mean page 148 of the 1986 reports. Other series include the *Industrial Cases Reports* (ICR) and the more general *Appeal Cases* (AC), *Weekly Law Reports* (WLR) and *All England Reports* (All ER).

PRESENTING THE CASE

The rules state that a tribunal shall sit in public but with exceptions on grounds of national security, confidential information, commercial damage other than through collective bargaining and where disclosure of information would be a breach of legislation.[15] A member of the Council on Tribunals is entitled to attend any hearing held in private. Where the hearing is in public, members of the public may observe and listen to the proceedings without any requirement to seek permission or give notice of attending.

Tribunals 'so far as it appears to be appropriate'[16] must seek to avoid formality and are not bound by normal rules of evidence. Moreover, subject to the rules, 'a tribunal may regulate its own procedure'.[17] However, note needs to be taken of actual practice.

In a case where sexual misconduct is alleged, the tribunal may issue a restricted reporting order under rule 14.[18] The power of the tribunal does not extend to excluding the press and such an order may be subject to judicial review. A similar provision exists in disability cases if personal information is being disclosed.[19]

Procedure

In practice, legal procedure is used. This means that the representative will proceed by examining witnesses (asking them questions). Each witness is examined, first, by the representative of the party for whom they, the witness, are appearing. Then they will be examined by the representative of the 'other side' (that is, cross-examined). At this stage the tribunal may well ask some questions. Finally, the witness may be re-examined by the representative of their own side. Parties have the right to give evidence, call and question witnesses and address the tribunal.[20] Tribunals have some discretion about procedure, but the typical hearing tends to follow a well-established pattern:

(1) Brief introduction by chairman. This will state the parties, and any representatives, the burden of proof and the relevant legislation.
(2) The respondent's case (if dismissal is not disputed – if it is, the applicant's case will come first):
    (a) short opening statement – this is not a legal right following changes in the regulations in 1980 and may be discouraged; and
    (b) the calling of witnesses: each witness undergoes:
        (i) examination-in-chief – from the respondent's representative;
        (ii) cross-examination – from the applicant's representative; and
        (iii) re-examination – by the respondent's representative.
(3) The applicant's case (as above); the applicant is likely to be a witness.
(4) Closing addresses from:
    (a) the applicant's representative; and
    (b) the respondent's representative.
(5) Tribunal adjourns.
(6) Tribunal announces its decision.

After cross-examination the tribunal may ask questions, although technically the responsibility for bringing out the facts and arguments lies with the parties. The purpose of re-examination is to enable the representative to deal with points arising out of the cross-examination. It is not an opportunity to introduce new evidence or arguments. Such attempts will either be blocked by the chairman or result in the other side being given another chance of cross-examination. More generally it will be difficult to spring new arguments at the tribunal hearing without someone raising the question of why they were not put in the original claim or original defence. Any significant documents sprung on the other party at the hearing are likely to cause objections. If there is a resulting adjournment costs could be awarded against the person producing the document. Tribunals will expect documents to have been exchanged beforehand, and to be put in as evidence with sufficient copies.

The essential features of the law of unfair dismissal are described in chapter 16 and the two-stage process emphasized. Here it must be noted, however, that the hearing does not follow this pattern. Instead, each witness is examined on all matters to bring out the evidence in its entirety. The only exception is likely to be the question of remedies. A chairman should indicate at the start of the hearing whether he wants to hear evidence on remedies, or whether this will be heard separately, and only if the finding is one of unfair dismissal *(Smith v Clarke)*. Evidence on any contributory fault is taken with the mainstream of evidence. Parties should take their evidence on remedies (for example, the applicant's attempts at mitigating loss, local unemployment, pay in any new employment or the respondent's ability to reinstate) to the first tribunal hearing in case the issue is dealt with at that hearing.

As already noted, certain types of case are governed by different procedures. Equal value claims, for example, are subject to a procedure which may involve a job evaluation expert preparing a report for the tribunal. Appeals by employers against improvement and prohibition notices (under the HSWA), against non-discrimination notices issued by the EOC and the CRE, and against training levies also have different procedures. In health and safety notice appeals the employer is the appellant and the inspector the respondent. In appeals against discrimination notices, the CRE or the EOC is the respondent.

Marshalling the evidence and arguments

Functioning effectively at the hearing requires the representative to be highly organized. A useful device is to have paper with the pages divided in half vertically. Questions for each witness can be entered in the left half, and answers in the right half. For one's own witnesses most of the questions can be written in advance, as can some of the questions for the opposition, especially if it is known in advance who their witnesses will be. The structure of the questions and answers should follow the tribunal's procedure for each witness, namely evidence-in-chief, cross-examination, tribunal questions and re-examination.

Giving evidence includes the right to present and read a signed, written statement. Written evidence (documents) in addition to any witness statement may also be admitted. Evidence submitted by the respondent is marked R1, R2, R3 and so on, and by the applicant A1, A2, A3 and so on. Such documents should include any that set out the terms and conditions of employment, details of pay and other benefits, including pension, in the job from which the applicant was dismissed, and any subsequent job(s), and evidence of social security benefits paid during any unemployment following dismissal. The applicant will need to give evidence of job search and should take copies of job applications and replies. Details of the cost of searching for a new job, or moving to a new job will be needed. When the respondent's last witness has been examined the applicant's case is put, and follows the same procedure. Finally, the parties have a right to sum up. The respondent, having the onus of proof, goes last. Summing up means succinctly putting the essential legal arguments and an evaluation of the evidence upon which those arguments rest, as well as trying to play down the significance of the other party's arguments and evidence. The tribunal will appreciate any attempts at clarifying the issues and evidence on the key points of the case. Finally, the tribunal should be asked to find in favour of the party summing up.

It is common for parties who are represented to cite authorities, that is, cases judged by the higher courts which decide principles and approaches as well as the facts of the particular case. The purpose is to persuade a tribunal that higher authorities have decided on an approach which you consider will help your case. Tribunals are a little defensive about criticism that they are unduly legalistic. Some chairmen may positively discourage the citing of cases as the EAT President did in *Anandarajah v Lord Chancellor's Department*, and as the Court of Appeal did in *British Gas Corporation v Woodroffe*. None will encourage it unless it is genuinely helpful and all will get irritated by a long closing statement punctuated by numerous case references. Against this background, having photocopies of the reports of cases, in order to save the tribunal the trouble of looking them up in the law reports, may be politic.

It should be noted that a failure to challenge the evidence of an opposition witness during cross-examination will mean that that evidence is established. Thus, a good representative will ensure that all points of disagreement are brought out during cross-examination. Moreover, all allegations need to be put in cross-examination. This may occasionally mean that the representative's own witness can 'adopt' the previous cross-examination if it covers all of the evidence which has to be put. This reduces the time spent on evidence-in-chief which would otherwise be highly repetitive. Another time-saving device is for a witness to be 'tendered', that is, offered up for cross-examination without giving evidence-in-chief. This might be done where the evidence of the witness would merely be repeating that already put by someone else. The right to re-examine remains. One witness may also simply confirm the testimony of another.

Costs[21]

The normal legal rule under which the loser pays the winner's costs does not apply. Costs will be awarded against a party only if that party acts frivolously (pursues a hopeless case), vexatiously (pursues a case in order to inconvenience the other party), abusively, disruptively or behaves unreasonably in some other way. The last-mentioned may include unreasonably causing postponements or adjournments. It is usual for tribunals themselves to determine the amounts of any award of costs rather than referring the matter to the county court for taxation, which would be slower and less responsive to the ability to pay of the party. Appeals can be made against the award of costs but an appeal solely against the amount would be unlikely to succeed.

AFTER THE HEARING

The decision

The tribunal will adjourn to make its decision. In most cases it will return to announce the decision and its reasons later the same day. Sometimes, if a lot of evidence has been given, or if there are complex legal issues, the decision might be reserved (that is, not announced). In both types of situation a written decision will be sent to the parties later. Decisions may be 'in summary form' except in discrimination cases and where the tribunal thinks full reasons are necessary to explain its decision although the parties still have a right to request full reasons.[22] Such a request can be made orally at the hearing or in writing within 21 days of the date on the tribunal's written summary decision. In the decision, the two-stage process mentioned earlier (that is fair reason, reasonableness) will be discernible. Decisions may be by majority. A public register is kept containing industrial tribunal decisions.

Reviews[23]

A tribunal may review its decision if there is a written request for a review within 14 days of the date of the tribunal's written decision, and the request is accompanied by reasons. The circumstances in which a tribunal may conduct a review are:

- if an error on the part of the tribunal staff caused a wrong decision;
- if a party did not receive notice of the hearing;
- if a person entitled to attend did not attend;
- if new, unforeseen evidence has become available; or
- if the interests of justice require it.

Where a chairman believes a review has no reasonable prospect of success they may refuse the application for review. The decision to conduct a review, however, is made by the tribunal.

Appeals

By contrast appeals are to a higher body – the Employment Appeal Tribunal – and must be on a point of law. Once an industrial tribunal has decided a fact, that fact can no longer be disputed. A point of law means in essence that the tribunal's approach to some matter was wrong. For example, it may not have followed higher authority on some point, or it came to a conclusion which was perverse in the sense that no reasonable tribunal could have arrived at it on the evidence available (see page 40).

The chairman's handwritten notes are typed and forwarded to the EAT when there is an appeal. Where an appeal is being launched on the basis that no reasonable tribunal could have come to such a decision on the evidence before it, an appellant will need to request notes of evidence. An appeal must be made within 42 days of the date of the tribunal's decision with full reasons.[24] Thus it is necessary to obtain full rather than summary reasons from the tribunal, and forward them to the EAT. Further appeals lie to the Court of Appeal (Court of Session in Scotland) and the House of Lords. Where EU law is involved, there may be an appeal to the ECJ.

Employer appeals against decisions in respect of health and safety notices lie with the 'divisional court' of the Queen's Bench Division (see pages 13–14).

Enforcement[25]

In the typical case the industrial tribunal decision marks the end of the legal process. For a few applicants, however, the process will be extended by action necessary to ensure the respondent complies with the tribunal's compensation award. The tribunals cannot enforce their own awards, so it is necessary to apply to the county court for an order, and ultimately the court will take steps to obtain settlement as with any normal debt.

Interest on industrial tribunal awards

An order which became operative on 1 April 1990 lays down rules for the payment of interest on industrial tribunal awards.[26] Interest is payable when awards remain unpaid for 42 or more days after the tribunal decision is promulgated. Costs, expenses, recouped amounts, national insurance and tax are excluded from the calculations for interest purposes. Interest also applies to the awards made by higher courts, for example, the Employment Appeal Tribunal, the Court of Appeal and so on. In the case of an appeal or review the commencement date for the calculation of interest is unaffected. The same is true where the amount of the award is varied on appeal. Where an appeal body decision is the first award made, the 42 days applies from the time of that decision. Interest is calculated on a simple and day-to-day basis at the current Bank of England base rate. The provisions applying to interest in discrimination cases are somewhat different (see page 125).

WORKED EXAMPLE OF UNFAIR DISMISSAL COMPENSATION

Details

(1) Gross weekly earnings are £225.
(2) Net weekly earnings are £150.
(3) Time between dismissal and hearing is 30 weeks of which:
    (a) the first 20 weeks unemployed, receiving £50 per week in social security benefits; and
    (b) the following 10 weeks employed with net earnings of £140 per week.
(4) The applicant's age is 55 years.
(5) Length of continuous employment prior to dismissal is six full years.
(6) There is no claim for any additional or special award.

Basic award

There is 1½ weeks' pay for each year of employment in the age category 41 years and over, so the basic award will be 6 × 1½ = 9 weeks' pay. Gross earnings, excluding non-contractual overtime, are taken, but there is a statutory maximum, currently £220. The calculation, therefore, is 9 × £220 = £1,980.

Compensatory award

This is in addition to the basic award.
(1) Net earnings were £150 per week.
(2) In the 30 weeks up to the hearing the applicant would have earned 30 × £150 = £4,500
(3) Against this has to be set net earnings of £140 per week for the 10 weeks in which the applicant was in a new job = £1,400. Any wages in lieu of notice in respect of the former job would have to be added to this *(Babcock FATA Ltd v Addison)*.
(4) Net loss of earnings = £4,500 − £1,400 = £3,100.
(5) Add to this £250 for loss of statutory rights, for example the loss of a right to claim a statutory redundancy payment in the next two years *(SH Muffett Ltd v Head)*.
(6) Add any expenses in looking for or travelling to new work (assume £50).
(7) Add any future losses that the tribunal accepts (say, 20 weeks × £10 = £200, because the applicant is £10 per week worse off in his current job).

The compensatory award is therefore £3,600.

From this, the State will recoup benefits paid for 20 weeks × £50 = £1,000, leaving a net payment of £2,600.

Format of tribunal decision on compensation

(1) Monetary award: £3,600 plus the basic award of £1,980 = £5,580.
(2) Prescribed element: this will exclude the basic award and those parts of the compensatory award not relating to the period of the prescribed element, that is, items (5) and (7) above and £100 (10 weeks × [£150 − £140]) from item (4) = £3,050.
(3) Period of the prescribed element: this is the period of 20 weeks between termination and the start of new employment that is, the period during which social security benefits were received.
(4) The excess of (1) over (2): thus £2,530 will be payable immediately while £3,050 must be withheld until the State has recouped £1,000 from it. Had the parties settled the compensatory award between themselves in the range £2,600 − £3,600 they would have both benefited at the State's expense. As it is, the respondent has to pay the full compensatory award of £3,600, while the applicant receives only £2,600.

Reduction of the compensatory award

Tribunals should reduce the compensatory award if they find that the dismissal was to any extent caused or contributed to by any action of the complainant. This may be a factor in misconduct and capability cases but will rarely apply to ill-health dismissals. The amount of the reduction should be what the tribunal considers just and equitable. An employer can rely only on information held by them at the time of the dismissal. However, there is a more general provision for the compensatory award to be what the tribunal considers just and equitable in all the circumstances, having regard to the loss sustained by the applicant as a result of the dismissal. This would allow for a reduction for conduct discovered, or even taking place, after the dismissal, as well as for a failure to mitigate losses.

Pension loss

A formula for calculating this is set out in a document produced by the industrial tribunal chairmen in consultation with the Government Actuary's Department.[27] It has no statutory force but provides useful guidance.

NOTES

1 ITA 1996, s 1 and the Industrial Tribunals (Constitution and Rules of Procedure) Regulations (SI 1993/2687).
2 ERA, s 92.
3 SDA, s 74; RRA, s 65; DDA, s 56.
4 Industrial Tribunal Regulations, Sched 1, rule 4(3).
5 The government Green Paper *Resolving Employment Rights Disputes: Options for Reform* (Cm 2707, HMSO, 1994) raised the prospect of increasing the (then) 14 day period and the change was effected in 1996.
6 IT Regulations, Sched 1, rule 13(3).
7 ITA 1996, s 18(2).
8 ITA 1996 s 16 and the Employment Protection (Recoupment of Jobseeker's Allowance and Income Support) Regulations 1996/2349.
9 ERA, s 203(3). There appears to be nothing to require a binding agreement under ACAS's auspices to be in writing.
10 IT Regulations, Sched1, reg 4(3).
11 ITA s 9.
12 IT Regulations, Sched 1, rule 7.
13 ITA s 6.
14 SI 1993/2687.
15 IT Regulations, Sched 1, rule 4.
16 Ibid, rule 9(1).
17 Ibid, rule 13(1).
18 ITA 1996, s 11.
19 ITA 1996, s 12; DDA, s 62; and the Restricted Reporting Orders in Disability Discrimination Act Cases Regulations (SI 1996/1757).
20 IT Regulations, Sched 1, rule 9(2).
21 Ibid, rule 12.
22 Ibid, rule 10(4).
23 Ibid, rule 11.
24 EAT Rules, rule 3(2).
25 ITA s 15.
26 ITA s 14 and the Industrial Tribunals (Interest) Order (SI 1990/479); but note that the Industrial Tribunals (Interest in Awards in Discrimination Cases) Regulations 1996/2803 are also relevant.
27 *Industrial Tribunals: Compensation for Loss of Pension Rights* (London, HMSO, 1990).

PART II

THE SUBSTANCE OF EMPLOYMENT LAW

F I V E

Employment Status and Continuity

The concepts of employment status and continuous employment are among the most important in the field of employment law. This is because they are often relevant in determining the scope of the legislation itself. Many statutory rights in the law of employment apply only where the worker is an employee with a specified length of continuous employment.

THE SIGNIFICANCE OF EMPLOYMENT STATUS

As noted, many employment rights (but not those under RRA, SDA and ERA, Part II (protection of wages)) are available only to employees (the definition of 'employee' is discussed below). Moreover, the legal duties of employers and workers may differ according to whether or not the worker is an employee or an independent contractor. For example, the employer will owe a stronger duty of care to an employee than to an independent contractor. Another point of significance is that an employer is vicariously liable for an employee's wrongful acts but not generally for those of independent contractors (on vicarious liability, see chapter 15). Finally there are tax and social security implications. An employee will be taxed under Schedule E (PAYE) while a self-employed person will have the more favourable regime of Schedule D. On the other hand, an employer will be required to pay national insurance contributions in respect of an employee, but not in respect of an independent contractor.

IS THE WORKER AN EMPLOYEE?

Definition of worker and employee

These terms are defined in a number of places within employment law. In the ERA, ' "employee" means an individual who has entered into or works under (or, where the employment has ceased, worked under) a contract of employment'.[1] A 'contract of employment' means a contract of service or apprenticeship.[2] By contrast, ' "worker" means an individual who works, or normally works or seeks to work (a) under a contract of employment, or (b) under any other contract whereby he undertakes to do or perform personally any work or services for another party to the contract who is not a professional client of his ...'[3]

The concept of a worker, being someone working under a contract of employment or some other contract to personally perform work, is also found in Part II of the ERA (protection of wages).[4] The key ingredient in a contract personally to perform work or services is personal service. The dominant purpose of the contract must be an obligation personally to perform work or services. The worker must be absolutely bound to perform all or some of the work (*Mirror Group Newspapers v Gunning*, a case under the SDA). Similarly, employment is defined in the SDA and RRA to include personal performance of work other than under a contract of employment.[5] However, these definitions are not universal in employment law. For example, the Transfer of Undertakings (Protection of Employment) Regulations 1981 define an employee as an individual working for another under a contract of service or apprenticeship 'or otherwise'.[6]

Nevertheless, generally, the traditional distinction has been between an employee employed under a *contract of employment* and an independent contractor employed under a *contract for services*, although it is clear from the cases that a worker does not have to fit into one or the other of these categories: he can be employed under a contract *sui generis* – a contract of its own kind (see, for example, *Ironmonger v Movefield*). Such a contract has been found in a number of cases where labour is provided by agencies. This was the position in *Ironmonger* and in *Construction Industry Training Board v Labour Force Ltd*. The pattern is shown in Figure 5.1 where A contracts with W to render services exclusively for E.

It should be stressed that there are possibilities other than those indicated in Figure 5.1. W could be employed by A, or even by E. Important considerations are whether there is mutual obligation between agency and worker and whether the agency can exercise control over the worker. If the answer is no, it is more likely that the worker will not be an employee of the agency. If he is also not an employee of the employer, he will be denied a range of statutory rights.

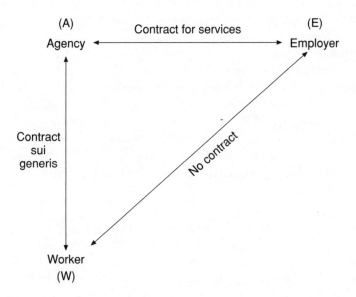

Figure 5.1   Possible contractual relationships where labour is supplied by an agency

Tests to determine employment status

The control test
The traditional test has been one of control: the test asks whether the employer can control the manner of the work. The premise upon which this is based is that an employer can control the manner in which an employee works but cannot control the method of work of an independent contractor *(Yewens v Noakes)*. This test, as a single test to be applied on its own, has become increasingly unreliable. What about professional employees who control their own work: an employer is unlikely to have the expertise to exercise control. On the other hand, small independent contractors working for a large client may find that the client dictates the method of the work.

The entrepreneurial test
This was put forward in *Market Investigations Ltd v Minister of Social Security* as the fundamental test. Was the worker in business on his own account, taking the risks and, where successful, reaping the profits? Or was he employed on a wage or salary doing his employer's business? The idea of the entrepreneurial test being 'fundamental' was later disapproved in

Nethermere (see below) – it is only one of a number of factors to be considered. In any case, there is a suspicion that the test really does little more than formulate the problem in a different way instead of helping to solve it.

The integration test

This was formulated in *Stevenson, Jordan and Harrison v MacDonald*. It asks the question: is the worker integrated into the organisation? Apart from the difficulty of defining what is meant by 'integrated', there are other problems attached to applying this test. For example, employees might be working from home and contractors working at the workplace. Important parts of the work process could be done by contractors. The complexities of modern-day work organization make this test unreliable as a single test.

The multiple test

Given the inadequacies of the 'single test' approach to establishing employment status, there began to be developed a multiple test. This, perhaps, is best seen in *Ready Mixed Concrete v Minister of Pensions and National Insurance*. The first test to be applied is personal service. Is the worker obliged personally to perform the work or service? The traditional control test is then brought in to play, and finally the question is asked, are the provisions of the contract consistent with it being a contract of service?

This last requirement leaves a lot of the answer missing and may be difficult to apply to modern employment conditions where some of the evidence points to the person being an employee and other evidence points to self-employment. Nevertheless, a number of criteria seem to have emerged. These need to be considered, but none of them is conclusive:

- the power to select, appoint, fix the place and time of work and fix the time of holidays;
- the power to suspend or dismiss;
- payment of a wage, sick pay and holiday pay (who pays them? a fixed payment for a specified period suggests a contract of employment; payment by task argues for a contract for services, but not conclusively);
- the right to exclusive service;
- the right to require the individual to work on the employer's premises;
- the employer owns the tools and means of production (but some employees by custom provide their own tools);
- who bears the risks and takes the profits (the entrepreneurial test)?
- is the work integrated into the business (the integration test)?
- the intentions of the parties and the label they put on their relationship;
- NI and tax arrangements (eg, is tax deducted *via* PAYE?);
- what contractual provisions are there?
- is there mutual obligation? *(Nethermere (St Neots) Ltd v Gardiner)*; and

- is the relationship genuinely one of self-employment or is there an attempt to avoid protective legislation?

In *Hall v Lorimer*, a tax case, it was stated that the process of determining employment status was not a mechanical exercise involving simply running through items on a checklist. The objective should be to paint a picture. In this case, the worker had worked customarily for 20 employers on assignments lasting one day. He had expenditure and took the risks of debt: he was self-employed.

One of the factors that has been prominent in a number of cases is whether there is a mutual obligation: to provide work and to perform it. In *Nethermere (St Neots) Ltd v Gardiner* the requirement was put thus: there must be an irreducible minimum of obligation on each side. Such obligation was found in *Nethermere* (a case involving homeworkers) but not in the employment agency case *Wickens v Champion Employment*.

It is trite law to say that the courts must look at the facts rather than the label attached by the parties since one or both of the parties may have an interest in presenting the employment relationship in one form rather than another *(Ferguson v Dawson; Oyston Estate Agency Ltd v Trundle)*. Nevertheless, a written contract expressly reflecting the intentions of the parties is good evidence *(Massey v Crown Life Insurance)* providing that the parties are not trying to alter the truth of the relationship by adopting a label *(Young & Woods v West)*. The matter will turn on the evidence: if the evidence is not there, there will be nothing to support the particular view. In *Parsons v Parsons*, the director was not an employee: there was no evidence (eg, wages etc) to show a contract of employment.

Whether employment status is a matter of law or fact

Significance of the distinction

Appellate courts are not entitled to interfere with the decisions of lower courts unless there has been a misdirection in law or the lower court has arrived at a decision that no reasonable court could have arrived at on the facts *(Edwards v Bairstow)*. Therefore, if employment status is a question of law it is appealable. If not, it is not appealable.

Case law

O'Kelly v Trusthouse Forte

FACTS
The court had to decide whether 'regular' casual workers employed by the hotel were employees. The industrial tribunal had decided that they were not: there was not enough mutual obligation to make them employees.

HELD (CA)

Employment status cannot be a question of law because of the scope for differing interpretations of the facts. Thus, following *Edwards v Bairstow*, the CA would not intervene.

Nethermere (St Neots) Ltd v Gardiner

In this case the CA held that homeworkers were employees. There was just enough mutual obligation. However, it is difficult to distinguish the evidence here from that in *O'Kelly* where they were not employees.

Lee v Chuang

It had been held that the construction worker in this case was not an independent contractor. The Privy Council reversed the decision because the finding was so at odds with the facts that no reasonable court would have so held.

Davies v Presbyterian Church of Wales

FACTS

A minister of the Church was dismissed. The question that arose was whether or not he was an employee. The court had to construe a written set of rules.

HELD (HL)

The question of employment status was a matter of law.

Santokh Singh v Guru Nanak Gurdwara

FACTS

The employment status of a priest turned on a combination of written and oral evidence. The industrial tribunal decided that he was not an employee.

HELD (CA)

The tribunal approach, weighing the totality of the evidence, was correct. The CA would not interfere.

It seems that *Davies* can be distinguished from *O'Kelly* and *Santokh Singh*. The construction of a written document is a matter of law. Applying the rules of interpretation, there should be only one answer. This contrasts with situations in which there is a mixture of oral and written evidence: here it is a question of fact which can be decided only by the court hearing the evidence.

Treating employment status as a question of fact has the merits of reducing the number of appeals and allowing the matter to be decided by the court hearing the evidence. However, it may mean that a 'rule of thumb' approach is taken and that there is a degree of inconsistency between tribunals, leading to uncertainty among practitioners.

PARTICULAR CATEGORIES OF WORKER AND THEIR EMPLOYMENT STATUS

There is no universal legal definition of 'worker' but in general the term includes not only those who have entered or work under a contract of employment but also those who personally carry out work or services. Five particular categories of worker whose employment status is sometimes in doubt are considered below: homeworkers, staff supplied by employment agencies, office holders, Crown servants and trainees.

Homeworkers

Homeworkers are not self-employed merely by virtue of working from home. Indeed, homeworking is now becoming more widespread because of information technology, so that homeworkers include managerial and technical staff as well as the more traditional makers of cuddly toys and garment repairers. To determine whether homeworkers are employees or working under contracts for services it is necessary to apply the normal range of tests.

It should be noted that what a tribunal decides is a contract for services for employment legislation purposes may not be so for Inland Revenue purposes. Definitions of employee and self-employed may differ between the two.

Workers provided by employment agencies

Clearly one can expect a contract for services between the agency and the organization in which the work is taking place. The key question, however, is whether the individual worker is an employee of that organization. Possibly the worker could be an employee of the agency. A further possibility is that the individual worker has a contract for services with the agency, and so is self-employed. Much will depend on the details of each particular case and the normal range of tests should be applied. As noted, the courts have sometimes found the worker to be employed under a contract *sui generis* (see page 76).

Office holders

This is a special category of people whose employment is not governed by a contract of employment. Judges, magistrates and other people holding public office or positions in voluntary bodies fall into this category. Definitions of 'worker' in the legislation do not extend to office holders. Some office holders may also have a contract of employment.

Crown servants

The traditional approach has been that a Crown servant was not employed under a contract of employment, but rather held office at the Crown's pleasure. Until recently the issue was not decided, although it did seem that Crown service and employment under a contract of employment were not incompatible. The intention of the Crown was thought to be a critical factor *(R v Civil Service Appeal Board ex parte Bruce)*. The High Court has now ruled that a civil servant works under a contract of employment *(R v Lord Chancellor's Department ex parte Nangle)*. In any case, the ERA expressly extends various employment rights to Crown servants so that they are treated as employees. Moreover, the Employment Act 1988 requires Crown servants to be treated as being under contracts of employment for the purposes of establishing liability in tort for industrial action, the right to hold a ballot before industrial action, the right not to be unjustifiably disciplined by a trades union and removal of immunity for industrial action to enforce union membership.

Trainees

There is no general legislation which determines the form of relationship governing the employment of trainees. Contractual matters are likely to be the main consideration, although contracts may not necessarily be contracts of employment. An existing employee undergoing part-time or full-time training will normally remain an employee under a contract of employment. If that training involves a secondment to some other organization (for example, as part of the employee's individual development programme) much will depend on the terms agreed but clearly continuity will need to be preserved for the purposes of accrued benefits.

The position is least clear where the individual is taken on as a trainee. Here the possibilities are that the trainee:

- is an employee of the company providing the training, in which case a contract of employment will exist (it should be noted that contract of employment is defined to include a contract of apprenticeship);
- is not an employee of the firm but may have a contract for training with the firm or with a training agency (the firm and the training agency would almost certainly have a contract of some kind with each other); or
- may have neither a contract of employment nor a contract for training; he or she may have a contract of its own kind or no contract at all.

Much will depend on the details of what was agreed.

For there to be a contract of any sort there will need to have been an intention to create legal relations. In the absence of a clear statement to the contrary, the courts will assume that there is no contract of employment and no contract for training *(Daley v Allied Suppliers Ltd)*. Where there is a contract, the label put on it by the parties will not necessarily be conclusive evidence of its real nature *(Young and Woods Ltd v West)*. The test developed is that of discovering the underlying purpose of the contract. If it is to create the standard employment relationship it will be a contract of service; if it is to provide general training and work experience it will be a contract for training; if it is a contract to teach a specific trade it will be a contract of apprenticeship *(Wiltshire Police Authority v Wynn)*. The Secretary of State may make an order specifying the status of people undergoing government-funded training. The order can state that they are to be treated as employees, trainees or 'in such other manner as may be specified'.[7]

The status of the apprentice is quite clear. An apprentice should have a written, signed contract of apprenticeship under which the employer agrees to teach them the trade. In return, the apprentice agrees to serve and learn. For the purpose of employment legislation the contract is treated as if it were a contract of employment for a fixed term. Because the apprentice starts as a minor, the contract as a whole must be beneficial if it is to be enforceable. The parties have only limited rights to end the contract during its term, although the position will be influenced by the contractual terms themselves (such as provision for termination by notice and provision for summary dismissal for gross misconduct). An apprentice may agree in writing to waive unfair dismissal and redundancy payment rights. The employer is obliged to provide written confirmation that the apprentice has satisfactorily completed his or her training, if this is the case (the dismissal of apprentices and the failure to offer jobs after expiry of apprenticeship are matters dealt with in chapter 17).

PARTICULAR CATEGORIES OF WORKER: SPECIFIC LEGISLATION

In addition to the general question of employment status already considered, there is the matter of legislation relating to various specific categories of worker. This legislation is now examined.

Foreign nationals

If an employer wishes to employ a foreign national, the first consideration will be whether or not a work permit is required. A work permit will not be required if the person is an EU national, or falls into one of a number of categories of Commonwealth citizen, for example those who can show that one of their grandparents was born in the UK. A limited number of others may work permit-free, for instance representatives of overseas firms. To be such a representative and thus be exempt from the need for a work permit the person's overseas business must still be fully operational at the time of entry *(R v Immigration Appeal Tribunal ex parte Lokko)*. It is not unlawful discrimination for an employer to require proof of the applicant's right to work in the UK *(Dhatt v McDonald's Hamburgers Ltd)*.

Generally, a non-EU national will require a work permit as well as meeting any other requirements, eg passport, visa etc. An employer wanting to employ such a person will have to apply for a work permit on his behalf, specifying the name of the worker and the job to be done. Permits are normally granted for jobs where skilled or professional workers are required (the category 'key worker' was widened with effect from 1 October 1991). An employer will need to show that the vacancy cannot be filled from normal sources, including from EU nationals. An application should be made at least eight weeks before employment is due to commence, and proof of the worker's skills, qualifications and experience should be provided. A new 'fast-track' application procedure was introduced in 1991 for cases which clearly merit approval. Offers of jobs to foreign nationals should be conditional upon them obtaining a work permit and meeting any other entrance requirements. Permission is also needed from the Department for Education and Employment if there is to be a change of job. A person entering the UK with a false permit is an illegal entrant under s 33 of the Immigration Act 1971 even if he did not know it was false and it was produced through the friend of a third party *(R v Home Secretary ex parte Kwan Fai Chan)*.

It is a condition of granting the permit that the worker must have terms and conditions no less favourable than other workers in the same job in that area. The worker will be covered by UK employment legislation in the same way as any other worker, including discrimination law. If the worker is in breach of the terms of the permit, any dismissal for this reason may fall under the heading of 'statutory bar' in dismissal law (see chapter 16). However, it will need to meet the test of reasonableness.

Continuing to work in breach of the conditions of the permit may make the contract of employment illegal, and therefore unenforceable.

It is a criminal offence under s 8 of the Asylum and Immigration Act 1996 for an employer to employ a person who does not have permission to work in the UK.

Children and young persons

In law, anyone under the age of 18 years is a minor, and anyone under the minimum age for leaving school is a child. Anyone over minimum school leaving age but under the age of majority is a young person.

As far as children are concerned, employment below the age of 13 is generally unlawful.[8] Employment in relation to children is defined to include working without reward providing the trade or occupation is carried out for profit.[9] A child must not lift, carry or move anything so heavy as is likely to cause injury to them.[10] Local authorities have powers to supervise the employment of children (for example, to require registration of employment) and may restrict or prohibit employment.[11] They can also pass bye-laws restricting the employment of children.[12] The precise legal requirements in relation to the employment of children can, therefore, vary from area to area.

The Employment of Children Act 1973 provides for regulations to be made to standardize the position nationally, but no regulations have yet been made.[13] Where children are employed in performances a set of regulations does apply.[14] The general legislation restricts not only the type of work on which children can be employed but also their hours. This is dealt with on page 231. On work experience, see page 269.

Much legislation relating to the employment of young persons was repealed by the Employment Act 1989.[15] The Act removed all specific statutory restrictions on the hours and holidays of young persons and removed some of the restrictions on the work that young people can do. However, it did not remove those restrictions on the employment of young persons which are necessary for health, safety and welfare purposes, for example in respect of working with dangerous machinery or hazardous substances. Anyone aged under 18 years is prohibited from working in places selling alcohol (except bars which are solely the subject of table licences) and in betting shops.[16]

In general, minors do not have the capacity to enter into a binding contract. They can, however, enter into such a contract if the contract is for 'necessaries' (that is, the supply of goods and services) and is for the minor's benefit. Thus, an employment contract will not be binding upon a minor unless the contract is, on the whole, beneficial to them, but will be binding upon the employer.

The government is currently reviewing the law relating to the employment of children and this review is expected to be complete by the end of 1998. The government has, however, already had to take steps to implement the EU Protection of Young People at Work Directive.[17] The Health and Safety (Young Persons) Regulations 1997 introduced various forms of health and safety protection for young workers.[18] The Children (Protection at Work) Regulations 1998 (operative 4 August 1998) will standardize various provisions relating to children's hours of work which are currently determined by local authority bye-laws and will make other changes.[19]

Women

The Employment Act 1989 lifted various restrictions on the employment of women, who may now, for example, work underground in mines.[20] Nevertheless, some protective legislation remains. There is still a prohibition upon employing women in certain lead-manufacturing processes; there are still restrictions under the Ionising Radiations Regulations and it remains unlawful to employ a woman in a factory within four weeks of her giving birth.[21] The full list is contained in Schedule 1 to the Employment Act 1989.

More generally, discrimination is lawful if it is necessary in order to comply with the requirements of existing statutory provisions concerning the protection of women or with relevant statutory provisions within the meaning of the Health and Safety at Work etc Act 1974.[22] In both cases the discrimination will be lawful only if it is necessary to protect women in relation to pregnancy, maternity or other circumstances giving rise to risks specifically affecting women.

Ex-offenders

Under the Rehabilitation of Offenders Act 1974, convictions do not have to be revealed if:

- they relate to offences included in the spent convictions scheme;
- the rehabilitation period has elapsed;
- no excluded offence has been committed during rehabilitation; and
- the sentence has been served.

There are minor exceptions to this last point. A further 'scheme' offence during a rehabilitation period creates a new rehabilitation period. The excluded offences, to which the scheme for spent convictions does not apply, are more serious ones attracting sentences of over 30 months. The maximum rehabilitation period for a scheme offence is 10 years.

The effect of completion of a rehabilitation period in relation to offences covered by the spent convictions scheme is that the conviction becomes spent. This means that the offences are to be treated as if they were not committed and the person as if not charged with or convicted of the offence. There are exceptions here for various legal proceedings. A job applicant can treat questions about their previous criminal record as excluding the spent convictions. If asked, 'Do you have a criminal record?' they can answer 'No', and a refusal to disclose a spent conviction cannot give rise to any legal liability. For example, it cannot constitute a breach of the term of trust in an employment contract. Moreover, spent convictions can be excluded from references, without the referee incurring any legal liability. However, a referee may include details of spent convictions providing that the information is true and the disclosure is done without malice. Dismissal on the grounds of a spent conviction or a failure to disclose one will be unfair. Refusing employment because of a spent conviction will also be unlawful. It is not just the spent conviction itself that is protected, but the circumstances surrounding it. Thus, a dismissal because of the nature of the offence which is the subject of the spent conviction would also be unfair. An employee may pursue an unfair dismissal claim or an action for breach of contract. It is not clear what remedy is available for a refusal of employment; an action for breach of statutory duty may be possible.

The right to be silent about spent convictions and the Act's protection against exclusion and dismissal are subject to numerous exceptions where suitability for employment is to be ascertained. The excepted professions, offices, employments and occupations include medical practitioners, barristers, solicitors, nurses, accountants, midwives, pharmacists, dentists, opticians, police constables, veterinary surgeons, firearm dealers, those involving access to minors and health service employment which involves access to patients. There are others and the Secretary of State has power to amend the list.[23]

Anyone applying for work in these occupations can be asked about spent convictions, must disclose them and can be refused employment on the basis of them or dismissed for them or failing to disclose them. Such dismissals will be permitted under the Rehabilitation of Offenders Act 1974 but must still stand the tests of unfair dismissal law. In the case of excepted employments, requests for references are not protected from questions about spent convictions. In such cases, the applicant (or referee) must be told that the exception order applies.

Anyone employed or seeking employment as an officer of a building society may be asked about spent convictions, but only with a range of offences connected with fraud, dishonesty or building society, company and related legislation. The person must be told that the order applies. Spent convictions may be the subject of questioning and grounds for exclusion or dismissal in the interests of national security, but again the individual must be told that the order applies.

As regards unspent convictions, a job applicant is under no general legal duty voluntarily to disclose them. However, the position may be different if a person is asked specifically about any unspent convictions and gives dishonest answers which are discovered later, although a dismissal in these circumstances will not necessarily be fair. Relevant questions are: how long ago was the conviction? What length of good service has there been with the employer? Is the offence relevant in any way to the job now being done? In general, is the employee now unsuitable for their job? Proper procedure will also need to be used.

It should be noted that the Police Act 1997 provides for the Secretary of State to issue certificates evidencing a person's criminal record or absence of criminal record but the relevant provisions are not yet in force.

CONTINUOUS EMPLOYMENT

Significance and computation

Various rules are set down for establishing whether or not a person's employment is continuous. Many employment law rights depend on a person having a minimum period of continuous employment, so that entitlement to use the legislation will be governed by whether there is the necessary length of continuous employment (it should be noted, however, that the two-year qualifying period for unfair dismissal applications is under challenge as being indirectly discriminatory on the ground of sex, and that the issue is currently before the ECJ). In addition continuity will be a factor determining the number of full years of employment for compensation purposes. An employer who establishes that there has been a break in continuity may succeed in barring the employee's claim altogether, or in reducing the compensation that has to be paid.

Employment means employment under a contract of service or apprenticeship, and the continuity provisions (except where they specifically relate to a change of employer; see below) apply to employment by one employer.[24] Once the fact of a contract of employment is established, and a starting date proven, employment is presumed to be continuous.[25] An employer would need to bring evidence to the contrary if he or she wanted to rebut the presumption. Continuous employment will begin on whatever date the contract specifies for the start of the employment rather than on the date when the performance of work begins. This will be true even if it is not a working day – the date specified might be the first day of the next month, and this might be a Sunday (see *The General of the Salvation Army v Dewsbury*). For the purpose of claiming a statutory redundancy payment, but not for claims for remedies for unfair dismissal etc, employment before the age of 18 years does not count towards continuous employment. Changes in the terms of contracts do not interrupt continuity of employment.

Two major issues which arise in the computation of continuous employment are:

- what counts towards continuity?
- what breaks continuity?

Until recently, continuous employment was accrued only by those employees working eight or more hours per week and a week did not count unless it was one in which the employee worked or was under a contract to work at least 16 hours (or eight hours if continuously employed for five years). Moreover, those working fewer than 16 hours required five years' continuous employment in order to qualify for statutory rights such as redundancy payments and eligibility to pursue an unfair dismissal application, whereas those working 16 or more hours required only two years. In *R v Secretary of State for Employment ex parte EOC*, however, the House of Lords held that this differential approach to qualifying periods amounted to indirect sex discrimination, since the vast majority of part-time employees are women.[26] Subsequently, the government legislated through the Employment Protection (Part-Time Employees) Regulations 1995 (the PTE Regulations) to remove the hours element from the computation of continuous employment.[27]

The position now is much simplified and is as follows:

> Any week during the whole or part of which the employee's relations with his employer are governed by a contract of employment counts in computing the employee's period of employment.[28]

In addition, in certain circumstances, there can be continuity during periods in which there is no contract of employment (see below).

Continuity preserved by contract or statute

An employer and an employee may agree, either expressly or impliedly, that the contract of employment will continue even in the absence of the employee. An express agreement may be found in cases of secondment, career break or maternity leave. Continuity in respect of the last of these (as far as the statutory period is concerned) is in any case preserved by statute, providing the woman returns to work, and the weeks also count. More problems are likely to be caused by cases involving long-term sickness or absence occasioned by employees serving prison sentences. Here, the general rule will be that the contract is taken as continuing unless terminated by the employer or employee. However, there is also the possibility that the contract may be frustrated. This is a useful argument for an employer to put, because if successful it means that there is no dismissal. Hence, no questions of unfair dismissal or redundancy arise. Frustration means that the contract comes to an end by force of law because one of the parties cannot perform it at all, or can only perform it on terms radically different from those originally appertaining. The reason is likely to be neither foreseeable nor the direct fault of the parties. Long-term illness and imprisonment are the main examples. There are some cases where it is obvious to all that the contract must be regarded as being at an end. There are others, however, which are less clear, for instance a prolonged illness where the outcome is uncertain. The EAT in *Egg Stores (Stamford Hill) Ltd v Leibovici* put forward a number of factors which should be considered in such cases:

- the length of previous employment;
- the expected future length of employment;
- the nature of the work;
- the nature, length and effect of the injury or illness;
- the employer's need for the work to be done and the need for a replacement to do it;
- the risk to the employer of a replacement employee acquiring employment protection rights;
- whether the employer has continued to pay the employee; and
- whether a reasonable employer could be expected to wait any longer for the employee to return.

An 18-month absence because of illness did not frustrate the contract in *Marshall v Harland and Wolff Ltd* because there was no evidence that the contract could not again be performed, or that it could be performed only in a way radically different from that originally intended. This was a large firm. On the other hand, a borstal sentence expected to last nine months did frustrate a four-year apprenticeship in a relatively small company (*FC Shepherd and Co Ltd v Jerrom*).

Statute specifically preserves continuity in a number of situations where there is no contract, and the weeks also count. First, absence due to injury or illness may result in continuity being preserved for up to 26 weeks. This would be in addition to any contractual sick leave. The same is true of absence due to pregnancy, although here the 26-week period can be extended through the provision of statutory maternity leave. Absence from work, without a contract, due to a temporary cessation of work (other than because of industrial action in which the employee takes part) does not break continuity, and also counts. What is temporary is a matter of fact for tribunal to decide *(Ford v Warwickshire County Council)*. The reason for any temporary cessation is not relevant to the question of continuity. It is also possible to have continuous employment in the absence of a contract where there is a custom or arrangement to that effect.

Strikes do not break continuity but neither do they count when computing the period of employment. They do count if the employee cannot work because of a strike by someone else. An employee dismissed during a strike and later re-engaged has his continuity preserved, but the days on strike do not count towards the period of employment. The days on strike postpone the start of the period of continuous employment. As regards lock-outs, there is no break in continuity and the days also count.

Whether there is continuity of employment in the absence of a contract has been a question which has given rise to a certain amount of case law. For example, in *Lloyds Bank v Secretary of State for Employment*, it fell to be decided whether an employment pattern of one week on and one week off allowed the preservation of continuity. It was held that continuity was preserved by arrangement or custom under the rules for dealing with continuity in the absence of a contract. However, this seems to be a set of circumstances where there was a subsisting contract which should have been tested against the hours requirements which operated at that time.

Where there has been a temporary cessation of work, the courts have considered and adopted more than one approach. In *Ford v Warwickshire County Council*, the applicant was a college lecturer. There were gaps in employment between dismissal in June and re-employment in September, but the employment continued over a number of years. The House of Lords, in holding that each of these gaps was a temporary cessation of work and that, therefore, there was continuity, adopted a mathematical approach by comparing the length of the gaps (short) with the length of the periods of employment (long). However, the Court of Appeal took a different approach in *Flack v Kodak Ltd*, stating that it was necessary to look at all the circumstances where the employment was intermittent and irregular, rather than taking a mathematical approach. In *Sillars v Charrington Fuels Ltd*, the two approaches were reconciled thus: the mathematical approach is suitable where the employment is regular, but otherwise the 'all the circumstances' approach is a better one.

The question of there being no contract because of the employee's sickness or illness came under consideration in *Donnelly v Kelvin International Services Ltd*. In particular, did 'incapable of work' (now in ERA, s 212(3)(a)) mean incapable of any work, or just the work that the employee was employed to perform? The EAT decided that the latter was the proper construction. In another case, *Pearson v Kent County Council,* the issue that arose was whether or not sickness or injury was in fact the reason for the gap between contracts. The complainant had terminated his old post on the ground of incapacity, but there was a delay in him starting his new post. Since the reason for this delay was not sickness or injury, he was not incapable of work 'in consequence of sickness or injury'.[29]

Changes of employer

The above description has related to continuous employment with one employer, but statute also makes provision for continuity to be preserved, in certain cases, when there is a change of employer. Where the respective employers expressly agree to continuity there is unlikely to be a problem. The difficulty is likely to arise where an employer finds unexpectedly that one of their employees can count employment with a previous employer and themself as continuous.

Statute preserves continuity where a business is transferred as a going concern, that is, including assets and goodwill. Another instance of continuity is where an employee transfers to an associated employer – where one firm controls the other, or both are controlled by a third person. Local authorities are to be treated as if they were associated for continuity for redundancy payments purposes.[30] Finally, continuity is preserved by statute if there is a transfer which falls under the Transfer of Undertakings (Protection of Employment) Regulations (see chapter 20). In the above situations an employer will need to check whether he has inherited any continuous employment. Continuous employment with a previous employer should be specified in the written particulars of terms of employment given to new starters (see chapter 8).

NOTES

1   ERA, s 230(1).
2   Ibid; see also TULR(C)A, s 295(1).
3   TULR(C)A, s 296(1).
4   ERA, Part II and s 230(3).
5   SDA, s 82(1); RRA, s 78(1). See chapter 6. The term 'workers' is not used in these Acts.
6   Regulation 2(1)
7   EA 1988, s 26. The Social Security (Employment Training: Payments) Order (SI 1988/1409) has been made under this section.
8   Children and Young Persons Act 1933, s 18; Children and Young Persons (Scotland) Act 1937.
9   1933 Act, s 30.

10 1933 Act, s 18.

11 Employment of Children Act 1973, s 2.

12 Children and Young Persons Acts 1933-69.

13 Employment of Children Act 1973.

14 The Children (Performance) Regulations (SI 1968/1728).

15 Employment Act 1989, s 10 and Sched 3.

16 Licensing Act 1964, s 170; Betting, Gaming and Lotteries Act 1963, s 21.

17 94/33/EC.

18 SI 1997/135.

19 SI 1998/276.

20 Employment Act 1989, Sched 2.

21 Factories Act 1961, ss 74, 128 and 131; Ionising Radiations Regulations, 1985 (Parts IV and V of Sched I); para 118 of the Approved Code of Practice under the Control of Lead at Work Regulations, 1980; Public Health Act 1936, s 205.

22 HSWA 1974, s 53. Relevant statutory provisions comprise Part I of the HSWA, health and safety regulations (including agriculture) and any other existing statutory provisions.

23 Rehabilitation of Offenders Act 1974; the list of exceptions is to be found in the Rehabilitation of Offenders Act 1974 (Exceptions) Order (SI 1975/1023) as amended by the (Exceptions) (Amendment) Order (SI 1986/1249) and the (Exceptions) (Amendment) (No 2) Order (SI 1986/2268).

24 ERA, s 218(1).

25 ERA, s 210(5).

26 In the earlier case of *Rinner-Kuhn* the ECJ had held that hours rules excluding employees from statutory sick pay (in Germany) could be indirect sex discrimination where part-time workers were predominantly female.

27 Employment Protection (Part-Time Employees) Regulations (SI 1995/31).

28 ERA, s 212(1).

29 ERA, s 212(3)(a).

30 Redundancy Payments (Local Government) (Modification) Order (SI 1983/1160) as amended.

Race and Sex Discrimination

This is the first of two chapters on discrimination law, a term which is not found in the legislation but which is a convenient description of an area of law. For the present purposes, it is taken primarily to mean sex, race and disability legislation, although other areas are considered.

Another preliminary point is that the EU context is very important in the discrimination area. Article 119 of the Treaty of Rome and the Equal Pay Directive are dealt with in chapter 11: here the significant point is the existence of the Equal Treatment Directive on access to employment etc and the fact that it has precedence over the UK's domestic legislation.[1]

GENERAL SCHEME AND SCOPE OF THE LEGISLATION

General scheme

Discrimination law is found in three principal pieces of legislation:

- the Sex Discrimination Act 1975;
- the Race Relations Act 1976; and
- the Disability Discrimination Act 1995.

The structure of race and sex discrimination law is quite similar, but with an important exception. Sex discrimination in respect of contract terms is covered by separate legislation – the Equal Pay Act 1970 – whereas race discrimination in respect of contract terms is dealt with alongside other race discrimination in the RRA.[2] Disability discrimination law is quite different from that relating to race and sex discrimination. Among other things, discrimination itself is defined in a different way in the DDA, and the defence available to employers is differently constituted.[3]

The general scheme of race and sex discrimination law is based upon a two-pronged attack on discrimination. This involves, first, an individual-level approach which provides remedies for those who suffer unlawful discrimination. Remedies are obtained by means of complaints to industrial tribunals. The second approach is a strategic one, where the aim is to give effect to public policy which seeks to eliminate discrimination. The vehicle for achieving this in the fields of both race and sex discrimination is action by a standing commission – respectively the CRE and EOC (on the roles of these Commissions see chapter 3). The general scheme of race and sex discrimination law is shown diagrammatically in Figure 6.1.

The strategic aspect of the legislation centres upon a number of unlawful acts which are not themselves defined as discrimination. These include discriminatory practices or advertisements and instructions or pressure to discriminate. Actions in respect of such unlawful acts are restricted to the commissions: they cannot be the subject of an individual complaint to an industrial tribunal. In contrast, the Acts define a number of areas of unlawful discrimination where the right of action lies with the individual (although the commissions may assist individuals). The legislation therefore makes unlawful two types of activity:

- unlawful discrimination, which may be the subject of complaints by individuals; and
- other unlawful acts, which may be the subject of action by the commissions.

A key concept in the scheme of race and sex discrimination law is that of discrimination itself. A distinction may be drawn here between the grounds of discrimination and the forms. The essence of this distinction and the categories within each of these two concepts are set out in Figure 6.2.

It should be noted that disability discrimination law does not distinguish between direct and indirect discrimination. Moreover, it seems likely that the concept of disability may itself be a source of considerable amount of case law, whereas the meaning of sex and race has unsurprisingly not created many difficulties of interpretation. Because of these and other differences between the DDA on the one hand and the SDA and RRA on the other, disability discrimination will be treated separately and is dealt with in chapter 7.

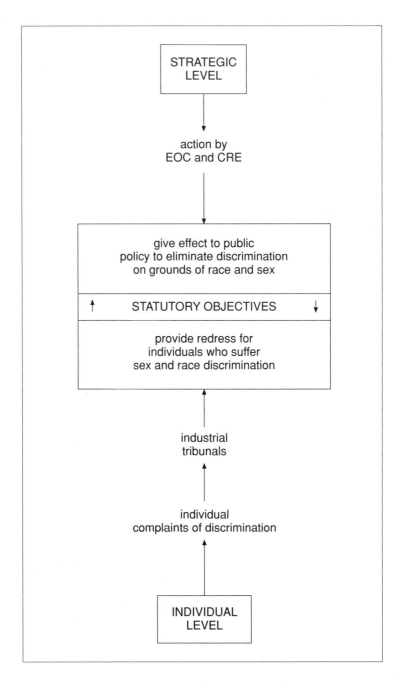

Figure 6.1   General scheme of race and sex discrimination law

The grounds

- 'On the ground of her sex'   SDA, s 1(1)(a)

- 'On the ground of his or her
  marital status'   SDA, s 3(1)(a)

- 'On racial grounds'   RRA, s 1(1)(a)

The forms

- Direct discrimination –

  'Treats her less favourably than
  he treats or would treat a man'   SDA, s 1(1)(a)

- Parallel provision in RRA   RRA, s 1(1)(a)

- Indirect discrimination –

  treatment which is irrespective   { SDA, s 1(1)(b)
  of race or sex but has a   { RRA, s 1(1)(b)
  discriminatory impact

- Victimisation, eg because the   { SDA, s 4
  individual has invoked the   { RRA, s 2
  legislation

Figure 6.2   Grounds and forms of unlawful race
and sex discrimination

The scope of discrimination law

The scope of discrimination law can be viewed in terms of:

- the breadth of the grounds of protection; and
- the extent of any exclusions.

The grounds

By the grounds of protection is meant race, sex, disability, religion, age, political views, union membership and sexual orientation. Here it will be seen that, in the main, UK law concentrates on race, sex and disability discrimination. The question, however, is not merely which grounds are protected, but whether the grounds themselves are adequately or restrictively defined.

A certain amount of case law has developed on the question of what constitutes 'racial grounds'. In the legislation, 'racial grounds' means colour, race, nationality or ethnic or national origins.[4] It does not expressly include religion, the only direct provision on this ground being in the Fair Employment (Northern Ireland) Acts of 1976 and 1989. However, in *Seide v Gillette*, Jews were held to be an ethnic group under the RRA, so where religion and ethnicity are closely linked there may be indirect protection on religious grounds.

The question of what is meant by an ethnic group was considered in *Mandla v Lee*. Here it was held that an ethnic group must be one that regards itself and is regarded by others as a distinct community by virtue of certain characteristics, among which the following are essential:

- a long, shared history; and
- a cultural tradition of its own.

In *Mandla*, applying this approach, Sikhs were held to be a group defined by ethnic origin and were thus covered by the RRA. By contrast, the relatively short history of the Rastafarians meant that they failed the test by not having a long, shared history *(Crown Suppliers v Dawkins)*. Gypsies have been held to be an ethnic group *(CRE v Dutton)*. The concept of disability is much more problematic than race or sex: see chapter 7.

Another aspect of the grounds is the coverage in terms of potential complaints. Both sex and race discrimination law apply to a category wider than employee (see chapter 5 on employment status). The Acts outlaw certain discriminatory behaviour 'in relation to employment' which is then defined to mean 'employment under a contract of service or of apprenticeship or a contract personally to execute any work or labour'.[5] While the jurisdiction is not restricted to employees, therefore, it is restricted to employment, and indeed, current employment. Thus, in *Navarajan v*

Agnew, a discriminatory reference from a former employer was not within the scope of the RRA: s 4(2) is limited to events occurring within the employment relationship because unlawful discrimination by an employer can be found only 'in the case of a person employed by him'. Similarly, a complaint about a discriminatory appeal against dismissal was not within s 4(2) because the complainant was not employed at the time of the appeal, and was not within s 4(1) because the appeal was not part of the recruitment process to which that subsection applies *(Adekeye v The Post Office (No 2))*. Moreover, there are other issues of scope. Omitting to offer employment can be unlawful discrimination.[6] However, a person proposing to buy a business is not in a position to make an offer of employment until he has actually bought the business. The offers made in *Swithland Motors v Clarke*, therefore, were not offers within the meaning of the RRA. Finally, in terms of the grounds of complaint, there is the question of the relationship between the individual and strategic functions of the legislation. Discriminatory advertisements can be the subject of action by the commissions, in race relations cases under RRA, s 29, but can they also be selection arrangements under s 4(1)(a) of the Act constituting grounds for complaints of unlawful discrimination by individuals? It seems not: only the CRE can take enforcement action in this area *(Cardiff Women's Aid v Hartup)*.

Exclusions

The general position is that there are few exclusions from the SDA and the RRA. In particular, it should be noted that no qualifying period of employment is necessary in order to bring a complaint and there are no requirements for workers to be working any minimum number of hours. The small firm exclusion under the original SDA was removed by the SDA 1986 following infringement proceedings taken by the European Commission *(Commission of the EEC v UK)*. However, special provisions apply to a small number of specific categories of employment and certain acts of discrimination are not unlawful. The latter include situations where being a member of a particular race or sex is a genuine occupational qualification (GOQ) for a job and positive action (such as single-sex training) to encourage members of a particular sex or particular racial groups to enter an occupation where they are under-represented. The Sex Discrimination and Race Relations codes of practice provide guidance in this area. The general principle, however, is that reverse discrimination (ie, discrimination in favour of the group which has been subject to discrimination in the past) is unlawful (see *Kalauke v City of Bremen*). Nevertheless, there is evidence in a recent ECJ decision of some departure from this principle. In *Marschall v Land Nordrhein-Westfalen* the ECJ considered a German law giving women priority in promotion where there were fewer women than men in a particular type of post. This applied where the candidates were equally suitable, as long as no reasons specific to the male candidate tilted the balance in his favour. The ECJ held this not to be a breach of the Equal Treatment Directive providing an objective assessment took account of all relevant criteria (none of which must be discriminatory) and overrode the female priority if on the balance of the criteria the man was stronger. Thus, positive discrimination is consistent with the Equal Treatment Directive where there is a properly applied 'saving' clause to protect a stronger, male candidate.

DIRECT DISCRIMINATION

The two principal requirements for success in an individual complaint of race or sex discrimination are:

- there has been an unlawful act (SDA s 6, RRA 4); and
- the act fits within the legislation's definition of discrimination (SDA, ss 1, 3 and 4; RRA, ss 1–2).

General discussion

The legislation: the Sex Discrimination Act
Direct discrimination on the ground of sex is defined as follows:

> A person discriminates against a woman in any circumstances relevant for the purposes of this Act if (a) on the ground of her sex he treats her less favourably than he treats or would treat a man ... '[7]

Direct discrimination on the ground of marital status is similar to that quoted above but 'on the ground of his or her marital status'[8]

Section 5(3) specifies the relevant circumstances for SDA, ss 1 and 3:

> A comparison of the cases of persons of different sex or marital status under section 1(1) or 3(1) must be such that the relevant circumstances in the one case are the same, or not materially different, in the other.

This appears to mean that like should be compared with like and has been used to justify the approach of the UK courts in cases (such as *Webb v EMO Air Cargo (UK) Ltd*) where discrimination is alleged on grounds of pregnancy. The approach, subsequently rejected by the ECJ, compared a pregnant woman with a 'sick man' (hence the 'sick man' approach).

Where a man is or would be treated differently according to his marital status, the woman should compare herself with a man of the same marital status.[9]

The Act applies equally to men as well as women: ie, a man can complain of sex discrimination.[10]

The legislation: the Race Relations Act

For direct discrimination on racial grounds, the RRA contains a provision which is similar to the SDA extract but refers to discriminating against 'another' and treating 'that other' less favourably.[11] Segregation on racial grounds is expressly stated to be less favourable treatment.[12] As noted, 'racial grounds' is defined to mean 'colour, race, nationality, or ethnic or national origins'.[13]

The case law

James v Eastleigh Borough Council

The general test for direct discrimination: *James v Eastleigh Borough Council*[14]

FACTS

Discriminatory concessions were applied to the price of entry to swimming baths: women aged 60 or over entered free, but men were required to be 65 or over to enter free. A man of 61 had to pay £0.75 to enter while a woman of 61 entered free of charge.

HELD (HL)

The question to be considered under SDA, s 1(1)(a) is: would the complainant have received the same treatment 'but for his or her sex'? (this is now labelled the 'but for' test). The answer in *James* was yes – if the complainant had been a woman instead of a man he would have been able to enter the baths free of charge.

Motive or intention is not a prerequisite for liability – it did not matter that the local authority running the baths had not intended to discriminate.

Any differential treatment arising out of a gender-based criterion – here, discriminatory state pension ages – must itself be discriminatory. Discriminatory state pension ages themselves are lawful because they are excepted from the EU Equal Treatment Directive on Social Security.[15]

Any material difference put forward under s 5(3) (in order to undermine the validity of the comparison) must be free of discrimination. Here, discriminatory state pension ages could not be used as a basis to argue that the cases were not comparable.

Webb v EMO Air Cargo (UK) Ltd

Direct discrimination on the ground of pregnancy: *Webb v EMO Air Cargo (UK) Ltd*

FACTS

The complainant was a replacement for someone on maternity leave. She herself became pregnant and was unable to cover for the absentee. She had already commenced employment before the discovery was made. The company dismissed her.

HELD (HL)

If the complainant was dismissed on the ground of pregnancy it was automatically unlawful sex discrimination (as per the ECJ in *Dekker*).

On the facts, the dismissal was because of non-availability rather than pregnancy, so did not constitute sex discrimination.

On reference to the ECJ to determine whether the dismissal was in breach of the Equal Treatment Directive:

HELD (ECJ)

It was a breach of the Equal Treatment Directive – the effects of pregnancy (such as non-availability) cannot be separated from pregnancy itself.

Dismissal for pregnancy is automatically unlawful sex discrimination: no comparison is required.

The case was then finally decided by HL according to the ruling of the ECJ. It should be noted that at the time of Mrs Webb's complaint, the option of an application under unfair dismissal law was not available because a two-year qualifying period applied. Regardless of what is finally settled about the validity or otherwise of qualifying periods more generally (see chapter 5), there is now no qualifying employment required in cases of pregnancy dismissals and a dismissal on the ground of pregnancy is automatically unfair.[16]

The different approaches to pregnancy and sex discrimination may be put thus:

- discrimination on the ground of pregnancy cannot be unlawful under the SDA because the SDA requires a comparison and no comparison is possible because only women can become pregnant. This early approach was soon abandoned as contrary to Parliament's intentions because it left a major gap in the protection offered by the Act.
- a comparison is required but that can be achieved by considering a man absent for reasons of illness. This 'sick man' approach held sway in the UK courts until the ECJ decisions in *Dekker* and *Webb*.
- since pregnancy applies only to women, discrimination on the basis of it is automatically unlawful sex discrimination. Moreover, pregnancy cannot be separated from the facts accompanying it, eg non-availability. This is the ECJ approach and seems to be the present position.
- nonetheless the Court of Session in Scotland subsequently held a woman dismissed on grounds of illness during pregnancy, in a situation where there was no entitlement to maternity leave, to be fairly dismissed on the ground of sickness absence *(Brown v Rentokil Ltd)*. This was because there was no 'protected period', an ECJ concept referring to the period for which a woman enjoys employment protection during maternity, under national laws. In the UK this period would begin with pregnancy and end with the expiry of maternity leave. The significance of this period is

that it appears to provide the limits of the ECJ 'automatic' discrimination rule in *Webb*. Thus, in dismissal post-maternity leave the 'sick man' approach is applicable as in *Larssan*. This, in effect, is an exception to the rule in *Webb*. There is also the residual possibility that the pregancy of a woman recruited solely for maternity cover could be an exception.

- In *Caledonia Bureau Investment and Property v Caffrey*, the EAT did not distinguish the protected period and found there to be automatic sex discrimination (as per *Webb*) despite the fact that the dismissal occurred post-maternity leave. It also decided that the dismissal was automatically unfair under ERA, s 99.

Showboat v Owens

Direct discrimination by means of dismissal for refusing to carry out an instruction to discriminate: *Showboat v Owens*
FACTS
A white manager of an amusement arcade was given an unlawful instruction to exclude young blacks from the arcade, ie an unlawful instruction to discriminate. He refused and was dismissed.
HELD (EAT)
This was a dismissal on 'racial grounds': the wording of the RRA is wide enough to extend protection beyond the person actually suffering the discrimination (see RRA, s 1(1)(a): 'a person discriminates against another ... on racial grounds ...').
The appropriate comparison is between how the employers treated the complainant and how they would have treated someone who had carried out the instruction.

Ministry of Defence v Jeremiah

Payments made to those suffering direct discrimination: *Ministry of Defence v Jeremiah*
FACTS
Men were required to perform dirty aspects of the work which women were not required to do. However, the men were paid extra for this work.
HELD (CA)
An employer cannot buy the right to discriminate.

Schmidt v Austicks Bookshops

Direct discrimination in dress codes: *Schmidt v Austicks Bookshops*
FACTS
Women were prohibited from wearing trousers at work.

HELD (EAT)

This was not sex discrimination: there was a dress code for both sexes. The dress requirements for the sexes do not have to be the same.

An employer has discretion in respect of dress codes, especially where the employee comes into contact with the public.

This approach was followed by the Court of Appeal in *Smith v Safeway plc.*

Burrett v West Birmingham Health Authority

FACTS

The complainant nurse was required to wear a hat which she felt was demeaning.

HELD (EAT)

The test for less favourable treatment is objective: how a reasonable person would view it (cf the subjective test – how the complainant views it) *(R v City of Birmingham ex parte EOC))*. NB: the employer in *Burrett* had a dress code for each sex, although the requirements for men did not include the wearing of a hat.

Mecca Leisure Group plc v Chatprachong

The need for evidence of less favourable treatment: *Mecca Leisure Group plc v Chatprachong*

FACTS

The employers rejected the complainant's application for promotion on the grounds that his English was inadequate. The complainant asked the employer to pay for language lessons so that he could improve his English and thus stand a better chance of being promoted.

HELD (EAT)

There was no evidence of discrimination because there was no evidence to show that a comparator had been or would have been treated differently.

Sexual and racial harassment[17]

Legislation

Harassment is not specifically mentioned in the legislation although there is an EU Recommendation and Code of Practice on sexual harassment which defines the concept thus:

'conduct of a sexual nature, or other conduct based on sex affecting the dignity of women and men at work' which:

- is 'unwanted, unreasonable and offensive to the recipient';
- is used to the recipient's detriment in respect of employment decisions; and
- creates 'an intimidating, hostile or humiliating work environment for the recipient'.[18]

The Recommendation goes on to note that such conduct could amount to a breach of the Equal Treatment Directive.[19]

Case law

Porcelli v Strathclyde Regional Council

This case is authority for the proposition that sexual harassment can constitute direct sex discrimination. Note, however, that there will need to be a comparison as in other cases of direct discrimination, and a detriment.

De Souza v Automobile Association

FACTS
Racial insults were overheard by a secretary or relayed to her.
HELD (CA)
The complainant was not treated less favourably since there was no intention nor could it be known that she would hear or find out.
A racial insult per se is not sufficient to constitute a detriment: there must be a disadvantage (but this could be in respect of psychological working conditions).
The test for less favourable treatment is objective: the reasonable worker.
NB: ultimately this case was decided on the basis that the complainant was not 'treated'.
On racial harassment see also *Burton v De Vere Hotels* (page 117).

Balgobin v Tower Hamlets

FACTS
Employees made allegations of sexual harassment but the employer's enquiry proved inconclusive. The employees returned to their former positions.
HELD (EAT)
Being required to work with an alleged harasser was not less favourable treatment on the ground of sex. The treatment was not less favourable because both sexes would have been treated the same and the reason for the treatment was the employer's inconclusive enquiry rather than the ground of sex.

Wileman v Milinec

FACTS
A director made sexual remarks to a number of women.
HELD (EAT)
The remarks have to be looked at in the context of each person. The industrial tribunal correctly refused to admit evidence of what the director said to women other than the complainant.
Each individual has the right to treat offensive remarks as a breach of the SDA (ie, a subjective approach).
NB: It can be seen that the courts are undecided over the issue of whether in determining detriment they should adopt a subjective or objective approach.

Stewart v Cleveland Guest (Engineering)

In this case the EAT held that exposure to nude pin-ups did not mean that the complainant was treated less favourably because such material is capable of being offensive to both sexes.

Bracebridge Engineering v Darby

This case is authority for the proposition that a single incident, if it is sufficiently serious, can constitute sexual harassment.

Wadman v Carpenter Farrer Partnership

Here the EAT states that the EU Recommendation and Code should be relied upon in situations where it can assist the court in deciding a case.

Conclusions on direct discrimination

- Under UK law the test is whether there has been less favourable treatment, and this requires a comparison with how another person was or would be treated.
- The comparison must be like with like – the relevant circumstances must be the same or not materially different.

- Following the House of Lords in *Webb*, pregnancy seems to be an exception to the comparison rule.
- No comparison is required by the Equal Treatment Directive for pregnancy cases, and perhaps more generally.
- Once direct discrimination is established, there appears to be no defence.
- The SDA and RRA do not deal expressly with harassment, but harassment fits into the scheme of the legislation through the concepts of direct discrimination and detriment. (Note also the Protection from Harassment Act 1997)
- Since harassment is to be judged as direct discrimination, a comparison is required (this may cause difficulty: eg, what if an employer harassed both sexes?).
- The EU Recommendation, which includes a code of practice, defines sexual harassment and can be used in domestic courts.

INDIRECT DISCRIMINATION

General points

The legislation

Indirect discrimination on the ground of sex is defined as follows:

> A person discriminates against a woman in any circumstances relevant for the purposes of this Act if ...

> ... he applies to her a requirement or condition which he applies or would apply equally to a man but:
> (i) which is such that the proportion of women who can comply with it is considerably smaller than the proportion of men who can comply with it, and
> (ii) which he cannot show to be justifiable irrespective of the sex of the person to whom it is applied, and
> (iii) which is to her detriment because she cannot comply with it.[20]

Indirect discrimination on the ground of marital status is similar to that above[21] as is indirect discrimination against members of a racial group.[22]

Examples from the case law

Price v Civil Service Commission

FACTS
The Civil Service Commission imposed a maximum age limit of 28 years for entry into a particular grade of work. The complainant was aged 35 years and

argued that a considerably smaller proportion of women than men could comply with this limit because of child-rearing activities during their 20s.

HELD (EAT)

There was a disproportionate impact.

The original industrial tribunal decision must be set aside.

The question to be determined is whether the impact was so disproportionate that the proportion of women able to comply is considerably smaller than the proportion of men.

The case must be remitted to another industrial tribunal to determine that question.

Note: the industrial tribunal to which the case was remitted decided that the proportion was considerably smaller and upheld that applicant's complaint.

R v Secretary of State for Employment ex parte EOC

FACTS

At the time of the case, employees working 16 or more hours per week who were seeking redundancy payments and/or to use unfair dismissal legislation were required to have two years' qualifying employment. Those employees working eight but fewer than 16 hours were required to have five years' qualifying employment. The vast majority of those working under 16 hours per week are women, and the EOC, as the body charged with supervising the legislation on sex discrimination, sought judicial review of the redundancy payments and unfair dismissal legislation on the basis that the different qualifying periods were discriminatory in contravention of EU law.

HELD (HL)

The EOC has *locus standi* to make the application.

The provisions in respect of redundancy payments (RPs) were:

- a breach of the Equal Treatment Directive since they constituted indirect sex discrimination;
- a breach of article 119 of the Treaty of Rome (the requirement for equal pay), since redundancy payments were pay for the purposes of the article.

The provisions in respect of unfair dismissal were a breach of the Equal Treatment Directive, again because they constituted indirect sex discrimination. It has yet to be decided whether unfair dismissal compensation is also pay for the purposes of article 119; if it is there will have been another breach of the article (in *Mediguard Services Ltd v Thame*, the EAT ruled that unfair dismissal compensation was pay).

Note: this case shows that the concept of indirect discrimination can apply to domestic legislation as well as to the rules imposed by employers.

Meade-Hill v The British Council

A mobility clause in a woman's contract of employment can be indirect sex discrimination because a considerably higher proportion of women than men are secondary earners who would be unable to relocate because of their husbands' jobs. Such a clause is a 'requirement or condition' which would have to meet the usual objective justification test. Moreover, it is applied for the purpose of SDA, s 1(1)(b) when it is put into the contract rather than when it is actually enforced. The purpose of SDA, s 77(5) is to allow a person to apply to the county court for the removal or modification of discriminatory contract terms without waiting for them to be enforced.

The meaning of key concepts

Requirement or condition

Home Office v Holmes

FACTS
The complainant was an executive officer, one of 250 in her department. When she returned to work after the birth of her first child she found it difficult to combine child-rearing and full-time work. After the birth of her second child, therefore, she wanted to return to work on a part-time basis. Her employer refused her request.
HELD (EAT)
The requirement to work full-time was a 'requirement or condition'.
The proportion of women who can comply with it is considerably smaller than the proportion of men who can comply with it.
The complainant had suffered a detriment.
A defence of justification had not been made out.
The industrial tribunal's decision in favour of the complainant would be upheld.
Note: This approach was confirmed by the Northern Ireland Court of Appeal in *Briggs v North East Education and Library Board.*

Perera v Civil Service Commission

FACTS
The complainant, who was Sri Lankan by birth, failed to obtain promotion despite having good qualifications.

HELD (CA)

A 'requirement or condition' must be an absolute bar ie a 'must'.

None of the criteria for promotion applied by the employer in this case amounted to an absolute bar.

COMMENT

This rule allows an employer to exercise discriminatory preferences as long as they do not amount to an absolute requirement. An example is given below in *Meer.*

Meer v London Borough of Tower Hamlets

FACTS

The case concerned a vacancy for head of the Borough's Legal Department. Ten criteria were set out in order to decide which applicants would be put on a 'long' short-list, one of the criteria being previous experience with the Borough of Tower Hamlets. The complainant, who was not 'long' short-listed, argued that this constituted indirect race discrimination.

HELD

Previous experience with the Borough was not a 'must' (following *Perera*), therefore it did not constitute a 'requirement or condition'. It was merely a factor taken into account.

Note: in fact eight out of the ten on the long short-list had no previous experience with the Borough.

In 1997, the EAT attempted to overrule the Court of Appeal's approach in *Perera* by stating that a requirement does not have to be an absolute bar: it is sufficient that it is more difficult for women to comply with it than men *(Falkirk Council v Whyte)*. The matter is likely to be resolved by the EU which has recently adopted a directive which defines indirect discrimination, in a way wider than the SDA, in terms of any 'provision, criterion or practice'.[23]

Enderby v Frenchay Health Authority

FACTS

A largely female group received lower pay than a largely male group. The employer argues that the reason is separate bargaining arrangements and that this is a historical factor. The complainants' argument is that this is indirect sex discrimination.

HELD (ECJ)

Where there is shown to be a disparate impact as here, a *prima facie* case of sex discrimination is made out.

In such circumstances, the burden falls upon the employer to justify the disparity.

COMMENT

The importance of the ECJ's decision lies in the shifting of the burden of proof if a *prima facie* case can be made out by the complainant; and also in the finding of indirect discrimination without there being any 'requirement or condition' (on the latter point see also *R v Secretary of State for Education ex parte Schaffer*). In both these respects the ECJ is interpreting EU law in a way that provides the complainant with better protection than the domestic law, although on the former point see *King v The Great Britain–China Centre*.

Note that *Enderby* is an equal pay case and is discussed in chapter 11. Only the indirect discrimination aspects have been considered above.

Note also the application of the concept of indirect discrimination to the matter of pay (not found in the Equal Pay Act).

Bhudi v IMI Refiners Ltd

The significance of this case is that it was decided by the EAT after the ECJ's decision in *Enderby*. It illustrates the continuing tension between the UK courts and the ECJ (also evident in the 'sick man' v automatic discrimination approach to discrimination on ground of pregnancy (see above)). The EAT held that notwithstanding the decision of the ECJ in *Enderby*, UK courts were not obliged to construe SDA, s 1(1)(b) in such a way as to remove the need for there to be a 'requirement or condition'. The reasons for this were as follows:

- the *Enderby* decision was solely about interpretation of article 119 of the Treaty of Rome and the Equal Pay Directive; and
- even if indirect discrimination could be established under EU law without there being a requirement or condition, there was no obligation on UK courts to distort the meaning of domestic legislation (see *Marleasing* – in chapter 2).

Considerably smaller proportion can comply

Three major issues arise in the interpretation of this part of the concept of indirect discrimination:

- what is the correct pool of people within which the comparison has to be made?
- what does 'can comply' mean?
- what is meant by 'considerably smaller'?

Jones v University of Manchester

The correct pool: *Jones v University of Manchester*

The Court of Appeal held that the correct pool was all those people to whom the requirement and condition was applied. That is, the pool should comprise all those who, in the absence of the requirement or condition, would be qualified for the post.

Mandla v Lee

Meaning of 'can comply': *Mandla v Lee*
FACTS
A Sikh boy was refused admission to a school because the wearing of a turban would breach the school's rules as regards uniforms. It was argued by the school that the boy could comply with the rules by not wearing a turban.
HELD (HL)
'Can comply' means that the complainant can comply in practice (or can comply consistently with the custom and culture of his racial group). It does not mean simply that it is physically possible for him to comply.

R v Secretary of State for Employment ex parte Seymour-Smith

Meaning of considerably smaller proportion: *R v Secretary of State for Employment ex parte Seymour-Smith*
FACTS
This was an appeal against the High Court's decision to refuse to grant judicial review of the Unfair Dismissal (Variation of Qualifying Period) Order 1985,[24] which increased the qualifying period of employment for unfair dismissal applications from one year to two.
The review was sought on the basis that the two-year qualifying period was unlawful because it was indirectly discriminatory and in breach of the Equal Treatment Directive. The High Court had found that the proportion of women who could comply with the qualifying period was 89 per cent of the male proportion and that this was not 'considerably smaller'.
HELD (CA)
There is a difference in the proportions and it is important not to exaggerate the weight to be attached to the word 'considerably' (this word is found in the SDA not in the ETD). The requirement was held to constitute indirect discrimination. The Secretary of State had not objectively justified the requirement.
COMMENT
For a number of reasons the Court of Appeal did not quash the 1985 Order. Moreover, there has been an appeal to the House of Lords which has resulted in a reference to the ECJ. In the meantime, the position in respect of the two-year qualifying period is unclear. Note that the Court of Appeal accepted that the complainant had *locus standi*, as the House of Lords had done in respect of the EOC in *R v Secretary of State for Employment ex parte EOC*.

Justifiable

Employers have a defence to indirect discrimination: that the discrimination can be justified on grounds unconnected with the sex or race of the complainant. In the early case of *Singh v Rowntree Mackintosh*, the test put forward was that justification meant 'reasonably necessary in the circumstances'. Under the influence of the ECJ, later case law developed the test into one of 'objective justification'.

Bilka-Kaufhaus v Weber von Hartz

FACTS
Part-time employees were excluded from the employer's occupational pension scheme.
HELD (ECJ)
The defence of justification requires 'objective justification' of the reasons for the discriminatory rule.
Here the reasons were not objectively justified and so the justification defence was rejected and the indirect discrimination was unlawful.

Hampson v Department of Education and Science

The leading domestic case which elaborates upon the objective justification defence is *Hampson v Department of Education and Science*.
FACTS
The complainant was a Hong Kong Chinese teacher refused qualified teacher status on entry to the UK because she had not been through the UK three-year training course. This requirement was maintained despite the fact that the complainant held an equivalent qualification and had considerable experience.
HELD (CA)
The requirement or condition – the three-year UK course – was not objectively justified.
The test is:

- whether there is a genuine organizational need (rather than mere convenience – *Steel v The Post Office*) – here, to have properly qualified teachers;
- whether the requirement or condition laid down meets that need; and
- whether the requirement or condition is reasonably necessary (ie, whether there is an alternative way of meeting the need) (here, an equivalent qualification).

Where the requirement can be justified as above, the discriminatory effects upon the complainant will then have to be weighed against the reasonable organizational needs of the employer. The test is set out diagramatically in Figure 6.3.
Note: this case went on appeal to the House of Lords on a different matter.

Detriment

The complainant who alleges indirect discrimination must demonstrate not only the existence of a requirement or condition and a considerably smaller proportion, but also that he or she has suffered a detriment. As *Clarke v Eley (IMI) Ltd* emphasized, the complainant must show that the detriment has been suffered because he or she cannot comply with the requirement or condition.[25] It should be noted that the concept of detriment also appears in the legislation as a discriminatory act (SDA, s 6(2)(b); RRA, s 4(2)(c)), meaning a disadvantage *(Ministry of Defence v Jeremiah)*. Apparently the concept means the same in both sections.

Figure 6.3 The test for objective justification in *Hampson v DES*

Conclusions on indirect discrimination

- Indirect discrimination is where a requirement is applied generally but has a discriminatory impact.
- It appears that a requirement or condition is not a prerequisite for indirect discrimination under EU law (in the circumstances of *Enderby*), but that it may still be so under domestic law.
- In UK law, a requirement or condition must be an absolute bar, but note *Falkirk Council* and the EU definition (see page 110). This leaves out of the reckoning any discriminatory preferences on the part of the employer.
- On considerably smaller proportion, there is little guidance on 'considerably', the correct pool comprises those who would be qualified for the post (excluding the effect of the requirement or condition) and 'can comply' means can comply in practice.
- Detriment simply means a disadvantage.
- The justification defence has four elements:
  - the employer's genuine need;
  - the requirement or condition meets that need;
  - the requirement or condition is reasonably necessary to meet that need; and
  - the employer's reasonable needs outweigh the discriminatory effect on the complainant.

UNLAWFUL ACTS

It was noted earlier that acts made unlawful by the legislation fall into two categories:

- discrimination; and
- other unlawful acts.

Discrimination by employers

The successful complainant will need to establish that a discriminatory act took place. This means that two separate parts of the legislation will have to be satisfied:

- the complainant will have to demonstrate that one or more acts falling within SDA, s 6 or RRA, s 4 took place; and
- the complainant will then need to establish that this constituted a form of discrimination (eg, direct discrimination) on one of the prohibited grounds (eg, sex).

The acts which are the basis of unlawful discrimination

These are set out below.

SDA, s 6(1) covers applicants:

> It is unlawful for a person, in relation to employment by him at an establishment in Great Britain, to discriminate against a woman:
>
> (a) in the arrangements he makes for the purpose of determining who should be offered that employment, or
> (b) in the terms on which he offers her that employment, or
> (c) by refusing or deliberately omitting to offer her that employment.

SDA, s 6(2) covers those already employed:

> It is unlawful for a person, in the case of a woman employed by him at an establishment in Great Britain, to discriminate against her:
>
> (a) in the way he affords her access to opportunities for promotion, transfer or training, or to any other benefits, facilities or services, or by refusing or deliberately omitting to afford her access to them, or
> (b) by dismissing her, or subjecting her to any other detriment.

RRA, s 4(1) covers applicants: this is in terms similar to SDA, s 6(1).

RRA, s4(2) covers those in employment. Here the coverage of the RRA is wider than that of SDA, s 6(2) by the addition of s 4(2)(a) which makes it unlawful to discriminate in the terms of employment which are afforded to the worker. The equivalent of this provision in relation to sex discrimination is found in the Equal Pay Act, so that the RRA covers in respect of race what the SDA and the EqPA combined cover in respect of sex.

Note that the definition of 'employment' extends beyond the contract of employment to include contracts 'personally to execute any work or labour' (SDA, s 82(1); RRA, s 78(1)). The legislation thus applies to a category of worker wider than employee. However, it will not include a former employee: see *Nagarayon*, pages 98–9.

The meaning of discrimination

The principal categories of discrimination – direct and indirect – have already been analysed in some detail. Here it is noted that there is a third category, victimization.[26]

Other unlawful acts

These are acts which the legislation makes unlawful but which do not fit within the definition of discrimination:

- discriminatory practices,[27] ie, a requirement or condition;
- discriminatory advertisements;[28]
- instructions to discriminate;[29]
- pressure to discriminate;[30] and
- aiding unlawful acts;[31]

Liability[32]

Anything done by a person in the course of his or her employment is to be treated as done by the employer as well as by him or her. This rule applies even if the employer did not know or did not approve of what was done. In earlier cases, a distinction was drawn between situations where the employee was wrongfully performing his duties, and those where employment merely provided an opportunity to perform a wrongful act (see *Irving v The Post Office* and *Cobham v Forest Healthcare NHS Trust*). This in effect applied the common law test for vicarious liability (see chapter 15). However, in *Jones v Tower Boot Co Ltd* the Court of Appeal ruled that the concept 'in the course of employment' is to be construed widely and is not restricted by the common law test. An employer has the defence that he did all that was reasonably practicable to prevent the employee doing what he did. A principal will be responsible, along with his agent, for anything done with his express or implied authority. It seems that an employer may also be responsible for discrimination by third parties. In *Burton v De Vere Hotels*, the EAT held the employer liable for racial harassment of the hotel's staff by the hotel's users. The employer was in a position to prevent the harassment but did not do so.

Discrimination by bodies other than employers

The SDA and RRA apply outside the employment field to cover discrimination in respect of the provision of goods and services. It must be noted here, however, that even within the employment field the legislation does not restrict itself to discrimination by employers. In both the RRA and SDA discrimination by the following is also unlawful:

- partnerships;
- trades unions;
- qualifying bodies (ie, bodies awarding qualifications);
- training organizations; and
- employment agencies.

EXCEPTIONS

Genuine occupational qualifications (GOQs)

Meaning
Where a particular sex or race is a requirement for the job it is regarded as a GOQ. This means that an employer can restrict recruitment to a particular sex or race without the discrimination being unlawful. However, GOQs are very narrowly drawn.

Where race is a GOQ[33]
Race can be a GOQ for purposes of authenticity in art, drama and catering and for the provision of personal welfare services. It should also be noted that (although it is not a GOQ) there is an exception for employment in a private household, although not if the discrimination takes the form of victimization.[34]

Where sex is a GOQ[35]
The circumstances in which sex may be a GOQ are where a particular sex is required:

- for reasons of physiology or authenticity;
- for reasons of decency or privacy;
- because close contact is necessary in a private household;
- because the location makes it impracticable to live elsewhere but on site and it is not reasonable to expect the employer to provide accommodation;
- single-sex hospitals, prisons etc;
- to provide personal welfare services;
- because duties are to be performed outside the UK in a country whose laws or customs prevent a woman doing her duties or doing them effectively; and
- because the job is one of two held by a married couple.

Case law

London Borough of Lambeth v CRE

The personal services GOQ under RRA applies where the individual is the direct provider of the service not where the person is in a managerial or supervisory capacity.

Tottenham Green Under Fives Centre v Marshall

In the first of two cases it was held that the test is whether personal services 'can most effectively be provided' by a person of that particular racial group (s 5(2)(d)). The test is not whether the services can only be provided by a member of that racial group. In the second case the issue was the relative importance of particular duties. Here it was decided that as long as the duty was not a sham or *de minimis*, the tribunal should have regard to it. However, it is not for the tribunal to determine the relative importance of duties.

Provisions relating to death or retirement (sex discrimination only)

Originally this was a blanket exception but following *Marshall v Southampton and South-West Hampshire Area Health Authority* and the Sex Discrimination Act 1986 the exception was narrowed to the present form.[36]

Marshall v Southampton and South-West Hampshire Area Health Authority

FACTS
The employer required Mrs Marshall to retire before the male retiring age of 65. She was dismissed at the age of 62. The blanket exception in the SDA appeared to rule out her complaint.
HELD (ECJ)
Discriminatory retirement ages were a breach of the Equal Treatment Directive. The SDA 1975 did not therefore give full effect to the ETD and was amended in the light of this by the SDA 1986.

Subsequent decisions of the ECJ have made it clear that discrimination in other matters relating to retirement is within the scope of the ETD. In *Bilka-Kaufhaus* (exclusion of part-timers from occupational pension schemes amounting to indirect discrimination) and in *Barber v Guardian Royal Exchange* (discriminatory ages for the payment of pensions in cases of early retirement) it was held that pensions are pay. Thus there is a breach of article 119 of the Treaty of Rome if there is less favourable treatment of one sex (unless, in the case of indirect discrimination, it is objectively justified). See chapter 11 for a discussion of equal pay.

Other exceptions

These are of relatively minor importance.

- acts done under statutory authority (both SDA and RRA) but limited in the SDA case to those protecting women from specifically female risks (SDA, s 51);
- special provisions relating to the police (SDA and RRA);
- acts to safeguard national security (SDA and RRA); a certificate from the Minister is sufficient evidence under SDA, but not apparently under the ETD (*Johnston v Royal Ulster Constabulary*);
- where under RRA, s 54(2) an appeal lies under some other enactment (in *Khan v General Medical Council* under the Medical Act 1983); there is a similar provision in SDA (s 63(2)); and
- special provisions relating to prison officers and ministers of religion (SDA only).

THE ROLE OF THE COMMISSIONS

Establishment and general duties

The commissions are intended to give effect to the strategic role of the legislation. The EOC is established under s 53 of the SDA with the following general duties:

- to work towards the elimination of discrimination;
- to promote equality of opportunity between the sexes; and
- to keep under review the working of the SDA and the EqPA and make proposals for their amendment where necessary or when required by the Secretary of State.

Following *R v Secretary of State for Employment ex parte EOC* it is clear that the EOC has *locus standi* to apply for judicial review of discriminatory elements of other legislation.

Similar provisions in respect of the CRE are found in RRA, s 43.

Specific duties

Various specific duties are then set out for the Commissions:

- carrying out research and education;[37]
- making annual reports to the Secretary of State;[38]
- drawing up and issuing codes of practice;[39] sex discrimination, equal pay and race relations codes have been issued;
- conducting formal investigations;[40]

- issuing non-discrimination notices;[41] a register of such notices must be kept (SDA, s 70; RRA, s 61).
- applying for injunctions to stop persistent discrimination.[42] (as a preliminary step, the commissions may present a complaint to an industrial tribunal); [43] and
- giving assistance to individuals (eg, representing them at industrial tribunals).[44]

The commissions are the only means by which enforcement action can be taken in respect of discriminatory practices, discriminatory advertisements, instructions to discriminate and pressure to discriminate (the 'other unlawful acts' on pages 116–17).

Codes of practice and positive action

Codes of practice give guidance on equal opportunities policies, monitoring and positive action. Positive action must be distinguished from reverse discrimination.[45] The former is lawful under both Acts, so that there can be training which is limited to a particular sex or racial group and encouragement given to job applicants. The qualification is that the particular groups are under-represented in the workforce. Reverse discrimination (such as restricting posts to groups discriminated against in the past) is unlawful.

Race Relations Code[46]
The code aims to give practical guidance to employers and others not only to help them understand the RRA and its implications but also to assist them in implementing policies to eliminate race discrimination and to enhance equality of opportunity. It deals not only with the responsibilities of employers but also with those of employees, trades unions and employment agencies. Employers' responsibilities are explained in terms of equal opportunities policies; recruitment and selection; promotion, transfer, training and dismissal; terms and benefits etc of employment; grievances; discipline; cultural and religious needs; and other matters.

Sex Discrimination Code
The EOC's Code of Practice was adopted in 1985.[47] It sets out the legal framework within which it operates and provides guidance on the role of good employment practices in eliminating sex and marriage discrimination and in promoting equality of opportunity. As regards the latter, it recommends the formulation and implementation of equal opportunities policies.[48]

Equal Pay Code

An equal pay code issued under SDA, s 56A came into force in March 1997. The central recommendation is that employers conduct an internal pay review in order to ensure that potentially discriminatory pay differences are objectively justified.

Status of codes of practice

These codes of practice may be seen as quasi-law: they are something stronger than advice and guidance but weaker than the law itself. A failure to observe a provision in a code will not render anyone liable to legal proceedings. However, in proceedings instituted under any of the relevant Acts (RRA, SDA or EqPA), codes of practice are admissible as evidence and where a tribunal considers the provisions of a code to be relevant, it must take those provisions into account.

APPLICATIONS TO INDUSTRIAL TRIBUNALS

Whether the application is in time

An application complaining of unlawful discrimination may be made to an industrial tribunal.[49] The tribunal will hear the complaint only if it is lodged within three months of 'the act complained of', unless it is 'just and equitable' to admit a late application.[50] There is provision for ACAS conciliation.

Establishing the date of 'the act complained of' has sometimes proved difficult, as the following case law illustrates.

Barclays Bank v Kapur

Whether the discrimination is a continuing act or a deliberate omission: *Barclays Bank v Kapur*
A discriminatory pension was an act extending throughout the duration of the contract and fell to be treated as occurring at the end of the contract (RRA, s 68(7)(a) and (b)). See also *Littlewoods v Traynor*, below.

Sougrin v Haringey Health Authority

Here the alleged discrimination was a refusal to upgrade the complainant. This was a deliberate omission under RRA, s 68(7)(c) and fell to be treated as occurring when it was decided.

Clarke v Hampshire Electro-Plating Co Ltd

Where the complainant did not within three months realise that he had a complaint: *Clarke v Hampshire Electro-Plating Co Ltd*

The complainant did not realise that he had a basis for complaint until more than three months after his application for promotion had been rejected. This was because his cause of action did not crystallize until a white person with fewer qualifications was appointed to the post for which he had been rejected, and this was more than three months later. It was held that the limitation period ran from the moment his cause of action crystallized rather than from the date his application for promotion was rejected.

Adekeye v The Post Office

Where there is discrimination after the date of the original 'act complained of': *Adekeye v The Post Office*

If a post-dismissal appeal is alleged to be discriminatory, this is a separate 'act complained of' for the purposes of the legislation, but note that, if the person is no longer employed, the complaint will not be within the scope of the legislation (*Adekeye v The Post Office (No 2)*: see page 99)

Littlewoods Organisation plc v Traynor

The failure of an employer to take agreed steps to remedy racial harassment was itself race discrimination and 'an act complained of'. Moreover, here it was a continuing act as in *Kapur.*

Matters of proof

Burden and standard of proof

King v The Great Britain–China Centre

The burden is upon the complainant.

However, it is rare to find direct evidence of discrimination, so courts may wish to draw inferences from the primary facts (but are not bound to do so: *Zafar v Glasgow City Council*) [51]

Thus, where there is a difference (here in race) and an act of discrimination, courts may infer unlawful discrimination in the absence of an adequate explanation by the employer (this seems to be similar to the view of the ECJ in *Enderby*:

see pages 110–11). The decision has to be taken on the balance of probabilities, bearing in mind that the burden is upon the complainant but also that complainants face difficulties in discharging the burden. The Court of Appeal's approach in *King* has been affirmed by the House of Lords in *Zafar*.

Discovery and disclosure

Statistics derived from monitoring (which is encouraged by the codes of practice) may be helpful and if so a tribunal may order disclosure (as in *West Midlands Passenger Transport Executive v Singh*). The test is whether the material is logically probative of the issue. This is possibly wider than the earlier test in *Nasse v Science Research Council*: disclosure will be ordered if the material is necessary to fairly dispose of the proceedings. Discovery and disclosure will be limited to documents already in existence. The employer cannot be ordered to prepare a new document *(Carrington v Helix Lighting)*. Finally, disclosure will not be ordered if it is oppressive, eg the information could be provided only at great expense or trouble *(West Midlands Passenger Transport Executive v Singh)*.

The question procedure

Statutory questionnaires may be used by complainants under SDA, s 74 and RRA, s 65 in order to elicit information as to why an employer has treated them in a particular way. No reply, or an evasive or equivocal reply, will allow a court to draw an inference, including the inference that there has been unlawful discrimination.

Remedies

The remedies available to a successful complainant are:

- a declaration of rights;
- compensation; and
- a recommendation that certain action be taken.

An example of a recommendation can be found in *Price v Civil Service Commission*. The recommendation was that the employer remove the discriminatory age limit on entry to a particular grade of work (see pages 107–8). However, a recommendation that the employer should offer the next vacancy to the complainant might lead to unlawful discrimination, and went too far *(British Gas v Sharma)*.

As regards compensation, it should be noted that:

- compensation is payable in respect of injured feelings;[52]

- aggravated damages may be payable because of the manner or motive of the employer's behaviour *(Alexander v Home Office; Noone v North-West Thames Regional Health Authority (No 2))* but not exemplary damages (*City of Bradford v Arora*, overruled in *Deane v Ealing Borough Council*);[53]
- compensation is now payable for unintentional indirect discrimination;[54]
- there is no limit on the compensation following *Marshall v Southampton and South-West Hampshire Area Health Authority (No 2)* where the ECJ held that there was no adequate remedy because of the statutory limit on compensation which then existed (the ECJ held that article 6 of the ETD required there to be procedures to deal with any wrongs suffered and that such procedures must provide for a proper remedy; subsequently the Race Relations (Remedies) Act 1994, the Race Relations (Interest on Awards) Regulations 1994, and the Sex Discrimination and Equal Pay (Remedies) Regulations 1993 removed the limits); and
- interest is payable in line with the Industrial Tribunals (Interest) Order 1990 and the Industrial Tribunals (Interest on Awards in Discrimination Cases) Regulations 1996.[18]

NOTES

1   76/207/EC, OJ 1976, L39.
2   RRA 1976, s 4(2)(a).
3   DDA 1995. Disability discrimination is defined in ss 1, 4 and 5. On the justification defence see s 5 and on reasonable adjustment, s 6.
4   RRA, s 3(1).
5   RRA, ss 4 and 78(1); and SDA, ss 6 and 82(1).
6   SDA, s 6(1) and RRA, s 4(1).
7   SDA, s 1(1)(a).
8   SDA, s 3(1)(a).
9   SDA, s 1(2).
10   SDA, s 2(1).
11   RRA, s 1(1)(a).
12   RRA, s 1(2).
13   RRA, s 3(1).
14   This is not an employment case but is included here because it establishes a test applicable to employment cases.
15   79/7/EC, OJ 1979, L6.
16   ERA, s 99. This contrasts with a refusal to employ because of pregnancy, where the complainant's only action would be under the SDA.
17   For discussion of the law of sexual harassment see Rubenstein, M, 'The Law of Sexual Harassment at Work', (1983) 12 ILJ 1. On good practice, see *Statement on Harassment at Work* (London, IPM (now IPD), 1992).

18 Article 1, EU Recommendation 92/131 of 27 November 1991 on the Protection of the Dignity of Women and Men at Work, OJ 1992 L49/1. A code of practice is annexed to the Recommendation.
19 Article 1 of the Recommendation cites possible breaches of articles 3, 4 and 5 of the ETD (76/207/EEC).
20 SDA, s 1(1)(b).
21 SDA, s 3(1)(b).
22 RRA, s 1(1)(b).
23 Burden of Proof in Sex Discrimination Cases, 1997.
24 SI 1985/782.
25 SDA, s 1(1)(b)(iii) in respect of indirect discrimination on the ground of sex. Similar provisions apply to marriage and race.
26 SDA, s 4; RRA, s 2.
27 SDA, s 37; RRA, s 28.
28 SDA, s 38; RRA, s 29.
29 SDA, s 39; RRA, s 30.
30 SDA, s 40; RRA, s 31.
31 SDA, s 42; RRA, s 33.
32 SDA, s 41; RRA, s 32.
33 RRA, s 5.
34 RRA, s 4(3).
35 SDA, s 7.
36 SDA, s 6(4).
37 SDA, s 54; RRA, s 45.
38 SDA, s 56; RRA, s 46.
39 SDA, s 56A; RRA, s 47.
40 SDA, s 57; RRA, s 48.
41 SDA, s 67; RRA, s 58.
42 SDA, s 71; RRA, s 62.
43 SDA, s 73; RRA, s 64.
44 SDA, s 75; RRA, s 66.
45 For guidance on positive action, including real case studies, see Race Relations Advisory Service, *Positive Action* (London, Department of Employment, 1994).
46 CRE, *Code of Practice for the Elimination of Racial Discrimination and the Promotion of Equality of Opportunity in Employment* (London, CRE, 1984).
47 EOC, *Code of Practice for the Elimination of Discrimination on the Grounds of Sex and Marriage and the Promotion of Equality of Opportunity in Employment* (London, HMSO, 1985).
48 Ibid, p14.
49 SDA, s 63; RRA, s 54.
50 SDA, s 76; RRA, s 68.
51 But note that when the Directive on Burden of Proof in Sex Discrimination Cases is implemented in the UK a tribunal will be required to find for the complainant in the absence of an adequate explanation by an employer where there is *prima facie* discrimination.
52 SDA, ss 65(1)(b) and 66(4): RRA, s 57(4).

53 However, the Law Commission, the statutory body responsible for advising on law reform, has recommended that exemplary damages (ie, punitive damages) should be available in race, sex and disability discrimination cases. Law Commission, *Aggravated, Exemplary and Restitutionary Damages* (London, No 247, 1997).

54 The Sex Discrimination and Equal Pay (Miscellaneous Amendments) Regulations (SI 1996/438) give tribunals the power to award compensation for unintentional indirect discrimination in employment cases where they decide it is just and equitable to do so. This is to bring the legislation into compliance with the ETD. Compensation in race discrimination cases is still not payable where there is unintentional indirect discrimination (RRA, s 57(3)).

55 The 1996 Regulations revoked the 1993 Sex Discrimination and Equal Pay (Remedies) Regulations and the 1994 Race Relations (Interest on Awards) Regulations.

Disability and Other Discrimination

This chapter is concerned with discrimination other than that on the grounds of sex and race. The principal area is disability, where a completely new legal framework is now operational. The statutory quota scheme and provisions for reserved occupations have been repealed. The chapter deals first with the new scheme. Thereafter it concerns itself with other grounds of discrimination – trades union membership, age, religion, political orientation and sexual preference.

THE DISABILITY DISCRIMINATION ACT 1995

Introduction

Like the SDA and the RRA, the new Act has an application which is not limited to the employment field. It covers:

- discrimination in relation to goods, facilities and services;
- discrimination in relation to the disposal and management of premises;
- access to education; and
- access to public transport.

In the employment field it provides for actions in respect of discrimination:

- against applicants and employees;
- against contract workers; and
- by trade organisations, such as trades unions.

The Act received the Royal Assent in October 1995 and the employment parts of it became operative in December 1996. There are regulations, a code of practice and guidance under the Act.[1]

Unlike the SDA, interpretation of the new Act has not been subject to the overriding supervision of the ECJ since there has been no Treaty article or directive governing this area. However, the amended Treaty of Rome (article 6A: see chapter 2) provides a basis for EU action against discrimination on grounds of disability. The ECJ will have a legal basis on which to interpret Member States' domestic legislation once there is an EU instrument (eg, a directive) adopted on the basis of article 6A.

Scope

The following exceptions and exemptions apply:

- small employers (fewer than 20 employees);
- national security;
- police;
- armed forces;
- prison officers;
- fire-fighters;
- employment ordinarily outside the UK;
- charities;
- statutory authority (eg, health and safety); and
- where the employer operates sheltered employment.

The Act provides no rights for the non-disabled. There is no age limit. Nothing in the Act forces an employee to disclose their disability, but the duty to make reasonable adjustments (see below) arises only once the disability is known. Nothing in the Act forces an employer to employ an employee who cannot do the job.

Meaning of disabled person

Complaints may be brought by disabled persons. A 'disabled person' means a person who has or had a disability. The definition of disability is central to the operation of the Act, and unlike race and sex discrimination, where definition is not particularly difficult, the concept of disability may prove troublesome.

A person has a disability if he has a physical or mental impairment which has a substantial and long-term adverse effect on his ability to carry out normal day-to-day activities. There are a number of concepts here:

Impairment

This is not defined but includes a physical impairment or condition. It extends to a mental impairment. However, mental illness is included 'only if it is a clinically well-recognised illness'.[2] This seems to require not just that the condition is clinically accepted by some within the medical profession, but rather that it is generally accepted within the profession. Overall, impairment seems to imply a medical status or condition.

Long-term adverse effects

The impairment must have lasted for 12 months, or can reasonably be expected to last at least 12 months, or can reasonably be expected to last for the rest of the life of the person concerned.

Normal day-to-day activities

These are:

- mobility;
- manual dexterity;
- physical co-ordination;
- continence;
- ability to lift, carry or otherwise move everyday objects;
- speech, hearing or eyesight;
- memory or ability to concentrate, learn or understand; and
- perception of the risk of physical danger.

The complainant will have to establish that he or she is or was a disabled person. This is likely to require them to adduce medical evidence to demonstrate the nature and extent of the impairment and its effects.

Special provisions are set out for:

- recurring and intermittent impairments;
- progressive conditions (eg, cancer, multiple sclerosis or muscular dystrophy);
- severe disfigurements;
- impairments controlled or corrected by medical or special aids;
- sight impairments and spectacles and contact lenses; and
- persons who were registered under the Disabled Persons (Employment) Act 1944, which is now repealed.

Unlawful discrimination under the DDA

Meaning of discrimination

Unlike the SDA and RRA, the new Act does not distinguish between direct and indirect discrimination. The burden and proof lies on the complainant to establish unlawful discrimination, ie, that there has been an act specified in the DDA which constitutes discrimination as defined. Discrimination means that for a reason which relates to the disabled person's disability, the employer treats the disabled person less favourably than he treats or would treat others to whom that reason does not apply, and the employer cannot show the treatment to be justified. The comparison will be between disabled and non-disabled or between people with disabilities of a different nature or extent.

Justification defence

The justification defence may be applied to any form of discrimination (*cf* the RRA and the SDA where it can be used only as a defence to indirect discrimination). For the justification defence to succeed, the reason for the treatment must be material and substantial. Moreover, the justification defence cannot be entered unless the employer has discharged his duty to make reasonable adjustments. On both these questions, the burden lies with the employer.

Duty to make reasonable adjustment

This is a potentially onerous duty for which the Act provides examples, the list not being exhaustive:[3]

- making adjustments to premises;
- allocating some of the disabled person's duties to another person;
- transferring a disabled person to another vacancy;
- altering the person's working hours;
- changing the workplace of the disabled person;
- allowing time off during working hours for rehabilitation, assessment or treatment;
- providing or arranging the provision of training;
- acquiring or modifying equipment;
- modifying instructions or reference manuals;
- modifying testing or assessment procedures;
- providing a reader or interpreter; and
- providing supervision.

The duty applies when a disability is known to the employer and where arrangements affecting opportunities or physical features of premises put the disabled person at a disadvantage in comparison with a non-disabled person. Where this is the case, the employer is under a duty to take such steps as are reasonable in all the circumstances, to prevent substantial disadvantage. A failure to comply is itself discrimination but the justification defence applies to the failure to discharge this duty as well as to the treatment of the disabled person if the duty is discharged.[4]

Factors in reasonableness will be practicability, effectiveness, financial and other costs, disruption to business, the employer's resources and the availability of financial and other assistance.

Unlawful acts of discrimination

The new Act is similar to the RRA here in including contract terms as well as non-contractual matters. The unlawful acts of discrimination towards applicants are in relation to:

- recruitment and selection arrangements;
- the terms on which employment is offered; and
- the refusal of employment.

For employees, unlawful acts of discrimination are in relation to:

- terms of employment;
- employment opportunities and benefits (eg, promotion and training);
- dismissal; and
- any other detriment.

Detriment, presumably, will be defined as disadvantage (as in *Ministry of Defence v Jeremiah*) and there seems to be no reason why harassment cannot be part of the concept of discrimination.

Applications to industrial tribunals

A disabled person may complain to an industrial tribunal that they have been subject to unlawful discrimination under the Act. The complaint must be made within three months of the act about which they are complaining. As with race and sex discrimination there is provision for the use of a statutory questionnaire to enable the complainant to obtain a clearer view of why he or she has been treated in the way they have, and to better formulate and assess their case. Unless the contrary is shown, a discriminatory advertisement will lead to an inference that the applicant has been refused employment because of his or her disability.[5]

Complaints may be settled by ACAS conciliation or by compromise agreements, so preventing the complainant continuing to an industrial tribunal. If the case is not settled, proceeds to a tribunal and is decided in favour of the complainant, the remedies are a declaration, recommendation and compensation. As with race and sex discrimination, compensation awarded for injury to feelings has no limit and may attract interest. Tribunals are required to provide extended rather than summary reasons for their decisions.

Liability lies with the discriminator but as with race and sex discrimination the employer will be vicariously liable, alongside the discriminator, if the discrimination is carried out by an employee in the course of his or her employment.

It seems likely that applications in cases of ill-health dismissal will be argued as either or both disability discrimination and unfair dismissal. The latter may be easier to prove but the former has no compensation limit. The duty to make reasonable adjustments is probably stronger than the duty to consider alternative work in capability cases under unfair dismissal legislation (on dismissal for medical condition/handicap, see chapter 16).

The National Disability Council (NDC)

The NDC represents the strategic dimension of the DDA but is not comparable with the EOC or CRE. This is because it is an advisory rather than an enforcement mechanism, and is without powers. Moreover, it is not permitted to advise on matters relating to the employment part of the Act. However, the government has stated that it will replace the NDC with a standing commission similar to the EOC and CRE.

STATEMENTS IN DIRECTORS' REPORTS

Under separate legislation, companies employing an average of more than 250 employees in the financial year must include in their directors' report a statement about the employment of people with disabilities.[6] This applies to disabled people generally and is not restricted to those formerly registered as disabled.

DISCRIMINATION ON GROUNDS OTHER THAN RACE, SEX AND DISABILITY

Union membership[7]

Employees are protected against dismissal and action short of dismissal on grounds of union membership or activity, or non-membership. In addition, there are provisions making it unlawful to refuse employment to a person because of union membership or non-membership. In all these cases, remedies are obtained by making an application to an industrial tribunal. Discrimination on union or non-union grounds is dealt with in chapter 21.

Age

There is no legislation in the UK specifically outlawing discrimination on the ground of age, but it is possible for age limits to constitute indirect sex discrimination as in *Price v Civil Service Commission* (see pages 107–8. The government prefers there to be a voluntary code governing this area rather than legislation.

Religion

The right not to be discriminated against on the ground of religious belief is enshrined in the European Convention on Human Rights 1950 (articles 9 and 14) and the Universal Declaration of Human Rights 1948 (article 2), but not generally in UK law. The exception is Northern Ireland, where the Fair Employment (Northern Ireland) Acts of 1976 and 1989 seek to offer protection for religious beliefs.

The 1976 Act defines discrimination as less favourable treatment on grounds of religious belief or political opinion, or victimization for taking action in respect of the legislation. The 1989 Act extended the definition to include indirect discrimination (see chapter 6 on the meaning of indirect discrimination).

In the UK generally, religious beliefs might be protected by the RRA if the persons holding those beliefs can be said to form an ethnic group. Thus Jews have been held to be a racial group (the test is laid down in *Mandla*; see page 98). Even if a religious community cannot be seen as an ethnic group, it may be protected by the RRA if discrimination on the ground of religion constitutes indirect race discrimination. This might occur, for example, if an employer refused to employ people who believed in a particular religion and those people made up a significant proportion of a particular ethnic group.

Political orientation

Again there is no general protection in the UK. The provisions in respect of political belief in the Fair Employment (Northern Ireland) Acts seemed to apply only in the context of discrimination on grounds of religion, but it now appears that protection against discrimination on the ground of 'political opinion'[8] is a separate and free-standing right under the Acts *(McKay v Northern Ireland Public Service Alliance)*.

Sexual preference

The European Convention on Human Rights (article 8) provides an international basis for protection against discrimination on grounds of sexual preference but there is no express protection in the law of the UK.[9] Indeed, it was held recently that the ban on employing homosexuals in the British armed forces was lawful (being neither irrational nor a breach of the ETD), although a warning was sounded that such a policy is increasingly out of step with modern-day thinking *(R v Ministry of Defence ex parte Smith)*. Moreover, in *P&S v Cornwall County Council*, the ECJ ruled that dismissal for proposing to undergo gender re-assignment surgery would be a breach of the ETD if not justified, so extending discrimination law protection to transsexuals. Some of the difficulties in this area are illustrated by the following two cases.

Saunders v Scottish National Camps Association

It was held in this case that it was fair to dismiss a maintenance handyman in a children's camp because of his involvement in a homosexual incident. This was 'some other substantial reason for dismissal' (see chapter 16). The employer's reasonableness has to be judged in the light of prevailing social attitudes even if these are based on prejudice.

Boychuk v Symons Holdings Ltd

Here the issue was not so much the sexual preference as the expression of that preference. The applicant wore provocative badges – with messages such as 'lesbians ignite' – contrary to instructions and warnings. The dismissal was again held to be fair for 'some other substantial reason' and turned on the employer's discretion to lay down a reasonable dress code which would not be offensive to fellow workers or customers.

More recently, the ECJ had to decide whether treating a person less favourably in respect of pay (here, concessionary travel) on the ground of their sexual orientation constituted a breach of article 119 of the Treaty of Rome, which sets down the principle of equal pay for equal work on the basis of sex. It was held that denying the benefit to the same-sex partner of a female employee, while conferring benefit on a different-sex partner was not discrimination on the ground of sex and did not breach article 119. First, a male employee with a male partner would have received the same treatment. Secondly, sexual orientation was not covered by article 119, which relates only to sex discrimination *(Grant v South-West Trains Ltd)*.

NOTES

1 There are parallels here with health and safety at work: see chapter 14. There are sets of DDA regulations on the meaning of disability (SI 1996/1455) and on the application of the Act to the employment field (SI 1996/1456).

2 DDA, Sched1, para 1(1).

3 DDA, s 6.

4 DDA, s 5.

5 DDA. s 11.

6 Companies Act 1985, s 235 and Sched 7, Part III

7 TULR(C)A, ss 137, 146 and 152.

8 Fair Employment (Northern Ireland) Act 1989, s 16(1)(a).

9 Since the European Convention is not part of UK law, it can be held to be irrelevant (as in *R v Ministry of Defence ex parte Smith*, where the court accepted that the Ministry's policy was inconsistent with the Convention). The Human Rights Bill 1997, once enacted, will alter the position by incorporating the European Convention into UK law.

The Contract of Employment: Formation and Sources

FORMATION OF THE CONTRACT OF EMPLOYMENT

Relationship to general contract law

Guiding principle

The guiding principle is to be found in the statement of Lord Evershed MR in *Laws v London Chronicle*:

> A contract of service is but an example of contracts in general, so that the general law of contract will be applicable.

The principle in practice

In practice, a contract of employment will come into existence only when the normal prerequisites for contractual relations are met, namely, offer and acceptance, capacity, consideration, intention to create legal relations and the absence of vitiating factors.

Offer and acceptance

Without an offer and acceptance there will be no contract of employment. The offer may be conditional, eg upon receipt of satisfactory references *(Wishart v National Association of Citizens' Advice Bureaux)* or the passing of a medical examination. As usual, an offer must be distinguished from an invitation to treat – advertising a job vacancy in a newspaper will be the latter *(Crosville Wales Ltd v Tracey)*. Even in the absence of a contract of employment there may be a collateral contract if work has been promised (see *Gill v Cape Contracts*, below).

Capacity

Parties to the contract must have the legal capacity to enter into a contract. This is not likely to be an important issue in the employment field, although it could arise in relation to minors (ie, those under 18 years of age). The general rule is that if a contract is, on the whole, for the minor's benefit, it will bind him or her. The capacity of Crown servants may also be relevant. However, the balance of authority is now clearly in favour of them being employed under a contract of employment *(R v Lord Chancellor's Department ex parte Nangle)*.

Consideration

Typically, the employee provides work and the employer provides wages or salary and perhaps other benefits, or the parties promise to provide these things. Where there is a wage increase, the employer's consideration appears to be more wages and the employee's the continuation of work *(Lee v GEC Plessey)*.

Intention to create legal relations

This is presumed because the context is a business rather than a personal relationship.

Absence of vitiating factors

There must be nothing which undoes the contract by making it void (ineffective) or voidable (capable of being rendered ineffective). Thus the agreement which forms the basis of the contract should be free from mistake, misrepresentation and illegality (on illegality, see below).

The form of the contract

A contract of employment can be entered into orally at common law, and statute has not intervened to alter this. However, as noted later, the contract must be evidenced in writing (see pages 142–8).

Collateral contracts and representations

It is possible that representations made by one of the parties and acted upon by the other may bring into existence a collateral contract which will exist even if the contract of employment has not itself been formed. This process is clearly illustrated by the case cited below.

Gill v Cape Contracts Ltd

FACTS
Cape Contracts promised Gill and others that if they came to work for them there would be at least six months' work. Gill and others terminated their positions elsewhere but before they could start with Cape, the firm withdrew its promise.
HELD (Northern Ireland High Court)
A promise of work for at least six months was a collateral contract. The defendant made representations on which the plaintiffs had acted in resigning their jobs. Damages would be awarded for breach of the collateral contract.
RATIO (the reason underlying the decision)
If a representation is made in the knowledge that the plaintiff will act upon it and it is intended that he should act on it, then this is a warranty. In the present case, there was a breach of warranty that if the men gave up their existing employment they would be employed by the defendant for a period of at least six months.
Note that no express finding was made as to whether a contract of employment had yet come into being. If it had (which seems unlikely) there would have been a remedy in the form of damages for breach of the main contract.

Illegality

General principle
The doctrine of illegality holds that a contract with purposes contrary to common law or statute, or with illegal consideration, is void.

Significance of the doctrine in employment law
If the contract of employment is void, not only are the contract terms not enforceable, but statutory rights depending on the existence of a contract of employment may also be unenforceable. There is the possibility here of an employer benefiting from his own wrongdoing by preventing the employee from exercising his legal rights.

The paradigm case: tax evasion
The paradigm case of illegality in employment law is probably an arrangement to pay the employee some or all of his wages without the deduction of tax. An example of such a case is given below.

Tomlinson v Dick Evans U-Drive Ltd

FACTS
The employee was engaged to run a car hire business. At some stage he was given an increase in wages amounting to £15 per week. Both employer and

employee knew that this sum was taken from petty cash and that no income tax was paid in respect of it.

HELD (EAT)

Even though unfair dismissal and redundancy rights were statutory, they depended upon and arose from the contract of employment. Where the contract was illegal, as here, those statutory rights would not be enforceable.

COMMENT

This was an early case – 1978 – and the EAT seemed to treat the contract as illegal without making any distinction between illegal purpose and illegal performance. Later cases also attach importance to whether or not the employee knew of the illegality, which he did here.

Illegal purpose or illegal performance?

The contract may not be void if its purpose is legal but its performance illegal.

Coral Leisure Group Ltd v Barnett

FACTS

Mr Barnett was taken on as a public relations executive but part of his job was to hire prostitutes for his employer's clients. The employer argued that the contract was void for immorality.

HELD (EAT)

The contract was not void. The purpose of the contract was not the hiring of prostitutes, nor was this a term of the contract.

COMMENT

It seems that the gravity of the illegality needs to be considered. Thus, it does not follow automatically that illegal performance (as distinct from illegal purpose) will result in the contract not being void, but it may do.

The leading case

The leading case in this area is presented below.

Hewcastle Catering Ltd v Ahmed

FACTS

The applicants were waiters at their employer's club. They – the employees – participated in their employer's VAT fraud, but did not benefit by doing so. When the employer was prosecuted, the employees gave evidence against him.

HELD (CA)

The contract was not void for illegality;

The doctrine of illegality should be applied only if the case proceeding would be 'an affront to the public conscience'.

The employer's defence of illegality is to be rejected if the employer is proportionately much more blameworthy than the employee.

COMMENT

This case seems to confirm a move towards a less harsh application of the doctrine when compared with, for example, *Dick Evans U-Drive* (although in that case the employee did benefit from the illegality, so the cases can be distinguished). In *Hewcastle*, there also seems to be acceptance of tax evasion as illegal performance rather than illegal purpose.

Temporary illegality

The question arises as to the legal position if the illegality is not a permanent feature of the contract, as in the case below.

Hyland v J H Barker (North West) Ltd

FACTS

A tax-free (and thus illegal) lodging allowance was paid to the employee for four weeks while he was working away from home. The duration of the employment contract was 16 years.

HELD

The whole contract was not void. All that was void was the contractual relationship during the four-week period in which illegal payments were made.

Continuous employment for the purposes of the various statutory provisions means continuously employed under a legal contract.

Therefore, the four-week period interrupted the applicant's continuity of employment (the effect was that the applicant did not have sufficient continuous employment for there to be tribunal jurisdiction over his complaint.)

Conclusions on the formation of the contract

- General contract law applies to employment contracts.
- Therefore, the usual characteristics must obtain – offer, acceptance, capacity, consideration, intention to create legal relations and the absence of vitiating factors.
- The contract of employment can be entered into wholly by oral means.
- Pre-contract representations can give rise to a collateral contract which is capable of being enforced.
- The doctrine of illegality applies but contracts will be void for illegality only if enforcement would be an affront to the public conscience.
- The employer's defence of illegality will not be available if the employer is substantially more to blame than the employee.

EVIDENCE

As noted, at common law the contract can be entered into orally, and statute has not altered this position. However, although the form of the contract may be oral, statute does require that to some extent it is evidenced in writing. The distinction here is important: statute is not requiring the contract to be in written form, merely that some of the details must be evidenced in writing.

Written particulars of employment

Legislation

The relevant legislation is found in Part I of ERA, the essential requirement being that:

> Where an employee begins employment with an employer, the employer shall give to the employee a written statement of particulars of employment ...[1]

The statement must be given 'not later than two months after the beginning of the employment'.[2]

Status of the written statement

The question of the status of written statements was addressed in *System Floors (UK) Ltd v Daniel.* The EAT made clear that the written statement:

> provides very strong *prima facie* evidence of what were the terms of the contract between the parties, but does not constitute a written contract between the parties.

However, the statement is not finally conclusive. There will be a heavy burden on the employer who wishes to show that the terms were different from those in the statement. The burden on an employee will be less heavy, but the statement will still be persuasive. The above views of the EAT were approved by the Court of Appeal in the following case.

Robertson v British Gas Corporation

FACTS
The employees challenged the accuracy of their written statements (sometimes referred to as s 1 statements) on the grounds that they did not reflect what was agreed at the commencement of employment as regards the payment of bonus.

HELD (CA)

The other evidence was preferred to the written statements which were held to be inaccurate evidence of the terms of the contract.

Note that the statements in this case were given seven years after the employment commenced. Normally statements are given on or shortly after commencement and are likely to be strong evidence.

A further issue arose in the next case.

Gascol Conversions Ltd v Mercer

FACTS

Here the court was asked to consider the position where the written statement was in the form of written terms of employment and was signed by the parties.

HELD

The document was a written contract to which the parol evidence rule applied, that is, no extrinsic evidence should supplant the written terms where these purport to be the full terms of the contract. If the document had been a written statement, the parol evidence rule would not be applicable.

Note that the distinction between signing a written contract and signing to indicate receipt of the written statement should be noted. The latter is common practice.

Requirements of the written statement

- Scope: the written statement must be provided to employees who have at least one month of continuous employment. Those ordinarily employed outside Great Britain are excluded, as are merchant seamen.[3]
- Method: the specified information has to be provided within two months of the employee commencing employment. The information can be provided in instalments, but certain parts of it must be contained in a single document.[4] Some specified parts of the information can be in reference documents rather than in the statement itself.
- The information to be provided: The information to be provided may be divided into that which has to be contained in the single document, other information which has to be given to the employee directly (ie, not by means of reference documents) and further information which can be provided by means of reference documents. Figures 8.1 to 8.3 set out the details.

In contrast to the information referred to in Figure 8.1, the information referred to in Figure 8.2 can be provided separately from the single document and not necessarily in one document.

- Names of employer and employee

- Date of commencement of employment

- Date of commencement of period of continuous employment (including that with any former employer)

- Details of remuneration

- Any terms relating to hours of work

- Any terms relating to holidays

- Job title or description

- Place of work

Figure 8.1 Contents of the single document under ERA s 1

Finally, certain information does not have to be given to the employee directly, but can be made available through reference documents to which he has access. This information is set out in Figure 8.3.

The employee must have 'reasonable opportunities' of reading the reference documents in the course of his employment or they must be made 'reasonably accessible' to him in some other way.

Where an employer (and any associated employer) employs fewer than 20 employees, details of disciplinary rules and the further stages of grievance and disciplinary procedures do not have to be provided. However, the first stage of the grievance procedure must still be communicated.

- Expected termination date if the employment is not 'permanent'.

- Details of any collective agreements, ie agreements between the employer and one or more trades unions (see chapter 22, see also *Lee v Plessey* for an example of the express incorporation of the provisions of a collective agreement via the written particulars).

- The first stage of the grievance procedure (a person or a position) and the first stage in defending against disciplinary action.

- Details relating to working abroad, if there are any.

- Whether a contracting out certificate applies under the Social Security Pensions Act 1975.

Figure 8.2   Other direct information under ERA s 1

- Any terms and conditions relating to sickness.

- Any terms and conditions relating to pensions.

- Any disciplinary rules.

- Any further stages in grievance and disciplinary procedures.

- Notice provisions.

Figure 8.3   Information which can be provided in reference documents under ERA s 1

- Changes in terms: these should be notified 'at the earliest opportunity' and not later than one month after the change.[5] This is merely a procedural requirement: it does not give the employer a right to make the change. The position will be that if the employer has no right to change the terms, the ERA provisions do not confer one (see *Burdett-Coutts*, where there was a formal letter notifying changes). Even if an employee assents to a change in the written statement, it will not be taken as assent to a variation in contract terms, especially if there is no immediate practical effect on the employee (as in *Jones v Associated Tunnelling* where there was a mobility clause introduced *via* a change in the written particulars). This approach was followed by the EAT in 1996 in *Aparau v Iceland Frozen Foods plc.*

- Changes of employer: a new statement must be issued upon a change of employer, although this is not required if there has simply been a change of name, or where continuous employment is preserved (eg, under the Transfer of Undertakings (Protection of Employment) Regulations 1981).

- Where there are no terms: if there are no terms in relation to a particular subject the statement should say so. However, a distinction must be drawn between those requirements which state simply that information must be provided (eg, in respect of pay) and those which state that information must be provided about the terms if there are any (eg, in respect of holidays). The former can be regarded as mandatory: they require information to be provided and signify that there must be such terms. The latter are not mandatory: such terms do not have to exist and if they do not, the only requirement is that their absence is stated.

- Where there is a written contract of employment: the legislation is silent on this point. Presumably such a contract can also be treated as a written statement if it meets the Act's requirements.

Failure to provide a written statement or provision of an incomplete or inaccurate statement

- An employee may make a reference to an industrial tribunal if there is a failure to comply with the Act.[6]

- Where a question arises as to what is to be included in the statement in order to comply with the Act, either the employer or employee may seek a reference.[7]

- An application may be made while the employment is continuing or within three months of the date on which the employment ceased. If it was not reasonably practicable for the application to be made within three months, it must be made within such a further period as is reasonable.

- The industrial tribunal will determine the particulars that should have been included. The meaning of this is illustrated through the following cases.

Mears v Safecar Security Ltd

Here the Court of Appeal stated (*in obiter*) that in the absence of agreement between the parties the tribunal could invent a term.

Eagland v British Telecommunications plc

The Court of Appeal disapproved of its earlier decision in *Mears*: the tribunal's role is to determine what was agreed by the parties. It is not the duty of the tribunal to interpret the terms or to invent terms where they are missing. Where there are no agreed terms, the tribunal should state this.

COMMENT

This appears to leave open the question of the legal position if one or more of the 'mandatory' terms has not been agreed. Is the contract void for uncertainty? Are any proceedings possible where an employer fails to specify one of the mandatory terms?

Note that although *Mears* was disapproved as indicated above, it remains authority for the fact that tribunals can deal with complaints of inaccurate as well as partial or absent statements.

Conclusions about written statements

- A contract of employment can be entered into orally but must be evidenced in writing in accordance with ERA, Part I.
- The written statement is not a contract but is good, although not conclusive, evidence of the terms.
- Information has to be provided to employees in writing within two months of them commencing employment. Some must be provided in a single document but other information can be provided in instalments and certain details can be provided by means of reference documents.
- The single document must contain the information set out in Figure 8.1.
- Changes in terms must be notified within a month.
- Remedies are obtained by application to an industrial tribunal.
- The tribunal's role is limited to determining what was agreed.

Itemized pay statements

The right conferred

Every employee has the right to a written pay statement on every payment of wages or salary.[8]

Exclusions

The following are excluded: employees ordinarily working outside Great Britain; merchant seamen; the police; and share fishermen.

What must be itemized?

- Gross amount of pay.
- Amount of any variable and fixed deductions and the purpose for which they are made (labels such as 'miscellaneous' will not suffice: *Milsom v Leicestershire County Council*).
- Net amount of pay.
- Where different parts of the net amount are paid in different ways, the amount and method of each part payment.

Fixed deductions

These can be aggregated if the employee is given a standing statement of fixed deductions, which is valid for up to 12 months. This must indicate the amount of each deduction, its interval and its purpose.

Enforcement

A failure to provide a statement means that an employee may apply to an industrial tribunal within three months of termination or such later period as is reasonable if it was not reasonably practicable to apply within three months. Where a statement has been provided, either employee or employer may apply. Remedies consist of a declaration that the statement had not been provided, or is incorrect, and an order that the employer pay up to the amount of unnotified deductions during the previous 13 weeks, this being penal and at the discretion of the industrial tribunal *(Scott v Creager)*.

Relationship to protection of wages under ERA

The remedy is not affected by whether or not the deduction is authorized under the wages protection provisions of ERA, but where there is an award under both provisions the aggregate must not exceed the amount of the deduction.

Other

An application under these provisions cannot be solely about the accuracy of any amount.[9]

EXPRESS AND IMPLIED TERMS

Contracts of employment contain express and implied terms.

Express terms

These are terms expressly agreed between the employee and employer.

Form

Express terms may be written or oral or partly written and partly oral. If the whole of the contract has been reduced to writing, the parol evidence rule may exclude evidence which adds to, varies or contradicts the written contract (see, for example, *Gascol Conversions v Mercer*). More usually, express terms will be written and oral, with the written terms embodied in various documents such as correspondence, works rules, notices and collective agreements. Providing that these documents do not purport to set out all the terms agreed between the parties, other evidence will be admissible.

Express terms and extrinsic evidence

The general rule is that where a term is expressed in unrestricted language, the courts will not imply a restriction. This would be an improper alteration to the meaning of a written term. The case below illustrates this point.

Nelson v BBC

FACTS
The contract stated that the employee would work when and where the Corporation demanded. In practice, he worked in the Caribbean Service. When this closed, it was argued that he was redundant, since he was employed only for the purposes of that one service.
HELD (CA)
The express term was in unrestricted language. On basic contract law principles, the court could not imply a term restricting the employee's employment to the one service. The decision of the lower court (EAT) was reversed.

However, extrinsic evidence can be properly used to amplify written terms which are incomplete, as shown in the next case.

Tayside Regional Council v McIntosh

FACTS
It was stated in a job advertisement and at a job interview that a clean driving licence was essential for the job. However, the written terms did not include this requirement. Later, the employee was dismissed when his licence was revoked.
HELD (EAT)
There was an express term requiring a clean licence.

The exercise of express terms

The principal question here is whether express terms, clearly stated, have to be exercised reasonably. This will be dealt with later when the interpretation of contract terms falls to be considered. For the moment, it should merely be noted that:

- the exercise of express terms in a harsh way may result in a breach of the general implied term of mutual trust and confidence (as per *Woods*);
- specific express terms (eg, mobility clauses) may be accompanied by specific implied terms (eg, reasonable notice as in *Akhtar*);
- the emerging test seems to be something narrower than reasonableness (see *White*); and
- classical contract theory would not admit to any such test: if a term is agreed, a party must abide by it.

Express terms in restraint of trade

Terms in restraint of trade in this context are express terms designed to protect the employer's business interests, particularly against post-employment activities by the employee. An example would be the employee setting up in competition with the employer.

These terms are sometimes known as restrictive covenants and are separate from any implied duties that the employee may have, such as the duty not to disclose confidential information, which also extends to the post-employment period (on these implied duties, see pages 182–6).

The doctrine of restraint of trade holds restraint clauses to be void unless:

- they are reasonable between the parties; and
- in the public interest *(Nordenfelt)*.

In *Esso Petroleum Co Ltd v Harper's Garage (Stourport) Ltd*, the House of Lords confirmed that the doctrine applies to the employment field and stressed the public interest aspect. In *Herbert Morris Ltd v Saxelby*, the House of Lords indicated that the validity of a restraint clause would be more difficult to establish in the employment field. This was because of the imbalance in bargaining power between employer and employee and the potential harm to the employee's livelihood.

An employer may protect two types of interest: trade secrets and customer connections *(Saxelby)*. The employer cannot restrict generally available information or the employee's skills and knowledge of the trade. Nor can the restraint extend further than is necessary to protect the employer's protectable interests: it must be what is reasonably necessary to give the employer adequate protection *(Saxelby)*.

A restraint clause will not be enforceable if it is void, because for example it seeks to protect the employer's non-protectable interests. If the restraint is too wide – in terms of the interests protected, time or geographical restriction – the offending clause can be severed if this is possible, so allowing the rest of the covenant to be enforced. If the covenant is ambiguous, it can be narrowed. There will be no enforcement if an employer is in breach of contract, for example by dismissing the employee wrongfully. The normal contract principle applies: a party in breach cannot benefit from enforcement of the contract terms. If the covenant is valid, the usual remedies will be an injunction or damages.

Mobility clauses and indirect sex discrimination

As noted in chapter 6, mobility clauses can amount to indirect sex discrimination requiring objective justification (see *Meade-Hill v The British Council*).

Implied terms

Terms may be implied from the facts of the particular employment or implied at common law wherever there is a contract of employment.

Terms implied from the facts of the particular employment

These are known as terms implied in fact. The courts will imply such terms where they are necessary to give business efficacy to the transactions as intended by the parties. The two ingredients here, therefore, are business efficacy and the intentions of the parties.

The business efficacy test asks whether it is necessary to imply a term in order to give effect to the contract, as the leading case below illustrates.

The Moorcock

FACTS
A vessel, *The Moorcock*, suffered damage because the owners of a wharf did not ensure that the wharf was safe. There was a contract between the owners of the vessel and the owners of the wharf.
HELD (CA)
To enable the contract to be fulfilled, it was necessary to imply a term of reasonable care on the part of the wharf-owners.

As regards the intentions of the parties, the 'officious bystander' test asks what the parties intended. To satisfy this test, the term to be implied must be so obvious that it goes without saying, so that if an officious bystander suggested its inclusion in the contract the parties would say 'of course' (*Shirlaw v Southern Foundries Ltd*).

Of course, the intentions of the parties may not be clear. Terms may be implied, therefore, from the conduct of the parties, from custom and from other sources such as collective agreements.

A term will not be implied simply because it is reasonable to imply it: rather, it must be necessary. Thus, in a case where a firm of solicitors made an offer of articles without specifying that it was conditional upon the passing of examinations, the Court of Appeal would not imply a term: it was not necessary to do so (*Stubbes v Trower, Still and Keeling*). Apparently, an implied term does not have to be one the parties would have agreed to: rather it is one that they would have agreed to if they were being reasonable (*Courtaulds Northern Spinning Ltd v Sibson*, where the contract was silent on location and mobility).

Terms implied into contracts of employment generally

These are known as terms implied as legal incidents of the employment relationship. They are dealt with more fully in the examination of the respective duties of employers and employees (see pages 175–87) but some important points of introduction are made here. The general authorities for this kind of implied term are *Lister v Romford* and *Sterling Engineering v Patchett*. In *Sterling* it was stated that:

> the phrase 'implied term' can be used to denote a term inherent in the nature of the contract [of employment] which the law will imply in every case unless the parties agree to vary or exclude it.[10]

These terms are implied irrespective of the intentions of the parties. An example here would be the term of mutual trust and confidence (*Woods v WM Car Services*).

What is the position where implied terms qualify clearly stated express terms?

United Bank Ltd v Akhtar

FACTS
The contract contained a clearly stated express term allowing the employer to move the employee to any of its UK branches. The employer ordered the employee to move from Leeds to Birmingham at six days' notice and refused a request for more time to be given.
HELD (EAT)
There was an implied term that reasonable notice would be given in exercising the express mobility clause and the employer had breached this term.
There was an implied term that mutual trust and confidence should be maintained. The employer was also in breach of this term.

See also *Prestwick Circuits Ltd v McAndrew*, another case in which the courts implied a term of reasonable notice in the exercise of an express mobility clause.

Is there a general implied term that express terms have to be exercised reasonably? The answer appears to be 'no' according to the EAT in *White v Reflecting Roadstuds Ltd*: there would be a breach of the express mobility clause itself if there were no reasonable or sufficient grounds for moving the employee; and in any case the term of mutual trust and confidence may be relied upon.

Classical contract theory would hold that express terms have primacy over implied terms but clearly *Woods, Akhtar* and *White* demonstrate some movement away from this principle.

Conclusions about express and implied terms

Express terms
- Express terms may be written or oral or a mixture of the two.
- Extrinsic evidence can be used to amplify an express written term but not to alter its meaning.
- There is no rule of law requiring clearly stated express terms to be exercised reasonably, but they may be qualified by implied terms, particularly the requirement for mutual trust and confidence.

Implied terms
- Implied terms are of two principal types: implied in fact (relating to the particular employment) and implied as incidents of the employment contract (implied generally).
- For a term to be implied in fact it must be necessary for the performance of the contract and in accordance with the parties' obvious intentions.
- Terms implied as incidents of the employment relationship may be implied irrespective of the parties' intentions.
- On the relationship between express and implied terms see pages 188–9.

INCORPORATION: PROCESS AND SOURCES

The process of incorporation

Both express and implied terms may be incorporated from various sources as well as being directly agreed.

Express incorporation

Here the employer and employee expressly agree that the individual contract will include some or all of the contents of a specified document or documents.

Implied incorporation

Terms may also be incorporated from various sources by implication.

Sources of incorporated terms

Collective agreements

Collective agreements are dealt with in more detail in chapter 22. For the moment it has to be noted that the parties to the employment relationship may expressly agree that some or all of the contents of a collective agreement shall form part of the contract of employment. *NCB v Galley* provides an example: the individual contract was subject to the 'collective agreement for the time being in force'. If terms are to be incorporated in the absence of express incorporation, there must be evidence of implied incorporation *(Young v Canadian Northern Railway Co)*.

The effect of incorporation is to make the incorporated term capable of being enforced at law through the contract of employment. This is so even though the source of the incorporated term, the collective agreement, will normally itself be unenforceable *(Marley v Forward Trust Group Ltd)* (on the legal status of collective agreements see chapter 22: they are presumed not to be legally enforceable).

There is no incorporation solely because an employer is a member of an employers' association which negotiated the collective agreement *(Hamilton v Futura Floors Ltd)*.

Incorporation will also be influenced by whether the parties had knowledge of the term. Terms will rarely be implied in fact in the absence of knowledge but that knowledge may be constructive (ie, what the courts will treat as known).

Which terms are suitable for incorporation? The principle appears to be that the term must be apt for expression as part of the contract of employment ie, suitable for expression as an individual (as distinct from a collective) right. Examples are given below.

NCB v NUM

The court would not find that a disputes procedure operated jointly by the union and employer was suitable for incorporation.

Alexander v Standard Telephone and Cables (No 2)

The court would not find a redundancy procedure suitable for incorporation. (But what about the individual's right to appeal against selection – could that be suitable?)

Note that the courts are not saying that procedures *per se* are unsuitable (disciplinary procedures can be contractual): rather they are unsuitable if they are of a collective nature.

However, in *Anderson v Pringle of Scotland Ltd*, the court was prepared to find a last in/first out redundancy procedure incorporated into the contract of employment.

Under TULR(C)A, s 180, a clause restricting the right to strike will have to state in writing that it is to be incorporated and there are other requirements. Beyond this, the clause will have to be incorporated by the words and/or behaviour of the parties when establishing the contract's terms.

Where collective agreements are in conflict, for example, a national agreement makes one provision and a local agreement another, there are no clear rules. A later agreement may have precedence. An agreement stating that it has precedence over other agreements may also have precedence.

How does an increase in pay or other benefits become incorporated? The following case provides an illustration.

Lee v Plessey

FACTS

A redundancy pay agreement led to an enhancement of redundancy payments. The employers argued that it could not be incorporated because of the absence of consideration.

HELD (High Court, QBD)

There was consideration. Settlement of the claim and continuation of employment were consideration for the increase, which was held on the facts to be incorporated.

Since collective agreements are presumed not to be legally enforceable, they are not usually drafted as legal documents, tending to be looser in their wording. How should such terms be interpreted once incorporated?

Hooper v British Railways Board

FACTS
Sick pay was to be paid until an employee returned to work. The employer argued that this was intended to apply only in the short-term.
HELD (CA)
Once a term becomes part of the contract of employment it is subject to literal construction. The Court of Appeal refused to admit extrinsic evidence, notably the employer's intentions during negotiations and actual practice.

What is the position if an employer terminates a collective agreement which has terms that have become incorporated? What is the status of those incorporated terms? They are still enforceable as part of the contract of employment unless there is agreed change, even though the collective agreement from which they came no longer exists *(Robertson v British Gas)*.

What is the position of the non-unionist in relation to the process of incorporation of terms from collective agreements? If the contract of employment of a non-unionist expressly states that terms from a collective agreement will be incorporated, then there will be incorporation.

Can an employee enforce the terms of a collective agreement other than through the incorporation process? The employee will not be able to enforce the agreement itself because he is not a party to it: the rule of privity of contract would apply. Nor is a union usually seen as an agent of the member. Certainly, a relationship of principal and agent does not arise out of the member/union relationship itself. However, it might be capable of being inferred from the particular facts *(Burton Group v Smith)*. The collective agreement might be seen as a standing offer which the individual employee is free to accept or reject *(Edwards v Skyways)*.

Custom and practice

Are custom and practice the same thing? The expression 'custom and practice' is used by managers and union officials as if the words are interchangeable. However, some distinctions can be made. Custom has a legal significance in that contracts are presumed to include it unless the parties state otherwise. Practice, in the sense of widespread practice, has no general legal significance unless it is a custom but could be relevant in, for example, tests of reasonableness. Practice over time in a specific employment is conduct, which may provide evidence of a term or acceptance of a change.

Sagar v Ridehalgh

General rules for incorporation: *Sagar v Ridehalgh*
FACTS
A deduction was made from the wages of a cotton weaver for bad workmanship. The employer argued that there was an implied contract term permitting this (the case pre-dated the wages protection provisions now found in the ERA).
HELD (CA)
There was such a term. It was implied, being incorporated from a custom of the trade.

What are the requirements for such incorporation?

- the custom must be certain (precise enough for the court to be able to identify what it is);
- it must be general (widely adopted);
- it must be reasonable;
- there should be evidence of knowledge of the custom; and
- there should be evidence of acceptance of the custom.

Custom may be incorporated without evidence of knowledge and acceptance (automatic incorporation) in some cases, particularly where the employee can be said to have accepted employment subject to it (see *Sagar*).

What if an employer wishes to change the customary method of working?

Cresswell v Board of Inland Revenue

FACTS
Staff carried out their work by dealing manually with files and records. The employers introduced a programme of computerization. The plaintiff argued that this constituted a breach of contract because there was an implied term that he could not be required to perform his duties other than in the manner established by custom and practice.
HELD (High Court, QBD)
The employers were not in breach of contract. There was no such implied term about custom and practice. The employee is under a duty to adapt to new methods and techniques, although if necessary, the employer must provide training.

Works rules

Not all works rules are contractual: disciplinary rules can be distinguished from those which are merely instructions as to how to perform the job

(Secretary of State for Employment v ASLEF (No 2)). The significance of the distinction between contractual rules and non-contractual instructions is that the latter can be changed unilaterally on reasonable notice while changes to the former require consent. There is possibly a third type of rule – a condition of employment. This is established unilaterally and, according to *Cadoux v Central Regional Council*, can be altered unilaterally. An example of a condition might be that it is a condition of your employment that you take your holidays at times agreed by your head of department.

A leading case on introducing new rules is set out below.

Dryden v Greater Glasgow Health Board

FACTS
The employers introduced a complete ban on smoking at work. The applicant was a long-time smoker who was unable to give up the habit.
HELD (EAT)
Introducing such a rule – one which an employee finds it difficult to comply with – does not constitute a breach of contract. There was no implied term giving a right to smoke and the employers were not preventing the employee from fulfilling her contractual duties. The smoking rule was within the realm of the employer's discretion.
Note that the context here should be considered, in particular the fact that the employer had a statutory duty to make the workplace safe.[11]

Disciplinary procedures
These may or may not be contractual, depending on the intentions of the parties. Where the procedure is contractual, it will be enforced in the normal contractual way, as the following cases show.

Dietmann v London Borough of Brent

FACTS
The plaintiff was a social worker. Following the death of a child under her supervision, a judicial enquiry found her to have been grossly negligent. Because of the thorough external enquiry, the employers dispensed with the disciplinary procedure and dismissed her.
HELD (CA)
The disciplinary procedure was contractual and the employers were in breach of contract (ie, the dismissal was wrongful; see chapter 16). The plaintiff was entitled to a remedy for loss of her contractual rights. An injunction would not be granted but damages were appropriate.

Stoker v Lancashire County Council

FACTS

The applicant was dismissed by his employer after his case had completed the in-house procedure of the polytechnic where he was employed. A further procedure within the local authority itself was dispensed with. The applicant claimed that the dismissal was unfair.

HELD (CA)

The dismissal is unfair. The employer's conduct fails the reasonable test under unfair dismissal law.[12] The disciplinary procedure was contractual and the applicant was entitled to his contractual rights. Denial of those contractual rights was unreasonable.

Note that breach of contract does not automatically mean that a dismissal will be unfair: this is a matter of fact for the industrial tribunal.

In both of the above cases the employer did not follow the full procedure because there had already been a thorough investigation of the case. The merits of this approach were not the issue, however. The issue for the court was whether there had been a breach of contract.

TERMS IMPOSED BY STATUTE

As noted, the terms of the contract of employment may be express or implied and may be agreed by reference to one or more specified documents (ie, incorporated). A further source of contract terms is statute, although it should be noted that statutory provision may or may not work through the contract of employment. In fact, most statutory employment rights are separate from the contract of employment. For example:

An employee has the right not to be unfairly dismissed by his employer.[13]

The statutory right not to be unfairly dismissed makes no mention of the contract of employment. Of course, the right is given only to employees, who are defined as working under a contract of employment, but the legislation does not insert the statutory right into the contract. The action for breach of the right does not lie in contract: it is an action under the statute.

The right to minimum notice periods is again expressed as a statutory right, so if the contract provides for two weeks when statute requires three, the statute applies. This is because s 203(1) of ERA states that any provision in an agreement (whether a contract or not) will be void if it conflicts with a provision of the Act.

The Equal Pay Act 1970 is the exception to the general rule that in the employment field statutory rights tend to be separate from the contract rather than expressed through it. The EqPA inserts a clause into the contract of employment, thus:

> if the terms of a contract ... do not include ... an equality clause they shall be deemed to include one.[14]

The equality clause then works to equalise terms between men and women. The Act, therefore, inserts a statutory right directly into the employment contract.

NOTES

1 ERA, s 1(1). The current provisions relating to written statements were substituted by the Trade Union Reform and Employment Rights Act 1993 (TURERA) in order to give effect to the Proof of Employment Relationship Directive (91/553/EEC), OJ 1991, L288/32.
2 ERA, s 1(2).
3 Ibid, ss 196 and 199.
4 Ibid, s 2(4).
5 Ibid, s 4(3).
6 Ibid, s 11(1).
7 Ibid, s 11(2).
8 Ibid, s 8.
9 Ibid, s 11(3)(b).
10 Presumably the parties would be able to exclude such a term only if it had its source solely in contract rather than also deriving its authority from, eg the law of negligence or from statute (such as the duty of care).
11 HSWA, s 2. See chapter 14.
12 ERA, s 98(4); see chapter 16.
13 Ibid, s 94(1).
14 EqPA, s 1(1).

N I N E

Recruitment, Selection and Appointment

Part II of this book attempts to follow the employment relationship from beginning to end but employment law is not organized in such a manner. The present chapter, therefore, examines an important part of the employment relationship – the recruitment, selection and appointment process – with a view to pulling together the various elements of law which impinge upon it.[1]

Discrimination is the main area of law likely to be relevant here but it must be borne in mind that there is specific legislation relating to particular types of employee (see chapter 5). There must be no discrimination at any stage of the recruitment, selection and appointment process. There are four types of discrimination which are unlawful:

- race;
- sex (including discrimination against married persons);
- union, that is, on grounds of union membership or non-membership; and
- disability.

Protection against union discrimination in the recruitment process was introduced by the Employment Act 1990 and protection against disability discrimination by the Disability Discrimination Act 1995. There is no legislation outlawing discrimination on other grounds (eg, age), but see chapter 7.

ADVERTISING JOBS

Disability, race and sex discrimination

Attention has already been drawn to the dangers of indirect discrimination – placing requirements upon candidates which have the effect of being discriminatory. By contrast, direct discrimination – treating someone less favourably than a person of the opposite sex, or of a different racial group – would occur where a job is not genuinely available irrespective of race or sex. Thus, in what must be one of the few cases where direct discrimination has been admitted in writing, a firm of solicitors wrote to a female applicant for a job saying that what they wanted was a man. The tribunal at the resultant hearing came to its decision without difficulty. Except in the limited circumstances where sex or race is a GOQ, such restrictions will be unlawful.

As regards sex discrimination – and similar provisions apply in relation to race – it is unlawful to publish or cause to be published an advertisement which indicates or could be taken to indicate an intention to commit unlawful discrimination. Use of job descriptions which have sexual connotations (for example, 'salesgirl', 'waiter', 'postman', and 'stewardess') are to be taken as showing an intention to discriminate unless the advertisement indicates to the contrary.[2] Thus, if both male and female terms are not used in the advertisement, it would be advisable to insert a phrase indicating that applicants of both sexes will be welcomed. There is no statutory requirement for job titles to be changed. However, occupational descriptions giving both sexes (for example, 'manager/ess', 'salesman/woman') or appearing in neutral form (for example, 'cowperson, with experience of milking and herd-rearing') make an employer's non-discriminatory policy clear. Where there are doubts about terminology (that is, fears that it might imply one particular sex) a phrase of the sort mentioned above might be inserted. In any case, where there is an equal opportunities policy, it might be helpful to draw attention to it. It is not advisable to advertise, as one employer who subsequently visited an industrial tribunal did, 'overhead crane driver/ess – to satisfy damn silly employment legislation'. As regards race relations, confining advertisements to areas or publications which would disproportionately exclude a particular racial group is likely to constitute unlawful discrimination.

An employer should not tell a publisher that an advertisement is lawful unless they know it to be so. Making such a statement knowingly or recklessly which is materially false or misleading constitutes a criminal offence punishable by fine. Advertisement for the purposes of both race and sex discrimination law includes every form of advertisement, whether public or not, and whether:

- in a newspaper or other publication;
- by television or radio;
- by display of notices, signs, labels, showcards or goods;
- by distribution of samples, circulars, catalogues, price lists or other materials;
- by exhibition of pictures, models or films;
- in any other way.[3]

This definition would seem to include careers advertising films, direct mail and in-company advertising as well as advertising in the public media. The legal requirements apply in relation to each advertisement. It should be noted that the placing of a discriminatory advertisement and the instructing of someone else to place such an advertisement are unlawful acts in themselves. The failure subsequently to offer a person a job on the grounds of sex or race would constitute a further unlawful act. Employers may target some of their publicity towards a particular sex or race where a particular sex or race is under-represented among the existing staff.

Union discrimination

It is unlawful to refuse someone a job on the grounds that they are, or are not, a trades union member. An advertisement containing such a requirement will not in itself be unlawful, but it will be taken as conclusive evidence that an unlawful act was committed if a non-unionist or union member is subsequently refused employment, does not have the required status as specified in the advertisement and makes a claim to an industrial tribunal. Any requirement that a person must agree to join or leave a union if appointed is also unlawful. Union discrimination is unlawful whether practised by an employer directly, or indirectly through an employment agency.

Claims are made to an industrial tribunal within three months against employers, employment agencies or both. Provision exists for joining parties to the proceedings (for example, a trades union insisting on union members only being recruited, or an employer if the original action is against an employment agency). Remedies are a declaration and such compensation as is just and equitable including injury to feelings. The tribunal can make a recommendation of action to ease the complainant's position, and increase the compensation if it is not complied with. Maximum compensation is £12,000. It should be noted that advertisement is defined widely to include any notice even if it is not made public.

Contracts of employment

Stating certain requirements in job advertisements will generally strengthen the employer's case if there is a subsequent dispute with the employee.

Telling applicants in advance that the organization operates a no-smoking policy, or that mobility is required, provides evidence that the individual knew these things before agreeing to become an employee, the inference being that these terms were accepted as part of the contract of employment (see chapter 8).

Application forms and further particulars

Application forms and further particulars also provide an opportunity to inform the employee in advance of his employment that certain requirements must be met. The employer will have records showing that the prospective employee has been sent these documents, and in the case of an application form the employee's signature indicates that he or she wishes to apply for the job, perhaps on the terms as stated. For example, an application form containing the words 'I agree to work shifts' and signed by the employee is strong evidence that this was an agreed term of the contract and could be important if the matter later turned out to be in dispute. There is some value, therefore, in specifying the main, and particularly any potentially controversial, terms.

It is possible for the application form itself to give the impression that it could be used in a discriminatory way. Thus, where questions about disability, sex or race are asked, it should be made clear that the reason is for equal opportunities policy monitoring purposes only or in order to ascertain whether the applicant will need a work permit. Moreover, care needs to be taken not to use the application form as a test of English literacy unless that can be demonstrated to be necessary for the job.

INFORMATION SUPPLIED BY APPLICANTS

It is a matter for the prospective employer to check the authenticity of data supplied by job applicants: *caveat emptor* – let the buyer beware. This may be done by asking the applicant for certificates proving that stated qualifications are actually held, by taking up references, by pursuing issues with the applicant at an interview, by testing and so on. If the employer does not make a reasonable enquiry any dishonesty on the part of the applicant which is discovered later, although not excused, may be more difficult to deal with. In any case there is a possibility of recruitment being negligent (see page 168). Other than in exceptional cases, there is no duty upon the job applicant to volunteer information about themselves except in response to direct questions *(Walton v TAC Construction Materials Ltd)*.

Under the Theft Act 1968, it is a criminal offence dishonestly to obtain a job and a person doing so may be prosecuted. When the dishonesty is discovered, dismissal may be justified but this is not automatically the case (see chapter 16). It can be useful for an application form to contain a statement whereby the applicant confirms the correctness of the information provided and acknowledges that deliberately providing false information could result in dismissal.

Where information is sought about criminal convictions, the provisions of the Rehabilitation of Offenders Act 1974 may apply (see pages 86–8). Where a medical report is required, the provisions of the Access to Medical Reports Act 1988 might apply.

Employers in large, multi-site organizations should be aware of the implications of recruiting strikers dismissed elsewhere in the organization. The effect of this is likely to be to bring those dismissals within the jurisdiction of the industrial tribunal (see page 450; *Bigham and Keogh v GKN Kwikform Ltd*). Employees would be under no duty to volunteer the information that they are ex-employees dismissed for taking industrial action.

INTERVIEWS AND TESTS

Interviews

The interview stage usually marks the appearance of the candidate on the employer's premises. Therefore, the employer's general duty of care as owner or controller of the premises is brought into effect. The main danger at this stage, however, is that employers act contrary to discrimination law. A problem is that the boundary between lawful and unlawful is not altogether clear. What is clear is that in an interview the candidates should not be asked different questions because they are of a different race or sex. This does not mean that all candidates must be asked the same questions. Interviewers may legitimately frame their questions in the light of what the candidate has said on an application form or in a letter of application.

The Sex Discrimination Code of Practice (para 23(c)) recommends that 'questions should relate to the requirements of the job'. In *Woodhead v Chief Constable of West Yorkshire Police*, questions asked (of a woman) about child-care and other domestic issues were not unlawful because they were relevant to the requirements of the job and were asked of all candidates, male and female.

One of the difficulties is that some of the matters which employers need to be reassured about could give rise to questions which lead to accusations of discrimination. For example, employers may wish to enquire about a woman's family circumstances as a means of judging the candidate's likely work commitment. This is a potentially discriminatory line of questioning which some would say is based on a stereotyping of women's roles. Similarly, employers will want to be sure that candidates from ethnic minorities have sufficient command of the English language. Again, such a line of questioning is potentially discriminatory. So too is questioning about union membership or non-membership. All that can be said is that evidence of such questioning may lead to unfavourable inferences being drawn by a tribunal. This has prompted some employers to drop such questions from interviews, and indeed to omit questions of this sort from application forms. It should be remembered that an industrial tribunal may well have the application forms of all of the candidates before it. It is quite likely that disclosure of these would be ordered by a tribunal if resisted. Finally, it should be noted that if interviewers are being called as witnesses there is nothing to stop their contemporaneous notes being submitted as evidence – doodles and all. A record of the proceedings of an interview could also provide evidence.

Tests

The main problem with testing is that the tests themselves may be discriminatory. This is less likely to be the case with sex discrimination but has been alleged in relation to race. Here it is said that testing in part reflects cultural values, so that candidates from cultures other than the dominant one are disadvantaged. Another way in which tests might be discriminatory is by setting educational standards which amount to indirect discrimination and which cannot be justified in terms of the job. A high standard of written English as a requirement to pass a test would be difficult to justify in relation to a job where little or no writing was needed and a considerably smaller proportion of people from ethnic minorities would be able to comply.

REFERENCES

There is no general duty on the part of an employer to provide a reference. However, an employer who agrees to provide a reference does have duties both to the recipient of the reference and to its subject.

Duties owed to the recipient of a reference

The reference provider owes a duty of care to the recipient of the reference. However, a disclaimer will protect against liability.

Duties owed to the subject of the reference

Spring v Guardian Assurance Ltd

FACTS
A reference from the former employer contained negligent misstatements which severely hampered the plaintiff's attempts to find another job.
HELD (HL)
The reference provider owes the subject of the reference a duty of care in the law of negligence.
The duty can arise from an implied term in the contract of employment even in the absence of any legal duty to provide a reference.
The duty applies even after the employee has left the employer's employment.
COMMENT
The House of Lords decision in *Spring*, reversing the Court of Appeal, can be seen as an application of the *Hedley Byrne* principles to the employment field.[4] First, there is an assumption of responsibility by the defendant; secondly, there is reliance by the plaintiff. These provide the basis for the 'special relationship' required by *Hedley Byrne*.
The subject of a reference may have other causes of action, depending on the facts. A negligent reference could constitute a breach of contract or a breach of promise. There may be scope for an action in defamation (ie, reputation) or in respect of injurious falsehood (ie, financial loss). However, a defence to defamation and injurious falsehood will be honest belief in the truth of the statements (qualified privilege). This would leave the plaintiff needing to show that there had been malice (malicious falsehood).

Meaning of a 'satisfactory' reference

Wishart v National Association of Citizens' Advice Bureaux

FACTS
The employer made an offer which was conditional upon the receipt of 'satisfactory' references. The references were received but the employer did not consider them to be 'satisfactory'. The prospective employee argued that a reasonable employer would have found them satisfactory.
HELD (CA)
'Satisfactory' in this context means to the satisfaction of the prospective employer. That is, a subjective test is to be applied rather than an objective one (what a reasonable employer would find satisfactory).

SELECTION

The carrying out of a discriminatory interview or test is not of itself unlawful. Apart from discriminatory advertisements and other unlawful acts the law is broken only where a person is denied access to a job on grounds of discrimination. If the selection is based heavily upon a discriminatory interview or test it is likely that selection will be unlawful. If selection is based on a number of factors, one of which is a discriminatory test, then the critical factor will be how much weight was put upon the test result. Where recruitment is done by word of mouth it may be discriminatory if it reduces the opportunity of members of a particular sex or race to apply for jobs. It may perpetuate the existing make-up of the workforce especially if it is the only method used. If the workforce is largely black, or largely white, in the context of a multi-racial labour market, using this method alone may be unlawful.

The freedom to discriminate positively has already been mentioned in relation to training. However, that freedom does not extend to the selection process. Restricting offers of jobs to those of a particular sex or race constitutes unlawful discrimination (but see pages 99–100). An industrial tribunal recommendation that an applicant (who had been unlawfully discriminated against in the recruitment and selection process) should have preferential treatment in future went too far *(Noone v North West Thames Regional Health Authority)*.

Another potential constraint on the selection process is procedure. In the public sector an abuse of procedure could possibly be open to challenge by means of judicial review. This could occur, for example, where recruitment is in breach of the principles of natural justice, as it would be if (some of) those doing the selection knew one of the candidates and favoured that candidate in the selection process.

Finally, recruitment could be negligent if a person appointed to a post proves to be unsafe in it. There is a common law duty to take reasonable care in making the appointment, especially with certain kinds of jobs. In *Hicks v Pier House Management Ltd*, the company employed a night porter at a block of flats, but did not adequately check his background. He had a long list of convictions and many spells in prison for theft and/or burglary. He went on to commit several burglaries at the flats which were in his charge. One of the tenants, who had been burgled, successfully sued the company for damages for negligence.

APPOINTMENT

The contract of employment

It is on appointment that the employer enters into what is the central relationship in employment law. Once the employer makes an offer and the candidate accepts, there is a contract of employment. The offer may be conditional in which case it expires if the condition is not met, as in *Wishart v National Association of Citizens' Advice Bureaux Ltd*, where satisfactory references were not provided. More generally, an offer terminates after a fixed period, if specified, or otherwise after a reasonable length of time has elapsed. It should be noted that the concept of a contract of employment has common law origins. There is no Act of Parliament determining that the employer–employee relationship shall be one of contract. In essence the contract is an agreement in which the employee agrees to work for wages and the employer agrees to pay for the work done. Exchange is at the root of the contract – there must be consideration for the services rendered. Describing the contract as an agreement (rather than a document) is a reminder that the contract is unlikely to be committed to paper. Even if there are no pieces of paper arising out of the employment transaction the contract is still enforceable. The absence of paper, however, may make it more difficult to establish evidence of the contract terms.

The contract begins when it is made – the date of the agreement (that is, once the employee accepts the employer's offer) – rather than when the employee actually starts to perform the work. Thus if either party changes their mind between agreement and the commencement of work the other party has a potential claim for breach of contract.

Sources of contract terms

As noted in chapter 8, the contract of employment comprises express and implied terms, incorporated terms and any terms imposed by statute.

Express terms
These will be directly agreed between the employee and employer either in writing (for example, the letter of appointment and a reply of acceptance) or orally (for example, at the end of the interview). The employee needs to know the standards of performance and conduct required and the consequences of not meeting them.

Implied terms
These may be terms implied into all employment contracts or terms implied to give effect to a particular contract. Prominent duties placed upon employees by general implied terms are care, co-operation (obedience) and fidelity, and on employers the duty to pay wages, take reasonable care and act in good faith (see chapter 10).

Terms imposed by statute
These are terms which Parliament has decreed will be put in contracts of employment generally, for example, contracts have an equality clause as a result of the Equal Pay Act 1970.

Incorporated terms

These are terms incorporated into the contract from various documents (eg, collective agreements, workplace rules and disciplinary procedures) and from custom and practice.

- Workplace rules: these should be non-discriminatory and be applied in a non-discriminatory way. Rules, other than job instructions, are likely to be contractual, especially those relating to discipline. They will either be expressly contractual or become contractual by the employer giving reasonable notice of them and the employee working under them.
- Custom and practice: where there are no express terms or other evidence on a particular point, custom or practice may be used to imply a term. This will be the case only where the custom is widely known, reasonable and certain (that is, precisely defined).
- Terms incorporated from collective agreements: it is appropriate to consider the relationship between the contract and any collective agreement which may have been made between the employer and one or more trades unions. Unless the parties specifically state otherwise, the collective agreement will not be legally enforceable. This emphasizes the key legal status of the contract of employment between the employer and the individual employee. An important feature of the contract, however, is the incorporation of terms from the collective agreement. Thus terms from the non-enforceable collective agreement may become incorporated into the individual contract of employment, and by being so become enforceable between the employer and individual employee. The incorporation is not automatic – it may occur expressly by terms in an individual contract being linked to a union agreement, or impliedly by the custom of wages and other terms being adjusted when changes occur in the collective agreement. These terms, therefore, are agreed by a union on behalf of the employee.

Although statute limits to some extent what can be included, much of the substance of the contract stems from what the parties themselves agree. The terms of contract, therefore, have a number of sources, and it is the totality of what is derived from these which constitutes the contract (see chapter 8).

Letters of appointment and other documents

It is clear from what has been said about the contract of employment that there is considerable potential for dispute about terms. Having unambiguous evidence of what was agreed is therefore important. A letter of appointment may be a key document, especially if it sets out some of the main terms, including anything perceived as an area of potential dispute.

Successful candidates might be encouraged to reply in writing stating that they accept the offer on the terms laid down in a letter of a particular date.

Special care needs to be taken in relation to three areas which often give rise to problems: location, hours of work and duties. In all three cases, as generally, an employer has much to gain by drawing the contract terms widely. This is because an employer may legitimately alter an employee's terms within the contract, but may be at risk of legal challenge if the alteration is not permitted by the contract. For example, if it is a term of an employee's contract that they will work at any of the health district's establishments, the employer (all other things being equal) will be free to effect the change. However, if it is a term of the contract that the employee works at a particular hospital, the employer may risk a legal challenge if he or she goes ahead. Similar problems often occur in relation to hours of work and duties. In relation to the latter, job descriptions may offer useful evidence of contract terms.

Another important document is one containing disciplinary rules. This should set out the dos and don'ts of employee behaviour indicating what sorts of punishments are likely, and in particular what may lead to dismissal. It is useful for employers to have evidence that the employee has received a copy of such rules. The law will then assume that the rules are known and the employer has a defence to claims that the employee did not know the rules. The clearer and more widely known the rules, the stronger is this defence. The documentation should also contain the disciplinary procedure. The rules themselves (which may include those posted on boards or at clocking stations or circulated as memos) will generally be taken to be part of the contract of employment. Procedural aspects may not be, although, depending on the facts, a disciplinary procedure can be part of the contract of employment (as in *Dietmann v London Borough of Brent*).

Disputes about contract terms

The courts may, in any dispute about the terms of a contract, imply a term. The aim is to decide what the parties intended, in the absence of express agreement. The approach taken is that such a term should be so obvious that the parties did not feel a need to state it expressly. In practice, it is often difficult in the absence of express provisions to decide what was intended by the parties. Sometimes evidence can be found in the terms of collective agreements, or in custom and practice. In other cases, the courts may simply imply what is reasonable. Thus, in *Coslett Contractors Ltd v Quinn*, they implied a term that expenses reasonably incurred in the course of employment would be reimbursed.

Courts will generally enforce contract terms without reference to their fairness to the respective parties, providing that the contract itself is not illegal, the terms are not contrary to public policy and are not made void by statute, and the contract was entered into willingly. In *Electronic Data Systems Ltd v Hubble* the Court of Appeal set aside (pending trial) a judgment of the High Court that the employee should pay a refund of training costs because he left within a specified time. This term had been contractually agreed but was potentially in restraint of trade. In the event, the case was settled without going to trial. Courts may restrict the operation of terms if they consider them too wide, especially if they are in restraint of trade or made under duress. In *United Bank Ltd v Akhtar*, where an employment contract had a widely drawn term allowing geographical mobility, the court implied a further term requiring the employer to give reasonable notice. Where a court finds a particular term of a contract is void, the remainder of the contract terms will still be enforceable if the offending term can be severed.

Types of contract

If the relationship is to be one governed by a contract of employment it will be necessary to determine the type of employment contract to be used. There are four principal types:

Permanent contract

This is the most usual type of employment contract. It is open-ended in that no date of expiry is fixed. The parties assume that the contract will continue indefinitely, although provision is made for termination by notice.

Fixed-term contract

A fixed-term contract has a definite starting date and a definite expiry date. Provision for notice to end the contract during its term does not prevent it from being a fixed-term contract. A fixed-term contract terminates when the expiry date is reached, and constitutes a dismissal.[5]

'Performance' contract

A contract discharged by performance is a contract of employment for the performance of a specific task. It terminates when the task is completed. The ending of the contract is not a dismissal.

Temporary contract

A temporary contract worker is employed for a limited period but not under a fixed-term contract or a performance contract. In general a temporary worker will have the same rights as a permanent employee if he or she acquires sufficient continuous employment. Dismissal of a temporary replacement for someone medically suspended or on maternity leave will normally be a fair dismissal.

Task contracts are clearly relevant where the job will last as long as the work itself, and the work lasts for an unspecified period of time – until completion. Because the ending of a task contract is not a dismissal, no question of redundancy or unfair dismissal arises. By contrast a fixed-term contract, upon expiry, constitutes a dismissal, but it may be shown to be fair if challenged (for example, because of redundancy). Some employers use rolling fixed-term contracts, annually renewing the contract for a further term (eg, renewing a three-year fixed-term contract annually so that it does not expire). Since task and fixed-term contracts end automatically – by completion of the work in the former case, and by completion of the term in the latter – notice is not required to bring them to an end. Notice would be required, however, to end them at an earlier stage.

Most contracts of employment are open-ended – they are assumed to continue indefinitely. Termination may be mutual, by the employee resigning, by the employer dismissing or by force of law – frustration of contract. Frustration of a contract occurs where one of the parties, for unexpected and unintended reasons, is unable to perform the contract in the manner agreed. Prison sentences and long-term sickness are the main examples in the employment field. Tribunals are reluctant to apply the concept of frustration because it has the effect of removing the employee's statutory rights to claim unfair dismissal. This arises out of the fact that frustration, and not dismissal, is the cause of termination. There have been occasional examples of frustration in employment law, as in *FC Shepherd and Co Ltd v Jerrom* where the Court of Appeal held that a borstal sentence of nine months frustrated a four-year contract of apprenticeship. There is no particular length of time by which frustration occurs – this will depend upon the circumstances of the case (see page 317).

Task and fixed-term contracts are types of temporary contract but temporary contracts can also be open-ended. The expectations of the parties are different from those where the contract is permanent. The legal position is not dissimilar, however, perhaps with one exception – temporary employees might have less protection in a redundancy. Otherwise, normal legal rights accrue with continuous employment and several temporary contracts nose to tail (or even sometimes with gaps in between) are treated as continuous. There is no legal requirement to make a temporary contract permanent at any stage unless this has been specifically agreed. However, in the long term it is possible that a stream of temporary contracts might suggest that in practice there has been a mutually agreed variation of the contract terms.

The term 'personal contract' has become increasingly prominent in the employment field. In one sense, all contracts of employment are 'personal' contracts since they are made between individual employees and their employer. That is not the sense in which the term is commonly used, however: it refers more to the method by which the terms of the contract are determined. Personal contracts are agreed directly by the individual employee and the employer rather than through any collective relationship: the normal context is where an employer is seeking to reduce union influence over terms and conditions of employment. The practice of enhancing terms for those on personal contracts or withholding increases from those not agreeing to them has resulted in cases in which action short of dismissal on union grounds has been alleged (see chapter 22).

NOTES

1 For useful, practical guidance see *The IPM Recruitment Code* (London, IPM (now IPD), 1990).
2 SDA, s 38; the race relations requirements are in RRA, s 29. There is also a presumption of discrimination in the DDA, s 11(2).
3 SDA, s 82(1); RRA, s 78(1). The definition in DDA, s 11(3) is equally wide.
4 *Hedley Byrne v Heller.* The ruling in this case extends the law of negligence to cover economic loss (as distinct from personal injury or damage to property) arising from negligent misstatements where there is a 'special relationship'. Such a relationship exists where one party relies on the statement of another and suffers economic loss, the advisor knowing that the advisee so relies. Consideration, eg a fee, is good evidence of a special relationship (as may be found between a client and professional advisor, eg lawyer or accountant).
5 ERA, s 95(1)(b).

The Contract of Employment: Terms, Interpretation and Change

The focus so far has been on the early stages of the employment relationship – recruitment, selection and appointment. The emphasis now shifts to the terms of employment, commencing in the present chapter with those terms inserted into all employment contracts – terms implied as incidents of the employment relationship (see chapter 8). The duties of the employer are examined, then those of the employee. Thereafter the chapter is concerned with questions of interpretation of the contract of employment and the matter of changes in terms and conditions of employment.

TERMS IMPLIED AT COMMON LAW: DUTIES OF THE EMPLOYER

The duty to pay wages

Nature of the duty

There is a general contract term to pay wages that are due. It should be noted, however, that wages may not always be the form of consideration. It could be commission, for example, or even the chance to earn wages. It should also be noted that where wages are payable there may not be a set amount. An example would be piecework, where pay varies according to the amount produced.

In normal circumstances wages are the consideration and a unilateral reduction will result in a breach of contract. This was the case in *Rigby v Ferodo* where the House of Lords refused to construe notice of a unilateral reduction in pay as notice of termination of employment.

What, however, if the wage reduction is indirect – arising out of a unilateral change in working practices? The following case is a good illustration.

Burdett-Coutts v Hertfordshire County Council

FACTS
The employer attempted to introduce amended terms of employment for school dinner ladies which in effect amounted to a pay reduction. The employees refused to accept the new terms but carried on working, albeit under protest.
HELD (High Court, QBD)
The dinner ladies were entitled to recover the unpaid wages payable under the original contract terms. They had not waived the employer's repudiatory breach by continuing to work.

Where there is no agreement as to amount, providing there is a reference to or an understanding that there will be payment, a *quantum meruit* action will be possible. This is a quasi-contract action in the law of restitution, under which the plaintiff sues for the amount deserved.

Situations in which the employee is not working

- Sickness: the traditional common law view was that the consideration for wages was service rather than actual performance of the work. This might suggest that wages are payable during illness, since the employee is still in the service of the employer. However, in *Mears v Safecar Security*, the Court of Appeal made it clear there is no presumption that sick pay is payable. Note that there are statutory provisions here in the form of statutory sick pay (SSP) (see chapter 11).
- Lay-off: this is where the employer has no work for the employee and sends him home. In the absence of dismissal and re-engagement, lay-off will amount to a suspension of the main terms of the contract of employment. There is no general common law power to lay-off without pay. Again, there are statutory provisions (see chapter 11).
- Short-time working: similarly, the employer has no general power to put the employee on short-time (ie, with reduced pay). In the absence of a contractual term permitting this and any agreement by the employee, the imposition of short-time working will amount to a breach of contract. See *Miller v Hamworthy Engineering* for an example. The statutory provisions in this area are dealt with in chapter 11.

- Industrial action: what is the position in contract law when the employee refuses to perform some or all of his duties under the contract in persuance of industrial action? A leading case is presented below.

Miles v Wakefield Metropolitan District Council

FACTS
Mr Miles was a registrar of births, marriages and deaths. His normal working week comprised 37 hours, including three hours on Saturday morning. He refused to perform his duties, which involved conducting marriage ceremonies, in the three hours on Saturday morning, as part of a campaign of industrial action. His employer deducted ³⁄₃₇ of his salary.
HELD (HL)
The employer was entitled to do this. The employee had no right to this pay because he had given no consideration during the three hours.

On this issue, see also chapter 23. The relationship with the wages protection provisions of ERA is considered in chapter 11.

The duty to exercise reasonable care

The main application here is in the field of health and safety at work (see chapter 15). However, the duty of care towards the subject and recipient of a reference should also be noted (see chapter 9).

The personal nature of the duty

Personal nature means that the duty is personal between the employer and employee. This has two principal implications. First, the employer cannot delegate the duty. Thus, if the employer arranges for someone else to perform the duty, the employer remains liable. Secondly, the duty is owed to the individual employee rather than employees in general. Thus the courts will look at the circumstances of the individual employee. If an employee has brought some personal handicap to the attention of the employer, the duty of care is likely to be greater. Thus, in *Paris v Stepney Borough Council*, eye protection was needed for a one-eyed person but not for those with two eyes. The duty of care was greater because of the increased risk of complete loss of eyesight.

Constituent parts of the duty

The leading authority for the existence of the duty and its constituent parts is *Wilsons and Clyde Coal*, reaffirmed in *McDermid*. The duty is to use reasonable care in providing:

- safe and adequate plant and equipment;
- safe premises;
- competent and safe fellow employees; and
- a safe system of work.

A recent example of a failure to provide a safe system of work can be found in *Walker v Northumberland County Council*. The employer was held liable for the stress suffered by the employee who experienced two nervous breakdowns and then retired on ill-health grounds. The plaintiff's area of work was understaffed and he had an excessive workload: he did not have a safe system of work. Moreover, after his first nervous breakdown, further psychiatric damage was reasonably foreseeable.

Most personal injury cases are founded in tort rather than contract. The duty of care can be found in the law of negligence as well as in the law of contract. In certain areas of health and safety, a civil action can also be based on breach of statutory duty (see chapter 15).

Duty to maintain mutual trust and confidence

The nature of the duty

An employer should not, without proper reason and cause, treat an employee in a manner likely to destroy or seriously damage the relationship of trust and confidence between the parties. This means that the employer is under a duty to act in good faith, or with respect, so as not to prevent the employee fulfilling his contractual duties. Taken with the employee's duty of fidelity, this gives rise to a relationship of mutual trust and confidence.

The case law

- Authority for the existence of the term: this can be found in a number of cases including *Robinson v Crompton Parkinson*, *Post Office v Roberts* and *Woods v W M Car Services*. In *Robinson*, the EAT observed that 'in a contract of employment ... there has to be mutual trust and confidence between master and servant'. In this case the employer falsely accused the employee of theft: a repudiatory breach.
- How wide is the term? In *Post Office v Roberts*, the EAT reviewed the authorities and concluded that the duty is not so wide that it requires the employer to treat the employee in a reasonable manner. This was a case in which the employer conducted an appraisal without due consideration of the employee's record.
- Is intention or bad faith a prerequisite for a breach of mutual trust and confidence? In *Woods*, the Court of Appeal confirmed the existence of the duty. Moreover, it made it clear that there is no requirement for an intention to repudiate: the courts should look at the employer's actual conduct.

In *Roberts*, it was of no relevance that the employer had not acted deliberately or in bad faith.

- Can a series of actions amount to a breach of mutual trust and confidence? In *Lewis v Motorworld*, the Court of Appeal held that a series of actions may cumulatively amount to such a breach even if each individual act taken alone might not be a breach. Here there were continuing criticism, threats of dismissal and other actions.

Other examples include the following:

Bracebridge Engineering v Darby

It was a breach of mutual trust and confidence not to treat seriously the employee's allegations of sexual harassment.

United Bank Ltd v Akhtar

It was a breach of mutual trust and confidence to exercise an express mobility clause in such a way that the employee could not fulfil his contractual duties (less than reasonable notice was given; moreover the employer exercised his discretion and did not provide financial assistance).

Note that a significant feature of the duty to maintain mutual trust and confidence is that there can be a breach of the duty even if an employer has the contractual right to enforce change. This is because the duty takes in the manner of implementation of change as well as its substance.

Other terms

Provision of work

The general common law position is that there is no duty to provide work:

> Provided I pay my cook her wages regularly, she cannot complain if I choose to take any or all of my meals out. *(Collier v Sunday Referee)*

Hence, in cases of dismissal, an employer can normally pay wages in lieu of notice.

The exceptions are where the opportunity to work is of the essence of the contract. For example:

- where publicity is important (eg, actors and singers) *(Clayton v Oliver)*;
- where the employee is engaged on piecework *(Devonald v Rosser; Langston v AUEW)*; and
- where the work is necessary in order to maintain skills (see *Provident Financial Group plc v Hayward* where a financial director was subject to a six-month notice period and a restrictive covenant. He was told not to come to work, thus being put on what is called 'garden leave').

Note that even in these exceptional cases the failure to provide work may not be a breach of contract if the employer has no work available.

Confidentiality

In *Dalgleish v Lothian and Borders Police Board*, an interdict (the Scottish equivalent of an injunction) was granted preventing the employers divulging employees' names and addresses to the local authority who were chasing community charge ('poll tax') defaulters, partly on the ground that this was confidential information.

The *Scally* principle

The House of Lords in *Scally v Southern Health and Social Services Board* upheld the finding that there was an implied contract term as follows. The employer must inform the employee where:

- terms of the contract had not been negotiated with the individual employee;
- the employee could avail himself of rights only by taking certain action; and
- the employee could not reasonably be expected to be aware of this term unless informed of it.

Reasonable opportunity for the employee to obtain redress of grievances.

It is an implied term of the contract of employment that an employer will reasonably and promptly afford a reasonable opportunity to his employees to obtain redress of grievances *(WA Goold (Pearmark) Ltd v McConnell)*.

Reasonably suitable working environment

An employer must provide and monitor for his employees, so far as is reasonably practicable, a working environment which is reasonably suitable for the performance by them of their contractual duties *(Waltons & Morse v Dorrington)*.

TERMS IMPLIED AT COMMON LAW: DUTIES OF THE EMPLOYEE

Duty to obey lawful orders

Authority for the term: *Laws v London Chronicle*

- It is a fundamental term of the contract that the employee must observe the lawful orders of the employer.
- Wilful disobedience is evidence of disregard for this term and so goes to the very root of the contract, justifying summary dismissal (ie, dismissal without notice – at common law, dismissal for cause).

Note that dismissal for cause will not automatically mean that the dismissal is fair under the statutory provisions relating to unfair dismissal. This is because the statutory test rather than the contractual test is the overriding one under those provisions.

Meaning of lawful orders

Lawful in this context means within (that is, permitted by) the terms of the contract of employment.

Instructions involving a crime

The employer's right to give orders to the employee clearly does not extend to instructing the employee to commit a crime, as the following case illustrates.

Morrish v Henleys

FACTS
The employee kept a record of the amount of fuel put into his vehicle. He entered the correct amounts but found that these were being altered by his manager, who then signed the record. The employee changed the altered figures so that the original, correct figures were recorded. The manager instructed the employee not to change the altered figures. The employee refused and was dismissed. The employer argued that the practice of altering the figures was common and that the employee had unreasonably refused to obey an order.
HELD (NIRC, the forerunner of EAT)
This was an untenable proposition. There was no breach of contract by the employee and he was unfairly dismissed.

Instructions involving a tort

It seems reasonable to assume that the position must be similar with instructions to an employee to commit a tort. What, however, if the instruction involves the *employer* in commiting a tort? As as an example, it is clear that an employer must not order an employee into danger since this would be both a crime under the HSWA and a tort in the law of negligence. Moreover, the employer would be in breach of the contract term of reasonable care, and probably that of mutual trust and confidence.

Instructions involving change

This issue is explored in more detail on pages 189–99. Here the aim is to note the general position when an employer orders an employee to perform new duties or to use new techniques, methods or equipment. The critical test at common law is whether the change is permitted by the contract. It may be permitted in four particular situations:

- Where there can be implied a general duty on the part of the employee to adapt to changed methods of doing the same work. *Cresswell v Board of Inland Revenue* and *MacPherson v London Borough of Lambeth* are examples, both involving computerization of the work.
- Where the change lies within the realm of the employer's administrative discretion and is not of the nature of a contractual change. The employee's duty to obey the employer's lawful orders underpins this.
- Where the contract terms are drawn widely enough to permit the change, eg a term requiring the employee to work at any of the company's sites according to the needs of the business.
- Where there is an express term of the contract giving the employer the right to change the terms, ie the company reserves the right to change the terms according to the needs of the business. In other situations, there will need to be consensual variation if the change is to be effected lawfully.

Note, again, that under the statutory provisions relating to unfair dismissal, a change of terms in breach of contract will not automatically make unfair any subsequent dismissal for refusal to obey. The statutory test has to be applied (see chapter 16).

Duty to give faithful service

Meaning and authority

The employee is under an obligation to 'faithfully and truly discharge his duty towards his employer' *(Boston Deep Sea Fishing v Ansell)*. The duty is to 'serve the employer faithfully within the requirements of the contract' *(British Telecommunications plc v Ticehurst)*. In particular, the employee should not put himself in a position where his interests conflict with the duty to the employer.

Note that the duty is not unlimited: see *Ticehurst*: 'within the requirements of the contract'.

Industrial action

Where the employee's aim is to prejudice the employer's business, there will be a breach of fidelity even if the employee is working to rule or working to contract. For example:

British Telecommunications plc v Ticehurst

'Going slow' and 'working to contract' were held to be a breach of fidelity.

Secretary of State for Employment v ASLEF (No 2)

The rules here were not contractual but 'working to rule' disrupted the railways (which was the intention) and was capable of being a breach of fidelity.

As noted earlier in *Miles* – the registrar who refused to perform marriages on Saturday mornings as part of industrial action – an employer may deduct from pay in respect of partial performance. In *Sim v Rotherham Metropolitan Borough Council* teachers would not perform their full duties and the employer deducted a percentage from their pay. However, in *Sim* the employees could recover their wages, but subject to the employer's right to equitable set-off of the amount representing the unfulfilled duties. The effect, therefore, was the same as in *Miles*, but with different reasoning.

Two further points should be made here, both of which emanate from *Ticehurst*. First, where (as in this case) the employee had discretion in their work (eg, being a manager), the discretion must be used to advance the interests of the employer rather than to frustrate them. Secondly, returning to the question of making deductions from pay, it is established that an employer does not have to accept partial performance. That is, the employer is entitled to make clear that only full performance will be accepted, and that in its absence there will be no pay whatsoever.

Secret profits

In *Boston Deep Sea Fishing* the managing director took a secret commission from suppliers. In effect, he obtained a personal fee for giving them a contract. Such conduct goes to the very root of the contract of employment and it was held that he had to account to his employer for these profits (ie, they belonged to the employer).

Disclosure of misconduct

To what extent is an employee under a duty to disclose misconduct to his employer? The first point to be noted is that a contract of employment is not a contract *uberrimae fidei* (utmost good faith) requiring complete and voluntary disclosure (*cf* an insurance contract). Except in the case of directors, there is not normally any fiduciary duty.

It follows from the above that the employee is not under any general duty to disclose his own misconduct, although he must not positively mislead his employer, since this would be a fraud (see *Bell v Lever Bros*). Is there, however, a duty to disclose the misconduct of others, ie fellow employees? The general rule is that there is no such duty, but it is clear from the case law that there may be a duty under certain circumstances. In *Swain v West (Butchers) Ltd*, the employee's contract contained an express term requiring him to do all he could to develop the company's interests. He was a senior employee. The Court of Appeal thought that there were certain cases where there was a duty to disclose the misconduct of others – similar in the case below.

Sybron Corporation v Rochem

FACTS
The employees, who were subordinates of the defendant, set up and operated rival businesses in competition with their employer. The defendant was a senior employee with a contractual duty to report on the state of the part of the business for which he was responsible.
HELD (CA)
Non-disclosure of fellow employees' misconduct was a breach of contract on the part of the defendant.
COMMENT:
The Court of Appeal followed the approach it had adopted in *Swain*. Critical factors again appeared to be the senior status of the employee and his specific contractual duties (here, to report on his area of the business).

Disclosure of an interest

Again, there appears to be no general rule requiring an employee to disclose an interest. However, it seems likely that an interest should be disclosed where it may conflict with the interests of the employer and that the duty to disclose may be greater for senior employees. In *Horcal v Gatland*, involving a director of the company, it was held that it was a breach of fidelity for an employee to have an interest in a firm transacting business with his employer without disclosing the fact.

Competition

The leading case relating to competition during employment is *Hivac v Park Royal Scientific Instruments*, which is particularly interesting for those who are fascinated by the manufacture of midget valves. The general rule is that the employee is free to do what he likes with his spare time. However, the rule is qualified thus: the employee is not free to cause definite harm to the employer.

A mere intention, expressed during employment, to leave and set up in competition is not a breach of fidelity *(Laughton v Bapp Industrial Supplies)*. However, trying to persuade a major client to transfer his business, albeit at some time in the future, clearly will be *(Marshall v Industrial Systems and Control Ltd)*. The same will apply to an employee tendering for the work of his own employer *(Adamson v B&L Cleaning Services Ltd)*. What distinguishes *Marshall* and *Adamson* from *Laughton* is that in both former cases the employees had already taken action which could be seen as being in competition with their employer, while in *Laughton* there was nothing more than an intention.

Post-employment, as noted, the doctrine of restraint of trade will hold such restrictions to be void unless there are legitimate interests to be protected and the restraint is reasonable *inter partes* and in the public interest.

Confidential information

An employee is under a duty not to misuse confidential information and the duty may continue post-employment. The leading case is *Faccenda Chicken v Fowler*. The duty of the employee is wider than that of the ex-employee. The latter has an implied duty not to misuse trade secrets and customer information. The former has in addition a duty not to misuse anything confidential arising out of the employment. However, employees have a right to exploit their knowledge and skills including knowledge and skills arising out of their previous employment.

Whether information is confidential will depend upon factors including:

- the nature of the employment;
- the nature of the information;
- whether the employer made it clear that it was confidential; and
- whether the information can be separated from other information which is in the public domain.

There is an exception to the general rule that an employee must not disclose confidential information. This is where it is in the public interest to do so.

In *Initial Services v Putterill*, an ex-employee disclosed price fixing which was illegal under the Restrictive Trade Practices Act 1956. He gave the information to a newspaper. The Court of Appeal, defining the scope of the public interest exception, thought that the employer's practice did not have to be illegal (as here): it was sufficient that it was an 'iniquity'. In *Lion Laboratories v Evans* the scope was defined even more widely: not necessarily misconduct, rather, a genuine public concern.

Another important issue in relation to the public interest exception may be the nature of the person to whom disclosure is made *(Putterill)*. For example, where disclosure was to be made to the Inland Revenue and an industry regulator, a company sought an injunction to prevent any disclosure whatsoever. The court granted an injunction but in terms preventing disclosure other than to the Revenue and regulator *(Re a Company's Application)*.

It should be noted that the Public Interest Disclosure Bill 1997 – a private member's bill which has government support – will, if enacted, provide protection for workers who disclose information in the public interest.

Inventions and intellectual property

The traditional common law position was that an employer was entitled to the benefit of inventions made by the employee if referable to their employment.

British Syphon Co Ltd v Homewood

FACTS
The employee was chief technician. He invented a new type of soda syphon although it was not his job to invent new designs. His contract contained no express term about inventions.
HELD
The invention belonged to the employer, because it had arisen out of the employment. This was part of the duty of fidelity.

The position in respect of inventions, and also copyright, is now regulated by statute. (See Chapter 24.)

Duty to show reasonable care and skill

The employee is under a general duty of care and skill (see, eg, *Harmer v Cornelius*) and may be required to indemnify his employer for any losses. In *Lister v Romford* the employee's negligence caused injury to a third party. His employer was vicariously liable for damages and it was held that the employee was under a duty to indemnify his employer for these.

Note that the employee is under a statutory duty to take reasonable care in relation to his own health and safety at work and that of others (HSWA, s 7).

THE INTERPRETATION OF CONTRACT TERMS

The normal canons of legal construction must be applied

As stated in *Laws v London Chronicle* and *Hooper v British Railways Board,* the contract of employment is but an example of the general law of contract. Thus, a literal construction will be enforced even where the contract term is incorporated from a loosely worded, unenforceable collective agreement (as was the case in *Hooper,* relating to sick pay).

Written documents

The parol evidence rule will apply where a written document purports to contain all the terms of the contract. That is, no extrinsic evidence will be admitted. Moreover, the interpretation of a written document will be a matter of law. Thus, in *Davies v Presbyterian Church of Wales,* a written document was construed as a matter of law to be something other than a contract of employment (see chapter 5).

The requirement for certainty

The principle of contract law that without certainty of terms a contract will be void is difficult to apply in the employment field where most contracts contain a mixture of oral and written terms. The more usual approach of the courts will be to imply a term. A stricter approach by the courts would probably make void large numbers of employment contracts.

Specific words followed by general words

Where specific words are followed by general words, the general words are to be interpreted in the light of the specific words. This is the *ejusdem generis* (of the same kind) rule.

The lecturer's duties shall be to lecture, take tutorials, set and mark examinations, do research, undertake administration and *perform such other duties as the head of department may require.* The emphasized words relate to duties of the same kind as those already specified, eg academic work, and would not extend, say, to cleaning the toilets.

Specific words not followed by general words

Where a list of specific items is not followed by general words, the list is usually treated as exhaustive, ie nothing apart from the items listed applies. The exception is where the items are preceded by the word 'include', eg duties will include loading, unloading, delivery, obtaining receipts and keeping records. If this stated 'duties will be', the list would be taken to be exhaustive.

The relationship between express and implied terms

Classical contract law holds that express terms have primacy over implied terms. As noted in *Nelson v BBC*, the courts will not imply a term where an express term is stated in unrestricted language because this would alter its meaning. However, they may imply a term where it amplifies an express term *(Tayside Regional Council v MacIntosh)*.

Moreover, important developments appear to be taking place in this area. The courts seem to have confirmed the existence of overriding implied terms, in particular the duty of reasonable care and the duty to maintain mutual trust and confidence *(Woods v W M Car Services)*. In addition, the courts have accepted that implied terms might qualify the way express terms are exercised.

The law does not go as far as requiring the reasonable exercise of express terms but it does require that the employee must not be prevented from fulfilling his contractual duties *(White v Reflecting Roadstuds)*. Thus there should have been reasonable notice of mobility in *United Bank v Akhtar*. The employer may be in breach of the express term itself if it is applied capriciously *(White)*.

A major issue in this area is the legal position where express and implied terms are incompatible.

Johnstone v Bloomsbury Area Health Authority

FACTS
The plaintiff, who was a hospital doctor, worked under a contract which stated expressly that his normal working week would be 40 hours. It also stated expressly that there would be an additional 48 hours on call. In practice, the on-call hours were regularly worked. The plaintiff argued that his actual hours of work had a detrimental effect on his health (not to mention the health of patients treated in his 88th hour), and that the requirement to work these hours was a breach of the employer's duty of reasonable care. The employers made an inter-locutory application to have the case struck out on the ground that it disclosed no cause of action.

HELD (CA) (by a 2:1 majority)
The employer's application is dismissed. Leggett LJ, dissenting, stated that the express term has primacy over the implied duty of care.
Browne-Wilkinson V-C stated that the additional 48 hours were an optional not an absolute right (because they were hours on call rather than necessary hours of work). It was not improper to imply a term that in exercising their discretion the employers should have regard to the health and safety of their employee. However, if there had been a blatant express term/implied term conflict, the former would have precedence.
Stuart-Smith LJ stated that the power to require 88 hours on average had to be exercised subject to other contractual terms, particularly that relating to health and safety (ie, the term of reasonable care).
COMMENT
The differing opinions in this case illustrate the tensions which occur in the debate in this area. Two of the three judges appear to uphold the principles of classical contract law.

Exclusion clauses

Anything restricting the operation of the ERA, unless it is provided for as an exception within the Act itself, will be void by virtue of s 203. Similar provisions apply to other legislation. More generally, the provisions of the Unfair Contract Terms Act 1977 apply, so making void exclusion clauses in respect of liability for death and personal injury and subjecting other exclusions to a test of reasonableness.

CHANGES TO TERMS AND CONDITIONS OF EMPLOYMENT

Preliminary points

Notification of changes to terms of employment is required under ERA, s 4, but this does not confer a right to make the changes. Nor is notification of change notification of termination of employment (such as to avoid a breach of contract) *(Burdett-Coutts v Hertfordshire County Council)*.

Another preliminary issue is that of consideration. If the change involves an increase (in, say, wages), consideration may be found in the settlement of the claim and a continuation of work *(Lee v Plessey)*. If the change involves a deterioration, then rescission of the old contract may be consideration for the new one.

For the purposes of the present analysis, three principal situations are identified:

- where change is non-contractual;

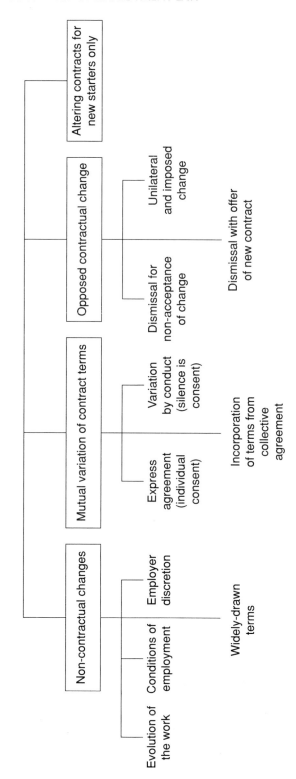

Figure 10.1 Changes to terms and conditions of employment

- where change is contractual but agreed; and
- where change is contractual but opposed.

These are presented diagrammatically in Figure 10.1.

It should be borne in mind that, even where a change is non-contractual or permitted by the contract, there may still be a breach of contract if the manner of its introduction causes a breach of mutual trust and confidence (see *Akhtar* and *White*).

Where change is non-contractual

These are circumstances in which the proposed change does not involve any alteration to the terms of the contract. There are four particular sets of circumstances.

Conditions of employment

Not all changes to terms and conditions of employment involve contractual changes. A distinction can be drawn between terms and conditions. The former may include the amount of holidays, the latter when the holidays may be taken. Terms are based on contractual agreement whereas conditions are laid down by an employer unilaterally – they are a condition of employment. The significance is that conditions may be altered unilaterally by the employer but changes to terms require mutual agreement. See *Cadoux* and *Dryden*. Changes in conditions may be seen as relatively minor, perhaps even as administrative changes. Clearly, however, changes made to, for example, the timing of holidays, method of payment or method of work may give rise to legal and/or industrial challenges. Nevertheless, it is submitted, an employer may argue that a change does not amount to a change in terms but is merely a change in conditions which lies within the legitimate authority of the employer.

Employer discretion over non-contractual benefits

Some benefits of employment may be neither terms nor conditions. They may be provided by an employer on a goodwill basis, with nothing specific sought in exchange. It follows that the withdrawal of such benefits may well be at the discretion of the employer.

This applies particularly to matters such as Christmas bonuses and the private use of company cars. In effect these are gifts made by management since the employee is not required to contribute anything to the organization in exchange. However, much will depend on the circumstances of the case; for example, use of a company car could be expressly agreed as a contractual term. Where something is required in exchange (for instance, good attendance as a qualification for entitlement to a bonus) the relationship assumes more of a contractual character. The provision of a non-contractual benefit is often accompanied by an express right to alter or withdraw the benefit.

Employer's right to vary terms

Where there is an express term of the contract giving the employer the right to vary the terms, there will be no breach of contract if a variation is made (subject to the way the discretion is exercised). However, an employer may not vary a term incorporated from a collective agreement by reserving a right to alter it by general instruction *(Lee v Plessey)*.

Widely drawn terms

Contract terms may be sufficiently wide to allow a change to be effected within the contract without any breach occurring. For example, if the employee's contract provides that they will work at any of the organization's sites, a change of location will be permitted by the contract. It is then a matter for the employer to ensure that the move is reasonably handled; that sufficient warning and perhaps financial assistance are provided *(United Bank Ltd v Akhtar)*. Another example is where a contract includes a description of specific duties but also provides that the employee will perform whatever else his manager may require. Courts will look at the reasonableness of such requirements, particularly in relation to the normal job duties and status of the employee. Therefore, a university lecturer with such a term in his contract need not feel unduly troubled about refusing a request to clean out the lavatory.

The courts will use common law principles looking closely at widely drawn terms and at anything involving penalties (eg, payments in relation to discrepancies; repayment of training costs). By doing this they have developed the practice of limiting the effect of what the parties have agreed. This happened in *Akhtar* where an implied term that there should be proper warning was found. In *Johnstone* there was no absolute right to require 88 hours of work (including hours on call) despite a contractual term to this effect. A lack of reasonableness can also give rise to a finding that the employer has breached that term of the contract which requires mutual trust and confidence. Finally, if a term is too widely drawn the courts may regard it as uncertain in its application. Although a valid term, the courts may nonetheless refuse to enforce it.

An employer will need to provide evidence of the existence of the widely drawn term(s) on which he is relying *(O'Brien v Associated Fire Alarms Ltd)*.

Evolution of the work

The contract of employment is not static – it is a social instrument which must reflect the working conditions of the day. The terms of employees will vary according to a number of factors including technology and the economic climate. Thus one can find an implied duty on the part of the employee to adapt to change, such as computerization (see *Cresswell and MacPherson*). The duties of employers may also evolve: for example, the duty of care will be updated in the light of new knowledge generally available about specific health and safety risks and preventive measures.

Note that a change permitted by the contract is not a breach just because it causes the employee loss *(Spafax Ltd v Harrison)* or is difficult to comply with *(Dryden)*.

Where change is contractual but agreed

Where, in contrast to the above, the change is contractual, a breach of contract can be avoided if there is an agreed variation of terms (once variation is agreed, the parties will be estopped from enforcing the original terms).

Express agreement

The contract of employment is at the centre of the employment relationship and changes in terms can easily give rise to problems. In law the contract is an agreement entered into voluntarily by the parties. In theory, the parties have equal status and power. The mutuality principle extends to changes in the terms – where both parties agree, the terms may be varied. This is known as mutual or consensual variation. Such variation occurs frequently and by definition is rarely problematic. For example, an employee agrees to a change in work location; the employer agrees to a financial package to compensate. This would be express agreement.

Variation by conduct

There are also situations in which changes are made unilaterally by one party but are accepted by the other party by implication. That is, they are not challenged, and over a period of time – unspecified, as is usual in law – it will be taken that 'silence is consent'. For example, an employee's hours are reduced from 32 to 26 per week. After initial protest the employee continues working until made redundant three years later. The change was agreed. The employee's conduct is interpreted as indicating acceptance of the change. However, the central question is whether or not the employee has accepted the change and courts will be reluctant to find acceptance where the change has no immediate and practical effect upon the employee *(Jones v Associated Tunnelling; Aparau v Iceland Frozen Foods plc)*. Courts will also be slow to find a consensual variation if the employee is threatened with dismissal for non-acceptance of a change which is to his detriment.

Incorporation of terms from collective agreements

Employers may also be able to make changes to contract terms by securing agreement with a trades union. Again, the change may be willingly agreed by a union or be accepted because the union is unable in practice to prevent it. The change will alter the contracts of employment of individual employees only if the terms of the collective agreement become incorporated into those contracts. This may be provided for expressly – where it is stated that contract terms will be as negotiated from time to time between the company and the trades union – or be implied. In the latter case, individual contract terms are altered in practice by collectively bargained changes. Contract terms may be altered by collective bargaining where, for example, employers have succeeded in negotiating work flexibility agreements with unions.

Where change is contractual and opposed

The legal position

Problems often occur when an employer wishes to change what is clearly a contractual term and this is against the wishes of the employee (and perhaps their union). Where agreement to the change is not forthcoming an employer may contemplate unilateral change. Generally speaking, any unilateral change which is not accepted opens the way for a claim that one or more of the contract terms have been breached. If the breach is substantial and the term is one which goes to the very root of the contract – pay, for example – the breach may be said to be a fundamental one. That is, the employment contract has been repudiated – the employer has, in effect, said that he or she no longer intends to be bound by the terms of the contract. Putting someone on a half-time, half-pay contract after a full-time, full-pay one was a pay cut and a demotion amounting to a fundamental breach of contract. The fact that a part-time contract was accepted afterwards did not mean that the change was affirmed. The employee accepted the employer's repudiation and brought the former contract to an end *(Hogg v Dover College)*.

The employee, faced with any breach of contract (whether a repudiatory (fundamental) breach or not) may elect to affirm the contract and continue. In doing so he or she can either accept the change, or reject it by standing on the original terms and suing for damages. Thus, in *Ferodo v Rigby*, where a wage cut was imposed on employees despite their opposition and the opposition of their union, the resulting breach of contract allowed them to sue for damages for the amount of the reduction. This was also the position in *Burdett-Coutts v Hertfordshire County Council.* Similarly, in the absence of an agreed variation of terms, an employee was entitled to claim lost pay caused by a shorter working week being introduced unilaterally by his employer *(Miller v Hamworthy Engineering Ltd)*.

If the breach is repudiatory, the employee can accept the repudiation and treat it as grounds for terminating the contract. In such circumstances the employee must at some stage choose between acceptance and affirmation. Provided he makes clear his objection to what is being done, he may continue to work and draw pay for a limited period of time without being taken to have affirmed the contract *(Marriott v Oxford Co-operative Society)*. However, in a later ruling – also by the Court of Appeal – it was stated that if the employee 'continues for any length of time without leaving he will lose his right to treat himself as discharged' *(Western Excavating (ECC) v Sharp)*. The EAT subsequently adopted the softer line of *Marriott* but noted that a prolonged delay in electing for acceptance of repudiation may be evidence of an implied affirmation *(WE Cox Toner (International) Ltd v Crook)*. After accepting repudiation, the employee may sue for damages or pursue a claim for compensation for unfair (constructive) dismissal, or both.

The employee has the right to treat the contract as terminated only if the breach is fundamental. Where the breach is not fundamental, the employee's action is to stand on the original terms and sue for damages.

Effecting the change: the employer's options

Can an employer ever defend a contractual breach as unlawful? There are three options here, all of which, ultimately, might need defending at law. First, an employer may give notice to the employee (that is, notice of termi-nation of contract) and offer a new contract containing new terms *(Gilham v Kent County Council)*. Continuity is automatically preserved for statutory purposes and can be preserved for other purposes by agreement. A second option is to enforce the change by informing the employee that if they do not accept it they will be dismissed with due notice. The third option is to impose the change and wait for the employee either to consent to it by his conduct or to commence legal proceedings.

Possible responses by employees

Whichever option the employer chooses it will result in a dismissal, although this will be true in the third case only if the breach is fundamental and is accepted as a repudiation. A fundamental breach will establish a constructive dismissal which may or may not be unfair. For a dismissal to be found fair, if it is challenged, an employer will have to demonstrate to a tribunal that there was a valid reason. A dismissal for unwillingness to accept contractual change constitutes 'some other substantial reason' under unfair dismissal law (see chapter 16). An employer will need to show that the business had a real need for change of the type that has been effected. For example, acute financial difficulties caused by a lack of competitiveness might warrant changes in the duties of employees in order to increase productivity and reduce unit costs and the fact that the change involved a breach of contract will not necessarily render the dismissal unfair (the test is statutory not contractual). Less dramatically, an employer wishing to introduce a no-smoking policy and dismissing someone who would not accept it might argue that the need to comply with s 2 of the HSWA was a substantial reason.

Once a fair reason is established, the fairness of the dismissal will then depend upon how it was handled. For example, were the need for and details of the change explained to the employee? Was there advance warning (if it was possible)? Was there assistance, if necessary (for example, where there is a change of location) or training (for instance, where duties are changed)? In addition, has the proper procedure been followed – has an opportunity been given to the employee to state his or her case?

The employee may respond in other ways (see Figure 10.2). Where the

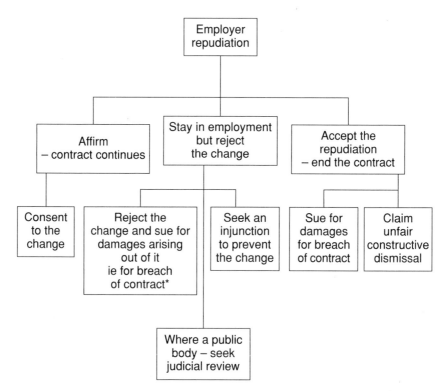

* An application in respect of unfair constructive dismissal may be possible
(see *Hogg v Dover College*)

Figure 10.2   The employee's options when an employer repudiates
the contract

contractual change is a wage reduction, an employee may be able to apply to an industrial tribunal under the wages protection provisions of ERA, that is, in respect of an unauthorized deduction. More generally, there is the possibility of suing for breach of contract. This will not be an option if the employer has dismissed with due notice, but will apply where a change has been unilaterally imposed. Dismissing with due notice for non-acceptance of change or by offering a new contract thus restricts the employee to a tribunal claim (if there is eligibility) and removes the prospect of a claim in respect of breach of contract. Claims in respect of breach of contract are dealt with in the common law courts – the county court and High Court – and since 1994 in the industrial tribunals (see chapter 3). The remedy is damages. In as much as an employee is able to claim damages for breach of contract these will normally be restricted to the notice period since the contract could have been ended lawfully if due notice had been given, although this principle was not accepted as applying in *Ferodo*.

There are also equitable remedies, namely injunctions and orders for specific performance. It is considered inappropriate to force continuation of an employment relationship when one of the parties is opposed to it, so specific performance is rarely granted. Trust and confidence would need to have been preserved between the parties and there would need to be some benefits arising from continuation. However, in a recent case the test applied was less stringent: the relationship had to be 'workable' *(Robb v London Borough of Hammersmith and Fulham)*. In any case, it would need to be established that damages would be an inadequate remedy. Sometimes a temporary injunction may be granted where breach of contract is alleged (see *Hill v CA Parsons* and *Irani* – wrongful dismissals (chapter 16) – and *Hughes v London Borough of Southwark* – change of work duties and location). On the other hand, the High Court would not grant an injunction in *MacPherson v London Borough of Lambeth* to stop the employer withholding pay because the employees would not operate a new computer. The employees were not able and willing to perform their contractual duties.

To decide whether an injunction should be granted the courts apply what is known as the balance of convenience test *(American Cynamid v Ethicon Ltd)*. The court asks:

- is there a serious issue to be tried?
- would damages provide an adequate remedy for the plaintiff if the injunction was refused but he or she subsequently succeeded at a full hearing of the case?
- would the employer be adequately compensated by damages if the injunction was granted but he or she subsequently succeeded at a full hearing of the case?

The court is not required to look at the relative strength of the parties' cases.

It will not be possible for employees to seek remedies of any sort for breach of contract, if the contract itself is illegal, for example, because the employee is a child, or because there was a deliberately illegal purpose such as defrauding the Inland Revenue. This would also prevent unfair dismissal and other claims such as sex discrimination although perhaps not if the employee was unaware of the illegality.

Many employees faced with a repudiatory breach of contract by an employer will prefer the simpler, quicker and cheaper route of claiming unfair constructive dismissal to processing a claim for damages. This may, perhaps, be less true where a claim for damages if compatible with continued employment, and where the legal services of a trades union are available (both of these applied in *Ferodo*). In practice, many employees will probably reluctantly accept the employer's imposed change because of the need to keep their job.

Where the employer is a public body, there is also the possibility of a decision being open to challenge by judicial review. There will have to be a public law issue at stake, otherwise the case would be a straightforward private law matter (for example, a claim for remedy for breach of contract) *(R v East Berkshire Health Authority ex parte Walsh)*. However, the decisions of local authorities to reduce wages by dismissing and offering new employment on inferior terms were subject to judicial review, although orders to quash them were not granted *(R v Hertfordshire County Council ex parte NUPE; R v East Sussex County Council ex parte NUPE)*. A decision to withhold the pay of teachers because they were unable to work when caretakers were involved in industrial action was quashed in *R v Liverpool City Corporation ex parte Ferguson*. A decision of the same council to declare redundancies (following the setting of an illegal rate) was also quashed *(R v Liverpool City Corporation ex parte Ferguson and Smith)* (see chapter 20).

Altering the contract terms for new starters

If an employer is worried about the response that existing employees and/or their trades union might make to a change in terms, there is the possibility of restricting the change to new entrants. The individual nature of the contract of employment makes this relatively easy to achieve. New entrants would be offered terms different in some way from those of existing staff. For example, new staff might have a wider term in relation to where the work is to be carried on – they may be required to work in more than one place or to transfer from time to time between places. Existing staff may have contracts specifying one place of work. Care would need to be taken in relation to any collective agreements. A confusing situation would arise if the employee's written particulars specified that terms were to be as determined from time to time by agreements with a union, whereas in fact one or more of the terms differed from that laid down in the collective agreement. It would need to be clear that the express incorporation of collectively bargained terms did not extend to the particular term(s) in question.

E L E V E N

Pay

This chapter attempts to draw together much of the law governing pay, particularly the statutory provisions relating to the payment of wages, equal pay and sick pay. Other aspects of pay are dealt with elsewhere: maternity pay in chapter 13 and redundancy and guarantee payments in chapter 19. Moreover, it should be noted that the Equal Pay Act, dealt with here, is concerned only with pay discrimination on the ground of sex: pay discrimination on the ground of race is covered in chapter 6 and on union grounds in chapter 21.

Key problem areas are those relating to the employee's entitlement to pay and to management's ability to make changes. These issues are much more likely to hinge upon questions of contract than upon the provisions of statute. Indeed, one of the notable features of the legal context within which pay and other terms are set is the relatively small amount of statute law governing specific terms. However, this situation is about to change as the EU Working Time Directive is implemented in the UK and the National Minimum Wage Bill 1997 is enacted.

The applicability of discrimination law to the recruitment process was considered in chapter 6 and it was noted that it covered discrimination in the terms offered. Once employment has commenced, it embraces the terms as applied. Continuing discrimination in relation to terms of employment is an act extending over the period of employment *(Barclay's Bank plc v Kapur).* It will be treated as if it were done at the end of the period of employment rather than at the time the decision was made. Race and sex discrimination law covers workers employed under a contract of employment as well as those who may not be employed under such a contract. The latter will be people under contracts personally to execute work or labour – contracts for services. In contrast, once employment has commenced, union discrimination law applies only to those working under contracts of employment (including contracts of apprenticeship).

Discrimination law as it relates to union membership, activity or non-membership is constituted differently from that relating to race and sex but may still cover pay discrimination in certain circumstances. It seemed as though granting a pay increase to members of one union but not to members of another might be unlawful *(National Coal Board v Ridgway)*, but the House of Lords subsequently overruled this decision (by a majority) in *Associated Newspapers Ltd v Wilson*. The right not to have action taken against him on union grounds included protection against omissions, but there could not be an omission where the employer was under no obligation to pay in the first place[1] (see chapter 21).

THE PAYMENT OF WAGES

Overview

For the purposes of this chapter the terms 'pay', 'wages' and 'salary' are used interchangeably. ERA defines wages as 'any sums payable to the worker in connection with his employment'.[2] What is to be included in this definition is described later (see pages 203–4). The European Court of Justice has also contributed to the definition of pay by developing what might be termed the European concept of pay (see pages 211–12).

The most significant point is that there is no legislation requiring a minimum level of pay generally, although the government has now introduced a National Minimum Wage Bill as a framework for the introduction of a generally applicable national minimum wage.[3] In the absence of legislation, employees cannot complain in law that their pay is too low. They can complain, however, if their pay is less than the amount due under their contract of employment, that is, if it is less than was agreed. If there is a dispute about what was agreed, the courts will rule on entitlement. Employees may also complain even where there is no dispute about entitlement if their employer has not paid them. The Industrial Tribunals Act 1996 provides for a ministerial order to allow industrial tribunals to deal with such contractual matters where they arise on termination of employment or can be brought alongside some other issue which is already within the tribunal's jurisdiction.[4]

The position in relation to deductions is quite different. This is provided for by legislation, although part of the statutory test is based upon contractual arrangements. ERA restricts the deductions that can be made from wages (or the payments that can be obtained from workers) and allows complaints to industrial tribunals about unauthorized deductions or payments.[5] Finally, there is legislation requiring itemized pay statements.

Deductions

Rights conferred
There is a general restriction on deductions and payments which applies to both manual and non-manual workers.[6] The rights conferred on workers are:

- not to have a deduction from wages that is not authorized or required by statute, a relevant provision of the worker's contract or by the worker in advance in writing;[7] and
- not to have to make a payment to the employer unless similarly authorized or required.[8]

In addition, rights are conferred on workers in 'retail employment' defined below:[9]

- not to have more than 10 per cent of gross pay deducted on any pay day as a result of cash shortages or stock deficiencies; and
- not to have to make a payment to the employer of more than 10 per cent of gross pay for the reasons mentioned above.

Statutory authorization will include such deductions as national insurance contributions and PAYE. A relevant provision of the worker's contract means that there must be a term of the contract permitting deduction, as there is in the case of occupational pension contributions. Moreover, the employer must provide a copy of that term, or notify it to the worker in writing in advance of any deduction. Posting a notice on a board where the worker has an opportunity to read it may amount to notification *(McCreadie v Thomson and MacIntyre (Patternmakers) Ltd)*. Neither contractual changes nor the worker's agreement can be used to authorize deductions retrospectively. Contractual terms or the worker's agreement in writing must precede not only the deduction (or payment) but also the conduct giving rise to the deduction (or payment) *(Discount Tobacco and Confectionery Ltd v Williamson)*.

Scope
As regards deductions and payments, ERA has general applicability. There are no hours restrictions or qualifying periods of employment. However, unlike previous legislation it does not actually specify whether any particular type of deduction is reasonable. It simply aims to prevent deductions being

made which have not previously been agreed. In this respect the law applying to pay is like much of the law relating to terms of employment more generally – it is imbued with the spirit of the doctrine of freedom of contract. This means that the parties can (up to a point) agree what they like: in the main the law will intervene only to enforce what was agreed.

The legislation applies to workers rather than employees, and so has a broad application similar to that of the law relating to sex and race discrimination and equal pay. A worker is defined in s 230(3) as someone working under:

- a contract of service;
- a contract of apprenticeship; or
- any other contract whereby the individual undertakes to perform personally any work or services for another party except where the other party is a professional or business customer or client.

Certain deductions and payments are excluded from the authorization rules of the Act by virtue of ss 14 and 16. These include the recovery of overpayments, agreed deductions to pay third parties (eg, union subscriptions or charities) and deductions relating to the worker's participation in industrial action (see *Sunderland Polytechnic v Evans* – deduction in respect of industrial action held to be outside the scope of the Act). A small number of occupations are excluded from the Act: those ordinarily working outside Great Britain, merchant seamen and the armed forces.

Meaning of wages

Wages mean 'any sums payable to the worker in connection with his employment' including a number of specific payments: fees, bonuses, commission, holiday pay or other emoluments (in all these cases, whether contractual or non-contractual), as well as various statutory payments, eg SSP, SMP and guarantee payments. Wages exclude advances of wages, expenses (see *SIP (Industrial Products)*), pensions, *ex gratia* payments on retirement or loss of office, redundancy payments and payments to the worker other than in his capacity as a worker. Benefits in kind are excluded unless they are vouchers, stamps or similar documents which have a fixed monetary value and are capable of being exchanged for money, goods or services (luncheon vouchers would be an example).

It is common for employment to be terminated by employers without notice but with wages in lieu of notice. If wages in lieu of notice are wages within the meaning of ERA, an application may be pursued under the Act. Otherwise, the matter could be pursued under the industrial tribunals' contract jurisdiction. The following case was settled at a time when contract cases were not within the tribunals' jurisdiction, so that an action would lie in the county court.

Delaney v Staples

FACTS

The complainant had been dismissed. On dismissal, she claimed that her employer owed her the following sums:

- commission and holiday pay £55.50; and
- wages in lieu of notice £82.00;

Nothing had been paid under either head and a complaint was made under the protection of wages provisions.

HELD (CA)

Non-payment of the holiday pay and commission was a deduction under the Act. It had not been agreed to by the employee and therefore was unlawful.

Wages in lieu of notice were not wages within the meaning of the Act. Therefore, the industrial tribunal had no jurisdiction. This was later affirmed by the House of Lords.

RATIOS

The Court of Appeal and subsequently the House of Lords decided that non-payment of wages is a deduction under the Act. This could be a situation where the deduction extinguishes the wage payment altogether, or there is non-payment of a specific payment (eg, commission and holiday pay in *Delaney*). The reasoning is based on what is now ERA, s 13(3) – what falls to be treated as a deduction – which refers to the amount paid being less than the amount payable, seemingly including a zero payment.

Wages in lieu of notice were held to be damages for breach of contract rather than wages. The reasoning is based on what is now ERA, s 27 – which defines wages as sums payable to the worker 'in connection with' his employment. The Court of Appeal took the common law view that wages are payment for the rendering of a service. Wages in lieu, by contrast, were a payment relating to termination.

The distinction drawn in *Delaney* emphasizes the importance of the particular facts in dismissal cases, as Figure 11.1 illustrates.

Provisions relating to 'retail employment'

In addition to the general restrictions on deductions and payments, there are special restrictions applicable to 'retail employment'. This term means the carrying out of retail transactions with the public, other workers or other individuals in a personal capacity or the collection of money in connection with such retail transactions. The term 'retail transaction' means the sale or supply of goods or the supply of services. The definition – found in ERA, s 17 – is therefore wider than just shop assistants: it includes many others handling money – bus conductors, drivers who collect fares, cashiers, ticket clerks and so on.

	EDT	Wages
Dismissal 1: notice given today to expire in four weeks' time (regardless of whether or not the notice has to be worked).	in 4 weeks	Yes
Dismissal 2: dismissal today without notice but with wages in lieu paid (four weeks' pay)	today	No

Figure 11.1   Type of dismissal: effect on EDT and wages

The provisions apply to deductions for cash shortages or stock deficiencies including those arising from the dishonesty or negligence of the worker. The restriction is not on the amount that can be recovered by the employer, but simply on the rate at which he can make recovery. The deduction is limited to 10 per cent of gross wages on any pay day although there is no limit at the termination of employment. Deductions, or the first of a series of deductions, must be made within 12 months of the employer's discovery of the shortage or deficiency, or from any earlier date when the employer ought reasonably to have made the discovery. If the deduction is one of a series arising from the same shortage the repayment may continue beyond the 12-month limit. Wages cannot be agreed as being net of cash shortages to avoid the 10 per cent rule.

The rules governing deductions also apply to repayments. That is, there must be statutory or contractual authorization or the worker's agreement in writing. In retail employment the demand must be in writing and made on a pay day, and the total liability must be stated before any repayment is received. The 10 per cent and 12-month rules apply. A worker's failure to repay removes the 10 per cent rule and there is no limit to the percentage deduction on termination of employment. The employer may take the usual steps for recovery providing that within 12 months of the discovery of the shortage or deficiency he has made a demand for repayment in the above manner. If the worker is still in that employer's employment any court order will be limited by the 10 per cent rule.

The time limit for complaint to a tribunal is three months or within such further period as is reasonable in a case where it was not reasonably practicable to apply within three months. The tribunal, if it finds for the applicant, will make a declaration to that effect. Any unauthorized deduction will have to be repaid in full. Any over-deduction (for example, more than the 10 per cent in the retail employment case) will result in repayment of the excess. Further attempts to recover the same amount from a worker after a tribunal order will be unlawful. The right of application to a tribunal replaces the worker's right to go to the county court over the matters contained in the ERA. Where the amount properly payable to the employee is disputed, a tribunal will need to determine this matter before deciding the issue of whether or not a deduction is lawful. An agreement excluding these rights will be void but an agreement made through ACAS or a compromise agreement will result in a complainant being unable to pursue their application at an industrial tribunal.

Other points

- Nothing in the above provisions lays down any rules about whether or not a deduction is fair. The only requirement is that it be agreed.
- As regards retail employment, nothing in the provisions limits the total amount repayable: only the rate of recovery is restricted.
- There is no statutory right to be paid in cash but if an employer pays his workers in kind, the payment will not be wages. Therefore a worker could claim that there has been an unlawful deduction. But what if the worker agreed to be paid in kind, so that no wages were due? Or if the employer provided vouchers with a monetary value, but which could be used only to buy specified goods and/or services from that employer?
- A dispute about whether an employer is entitled under the contract to deduct for a particular reason, or how much can be deducted *(Fairfield Ltd v Skinner)* remains a matter of contract. However, an industrial tribunal may have to address these matters under the ERA (this was seen as giving the tribunals a contract jurisdiction 'by the back door' before they were formally given one in 1994).
- Where there is an agreement about deductions which includes the amount which may be deducted, common law requires the amount to be a reasonable pre-estimate of loss (rather than in the nature of a penalty).

Manner and frequency of payment

Manner of payment

There has been much interest in this area in recent years as government and employers have recognized the financial and security gains to be made from payment other than in cash. The various Truck Acts gave manual workers a right to be paid in cash (coin and notes) and so these were seen as an obstacle. The Wages Act 1986 repealed them.

The repeal of the Truck Acts means that manual workers no longer have a statutory right to be paid in cash. The issue is subject entirely to matters of employment contract and union–employer negotiation. It may well be that those employees paid in cash before 1 January 1987 have an implied term in their contracts that cash will be the method of payment. Cashless pay, therefore, may result in claims for damages for breach of contract or, perhaps less likely, in resignations followed by tribunal applications for compensation for unfair constructive dismissal. For employees starting on or after 1 January 1987 employers are likely to insist on cashless pay as part of the contract, unless unions can persuade them otherwise.

The abolition of the manual worker's statutory right to be paid in cash also raises the question of payment in kind. How does modern law deal with this? The answer is that it does not deal with it directly. Rather, ERA defines what is meant by wages (see above). Anything else, such as payment by cans of beer, bags of potatoes or car components will not constitute wages. Therefore, it follows that due wages will not have been paid, leaving an entitlement to claim under contract for damages for non-payment or under statute in respect of an unlawful deduction (but note the queries raised earlier).

Frequency of payment

None of the above changes introduced by the Wages Act 1986 affect the frequency of pay (weekly or monthly) which remains a matter of contract and collective bargaining. Nor, indeed, is there any law in this area other than the terms of the contract of employment. Thus it is open to the parties to agree whatever frequency they wish. Courts might intervene, however, if an employee were foolish enough to agree that they would accept payment once a year, on the grounds that there had been duress or conceivably that such a frequency breached an implied term of reasonable frequency. In any case, at what stage does this amount to non-payment?

Overpayments

Occasionally employers may pay an employee more than he or she is due. This may arise purely through arithmetic error, or through incorrect interpretation of legal or other requirements (in relation to tax, pensions or national insurance for instance). The law generally distinguishes between these two types of case, seeing the former as a genuine mistake which all of us are allowed to make from time to time. In such circumstances the employee will be required to make good the overpayment. In the second type of case the employer may be held to be culpable and the money may not have to be repaid.

The position is not clear-cut. Even where there has been a mistake of fact rather than a mistake of law, *prima facie* allowing recovery, there are considerations: the length of time which elapsed between overpayment and discovery, whether the employee knew that they had money not due to them and whether the employee had relied upon the money (that is, spent it). Where the time period is long, the employee did not know and there has been reliance, the employer's position will be at its weakest. The leading case is set out below.

Avon County Council v Howlett

FACTS

This was an action by the employer to recover overpayment of salary amounting to £1007. The employee's defence was estoppel by representation: the employer had represented the payments as salary and should not now be allowed to argue otherwise. Using this doctrine, the employee argued that he had relied upon (ie spent) only half the amount, but that none was recoverable (in fact, all of it had been spent). The employer's error was a mistake of fact.

HELD (CA)

The employee's defence succeeded – none of the money was recoverable by the employer.

Estoppel by representation is a rule of evidence precluding the representor (here the employer) from relying on facts contrary to his own representation (he could not now say that what he said was salary was not salary).

The defence of estoppel is not capable of being applied *pro tanto* (in part) – thus where the defence is successful, none of the money can be recovered.

The law of restitution holds that a plaintiff (here the employer) is estopped from asserting his claim if the following conditions are satisfied:

- the plaintiff made a representation of fact which led the defendant (the employee) to think that the money was his own;
- the defendant, *bona fide* and without notice of the plaintiff's action, must have consequently changed his position (ie, relied on the money); and
- the payment must not have been primarily caused by the fault of the defendant.

All these conditions were met in *Avon*. However, the court noted, *in obiter* (in passing, and not as part of its decision) that the plaintiff could have pleaded facts in support of retention of the whole sum by the defendant being inequitable, but failed to do so.

As noted, the general position in the law of restitution is that payments made by mistake of fact are recoverable. In *Lipkin Gorman v Karpnale Ltd* – not an overpayment of wages case – the House of Lords considered the use of the estoppel defence in cases such as *Avon* and concluded that the defence of change of position (ie, reliance) was preferable. This would allow recovery of any unspent amounts rather than requiring an outcome on an all-or-nothing basis.

An employee keeping quiet about an overpayment, or spending the money knowing there has been a mistake, could be committing a theft under the Theft Act 1968.[10]

In reclaiming repayment of overpaid monies, due regard will need to be given to the pay of the employee. There is no legislation on this point, but clearly as a matter of contract the employee has a right to expect that he or she will not be put in financial difficulties as a result of what was, after all, a mistake made by the employer rather than the employee.

Pay during statutory notice period

By virtue of ERA, s 88 an employee must be paid during his statutory notice period. This includes when the 'employee is incapable of work because of sickness or injury' (s 88(1)(b)). The right to be paid does not apply if the notice to be given by the employer exceeds the statutory requirement by one or more weeks (s 87(4)).

EVIDENCE

Pay statement

The wages provisions of ERA do not affect the employee's rights under ERA to have an itemized pay statement.[11] This is a right to have deductions notified, compared with the right not to have unauthorized deductions made. ERA requires the employer to provide an itemized pay statement on or before the time of payment of wages or salary. It must show:

- the gross amount of wages or salary;
- the amount of any variable or fixed deductions and the purposes for which they are made;
- the net amount of wages or salary payable; and
- where different parts of the net amount are paid in different ways, the amount and method of each part payment.

Separate details of fixed deductions need not be given providing the employee has been issued with a standing statement of fixed deductions. This must be issued at least every 12 months, and updated as necessary.

An employee may apply to an industrial tribunal in order to have determined what should be included in the itemized pay statement or standing statement of fixed deductions. If the employee is no longer employed by the employer the application must be made within three months of termination. The tribunal must make a declaration if they find unnotified deductions, and may order the employer to pay a sum amounting to the total of any such deductions made in the 13 weeks preceding the tribunal application.

As already indicated, there is no qualifying period of employment needed for the ERA's wages protection rights. This is also true for the right to have an itemized pay statement.

Written particulars

The requirements in Part I of ERA are set out in chapter 8. Here it is merely noted that the particulars must include details of:

(a) the scale or rate of remuneration or the method of calculating remuneration,
(b) the intervals at which remuneration is paid (that is, weekly, monthly or other specified intervals) ...

and of any terms relating to holiday pay, sick pay and pensions.[12]

EQUAL PAY

The European Union context

The Treaty of Rome

Article 119 of the Treaty of Rome establishes the principle of 'equal pay for equal work'. *Defrenne v SABENA (No 2)* is authority for the view that article 119 is directly applicable in Member States, ie it can be relied upon as the basis for an independent cause of action. An example of such an action can be found in *Secretary of State for Scotland v Wright*. This case was commenced in an industrial tribunal on the basis of article 119 and related to the exclusion of part-time employees from a contractual redundancy payments scheme. Similarly in *Worringham v Lloyd's Bank Ltd* an enhanced gross salary for men to compensate for pension contributions which they had to pay, but which women did not pay, constituted a breach of European law, notwithstanding the exception in the UK legislation. That exemption has subsequently been narrowed considerably by the Sex Discrimination Act 1986 so that pay provisions relating to retirement and concerning demotion, dismissal, promotion, transfer or training must not be discriminatory.

The Equal Pay Directive[13]

The Equal Pay Directive (EPD) explains what the principle of equal pay, as set out in article 119, actually means: no discrimination with regard to remuneration where the work is the same or of equal value (EPD, article 1). There is no decided case on whether the EPD has direct effect, ie whether it can be used 'vertically' by public sector workers against a state employer. What is clear is that it requires Member States to give effect to the equal pay principle through their own legislation.

In 1982, the Commission of the EU took infringement proceedings against the UK on the basis that the Equal Pay Act 1970 did not fully meet the requirements of article 119 of the Treaty of Rome and the EPD *(Commission of the EC v UK)*. The reason was that the Act had no provision for a woman to claim equal pay on the basis of her work being of equal value to that of a male comparator. At the time, claims had to be based on there being 'like work' or 'work rated as equivalent' under a job evaluation scheme. If a claim could not be fitted into one or the other of these categories, it could not be the basis of an action under the EqPA. The Equal Pay (Amendment) Regulations 1983 introduced a right to claim using a comparison based on the work being of equal value.[14]

The European concept of pay

The general point here is that the EU has adopted a wide definition of pay, so giving article 119 of the Treaty of Rome a wide application. Pay includes any 'consideration'. Examples include:

- differences in pensionable age and in benefits payable under an occupational pension scheme *(Barber v Guardian Royal Exchange Assurance Group)*;
- statutory sick pay *(Rinner-Kuhn)*;
- redundancy payments in a collective agreement *(Kowalska)*;
- discrimination in travel concessions for retired employees (*Garland v British Rail Engineering Ltd* – ultimately this case was decided under UK law: there was a breach of EqPA); and
- statutory redundancy payments *(Barber)*

The implications of this approach are as follows. First, any employer excluding a category of employee from any benefit which fits within the EU definition of pay (eg, pensions) where that category is predominantly made up of one sex (eg, part-time employees, who are mainly women), will be in breach of article 119. Secondly, the same will apply to a Member State which has legislation excluding such a category or imposing stricter service requirements upon them (*R v Secretary of State for Employment ex parte EOC*). The differential qualifying periods for part-time and full-time employees in respect of statutory redundancy payments and unfair dismissal compensation were held to be indirect sex discrimination. In the case of redundancy payments, since redundancy payments were pay under article 119 *(Barber)*, there was also a breach of the Treaty. The question of whether unfair dismissal compensation was also pay under article 119 was not decided, although in a subsequent case, the EAT held that it was *(Medigard Ltd v Thame)*.

The Equal Pay Act: the equality clause

The mechanics of the Act

The Act works by inserting an equality clause into the contract of employment: the terms of the contract 'shall be deemed to include' an equality clause if there is not one already (s 1(1)). The Act deals with any 'provision which relates to terms (whether concerned with pay or not)' so that the equality clause is capable of equalizing any contractual term as between a woman and her male comparator.

The effect of the equality clause is such that:

- if a man has the benefit of a contractual term but a woman does not, the woman's contract shall be treated as having a corresponding term; and
- if a woman's term is less favourable than a man's, the woman's term shall be treated as modified to make it no less favourable. The wording of the Act is important here: 'if... *any term* of the woman's contract is... less favourable ...' (emphasis added). The point at issue in *Hayward v Cammell Laird Shipbuilders Ltd* was whether the comparison ought to involve the particular term (here, pay) or the overall contractual package. The House of Lords held that the Act required the particular term in the woman's contract to be compared with the corresponding term in the man's contract.

Where the equality clause operates

The equality clause is inserted if a woman is 'employed' (s 1(1)). The word 'employed' is defined in s 1(6) to mean employed under a contract of service or apprenticeship, or 'a contract personally to execute any work or labour'. This is a category wider than 'employees' (see *Quinnen v Hovells*).

The equality clause will operate only if the man and woman are in the 'same employment'. This is defined in s 1(6) to mean:

- employed by the same or an associated employer at the same establishment; or
- employed by the same or an associated employer at different establishments but where 'common terms and conditions of employment are

observed'. That is, terms and conditions must be common to both establishments.

However, the EAT has held that article 119 allows a wider class of potential comparators than the EqPA *(Scullard v Knowles)*. This is on the basis of the ECJ's decision in *Defrenne v SABENA (No 2)* where it was stated that article 119 covers 'cases in which men and women receive unequal pay for equal work which is carried out in the same establishment *or service*' (emphasis added).

An associated employer is one who controls or is controlled by the other. In addition, where the complainant's establishment and comparator's establishment are both controlled by a third employer, these will be associated employers.

Leverton v Clwyd County Council

Here the House of Lords held that the test for common terms was whether common terms applied generally (or for a specific class of employee) and not whether the terms were actually similar.

British Coal Corporation v Smith

The House of Lords held that common terms means broadly similar terms. There should be a broad similarity between the terms and conditions of the comparator and the terms that apply or would apply to similar employees at the complainant's workplace.

Macarthys v Smith

On a literal construction, the EqPA seems to require a man and woman to be contemporaneously employed if they are to be compared. However, EU law will allow a woman to compare herself with an actual predecessor (so held the ECJ). (It is not provided under the Act for comparison to be made with a 'notional' man ie to argue that a man doing the same job would have been paid more.)

There are three types of comparison which may provide the basis for establishing a difference in contract terms and invoking the equality clause:

- like work (s 1(2)(a));
- work rated as equivalent (s 1(2)(b)); or
- work of equal value (s 1(2)(c)).

These are discussed in more detail below but first it should be noted that an equality clause will not operate if an employer can establish a material factor defence:

> An equality clause shall not operate ... if the employer proves that the variation is genuinely due to a material factor which is not the difference of sex. (s 1(3))

Note that the word 'variation' is somewhat confusing here, meaning the difference between the man's contract and the woman's in respect of the particular term being compared.

Equal Pay Act like work, work rated as equivalent and work of equal value

Like work

'Like work' means that the work must be 'of the same or a broadly similar nature' and that any differences between the woman's work and the man's work must not be 'of practical importance in relation to terms and conditions of employment'. In comparing the work, regard should be had to the frequency of any differences in practice, their nature and extent.[15]

In *Capper Pass Ltd v Lawton*, it was emphasized that the question of whether the work was 'like work' had to be answered in two stages. First, is it the same or broadly similar? Secondly, if there are differences, are they of practical importance. A broad-brush approach is appropriate, ignoring any trivial differences. The burden of proof is upon the employee to demonstrate that the work is the same or broadly similar, but upon the employer to show that any differences are of practical importance *(Coomes (Holdings) Ltd v Shields)*. Responsibility can be a difference of practical importance but the emphasis in respect of any difference must be upon the work that is actually performed rather than what could be done under the contract *(Eaton Ltd v Nuttall; Electrolux Ltd v Hutchinson)*. The issue arising in *Dugdale v Kraft Foods Ltd* was whether the time at which the work was performed was a factor in determining whether or not work was 'like work'. It was held that in considering differences, the time at which the work was done should be disregarded.

Work rated as equivalent

This comparison can be made where the man's job and the woman's job are different but have been given equal values under a job-evaluation scheme

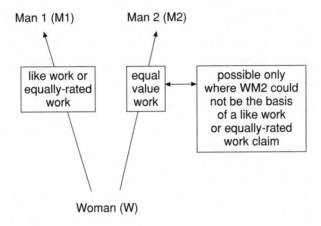

Figure 11.2 Equal pay: the comparison in *Pickstone v Freeman's*

which takes into account factors such as effort, skill and decision-making responsibility. The scheme itself must not be discriminatory.[16] Moreover, it must be analytical and objective *(Bromley v H&J Quick Ltd)*. Nothing outlaws the use of physical effort as a factor, but using average male effort as a reference point would be a breach of the Equal Pay Directive. Non-discriminatory job-evaluation schemes will include factors in relation to which both sexes show aptitude *(Rummler v Dato-Druck)*.

Work of equal value

This provision in EqPA, s 1(2)(c) was inserted by the Equal Pay (Amendment) Regulations 1983 following the ECJ ruling in *Commission of the European Communities v UK.* The comparison applies where the work is not 'like work' or 'work rated as equivalent'.

The question arises as to the legal position where a woman and a man are employed on 'like work' and paid the same, but where the woman is paid less than another man performing work of equal value. On a literal construction of s 1(2)(c), she appears to be barred from making an application. However, in *Pickstone v Freemans plc*, the words of the Act were construed (in a rather tortuous way) by the House of Lords to give effect to the EPD: an application is barred only where the work of the comparator does not fit into the like work or equally rated work categories. Figure 11.2 illustrates this interpretation.

Presumably if the WM2 comparison permitted a like work or equally rated work claim the complainant would pursue such a claim rather than the more difficult equal value variety. The conclusion, therefore, is that the primary purpose of this interpretation is to give effect to the EPD rather than to actually make sense.

Finally, in respect of equal value cases, it appears that there is nothing to stop an employer introducing a job-evaluation scheme after an equal value claim has begun. Subject to what was said earlier about such schemes, its results will be admissible as evidence *(Dibro Ltd v Hore)*.

Equal Pay Act: the material factor defence

Meaning
If the complainant employee establishes a comparison (like work, work rated as equivalent or equal value) and that there is a difference in contractual terms (a 'variation' between the contracts in the words of s 1(3)), the defendant employer is given an opportunity to enter a defence. The defence is that the difference in contract terms (the 'variation') is due to a material factor other than the difference of sex.

Mechanics of the material factor defence
A successful material factor defence stops the equality clause from working (s 1(3)). The difference in terms is thus lawful.

Interpretation
There is a technical distinction between the defence in like work and work rated as equivalent cases on the one hand and equal value cases on the other. With like work and work rated as equivalent comparisons, the material factor must be a 'material difference' between the cases: with equal value comparisons the material factor may be a material difference. The reason for this distinction is that in the early cases the material factor defence was restricted to personal differences (see *Clay Cross (Quarry Services) v Fletcher*, below): the aim with the 1983 Equal Value Regulations was to allow a wider defence. In practice, 'material difference' has been interpreted in a wide way (eg, by the House of Lords in *Rainey*, see below) so that the distinction is probably of little or no practical importance.

The scope of the material factor defence is not defined in the Act, not even in the form of a non-exhaustive list. The early cases stressed the importance of personal factors: skill, experience, qualifications, output and training *(Clay Cross (Quarry Services) v Fletcher)* (CA, 1978). In the same year, however, the EAT accepted that different hours of work (part-time as opposed to full-time) were a material difference because of the differential contribution made towards offsetting the firm's overhead costs *(Handley v H Mono Ltd)*. By 1981 the EAT, after a reference to the ECJ, decided that a difference in hours (full-time rather than part-time) was not in itself a material difference, but could be if it gave economic advantages to the employer *(Jenkins v Kingsgate (Clothing Productions) Ltd (No 2))*. Thus material difference could include economic factors, an interpretation later confirmed in *Rainey v Greater Glasgow Health Board*. In reviewing the issues, the House of Lords concluded in *Rainey* that limiting material factors to personal factors was too narrow a view. It held that market forces could be a material factor, here the need to pay men more than women to recruit them. 'Material difference' meant that the difference was 'significant and relevant'. A material factor cannot comprise anything which amounts to direct sex discrimination because this would not be a difference explained by factors other than sex *(British Coal Corporation v Smith)*. See also *Ratcliffe v North Yorkshire County Council* where pay reductions to enhance competitiveness were held to be based on sex.

Returning to personal factors, it must be shown that these are relevant to the performance of the work. In *Danfoss* the issue was flexibility and training: in *Nimz* it was seniority (ie, length of service) and in particular the respective treatment of part-time and full-time employees. Red-circling can be a material factor. This is where an individual or a group of individuals have their pay protected for a period of time when they are transferred to a job with a lower rate of pay. This may happen, for example, as a result of an employee's ill-health. However, whatever the reason for the red-circling, it must not be based on sex discrimination (it was in *Snoxell v Vauxhall Motors*, and therefore did not constitute a material factor). Different hours of work can be a material factor. When an industrial tribunal is comparing a woman's pay with that of a man whose work is of equal value, the tribunal may take into account that their notional hourly rates of pay are similar but that she both works shorter hours and is entitled to longer holidays in order to infer that the difference between their annual salaries is genuinely due to a material factor other than sex *(Leverton)*.

Where the material factor is independent of sex but adversely affects women, it must be objectively justified (see *Bilka-Kaufhaus* and *Rainey*). However, in *Strathclyde Regional Council v Wallace*, the House of Lords made it clear that there is no need for objective justification where the material factor does not have a disparate impact (because in such cases there is no sex discrimination). In effect, the EqPA now embraces indirect pay discrimination. The test for objective justification is the same as for indirect sex discrimination, ie that laid down in *Hampson v DES (Rainey)*. Examples of indirect pay discrimination, needing to be objectively justified include:

- exclusion of part-time employees from an occupational pension scheme *(Bilka-Kaufhaus)*;
- exclusion of the same category from rights under redundancy payments and unfair dismissal legislation *(R v Secretary of State for Employment ex parte EOC)*; and

- differential pay structures for largely male and largely female groups (*Rainey*).

Separate collective bargaining arrangements can explain a difference but do not in themselves justify it (*Enderby v Frenchay Health Authority*). This appears to be a more demanding approach than that taken in earlier cases such as *Reed Packaging v Boozer*. Where indirect discrimination is alleged and a predominantly female group is paid less than a predominantly male group (thus establishing discrimination *prima facie*), the burden of proof shifts to the employer to show how the difference in pay is objectively justified (*Enderby*). It seems that, where the difference is only partly justified, there can be a partial material factor defence (again *Enderby*).

In *Birds Eye Walls v Roberts*, a case taken on the basis of article 119 of the Treaty of Rome, the equivalent of a material factor defence was the aim of equalizing total pensions (ie, state and company pension combined) for those retiring on ill-health grounds. To achieve this aim, the company paid women aged 60–64 years a smaller occupational pension to allow for the fact that they received a state pension while men did not (the 60/65 differential in the state pension age being lawful). The ECJ held that there was no breach of article 119. It seems that the ECJ was taking more of a total package approach here, compared with the term-for-term approach of the EqPA (evidenced by the House of Lords decision in *Hayward v Cammell Laird Shipbuilders Ltd*).

Applications to industrial tribunals, proof and remedies

Applications for industrial tribunals

Under the EqPA, an application to an industrial tribunal may be made by the complainant, the employer or the Secretary of State. This may be done while the employment continues or within six months of its termination. There are no hours or length of employment qualifications attached to making an application. The courts may also refer equal pay cases to industrial tribunals.

The EqPA and the SDA are to be viewed as complementary but mutually exclusive. The former deals with contractual terms, the latter with non-contractual issues. As with the SDA, complaints may be made by men as well as women.

Procedure in equal value cases

A separate procedure exists for equal value cases.[17] The industrial tribunal must not determine the issue of equal value if there are 'no reasonable grounds' for determining it (including an unequal rating under a non-discriminatory job-evaluation scheme).[18] Where the tribunal proceeds, it may commission a report of a job-evaluation study by an independent expert (drawn from a panel set up by ACAS) (until 1996 it was mandatory for the tribunal to do this).

An employer must be allowed to argue a material factor defence at the outset (ie, prior to any independent expert being asked for a report) as well as later.[19]

Proof

The proof of establishing that they are employed in the same employment and of justifying the comparison lies with the complainant, but the employer's responsibility to establish that any differences are of practical importance in like work cases has also been noted. Similarly, where the complainant establishes that a predominantly female group is paid less than a predominantly male group, the burden switches to the employer to explain why. Originally formulated in *Danfoss*, this is now set out as a two-stage test in *Enderby*:

- the complainant must establish the difference (ie, *prima facie* discrimination);
- the defendant must justify the difference objectively.

More generally, the burden falls upon the employer to demonstrate a material factor as a defence.

Note that domestic legislation requires a woman to use one or more individual comparators as the basis for her case. In *Danfoss*, the ECJ stated that it was sufficient for the complainant to show a statistical imbalance between men's and women's pay to throw the burden onto the employer to justify the imbalance. The context was one in which discretionary elements of pay were being distributed between individuals on a basis which was not clear.

Remedies

Damages and arrears of remuneration are payable for a period of up to two years prior to the proceedings being instituted. Damages are payable where no term corresponding to that of the man's contract exists; arrears are payable where the term is less favourable. A tribunal must make a declaration if they find that an equality clause exists preventing less favourable treatment. Interest is payable under the Industrial Tribunals (Interest on Awards in Discrimination Cases) Regulations 1996.[20]

There may be some doubt about the legality of the two-year limit on the amount of damages or arrears payable under the Act. If such an amount were not fully to compensate the complainant for the discrimination, the limit might be in breach of article 6 of the Equal Treatment Directive (as in

Marshall (No 2)). The government did not remove this limit when it introduced the 1993 Remedies Regulations following the ECJ's ruling in *Marshall (No 2)*.

It should be noted that the victimization provisions in SDA, s 4 apply to the EqPA as well as to the SDA.

Finally, there are some exceptions to the Act where terms are affected by laws regulating the employment of women or affording special treatment to women in connection with pregnancy or childbirth. Terms relating to death or retirement are excluded except for access to occupational pension schemes and retirement terms relating to promotion, transfer, training, dismissal or demotion.[21]

Sex equality and pensions

There is a growing body of case law in this area, based upon the fact that pensions are pay under article 119 of the Treaty of Rome. New equal treatment rules were introduced by the Pensions Act 1995 and supplemented by the Occupational Pension Schemes (Equal Treatment) Regulations 1995.[22] There must be equality of access to schemes and equality of benefits.

The effects of the *Barber* decision were limited to actions which had already commenced at the time of the decision. This was a public policy stance taken by means of a protocol attached to the Maastricht Treaty and subsequently confirmed by the ECJ in *Ten Oever* (see chapter 2). However, while this appears to deal with the entitlement to equal benefits, it is not clear that it applies to entitlement to equal access and in *Magorrian v Eastern Health and Social Services Board* the ECJ made clear that it does not. The relevant starting point is when article 119 was declared to have direct effect (8 April 1976 in *Defrenne v SABENA*). Thus, part-time workers denied access to occupational pension schemes can rely on length of employment from that date when they join their employer's scheme, notwithstanding the EqPA's limit of two years' arrears or damages. However, the time limit for applications under the EqPA is six months if the employee is no longer employed by that particular employer, and in *Preston v Wolverhampton Health Care NHS Trust*, the Court of Appeal upheld this limit. However, the House of Lords has now referred the matter to the ECJ.

STATUTORY SICK PAY

Background

The statutory sick pay (SSP) scheme was first introduced in 1983.[23] It made employers legally responsible for administering SSP for the first eight weeks of sickness. In 1986, the scheme was extended to cover the first 28 weeks of sickness. Employers acted as state agents and were reimbursed by the government through reduced NI contributions and, if necessary, through the PAYE system. Initially reimbursement was in full, later reduced to 80 per cent. From 1985 employers were given compensation for NI contributions on SSP, but this was later abolished.[24] The position since April 1994 is that employers have had to meet the full cost of SSP for their employees.

Until April 1995 a relief scheme existed for small employers. These were defined in terms of combined employer and employee NI liability: from April 1994 the figure was £20,000.[25] This applied to the last complete tax year before the days to which the claim for SSP related. Reimbursement of SSP was payable once the employee had been absent through sickness for four weeks.

This scheme has now been abolished and there is once again a system of general relief applicable to employers irrespective of their size. However, the relief is triggered only once a threshold is passed. The relevant provisions are made under the Statutory Sick Pay Act 1994 (s 3(3)) and given effect by the SSP Percentage Threshold Order 1995.[26] Article 2 of the Order provides for reimbursement of SSP where its amount exceeds 13 per cent of the employer's NI liability in any income tax month. The reimbursement is in full but comprises only the amount by which SSP exceeds the 13 per cent figure.

Eligibility

There has to be a period of four or more consecutive days of incapacity for work before there is entitlement to SSP. Incapacity for work means that the employee is incapable through 'disease or bodily or mental disablement of doing work which he can reasonably be expected to do under [his] contract'.[27] Two periods of incapacity are linked and treated as one if the gap between them is less than eight weeks. SSP applies only to employees, who are defined as those working under a contract of service or holding an office where emoluments are chargeable for income tax Schedule E purposes. There are no qualifying periods of employment or hours requirements.

There are a number of people who fall within the above definition but who are nonetheless excluded from entitlement to SSP. These are:

- people who have reached state pensionable age;
- those on contracts for three months or less (but there are some exceptions);
- anyone below the SSP minimum earnings level (see below);
- people who were ill prior to starting work;
- those becoming ill after the commencement of a strike;
- people in legal custody;

- anyone who has used up his full entitlement to SSP;
- people abroad outside the EU;
- pregnant women who are within the disqualification period (see chapter 14 on statutory maternity pay); and
- people who have recently had other state benefits, eg maternity allowance.

A person excluded from entitlement to SSP may be able to claim other social security benefits.

SSP stops after 28 weeks. Anyone who is still incapacitated in the 29th week will transfer to incapacity benefit. Employers must issue transfer forms to employees after 22 weeks. An employee changing employers after receiving SSP has a right to a record of SSP from their former employer. This is known as a leaver's statement (form SSP1(L), although employers may use their own computerized version of the form if they wish).

Rate of SSP

The rate from 6 April 1998 is £57.70 per week. Those earning less than a lower earnings limit (currently £64) have no entitlement to SSP. In *Rinner-Kuhn v FWW Spezial-Gebaudereinigung GmbH & Co KG*, the ECJ decided that excluding part-timers from (German) SSP amounted to unlawful sex discrimination where the part-timers were almost all women, unless the exclusion could be objectively justified by factors unrelated to sex. The UK legislation may therefore be unlawful (see *R v Secretary of State for Employment ex parte Equal Opportunities Commission*).

The earnings figure is gross and covers any payments to the employee on which NI contributions are due. It is not, therefore, restricted to basic pay. An average is taken over the eight weeks prior to the commencement of the period of incapacity. Any contractual payments made to the employee during incapacity may be offset against SSP liability. SSP is payable for each employment contract – an employee may be doubly entitled if they meet NI and other requirements.

SSP is taxable and subject to NI deductions and is usually paid in the same way as wages. It is payable for periods of at least four consecutive days. The days must be ones on which the employee would have worked if they had not been sick. These are known as qualifying days. Employers may designate any number of days per week (from one to seven) as qualifying days, but the more qualifying days per week the lower the daily rate of SSP. Nothing is paid for the first three (waiting) days.

Statutory sick pay is a minimum. Nothing in the regulations prevents a scheme being operated with higher level of payments.

Notification and evidence of incapacity

Notification of incapacity

How and when an employer should be notified of an employee's incapacity is not laid down statutorily. Rather, employers are told what they cannot do. They cannot:

- require notification before the end of the first day of incapacity;
- demand notification from the employee personally;
- require notification to be given by means of completion of a particular form;
- require medical evidence (for notification purposes – they may require it later); or
- demand notification more frequently than once a week.

Late notification is allowable only if there is 'good cause'[28] and SSP can be withheld if there is no good cause. There is an absolute limit of 91 days after incapacity, beyond which notification is not allowed.

Evidence of incapacity

Employers may seek reasonable evidence of incapacity in order to determine whether or not an employee is entitled to SSP, and if they are so entitled, to determine duration. Since self-certification was introduced in 1982, employees have not required a doctor's certificate to support their absence from work for the first seven days. Those absent for four to seven days are normally required to fill in a self-certification form. There is no strict legal requirement for this, it is simply part of the process by which an employer gathers evidence. Employers may design their own forms for this purpose. Since no SSP is payable for the first three days of incapacity, there is no legal basis whatsoever for self-certification for these days.

As noted, the regulations say little more than that an employer should obtain reasonable evidence of incapacity and leave them to design their own form. Not surprisingly there have been cases where trades unions have objected to the forms used. For example, some forms require the following:

- completion in the presence of a foreman or supervisor;
- details of illness;
- doctor's name and address;
- the information on the form to be correct if there is to be a payment;
- agreement to the doctor providing medical information; and
- the form to be completed accurately, otherwise disciplinary action may be taken.

Trades unions argue that such forms are not reasonable and that the only information needed is name, employment identification, first and last days of absence and brief reasons for absence. They say that requiring details of illness gives rise to problems of diagnosis by unqualified people and of breach of confidentiality. Ultimately, a failure to pay SSP because the employer felt insufficient or incorrrect information had been given could be challenged through the social security appeals process (see below). Any disciplinary action might be open to challenge through normal legal channels (for example, claims for damages for breach of contract or for compensation for unfair dismissal).

Certain rules are laid down in relation to evidence from doctors. Regulations prescribe the form of statement to be issued by a doctor.[29] The statement must advise whether the employee should or should not refrain from work. Any period during which the employee should refrain from work – up to six months, or longer in certain circumstances – must be stated. Such medical evidence cannot be required in relation to the employee's first seven days in any period of incapacity.

Disputes

If an employer refuses to pay SSP, an employee has the right to ask for a statement showing:

- for which day(s) the employer intends to pay SSP;
- how much the employer intends to pay per day; and
- why the employer thinks SSP is not payable for other days.

Where the reason for non-payment is that the employee is excluded from SSP or has exhausted their entitlement, the employer should inform the employee using the appropriate DSS form – the 'change-over' form, SSP1. Other reasons for non-payment are late notification, doubts about the genuineness of the incapacity and a refusal to do lighter (contractual) duties.

It is normal practice for employees to use the established grievance procedure where there are disputes over SSP. If an employee is not satisfied with the outcome of this, however, they may appeal to a DSS adjudication officer, providing this occurs within six months of the first day of disputed SSP liability. Thereafter there are rights of appeal to a social security appeals tribunal (SSAT) and a social security commissioner, after which appeals on points of law lie with the Court of Appeal (Court of Session in Scotland) (some decisions can be made only by the Secretary of State for Social Security and are therefore not appealable). A failure to pay SSP when payment is required by the decision of an adjudication officer, an SSAT or a commissioner will not only be a criminal offence punishable by a fine but will allow the employee to enforce payment through the county court. If an employer is insolvent or defaults on payment, an employee may claim SSP from the NI fund.

Criminal offences

The following are criminal offences, punishable by a fine except where otherwise indicated:

- failure to pay SSP within the time allowed following the formal decision of an adjudication officer, an SSAT or a commissioner;
- failure to provide information required by one of the above;
- failure to keep the required records;
- failure to provide the employee with a change-over form (form SSP1);
- failure to provide the employee with a leaver's statement (form SSP1(L)).

NATIONAL MINIMUM WAGE

The National Minimum Wage Bill 1997, once enacted, will give the Secretary of State the legal power to set a figure for the NMW and will provide a statutory basis for the Low Pay Commission (LPC). The minimum wage protection will apply to workers and specifically includes agency workers (see chapter 5 on employment status). The Bill prohibits a differentiation in NMW rates, so enshrining the principle of a single rate, but would allow the Secretary of State to exclude workers aged less than 26 years. The LPC will provide the detailed information upon which the Secretary of State decides the NMW figure and will monitor the working of the legislation. Employers will be required to keep records and a worker with reasonable grounds for thinking that he or she is not being paid at least the NMW will have a right to see those records. Applications by workers refused their rights will lie with the county courts and industrial tribunals. Where the application relates to a breach of the requirement to pay the NMW the action will be in contract or under the ERA wages deductions provisions. There will also be enforcement officers authorized to act on behalf of workers. Finally, there will be a range of criminal offences.

NOTES

1 TULR(C)A, s 146 and ERA, s 235(1). The latter section states that 'act' and 'action' are to be treated as including 'omission'.
2 ERA, s 27(1).

3   Until the provisions were repealed by TURERA, the Wages Act 1986 provided for minimum wages in certain industries and services. It should be noted that the provisions of the Agricultural Wages Act 1948 were not repealed, so that minimum wages still apply in agriculture.

4   ITA 1996, s 3 brought into operation by the Industrial Tribunals Extension of Jurisdiction (England and Wales) Order (SI 1994/1623) (SI 1994/1624 applies to Scotland).

5   ERA, Part II.

6   Previous legislation, notably the various Truck Acts and related measures, applied only to manual workers.

7   ERA, s 13(1).

8   Ibid, s 15(1).

9   Ibid, ss 18, 20 and 21.

10 Theft Act 1968, s 5(4).

11 ERA, s 8.

12 Ibid, s 1(4).

13 75/117/EC, OJ 1975, L45.

14 Equal Pay (Amendment) Regulations (SI 1983/1794) issued under the European Communities Act 1972.

15 EqPA, s 1(4).

16 Ibid, s 1(5).

17 See the Industrial Tribunals (Constitution and Rules of Procedure) Regulations 1993, reg 8 and Sched 2.

18 EqPA, s 2A. The 1996 change was made by the Sex Discrimination and Equal Pay (Miscellaneous Amendments) Regulations (SI 1996/438).

19 Industrial Tribunal Regulations 1996, reg 8, Sched 2, rule 9(2E).

20 SI 1996/2803.

21 EqPA, s 6. This exception was narrowed by SDA 1986, s 2.

22 SI 1995/3183. The EU framework for occupational pension schemes comprises the Equal Treatment Directive on Occupational Social Security (86/378/EC, OJ 1986, L225) as well as art 119 of the Treaty of Rome and the EPD.

23 Now found in Social Security Contributions and Benefits Act 1992, ss 151–163; and Statutory Sick Pay (General) Regulations (SI 1982/894).

24 Statutory Sick Pay Act 1991.

25 Statutory Sick Pay (Small Employers' Relief) Regulations (SI 1991/428); and SSP (Small Employers' Relief) (Amendment) Regulations (SI 1994/561).

26 SSP Percentage Threshold Order (SI 1995/512); article 5 of this Order revoked the Small Employers' Relief Regulations 1991. See also SI 1995/513.

27 Social Security Contributions and Benefits Act 1992, s 151(4).

28 SSP (General Regulations) 1982, Reg 7(2).

29 SSP (Medical Evidence) Regulations (SI 1985/1604).

Hours of Work, Holidays and Time Off

HOURS OF WORK

General statutory provisions

There is no UK legislation operating to generally determine hours of work. Hours will depend upon contractual arrangements. However, the EU Working Time Directive should have been given effect by Member States by 23 November 1996; therefore legislation should be in place. Implementation was delayed in the UK by the government challenging the lawfulness of the directive.[1]

As regards hours of work, the Working Time Directive requires Member States to enact legislation providing for:

- a minimum daily rest period of 11 hours (article 3);
- a rest break if the working day is longer than six hours (article 4);
- a weekly rest period of 24 hours in addition to the 11 hours already specified (article 5);
- maximum weekly hours, including overtime, of 48 (article 6); and
- control over night work (articles 8–12).

An employer who 'intends to organize work according to a certain pattern' must take account of 'the general principle of adapting work to the worker' (article 13).

However, there are various exceptions – 'derogations' in EU terminology – and in particular the right of Member States to opt out of article 6 (maximum working week) if certain conditions are met, including worker agreement. The Working Time Directive also covers holidays: see below.

Now that the Working Time Directive has been declared lawful by the ECJ, there will have to be substantial new legislation in the UK to give effect to it. Regulations are expected to operate from October 1998.

Sunday working

The increased freedom to trade on Sundays has resulted in legislation to protect two groups of workers from being compelled to work on Sundays. These are shop workers and betting workers. The provisions are now to be found in ERA.

Shop workers

Liberalization of the regime governing Sunday trading was accompanied by protection for shop workers.[2] They are given the right to refuse to work on Sunday. 'Shop worker' is given a wide definition: an employee who is or may be required under his contract to do shop work.[3] 'Shop work' is work in or about a shop in England and Wales on a day when the shop is open for the serving of customers. Shop includes retail trade premises, defined to include hairdressers, retail hire shops and retail auctions, but not the catering trade and places of amusement. The definition of shop worker is probably wide enough to include store management and those in warehouses attached to stores, and possibly cleaning and maintenance staff. It seems unlikely to include head office staff, those in distribution depots, drivers delivering to the store and area or regional management.

Two types of employee are protected: 'protected shop worker' and 'opted-out shop worker'. Protected shop worker[4] status is achieved in one of two ways: either:

- immediately prior to the commencement of this section of the Act the person was a shop worker not employed only to work on Sundays;
- he has been continuously employed from then until the 'appropriate date' (which would be his EDT in the case of a dismissal); and
- throughout this period he has been a shop worker;

or:

- the person has not, and may not be required to work Sundays under his contract of employment;
- he could not be so required even in the absence of the legislation; and
- he is a shop worker.

Thus a 'protected shop worker' is either one who was employed as a shop worker prior to the commencement of the legislation (ie, an existing shop worker, who is automatically protected) or someone who cannot under his contract of employment be required to work on Sundays. Protected shop workers can opt-in to Sunday working, thus losing their protected status. An opted-out shop worker is a shop worker who is not protected but elects to opt out of Sunday working. They may be unprotected because they started employment after the commencement of the legislation or because they had given up their protected status by opting-in.

Any worker who under his contract can be required to work on Sunday must be given an explanatory statement by his employer. A prescribed form is set out in the Act.[5] The various protections of the Act apply once a period of three months has elapsed. The statement must be given within two months of the person becoming a shop worker, but there is no need to provide it if within that time the employee has given him an opting-out notice.

Protected and opted-out shop workers are given the following rights:

- the right not to be dismissed for refusing to work on a Sunday;
- the right not to be dismissed for reason of redundancy with selection because of a refusal to work on a Sunday; and
- the right not to suffer detriment (ie, something less than dismissal) on the same ground as above.

ERA, s 108(3) and 109(2) provide that there is no qualifying employment required for the rights under the Act, nor any upper age limit for applicants.

The right to opt-out is a subsisting right which can be exercised at any time by a shop worker who is neither protected nor already opted-out. There is a similar right to opt-in. Both rights are subject to the notice being in writing.

Agreements to exclude the rights conferred under the Act will be void (s 203) except where they result from ACAS conciliation or where the agreement is a 'compromise agreement'.

Where the employee prior to the legislation was contractually required to work Sundays the ERA overrides the contractual requirement by making it unenforceable (s 37).

Betting workers
ERA provides rights for betting workers in respect of Sunday working. The provisions are identical to those in relation to shop workers.

Specific occupations[6]

There is a small number of occupations whose hours of work are controlled by specific legislation: sheet glass workers, transport workers and agricultural workers.

Overtime

Hours of work will be in accordance with the contract of employment. Usually, this will provide for some normal or standard number of hours per week, beyond which hours constitute overtime. The rate at which overtime is paid, is, like ordinary pay, not governed by legislation. Rather it is a matter of contract.

The requirement to work a reasonable amount of overtime may be a term of the contract. Whether an employee can lawfully refuse to work overtime in these circumstances will depend on such factors as the number of hours overtime sought by the employer, the frequency of overtime working, the extent of advance notice given by the employer, any health and safety considerations and the need of the business for the overtime. It is doubtful that an employer can lawfully require an employee to work for so many hours that there would be a foreseeable risk of injury to his health *(Johnstone v Bloomsbury and Islington Health Authority)* (see pages 188–9).

Even where an employee is required to work a reasonable amount of over-time as part of the contract of employment the overtime worked will not necessarily be of a contractual nature. This will be true even if the overtime is frequent, regular and substantial. The test of whether overtime is contrac-tual is whether the employer must provide it and the employee must work it *(Tarmac Roadstone Holdings Ltd v Peacock; Lotus Cars Ltd v Sutcliffe)*. Thus, even if the work the overtime is intended to produce is not there, the employer must pay and the employee must be available. Contractual over-time is characterized by overtime pay being included in pay during absence (for example, for sickness or holidays).

The significance here is that if overtime is contractual it will count for the purposes of calculating a week's pay in the computation of statutory redun-dancy payments and other payments (eg, unfair dismissal compensation). The provisions relating to a week's pay are found in ERA ss 220–229 and are dealt with in chapter 19 (redundancy payments). Overtime is not generally defined, but there is a concept 'normal working hours' in ERA, s 234. 'Working hours' is the more general legal concept meaning hours of work as determined by the contract of employment.[7]

Evidence

If there are any terms of employment relating to hours of work, these must be specified in the written particulars provided under ERA, s1 (see pages 142–7). There do not have to be any such terms, but if there are not any this fact must be stated in the particulars.

Children and young persons

A child is a person under the minimum school leaving age, approximately 16 years depending on date of birth. A young person is beyond minimum school leaving age but below the age of majority (ie, under 18 years).[8] Under the Children and Young Persons Acts 1933–1969 there are various restrictions on the hours of work of children:[9]

- they must not be employed before school hours on a school day;
- they must not be employed before 7.00 am or after 7.00 pm on any day; and
- the maximum number of hours on any school day or Sunday is two.

Local authorities have the power to make bye-laws extending the regulation.

In contrast, the general restrictions on the hours of work of young persons were repealed by the Employment Act 1989.[10] However, the EU Directive on the Protection of Young People at Work 1994 requires Member States to bring into force domestic legislation or give effect through collective agreements no later than 22 June 1996.[11] The Directive includes provisions relating to working time, night work, rest periods and breaks but by article 17 exempts the UK for four years (from 22 June 1996) from some of the key requirements. Nevertheless, minimum rest periods of two days a week will be needed to give effect to article 10(2) and minimum rest periods of 12 hours in every 24 to give effect to article 10(1)(b); the UK four-year opt-out applies to neither of these. Nor does it apply to breaks: where working time exceeds 4 hours, a break of 30 minutes is stipulated, if possible to be taken as a single break (article 12).

The provisions of the Young Persons Directive also embrace the employment of children. Here there is existing UK legislation as noted above, but the UK opt-out extends to article 8(1)(b) which limits the working week of children to 12 hours in term-time, with a two-hour daily maximum.

As noted above (see page 86) the government is reviewing the law as it relates to the employment of children and has introduced two new sets of regulations in response to the EU Directive.

Women

The restrictions on the hours of work of women were removed by SDA 1986, s 7. However, some protection in respect of pregnancy or maternity or other specifically female matters is contained in SDA 1975, s 51. This allows discriminatory statutory provisions: an example would be the Maternity (Compulsory Leave) Regulations preventing women working or being permitted to work in the fortnight immediately after childbirth[12] (see chapter 13).

Excessive hours and the health of the employee

The *Johnstone* case was noted on pages 188–9. The essence of the plaintiff's case was that the employers were in breach of their duty of care. That case did not go to trial, but the same issue was argued in *Walker v Northumberland County Council*, albeit on different facts. Here the failure to provide adequate resources for a manager meant there was not a safe system of work: the duty of care was not fulfilled (see pages 289–94).

HOLIDAYS

General statutory position

Again, there is no general statutory provision in the UK: the matter will depend on contractual arrangements. As with pay, there is generally no legal remedy for the employee's complaint that he does not have sufficient holidays. Disputes over holidays, therefore, are more likely to be about entitlement (ie, what was agreed) or timing, or perhaps failure to return to work on time. The EU adopted a Council Recommendation in favour of four weeks' annual paid holidays as early as 1975.[13] The Working Time Directive 1993 takes the matter much further by requiring annual leave of at least four weeks to be the subject of domestic legislation or collective agreements by 23 November 1996 (article 7). However, there is an optional transitional period of three years from that date before Member States have to comply fully with the article as long as minimum annual holidays during that period are set at three weeks (article 18).

Bank and public holidays

The Banking and Financial Dealing Act 1971 confers the right to suspend financial dealings on bank holidays but does not impose any statutory duty on other employers to observe these holidays. New Year's Day and May Day are bank holidays by Royal Proclamation. Christmas Day and Good Friday are public holidays at common law by custom. None of these provisions requires an employer to pay the employee: this is a contractual matter. However, in the absence of an express term or custom to the contrary, it is possible that there is an implied term requiring payment. Clearly this will not be the case in those industries (such as hotels and catering) where bank holidays are traditionally busy work periods although there might be an implied term that there will be paid time off in lieu.

Holidays during notice period

Under ERA, s 88(1)(d), an employee must be paid when on holiday during any notice period. This does not apply if the notice required to be given by the employer exceeds the statutory amount by one or more weeks (s 87(4)).

Specific occupations

Provisions are made for minimum holiday entitlement in the Agricultural Wages Act 1948 and Agricultural Wages (Scotland) Act 1949.

Evidence

Written particulars under ERA, s 1 must contain details of any terms relating to holidays and holiday pay such that entitlement can be calculated, including accrued entitlement on termination. It is not mandatory that there are terms relating to holidays, but if there are none, the written statement must say so.

TIME OFF

General position

Employment legislation provides for time off – sometimes with pay and sometimes without – in a number of different circumstances:

- ante-natal care and maternity leave (pages 244–53 and 249–50);
- trades union activities and duties (pages 438–40);
- union safety representatives (pages 273–4);
- to look for another job or arrange retraining when given notice of redundancy (pages 363–6);
- public duties;
- jury service; and
- reserve forces services.

The last three of the above are dealt with below.

Time off for public duties[14]

An employee is entitled to time off for duties arising out of holding one of the following public positions:

- justice of the peace;

- member of a local authority;
- member of a statutory tribunal;
- member of an NHS trust or authority (including a family health services authority;[15]
- member of the National Rivers Authority;
- member of the governing body of an educational establishment maintained by a local authority, a grant-maintained school or a higher education corporation; or
- member of a board of visitors for prisons, remand centres and so on.

The amount of time off is what is 'reasonable in all the circumstances'. There is no obligation upon an employer to pay for the time off. Any employee refused time off may apply to a tribunal within three months. The tribunal may make an award which is 'just and equitable' taking into account any loss sustained and the infringement of rights.

In deciding whether reasonable time off has been permitted, the industrial tribunal has to consider the competing needs of the employee for time off and the employer for the employee's service (s 50(4). The sole issue for the tribunal to decide is whether reasonable time off has been permitted – it cannot go further or attach conditions to the time off *(Corner v Buckinghamshire County Council).*

Other provisions

There is no general legislation but specific provisions exist in relation to jury service and service in the reserve forces. The Juries Act 1974 requires that a person summoned to attend for jury service be given time off for that purpose unless within an excepted category. Application may be made to be excused jury service. Members of the reserve forces who are called up to serve in the armed forces have their rights protected under the Reserve Forces (Safeguard of Employment) Act 1985: the returning employee must be re-employed by his employer (The general framework governing reservists is to be found in the Reserve Forces Act 1996).

As a result of the EU Directive on Parental Leave the UK has until December 1999 to bring in its own legislation in this area.[16] It is left to individual Member States to decide whether such leave will be paid or unpaid and, if the former, how it will be financed. Parental leave is an entitlement of a given duration for fathers and mothers consequent upon the birth of a child. It applies to the period following maternity leave and is distinguished from maternity leave which is available exclusively to women and is specifically designed to protect the health of the mother and the new-born child. Parental leave can be taken over a long period. The EU Directive gives a minimum of three months' unpaid leave after the birth or adoption of a child, to be taken within eight years of the birth or adoption. In addition, there will be time off for child illnesses and family emergencies.

NOTES

1 93/104/EC, OJ 1993, L307/18. The Directive is based on article 118A of the Treaty of Rome which relates to health and safety at work and is subject to majority voting in the Council of Ministers. The former UK government view was that the Directive is concerned with terms and conditions and therefore should be subject to unanimous voting. However, the ECJ rejected this view.
2 The protective provisions are in ERA, ss 45 and 101.
3 ERA, s 232.
4 ERA, s 36.
5 ERA, s 42.
6 See the Transport Act 1968, Part VI; and the Hours of Employment (Conventions) Act 1936, s 3 (hours of work in automatic sheet-glass works). Agricultural Wages Board orders may also regulate hours (Agricultural Wages Act 1948, s 3).
7 See, for example, ERA, s 52(3).
8 The EU definitions are somewhat different: a child is a person under 15 years or below minimum school leaving age; a young person is a worker under 18 years; and an adolescent is someone who is at least 15 years but under 18 (Young Workers' Directive, article 3). The government is currently reviewing the law relating to the employment of children. The review is expected to be complete by the end of 1998.
9 See in particular the 1933 Act, s 18(1).
10 EA 1989, s 10 and Sched 3. Protective legislation affecting the health and safety at work of young persons was not repealed.
11 94/33/EC, OJ 1994, L216/12.
12 The Maternity (Compulsory Leave) Regulations (SI 1994/2479), made under the European Communities Act 1972.
13 Council Recommendation 75/457/EC, OJ 1975, L199.
14 ERA, ss 50–51.
15 Previously family practitioner committees (NHS and Community Care Act 1990, s 2).
16 96/34/EC.

Maternity

This chapter aims to draw together the various legal provisions relevant to maternity. These provisions cover health and safety at work, maternity leave and pay, sex discrimination and dismissal. The starting point is health and safety at work.

HEALTH AND SAFETY AND WORK

The legal framework

An employer's duties towards a pregnant employee comprise:

- those duties which apply to any employee; and
- those duties which apply specifically to the pregnant employee.

Prominent among both types of duty is the statutory requirement for an employer to carry out a risk assessment. In addition, in certain circumstances the employment of a pregnant woman is prohibited.

An employer's health and safety duties in the maternity context are not restricted to the period of pregnancy. They may also apply to the post-natal period and more specifically to the period during which the mother is breastfeeding.

The legal framework governing health and safety at work comprises:

- the general statutory duties of employers and others;
- the specific statutory duties of employers and others; and
- a duty of care at common law

Breach of the statutory duties is a criminal offence and may also provide the basis for a civil action. The Management Regulations requiring maternity risk assessments cannot generally be used for this purpose but they can be so used in respect of risks subject to a maternity risk assessment.[1] The failure to take reasonable care may be negligence and/or a breach of contract, again opening up the possibility of an employer being sued for damages. Figure 14.1 shows the legal framework for health and safety in diagrammatic form, indicating the provisions which relate to maternity. The law of health and safety at work is discussed more generally in chapters 14 and15.

Risk assessment

The requirement to assess risks

The Management Regulations impose a general requirement upon employers to conduct 'a suitable and sufficient assessment of ... the risks to the health and safety of his employees to which they are exposed whilst at work ...'[2] This general requirement includes a specific obligation, where the workforce includes women of child-bearing age, to assess the health and safety risks which, because of her condition, might be exposed to 'a new or expectant mother' or her baby.[3] New or expectant mothers are:[4]

- pregnant employees;
- employees who have given birth during the previous six months; or
- employees who are breastfeeding.

In conducting a risk assessment, employers will need to take into account only risks that might arise from any processes or working conditions, or physical, biological or chemical agents. They are also required, however, to address specific risks. These risks are risks which are set out in annexes to the EU Protection of Pregnant Workers Directive 1992.[5] In conducting a maternity risk assessment, employers will have to consider these risks as well as any others which might arise.

Employers will not have to consider risks from infectious or contagious diseases when the level of risk is no higher than that which a new or expectant mother might be expected to face outside the workplace.

The hierarchy of preventive measures

Once it is apparent that there is a maternity health and safety risk, an employer must adopt preventive measures to comply with health and safety legislation. If the risk cannot be avoided, the employer must 'alter' the employee's 'working conditions or hours of work' so that it can be avoided.[6] If this is not 'reasonable' the employer will then have to consider whether there is 'suitable alternative work' for the employee.[7] Where there is no suitable alternative work, the employee will have to be suspended. It can be

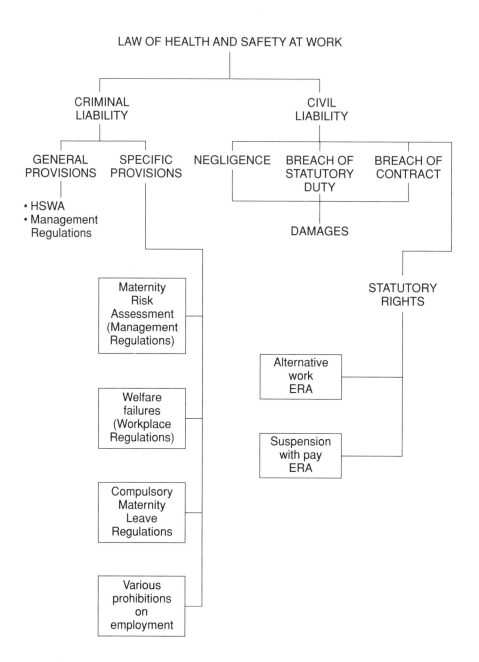

Figure 13.1 The legal framework for health and safety at work indicating the provisions which relate to maternity

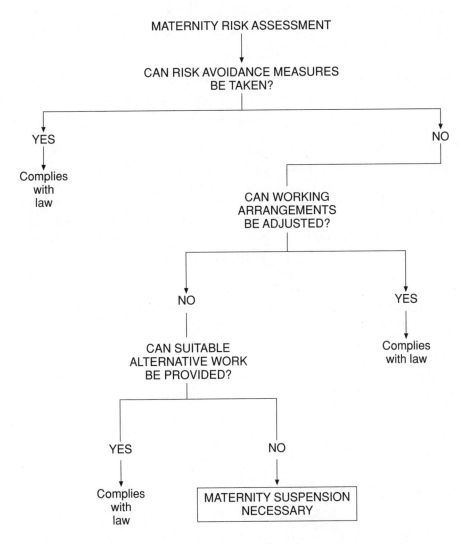

Figure 13.2 Maternity: the hierarchy of preventive measures

seen, therefore, that there is a hierarchy of preventive measures, as illustrated in Figure 13.2. The specific meanings of 'suitable alternative work' and 'suspension from work on maternity grounds' are considered below.

Nothing requires an employer to alter working conditions or hours or suspend the employee until the employee notifies him that she is pregnant, has given birth within the last six months or is breastfeeding. Moreover, the employer is not required to maintain the altered working conditions or hours or suspension unless the employee provides medical evidence within a reasonable time of any written request to do so. The requirement here, therefore, is triggered by the employer's written request. The employer will not need to maintain the altered arrangements or suspension once he knows that the employee is no longer a new or expectant mother or if he cannot establish whether she remains so.

Carrying out a maternity risk assessment

Much of the guidance available on carrying out general risk assessments is relevant here, but with some additional, specific considerations.[8] First, however, it should be noted that the maternity assessment must be suitable and sufficient. This is because the maternity assessment is not a separate assessment, but rather, part of the general assessment. If it does not reach this standard, there will be a breach of the general requirements.

The maternity risk assessment should be such as to identify the hazards including those specifically affecting women, which form a non-exhaustive list within the Directive. The specified hazards are set out below in Table 13.1. The risks associated with these and any other hazards must then be evaluated. Risk means the likelihood of the hazard causing illness or injury and the likely severity of the illness or injury that may be caused. A suitable and sufficient assessment will be one that identifies any 'significant' risks arising from the work.[9] Such risks having been identified, an employer will then have to determine the preventive measures that are necessary, record the assessment (unless that employer employs fewer than five employees: reg 3(4)) and implement the preventive measures. As noted, these measures may include the provision of suitable alternative work or the suspension of the employee on full pay.

Suitable alternative work

There is no requirement to provide suitable alternative work where it does not exist. However, a failure to provide it where it does exist will constitute an automatically unfair dismissal if the employee is then dismissed (see pages 257–9). Moreoever, the right to be offered suitable alternative work where it exists is a free-standing right of the employee. A failure to offer it can be the basis of an application to an industrial tribunal which, if successful, may result in the employer having to pay the employee compensation. The amount will be what the tribunal considers 'just and equitable in all the circumstances' bearing in mind the infringement of the employee's rights and any resultant loss sustained by the employee. The absence of suitable alternative work brings into play a maternity suspension.

Suitable in respect of the employee means that the work must be 'suitable in relation to her and appropriate for her to do in the circumstances' and that the terms and conditions must not be 'substantially less favourable' than those applying to her normal work.[10]

Table 13.1 *Maternity risks specified in the Pregnant Workers Directive*

- AGENTS

Physical agents where these are regarded as agents causing foetal lesions and/or likely to disrupt placental attachment, and in particular:

(a) shocks, vibration or movement;
(b) handling of loads entailing risks, particularly of a dorsolumbar nature;
(c) noise;
(d) ionizing radiation;[1]
(e) non-ionizing radiation;[1]
(f) extremes of cold or heat; and
(g) movements and postures, travelling – either inside or outside the establishment – mental or physical fatigue and other physical burdens connected with the work activity of the worker. Physical agents also include work in hyperbaric atmosphere, such as pressurized enclosures and underwater diving.

Biological agents specified elsewhere[2] in so far as it is known that these agents or the therapeutic measures necessitated by such agents endanger the health of pregnant women and the unborn child. Only toxoplasma and rubella virus are specifically mentioned.

Chemical agents
These are various agents listed elsewhere[3] and:
(a) mercury and mercury derivatives;
(b) antibiotic drugs;
(c) carbon monoxide; and
(d) chemical agents of known and dangerous percutaneous absorption; and
(e) lead and lead derivatives in so far as these are capable of being absorbed by the human organism.

These agents are included in so far as it is known that they endanger the health of pregnant women and the unborn child.

- PROCESSES
Various industrial processes listed elsewhere.[4]

- WORKING CONDITIONS
Underground mining work.

Notes:
[1] See 80/836/Euratom, OJ 1980, L246/1.

[2] See the Directive itself, Annex I, and 90/679/EEC, OJ 1990, L374/1.
[3] See the Directive itself, Annex I, and 67/548/EEC, OJ 1967, L196/1 and Annex 90/394/EEC, OJ 1990, L196/1.
[4] See Annex I to 90/394/EEC, OJ 1990, L196/1.

Prohibition of employment of pregnant employees

Maternity suspension

Where there is no suitable alternative work, the employee is to be suspended with pay ('suspension on maternity grounds').[11] This contrasts sharply with the former legal position where it was fair to dismiss a pregnant woman on health and safety grounds, although it might nevertheless have amounted to unlawful sex discrimination. The maternity suspension comes into play where the suspension is in consequence of a statutory requirement or a provision in an approved code of practice under the HSWA (the relevant provisions here are specified in a Ministerial Order: currently these are the provisions of the Management Regulations relating to maternity risk assessments and night work).[12]

Where an employer suspends a woman on the ground of her incapacity to perform the work, this will not be a suspension on maternity grounds. The woman will be absent for ill-health reasons and, if eligible, will receive statutory sick pay (SSP). A dismissal here would be likely to be caught by the unfair dismissal provisions relating specifically to pregnancy.[13] Again, this contrasts sharply with the former legal position where a dismissal on the ground of incapacity to perform duties was expressly excluded from the protection of those specific unfair dismissal provisions, although not necessarily from the unfair dismissal provisons more generally and not from the law of sex discrimination.

A woman suspended on maternity grounds as defined earlier is entitled to be paid during the period of the suspension. The remuneration will be a week's pay in respect of each week of suspension, a week's pay being defined in ERA, ss 220–229[14] (see pages 378–80 where the concept is explained). There appears to be no specific limit on the duration of maternity suspension.

Any contractual payments made by an employer can be offset against the payments made in compliance of the statutory requirements, and *vice versa*. Where a woman is not paid part or all of the remuneration due under the statute, she may make an application to an industrial tribunal. If successful, the tribunal will order arrears of remuneration.

Nightwork

The Management Regulations require that an employee who is a new or expectant mother should be suspended from work if:

- she works at night; and
- a medical certificate states that it is necessary for her health and safety that she should not do so.

The medical certificate may identify a period of time. The first step should be to consider the possibilities of suitable alternative work during the day. Where a suspension proves to be necessary, it operates as discussed above and for the period necessary to protect the employee's health and safety. Dismissal of the employee because her employment would be unlawful is itself likely to be unlawful, as the following case illustrates.

Habermann-Beltermann

FACTS
HB was employed as a night worker: this was a contractual term. Shortly afterwards, it was discovered that she was pregnant. German law makes night work unlawful during pregnancy and the employers dismissed her. They argued, first, that their contract with HB was void because it was illegal, being in breach of German law. In the alternative, they argued that the contract was voidable because of mistake, ie that they were entitled to treat the contract as void because they entered into it not knowing she was pregnant when in fact she was.
HELD (ECJ)
The employer's arguments were rejected. German law was in breach of the EU Equal Treatment Directive by allowing the dismissal of a pregnant night worker on the ground that her employment conflicted with German law.

Compulsory maternity leave

The Maternity (Compulsory Leave) Regulations 1994 prohibit an employee from working or being permitted to work by her employer during the two weeks commencing with the day of childbirth.[15] Childbirth means the birth of a living child or the birth of a child whether living or dead after 24 weeks of pregnancy. An employer in breach of the Regulations is liable to a fine on summary conviction not exceeding level two on the standard scale (currently £500). Enforcement is by the HSE or the local authority depending upon the type of workplace (on the allocation of inspection and enforcement duties, see chapter 14). It should be noted that the employees prohibited from working under these regulations are those entitled to maternity leave under Part VIII of ERA. An employee without such a right (eg, because of a failure to meet the ERA notification requirements) will not be prohibited.

Other prohibitions

It will not be unlawful to take action in order to comply with relevant health and safety provisions or existing statutory protection for women. However, the protection must relate to pregnancy or maternity or other risks specifically affecting women.[16] In addition, EA 1989 provides that the operation of certain specified provisions protecting women will not be unlawful sex discrimination.[17] These are set out in Table 13.2.

Welfare facilities

Under the Workplace Regulations 1992, 'suitable and sufficient rest facilities shall be provided at readily accessible places'.[18] More specifically, suitable facilities have to be provided for pregnant women or nursing mothers to rest.[19] The ACOP explains that these facilities should be conveniently located in relation to sanitary facilities and where necesssary, should include the facility to lie down.[20]

Table 13.2 *Protective provisions in Schedule 1 of the Employment Act 1989*

- Factories Act 1961, ss 74, 128, 131 and Sched 5
- Public Health Act 1936, s 205
- Manufacture of Paints and Colours Regulations 1907, reg 3
- Smelting of Material Containing Lead etc Regulations 1911, reg 10
- Indiarubber Regulations 1922, reg 1
- Electric Accumulator Regulations 1925, reg 1(ii)
- Pottery (Health and Welfare) Special Regulations 1950, reg 6(1)(i)–(iv)
- Ionising Radiations Regulations 1985, Parts IV and V of Sched 1
- Air Navigation Order 1985, article 20/8 so far as it relates to pregnancy
- Control of Lead at Work Regulations 1980, ACOP, para 118
- Merchant Shipping (Medical Examination) Regulations 1983, reg 7 (medical standards in notice M1131) (Part X so far as it relates to gynaecological conditions and Part XI)

MATERNITY LEAVE

Types of maternity leave

There are now four types of maternity leave.

Basic maternity leave (the 'maternity leave period')[21]
This is the new right for pregnant employees, which was introduced in 1994. It lasts for 14 weeks with exceptions (see below) and there are no

requirements in respect of length of employment or hours of work. Only employees are eligible (see chapter 5 on employment status).

Extended maternity leave[22]

The existing scheme, now modified, provides a right to extended leave. This commences at the termination of basic maternity leave and ends no later than 29 weeks after the expected week of childbirth (EWC). As before, an employee must have at least two years' continuous employment with her employer in order to qualify for this right, but there are no longer any hours restrictions. Therefore, part-time employees with at least two years' such employment will have an entitlement.

Compulsory maternity leave

This is the name given to the two weeks commencing with the day of child-birth during which the employer is prohibited from employing the employee. Breach of this prohibition is a criminal offence. See above.

Contractual maternity leave

Contractual maternity leave is that agreed by the parties – employer and employee – either orally or in writing. Where there is a maternity agreement between an employer and a trades union, some or all of its terms may be incorporated into the contracts of individual employees (on incorporation, see pages 153–9).

Relationship between contractual and statutory maternity leave

The employee cannot have her statutory right reduced by agreement, nor can she aggregate her statutory and contractual rights. However, she can pick and choose from the combined statutory and contractual package, that is, she can pick the best from each to form a 'composite right'.[23] An example would be combining contractual maternity pay with statutory protection of non-contractual fringe benefits. Contractual rights may be implied as well as express. They may exist in the absence of any statutory rights, and *vice versa*. In *Lucas v Norton of London Ltd*, the employee had no right to statutory leave because she had not complied with the notification requirements, but the EAT found an implied contractual term giving a right to maternity leave.

Basic maternity leave

Duration

Basic maternity leave is generally for 14 weeks, but with the following exceptions:[24]

- if childbirth occurs after basic maternity leave, the leave continues until childbirth;
- if the woman is dismissed during basic maternity leave, the leave will end on dismissal;
- if the woman is prevented by law from working at the expiry of basic maternity leave, the leave will continue. An example would be where childbirth occurs at the end of the period of basic maternity leave: under these circumstances the woman will be prohibited from working for the next two weeks (see page 243).

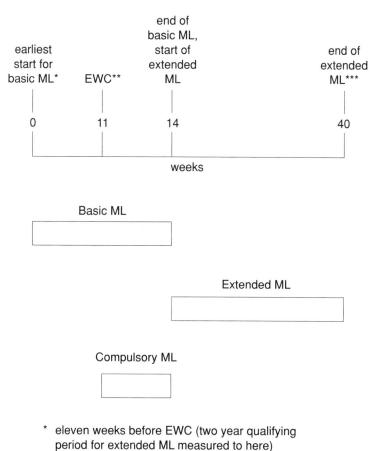

Figure 13.3 Types of maternity leave

Eligibility

To be entitled to maternity leave, the woman must be an employee. There are no length of employment or hours requirements but the information and notification procedures set out below must be followed. Few categories of employee are excluded from the right to basic maternity leave: only those ordinarily working outside Great Britain, those employed in share fishing and those employed in the police service.[25]

Commencement

Basic maternity leave commences on the date the employee notifies the employer as the date she intends to start the leave.[26] This must be no earlier than the 11th week before EWC.[27] The employee must notify the employer of the date at least 21 days in advance of the date, or, if that is not reasonably practicable, as soon as is reasonably practicable. The EWC starts at midnight on Saturday night – it is not the same as a pay week.[28]

Where childbirth occurs before the notified date or before any date has been notified, basic maternity leave starts on the day of childbirth.[29] It is also allowed where maternity absence starts before the notified date. In such cases the leave begins on the first day of absence, providing this is no earlier than the beginning of the sixth week before the EWC. In the two sets of circumstances above, notice must be given as soon as is reasonably practicable.

Information and notification arrangements

A woman will lose her right to basic maternity leave if she does not comply with the legal notification and information requirements. A woman must notify her employer of the date she intends to commence her basic maternity leave.[30] This must be done at least 21 days before the date, or, if, this is not reasonably practicable, as soon as is reasonably practicable. The notification must be in writing if the employer so requests.

The employee must:[31]

- inform the employer that she is pregnant;
- state the EWC (or the date of actual childbirth if this has already occurred);
- provide the above information in writing;
- provide her employer with a medical certificate stating the EWC if her employer so requests; and
- provide the above information at least 21 days before the start of her basic maternity leave or if this is not reasonably practicable as soon as is reasonably practicable.

Pay and conditions during the maternity leave period (basic maternity leave)

During the maternity leave period, an employee is entitled to 'terms and conditions of employment which would have been applicable to her if she had not been absent'.[32] This is a central provision which has one major exception – remuneration. In other words, an employer is not required by statute to pay the remuneration that would have been applicable. This is because statutory maternity pay (SMP) – dealt with below – is likely to be payable (where it is not payable, there may be an entitlement to maternity allowance). However, there may be a contractual entitlement to be paid the normal amount of remuneration. Paying something less than normal remuneration during maternity leave does not amount to sex discrimination under EU law *(Gillespie)*

The meaning of the term 'remuneration' is clearly of considerable importance. The significance is that anything that is not remuneration (ie, non-remuneration benefits) must be maintained. The term is not defined in relation to maternity leave but is used elsewhere in ERA, notably in ss 220–229 which deal with computation of 'a week's pay'. However, it is not defined there either, but there is the benefit of some case law. Wages, salary, contractual commission and bonuses are thought to be remuneration but benefits in kind are not (eg, company cars, health care and insurance). Pensions are not thought to be remuneration, but contributions must be paid and the weeks count as pensionable service.[33] This applies only to periods of paid maternity leave, ie the period of statutory or contractual maternity pay. Related rights including contractual sickness and unemployment benefits must also be maintained.

Continuity of employment is embraced by the wording of s 71 of ERA. Terms and conditions are to be as if the employee had not been absent. Thus, the contract is deemed to subsist, presumably for both statutory and contractual purposes.

Right to return

As noted, the contract subsists. No notice of return is required since the return is automatic: the maternity leave period ends after 14 weeks. However, if the return is to be early – ie, before 14 weeks have elapsed – the employee must give at least seven days' notice.[34] If such notice is not provided, the employer may postpone the return in order to obtain seven days' notice, although the postponement cannot delay the return beyond the end of the maternity leave period. An employee returning early and prior to the postponed date will not be contractually entitled to remuneration for the period between her return and the postponed date.

The date of return can be postponed by the statutory extension of the maternity leave period. This may be where the birth has been late, where the employee is prevented under statute from performing her work, or where the compulsory maternity leave regulations apply.

Rights on return

These are protected by the general requirement that everything apart from remuneration must be maintained. If there is a redundancy during the maternity leave period, however, a dismissal may be fair. The test will be whether continued employment is not practicable by reason of redundancy. If there is a suitable vacancy, the employee has a right to be offered it, and this may be with her employer, an associated employer or a successor employer. A failure to offer suitable alternative employment will mean that any dismissal will automatically be unfair.[35]

An offer of alternative work must take effect immediately the old contract ends and be made before the old contract ends. The work must be suitable and appropriate in the circumstances and on not substantially less favourable terms and conditions of employment.

Disputes

A breach of terms or conditions (ie, non-remuneration), whether during or on return from maternity leave, may allow an action for breach of contract or possibly a complaint of unfair constructive dismissal (see chapter 16). The failure to pay remuneration, as noted, is not unlawful in terms of the ERA nor in breach of EU law (see *Gillespie*, page 248). Conceivably, however, it could involve a breach of the SDA or the EqPA.

The denial of the right to return constitutes a dismissal and such a dismissal is likely to fall under the maternity dismissal provisions of ERA, s 99, so removing the need for two years' qualifying employment. Such dismissals are also automatically unfair. In addition, a complaint under the SDA may be possible.

Extended maternity leave

Extent and commencement

Extended maternity leave commences at the end of the maternity leave period and continues up to 29 weeks after the beginning of the week of childbirth.[36]

Eligibility

Eligibility is the same as for the maternity leave period except:

- the employee must have two years' continuous employment measured at the beginning of the eleventh week before the EWC; and
- the employee must notify her employer in writing at least 21 days before the maternity leave period starts that she intends to exercise her right to extended leave.

It should be noted that eligibility for basic maternity leave is a prerequisite for extended leave. Moreover, there is no hours requirement, so the right will be available to part-time employees as well as those working full-time.

Pay and conditions during extended maternity leave

The first question to determine here is whether the contract subsists during extended maternity leave. This seems to be a contractual matter: if there is no termination, the contract subsists. Thus in *Institute of the Motor Industry v Harvey*, the EAT thought that, where a woman gives notice of her intention to take maternity leave, the contract is likely to continue during that leave unless terminated by agreement, resignation or dismissal. In the subsequent case of *Hilton Hotels v Kaissi*, the EAT held it to be a matter of contract rather than statute as to whether the contract subsisted. There was no evidence in *Kaissi* of any agreement or other action to bring the contract to an end, therefore it subsisted. However, the EAT held in *Halfpenny v IGE Medical Systems Ltd* that in the absence of an agreement to keep the contract in being, the contract would be kept in being only to allow the exercise of the statutory right to return. If that was lost, the contract would end automatically, (ie, not by dismissal). This line of reasoning was doubted in *Caledonia v Caffrey*.

Another issue is whether continuity of employment is preserved for statutory purposes such as qualifying employment for various statutory rights (eg, redundancy payments). The answer is that continuity is expressly preserved.[37] The position in respect of pension rights is the same as with the maternity leave period.

Right to return

The right to return is expressly stated in ERA, s 79. However, there are notification provisions and two separate notices may be required:

- Written confirmation of the intention to return (s 80(2)) must be given no earlier than 21 days before the end of the maternity leave period if the employer requests it.
- The employer's request must be in writing and must indicate that rights under s 79 will be lost if the request is not complied with in the required time.
- The employee must comply within 14 days or, if this is not reasonably practicable, as soon as is reasonably practicable.

There must be notification of the date of return (s 82(1)) at least 21 days before the date of return. The notification must be in writing and it is mandatory – it is not dependent upon a request by the employer.

There is no escape clause here for a late notification so a notice say, 14 days beforehand will not count even if it was not reasonably practicable to give it earlier. For an example of a case where the right to return was lost because of a failure to give proper notice of the date of return see *Lavery v Plessey*.

However, if the contract subsists during extended maternity leave, as in *Kaissi*, an employee who has no statutory right to return and is prevented from returning will be able to make an unfair dismissal application. This happened in *Kaissi* and resulted in a finding of unfair dismissal.

The return to work may be postponed for up to four weeks:[38]

- by the employer for 'specified reasons'; or
- the employee on medical grounds.

The return can be postponed if there is an interruption to work (eg, by a strike). The postponement can last until the interruption is over.

Return does not necessarily mean a physical return. It is sufficient that the woman has exercised her right to return by giving notice of return under ERA, s 82, even if on the notified day of return she is ill and unable to work *(Crees v Royal London; Greaves v Kwik Save)*.

Rights on return

The employee has the right to return to the same employer or successor and in the same job. A job is defined in relation to an employee to mean 'the nature of the work which he is employed to do in accordance with his contract and the capacity and place in which he is so employed.'[39] The terms and conditions must be no less favourable than if the employee had not been absent.

Continuity of employment is preserved for statutory purposes and the weeks on extended maternity leave also count.[40] Moreover, statute provides for continuity of contractual rights by stating that the period commencing on return shall be continuous with the period prior to the commencement of extended leave. However, while statute preserves contractual continuity, it does not require contractual terms to operate during the leave: this will be a matter for the contract itself (the pension position is as described earlier in relation to the maternity leave period).

A potential difficulty arises where the employee has neither a contractual nor a statutory right to maternity leave. This occurred in *Mitchell v The Royal British Legion Club*. The employee resigned, had her baby and returned after 16 weeks' absence. The EAT held that she had continuous employment by virtue of what is now ERA, s 212(3) – the provisions which preserve continuity for statutory purposes where there is no contract. Under s 212(3)(d) her continuity was preserved, and the weeks counted, because she was absent due to pregnancy or childbirth. Absences of up to 26 weeks may be protected by this provision.

Where there is a redundancy during extended maternity leave, the provisions are similar but not quite the same as those which apply to the maternity leave period. There is a difference in the timing of the offer and the start of any new contract and a difference in the mechanics of how a failure to offer a suitable vacancy becomes unfair. The denial of the right to return is a dismissal by virtue of s 96 and s 99(4) makes the failure to offer suitable alternative employment (where there is any) automatically unfair.

The only question for industrial tribunals in these redundancy cases is whether or not there was a suitable vacancy. If the answer is yes, any dismissal will be automatically unfair. An example of such a case is *Community Task Force v Rimmer*. The vacancy situation has to be judged once the intention to return has been notified rather than when the date of return has been provided. This is because the right to return is triggered by the notification of intention to return. Notifying the date is the means of exercising the right. Thus, a permanent replacement recruited during an employee's extended maternity leave after her intention to return had been notified but prior to notification of her date of return was evidence of a vacancy. Since it was not offered to the complainant her dismissal was automatically unfair *(Phillip Hodges and Co, Solicitors v Kell)*.

A question arises as to the position where an employee wishes to return on a different basis, for example, on a part-time rather than a full-time basis. The answer is that the employee can exercise statutory or contractual rights, so that any change agreed by the employer and the employee should satisfy the statutory provisions. In *Bovey v The Hospital for Sick Children* the employer agreed to a return on a part-time basis, but only in a lower grade. The employee had no right to insist on returning in a part-time capacity on her old grade. Note, however, that any rule detrimental to part-time employees is capable of being indirect sex discrimination and should be objectively justified.

Disputes

The denial of the right to return constitutes a dismissal under ERA, s 96 (or, in the context of redundancy, s 137). There are, however, two exceptions where such a denial will not constitute a dismissal. First, there is a small employer exception. This is where the employer and any associated employer(s) have five or fewer employees, where it is not reasonably practicable to allow the employee to return and where there is no suitable alternative employment. Secondly, there is a general exception. This is where it is not reasonably practicable to allow return, where an offer of suitable alternative employment has been made, and where that offer has been accepted by the employee or unreasonably refused. The offer must be in respect of suitable and appropriate work on terms and conditions not 'substantially less favourable' than those applying prior to maternity leave. The burden of proof lies upon the employer to show that one of the exceptions applies.

The denial of the right to return will constitute a dismissal only if the employee has a right to return. Where that right is lost because of a failure to give proper notice, as in *Lavery*, there is no 'deemed' dismissal. Moreover, the Court of Appeal held in *Lavery* that there was no 'ordinary' dismissal either.

Continuity is preserved for statutory purposes even if the employee returns to a different job and, on calculating the end of extended maternity leave, the 29 weeks is to be measured from the actual date of childbirth and not from the expected week *(Woolworths v Smith)*.

Where there is a breach of terms and conditions during or after maternity leave, this will be a contractual matter. Depending on the significance of any contractual breach, there could arise a complaint of unfair constructive dismissal. There might also be equal pay considerations (eg, if sick pay terms exclude maternity) or sex discrimination.

MATERNITY PAY

Maternity allowance[41]

This is a social security benefit paid by the DSS. A person who is not entitled to statutory maternity pay (SMP) may be entitled to maternity allowance if they have paid the required number of national insurance contributions.

Statutory Maternity Pay

Background
Statutory maternity pay arrangements were completely remodelled in the Spring of 1987 along the lines of the statutory sick pay scheme.[42] From 6 April 1987 employers were given responsibility for paying SMP to their employees. An employer can recover 92 per cent of his SMP payments by deductions from NI contributions. Small employers (with NI contributions of £20,000 or less) receive additional assistance.[43]

During the 13-week core period of payment of SMP – starting six weeks before the expected week of confinement (EWC) – a woman is excluded from any right to receive SSP regardless of whether or not entitled to SMP. More generally, SSP and SMP cannot be paid at the same time. Statutory sick pay is regarded as terminated the day before entitlement to SMP begins or, where there is no entitlement, would have begun if the woman was qualified.

Eligibility
To qualify for SMP, a woman, who has ceased to work for her employer because of pregnancy or confinement, must:

- have been continuously employed by the same (or an associated) employer for 26 weeks; the continuous employment must extend into the qualifying week – the 15th week before EWC;
- have had normal weekly earnings during the last eight of the 26 weeks at a level not less than the lower earnings limit for NI contributions;[44]
- have reached, or been confined before reaching, the start of the 11th week before the EWC;
- have given notice to her employer (see page 256); and
- have supplied medical evidence of the EWC (see page 256).

It should be noted that employers must pay SMP to an employee who qualifies regardless of whether she will be returning to work with them after the baby is born. An employee is a person whose earnings attract a liability for employee's Class 1 NI contributions, or would do if they were high enough (social security and tax institutions do not necessarily adopt the same criteria for defining employee as might be adopted by an industrial tribunal). Whoever is liable to pay the employer's share of the Class 1 contribution is to be treated as the employer.

A woman will not be entitled to SMP if:

- she was not employed by her employer (or an associated employer) during the qualifying week;
- she does not have 26 weeks' continuous employment;
- her earnings are below the NI minimum;
- her notice is late and it was reasonably practicable for her to give it in time;
- she does not provide medical evidence;
- she is a foreign-going mariner whose employer pays NI contributions at a special rate;
- she is in legal custody; or
- she is serving as a member of HM Forces.

An employee is not entitled to SMP at all if at the start of the SMP payment period there is no entitlement. Even where there is an entitlement, SMP may not be payable for certain weeks – such as after the woman's death, or if she is in legal custody. Where a woman works for her employer beyond the sixth week before the EWC she will lose SMP for those weeks (at the lower rate, providing that at least six weeks of entitlement remain). This will not apply if she works for some other employer before the EWC. Any work post-EWC – whether for the same or some other employer – will result in SMP not being payable for that particular week. Once SMP is paid, an employee must notify her employer of any changes, such as starting to work for another employer, or being in legal custody.

Where an employee is fairly dismissed because of pregnancy the period of continuous employment is treated as not having been terminated. Such circumstances are where it is impossible for the employee to do her job properly because of pregnancy, or where it would be a breach of law (for example, the HSWA) for her to continue working. There must be no alternative work available on terms which are not substantially less favourable that those relating to the original work. A fair dismissal, therefore, does not prevent qualification for SMP.

Where a dismissal is unfair and the employer has failed to establish a reason, SMP will still be payable if the dismissal was solely or mainly for the purpose of avoiding the payment of SMP. If an employer demonstrates some other reason for the dismissal, but the dismissal is nonetheless unfair, the compensation awarded is likely to take into account the loss of SMP (the law on unfair dismisssal is described in chapter 16).

If pregnancy ends other than by a live birth before the 28th week of pregnancy, no SMP is payable, although SSP might be. However, if this happens after the start of the 12th week before the EWC, SMP is payable.

Payment of SMP

Maternity pay is payable for up to 18 weeks. It cannot start earlier than the 11th week before confinement, nor later than the start of the week after the birth. There is thus a fixed period of 13 weeks, and a period of five weeks which can be taken earlier, later or a combination of the two. A woman will need to cease work at least six weeks before the EWC if she is to obtain the full 18 weeks' maternity pay. There are two rates of pay, the higher of which is 90 per cent of normal weekly earnings in the last eight of the 26 weeks mentioned earlier. A woman is entitled to six weeks on the higher rate, followed by 12 weeks at the lower rate (a flat amount of £57.70 from 6 April 1998).[45]

Wages during maternity leave, company maternity pay and company sick pay can be offset against SMP, but these are the only payments that can be.

Like SSP, SMP applies to earnings rather than basic pay, and applies to each employment contract. SMP could be paid twice to one employee, therefore, if that employee worked for two employers or under two contracts (ie, with two sets of NI contributions) for one employer. SMP is subject to tax and NI contributions. Unlike SSP, however, it is payable only for full weeks – there is no daily rate. Thus, where entitlement is lost for part of a week, the whole week's entitlement is lost.

Payment can be made in the same way as wages, or by means of a lump sum. It can also be paid through a third party (such as an insurance company) although the liability remains with the employer. A woman may claim SMP from the National Insurance Fund if the employer is insolvent or defaults on payment.

Notification and evidence of maternity[46]

A woman must give her employer at least 21 days' notice, in writing if so requested, that she will be absent because of pregnancy or confinement, unless it is not reasonably practicable to give such an amount of notice. Evidence of birth or confinement will be necessary, usually in the form of a maternity certificate (form MAT B1). This is not normally issued earlier than 14 weeks before the EWC. The evidence should be provided no later than the end of the third week of payment of SMP, although this can be extended by a further ten weeks if an employer accepts the reason for delay. Where notification is outside the 21-day period and it was reasonably practicable to notify in time, SMP may be withheld.

Disputes

Refusal to pay SMP may be challenged. An employer refusing to pay SMP should, if asked for a written statement, complete form SMP 1 and in doing so state the reason(s) for the refusal. The statement must show the weeks for which SMP is payable, how much SMP is payable per week and why no SMP is payable for other weeks. The form should be given to the employee within seven days of the decision being made. The maternity evidence should be returned to the employee. Some disputes might be avoided if employers make clear to their employees:

- when the employee must notify her intention to stop work;
- the flexibility of the SMP payment period and the employer's need to know the period chosen; and
- what evidence of birth or confinement is required and when it is required.

If there is a dispute, the employee should process it through the normal grievance procedure. However, if the employee is still dissatisfied an appeal may be made to a DSS adjudication officer. Thereafter, appeal may be made to an SSAT, a social security commissioner and (on a point of law only) to the Court of Appeal (Court of Session in Scotland).[47] Some decisions, however, can be made only by the Secretary of State for Social Security and are not therefore appealable. These are, whether:

- employment is continuous;
- amounts under separate contracts with the same employer can be added;
- an employee is entitled to compensation for national insurance contributions on SMP;
- one person is an employer or employee of another and over what period (this also applies in the case of SSP);
- an employer is entitled to recover SMP payments and, if so, how much; and

- two or more employers should be treated as one for SMP purposes (this also applies to SSP).

Criminal offences
The following are criminal offences.

- failure to pay SMP in time following a decision of an adjudication officer, an SSAT, a social security commissioner or the Secretary of State for Social Security;
- failure to provide information to the statutory agencies;
- failure to keep the required records, namely dates of maternity absences, copies of maternity certificates and records of weeks during the SMP payment period when no SMP was paid, and the reasons for non-payment (records must be kept for three years); and
- falsifying documents for the recovery of SMP or NI contributions on SMP.

Interrelationship of basic maternity leave and SMP
An employee entitled to basic maternity leave but not extended leave (ie, entitled to 14 weeks' leave) will not be able to take up her entitlement to 18 weeks' SMP because absence from work beyond 14 weeks will be unauthorized, while returning to work will remove entitlement to SMP.

DISMISSAL ON GROUNDS OF PREGNANCY OR CHILDBIRTH

The scheme of unfair dismissal law

This is dealt with in chapter 16 but briefly comprises the need for an employer to demonstrate one of the reasons for dismissal laid down in s 98 of ERA and for the tribunal to be convinced that the dismissal for that reason was reasonable in all the circumstances.[48] In the general case, an employee must have two years' continuous employment in order to acquire rights under unfair dismissal law. The following sections indicate how dismissal for reasons of pregnancy or childbirth differ from the general unfair dismissal requirements.

Dismissal on grounds of pregnancy or childbirth[49]

Meaning of 'dismissal on ground of pregnancy or childbirth'
The meaning of this term is found in ERA, s 99:

- pregnancy or any other reason connected with it;

- dismissal which ends the maternity leave, where the reason is childbirth or anything connected with it;
- dismissal after maternity leave because the employee took maternity leave or the benefits thereof;
- dismissal because of a relevant requirement or recommendation in the context of maternity suspension; and
- dismissal which ends the maternity leave by reason of redundancy where a suitable vacancy exists but is not offered.

Note that maternity leave here refers to the 14-week maternity leave period (or basic maternity leave) under s 71.

Where a dismissal is related to maternity, but falls outside s 99, this is covered in chapter 16. These may be dismissals for incapacity, ill-health or absence.

Automatically unfair

As noted, the general test for unfair dismissal involves two stages: reason and reasonableness. Here, it must be emphasized, the second stage is not applicable. Once it is established that the reason for dismissal is one of the factors listed above (ie, one of those found in s 99) the dismissal is automatically unfair: no reasonableness test is to be applied. In *Caledonia Bureau Investment and Property v Caffrey*, the EAT held a pregnancy-related illness dismissal to be automatically unfair despite the fact that it occurred post-maternity leave.

Absence of qualifying period

Another important difference from the general case is the absence of any requirement for a two-year period of qualifying employment. The upper age limit for unfair dismissal cases is also removed.[50]

Dismissal on ground of redundancy with selection on the basis of pregnancy or childbirth

This is defined (ERA, s 105) in terms of the first four of the five s 99 categories. Again, once redundancy is demonstrated and the reason for selection is shown to be pregnancy or pregnancy related, the dismissal will be automatically unfair. There must be at least two candidates for redundancy, in the same undertaking. The word undertaking is not defined here but is taken to mean organization. Regulation 2(1) of the Transfer of Undertakings (Protection of Employment) Regulations defines undertaking to include 'any trade or business'). The employees must be in similar positions. ERA, s 235(1) defines position as status, nature of work and terms and conditions of employment – taken as a whole. Again there is no qualifying period or upper age limit (ERA, ss 108(3) and 109(2)).

In a case prior to the introduction of these provisions, the House of Lords were prepared to find that a dismissal in a redundancy context was in fact a dismissal on the ground of pregnancy, so coming within the ambit of the predecessor of ERA, s 99 (EP(C)A, s 60) *(Brown v Stockton on Tees Borough Council)*. There may be less need for such an approach since selection for redundancy is now expressly outlawed, but the reason for dismissal will remain a question of fact for the tribunal.

Written statement of reasons for dismissal[51]

This is dealt with more generally in chapter 16. However, it is important to note here that the general provisions are varied for maternity cases, and in two ways:

- the two-year qualifying period for entitlement to the right to be provided with a written statement of reasons for dismissal is removed in the maternity case.
- in the general case, an employer needs to provide a written statement only if requested to do so. In the maternity case, it is mandatory that the employer provides it.

These two differences apply where the employee is dismissed while pregnant or dismissed after childbirth such that the dismissal ends her maternity leave period.[52]

OTHER MATERNITY PROVISIONS

Time off for ante-natal care[53]

Eligibility
There are no service or hours requirements but the woman must be an employee and have an appointment for ante-natal care. For any second or subsequent appointment, she must produce evidence of both pregnancy and the appointment if the employer so requests.

Nature of the employee's right
The employee is given a right not to be unreasonably refused time off, with pay, during working hours for the purpose of ante-natal care. Working hours means contractual hours (s 55(4)).

Complaint and defence
An employee may complain to an industrial tribunal that she has been unreasonably refused ante-natal time off or pay for such time off. Employers

may defend such cases on the basis that their refusal to grant paid time off was reasonable.

Complaints must be made within three months of the date of the appointment to which the complaint relates, or such other period as is reasonable in cases where compliance with the three-month rule was not reasonably practicable.

Remedies

Where the complaint is upheld, the industrial tribunal will make a declaration and order an employer to pay for time off taken without pay or for time off that was refused.

Employer's right to dismiss temporary replacement

This is provided for under ERA.[54] The dismissal of a temporary replacement for a woman on maternity leave is expressly stated to be a dismissal for 'some other substantial reason' (SOSR) under unfair dismissal law.[55] This means that the first stage of the two-stage unfair dismissal test is passed. However, the dismissal will still have to meet the requirement for reasonableness under s 98(4). The employer's right to have the reason treated as SOSR will apply only if the temporary replacement is informed in writing at the outset that they will be dismissed when the absent employee returns.

Maternity and discrimination law

Matters relating to maternity may be capable of falling within the scope of discrimination law. The discrimination law framework was set out in chapter 6 and the question of whether discrimination on the ground of pregnancy constitutes sex discrimination was addressed. As noted, dismissal on maternity grounds is likely to be unfair under unfair dismissal law: the question is whether it is also unlawful discrimination under the SDA and/or EU law.

An important consideration here is where the employer's behaviour is not covered by unfair dismissal law at all, for example, because it relates to recruitment. Here the employee's only complaint will lie under the SDA (or possibly directly under EU law). Another area where discrimination law might be important is where a dismissal is related to maternity but not specifically covered by ERA, s. 99. This would include pregnancy-related illness after the expiry of maternity leave causing either unacceptable levels of absence or substandard work performance.

A final area where discrimination law may bite in relation to maternity is the reduction in benefits and services during maternity leave. This could be a breach of the Equal Pay Act and/or article 119 of the Treaty of Rome.

However, in *Gillespie*, the ECJ ruled that the latter is not the case. EU law does not require pay to be maintained in full during maternity leave. The only requirement is that contained in the Pregnant Workers Directive, ie pay must not be below the minimum level of sick pay.

NOTES

1 Management of Health and Safety at Work Regulations (SI 1992/2051), reg 15(1). These regulations are issued under the HSWA. The same applies to the general duties in the HSWA. Regulation 15(2) of the Management Regulations disapplies reg 15(1) in respect of maternity risks.

2 Management Regulations, reg 3(1).

3 It should be noted that the maternity-specific provisions were introduced into the Management Regulations by the Management of Health and Safety at Work (Amendment) Regulations (SI 1994/2865). The HSE has produced guidance, *New and Expectant Mothers at Work: A Guide for Employers* (HSE, 1995).

4 The term is defined in reg 1(2).

5 92/85/EC, OJ 1992, L348/1 See Annexes I and II.

6 Management Regulations, reg 13A(2).

7 It is here that the requirements of the Management Regulations dovetail with the provisions of the ERA. The Management Regulations require risk avoidance by adjusting the work. Where this cannot be done, ERA, s 67 requires any suitable alternative work to be provided. Where there is none, the employee will be suspended on maternity grounds on full pay (ERA, s 66).

8 For general guidance see Bateman, M, King, B and Lewis, P, *The Handbook of Health and Safety at Work* (London, Kogan Page, 1996). Chapter 8 deals specifically with risk assessments.

9 Management Regulations, Approved Code of Practice, para. 9.

10 ERA, s 67.

11 ERA, ss 66 and 68.

12 Under ERA, s 66(2). See the Suspension from Work (On Maternity Grounds) Order (SI 1994/2930).

13 ERA, s 99.

14 By virtue of ERA, s 69(1).

15 The Maternity (Compulsory Leave) Regulations (SI 1994/2479) reg 2. These regulations are issued under the European Communities Act 1972.

16 SDA 1975, s 51.

17 EA 1989, s 4 and Sched 1.

18 Workplace (Health, Safety and Welfare) Regulations (SI 1992/3004), reg 25(1).

19 Ibid, reg 25(4).

20 Para 237 of the ACOP accompanying the Workplace Regulations.

21 ERA, ss 71 and 73.

22 ERA, s 79.

23 ERA, ss 78 and 85.
24 ERA, s 73.
25 ERA, ss 196, 199 and 200.
26 ERA, s 72.
27 ERA, s 74(2).
28 ERA, s 235(1).
29 ERA, ss 72 and 74.
30 ERA, s 74.
31 ERA, s 75.
32 ERA, s 71(1).
33 Social Security Act 1989, Sched 5 This was to give effect to the EU Equal Treatment in Occupational Social Security Directive 86/378/EC.
34 ERA, s 76.
35 Under ERA, s 99(1)(e).
36 ERA, s 79(1).
37 ERA, s 212(2).
38 ERA, s 82.
39 ERA, s 235(1).
40 ERA, s 212(2).
41 Social Security Contributions and Benefits Act 1992, s 35.
42 Social Security Act 1986 and Statutory Maternity Pay (General) Regulations (SI 1986/1960). Provisions relating to SMP are currently to be found in the Social Security Contributions and Benefits Act 1992, ss 164–71.
43 See the Statutory Maternity Pay (Compensation of Employers and Miscellaneous Amendment) Regulations (SI 1994/1882). See also SI 1995/566 and SI 1996/668.
44 In *Banks v Tesco Stores* an industrial tribunal rejected an application based on the argument that this exclusion was indirect sex discrimination. However, the case is on appeal and in a separate action the Pensions Ombudsman held exclusion from an occupational pension scheme to be indirect pay discrimination in breach of article 119 (*Shillcock v Uppingham School*, also on appeal).
45 The Social Security Maternity Benefits and Statutory Sick Pay (Amendment) Regulations (SI 1994/1367).
46 Statutory Maternity Pay (Medical Evidence) Regulations (SI 1987/235).
47 Social Security (Adjudication) Regulations (SI 1986/2218).
48 ERA, s 98(4).
49 ERA, s 99.
50 ERA, ss 108(3) and 109(2).
51 ERA, s 92.
52 ERA, s 92(4).
53 ERA, s 55.
54 ERA, s 106. Similar provisions are found in this section in relation to employees who replace someone absent because of medical suspension under ERA, s 64.
55 ERA, s 98(1)(b).

F O U R T E E N

Health and Safety: General Statutory Requirements

The purpose of this chapter is to describe the general legal framework of health and safety at work in terms of the criminal law and its enforcement. The civil process is described in chapter 15.

INTRODUCTION

Background[1]

The first legislation on health, safety and welfare was at the beginning of the nineteenth century, the focus being on health and welfare rather than safety.[2] In particular, there were restrictions on hours of work and provisions for cleanliness and ventilation. The legislation had limited effect: not only was it restricted in its scope, but there was no proper mechanism for enforcement. Voluntary, unpaid inspectors were appointed by local magistrates. Subsequent legislation prior to 1833 suffered from the same defects.

The Factory Act 1833 empowered the government to appoint paid factory inspectors but the numbers appointed were limited and the Act applied only to textile mills. Again, the legislation dealt with health and welfare, but not safety. However, the new inspectors quickly became aware of the problem of accidents and realised that the failure to fence and guard machinery was a major factor. The government called for a report on the issue and the inspectors provided this in 1841, arguing the case for safety legislation. Social reformers were in support of the case and attention was drawn to the issue indirectly in 1840 when Lord Shaftesbury took successful legal action for damages in negligence on behalf of an employee injured in a factory accident *(Cotterell v Stocks)*.

In fact it was the Coal Mines Act of 1842 which contained the first safety provision. However, the principal development was contained in the Factories Act 1844. This included prohibition on the cleaning of machinery that was in motion, required the fencing of certain machinery and provided for the reporting of accidents. Opposition by employers led to the 1844 Act being weakened by an amending Act in 1856 in respect of its fencing requirements.

The inspectorate developed in strength but from the outset adopted the method of working by persuasion and conciliation that remains one of its hallmarks. Legal action was used only when everything else had failed. Over many years there was a general extension of legislation to cover different types of workplace and different types of process. However, the effect was separate legislation for mines and quarries, agriculture and factories, and gaps in the legislation meant that not all employees had protection. There was a multiplicity of legislation even as regards factories, the first consolidation not occurring until the Factory and Workshop Act of 1901. By this time it was apparent that the inspectors were adopting a cautious approach to prosecution, and that in any event prosecution on a large scale would be administratively impracticable. Against this background, the development of the civil law was particularly important. Employees became able to use the statutory duties as a basis for civil actions for damages. The first succesful action for damages for breach of statutory duty was in 1898 *(Groves v Lord Wimborne)* (see chapter 15 on civil liability).

There were, of course, problems of interpretation such as: what was 'dangerous' machinery within the meaning of the Factories Acts. Major reforms removing outdated distinctions – such as that between textile and non-textile factories – were effected through the Factories Act 1937. This and subsequent amending legislation was then consolidated in the Factories Act 1961, parts of which are still operative. The first legislation relating specifically to shops was 1886 and offices 1960.[3] The Offices, Shops and Railway Premises Act 1963 consolidated the legislation. The principal legislation governing mines and quarries is the 1954 Act.[4]

Finally, there have been two major developments in the last 25 years. First, the patchwork history of health, safety and welfare legislation that extended over 172 years was reformed in 1974 by the HSWA. The new legislation was all-embracing in its coverage, removing the distinctions between different types of workplace and placing general duties upon employers, employees and others (see below). The intention was to replace the old, workplace-specific legislation with regulations issued under the 1974 Act, and to encourage employers, employees and others to take more responsibility for health and safety at work. Consequently, there has been increased emphasis on the management of health and safety at work. The 1974 reforms were based upon an analysis of the shortcomings of the old legislation carried out by the Robens Committee of Inquiry during the early 1970s.[5]

The second major development has been caused by the UK's membership of the European Union and the commitment of the European Union to the improvement and harmonization of health, safety and welfare in the Member States (see chapter 2). One effect of this has been to modify the more generalist approach of the HSWA by requiring detailed, prescriptive regulation. To date, this has been achieved mainly by issuing regulations under the HSWA.

The current statutory provisions are examined later in this chapter. Prior to this, however, it is necessary to consider some of the key words and phrases used in the legislation. An understanding of these is required if the duties laid down in the legislation are to be translated into actual management practice. The first step is to describe the legal framework.

The legal framework

Breach of statute law in this area gives rise to criminal offences, with prosecutions taken by the Health and Safety Executive or the appropriate local authority, and to claims for damages by injured parties for breach of statutory duty. Civil claims for such breaches are not, however, permitted on the basis of the general sections of the HSWA nor on the basis of the Management of Health and Safty at Work Regulations with the exception of maternity risks.[6] Nevertheless, injured parties might be able to sue for damages for negligence (see chapter 15). Much of the legislation laying down specific duties is in the form of regulations made under one of the major Acts, predominantly the HSWA, although some specific duties are laid down in the major Acts themselves. Regulations have the full force of law and are frequently backed by approved codes of practice. These have the object of providing practical guidance on the requirements contained in ss 2–7 of the HSWA, or in regulations, or in any of the existing statutory provisions. Approved codes of practice have a specific status (see page 268).

In addition to the statutes, the common law imposes duties upon employers (and employees). A major source of these duties is the law of tort (civil wrongs) under which an employer has a duty of care arising out of his or her position as employer and as owner or controller of premises. Thus, where the employer is also the owner or controller of premises his duty extends to people who are not employees. The duty of care towards employees is also found as part of the employment contract. It should be noted that criminal proceedings may be taken under the common law. Where negligence is gross, or behaviour reckless, a prosecution for manslaughter may occur. (see page 285) The prosecution would need to establish that the accused was aware of an obvious and serious risk as well as being guilty of the act or omission itself. Where senior employees who are in control of the organization were aware of such a risk and allowed such acts or omissions to occur, a charge of corporate manslaughter may accompany the charges against individuals. This happened in the prosecution following the capsizing of the ferry *Herald of Free Enterprise* and also in the *Lyme Bay* canoeing case, although the prosecution was successful only in the latter.

A number of features of legislation in the health and safety field are worth stressing. First, the law is often invoked, particularly in respect of the more serious cases. Secondly, one incident often gives rise to two separate cases – a civil case, pursued in the High Court or county court, and a criminal case, usually prosecuted in the magistrates' court (but sometimes the Crown Court). Thirdly, different parts of the legislation set different standards. Thus, some requirements are mandatory (that is, there is an absolute duty) and others need to be met as far as is practicable or as far as is reasonably practicable. Finally, health and safety is an area where EU law plays an increasingly important role. EU health and safety legislation is subject to the qualified majority voting process in the Council of Ministers (see chapter 2).

LEGAL TERMINOLOGY

Standards of care

Absolute

Where the statute states that something 'shall' or 'shall not' be done, there is an absolute requirement to comply. No test of practicability, nor indeed any other test, is to be applied. For example, the Provision and Use of Work Equipment Regulations 1992 state that:

> every employer shall ensure that work equipment is maintained in an efficient state, in efficient working order and in good repair.'[7]

Similarly, under the Management Regulations, 'every employer shall make a suitable and sufficient assessment ...[8]

Practicable

If the requirement is that a duty is to be fulfilled so far as is practicable, it is the responsibility of the person on whom the duty is placed to meet their obligaton as far as the current state of knowledge and invention allows. The burden of proving that the standard was met lies with the accused.[9] An example taken from the Management Regulations is: 'so far as is practicable', employees exposed to serious and imminent danger must be informed of the hazard and the protective measures.[10] A variant of this standard is the requirement to use the 'best practicable means'. The meaning of 'practicable' is dealt with on pages 270–71.

Reasonably practicable

'Practicable' implies a standard that is less strict than the absolute, and 'reasonably practicable' is less onerous than practicable. The quantum of risk is placed in one scale and the cost, inconvenience etc of preventive measures placed in the other. The onus of proof lies with the accused, but the test is the balance of probabilities. The general duties of employers in the HSWA are an example of the use of this standard.[11] The meaning of reasonably practicable is dealt with on pages 270–71.

Work and employment

The issue and significance of employment status was dealt with in chapter 5. A second issue which arises is whether the act or omission giving rise to the injury occurred at work, and, if at the workplace, whether it occurred during the course of work. The HSWA defines 'work' to mean 'work as an employee or as a self-employed person'.[12] An employee is at work when 'in the course of his employment'.[13] The definitions leave a lot of room for interpretation and the issue has been much considered in cases concerning civil liability (see chapter 15). These are not necessarily authority for criminal law and in one case a person driving to his place of work but already on the employer's internal road system just under 20 minutes before the start of his shift was held to be not in the course of his employment *(Coult v Szuba)*.

Other definitions

Personal injury

This is defined to include 'any disease and any impairment of a person's physical or mental condition'.[14] This is a very wide definition and one that is of considerable importance in view of the increasing incidence of stress-related illness arising out of overwork.

Competent person

Where there is a requirement to appoint such a person, the specific regulations and any associated materials (ACOPs or guidance notes) may provide assistance as to what is needed. There is no universal definition (see page 275).

Codes of practice and guidance notes

Approved codes of practice

A code of practice is defined to include 'a standard, a specification and any other documentary form of practical guidance'.[15] The HSC is empowered under the HSWA to approve and issue codes of practice (ACOPs).[16] The aim of such codes is to provide practical guidance on how to comply with the statutory requirements. The HSC must obtain the consent of the Secretary of State, after consulting appropriate bodies including government departments. Codes do not have the full legal status of Acts, Regulations or Orders (see chapter 1) but neither are they merely advisory. Rather, they can be seen as quasi-legal. A person will not be liable simply because they failed to observe the provisions of a code and this will be the case under both criminal and civil law. However, in criminal proceedings the breach of an ACOP, where the person is alleged to have committed an offence in respect of a matter to which the code relates, will cause the code to be admissible in evidence. Moreover, breach of the code will be taken as proof of a failure to comply with the statutory provisions unless the accused can show that compliance was achieved by some other equally satisfactory means.[17] Thus a breach of an ACOP creates a presumption of guilt which the accused must then rebut to establish their innocence. It seems unlikely that anyone following the provisions of an ACOP would be successfully prosecuted. Nothing is said about the status of ACOPs in civil proceedings but it seems likely that a breach would provide *prima facie* evidence of negligence. A successful defence would require the defendant to bring evidence to the contrary.

Guidance notes

In contrast to codes, guidance notes have no legal standing. However, they contain detailed practical guidance on how to comply with the statutory provisions, and are generally regarded as very useful supplementary material for those who have statutory duties. An important consideration is their use as evidence of the state of knowledge. Since the guidance is authoritative, being produced by the HSC, it is likely to be regarded as good evidence of what is known about particular risks and preventive measures at the time of issue. Thus it would be difficult for an employer to succeed with the argument that he was unaware of a risk if that risk and suitable preventive or control measures were dealt with in a set of guidance notes. For ease of access, the HSC publishes regulations, any ACOP and guidance notes in one booklet. The example overleaf is taken from the Workplace (Health, Safety and Welfare) Regulations, ACOP and Guidance Notes, 1992.

Example of integrated regulations, ACOP and guidance notes

Regulation 7
(1) During working hours, the temperature in all workplaces inside buildings shall be reasonable.'
ACOP
'43 The temperature in workrooms should normally be at least 16 degrees Celsius ...'
Guidance
[The guidance note contains details of relevant sources and indicates other, related statutory duties.]

GENERAL STATUTORY DUTIES

Health and Safety at Work etc Act 1974

General duty of employers to their employees
The philosophy behind this legislation is that the duties of employers should be set out in broad terms covering all sorts of employment situations – shops, offices, factories etc. The Act covers all persons at work except domestic servants in private households. Sets of regulations issued under the Act then deal with different types of work situations or different health and safety issues.

It should be noted that all those receiving training or work experience from an employer in the workplace, and who are not employees, are deemed to be employees for the purposes of health and safety legislation.[18]

The essence of the HSWA is a general duty imposed upon employers which requires them 'to ensure, so far as is reasonably practicable, the health, safety and welfare at work' of all their employees.[19] This general duty includes health and safety in relation to the:

- provision and maintenance of plant and systems of work;
- arrangements for use, handling, storage and transport of articles and substances;
- maintenance of the place of work and access to and egress from it; and
- working environment;

and includes the duty to provide:

- adequate welfare facilities; and
- necessary information, instruction, training and supervision;

and to consult with union safety representatives if there are any. A notice containing the main provisions of the Act must be posted.[20]

Employers must prepare a written statement of their policy with respect to the health and safety at work of their employees, and show it to an inspector if requested to do so. The statement must indicate the organization and arrangements in force to give effect to the policy and must be revised as often as is appropriate. The statement, and any revision of it, must be brought to the notice of all the employees.[21] There is a provision for exceptions, but the only exemption granted to date is for employers who employ fewer than five employees.[22] The number of employees relates to the undertaking rather than the site or establishment, and trainees count as employees for the purposes of these and other health and safety requirements. The HSC has produced a leaflet *Writing a Safety Policy Statement: Advice to Employers* (HSC6).

By virtue of s 235 of, and Sched 7 to, the Companies Act 1985, the Secretary of State has power to prescribe by regulations information to be contained in directors' reports about a company's arrangements for ensuring the health, safety and welfare of its employees, but this power has not yet been invoked.

Where, under the HSWA,[23] a safe system of work for the employer's own employees involves giving information and instruction to persons other than his or her own employees (the employees of a contractor, for instance) it must be given *(R v Swan Hunter Shipbuilders Ltd and Telemeter Installations Ltd)*. Thus, employers have a duty to provide relevant safety information to the employees of other employers working on their premises.

Meaning of 'practicable' and 'reasonably practicable'

'Practicable' means something less than physically possible. It means feasible – possible in the light of current knowledge and invention. Where the requirement is that something should be as safe as is reasonably practicable this means that the duty must be performed unless it is unreasonable to do so *(Marshall v Gotham and Co Ltd)*. The word 'reasonably' requires that a comparison be made between the risk of injury (including the severity of any injury which might occur) and the time, trouble and expense of preventive action. If there is gross disproportion between them (that is, the risk is insignificant compared with the preventive measures needed), the defence that an employer has done what was reasonably practicable will succeed *(Edwards v National Coal Board)*. Because reasonably practicable involves weighing the risks against the costs of prevention, employers will need to adduce evidence about the risks and costs involved, so influencing what is reasonably practicable. For example, in assessing the likelihood of risk a relevant consideration would be the length of time the employee is exposed to the risk. When considering preventive measures, doubts about the efficacy of those measures in reducing risk may be of relevance. The onus of proof lies upon the accused to show that it was not practicable or reasonably practicable to do more than was done.[24]

Duties owed to non-employees

The HSWA operates where people are at work rather than by specifying particular types of workplace. It therefore covers all premises including vehicles, movable structures and offshore installations. Under the Act employers have a responsibility to show the same standard of care towards non-employees (such as visitors and contractors) as they are required to show to their employees and, as noted, this duty includes provision of information and instruction *(Swan Hunter)*.[25] The duty is not restricted to the employer's premises. A self-employed person has similar duties. Both the self-employed and employers may be required to provide information to non-employees about the way in which their undertakings might affect such people's health and safety.

Persons who have 'to any extent, control of premises'[26] (but not domestic premises), or control access to or egress from such premises, have duties to persons other than employees and must take such measures as are reasonable for a person in that position to take, as far as is reasonably practicable. This does not extend to taking measures to guard against unexpected events *(Austin Rover Group Ltd v HM Inspectorate of Factories)*. Whether precautions in relation to someone else's use of the employer's premises are reasonable will depend upon:

- the employer's knowledge of the anticipated use of the premises; and
- the extent of control and knowledge of actual use.

In *Austin Rover*, contractors' employees were in breach of safety rules and the controller of the premises (Austin Rover) could not reasonably have been expected to foresee and to guard against this.

The Act also covers control of emission into the atmosphere of noxious or offensive substances from prescribed premises. These are premises and substances laid down in the Health and Safety (Emission into the Atmosphere) Regulations 1983 as amended.[27] The duty imposed is to use the 'best practicable means' for preventing the emission and to render harmless or inoffensive any substances emitted. (Part I of the Environment Protection Act 1990 and regulations thereunder contain further controls over air pollution).

Duties of designers, manufacturers and others

Duties are also placed upon designers, manufacturers, importers and suppliers to require the safe design and construction of articles, testing and examination and the provision of information indicating the designed use and precautions needed to avoid risks. Designers and manufacturers must carry out necessary research. Those erecting or installing articles are also responsible for safety. Parallel requirements exist in relation to manufacturers, importers and suppliers of substances. The standard of care is what is reasonably practicable to achieve safety and the absence of risks to health. This section of the Act has been stengthened by the Consumer Protection Act 1987.[28] Manufacturers and others must now consider reasonably foreseeable risks. Moreover, these risks are to be considered in relation to handling, maintenance and storage, as well as use. The requirement to provide health and safety information is also widened so that it covers revision (for example, in the light of new knowledge), applies not just to use, and covers situations such as foreseeable errors by users. Manufacturers and others must also take account of non-domestic premises other than workplaces to which they supply substances. As a result of the Control of Substances Hazardous to Health (COSHH) regulations there is now a much clearer onus upon employers to obtain health and safety information, and data provided by suppliers are a major source.

Duties of employees

As noted in Chapter 10, employees have a common law duty to go about their work with reasonable care. This is supplemented by the 1974 Act which lays upon employees a statutory duty of reasonable care towards themselves and those who may be affected by their acts or omissions.

There is also a statutory duty to co-operate with the employer or any other person in meeting the statutory requirements. Reasonable care includes the use of equipment provided for employees' safety. The employer must make sure that employees know of the equipment and must take steps, as far as is reasonably practicable, to get them to use it. Standards for personal protective equipment are now set down by an EU directive so that it is important for the equipment to meet these standards if a successful defence is to be raised by an employer. The duties of employees include not intentionally or recklessly interfering with or misusing anything provided for health, safety and welfare purposes in pursuance of the statutory provisions (this is a duty placed upon all persons and not just employees).

Individual employees can be, and occasionally are, prosecuted by the inspectors under these provisions. Moreover, as noted below, senior managers, as well as the organization, may be liable under the HSWA where they consented to or connived at the commission of an offence or neglected their duties.[29]

No charge may be made for anything done or provided in respect of any specific requirement of health and safety legislation.[30] Anything necessary as a result of an employer's PPE assessment is a specific requirement.

Safety representatives[31]

Regulations under the Act allow a recognized trades union to appoint safety representatives, with specified functions:

- to investigate potential hazards, dangerous occurrences and the cause of accidents;
- to investigate and process members' complaints about health and safety at work;
- to deal with management over general questions of health and safety;
- to carry out workplace inspections;
- to represent members in discussions with inspectors;
- to receive information from the inspectors; and
- to attend meetings of health and safety committees.

The Safety Representatives and Safety Committees Regulations have been extended by the Management Regulations of 1992. There is now a specific duty placed upon employers in respect of consultation with safety representatives and the provision of facilities and assistance. The duty to consult, as laid down in the Management Regulations, covers:

- any change which may 'substantially' affect employees' health and safety;
- the appointment of a competent person to assist with health and safety;
- the appointment of a person responsible for implementing emergency plans;
- information and training requirements; and
- the introduction of new technology.[32]

A code of practice and guidance notes give further detail. As far as is reasonably practicable a safety representative should have been employed by their employer for the previous two years, or have had at least two years' experience of similar employment.[33] Employers must provide safety representatives with facilities for inspections, including the opportunity for independent investigation and discussion. However, employers are entitled to be present during inspections.[34] Safety representatives can have access to any documents kept by their employer for statutory health and safety purposes, except those relating to the health and safety of individuals, and in general are entitled to information which it is necessary for them to have to perform their duties. Safety representatives are not entitled to information where:

- disclosure would be against the national interest;
- disclosure would result in contravening a statutory prohibition;
- it relates to an individual (unless the individual gives their consent);

- apart from health and safety effects, the information would cause substantial injury to the employer's undertaking, or where the information was supplied to the employer by some other person, to the undertaking of that other person; or
- information was obtained for the purpose of any legal proceedings.

Disclosure is restricted to documents or parts of documents which relate to health, safety or welfare.

Safety representatives are the appropriate people to receive information from the inspectors about particular occurrences in the workplace, and any action that inspectors take or propose to take. Safety representatives are given a right to time off in order to perform their functions, and also for training.

A separate code of practice covers time off for training.[35] This states that basic training should be provided as soon as possible after appointment. There should also be further training for any special responsibilities or changes in legislation or work circumstances. Training should be approved by the TUC or the independent trades union to which the safety representative belongs. However, the code does not have full legal status: the law requires such training as may be reasonable in all the circumstances. While such circumstances include the code, the ultimate test is reasonableness. Thus in *White v Pressed Steel Fisher Ltd* the employer was reasonable in refusing time-off for union safety representative training when it preferred its own in-company course.

The code states that basic training should include the role of safety representatives, and safety committees. These should be related to the legal requirements, the nature and extent of workplace hazards and precautions and the employer's health and safety policy. The training should also develop skills, for example, accident and incident investigation, conduct of inspections and use of legal and official sources. Management should be provided with a copy of the syllabus on request. Normally, a few weeks' notice should be given of the names of safety representatives nominated to attend a course. The numbers should be reasonable taking into account the availability of courses and the operational requirements of the employer. Union training for safety representatives should be complemented by employer training which should focus upon the technical hazards of the workplace, relevant precautions for safe methods of work and employer organization and arrangements for health and safety.

A safety representative may complain to an industrial tribunal if refused reasonable time off or refused pay for such time off. Where at least two safety representatives request it in writing, an employer is required to establish a safety committee. The overall function of such a committee is to keep health and safety measures under review.[36]

Management of Health and Safety at Work Regulations 1992[37]

Introduction

With the exception of merchant shipping, these regulations apply to all workplaces and workers (including the self-employed). They flesh out some of the basic principles already established in the Health and Safety at Work Act and are accompanied by an Approved Code of Practice (ACOP) which gives some detail of how to comply with the Regulations.

Regulation 3: risk assessment

Employers (and the self-employed) must make 'suitable and sufficient' assessments of the risks to employees and others who may be affected by their work activities in order to identify the measures necessary to comply with the law. Significant findings must be recorded where there are five or more employees.

Unfortunately the ACOP does not give illustrations of risk assessments but it does stress that it should normally be a straightforward process with specialist skills and quantitative techniques only necessary in the more complex situations, eg chemical plants, nuclear installations.

Regulation 4: health and safety arrangements

Arrangements must be made through planning, organization, control, monitoring and review for putting the measures identified under reg 3 into effect. Again these must be recorded where there are five or more employees.

Regulation 5: health surveillance

This may be required if problems are likely and there are valid techniques for detecting them.

Regulation 6: health and safety assistance

Employers must appoint one or more 'competent' persons to assist them in undertaking measures to comply with the law. The numbers, time available and resources must be adequate for the size and risks of the undertaking.

'Competence' is regarded as a knowledge and understanding of the work involved and health and safety principles and practices together with the capacity to apply this.

Formal competence-based qualifications provide a guide but in simple situations an understanding of relevant practices, a willingness and ability to learn and an awareness of one's own limitations may be sufficient.

Small employers may appoint themselves if they are competent.

Regulation 7: procedures for serious and imminent danger and danger areas

Procedures must be established and put into effect for foreseeable emergencies including sufficient competent persons to implement evacuations if necessary. Where specific danger areas are identified (eg, due to electrical or chemical risks) access to these must be restricted.

Regulation 8: information for employees

Employees must be given 'comprehensible and relevant information' on risks they are exposed to, appropriate countermeasures, emergency arrangements and other special procedures.

Regulation 9: shared premises

Employers sharing workplaces (temporarily or permanently) must co-operate, co-ordinate and inform each other on health and safety matters.

Regulation 10: persons working in host employers' or self-employed persons' undertakings

The host must give visiting employers comprehensible information on risks arising out of or in connection with the host's undertaking and measures taken by the host to comply with the law (where this relates to visiting employees).

Hosts must also ensure visiting workers are given instructions and information on risks and emergency/evacuation procedures.

Regulation 11: capabilities and training

Employees must be given adequate health and safety training following recruitment, transfer, responsibility change or the introduction of new or changed equipment, technology or systems of work.

Account must be taken of health and safety capabilities in entrusting tasks to employees.

Regulation 12: employees' duties

Employees must use machinery, equipment etc in accordance with their training and instructions. They must also report dangers or shortcomings which affect them or arise out of their work.

Regulation 13: temporary workers

Information must be given to contract staff or agency employees on special safety-related qualifications or skills needed and any health surveillance required before they commence duties.

Agencies must be given such information and pass it on to their employees.

Regulations 14–17
The remaining regulations allow exemption certificates to be issued in certain defence-related situations; exclude civil liability; and modify the SRSC Regulations as indicated earlier. The regulations apply to Great Britain and to certain premises and activities outside Great Britain.

Recording and reporting

Introduction
The occupier of a workplace – usually the employer – is required to keep particular registers and must display certain forms and notices under the various safety statutes. The HSE issues a comprehensive, free catalogue of its publications[38] and a complete list of forms can be obtained free of charge from any HSE enquiry point. The requirements include the following items:

- to display the HSWA poster or distribute equivalent leaflets;
- notification of accidents form; employers will probably need a supply of these; copies of the form can be used as a book;
- an accident book, for DSS purposes;[39] and
- an up-to-date certificate of insurance: this must be displayed by virtue of the Employers' Liability (Compulsory Insurance) Act 1969 (see chapter 15).

In addition, there are specific requirements under particular sets of regulations as well as under the main Acts themselves. The Factories Act, for instance, requires registers showing the testing, inspection and examination of chains, ropes and lifting tackle. A failure to display notices, submit forms or keep registers is a criminal offence.

Under the Factories Act 1961 and the Offices, Shops and Railway Premises Act 1963 an employer will need to register his occupation of premises with the relevant authority using the prescribed form.

Reporting of Injuries, Diseases and Dangerous Occurrences Regulations 1995 (RIDDOR)
These regulations create a legal obligation to report certain incidents to the relevant enforcing authority: fatalities and major injuries; dangerous occurrences; diseases; and injuries causing more the three days' incapacity.[40]

ENFORCEMENT OF THE LAW

The Health and Safety Commission (HSC)[41]

Constitution

The HSC is a body corporate established by the HSWA. It consists of a chairman and six to nine other members, chairman and other members being appointed by the Secretary of State for Employment. Before appointing the members (other than the chairman) the Secretary of State must consult organizations of employers (in respect of three members), organizations of employees (in a further three cases) and local authorities and other bodies concerned with health, safety and welfare (with regard to the remaining three). The HSC began to operate in 1974.

Duties[42]

The Commission is under a duty 'to do such things and make such arrangements as it considers appropriate' to give effect to the Act's general purposes. Principally, these are:

- to secure the health, safety and welfare of persons at work; and
- to protect those not at work from the activities of those at work.

More specifically, it has a duty:

- to assist and encourage persons concerned with matters relevant to the HSWA's general purposes to further those purposes;
- to make arrangements for and encourage research, publication of research findings, provision of information and training in relation to the Act's purposes;
- to provide an advisory and information service for those concerned with the Act's purposes; and
- to make proposals for regulations.

The HSC plays a major role in proposing and shaping new legislation, particularly in the context of EU directives.

The Commission reports to and is under the direction of the Secretary of State. In 1993, the government directed the Commission to undertake a review of health and safety legislation to determine whether the legislation could be reduced and simplified. The results and implications of this review are discussed in Bateman, King and Lewis.

Powers[43]

The Commission has the power to do anything (except borrow money) which 'is calculated to facilitate, or is conducive or incidental to' the performance of its functions. This includes appointing persons or committees to provide it with advice. A number of such committees have been formed covering particular classes of hazards and particular industries, and *ad hoc* committees may be established to deal with specific problems.

The HSC may issue codes of practice and guidance notes as described earlier (see pages 268–9). It may also set up investigations and enquiries, for example, where there has been an accident or occurrence, if this will assist it in its statutory duties. For there to be an enquiry, the consent of the Secretary of State is required. The report of an enquiry or investigation may be made public in part or in whole. An enquiry is a formal device with a statutory procedure.[44] The matter under consideration is likely to be of public interest. In contrast, an investigation may be less formal and the investigator has freedom to determine the procedure. Nevertheless, rules of natural justice must be followed and evidence should be taken from anyone able to make a positive contribution.

The Health and Safety Executive (HSE)

Constitution and functions
The HSE is a body corporate consisting of three people one of whom is appointed by the Commission, with the approval of the Secretary of State, to be director. The other two members are also appointed by the Commission with the approval of the Secretary of State, but after consultation with the director.[45] The Executive exercises the functions of the Commission and is directed by the Commission. Thus, the HSE is the operational arm of the HSC. However, the Commission cannot direct the Executive on the enforcement of the law in any particular case.[46]

Structure of the HSE
Its basic job of inspections and work in the field is done by its Field Operations Division which incorporates the former Factory, Agricultural and Mines and Quarries Inspectorates and the Employment Medical Advisory Service (EMAS). The HSE is now responsible for the work formerly done by the Railway Inspectorate and for offshore oil and gas safety. Other divisions of the HSE (eg, health policy) provide back-up services in relation to both policy and operations. National interest groups for particular industries exist to provide specialist information.

Method of working
A major feature of the inspection process is the advice and encouragement given to employers to improve health and safety. Although the inspector carries a big stick, the day-to-day role is very much one of reasoning and persuasion. The aims are to establish what is going on, to encourage improvements, find out how the legislation is working and to assess new

technological developments. A principal consideration is whether there is a commitment to health and safety – has management organized a system, and is it monitored and, if necessary, modified? The statutory written health and safety policy is the framework within which the HSE carries out its inspections. An assessment of management's ability to organize and maintain a safe workplace is formally recorded at the end of the inspection. Where there are problems, the improvement notice (see below) is a useful device. The average manager is likely to come into contact with an inspector at some stage: it could be through a routine inspection, because of an accident or complaint, or because the HSE is carrying out a special study or survey (eg, of small firms).

A report by the National Audit Office in 1994 suggested that the HSE was understaffed.[47] The report showed that the Executive had failed to assess 132 out of 331 reports on major hazard sites in the UK. Some 300 further reports were expected to be submitted in the following two years, threatening to increase the backlog.

Employment Medical Advisory Service

Next, there is the medical arm of the HSE, the Employment Medical Advisory Service (EMAS).[48] This has a field staff of employment medical advisors (doctors) and employment nursing advisors (nurses). For statutory purposes the employment medical advisors have the same powers of entry and investigation as inspectors. The role of EMAS includes research, the provision of health advice and information and the medical examination of people working on hazardous operations. An employment medical advisor cannot force a person to be examined against his will.

The public information role of the HSE and the HSC

Finally, there is the public information role of the HSE and the HSC. They play a major role in the supply of information about health and safety at work. Their very large output ranges from detailed technical publications to free basic information leaflets. The HSE has public enquiry points and a fax information service.

The criminal process

Notices and prosecutions

Enforcement is principally by the HSE, although local authorities are responsible for enforcement in certain premises and for enforcing the implementation of general fire precautions. The Commission retains responsibility for guiding enforcement agencies which are outside the HSE. The allocation of enforcement responsibilities is determined by the Health and Safety (Enforcing Authority) Regulations 1989, issued under the HSWA.[49]

These increased the local authorities' coverage by reallocating premises including those used for leisure and consumer services, churches and other places of religious worship, and premises used for the care, treatment and accommodation of animals.[50] Certain lower risk construction work carried out in premises where local authorities already had enforcement responsibilities was also reallocated. The 1989 Regulations allocate to local authorities responsibilities for enforcing the HSWA and relevant statutory provisions, subject to certain specific exceptions, in all premises where the main activity is listed under Sched 1 to the Act. Broadly speaking, local authorities have responsibility under the 1989 Regulations for:

- premises where the main activity is the sale or storage of goods for retail or wholesale distribution;
- office activities;
- hotels and catering; and
- places of entertainment.

It should be noted, however, that the 1989 Regulations allocate to the HSE sole responsibility for the enforcement of s 6 of the HSWA in relation to articles and substances for use at work including at those premises where the local authority would enforce the remaining provisions of the 1974 Act.

In terms of local authority enforcement, the principal role is performed by district councils and usually by the department which has an environmental health function. In addition, county councils (in England and Wales) and regional councils (in Scotland) have responsibilities such as those in relation to petroleum licensing, certain explosives including fireworks, and the packaging and labelling of dangerous substances in consumer premises. Enforcement in these areas is carried out by trading standards officers or fire authorities as appropriate. Some of these 'county' functions, however, are performed at district level, for instance where the district is a metropolitan one or a London borough. If there is doubt about whether enforcement is in the hands of the HSE or a local authority (or which local authority), employers can check with the HSE. In each HSE area there is an enforcement liaison officer.

If there is a breach of duty an inspector may serve an improvement notice, or a prohibition notice, or may prosecute. An improvement notice will apply where the inspector alleges a breach of statutory duty. The inspector will describe in the schedule to the notice the practical steps which should be taken. The notice will specify a time period within which the improvement(s) must be made, although this is often negotiable. An employer may appeal to an industrial tribunal within 21 days against either the allegation of a breach or the shortness of the time period if, for example, this would cause undue difficulty for the production process. The appeal has the effect of suspending the notice. Very few employers appeal, and, of those who do, very few succeed. This is not surprising: the HSE inspector is not only a health and safety expert but also has the full technical, medical and research backing of the HSE at his disposal. Where an inspector believes that there is a risk of serious personal injury he may serve a prohibition notice, which can have immediate effect. There is again a right of appeal but this does not suspend the notice unless an industrial tribunal so directs. The normal industrial tribunal costs rule does not apply.[51] In these cases costs may be awarded against the losing party at the tribunal's discretion. Because the Crown cannot prosecute the Crown, the HSC issues Crown notices where improvement or prohibition notices would be used (in the Civil Service for example) although these have no legal force.

Any breach of the general duties in the 1974 Act or of specific duties under other health and safety legislation is a criminal offence, as is obstructing an inspector or giving him false information. An employer will be liable for the acts of his or her employees during or arising out of the course of their employment. Where an offence is committed with the consent or connivance of, or due to the neglect of, any director, manager, secretary or other similar officer, the individual as well as the organization is to be held guilty.[52] Thus, in *Armour v Skeen* the inspector prosecuted a senior employee because he had been given the responsibility for drawing up the health and safety policy, but had not done it. However, in *R v Boal* it was held by the Court of Appeal that the assistant general manager of a book-shop was not a 'manager' within the meaning of s 23 of the Fire Precautions Act 1971.[53] Within the Act, and the same can be said about the HSWA, the term 'manager' means managers who have corporate responsibility and are thus directing the policy of the organization.[54] A manager in such a position may be individually liable. The other basis for the individual liability of managers lies in the duties placed upon employees, and here the duties of a manager may be more onerous because his acts and omissions may be capable of causing greater injury than an 'ordinary' worker (eg, by instructing subordinates to use incorrect or faulty equipment, or unsafe methods of working). The legislation does not lay duties upon managers as a category: rather the duties are laid upon employers, employees and others.

Where there is a breach of an approved code of practice issued under the HSWA this will be taken (in criminal proceedings) as conclusive proof of a contravention of a requirement or prohibition unless the court can be satisfied that there was compliance by some other method.[55] Prosecution for breaches of the HSWA is limited to inspectors save for permission otherwise by the Director of Public Prosecutions; nor can the Act be used for the purposes of civil claims, that is for breach of statutory duty. Regulations under the HSWA and legislation enacted prior to the HSWA can be used for civil purposes unless they state otherwise.

A successful prosecution for a breach of the HSWA requires proof beyond all reasonable doubt, as in criminal cases more generally. Thus, the relevant enforcement authority may decide not to prosecute if they conclude that the evidence is not strong enough. This was the case in relation to the *Piper Alpha* oil platform disaster in the North Sea in 1988, which resulted in the death of 167 men.

Powers of inspectors[56]

The powers of the inspectors are substantial. They have the right to:

- enter premises;
- make examinations and inspections;
- take samples;
- take possession of articles and substances;
- take measures and photographs;
- make recordings;
- keep things undisturbed;
- have something tested, removed or dismantled;
- obtain information and have answers to questions; and
- inspect and copy any entry in documents to be kept under statute.

Facilities and assistance must be provided for inspectors in connection with any of the above. Inspectors have any other powers necessary to fulfil their responsibilities. Where there is 'imminent danger of serious personal injury' an inspector may seize an article or substance and render it harmless.[57] An inspector does not need to give prior notice of a visit but an employer or occupier of premises is entitled to see proof of an inspector's identity prior to entry. An inspector may disclose relevant information to anyone who is a party in civil proceedings.[58]

Where an inspector exceeds his powers, there can be a civil action against him. Enforcing authorities have the power to indemnify their inspectors in such cases.[59]

Powers of the courts

Maximum penalties for different types of offence are laid down in the HSWA. On summary conviction the maximum is £5,000 (ie, level 5; see page 18) except for those offences set out in the Offshore Safety Act 1992. Despite its specific title, this Act makes some generally applicable changes to penalties for certain offences under the HSWA.

In the magistrates' courts (the sheriff court in Scotland), fines of up to £20,000 may be imposed for breaches of:

- ss 2–6 of the HSWA;

- an improvement notice;
- a prohibition notice; and
- a court remedy order.

According to the HSE, 25–33 per cent of prosecutions are for such breaches.[60] There can be imprisonment of up to six months for breach of a notice or a court remedy order. The time limit for commencement of prosecution for a summary offence is six months.

In the Crown Court, there are no time limits for commencement of prosecution for indictable offences. There can be imprisonment for up to two years for certain offences including breach of a notice or court remedy order. A company director convicted of an indictable offence may be disqualified from being a director under the Company Directors Disqualification Act 1986.

In the Crown Courts, on indictment, the fines are unlimited. In addition, the courts can order specific forms of action in order to ensure safety.

In all courts, a fine relates to a particular offence. It is quite common for an incident to give rise to more than one offence. Fines totalling £750,000 have been recorded (BP, 1987) and, unlike in civil cases, employers cannot insure against criminal liability. An example of multiple penalties is given below (prior to the 1992 increases in fines). Fines and imprisonment are not necessarily alternative penalties: they may be used together.

- *Company:* company machine not securely fenced £25,000; failure to register a factory £500; and breach of a prohibition notice £1,000
- *Managing director:* machine not securely fenced £15,000; failure to register a factory £500; and charge of manslaughter to lie on file.
- *Director:* machine not securely fenced £5,000; and one year prison sentence suspended for two years.[61]

Employer defences

An employer's defence will be that there is no breach of statutory duty. For example, it might be maintained that there is little or no risk, therefore what has been done in the way of prevention is all that is reasonably practicable. An employer is unlikely to be successful in arguing that financial difficulties facing the firm mean that safety improvements cannot be afforded. Some of the statutory provisions provide for a defence of due diligence. For example, under the Control of Substances Hazardous to Health (COSHH) Regulations 1994 it is provided that 'it shall be a defence for any person to prove that he took all reasonable precautions and exercised all due diligence' to avoid committing an offence.[62] The burden of proof will lie with the accused; the test of proof will be the balance of probabilities. The issue will be a matter of fact for the court to decide.

Manslaughter

The criminal process is not restricted to enforcement of the statutory provisions: criminal cases can be based on breaches of the common law. In particular, where there is gross negligence at common law, there can be a prosecution for manslaughter and the accused may be an individual or a corporation. There have been a number of successful manslaughter prosecutions of individuals, but only one of a corporation: in the *Lyme Bay* canoe case. The successful prosecution of a corporation requires it to be shown that at least one of the company's 'controlling minds' was grossly negligent about an obvious risk of death or injury. It is not sufficient to show that there was collective negligence in the sense that a number of people were each responsible for part of the negligence. This helps to explain the unsuccessful prosecution of P&O European Ferries following the sinking of the *Herald of Free Enterprise.*

NOTES

1 A useful source, and one that has been relied upon here, is *The Development of Factory Legislation* (Royal Society for the Prevention of Accidents, undated (but no earlier than 1963), General Information Sheet No 8). On health and safety more generally, see Bateman, King and Lewis, *The Handbook of Health & Safety at Work* (Kogan Page, 1996).

2 The Health and Morals of Apprentices Act 1802.

3 Shop Hours Regulation Act 1886 and Offices Act 1960.

4 Mines and Quarries Act 1954.

5 See *Report of a Committee*, Chairman Lord Robens (1972).

6 HSWA, s 47; and Management Regulations, reg 15.

7 Provision and Use of Work Equipment Regulations (SI 1992/2932), reg 6(1).

8 Management Regulations, reg 3(1).

9 HSWA, s 40.

10 Management Regulations, reg 7(2).

11 See, for example, HSWA, s 2.

12 HSWA, s 52(1).

13 *Loc cit.*

14 HSWA, s 53(1).

15 *Loc cit.*

16 HSWA, s 16.

17 HSWA, s 17.

18 The Health and Safety (Training for Employment) Regulations (SI 1990/1380). There are additional health and safety safeguards for young people: see the Health and Safety (Young Persons) Regulations (SI 1997/135).

19 HSWA, s 2(1).

20 The poster is entitled 'Health and Safety Law: What You Should Know'. The requirement to display it (or to distribute leaflets with the same title) arises out

of the Health and Safety (Information for Employees) Regulations (SI 1989/682).

21 HSWA, s 2(3).

22 The Health and Safety Policy Statements (Exception) Regulations 1975.

23 HSWA, s 2(1) (general duty), s 2(2) (a) (safe system of work), and s 2(2) (c) (information and instruction).

24 HSWA, s 40.

25 HSWA, s 3(1).

26 S 4(2).

27 SI 1983/943 as amended by SI 1989/319. The Alkali etc Works Regulation Act 1906 and other provisions require that certain works must be registered with the Secretary of State for the Environment. The registration system was modified recently by SI 1989/318.

28 HSWA, s 6; Consumer Protection Act 1987, s 36 and Sched 3.

29 HSWA, s 37.

30 HSWA, s 2.

31 Safety Representatives and Safety Committees (SRSC) Regulations (SI 1977/500). Consultation rights are given to employees by the Health and Safety (Consultation with Employees) Regulations 1996.

32 Management Regulations, reg 17 and Schedule.

33 SRSC reg 3(4).

34 SRSC reg 5.

35 Code of Practice on Time Off for the Training of Safety Representatives. This was issued under reg 4(2)(b) of the SRSC Regulations (London, HSC, 1978).

36 HSWA, s 2(7).

37 Management Regulations (SI 1992/2051).

38 *Publications in Series* (London, HSE, 1990). Requirements relating to the display of posters were rationalised by the Health and Safety Information for Employees (Modifications and Repeals) Regulations 1995.

39 Social Security (Claims and Payments) Regulations (SI 1979/628). The HMSO book is form BI510. Other documents are acceptable if they contain the same information.

40 For further detail, see Bateman, King and Lewis, *The Handbook of Health & Safety at Work* (Kogan Page, 1996), pages 194–199.

41 HSWA, s 10 and Schedule 2.

42 HSWA, ss 1, 11 and 12.

43 HSWA, ss 11, 13, 14 and 16.

44 The Health and Safety Inquiries (Procedure) Regulations 1975.

45 HSWA, s 10 and Sched 2.

46 HSWA, s 11(4).

47 *Enforcing Health and Safety Legislation in the Workplace* (report from the National Audit Office, London, HMSO, 1994).

48 HSWA, Part II.

49 HSWA, s 18.

50 The Health and Safety (Enforcing Authority) Regulations 1989.

51 The normal rule is that costs will be awarded only where a party acts frivolously, vexatiously, abusively, disruptively and otherwise unreasonably in

bringing or conducting their case (Sched 1, rule 12 to the Industrial Tribunals (Constitution and Rules of Procedure) Regulations 1993). Another procedural difference is that because the criminal law is involved an appeal against the decision of an industrial tribunal lies with the Divisional Court of the Queen's Bench Division of the High Court (see chapter 1) instead of with the EAT.

52 HSWA, s 37.

53 He was not a 'manager of the body corporate' (Fire Precautions Act 1971, s 23) because he had no responsibility for corporate policy and strategy. The Court of Appeal had a duty under s 2(1) (a) of the Criminal Appeal Act 1968 to allow an appeal if a conviction was unsafe or unsatisfactory.

54 HSWA, s 37.

55 HSWA, s 16.

56 HSWA, s 20.

57 HSWA, s 25.

58 HSWA, s 28(9).

59 HSWA, s 26. Actions against inspectors, the HSE and the HSC may be possible through the Parliamentary Ombudsman and through an application for judicial review.

60 HSE Press Notice E189: 92, October 1992.

61 *Works Management*, April 1990, page 5.

62 COSHH Regulations 1994, reg 16.

Health and Safety: Civil Liability

In chapter 14 it was seen that the cornerstone of health and safety law is the framework provided by the HSWA, and in particular the general duties it imposes. It was seen that the HSWA establishes a criminal law system for dealing with health and safety matters but does not provide a basis for civil actions. Civil actions are likely to be founded in the common law of negligence or breach of statutory duties other than those in the HSWA. In addition, there is an overlap between health and safety and the wider law of employment in respect of employee protection on health and safety grounds and questions of health and safety discipline. All these areas of civil law form the substance of the present chapter. The starting point is the civil process under common law, beginning with the different courses of action that are available.

DUTIES OF EMPLOYERS AND OTHERS AT COMMON LAW

Types of action

An injured person may have three types of possible legal case under the common law, all of which involve a claim for damages:

- breach of statutory duty (this constitutes a tort);
- breach of contract (through negligence); or
- negligence in tort.

In the absence of provision to the contrary, civil action can be taken for breach of a duty contained in a statute by someone injured as a result of the breach. In fact, there is such provision to the contrary in the HSWA so that breaches can be subject to legal action by the enforcement agencies but cannot be used as a basis for civil claims.[1] The same is not true of earlier legislation still in force, such as the Factories Act 1961. Thus employees may take a case on the basis of breach of statutory duty if a claim on the basis of negligence is ruled out, and *vice versa*. It should be noted that employer defences in the statute are in respect of criminal proceedings. They relate only indirectly to civil cases.

The basis of a worker's claim for damages arising out of an employer's negligence is as follows:

- the employer owes the worker a duty of care;
- the employer has not fulfilled that duty; and
- as a result, the worker has suffered injury or damage to health.

The origin of the duty of care is found in the law of tort (civil wrongs: see pages 7–8). The liability of the employer which arises in this respect is in tort. However, a duty of care also flows from the contract of employment, so an action for damages for breach of contract would also be possible in cases where the relationship is governed by such a contract. Nevertheless such actions are rare because the basis for the action is narrower. Actions for damages in tort are not limited to parties to a contract and encompass provision for greater damages. Even where there is a contract of employment the duty of care in the law of tort does not arise from the fact of contractual relations: it arises from the fact of the employee working for the employer. The employer's liability goes beyond situations where the employee is acting in the course of their employment. The test is whether the circumstances were within the control of the employer.

The duty of care

The concept of reasonable care
Employers have a duty of reasonable care for the safety of their employees, and the responsibility extends to the premises of third parties to which they send their employees. They also have a duty of care towards independent contractors, although the degree of care is less in such cases. The duty of reasonable care is part of a general duty which the common law imposes upon everyone in order to provide protection against injury. The word 'injury' here tends to mean physical or mental injury or harm to property – protection against economic loss (such as loss of livelihood) is much more restricted unless it flows from injury to the person or his or her property.

The employer's duties are a particular application of the general duty to take reasonable care.

What is meant by 'reasonable care'? In general it means avoiding acts and omissions which a person can reasonably foresee would be likely to injure their neighbour *(Donoghue v Stevenson)*. A neighbour is anyone who is so affected by my acts or omissions that I ought reasonably to have these effects in mind. Liability arises, therefore, where there is not reasonable care to prevent reasonably foreseeable risk. Foresight has to be assessed on the basis of what is known (or should reasonably be known) at the time. Therefore, courts may set a date by which a reasonable employer would have been aware of a particular risk and have taken precautions (1 January 1978 in the case of vibration white finger: *Bourman v Harland and Wolff plc)*. The employer cannot delegate his duty of care – it is a personal duty and he will be liable even if the job of fulfilling the duty has been given to an employee (see vicarious liability, pages 296–8). An employer in breach of the duty of care at common law will be committing the tort of negligence, for which the usual remedy is an award of damages (see pages 299–301). The key requirement is that the employer (or other duty-holder) must be at fault. There will be no liability if there is no negligence – for example, if the risks could not have been foreseen, or were not under the duty-holder's control. (The position is different where the action is founded on a breach of statutory duty: see, for example, *Morris v Breaveglen Ltd* where the employer was liable even though the employee was under the control of a temporary employer.)

The test is an objective one (what the reasonable person would have done) rather than a subjective one (what the judge thinks is reasonable). The approach is to weigh the risks of injury against the costs and other drawbacks of the preventive action. It follows that the degree of care required is determined by balancing risk against the actions necessary to prevent or reduce it. Risk is judged in terms of how likely it is that an injury will occur and how serious it would be. The cost of preventive action will figure highly in the equation. The degree of care may vary according to the worker, for example how experienced they are, because this affects the likelihood of the injury occurring. Furthermore, in a case where the employee had only one eye, it was held that the duty of care was heavier because the seriousness of any injury to that person's eye was greater than for the normal employee *(Paris v Stepney Borough Council)*. If the injury is caused by a manufacturing fault, the employer will not, ultimately, be liable if they could not reasonably tell that something was wrong. However, if the employer knew that there was something wrong and kept the machine in use they will be in breach of their duty of care. The Employers' Liability (Defective Equipment) Act 1969 provides that, where an employee suffers injury in the course of their employment in consequence of a defect in equipment provided by their employer and the defect is wholly or partly attributable to the fault of a third party, the injury will be deemed to be attributable to the negligence of the employer. This leaves the employer to recover damages from the third party, for example the manufacturer of the machine.

The duty of care may be divided into a number of specific parts:

- safe premises;
- a safe system of work;
- safe plant, equipment and tools; and
- safe fellow workers.

Safe premises

An employer is under a duty to provide a safe place of work but not absolutely, since the approach already discussed involves weighing risks against costs and inconvenience in order to determine the standard of care that is reasonable. Thus, although there is an obvious danger of electrocution where employees work near live rails, it would not be reasonable to require the current to be switched off every time there were minor repairs to be done, since this would cause substantial disruption to the working of the railway *(Hawes v Railway Executive)*. Where exceptional expenditure is needed in order to achieve a safe workplace, it will not be required if the risk is slight (eg, the danger of slipping on an oily, wet floor: *Latimer v AEC*) but is likely to be required if there is imminent risk of death or serious injury (eg, the danger of falling from a height: *Bath v British Transport Commission*).

If the employees' workplace is unsafe because of a third party and the employees' supervisor is aware of it but does nothing, the employer as well as the third party may be liable. This might occur where the employer is a subcontractor on a building site and his employees are working in unsafe conditions because of an act or omission by the main contractor, as in *Smith v Davies*. The duty of care is not removed because the employee is working on someone else's premises, nor because these premises are in another country *(Square D Ltd v Cook)*. Rather, what can reasonably be expected of the employer is less onerous. If the work is lengthy or poses an unusual hazard, it may be reasonable to require an inspection.

If an employer knows of a hazard, or should have known about it, and fails to take precautions in a reasonable time, he may be in breach of his duty of care. An adequate maintenance and housekeeping system, therefore, is an important consideration in ensuring that the duty of reasonable care is discharged. The duty to provide a safe place of work extends to providing safe access and egress.

A safe system of work

Part of a safe system of work is the provision of safety equipment. In *Crouch v British Rail Engineering Ltd,* the duty of care was not fulfilled by making safety goggles available for collection from a point about five minutes away. The lack of immediate availability encouraged risks to be taken. In *Pape v Cumbria County Council,* the employers provided gloves for cleaners handling chemical cleaning materials but the duty of care went beyond this; it extended to warning the cleaners about handling such materials with unprotected hands and instructing them as to the need to wear gloves at all times. The COSHH Regulations 1994 now require these steps to be taken.

In general, a safe system of work means that working practices should be safe. This implies that there should be adequate training, safety equipment and supervision, and may require the employer to provide incentives or take disciplinary action.

Supervisors cannot be expected to watch all of their employees all of the time. Nor are they expected to tell the employee what is obvious and commonsense in terms of precautions *(Ferner v Kemp).* Thus, an employer was not liable for not issuing new safety boots: it was the employee's duty to know that his old ones needed replacing *(Smith v Scot-Bowers).* However, where there is a danger which the employee cannot reasonably be aware of, the employer should reduce the risks and/or warn the employee.

Where employees ignore safety precautions (eg, because they slow the work and reduce the bonus) employers may be liable if they do not enforce discipline or make adjustments to pay or time *(Broughton v Lucas*: the employer was 75 per cent liable where the employee ignored safety precautions). Similarly, where employees refuse to wear safety clothing (eg, because it is uncomfortable), the employer must take all reasonable steps to get them to co-operate, especially if the risks are not obvious *(Crookall v Vickers Armstrong*; *Bux v Slough Metals).* This might include personal instruction, personal issue of the equipment, periodic checks as to use in practice, incentives, disciplinary action and safety awareness training. As a result of the PPE Regulations, the employer has a statutory duty not only to provide safety equipment but also to take all reasonable steps to ensure it is used.

On the other hand, there is no duty to stand over an experienced worker, so once instructions are given and proper equipment provided there may be nothing more that an employer can be expected to do *(Woods v Durable Suites).* Nor, where the risk is obvious and the employee knows that safety clothing is available and will make the work safer, is there any liability on the part of the employer for not telling the employee what he already knows if he chooses not to wear the safety clothing and is injured *(Qualcast v Haynes;* followed in *James v Hepworth & Grandage).* The rule that an employer does not have to tell an experienced, skilled worker to wear safety equipment (here a safety belt when working at a height of almost 100 feet above the ground) was also upheld where the employer did not have the equipment available. This was because when belts had been provided in the past they had not been worn. On these facts, the provision of belts and attempts to secure their use would not have affected the outcome and the employer was not held to be liable *(McWilliams v Arrol)*. This case illustrates that the injury has to be caused by the employer's failure. Here there was no causation because the belt would not have been worn even if provided.

In general, an employer should ensure that:

- the employee is warned about risks;
- the employee is instructed as to the precautions to be taken;
- safety clothing or equipment is available;
- the employee is issued with the clothing or equipment or knows it is available; and
- reasonable steps are taken to secure employees' co-operation in using safety equipment or clothing.

It is submitted that these factors apply as much to safe working procedures as they do to clothing and equipment. Establishing safe working procedures, instructing employees that they must be followed, instructing them in their use and checking periodically for actual use may demonstrate that an employer has taken reasonable steps to secure a safe system of work.

It should be noted that a safe system of work is one that avoids mental as well as physical risk. Therefore, a system in which a manager is under-resourced and overworked will not be a safe system where the manager makes his position known to his employer and there is a reasonably foreseeable risk of psychiatric damage *(Walker v Northumberland County Council)*.

Safe plant, equipment and tools

The question is again one of balancing risk against expense and effort. The precautions generally taken in the particular industry will provide some evidence of what is appropriate, but employers will not be able to hide behind a general practice of inaction *(Thompson v Ship Repairers; Baxter v Harland and Wolff)*.

Part of the duty of care will be met by adequate testing and maintenance, and ultimately renewal of plant. Thus, employers should periodically check the functioning of plant, equipment and tools (for example, the functioning of an electric drill: *Bell v Arnott and Harrison*).

Another aspect of the duty of care in respect of plant, equipment and tools is the need to keep up to date with relevant health and safety knowledge, especially that published by trade journals and official sources such as the HSC *(Ransom v McAlpine)*. The significance of this stems from the fact that the availability of knowledge determines the date from which the employer should have known about a risk and taken appropriate precautions.

Where there are hidden defects, the employer would not be liable at common law but the manufacturer probably would be *(Davie v New Merton Mills)*. However, the Employers' Liability (Defective Equipment) Act 1969 places strict liability on the employer (ie, no negligence is required), leaving the employer to seek redress against the manufacturer or other negligent party *(Clarkson v Jackson)*. Equipment includes plant, machinery, clothing, vehicles, ships and aircraft. It also extends to materials with which the employee is working: paving slabs in *Knowles v Liverpool City Council*.

Safe fellow workers

Fellow workers will generally be safe if they are competent to perform the work and are properly instructed and supervised. Fulfilling the duty of reasonable care means, therefore, that an employer should:

- select suitably qualified people to do the job *(Birnie v Ford)*;
- provide adequate training; and
- provide instruction and supervision which is competent in terms of safety.

The requirements for training, instruction and supervision may be greater where the worker is young and inexperienced and employers need to take extra care in order to be sure that immigrant workers have understood what they must do *(Hawkins v Ross)*.

Although a worker may be competent and properly instructed, he nevertheless may constitute a risk because of general behavioural characteristics. Employers may be liable if they know that someone presents such a risk but take no action *(Ryan v Cambrian Dairies*, bullying; *(Hudson v Ridge*, practical jokes).

Similarly, in assessing the risks, an employer should not limit himself to contemplating the risks faced by the prudent, alert and skilled workman going about his task. The risks facing the careless worker may also be reasonably foreseeable (see *Uddin v Associated Portland Cement Manufacturers Ltd* for an example of where this principle has been applied).

Negligence

Negligence occurs where there is a breach of the duty of care. In terms of the above definition of the duty of care this means that the actions taken by an employer to prevent or reduce risk were inadequate for the level of risk which was reasonably foreseeable. It should be noted that an employer cannot use a contract term or a notice to exclude or restrict liability for death or personal injury resulting from negligence.[2] The onus of proof of negligence lies with the plaintiff, who must also show causation, that is, that the negligence caused the injury, and that the employer had a reasonable and safer alternative to what they did. However, in the absence of an explanation of the cause of the injury there is what almost amounts to a presumption of negligence. This is because courts may infer from the immediate facts of the case that negligence occurred. It is particularly likely where *res ipsa loquitur* (the thing speaks for itself). Therefore, the plaintiff can establish a *prima facie* case on the immediate facts even if there is no direct proof that a negligent act or omission caused the injury. This discharges the plaintiff's burden of proof, leaving the defendant to rebut the inference of negligence by showing that the cause of the injury was not negligence.

If the action is against the defendant in the capacity of employer it will need to be established that the plaintiff was acting in the course of their employment when they received their injury. Where the injury was sustained in working hours on the employer's premises this is likely to prove difficult to challenge, especially if the employee was performing tasks in the employer's interest. Acting in the course of employment means carrying out acts which have been authorized by the employer, as well as some that have not been authorized, in order to fulfil contractual obligations (see page 297). The latter, however, must be connected with authorized acts in that they can be regarded as ways of performing such acts. Anything normally and reasonably incidental to a day's work, such as going to the toilet, to the canteen or to collect tools or materials, will also be included.

In contrast to the above, there was breach of statutory duty under the Offices, Shops and Railway Premises Act 1963 even though an employee had no authority to be where he was. The legislation applies regardless of whether an employee is in the course of his employment. Since there was no warning of danger there was no contributory negligence on the part of the employee *(Westwood v Post Office)*. Similarly in *Uddin* there was a breach of s 14 of the Factories Act 1961 where the employee was injured on unfenced machinery while trying to catch a pigeon. More recently, in *Smith v Stages and Darlington Insulation Co Ltd*, the House of Lords set out guidelines for helping to decide when travel associated with work is in the course of employment.

An employee paid wages (rather than a travelling allowance) to travel in their employer's time to a workplace other than their regular workplace will, *prima facie*, be acting in the course of their employment. The guidelines are as follows:

- travelling from home to a regular workplace will be in the course of employment if the employee is compelled by the contract of employment to use the employer's transport, unless there is an express condition to the contrary.
- travelling in the employer's time between workplaces will be in the course of employment.

- receipt of wages (as distinct from a travelling allowance) is indicative of travel being in the course of employment.
- travel in the employer's time from home to a workplace other than the regular workplace will be in the course of employment.
- incidental deviation or interruption to a journey taken in the course of employment will not take the employee out of the course of employment, but anything more would do.
- return journeys are to be treated on the same footing as outward journeys.

Where the action lies against the defendant in the capacity of occupier of premises the test is again whether there has been a breach of the duty of care. As a result of the Occupiers' Liability Act 1957, a statutory duty of care is owed to persons authorized to be on the premises.[3] The occupier's actual degree of control over the premises will be an important factor in determining liability. The Occupiers' Liability Act 1984 defines the duty owed to trespassers.

Vicarious liability[4]

It is a rule of law that an employer is liable to persons injured by the wrongful acts of his employees if committed in the course of their employment. This is known as vicarious liability. The injured party may sue the employer and/or the employee, knowing that employers are required to have insurance cover as a result of the Employers' Liability (Compulsory Insurance) Act 1969.

Where the injured person sues the employer directly, negligence on the part of the employer must be demonstrated. Where the injured person sues the employer vicariously, negligence on the part of the employee must be shown. Once shown, the employer is strictly liable, ie no fault on the part of the employer needs to be demonstrated. The right of non-employees to sue an employer vicariously is long-established in common law; the employee's right to sue directly stems from the Law Reform (Personal Injuries) Act 1948. Where an employer is sued vicariously he may obtain an indemnity from the employee who committed the wrongful act *(Lister v Romford Ice and Cold Storage)*.

A prerequisite for vicarious liability is the committing of a legal wrong – a tort, breach of contract or crime. An error of judgment, an Act of God or some unexpected event will not fall into this category. The employee's wrongful act must be in the course of his employment. This means that the employee must be engaged in performing his contractual duties, albeit in an unauthorized way. Acts which are normally and reasonably incidental to an employee's work – such as going to the toilet or to a canteen – are also included. The following selection of cases illustrates where the dividing line is drawn in this matter.

Acts which were in the course of employment

- A tanker driver causing an explosion by smoking while unloading petrol, despite a clear prohibition – the employee was performing his duty to unload petrol *(Century Insurance Co v Northern Ireland Road Transport Board)*;
- a works doctor failed to give proper advice to his employer and another employee died from cancer as a result *(Stokes v GKN)*;
- a solicitors' clerk swindled his employer's clients under cover of his duties *(Lloyd v Grace Smith)*;
- a driver took an extended route and caused an injury while doing so: he was employed as a driver *(Williams v Hemphill)* (but note that such an act may be regarded as the employee engaging in a 'frolic of his own');
- a milkman took on a boy to help him with his round: he was going about his contractual work *(Rose v Plenty)*; and
- a resident porter who stole tenants' property: it was his job to look after the property *(Nahhas v Pier House)*.

Acts which were not in the course of employment

- A driver employed to carry his employer's employees carried the employees of other employers, despite a prohibition, and injured them: it was not his job to carry other employer's employees *(Conway v Wimpey)*;
- a bus conductor drove a bus in the depot and caused injury: it was not his job to drive buses *(Iqbal v London Transport)*;
- a postman wrote insulting messages on letters: it was not his job to do so *(Irving v The Post Office,* but this may no longer be good law: see *Jones v Tower Boot* on page 117); and
- a cleaner made unauthorized telephone calls while on a client's premises: it was not part of the employee's job to make telephone calls *(Heasmans v Clarity Cleaning)*.

Practical jokes are likely to be outside the course of employment, but may not be if carried out by an employee abusing his authority over a subordinate *(Chapman v Oakleigh Animal Products; Bracebridge v Darby)*.

Vicarious liability is a principle extending beyond personal injury. There can be liability for breaches of contract by an employee unless the employee enters into the contract without actual or apparent authority – in which case the employee would be liable for breach of warranty of authority, or for fraud if there is an intention to deceive.

There is also vicarious liability for crime. Usually the employee is convicted while the employer is liable for damages. Examples include the delivery driver who exceeds the speed limit in the course of his deliveries and the resident porter who steals the tenants' property instead of protecting it (*Nahhas*: see above), but there was no liability for the cleaner who made telephone calls from the client's office (*Heasmans*: see above).

The vicarious liability of employers is stronger in respect of employees than in relation to independent contractors. This is explained historically by the fact that an employer can instruct his employee as to the manner of the work but cannot so instruct an independent contractor. Therefore there is less control, and accordingly, less responsibility. This was the origin of the 'control' test to determine whether a worker was an employee or an independent contractor. In practice, under modern-day conditions, the distinction is less easy to draw. Professional employees determine their own methods of work, while small contractors working for a major business organization may be instructed in detail. The legal test has developed therefore into a multiple test:

- is there a requirement for personal service?
- what is the degree of control?
- are the other characteristics of the relationship consistent with a relationship based upon a contract of employment *(Ready Mixed Concrete v Minister of Pensions)* (see pages 78–9)?[5]

Vicarious liability for contractors arises when the contractor is employed to do work which creates a danger for the public and when the work is done negligently *(Walsh v Holst)*. This might arise, for example, where a contractor is brought in to construct a new building and does so negligently. However, there will be no liability for contractors where the injury is incidental to rather than inherent in the work: for example, the employer's employee stands on a plank with a nail in it, left by the contractor *(Taylor v Coalite)*. Negligent selection or supervision of contractors will give rise to direct rather than vicarious liability.

Duties of occupiers and suppliers

Just as the employer's duty of reasonable care is part of the wider responsibility laid down in law, so too are the duties of occupiers and suppliers. These are duties owed to non-employees, eg visitors and users. Where the occupier or supplier has substantial control, the duty of care may be as great as that of an employer *(Garrard v Southey)*, but generally their duties are less strict because visitors and users are not their employees *(Jones v Minton)*.

The civil liability of occupiers is laid down in the Occupiers' Liability Acts of 1957 and 1984 (in Scotland, an Act of 1960). The legislation covers land, buildings and structures (fixed or movable, such as vehicles and scaffolding) and in England and Wales distinguishes between the lawful visitor and the trespasser. An occupier is the person in immediate occupation or control, although control (and hence liability) may be shared. The occupier is not necessarily the owner.

The duty of the occupier is to take reasonable care to ensure that lawful visitors are reasonably safe in using the premises for the agreed purposes of their visit. Business occupiers cannot exclude liability for death or injury by negligence (Unfair Contract Terms Act 1977). Historically this was done through exclusion notices. Typically the occupier must warn the lawful visitor about known hazards which the visitor is unaware of or cannot avoid. The degree of care must be what is reasonable in the circumstances.

Where the hazard is apparent, the visitor will be under a duty to take more care, and where the visitor is a contractor, the occupier is entitled to assume that the contractor will take all appropriate precautions against the risks of his own trade. Providing the contractor has been selected with reasonable care (and properly supervised if the occupier is the main contractor), the occupier will not be liable for the contractor's negligence (except in Scotland).

Where the visitor is a trespasser, the law imposes a lesser duty upon the occupier (except in Scotland). If the occupier knows or ought to know of the danger, knows someone may be near it and knows that he ought reasonably to offer some protection, he must take reasonable steps to prevent the trespasser being injured. Warnings are one such step. Trespassers whose presence is condoned are likely to be regarded as lawful visitors.

The duties of suppliers are parallel to those of occupiers. There will be liability if all reasonable care is not taken, eg for defective design, faulty workmanship or inadequate information, advice or warning for users. The liability may be reduced or removed if the product is used for an unintended purpose or where the user or his employer may be expected to test the goods himself. Anyone suffering personal injury as a result of a defect in a product may sue under the Consumer Protection Act 1987. Liability attaches to the producer: that is, the manufacturer, 'own brander' or, if outside the EU, the importer. There is strict liability unless the defendant can show that the state of scientific knowledge at the time did not enable him to discover the defect.

LITIGATION

Actions for damages

The Law Reform (Personal Injuries) Act 1948 gave employees the right to sue their employer by abolishing the principle that employees in common employment accepted the risks of their work. In the process, vicarious liability was allowed. The general rule now is that employers (principals) will be liable for the acts and omissions of their employees (agents), that is, they will be vicariously liable. The limiting factor is that the employee's act or omission must be in the course of employment or linked with it in the ways described above (page 297). Moreover, the courts have held that the person entitled to tell the employee how to do work would generally be liable for that employee's negligence, even if the employee is an employee of another company (see *Sime v Sutcliffe Catering (Scotland) Ltd*).

Vicarious liability does not mean that individual employees, whether managers or not, cannot be sued, since under the contract of employment (and in tort) the employee has a duty of reasonable care. In practice, however, the likelihood of a civil action is quite small since the sums involved in damages claims are larger than an individual could normally pay. The position would be entirely different if the individual had insurance cover. Most employers accept vicarious liability as a fact of life and the necessary insurance as an unavoidable cost of production.

The fact that a worker has not complained does not prove that the work-place is safe or that he thinks it is safe. Nor, on the other hand, does a complaint prove that it is unsafe. Complaints or their absence may help or hinder an action for damages, but are unlikely to be conclusive. If a specific complaint is made the employer must investigate and, if it is found to be justified, he must take action if he is to avoid liability. If there is a clear complaints procedure an employee may be partly responsible for his own injury if he does not use it properly and as a result the employer does not take the necessary precautions *(Franklin v Edmonton Corporation)*.

The time limit for commencement of claims is three years from the time of knowledge of the cause of action.[6] The time of knowledge will be the date on which the cause of action occurred or the date on which the plaintiff knew or should have known there was a significant injury and that it was caused by the employer's negligence. Where the person is fatally injured, the three years can be applied from the time of death or from the date of the personal representative's knowledge, whichever is later. Other exceptions are possible on grounds of equity.

Employers must be insured against such actions as a result of the Employers' Liability (Compulsory Insurance) Act 1969. The insurance must cover injury and disease arising out of and during the course of employ-ment. Cases will be heard in the county courts or High Court (see page 13 for details of the allocation criteria). Convictions (for instance, under the HSWA) are admissible as evidence: therefore, they can be cited as indicating civil liability. A breach of an approved code by an employer also substantially assists the plaintiff in discharging the burden of proof. A plaintiff may want to see the accident report in an attempt to establish their case. Such reports will be protected from disclosure by legal professional privilege only where use in possible litigation was the 'dominant purpose' of the report *(Waugh v*

British Railways Board). The dominant purpose of accident reports is usually to establish why the accident happened, so there may not be protection against disclosure. The plaintiff may also obtain information from an inspector.[7] Where the employer seeks a medical report, the provisions of the Access to Medical Reports Act 1988 may apply and, where the employee seeks medical information from a health professional, the Access to Health Records Act 1990 may be relevant.

Finally, the Civil Liability (Contribution) Act 1978 allows the plaintiff to take action against any of the tortfeasors (those who have allegedly committed torts), leaving the defendant to claim from others who contributed to the tortious act.

Damages are divided into special and general. The former covers provable loss to the date of the trial – loss of earnings, damage to clothing and so on. The loss of earnings is net loss. The general damages cover the remaining forms of loss such as pain and suffering before and after the trial and future loss of earnings. The broad aim is restitution – putting the injured person back where they were before the accident happened, in as much as money can do this *(British Transport Commission v Gourlay)*. Where appropriate, a money value will be put on disfigurement, loss of enjoyment of life, nursing expenses and the inability to pursue personal or social interests.

Under the Fatal Accidents Act 1976, certain dependent relatives can claim for the financial loss they suffer but not in England and Wales for the shock, grief and so on that they experience. Since 1985 a plaintiff may seek provisional damages and may return to apply for further damages in due course. However, the courts cannot declare that if a person dies before making that further claim their surviving dependents will have an entitlement to claim under the 1976 Act *(Middleton v Elliott Turbomachinery Ltd)*. Under s 17 of the Judgments Act 1838 interest is payable on damages, but only from the date of that judgment in which the amount of damages is determined. Where there has been a split trial, interest is not backdated to the judgment on liability *(Lea v British Aerospace plc)*. A number of statutory social security benefits are deductible from awards of damages. This principle does not extend, however, to benefits under an occupational pension scheme *(Smoker v London Fire and Civil Defence Authority)*. The principle laid down by the House of Lords in *Parry v Cleaver* is that the fruits of money set aside in the past, through private insurance, cannot be appropriated by the tortfeasor. Nevertheless, employers and insurance companies are at liberty to draft pension schemes in such a way as to negate the effect of this principle.

Defences

The burden of proof of liability lies upon the employee but the employer may reduce or remove liability by succeeding with one or more defences.

Despite the employer's duty of care, there is also a duty on the part of the employee, and where the employee is partly to blame there is said to be contributory negligence.

Contributory negligence

An employer may argue that the injured person was careless or reckless and was solely or partly to blame for their own injuries by, for example, ignoring clear safety rules. Contributory negligence might include contribution to the seriousness of the injury by the failure to wear available safety equipment. Where the injured person is partly to blame, the Law Reform (Contributory Negligence) Act 1945 requires that the damages be reduced rather than the claim defeated.

Courts will apportion liability according to the degree of fault. Accidental errors are distinguished from failure to take reasonable care *(Hopwood v Rolls Royce)* and recklessness or disobedience tend to be viewed seriously. Where the action is in respect of a breach of strict statutory duty rather than negligence, the impact of the employee's conduct (in terms of reduced damages) may be less (see below).

There was no contributory negligence where an employee misjudged whether he could safely lift a load *(Gallagher v Dorman Long)*, nor where a lapse of concentration resulted in the employee falling through the top of an unguarded tank *(Donovan v Cammell Laird)*. Nevertheless, there may be contributory negligence where employees fall over objects on the floor or otherwise act carelessly, work in obviously dangerous conditions *(Campbell v Harland and Wolff)* or would not have used safety equipment even if had been provided *(Simmons v Walsall Conduits)*. The most serious contributory negligence is likely to be a breach of safety rules (see *Qualcast v Haynes*).

In actions for breach of statutory duty the test for contributory fault is stated as being recklessness rather than mere carelessness *(Foster v Flexile Metal; McGuiness v Key Markets)*, but in practice it is difficult in a number of contributory negligence cases to see how the employee has been reckless (eg, *Mullard v Ben Line Steamers*).

Injuries not reasonably foreseeable

An employer may argue that the type and/or the extent of injuries sustained by the plaintiff were not reasonably foreseeable as a result of the employer's breach of duty of care. The plaintiff has the burden of proof in demonstrating that such injuries could be foreseen as arising out of that particular negligence. The employer's defence may be that the injuries were caused by an Act of God, that is, something beyond normal expectation and control. An employer may argue remoteness – that the injury was not in a category which could have been foreseen, the reason being that some unforeseen factor(s) intervened in the situation. There must be reasonably foreseeable cause and effect *(Overseas Tankships v Morts Dock (The Wagon Mound))*.

Delegation

An employer cannot exclude liability by delegating his duty to an employee *(Driver v Willett)*. However, delegation might be a complete defence where the employee delegated to perform the duty is solely to blame for his own injury *(Manwaring v Billington)*. In other cases liability is likely to be shared *(Boyle v Kodak)*. Where the duty is delegated to contractors, the question is whether reasonable care was taken in selecting and relying upon that contractor *(McDermid v Nash)*.

Voluntary assumption of risk

In extreme cases an employer may succeed in escaping liability on the grounds that the employee had consented to taking risks as part of the job – risks other than those inherent in performing the job as safely as is reasonable practicable. This defence – *volenti non fit injuria* (one who consents cannot complain) – is argued on the basis of the plaintiff's knowledge and acceptance of the likelihood of the occurrence of a tortious act. It can apply to negligence but cannot apply to breach of statutory duty because the effect would be to allow the employee to contract out of Parliamentary protection.

Injury not sustained in the course of employment

It may be argued that the injury was not sustained in the course of employment. This could be because:

- the injury was not sustained at work at all; or
- it was sustained at work and during working hours, but the employee was performing unauthorized acts, which could not be regarded simply as unauthorized ways of performing authorized functions (a defence to liability here will be an express prohibition; such a prohibition will not, however, remove liability as regards unauthorized methods of performing authorized tasks).

Absence of vicarious liability

An employer may try to avoid liability by arguing that they are not vicariously liable. In cases of alleged vicarious liability it has to be established, first, that the employee is liable; and, secondly, that the employer is vicariously liable for the employee's act(s) or omission(s). There may not be liability for the actions of an employee in the following situations:

- where the employee is 'lent' to another employer and is working for, and under the control of that other employer: vicarious liability may be transferred in such cases, the question of control being paramount;
- where the employee knows (or should have known) that what they have done is expressly outside the limits of their authority; or

- where the actions of the employee are excessive, for example a security guard who uses excessive violence against an intruder.

EMPLOYMENT PROTECTION IN HEALTH AND SAFETY CASES

Right of employees not to suffer detriment or dismissal

There are important provisions in the ERA which aim to protect employees from action by employers taken against them on grounds of health and safety at work.[8] The employee has a new right not to suffer detriment and the existing right not to be unfairly dismissed is strengthened by making dismissal in health and safety cases automatically unfair and by removing the two-year continuous employment qualification. In addition, selection for redundancy on health and safety grounds is also automatically unfair and again there is no qualifying period of employment required before an employee can exercise his or her right.

The health and safety activities which are protected are:

(1) carrying out health and safety activities having been designated by the employer to carry out such activities;
(2) performing or proposing to perform functions as a union safety representative or safety committee member when holding such a position;
(3) bringing to the employer's attention work circumstances which the employee reasonably believed were harmful or potentially harmful in situations where there is no safety representative or committee or where it was not reasonably practicable to raise the matter by those means;
(4) leaving or proposing to leave or refusing to return to work where the employee reasonably believed there was serious and imminent danger which he could not reasonably be expected to avert; and
(5) taking or proposing to take appropriate steps to protect himself or others from what he reasonably believed was serious and imminent danger.

Both (4) and (5) are capable of being regarded by managers as a breach of discipline (eg, refusing to work or to obey an order). See pages 307–8 for the common law position. First-aiders are likely to be included under (1) above. In (2) the representative or member must be either a statutory or employer-recognized representative or committee member. Under (3), the employee, when bringing matters to the employer's attention, must use 'reasonable means'. In (4) the right to refuse to return applies only while the danger persists; and in (5) the 'appropriate steps' will depend on all the circumstances applying, including the employee's knowledge and the facilities and advice available at the time. An employer has the defence that the employee's steps (or proposed steps) were (or would have been) so negligent that the employer reasonably responded in the way he did. The Minister may by Order extend these rights to trainees who are not employees and the government intends this to be done. Where the person dismissed is a safety representative, safety committee member or some other designated health and safety person, compensation will be at the enhanced level applied in cases of dismissal for union or non-union reasons. Interim relief is also available.[9]

The onus will be upon the employer to show why the dismissal or other detrimental act was taken and the provisions restricting the unfair dismissal rights of those taking industrial action are removed where the dismissal is on health and safety grounds.[10]

Suspension from work on maternity grounds

An employee is suspended from work on maternity grounds when she cannot work because of a specified statutory requirement or because of a specified recommendation in an approved code of practice under HSWA, s 16. Where there is suitable alternative employment the employee has a right to be offered it before any suspension. Where suspension occurs, the employee has a right to be paid during that suspension.[11] (See page 242).

Medical suspension or dismissal

Under ERA, an employee, or someone in Crown employment, who is suspended on medical grounds, has a right to be paid for up to 26 weeks. They must be suspended under a statutory requirement or under a code of practice issued or approved under s 16 of the HSWA and specified in ERA, s 64(3).[12] The qualification is one month's continuous employment.[13] An application may be made to an industrial tribunal within the usual three-month period. The employee must be available for work and not incapable of work because of illness or injury.

Where a suspension does not fall under the ERA provisions, the employee may be able to mount a challenge on the grounds of breach of contract, possibly resigning and claiming constructive dismissal. The employee would have much less chance of success in cases where the suspension was with pay. If a dismissal is ultimately effected it will be subject to the usual requirements of unfair dismissal law provided that the employee has two years' qualifying employment (the qualifying period will be only one month if the dismissal is for a reason which would otherwise give rise to a medical suspension under ERA). First, is there a fair reason? Breach of statute is one of the reasons laid down. Secondly, has the employer behaved reasonably? In this respect proper procedure is important as is investigation of the possibilities of a transfer to other work if the organization is sufficiently large.

In cases where the fitness of the employee is in dispute the provisions of the Access to Medical Reports Act 1988 may be of relevance. A further problem may arise where colleagues refuse to work with a person because of medical factors. AIDS is a particular example. What if, despite medical evidence to the contrary, employees will not work alongside an AIDS virus carrier? In the event of a dismissal a tribunal would have to be convinced that this was a substantial reason for dismissal and that the dismissal was altogether reasonable (see chapter 16).

Industrial tribunals

Employment protection matters in relation to health and safety at work are dealt with by industrial tribunals. The jurisdiction of industrial tribunals is found in UK statutes, but it now appears that complaints may be pursued directly on the basis of European law in the absence of a UK statutory right. A common law jurisdiction was added in 1994 but this excludes claims for damages in respect of personal injuries.[14] The current jurisdiction of industrial tribunals on the basis of UK statutes, and in respect of health and safety at work is:

- appeals against improvement and prohibition notices;
- time off work with pay for union safety representatives;
- the right to receive pay while suspended on medical grounds;
- the right to receive pay while suspended on maternity grounds; and
- the right not to be dismissed or suffer other detriment in health and safety cases.

Appeals against industrial tribunal decisions can be made to the Employment Appeal Tribunal (EAT) in most cases only on a point of law (that is, not generally on the grounds that the tribunal got its facts wrong). Appeals against industrial tribunal decisions on matters relating to improvement and prohibition notices lie, as noted earlier, with the Divisional Court of the Queen's Bench Division (see chapter 1).

SAFETY DISCIPLINE

Disregard of safety rules or procedures

Employees who disregard safety rules and procedures may be subject to discipline, including dismissal, in the same way as if there were a breach of some other type of rule (on discipline generally, see chapter 16). All the usual requirements laid upon employers need to be met: rules must be reasonable, applied consistently and fairly, and communicated to employees and the procedure for handling disciplinary breaches must be reasonable. A dismissal for a safety breach would need to be defended in the light of the normal requirements of unfair dismissal law.

An employer may seek to change existing safety rules or introduce new rules. If the change is a direct result of new legislation, the employer will be under a duty to meet the statutory requirements. Where the change stems from a policy change rather than a change in legislation an employer will need to consider the existing terms of employment and whether the change can represent a breach of contract. The procedure for implementation (advance warning, consultation and so on) may be important. For example, employers introducing no-smoking policies might justify their actions on the basis of their general duties under the HSWA, provide employees with evidence to support this, give advance warning, perhaps survey employee opinion or consult in other ways and provide some facilities for smokers after the rule becomes operative.

Refusal to work on grounds of lack of safety

Apart from where the ERA provisions apply (see above), what is the legal position if an employee refuses to work because what they are being asked to do seems to them to be unsafe? On the one hand the employee has a contractual and statutory duty to take reasonable care, so that they may feel that they will be in breach of such a duty. On the other hand, they are required by the terms of their contract of employment to obey the lawful commands of their employer. The critical question here is whether the employer's command is lawful. This means it must not only be within the terms of the contract, but also must not involve the employee engaging in a criminal act, or indeed being unable to act with due care. The problem is that opinions may well differ and neither party is likely to be able to wait for a legal ruling. The advice of specialists (safety managers, union representatives and perhaps even factory inspectors) is about as far as one can go. If there is a refusal to work the matter may then become a disciplinary one.

As part of their contractual duty to provide their employees with a safe system of work and take reasonable care of their safety, employers must investigate all *bona fide* complaints about safety brought to their attention by employees *(BAC Ltd v Austin)*. Failure to do so could give grounds for an employee to resign and claim unfair constructive dismissal. A failure to take complaints seriously could also amount to a breach of the term of mutual trust and confidence (see pages 178–9), again opening the way to a claim of unfair constructive dismissal (see *Bracebridge v Darby*: failure to deal with a complaint of sexual harassment). If the employee chooses to stay but refuses to do the work, the question of whether or not the employer is in breach of a contractual term or a statutory duty will not be conclusive in determining the fairness or otherwise of any consequent dismissal. The test will be reasonableness *(Lindsay v Dunlop Ltd)*. Relevant factors may include the attitude of other employees in the same position and what steps the employer is taking to deal with the safety problem. Employers might fare better if they did not treat refusal to work on safety grounds as straightforward disobedience. Dismissing for refusal to work before there has been a proper investigation of the employee's complaint and before the results of that investigation have been communicated to the employee may well be unfair. Any employee with a special condition ought to be treated as sympathetically as possible and alternative duties considered, especially if the condition is likely to be temporary. Pregnant women anxious about the effects of working at VDUs might fall into this category.[15]

In *Piggott Brothers and Co Ltd v Jackson*, an employer's failure to get a definitive explanation of the cause of the employees' symptoms (experienced as a result of exposure to fumes) was held to amount to unreasonableness. This was so even though ventilation had been improved and the problem had been investigated by HSE inspectors who thought it was a 'one-off' that had ceased to exist. Dismissals for refusal to work were held to be unfair. The Court of Appeal would not disturb these findings – the decision was a permissible option on the facts.

NOTES

1 HSWA, s 47. There is a similar restriction on civil liability in the Management of Health and Safety at Work Regulations (the Management Regulations), reg 15.
2 Unfair Contract Terms Act 1977, s 2.
3 Occupiers' Liability Act 1957; and Occupiers Liability (Scotland) Act 1960.
4 The rules described here relate to the common law test for vicarious liability. The test may be different when set in a statutory context: see *Jones v Tower Boot Co Ltd* on page 117.
5 Limitation Act 1980.
6 Under s 28(9) of the HSWA.
7 ERA, ss 44 and 100.
8 On the general provisions in relation to unfair dismissal, including interim relief, see chapter 16.
9 This is done by TURERA, Sched 8, paras 76 and 77 amending the Trade Union and Labour Relations (Consolidation) Act 1992, ss 238 and 254.
10 ERA, s 68. Provisions are specified when contained in a Ministerial Order issued under ERA, s 66(2).

11 ERA, s 64. The provisions specified in s 64(3) are the Control of Lead at Work Regulations (SI 1980/1248), reg 16; the Ionising Radiations Regulations (SI 1985/1333), reg 16; and COSHH Regulations 1994, reg 11.

12 On the rules for continuous employment see ERA, ss 210–219. Major changes were effected through the Employment Protection (Part-Time Employees) Regulations (SI 1995/31). There is no longer any hours requirement for the accrual of continuous employment. Thus, part-time employees now qualify for various statutory rights.

13 Industrial Tribunals Act 1996, s 3; and the Industrial Tribunals Extension of Jurisdiction (England and Wales) Order (SI 1994/1623) (SI 1994/1624 for Scotland).

14 On this see (1990) 433 *IDS Brief* 10.

SIXTEEN

Wrongful and Unfair Dismissal

This chapter is concerned principally with the law of unfair dismissal. However, apart from an unfair dismissal complaint there are two other types of legal action which may be taken by a person who is dismissed. These are, first, the use of public law, and secondly, suing for remedies for breach of contract. Where that breach of contract relates to dismissal it is known as wrongful dismissal.

This chapter starts by distinguishing between wrongful, unfair and public law dismissals. Thereafter, it deals exclusively with the law of unfair dismissal.

DISTINGUISHING THE CONCEPTS: WRONGFUL AND UNFAIR DISMISSAL

Wrongful dismissal

A wrongful dismissal is one where the dismissal is in breach of contract. Remedies can be sought by anyone who is employed under a contract of employment. There are no qualifying rules in relation to, for example, age, number of hours worked or length of employment. The remedies are sought from the employer. The basis of the case would be that the employee has been dismissed, and that the dismissal is in breach of one or more of the terms of the contract. Thus, a dismissal with less than the required contractual notice would be wrongful (as would be one with less than the statutory minimum notice if greater) unless the employee agrees to wages in lieu (the law tends to regard wages in lieu as damages for breach of contract). A dismissal during the term of a fixed-term contract which had no provision for termination by notice during its term would also be wrongful dismissal. So too would be a dismissal without the employer going through contractual appeals machinery, or through the disciplinary procedure as a whole if that were contractual (see *Dietmann v London Borough of Brent*). The manner of the dismissal may involve a breach of the term of trust: for example, dismissal in a blaze of publicity amidst unsubstantiated allegations of dishonesty.

Damages are the principal remedy available for wrongful dismissal, but where the employer had the right under the contract to terminate it with notice the damages will be limited to wages for the contractual notice period (or minimum statutory notice period if longer). Where the employer had no such right of termination – such as under a fixed-term contract with no provision for termination by notice during its term – the damages will not be so limited. In this case they will relate to the unexpired part of the term. An employee may be able to recover 'stigma damages' where an employer conducts business in a dishonest way, making it more difficult for the employee to obtain other work. This is potentially a breach of mutual trust and confidence and damages would be payable where it is foreseeable that the breach would damage the employee's reputation *(Malik v Bank of Credit and Commerce International SA (in compulsory liquidation))*.

A second remedy sometimes sought in wrongful dismissal cases is an injunction, that is, an order temporarily preventing the dismissal from being effected. The courts will only exceptionally grant such injunctions because it is not thought desirable to order even temporary performance of a contract of employment against the wishes of one of the parties. Special circumstances need to apply, as they did in *Hill v CA Parsons and Co* in 1971. Recently, there is some evidence that the courts may be more willing to grant such injunctions. In *Irani v Southampton and South-West Hampshire Area Health Authority* there were again special grounds: there was still confidence between employer and employee, a disputes procedure was available, and damages would not have been adequate as a remedy. An injunction was also granted in *Powell v London Borough of Brent*. The injunctions in *Hill, Irani* and *Powell* were all temporary. There are established rules for how courts will deal with applications for temporary injunctions. The test is known as the 'balance of convenience' test. Briefly, this involves establishing whether there is a serious issue to be tried and which of the parties would be worse affected by an adverse interim ruling of the court if they were ultimately successful in an action for damages. The court is not required to look, at this stage, at the relative strength of the parties' cases *(American Cyanamid v Ethicon Ltd)*.

Contract law provides a third remedy – an order for specific performance of the contract other than on the temporary basis described above. In relation to the employment field this is of only theoretical interest.

It should be noted that there is no wrongful dismissal where the contract of employment entitles the employer to dismiss without notice on payment of a sum in lieu of notice and the employer dismisses summarily. If the payment in lieu is not made the employee's action is for a sum due under the contract and not damages for a breach (Abrahams v Performing Rights Society).

Unfair dismissal

The essence of the law of unfair dismissal is the right of the employee not to be unfairly dismissed by his employer. In deciding cases, industrial tribunals go through a two-stage process. They ask:

- has the employer established a fair reason for the dismissal?
- did the employer act reasonably or unreasonably?

The statute defines fairness rather than unfairness. The fair reasons for dismissal – the first stage of the process – are:

- the capability or qualifications of the employee;
- the conduct of the employee;
- the employee was redundant;
- the employee could not continue in his work without contravention of a statutory duty or restriction; and
- some other substantial reason (SOSR).

A dismissal will be excluded, and in effect fair, if it can be shown that its purpose was to safeguard national security.[1] If an employer cannot establish a fair reason his case will fail. On the other hand, if a tribunal is satisfied that one of these reasons has been shown, it must then decide whether the employer acted reasonably or unreasonably in treating it as a sufficient reason for dismissal. The second stage of the process, therefore, is a test of reasonableness. The statute says little about reasonableness except that tribunals must take into account 'the size and administrative resources of the employer's undertaking' and decide the issue 'in accordance with equity and the substantial merits of the case'.[2] In practice, reasonableness comes down to proper procedure, consistency and the appropriateness of dismissal as the form of disciplinary action to be taken. The last of these involves consideration of the severity of the employee's offence as well as any mitigating factors such as length of employment, good record, provocation and domestic or personal difficulties.

The onus of proof for establishing a fair reason lies with the employer. The employee, may, however, wish to bring evidence and put arguments in order to challenge the reason put forward. On reasonableness, the onus of proof is neutral. Both parties will need to present arguments and evidence on this point. If the act of dismissal itself is denied the employee will be responsible for establishing dismissal within the statutory meaning. The employee will also be responsible for proof of loss for compensation purposes. Other than in the case of dismissal on the ground of pregnancy or childbirth (which are automatically unfair and require no qualifying employment), applications relating to dismissals on the ground of sex (or race) discrimination will require an employee to have two years' continuous employment in order to be able to use unfair dismissal law. Here the onus of proof of the reason for the dismissal is upon the employer. Those without the qualifying employment will be restricted to use of the discrimination legislation, where the onus of proof is on the complainant.

Not all unfair dismissal cases fall within the above general scheme: there are some special cases where dismissal is automatically unfair once the reason is established (see pages 327–8). That is, no test of reasonableness is to be applied. There is no period of qualifying employment required in these cases and nor does the upper age limit for applicants apply. There are also special considerations where industrial action is involved (see pages 328–9).

Public law remedies

These derive from the fact that the jurisdiction of the High Court includes the exercise of supervision over inferior courts, tribunals and public officials (see page 14 for a fuller description). Where a person's rights are affected by a decision made by 'someone empowered by public law' judges may enforce duties or quash decisions if they are, for example, illegal, irrational or procedurally deficient (*Associated Provincial Picture Houses Ltd v Wednesbury Corporation*; *Council of Civil Service Unions v The Minister for the Civil Service*). Such judicial review has an advantage over unfair dismissal law for the dismissed person in that it allows the dismissal to be permanently reversed. The general rule is that this remedy is available only where there is no other means of challenging the decision in question. Exceptionally, however, courts will depart from this rule, as in *Calveley v Merseyside Police*, where decisions to dismiss were quashed by the Court of Appeal, despite the fact that the complainants had a right of appeal to the Secretary of State under their disciplinary procedure and were exercising it. The High Court had refused to order that the dismissal be quashed because all other available remedies had not been exhausted, but the Court of Appeal thought that the serious breach of disciplinary procedure involved in the case justified an exception.

The availability of public law remedies in the employment field is not restricted to employees (people working under contracts of employment). Thus, a self-employed contractor or a public office holder, such as a magistrate or a member of a health authority, would be able to seek such remedies if they were dismissed from their positions. For judicial review to be used by a public sector employee they will have to show that their terms and conditions were in some way statutorily controlled, and that the dismissal was in conflict with the public body's statutory restrictions on dismissal. Thus in *R v Liverpool City Corporation ex parte Ferguson and Smith* the applicants were teachers whose pay and conditions were statutorily underpinned, and the decision to dismiss was in conflict with the fact that a local authority cannot dismiss when the reason is grounded in illegality (in this case the setting of an illegal rate).

UNFAIR DISMISSAL: EXCLUSIONS

The following are excluded:

- anyone who is not an employee (see chapter 5);
- anyone who has reached normal retiring age: where there is a normal retiring age and it is the same for men and women, that age applies even if it is different from 65; in any other case 65 will apply;[3]
- anyone with less than two years' employment with their present employer (although the service requirement is currently being challenged as indirect sex discrimination: see page 112);
- anyone who at the time of dismissal was taking part in unofficial industrial action;
- anyone who is the subject of a certificate excepting them from the legislation in the interests of national security or confirming that they have been dismissed for that same reason;
- anyone in specified occupations, namely share fishing and the police service;
- those who ordinarily work outside Great Britain;
- those with contracts for a fixed term of one year or more who have agreed in writing to waive their rights;
- those covered by a dismissal procedure which is exempted from the legislation by Ministerial Order;
- anyone who has made an agreement to refrain from proceeding further with or making a complaint to a tribunal 'where a conciliation officer has taken action'[4] or where a 'compromise agreement' has been reached;[5] and

- anyone whose employment contract has an illegal purpose. However, illegal performance of a contract which has a lawful purpose might not result in the contract being void. A relevant question is whether the employee knew of the illegality and the respective blameworthiness of employer and employee (see chapter 8).

There is no continuous employment qualification or upper age limit for dismissals on the following grounds:

- trades unionism or non-unionism;
- health and safety;
- assertion of a statutory right;
- pregnancy and childbirth;
- carrying out the functions of an employee representative (see chapter 18);
- refusal to work on Sundays (shop and betting workers);
- carrying out the functions of trustee of an occupational pension scheme; and
- redundancy where selection is for one of the above reasons.

However, an employee with less than two years' continuous employment will have the burden of proof of reason for the dismissal. Dismissals on the above grounds are automatically unfair (see pages 327–8). The employment qualification is one month where the dismissal is on medical grounds specified in s 64 of ERA.

Continuous employment begins on the date specified in the contract of employment, even if this is not a working day, rather than when the employee actually starts to do the work *(General of the Salvation Army v Dewsbury)*.

Normal retiring age (NRA) means contractual retiring age where there is one which is strictly applied. A contractual retiring age which is not strictly applied creates a presumption that the NRA is the same. In such circumstances, and also where there is no contractual retiring age at all, the overall test is the reasonable expectation of employees *(Waite v GCHQ)*. The reference group for establishing NRA will be determined by the 'position' held by the employee.[6] 'Position' means the status as an employee and the nature of the work and terms and conditions taken as a whole: *(Hughes v DHSS)*. An NRA in excess of 65 will allow unfair dismissal claims up to that NRA. This contrasts with redundancy where eligibility for redundancy payments is restricted to those who have not reached 65 years even if the NRA is in excess of 65.

UNFAIR DISMISSAL: MEANING OF DISMISSAL AND EFFECTIVE DATE OF TERMINATION

Meaning of dismissal

Where the words used are unambiguously those of dismissal or resignation, they alone may be sufficient to determine the issue. However, the context may also need to be taken into account. Even words which are unambiguous may not represent real intentions when spoken (or shouted) during a heated exchange *(Sovereign House Security Services Ltd v Savage)*. Thus some short period of cooling-off might be reasonable before the decision becomes final. This gives the parties an opportunity to communicate with each other.

Agreements to exclude unfair dismissal rights are void (but see the ACAS conciliation officer and 'compromise agreements' exceptions on pages 53–6). A mutual termination by consent, to avoid the act of dismissal, was such an agreement and was therefore void according to the Court of Appeal in *Igbo v Johnson Matthey (Chemicals) Ltd.* However, if an agreement to terminate is made with the proper advice and no duress it is a valid mutual termination and no question of dismissal arises *(Logan Salton v Durham County Council)*.

Dismissal is defined as:

- termination of the contract by the employer with or without notice;
- the expiry of a fixed-term contract without renewal;
- constructive dismissal; and
- a failure to permit a woman to return to work after confinement.

A constructive dismissal is termination by the employee, with or without notice, in circumstances where the employee is entitled to terminate the contract without notice because of the employer's conduct. These are circumstances where the employer is guilty of gross misconduct as a result of which the employee has a right to resign and claim that he has been unfairly dismissed. It is important to note that the onus of proof will be upon the applicant to demonstrate that there has been a dismissal within the statutory meaning. The test is whether there has been a fundamental breach of contract *(Western Excavating (ECC) Ltd v Sharp)*. This, however, establishes only the fact of dismissal, and not its fairness or otherwise.

Perhaps surprisingly, constructive dismissals are not automatically unfair *(Savoia v Chiltern Herb Farms Ltd*; see also *Vose v South Sefton Health Authority)*. The employer may argue that it was necessary to change the contract of employment unilaterally in the interests of the business. This would have special weight if the business was in trouble or had to make specified savings. Other breaches would be less easy to defend, for example, breach of trust (an implied contractual term: *(Woods v WM Car Services (Peterborough) Ltd)*, abusive language, failure to provide proper safety arrangements or reducing an employee's pay and/or status.

The employee does not have to resign and claim constructive dismissal (ie, accept the employer's repudiation of contract). He can affirm the contract, either accepting the change, or rejecting it but carrying on working and suing for damages *(Ferodo Ltd v Rigby)*.

Next, there is the position of the woman who is refused her right to return to work after confinement. This is part of the statutory definition of dismissal. It will not be treated as dismissal, however, if the employer has five or fewer employees and it was not reasonably practicable to allow her to return to work or offer her alternative employment on 'terms not substantially less favourable to her'.[7] Nor will it be a dismissal, irrespective of the size of the firm, if it is not reasonably practicable to take her back, but she is offered alternative employment which she unreasonably refuses. The onus is upon the employer to show that there was no dismissal.

Finally, it should be noted that the expiry of a fixed-term contract is itself a dismissal. Such a contract must have definite starting and finishing dates, although there may be provision for termination by notice within its period *(BBC v Dixon)*. This contrasts with a 'task' contract which is discharged by performance. Its expiry does not constitute a dismissal *(Wiltshire County Council v NATFHE and Guy)*.

Effective date of termination

The effective date of termination (EDT) is when any notice expires or, if there is no notice, the actual date of termination. For the woman refused her right to return to work the dismissal is taken as having effect on the notified day of return. Where notice given by the employer is less than the statutory minimum, the EDT (for the purposes of qualifying employment for unfair dismissal and written reasons claims, and the calculation of the basic award) becomes the date on which the statutory minimum notice would have expired. In constructive dismissals the EDT is at the end of whatever period of notice the employer would have had to give if he had dismissed on the date of the employee giving notice or terminating (whichever applied).

Frustration of contract

Sometimes the contract of employment can end because one party is no longer capable of performing it in the way the parties envisaged. This is called 'frustration'. The circumstances are likely to be external, unforeseen and not the fault of either party *(Paal Wilson & Co v Partenreederei)*. Long-term illness is an example. A borstal sentence was frustration in *FC Shepherd & Co Ltd v Jerrom*. The contract may be said to be frustrated after the passage of time. The significance of frustration is that it is not a dismissal, therefore no question of unfair dismissal or redundancy would arise.

FAIR REASONS

Capability

It is fair to dismiss an employee on the grounds of capability or qualifications, but subject to the test of reasonableness. Capability refers to 'skill, aptitude, health or any other physical or mental quality'. Qualifications means any 'degree, diploma or other academic, technical or professional qualification'.[8] In practice, dismissals on the grounds of capability fall into two categories: those involving incompetence and those involving ill-health. Where incompetence reflects the fact that the employee is working below capacity rather than a lack of ability the issue is to be treated as one of misconduct rather than one of capability *(Sutton and Gates (Luton) Ltd v Boxall)*. Loss of confidence in an employee, more likely in a management position, can amount to incapability. The overall test for incapability as a reason is that the employer must have an honestly and reasonably held belief that the employee is not competent, and have reasonable grounds for that belief *(Taylor v Alidair Ltd)*.

Conduct

This ranges from the mundane (clocking offences, theft, drunkenness, fighting) to the more unusual (having long hair, not wearing a tie properly, and even losing the company cat). The Employment Appeal Tribunal (EAT) has set out what it considers is the correct approach for tribunals to take. Known as the *British Homes Stores v Burchell* test and endorsed by the Court of Appeal in *W Weddell and Co Ltd v Tepper*, it requires the tribunal to ask:

- did the employer have 'a reasonable suspicion amounting to a belief' that the employee had committed the misconduct, at the time the dismissal decision was taken?
- did the employer have reasonable grounds for this belief?
- did the employer carry out a reasonable investigation?

These three requirements – belief, reasonable grounds and reasonable investigation – are widely applied by tribunals. As a result there is a duty imposed upon employers to handle misconduct cases with some care, although they will not be expected to establish an employee's guilt beyond all reasonable doubt as would be necessary in the Crown Court.

Certain offences normally attract the label 'gross misconduct':

- theft, fraud. deliberate falsification of records;
- fighting, assault on another person;
- deliberate damage to company property;

- serious incapability through alcohol or being under the influence of illegal drugs;
- serious negligence which causes unacceptable loss, damage or injury;
- serious acts of insubordination; and
- working for a competitor or otherwise damaging the company's commercial interests.

What constitutes gross misconduct is a matter of fact for tribunals to decide *(Dalton v Burton's Gold Medal Biscuits Ltd)*: there is no definition in law. Gross negligence, in the absence of any element of intention, does not amount to gross misconduct *(Dietmann v London Borough of Brent)*.

Redundancy

Redundancy is defined for the purposes of unfair dismissal law and redundancy payments as a dismissal which is 'attributable wholly or mainly to':

- an actual or intended cessation of business, either generally, or in the place in which the employee is employed; or
- an actual or expected diminution in the requirements of the business for employees to carry out 'work of a particular kind', either generally, or in the place in which the employee is employed.[9]

The concept of redundancy is explored in greater depth in chapter 17.

The expiry of a fixed-term contract could be dismissal for redundancy if redundancy was the reason for non-renewal.

Redundancy is essentially a management prerogative, and in the absence of bad faith there will normally be no challenge to it *(Moon v Homeworthy Furniture (Northern) Ltd)*. The fact of needing fewer employees is what matters; once this has been established few tribunals will put the reasons under a microscope. The statutory rights of unions in this field are limited to advance warning and consultation; there is no legal right to a share in decision-making.

A properly carried out dismissal by reason of redundancy will be a fair dismissal, although the employee, if qualified, may be entitled to a statutory redundancy payment (see chapter 19).

'Properly carried out' in this context means that the dismissal passes the general test of reasonableness, and in addition satisfies the selection requirements laid down in the statute. These are that selection must not be:

- because of the employee's proposed or actual union membership or activities;
- because of union non-membership;

- on the ground of pregnancy or childbirth;
- because the employee asserted a statutory right; or
- because certain health and safety reasons or other reasons specified in ERA s 105 applied.

If the selection fails on any of these points the dismissal is automatically unfair, and the stage two test of reasonableness is not applied. Otherwise, reasonableness must be judged, and this can include selection criteria *(Bessenden Properties Ltd v Corness)*. Selection on the grounds of race or sex will not be reasonable and will also be unlawful discrimination. The question of unfair dismissal for redundancy is dealt with in chapter 17.

Contravention of statutory duty or restriction

This reason is likely to apply, for example, to people who drive on the public road as part or the whole of their job. Disqualification from driving means that they cannot do this job without a breach of law. More generally the employer should check that there would in fact be a breach of statute if the employee continued to do his normal job and seek expert advice if there is any doubt. Secondly, can the job be done by that person in any other way, for example, by using public transport? If driving is only a small part of the job this may be feasible. Moreover, the general stage two test of reasonableness applies: has the employee been warned of the risks of losing his job if he loses his licence? Has the employer looked at the possibility of alternative work? Has proper procedure been invoked? Are there mitigating factors such as a good record and long service?

Some other substantial reason (SOSR)

The dismissal of a temporary replacement for someone on maternity leave or someone suspended on medical grounds specified in ERA, s 64 would be a dismissal for SOSR if the replacement was informed in writing at the outset that they would be dismissed on the return of the absent employee. A dismissal for economic, technical or organizational reasons arising out of the transfer of an undertaking is also a dismissal for SOSR.

The main application of SOSR, however, is where the employer seeks to change employees' terms and conditions of employment unilaterally as a result of some form of reorganization. The justification for doing this, which is usually accepted by tribunals, is the need for business efficiency or financial saving *(Hollister v National Farmers' Union)*. The financial problems facing firms in recent years have greatly influenced tribunals in this respect but management will need to show a sound business reason for introducing the change, and evidence of some advance consultation with employees. Moreover, anyone dismissed for not agreeing to the change will need to be given due procedural rights – investigation of their circumstances, warnings, right to put their case, right of appeal etc. In other words, the test of reasonableness will have to be satisfied. It is possible that an employee may justifiably resign as a result of the employer's actions, and claim constructive dismissal. A finding of constructive dismissal may result, but it will not necessarily give rise to an unfair dismissal. Where the reorganization leads to a requirement for fewer employees this will be a redundancy. The employee who is confronted by an imposed change in terms and conditions of employment (eg, a wage reduction) may of course invoke common law procedures in order to obtain a remedy. In the light of the employer's repudiation of contract the employee may continue working and sue for damages for the breach *(Ferodo Ltd v Rigby)*. Changing terms by terminating existing contracts and offering re-engagement on new terms removes the threat of common law actions but may open the door to unfair dismissal claims as in *Gilham v Kent County Council.*

The expiry of a fixed-term contract can be SOSR. The employer will need to show that he had a genuine need for a fixed-term contract in the first place and why that reason has ceased to operate. The dismissal would then have to stand the test of reasonableness. As noted earlier, a dismissal as a result of the expiry of a fixed-term contract could be for reason of redundancy rather than SOSR.

SOSR could include the dismissal of people with personal characteristics that are unconventional or socially unacceptable. Such people have little protection unless the characteristics have no bearing at all on the work situation. In fact, employers can nearly always argue that such factors do have a bearing because, for example, of the effect on relationships with other employees and/or customers. Because of this it remains to be seen whether the dismissal of AIDS virus carriers will be unfair. The dilemma for people with something to hide is that hiding it may help them obtain a job, but after discovery by the employer the deceit may count against them in any unfair dismissal claim. The Rehabilitation of Offenders Act 1974 offers protection in certain employments to some of those who have criminal records (see pages 86–8).

REASONABLENESS

Meaning

'Reasonableness' is not defined but the ACAS Code on Disciplinary Practice and Procedures in Employment, and a wealth, if not a surfeit, of case law provide a clear indication of what is meant.[10] In short it means:

- following proper disciplinary procedure, including carrying out a reasonable investigation;
- being consistent in the application of discipline;
- that the disciplinary action taken needs to be appropriate for the particular case or, to borrow a phrase from criminal law, the punishment must fit the crime; and
- taking into account any mitigating circumstances (eg, long service, good record, provocation, domestic or personal problems).

The standard of proof required is that facts need to be established on the balance of probabilities.

A breach creates no liability, but the Code is admissible in evidence in a case under the Act and must be taken into account by a tribunal where relevant. This means, for example, that a hiccup in a disciplinary procedure (eg, a failure to investigate properly) does not in itself render the employer liable. However, if the employee is dismissed and applies to a tribunal claiming that he was unfairly dismissed, the breach of code is admissible and must be considered by the tribunal if relevant. The Code deals with both rules and procedures. The former set standards of conduct at work, the latter provide means of dealing with a failure to meet those standards.

The general test

The approach to be adopted, as laid down by the appellate courts, is as follows:

- the tribunal should not put itself in place of the respondent and say what it would have done if it, the tribunal, had been the employer;
- rather, it should note that for any disciplinary offence there will be, among employers, a range of reasonable responses *(British Leyland (UK) Ltd v Swift)*; and
- the tribunal should ask itself if the response of the employer before it falls within that range.

If it does the employer has behaved reasonably. If, on the other hand, no reasonable employer would have behaved in that way, the employer before it has behaved unreasonably.

In *W Devis and Sons Ltd v Atkins* it was decided that post-dismissal evidence not connected with the reason which the employer gave for the dismissal could not be admitted except in the determination of compensation (this contrasts sharply with the common law position which applies in judging whether a dismissal is wrongful: see *Boston Deep Sea Fishing v*

Ansell). Similarly the test of reasonableness is to be applied to the employer's behaviour at the time of the dismissal, on the basis of the facts that he had at his disposal, or should have had if a reasonable investigation had been carried out, including those emerging during any period of notice. However, post-dismissal facts which emerge during any internal appeal can be taken into account in deciding reasonableness *(West Midlands Co-operative Society Ltd v Tipton)*. Ultimately, reasonableness is a question of fact for the tribunal to determine *(Union of Construction, Allied Trades and Technicians v Brain)*.

Disciplinary rules

The ACAS Code states that:

- rules should be reasonable;
- they should be readily available;
- management should do all it can to ensure that employees know and understand them; and
- management should make employees aware of the likely consequence of breaking any particular rule.

Faced with an industrial tribunal, management will want to be able to give positive answers on these points. From the employee's point of view, however, each of the above provides a potential mitigating factor to be offset against the breach of discipline.

Management should be in a position to provide a tribunal with a copy of the disciplinary rules, as well as with evidence that the dismissed employee had the rules drawn to his attention. If rules are not communicated properly the employee will have the defence that he did not know of a particular rule. That argument will be difficult to sustain if the employer has evidence (eg, signature for receipt) that a rulebook was given to the employee. The assumption in law is that the employee will have read the rules. Possibly, if the rules are unclear, he can argue that he knew of the rule, but had not been told that he could be dismissed for breaking it. An employer should be ready to demonstrate that the rules are fully applied in practice and are applied in a consistent and non-discriminatory manner. Establishing this should form part of the disciplinary investigation *(West Midlands Travel Ltd v Milke and Poole)*. If it can be shown that management often turned a 'blind eye' to breaches of rules there may be doubts about the reasonableness of dismissing. Good disciplinary rules will clearly distinguish, by examples, between gross misconduct (usually subject to dismissal) and other misconduct, and will provide sufficient flexibility to allow mitigating circumstances to be considered *(Hadjioannou v Coral Casinos Ltd)*.

Disciplinary procedures

The ACAS Code states that procedures should be speedy and in writing. They should indicate the range of disciplinary action and specify which levels of management have authority to take particular action. Immediate superiors should not have power to dismiss without reference to senior management. The ACAS Code envisages a system of warnings which is typically in four stages:

- a formal oral warning for minor offences;
- a written warning for subsequent minor offences or a more serious offence;
- a final written warning (or a disciplinary suspension) for further misconduct, making clear that dismissal may follow if there is not adequate improvement; and
- dismissal if there is not adequate improvement.

Sometimes the procedure may be entered at the second or third stage if there is serious misconduct and of course the right exists to dismiss summarily for gross misconduct. Previous warnings may be relevant to dismissal even if they were for different reasons. An employer can take into account:

- the substance of previous warnings;
- how many previous warnings there have been;
- the date(s) of previous warning(s); and
- the period of time between warnings (*Auguste Noel Ltd v Curtis*).

The ACAS Code goes on to lay down a number of requirements which have become quite prominent in the deliberations of industrial tribunals:

- the employee has a right to know the charges against him, and to have an opportunity to state his case – principles derived from the concept of 'natural justice' (see *Pritchett and Dyjasek v J McIntyre Ltd*, however, in which these requirements were not met but the dismissal was nevertheless judged to be fair).
- he has a right to be accompanied by a union representative or some other person.
- except for gross misconduct there should be no dismissal for a first offence. Instead, a system of oral and written warnings should be used. A warning, however, is not just a general exhortation to improve. It spells out the offence and indicates what will or may happen if it recurs, or if there is no improvement.
- there should be a careful investigation before any disciplinary action is taken.

- the reasons for the choice of disciplinary penalty should be explained to the employee.
- the employee should be given a right of appeal, and told of his right, and how to exercise it.

The ACAS Code distinguishes between suspension with pay while an alleged breach is being investigated, and the use of suspension without pay as a disciplinary penalty. Criminal offences outside employment should not be taken as automatic reasons for dismissal. The main consideration is whether it makes the employee unsuitable or unacceptable in his employment. Records of disciplinary breaches should be kept, as should details of warnings (including oral ones) and disciplinary penalties. Although records may be kept, the slate ought to be wiped clean after a period of satisfactory conduct. The length of the period is not specified in the ACAS Code.

Tribunals have added the chance to 'make good' or improve to the questions they are likely to ask of an employer. They have also been influenced by the principles of natural justice (see above). These include the requirement that nobody should be a judge in their own interest. This is significant particularly in relation to appeals. It prevents those taking the original decision from being involved in any subsequent appeal against that decision. An appeals body should act in good faith *(Khanum v Mid-Glamorgan Area Health Authority)*. Refusal to grant a right of appeal which is part of the contract of employment may lead to a finding of unfair dismissal *(West Midlands Co-operative Society Ltd v Tipton*; but see *Batchelor v British Railways Board)*.

Where there is gross misconduct an employer may dismiss summarily (at common law, 'with cause'). However, this does not mean that proper procedure can be dispensed with; an opportunity to explain will be necessary *(W & J Wass Ltd v Binns)*. There should always be a full investigation and a chance for the employee to put his case. Typically, the employee will have been sent home following his misconduct. A period of suspension, therefore, can be used to gather the facts, hear the employee's side of the story and arrive at a decision. That decision would not be at risk, if the employee's misconduct is criminal, simply by virtue of an acquittal in the Crown Court. The court and the tribunal are deciding different issues, and different degrees of proof are necessary. An employee may be not guilty, but the employer may still have dismissed fairly.

Taking into account the 'size and administrative resources of the ... undertaking' may affect such factors as the offering of alternative work, but is not an excuse for the absence of a proper investigation.

For many years, tribunals applied the 'any difference' test to breaches of procedure in order to determine whether or not a dismissal was fair *(British Labour Pump Co Ltd v Byrne; W&J Wass Ltd v Binns)*. This test asks whether the proper application of procedure would have made any difference to the outcome. For example, would dismissal have been averted if the applicant had had an opportunity to state his case, or if a warning had been given? Often the answer was that it would have made no difference, or at best that it would have delayed the dismissal (eg, pending fuller investigation). As a result of the House of Lords ruling in *Polkey v AE Dayton (Services) Ltd*, however, the application of the 'any difference' test is normally likely to be restricted to questions of compensation. A reduction can be made to reflect the chance that a dismissal would still have occurred even if the correct procedure had been followed. This '*Polkey* reduction' is separate and distinct from any reduction for contributory fault. The substantive matter of the fairness or otherwise of the dismissal will be decided according to what the employer did rather than he might have done. The correct statutory tests are fair reason and reasonableness. The *Polkey* decision is a reminder, therefore, that the lack of a proper procedure does not mean that a dismissal is automatically unfair *(West Midlands Co-operative Society Ltd v Tipton)*.

Exceptionally, an employer may be able to dispense with the procedural niceties on 'no difference' grounds and still be reasonable. Until recently, it was thought, on the basis of *Polkey*, that this required an employer to make a conscious decision that the normal procedural steps would be futile and that the decision should go ahead without them. It was believed that the appropriate test was whether the employer was reasonable in arriving at this conclusion. In *Duffy v Yeomans*, however, it was made clear by the EAT that, while reasonableness is the correct test, there is no requirement for an employer to make a conscious decision to dispense with procedure. As long as the failure to operate procedure can subsequently be judged as a reasonable course of action on the basis of what was known (or should have been known) at the time of dismissal, the dismissal will not be unfair because of it. Thus the test is the objective one of a reasonable employer, not the subjective one of whether the employer applied his mind to the matter at the time. A procedural deficiency can be remedied on internal appeal by a rehearing of the case but not merely by a review *(Whitbread and Co plc v Mills)*.

Consistency

The reference in the statute to 'equity' has been taken as the basis for the need for consistency of treatment as part of reasonableness. Where comparisons are drawn with how other people have been treated in the past, including elsewhere in the organization, consistency is to be applied to the organization and not to individual managers *(Post Office v Fennell)*. If more than one person is being dismissed as a result of an incident:

- are they being dismissed for the same offence?
- are there any differences between the cases, eg, past records, mitigating factors? *(Eagle Star Insurance Co Ltd v Hayward)*.

In practice, some degree of inconsistency may be reasonable if the facts of different individual cases can be distinguished, as in *British Steel Corporation v Griffin*.

SPECIAL CASES

The two-stage process of unfair dismissal law involves the establishing of a fair reason, and the satisfying of the test of reasonableness, but as noted, some dismissals are not subject to this process.

Automatically unfair dismissals

In certain cases the legislation instructs that dismissals are to be regarded as automatically unfair once the reason for dismissal is established. This applies to:

- dismissals on grounds of proposed or actual trades union membership or activity, proposed or actual non-membership; or because the employee was an employee representative (or a candidate for such a post) and performed or proposed to perform the functions or activities of that post (see chapters 18, 20 and 21);
- dismissal for refusing to work on Sunday (shop and betting workers);
- dismissal in health and safety cases;
- dismissal for asserting a statutory right;
- dismissals on grounds of pregnancy or childbirth;
- dismissal for carrying out the functions of trustee of an occupational pension scheme; and
- dismissal by reason of redundancy with selection on any of the above grounds.

Dismissal on the grounds of union activitiy or membership or non-union membership are not subject to the requirement for qualifying employment nor to the usual age limits. If the applicant has the normal qualifying employment the onus of proof lies with the respondent *(Shannon v Michelin (Belfast) Ltd)*. Otherwise, it lies with the applicant *(Smith v The Chairman and Other Councillors of Hayle Town Council)*. Even in the former circumstances, however, the applicant will have to adduce evidence that the reason for dismissal was trades unionism, as well as rebutting the employer's reason.

The statute says that union activities must be at the 'appropriate time' if they are to be protected – namely, outside working hours, or in working hours with the employer's agreement or consent – but does not say what constitutes such activities. The courts have interpreted the term narrowly, for example, by ruling that these activities do not include the actions of the union itself *(Therm-A-Stor Ltd v Atkins)* or the acts of a union member not done formally within the union's responsibility *(Drew v St Edmundsbury Borough Council)*. However, in *Fitzpatrick v British Railways Board*, dismissal for past union activities elsewhere was interpreted by the Court of Appeal as being dismissal because of a fear that such activities might be repeated in the present employment. Thus the dismissal was on grounds of trades union activity and was automatically unfair.[11] A non-unionist has the right not to be dismissed for refusing to make a payment (eg, to a charity) in lieu of a union subscription.

Dismissal on the ground of pregnancy or childbirth is dealt with on pages 257–9 and dismissal in health and safety cases on pages 304–6. Dismissal on grounds of an assertion of a statutory right is another type of dismissal which is automatically unfair. This applies where the employee brings proceedings against his employer in order to enforce one of his statutory rights or alleges that the employer has infringed such a right. The rights protected are a very wide range of statutory rights. Discrimination law is excluded because provisions with a similarly protective motive are contained in the RRA and the SDA. It is of no consequence that the employee does not have the right or that the right has not been infringed: the protection applies as long as the complaint is made in good faith. The employee does not have to specify the right but must make it reasonably clear to the employer.

Dismissal in connection with industrial action

Dismissal in connection with a lock-out, strike or other industrial action is largely excluded from unfair dismissal law. Where there are union members and the strike is unofficial, tribunals have no jurisdiction whatsoever. This is because an employee has no right to claim that he was unfairly dismissed if at the time of his dismissal he was taking part in unofficial industrial action.[14] Where the strike is official, or all the strikers are non-unionists, tribunals have a limited jurisdiction. If everyone is treated the same, no complaint of unfair dismissal can be heard. If, however, some are dismissed and others are not, there is a possible unfair dismissal claim. The selectivity must apply, however, at the time of the complainant's dismissal, rather than from the beginning of the strike. Thus, if 100 people go on strike and all are still on strike a month later, the dismissal of the six strike leaders may give rise to unfair dismissal claims. The dismissal of all 100 will not. Moreover, if

40 had returned to work after a month, the dismissal of the remaining 60 would not give rise to claims, since there was no selectivity among those on strike at the time of the dismissal.

Where all strikers are dismissed, but only some are re-engaged, the critical factor will be the time interval between the dismissal of those re-engaged and their re-engagement. If this period is three months or more, none of the people who have not been re-engaged will have a claim. Whether a person is taking part in industrial action is a matter of fact for the tribunal to decide *(Coates and Venables v Modern Methods and Materials Ltd)*. The law regards a strike as a breach of contract *(Simmons v Hoover)*. The legal aspects of industrial action are dealt with in more detail in chapter 23.

Dismissals in connection with transfers of undertakings

Finally, there is the question of dismissals in connection with the transfer of undertakings. Regulations issued under the European Communities Act 1972 apply where there is a transfer but not where there is simply a change in the ownership of share capital. Undertaking includes 'any trade or business'.[12] Contracts of employment automatically transfer with the business, as do rights and duties under the contract, including continuity of employment. Dismissals arising out of the transfer are automatically unfair, unless there is some economic, technical or organizational reason for them 'entailing changes in the workforce'.[13] Such a reason, including redundancy, would constitute SOSR. Thus, the mere change of identity of the employer does not give an employee the right to resign and claim unfair dismissal or redundancy. However, a detrimental and substantial change to the employee's working conditions will give a right to claim unfair dismissal. On the law relating to the transfer of undertakings more generally, see chapter 20.

UNFAIR DISMISSAL REMEDIES

Reinstatement and re-engagement

Reinstatement, re-engagement and compensation are the remedies laid down in the statute, in that order of priority. Reinstatement means the complainant is treated in all respects as if they had not been dismissed. Re-engagement can be with the employer, an associated employer or with a successor of the employer, and must be in comparable or other suitable employment. Unless there has been contributory fault on the part of the applicant re-engagement should be on terms as favourable as reinstatement. In making an order for reinstatement or re-engagement the tribunal must consider:

- the complainant's wishes;
- whether it is practicable for the employer to comply with the order – only exceptionally will engagement of a permanent replacement prior to the hearing be admissible as a defence; and
- if there was contributory fault, whether it is 'just' to make the order.

Compensation is the remedy in the vast majority of cases.

Compensation

There are three types of award:

- basic award;
- compensatory award; and
- an additional award ('special' award in cases involving dismissal for union or non-union reasons).

Interest is payable on industrial tribunal awards (see page 69). The basic award uses a formula which takes into account the employee's age, length of employment and gross weekly pay. A week's pay for those whose pay does not vary with output means the amount payable under the contract of employment. Non-contractual overtime is thus excluded. For those whose pay varies with output, those who work shifts and those with no normal hours, a 12-week average is taken. The concept of a week's pay is dealt with more fully below (see pages 378–80). The basic award formula is the same as that used to calculate a statutory redundancy payment except that employment below the age of 18 years counts for the basic award but not for redundancy payment purposes. There is entitlement to half a week's pay for every year of employment under the age of 22, one week's pay from 22 but under 41, and one and a half weeks' pay from 41 years on. The maximum number of years which can be counted is 20, making the maximum number of weeks' pay 30. The limit on weekly earnings to be taken into account is currently from 1 April 1998 is £220 – this is reviewed annually but not necessarily increased – so the maximum basic award is £6,600. The award can be reduced because of the employee's conduct before dismissal, or because the employee unreasonably refused an offer of reinstatement. If the employer is insolvent, the basic award (but not the compensatory, additional or special awards) may be paid out of the National Insurance Fund. In an unfair dismissal where the reason for dismissal is redundancy the employee will not be entitled to both a statutory redundancy payment and the unfair dismissal basic award. If the employee unreasonably refused suitable alternative employment or accepted renewal of contract and has no entitlement to a redundancy payment because of this, the basic award of unfair dismissal will be equal to two weeks' pay.

By contrast the compensatory award draws more on the principles used in common law damages claims than any statutory formula. The amount depends on the loss suffered and any projected future loss that the tribunal is prepared to take into account. The main heads were set out in *Norton Tool Co v Tewson*:

- actual loss of wages and benefits up to the hearing;
- future loss of wages and benefits;
- loss arising from the manner of dismissal (such as damaged job prospects arising out of damaged reputation);
- loss of statutory protection because qualifying employment for employment protection will have been lost (a sum of £250 is normally awarded); and
- loss of pension rights: the industrial tribunal chairmen (in consultation with the Government Actuary) produced guidelines in 1990 on how to calculate compensation under this head.[14]

The tribunal must raise these heads but the onus of proof of loss lies with the applicant *(Tidman v Aveling Marshall Ltd)*.

The applicant must mitigate their loss, for example by looking for another job and by not preventing the employer from complying with a tribunal reinstatement or re-engagement order. If the employer wishes to allege a failure on the part of the employee to mitigate loss the onus is on the employer to prove such failure *(Bessenden Properties Ltd v Corness)*. In practice the onus is often put on the employee to show mitigation, as was done by the EAT in *Scottish and Newcastle Breweries Ltd v Halliday*. The compensatory award can be reduced if there has been contributory fault or to reflect the *Polkey* factor. The maximum award is currently £12,000 (see pages 70–71 for a worked example of unfair dismissal compensation).

Where the applicant is re-engaged or reinstated but the terms of the order are not fully complied with there may be an award according to loss sustained. Where the reinstatement or re-engagement is not effected this award is additional to the basic and compensatory payments, and is at the tribunal's discretion:

- 26–52 weeks' pay in dismissals on ground of race or sex; and
- 13–26 weeks' pay in all other cases, except dismissals for unionism or non-unionism which are treated differently (see below).

Such extra compensation is payable only where an employer's compliance with the tribunal order is practicable. The maximum earnings limit applies here so the additional award cannot exceed £11,440 (52 weeks × £220 per week). Thus, in unfair dismissals other than those arising out of unionism or non-unionism the maximum compensation payable – all three awards together – is £30,040.

There is no provision for an employer to be compelled to reinstate or re-engage a dismissed employee. Nor can an industrial tribunal order for reinstatement or re-engagement be the basis of an ordinary damages claim in the courts (which would not be subject to unfair dismissal compensation limits). The only compensation payable for failure to comply with a tribunal order is an additional award by the tribunal itself *(O'Laoire v Jackel International Ltd)*.

Where the dismissal is for union or non-union reasons (including selection for redundancy on these grounds) there is a minimum basic award of £2,900. The compensatory award is again based on loss, but there is a special rather than an additional award. The special award is calculated as follows.

- where the tribunal refuses to order re-employment, 104 weeks' pay subject to a minimum of £14,500 and a maximum of £29,000;
- where the tribunal makes an order for re-employment but the employer fails to comply without showing that it was not practicable to comply, 156 weeks' pay or £21,800, whichever is the greater, with no maximum; and
- in both of the above cases a week's pay is not subject to the statutory earnings limit of £220.

The special award may be reduced because:

- of the employee's conduct before dismissal;
- the employee refused an offer of reinstatement; or
- the employee prevented the employer complying with an order for reinstatement or re-engagement.

Either the applicant or respondent may claim that the respondent was induced to dismiss by trades union industrial action or the threat of it. If such pressure was put upon the respondent employer because the applicant would not join a union, that union may be included as a party in the proceedings. This process, known as joinder, may result in the union being ordered to pay part or all of the compensation.

Interim relief

This is a rarely sought remedy which was devised to take the heat out of dismissals for union reasons, and to give recognition to the fact that such dismissals involved a breach of the right to freedom of association. It was thought that these dismissals were particularly likely to lead to industrial disputes. Dismissals for non-unionism were later included in the provisions, as were dismissals on certain health and safety grounds, dismissals for carrying out the functions of an occupational pension scheme trustee and dismissals for performing the duties of an employee representative.[15] An employee dismissed on the above grounds may apply to an industrial tribunal no later than seven days after the effective date of termination. In the case of dismissal for union reasons the relevant union must provide a certificate confirming that the applicant was a member of, or proposed to join, that union, and must state that in their view the reason for the dismissal was as alleged. The tribunal must decide whether it is 'likely' that it would find it an unfair dismissal at the full hearing. 'Likely' means more than a reasonable chance – it means a 'pretty good' chance *(Taplin v C Shippam Ltd)*. If this is the tribunal's assessment it must say so, and explain its powers. It will then ask the employer if he will agree to reinstate or re-engage the applicant and if there is agreement it will make an order to that effect. If the employer fails to attend, or refuses to reinstate or re-engage, the tribunal 'shall make an order for the continuation of the employee's contract of employment'. This will include all remuneration, benefits and continuity, but will exclude the requirement to work. It will last until a full hearing of the case takes place.

USE OF ACAS ARBITRATION

Employers and employees may prefer, however, to settle their differences through voluntary third party adjudication, although the statutory provisions are not abrogated by them doing so. In particular, they may wish to use ACAS arbitrators. The advantages of this method include the following.

- Speed: an on-site arbitration hearing and decision can be achieved more quickly than an industrial tribunal hearing and decision.
- Informality: arbitration procedures involve the presentation of cases but legal procedure is not used and the arbitrators are often not lawyers.
- Flexibility: the terms of reference can be drawn to take into account local industrial relations circumstances, for example, rules, custom and practice.
- Greater emphasis on reinstatement or re-engagement where the dismissal is held to be unfair. This is because the parties have agreed in advance to accept the arbitrator's decision. The decision of an industrial tribunal is seen as being imposed from outside. Moreover, the speedier handling of the case makes such remedies easier to achieve.

Personnel managers, employees and any union officials may feel more at home with this system and may prefer a private hearing to a public tribunal. On the other hand, some employees may positively welcome the chance that a tribunal gives them to air their grievance in public.

The government is in favour of encouraging wider use of voluntary dispute resolution such as arbitration.[16] A major consideration is the need to control public expenditure in the light of the rapidly increasing aggregate cost of the industrial tribunal system. The functioning of the tribunal system is discussed in chapter 26 and the public policy issues arising therefrom are considered in chapter 28.

WRITTEN STATEMENT OF REASONS FOR DISMISSAL

General provisions

An employee has a legal right to request (orally or in writing) and obtain from their employer a written statement of the reasons for their dismissal.[17] This right is given to those with two years' or more continuous employment with their employer prior to termination, although the qualifying period is currently subject to challenge on the grounds that it amounts to unlawful indirect sex discrimination *(R v Secretary of State for Employment ex parte Seymour-Smith)*. There is also an exception in maternity cases (see below).

The claim for compensation for failure to give written reasons is usually made on the same application form as the unfair dismissal complaint itself and must reach the Regional Office of the Industrial Tribunals within three months of the EDT (on EDT, see page 317) The respondent employer has 14 days in which to reply to the request for written reasons.

Where there is an unreasonable failure to comply, or where the particulars of reasons are inadequately stated or untrue, a tribunal may make a declaration as to the reasons for the dismissal but must make a penalty award of two weeeks' pay. The week's pay is gross and since the right to have written reasons is separate from the right not to be unfairly dismissed there is no percentage deduction for any contributory fault on the part of the employee. The award will be made at the end of the hearing of the substantive unfair dismissal complaint.

Provisions relating specifically to maternity

The general provisions are varied in maternity cases in two ways. These two differences apply where the employee is dismissed while pregnant or dismissed after childbirth such that the dismissal ends her basic maternity leave. First, the two-year qualifying period is removed in maternity cases; secondly, it is mandatory for the employer to provide written reasons in such cases. In the general case, an employer is required to provide written reasons only if requested to do so by the employee. In maternity cases it is mandatory that the employer provides them – the employee does not need to make a request.

NOTICE PERIODS

ERA lays down minimum notice periods.[18] The right is given to those employees with one month or more of continuous employment, and is as follows.

- if the continuous employment is less than two years: one week's notice; and
- one week's notice per year of continuous employment from two years to 12.

The minimum legal notice to be given where length of employment exceeds 12 years is still 12 weeks. The minimum notice which has to be given by the employee to the employer is one week. This does not increase with length of employment. Contractual arrangements may add to the statutory minimum on either side (for the purposes of notice, a week does not have to be a 'pay' week as defined in ERA, s 235(1).

Fixed-term contracts of one month or less will attract the legal minimum notice only if the employee has already worked continuously for three months. Task contracts expected to last three months or less will be excluded unless there is already three months' continuous employment. The notice rights apply to those fixed-term contracts with provision for termination by notice within the fixed-term, but do not apply to Crown servants. Notice may be waived or payment in lieu accepted.[19] The right to terminate without notice because of the other party's repudiation is not affected. The employer must pay the employee during the notice period even if the employee is incapable of work because of sickness or injury or if there is no work, providing, in the latter case, that the employee is 'ready and willing to work'. Also, the employee must be paid if absent on holiday 'in accordance with the terms of his employment relating to holidays'.[20]

Where there is a contractual right to terminate summarily and make a payment, a dismissal without notice will not be wrongful (see page 310).

For infringement of notice rights the remedy is to sue through the courts or tribunals for wrongful dismissal, ie dismissal not in accordance with the terms of the contract. In this respect pay in lieu of notice is regarded as damages for breach of contract (Delaney v Staples).

Under common law there can be an agreement for withdrawal of the notice or an agreement to defer it (see *Mowlem (Northern) Ltd v Watson*). Where in a redundancy employees stay back to assist in an orderly run down of plant, it is common for employers to make retention payments.

Where there is a conflict between the notice provisions in the contract and those required by the legislation, such that contractual notice is less than statutory notice, the statute will prevail since any agreement restricting the operation of the legislation is void.[21]

NOTES

1 ERA, s 193; but some dismissals, eg those on health and safety grounds, cannot be excluded.

2 ERA, s 98(4).

3 Sex Discrimination Act 1975, as amended by SDA 1986, s 3.

4 ERA, s 203(2)(e).

5 ERA, s 203(2)(f) and (3).

6 ERA, s 235(1).

7 ERA, s 96(4).

8 ERA, s 98(3).

9 ERA, s 139.

10 ACAS, *Code of Practice, Disciplinary Practice and Procedures in Employment*, (London, HMSO, 1998). See also: ACAS, *Discipline at Work* (London, Advisory, Conciliation and Arbitration Service, 1987).

11 Under EP(C)A, s 58(1)(b). Now TULR(C)A, s 152(1)(b).

12 Transfer of Undertakings (Protection of Employment) Regulations (SI 1981/1794), reg 2(1).

13 Transfer of Undertakings (Protection of Employment) Regulations, reg 8(2).

14 *Industrial Tribunals: Compensation for Loss of Pension Rights* (London, HMSO, 1990).

15 TULR(C)A, s 161; and ERA, s 128.

16 *Resolving Employment Rights Disputes: Options for Reform* (Cm 2707, HMSO, 1994). The Employment Rights (Dispute Resolution) Act 1998 ss 7–8 provides for an arbitration scheme to be operated by ACAS.

17 ERA, s 92.

18 ERA, ss 86–91.

19 ERA, s 86(3). These are not the same. It is submitted that there need be no payment in lieu where a party waives their right to notice since the other party is not in breach of contract by terminating without notice. The more common situation is where a payment is accepted instead of the notice. It seems that the waiving of notice rights applies only to contractual rights and does not apply to the qualifying right for a redundancy payment or for the purpose of calculating a redundancy payment. In such cases ERA, s 145(5) would postpone the relevant date even if the employee accepted pay in lieu or waived his right to notice (*Staffordshire County Council v Secretary of State for Employment*).

20 ERA, s 88(1)(d) (in respect of employments for which there are normal working hours). The employee must be paid in such circumstances regardless of whether notice is given by the employer or the employee. However, this will not be the case where the notice which must be given by the employer is at least one week more than the statutory minimum (s 87(4)).

21 ERA, s 203(1).

Redundancy and Unfair Dismissal

It has been noted that redundancy is a form of dismissal; as a result, it is subject to the law of unfair dismissal. In practice, the most common challenge in law to an employer's redundancy decision is an unfair dismissal claim. Therefore, this chapter identifies good practice and the requirements of the law in relation to how the individual employee should be treated in a redundancy.

THE CONCEPT OF REDUNDANCY

The legal definition of redundancy

Redundancy is a concept familiar to everyone in the employment field – employees, employers, union officials, lawyers and others – although not everyone would necessarily define it in the same way. In law, redundancy is defined as a dismissal which is 'attributable wholly or mainly to':

(a) an actual or intended cessation of business, either generally or in the place in which the employee is employed; or
(b) an actual or expected diminution in the requirements of the business for employees to carry out 'work of a particular kind', either generally or in the place in which the employee is employed.[1]

The cessation of work or diminution in requirements can be temporary or permanent.[2]

The above definition causes few problems where a whole business closes or where a site closes and the employee contractually can be required to move elsewhere in the company. Where a site closes and the employee is under no contractual duty to move, there will be a redundancy unless an offer of alternative employment (which meets the legal requirements) is accepted. An unreasonable refusal of an offer of suitable alternative employment will lose the employee his or her right to a statutory redundancy payment. Where there is no closure, partial or total, the test is whether the employer requires fewer employees to carry out 'work of a particular kind'. The most difficult case here is where the employer does not require fewer employees in aggregate, but wants fewer to carry out one particular type of work and more to carry out another. Whether changes in technology, systems and duties amount to a change in the 'particular kind' of work will be a matter of fact and degree for the industrial tribunal. The replacement of a plumber by a heating technician was a redundancy. The 'particular kind' of work done by plumbers was different from that done by heating technicians *(Murphy v Epsom College)*. Similarly, the replacement of one type of doctor by another was a redundancy (in the context of the transfer of an undertaking: see chapter 20) in *Porter v Queen's Medical Centre (Nottingham University Hospital)*. On the other hand, the replacement of an older barmaid by a younger one, in the context of the refurbishment of a public house, was not *(Vaux and Associated Breweries Ltd v Ward)*. The type of work was still barmaids' work. Redundancy will not be the reason for dismissal where there is a background of work changes if the dismissal does not arise out of the changes. In *Hindle v Percival Boats Ltd* there was a change in technology but the dismissal was on grounds of capability which did not stem from the change.

Three important preliminary points need to be made about the position of redundancy in law. First, it should be noted that redundancy is a form of dismissal. In industrial life a distinction is often drawn between dismissal (ie, the sack, for, say, misconduct) and redundancy, which by implication is not seen as 'dismissal'. In law, 'dismissal' is the umbrella concept covering termination by the employer. Redundancy is one form of dismissal. The fact that a redundancy is voluntary will not prevent it from being a redundancy in law as long as the termination is by means of dismissal, rather than by mutual agreement *(Burton, Allton and Johnson Ltd v Peck)*. Retirement under an early retirement scheme is likely to be a mutual termination *(Birch and Humber v University of Liverpool)* but termination as a result of volunteering under a redundancy scheme should be a redundancy, even if there is early payment of retirement benefits (see pages 387–8 with respect to the tax position).

Secondly, the key to the definition of redundancy is not the fact that the amount of work has diminished, but rather that the employer requires fewer employees.[3] The test for redundancy, therefore, is whether fewer employees are needed. Three types of situation were specified by the Court of Appeal in *McCrea v Cullen and Davidson Ltd*:

(a) the work has diminished, so fewer employees are needed;
(b) the work has not diminished, but new technology has reduced the demand for employees; or
(c) the work has not diminished, but reorganization leads to fewer employees being wanted (ie, past over-manning).

All of the above situations constitute redundancy. In general, the redundancy test of fewer employees has been applied to the jobs being done by those made redundant. The exception has been the practice of bumping or indirect redundancy, where if a particular job is to go, the occupant might move to another job, and the person so displaced be made redundant *(W Gimber and Sons Ltd v Spurrett)*. However, this approach has now been rejected by the EAT in *Church v West Lancashire NHS Trust* where it was held that 'work of a particular kind' relates to the work that had been done by the dismissed employee.

The function test (involving examination of what the employee actually did) had already given way to a contract test. The Court of Appeal ruled, that the fewer employees test should be applied to the work that could be done under the contract rather than to the job actually being done *(Haden Ltd v Cowen)*. Thus how widely or narrowly 'work of a particular kind' is defined may depend upon how widely or narrowly the contract terms are drawn. More recently, the EAT appears to have rejected both function and contract tests, substituting in *Safeway Stores Ltd v Burrell* the overall requirements of the employer. This seems to have the effect of defining 'work of a particular kind' as the entire operation of the employer, or the entire operation in a particular place. In *Church*, the EAT rejected its own approach in *Safeway*, arguing for a blend of contract and function, as applied by the Court of Appeal to the question of place of work in *High Table* (see below). In an earlier case, it seemed that a distinction had to be drawn between a contract which defines a specific place of work but permits an employer to alter the place of work, and one which defines place of work broadly to include more than one geographical site. In the latter, it appears that closure of the site at which the employee is working would not constitute a redundancy, while in the former it would, notwithstanding the mobility clause *(Bass Leisure Ltd v Thomas)*. In *High Table Ltd v Horst*, however, the Court of Appeal thought that it could not 'be right ... to let the contract be the sole determinant'. The factual circumstances would decide the issue and the contract might be helpful. A purely contractual test would mean that an employee with a mobility clause in his contract would have a genuine redundancy claim defeated.

A third factor of considerable importance is that the law accepts redundancy as a legitimate management decision. As noted in chapter 16, redundancy is one of the specified fair reasons for dismissal in the statute containing the unfair dismissal provisions. Essentially, the redundancy decision is a management prerogative and in the absence of bad faith there will normally be no challenge to it *(Moon v Homeworthy Furniture (Northern) Ltd)*. Altogether this means that there is no check in law on management dismissing for the reason of redundancy, providing that redundancy is the real reason for the dismissal and that the procedure adopted conforms to the legal requirements (see chapter 16). An exception to this occurs in the realm of public law. The redundancy decision of a public body may be quashed on judicial review, as was the case when Liverpool City Council set an illegal rate in 1985 *(R v Liverpool City Corporation ex parte Ferguson and Smith)*. In the field of private law, an employee may seek an injunction to prevent redundancy but is unlikely to succeed unless there are some special factors at work. There were no such factors in *Alexander v Standard Telephones and Cables plc*. A relevant question in applying the balance of convenience test would be whether there was any work for the employee to do.[4]

Reorganization

It is important to distinguish the concepts of redundancy and reorganization. The latter is a common occurrence in industry but is not a concept to be found in employment law. The legal implications of reorganization, if there are any, will depend upon the facts of the particular case. Thus, reorganization may involve redundancy, which is governed by legal rules, but equally, it may not. It may involve a change of employer – where there is a substantial amount of law – but equally it may not. It may involve changes in terms and conditions of employment, where a key consideration is likely to be what is permitted under the terms of the contract of employment. Where reorganization results in short-time working or lay-offs there are separate provisions.

One of the most common features of a reorganization is a change in work practices. This may involve increased flexibility of tasks, hours of work or location, but does such reorganization constitute a redundancy? The purpose of such changes is often to reduce unit costs and a major component of the saving is usually employment costs. If that is achieved by employing fewer people, the reorganization involves redundancy. Two cases illustrate the distinction which needs to be made. Reorganization was not a redundancy in *Johnson and Dutton v Nottinghamshire Combined Police Authority* because although there were changes in terms – hours of work – no fewer employees were required. In contrast, reorganization was a redundancy in *Bromby and Hoare Ltd v Evans* where employees were replaced by self-employed contractors. The employer required fewer employees. Consequently redundancy legislation was brought into play in the latter case.

REDUNDANCY AS A REASON FOR DISMISSAL

Because redundancy is one of the fair reasons for dismissal, a properly carried out dismissal by reason of redundancy will be a fair dismissal, although the employee, if qualified, may be entitled to a statutory redundancy payment. Properly carried out in this context means that the dismissal passes the general test of reasonableness, and in addition satisfies the selection requirements laid down in the statute (see below). The expiry of a fixed-term contract could be dismissal for redundancy if redundancy was the reason for non-renewal as it was in *Association of University Teachers v University of Newcastle upon Tyne* where the funding for the course taught by the teacher had ceased.[5] This contrasts with the position in *North Yorkshire County Council v Fay* where a teacher's fixed-term contract was not renewed when the post was filled on a permanent basis. This was a dismissal for 'some other substantial reason' rather than for redundancy. Expiry of an apprenticeship constitutes dismissal, but failure to appoint to a post will most likely be a fair dismissal for SOSR. Such a situation is not a redundancy and there is no obligation to offer a post *(North East Coast Shiprepairers v Secretary of State for Employment)*.

Redundancy is a management decision and unless there is bad faith or illegality it is unlikely to be susceptible to legal challenge. There cannot be any inquiry into the reasons for redundancy or into the rights and wrongs of it *(Moon v Homeworthy Furniture (Northern) Ltd)*. However, in *Delanair Ltd v Mead* the EAT stated that an employer must carry out an assessment of the needs of the business to see if it is practicable to perform the work with fewer employees, otherwise there would be no diminution in the requirement for employees (ie, no redundancy). This was in the context of reduced staffing for cost-saving reasons. In *Orr v Vaughan* the EAT went further, holding that in making such an assessment the employer must act on 'reasonable information reasonably acquired'. More recently, in *James W Cook (Wivenhoe) Ltd v Tipper* the Court of Appeal stated that tribunals must not investigate the commercial and economic reasons for redundancy. However, they were entitled to examine whether the dismissal was genuinely on the grounds of redundancy and to require that the redundancy decision was based on proper information. In practice, the fact of needing fewer employees is what matters; once this has been established few tribunals will put the reasons under a microscope. The statutory rights of unions in this field are limited to advance warning and consultation; there is no legal right to a share in decision-making.

A change of employer within the meaning of the Transfer of Under-takings (Protection of Employment) Regulations does not constitute dismissal; instead, continuity is preserved and terms and conditions are transferred. Where there is a dismissal for redundancy, either by transferor or transferee, and it arises out of the transfer, it would need to be justified on economic, technical or organizational grounds (see chapter 20).

SELECTION FOR REDUNDANCY

As already noted, a genuine redundancy properly carried out should not give rise to a claim let alone a finding of unfair dismissal. However, various aspects of the handling of redundancy are covered by the legislation and employers do from time to time fall foul of them. The main area which gives rise to problems is selection. Certain grounds of selection are automatically unfair.

Automatically unfair selection

Selection must not be because of the employee's proposed or actual union membership or activities or because of proposed or actual union non-membership; it must not be on grounds of pregnancy or childbirth, or on grounds of health and safety or for asserting a statutory right. It must not be for carrying out the functions of trustee of an occupational pension scheme, for carrying out the duties of an employee representative nor, in the case of shop and betting workers, for refusing to work on a Sunday. If selection fails on any of these points the dismissal is automatically unfair, and the stage two test of reasonableness is not applied.[6] An employer has no defence to selection on these grounds once established. It should be noted that the provisions relating to agreed procedures and customary arrangements have been repealed.[7]

The provisions on automatically unfair selection are brought into play where the circumstances constituting the redundancy apply equally to two or more employees, one of whom is not made redundant.[8] That is, there must be at least two candidates, one of whom is not chosen. The relevant unit is the undertaking and the employees must hold similar positions. Different grades or classes are not likely to be similar positions (Robinson v Carrickfergus Borough Council; Power and Villiers v A Clarke & Co).

Until recently, the law of unfair dismissal did not provide that selection for redundancy on grounds of pregnancy was automatically unfair. However, the House of Lords decided in Brown v Stockton on Tees Borough Council that the selection of a woman for redundancy because she was pregnant did constitute an automatically unfair dismissal. Employers must disregard the inconvenience of having to grant maternity leave. The Trade

Union Reform and Employment Rights Act 1993 amended the legislation to make this clear.

As regards trades union reasons, selection of shop stewards for redundancy because the employers believed (on the basis of the stewards' past activities) that they would engage in disruptive activities in the future was dismissal for redundancy on the grounds of trades union activities. It was held that the dismissals were automatically unfair *(Port of London Authority v Payne).*[9] Where redundancy is argued but is not the principal reason for the dismissals, the finding is likely to be dismissal on trades union grounds. This happened where 20 people were made redundant in a situation where there was a need for 13 fewer people, in order to include seven union members in the redundancy. The company then recruited seven replacements *(Controlled Demolition Group Ltd v Lane and Knowles).*

The automatically unfair reasons for selection set out above do not require the employee to have any qualifying period of employment, nor is there any upper age limit for complaints.

Where selection is not automatically unfair: the reasonableness test

Other than in the automatically unfair selections mentioned above, reasonableness must be judged,[10] including the selection criteria *(Bessenden Properties Ltd v Corness).* If a redundancy is not reasonable it becomes an unfair dismissal. The general test is that the employer's selection must fall within a band of reasonable responses (see below). It will be unreasonable only if no reasonable management would have made that selection *(N C Watling v Richardson; BL Cars Ltd v Lewis).* Thus, the criteria must not be vague *(Graham v ABF Ltd).* Preference may be given to the disabled so that they are not made redundant but the general test of reasonableness still must be applied *(Seymour v British Airways Board).*

There is unlikely to be unfair selection if some employees are kept on by a liquidator to achieve an orderly winding-up of the company while the rest of the workforce is made redundant *(Fox Brothers (Clothes) Ltd v Bryant).*

The fact that selection is based on customary arrangements in the trade or industry, or is according to a procedure agreed with a trades union, will not of itself make the selection reasonable. The general test of reasonableness must be satisfied and there is the possibility of an agreed procedure or customary arrangement being unreasonable. A customary arrangement failed the test in *NC Watling Ltd v Richardson* because it gave insufficient weight to length of employment – the employers were not entitled to put their contracts into watertight compartments when selecting. In *Graham v ABF Ltd* the selection criteria under an agreed procedure were not specific enough.

What if the employer selects on the basis of age, for example, selecting everyone aged 60 or over? As noted in chapter 6, there is no age discrimination legislation, but conceivably selection on grounds of age alone might not pass the reasonableness test in unfair dismissal law.

Length of employment has traditionally been adopted as a selection criterion, often using the principle of last in/first out (LIFO) which should be based on continuous rather than accumulated service – the latter might include breaks in employment *(International Paint Co Ltd v Cameron)*. Whatever the criteria for selection, however, there should be a proper analysis of the available information, so that it is clear how, by whom and upon what basis the selection was made *(Bristol Channel Ship Repairers Ltd v O'Keefe; Grieg v MacAlpine)*.[11] But it would be imposing too great a burden on employers to require them to prove that the information on which they made their selection was accurate – employers need establish the fairness of selection only in general terms *(Buchanan v Tilcon Ltd)*.

LIFO has been a widely used criterion for redundancy selection for a number of reasons. It is least likely to result in worker resentment, conflict with trades unions and unfair dismissal claims. It enables experienced workers to be retained and so helps to maintain stability. It is also relatively cheap, because younger, shorter-serving employees are made redundant. Finally, it lends itself to a flexible approach, because it can be tempered by managerial interest criteria or applied only to particular parts of the workforce. Nevertheless, many employers see LIFO as too blunt an instrument, leaving them with minimal control over who goes and offering them little chance of ensuring that the best people stay. Some feel that it also adds to pay pressures, since most employees know that they are safe from redundancy and consequently are prepared to push for wage increases even though some jobs might be lost.

It is not surprising in the more competitive conditions of recent years that in selecting people for compulsory redundancy there has been a move away from the principle of last in, first out towards systems which give greater weight to the skills and experience which need to be retained in order to maintain an effective and balanced workforce.[12] The criteria used include:

- skills and/or qualifications, including experience and training;
- length of employment (seniority);
- standard of work performance including abilities, aptitude, adaptability and reliability;
- attendance record;
- disciplinary record;
- personal and/or domestic circumstances, such as ill-health;
- age; and
- those who are disaffected, eg have poor promotion prospects.

Where redundancy is voluntary, criteria adopted have included, additionally, seniority (but first in, first out) and date of volunteering.

It will be important for management to have accurate information where, for example, absence or disciplinary records are being used as criteria. Management should know and take account of the reasons for absence *(Paine v Grundy (Teddington) Ltd)*. The criteria must be reasonable and not in breach of any statute (eg, by being discriminatory on grounds of sex). They must also be applied reasonably, ie in a consistent and careful manner, again without breach of any statutory provisions.

Overall, some recognition of length of employment is likely to be regarded as reasonable, but so too would be its tempering with business requirements such as the need to keep employees with particular skills, good records, flexible attitudes etc. Tribunals will want to identify the candidates for redundancy and to know the criteria used for selection between them. They will also want to know how the selection was operated, and by whom. In general, they will look for an objective approach, which includes taking into account length of employment.

Employers may find that performance appraisal schemes provide a useful structure for establishing fair and objective selection criteria and that the use of appraisal data can help to ensure that the act of selection is not itself unfair. Aspects such as skills and qualifications, standards of work, aptitude and attendance and disciplinary record may be considered alongside the traditional factor of length of employment. Alternatively, employers may wish to devise a special, separate performance assessment for redundancy selection purposes. This would have the advantage of not putting at risk the dialogue and development which is supposed to be part of a regular appraisal system. Moreover, where appropriate, the assessment criteria could be different. If such an approach is administered fairly it should protect an employer from a tribunal finding of unfair dismissal for redundancy. Above all, an employer must be able to defend the criteria chosen and the manner of application.

Management may feel it is worthwhile to provide a system of appeal against redundancy selection, although a failure to do this will not in itself make a redundancy dismissal unfair *(Robinson v Ulster Carpet Mills Ltd)*.[13] In a unionized setting this might be a joint committee of management and union. In non-union situations, an appeal might lie to management at a more senior level. The right to appeal would be available to any individual selected for redundancy. Experience suggests that providing in-house opportunities for aggrieved employees in this way reduces the risk of claims being made to industrial tribunals.

Race and sex discrimination

Selection for redundancy could constitute race or sex discrimination under the RRA 1976 or the SDA 1975 as well as being an unfair dismissal (see chapter 6). This could be direct or indirect discrimination. Indirect discrimination is where a requirement or condition is applied and the proportion of one sex or race which can comply with it is considerably smaller than the proportion of the other(s). For example, selecting temporary staff for redundancy might amount to indirect sex discrimination if these employees were predominantly female. Selecting part-timers almost certainly will since the vast majority of part-time employees are women. In *Clarke v Eley (IMI) Kynoch Ltd* the dismissal of part-time employees was held to be unlawful sex discrimination and unfair dismissal. The unfair dismissal finding was because the employer's selection failed the reasonableness test. Another issue is whether the application of the LIFO principle can amount to indirect sex discrimination, especially in areas to which women have gained access only in recent years. The EAT rejected such claims in *Brooks v London Borough of Haringey*; LIFO was justified by a common sense need for length of service to be taken into account. The EAT commented that 'length of service is an essential ingredient in any redundancy selection, save in the most exceptional cases'. Thus, length of service as a selection criterion was assumed to be justifiable notwithstanding its indirectly discriminatory effect. The EAT also rejected claims that the exclusion of some largely male areas from the redundancy exercise was unlawful indirect discrimination since these areas were open to recruitment from both men and women.

Selection: types of complaint

The above analysis shows that such complaints may be made on three bases. An employee may be able to mount two separate unfair dismissal challenges to the employer's selection decision, one on specific grounds (eg, on health and safety grounds) the other on the basis of unreasonableness (eg, the criteria adopted). In addition, a case of unfair selection on grounds of race or sex may be possible under the RRA or the SDA.

REASONABLENESS

Aspects other than selection

The reasonableness factor extends beyond selection to any other relevant issues. A main one in practice is lack of consultation. If redundancy becomes necessary 'the employer will normally not act reasonably unless he warns and consults with any employees affected, or their representative' *(Polkey v AE Dayton (Services) Ltd)*. The drift of the rulings in this and other cases is that consultation is required in the ordinary, normal case.[14] The logic is that consultation is necessary so that an attempt can be made to see if the needs of the business can be met without the dismissal and, if not, whether the position of the employee can be improved. However, a failure to consult does not render an otherwise fair redundancy automatically unfair – the ultimate test is reasonableness. If a tribunal concludes that the employer reasonably took the view at the time of dismissal that the exceptional circumstances of the case would make consultation futile, it can find reasonableness even in the absence of proper procedure *(Polkey*; see, eg, *Spink v Express Foods Group Ltd)*.

The size and administrative resources of the undertaking may affect the nature or formality of the consultation process but cannot excuse the lack of any consultation at all *(De Grasse v Stockwell Tools Ltd)*. Consultation with the individual still may be required even where there is negotiation with a union. The individual employee may not know about the content of negotiations prior to a settlement *(Huddersfield Parcels Ltd v Sykes)*. Failure to consult a recognized union as required by the Trade Union and Labour Relations (Consolidation) Act 1992 (see pages 355–7) will not in itself make a dismissal for redundancy unfair *(Atkinson v George Lindsay & Co*; see also *Hough v Leyland DAF Ltd)* but it can be included as part of the reasonableness test.

An employer should take into account all relevant circumstances, not just those directly relating to or surrounding his grounds for dismissal *(Vokes Ltd v Bear)*. Thus, it would be unreasonable not to consider alternative work where there is a possibility. An employer should do what he reasonably can to seek alternative work *(Thomas and Betts Manufacturing Ltd v Harding)* but if the company is part of a group he is not obliged by law to look for job opportunities elsewhere in the group *(MDH Ltd v Sussex)*. Ultimately there is no obligation to provide alternative work *(Merseyside and North Wales Electricity Board v Taylor)*. An employer's behaviour is not likely to be reasonable if the alternative work is not genuine *(Oakley v The Labour Party)* or is offered on unreasonable terms *(Elliott v Richard Stump Ltd)*. Dismissal for refusal to accept alternative work on unreasonable terms is likely to be unfair. The principle decided in the early cases – before the onus of proof of reasonableness was taken off the employer and made neutral – remains valid: a reasonable employer will see if he can offer other employment as an alternative to redundancy *(Barratt Construction Ltd v Dalrhymple)*. The fact that an employer requires applications for alternative work rather than offering it (in the context of a reorganization) may not be unreasonable *(Rennie v Grampian Regional Council,* where an offer had already been made but was rejected as unsuitable).

Next there is the special case of an employer's refusal to take a woman back after maternity leave, where the reason for the refusal is redundancy. The woman must be offered an alternative job if the employer, his successor or any associated employer has a suitable vacancy. The alternative work must be 'suitable in relation to the employee and appropriate for her to do in the circumstances'. The terms and conditions must not be substantially less favourable to her than those under her original contract.[15] Where there is a suitable vacancy which is denied to the woman, she will have been dismissed and the dismissal will be automatically unfair.[16] Indeed, in *John Menzies GB Ltd v Porter* the EAT held the dismissal to be automatically unfair because the employers did not give proper consideration to the search for alternative employment. Where there is no suitable vacancy, there will be a dismissal for redundancy. Where the employer and any associated employer has five or fewer employees and there is no suitable vacancy, there will be no dismissal for the purposes of unfair dismissal law but there will be a dismissal for redundancy for redundancy payments purposes.[17]

The general test

The general test of reasonableness in relation to unfair dismissal claims is 'how a reasonable employer in those circumstances in that line of business would have behaved' *(N C Watling v Richardson)*. However, employers will respond in different ways to a particular set of facts; thus, there will be a range of reasonable responses.[18] An employer' s response will be reasonable if it falls within this range. Unreasonable means that no reasonable employer would have responded in that way. In the context of redundancy, dismissal will not normally be reasonable unless there has been advance warning, consultation with employees and/or their representatives, fair selection and reasonable steps to avoid or minimize redundancy *(Polkey)*. In 1982 the EAT laid down some guidelines in *Williams v Compair Maxam Ltd*.

- An employer should give as much warning of impending redundancies as possible.
- There should be consultation with trades unions to ensure fairness and a minimum of hardship. Employers should seek to agree selection criteria with unions and to check that selection has been carried out according to the criteria.
- As far as possible the factors used in selection should be objective rather than subjective, eg attendance record, job performance, experience and length of service.
- There should be fair selection in accordance with the criteria and consideration of any union representations over selection.
- An employer should seek alternative employment instead of redundancy.

An employer should depart from the above only where there is a good reason.

This case was decided at a time when the EAT's prescriptive role was at its high point and, as is often the case, guidelines came to be taken as requirements. Subsequent decisions of the EAT put the matter in perspective, although the *Compair Maxam* principles remain good practice and are relevant to the question of reasonableness. Nevertheless, the absence of one or more of them will not necessarily lead to a finding of unfair dismissal; it will depend upon the circumstances of the case *(Grundy (Teddington) Ltd v Plummer and Salt; Rolls Royce Motors Ltd v Dewhurst)*. Also, the principles need to be applied with caution where the size and administrative resources of the employer are minimal *(Meikle and McPhail (Charleston Arms))*. In fact, they are likely to be applicable mainly, perhaps only, in the context of substantial redundancies and where there is an independent, recognized trades union *(A Simpson and Son (Motors) v Reid and Findlater)*.

There is no code of practice governing redundancy, the 1972 Industrial Relations Code of Practice having been revoked in 1991. The main procedural requirement of the code had been that management should, in consultation with employee representatives, seek to avoid redundancies. The code stated that where redundancy proved necessary, various matters should be considered, including the following:

- the use of voluntary redundancy,[19] retirement and transfer;
- the phasing of the rundown of employment; and
- offers of help to employees in finding work with other employers.

In the absence of the code, it will be for industrial tribunals to decide whether any of these matters are relevant to the question of reasonableness when determining claims in relation to unfair dismissal for redundancy.

The effect of a procedural slip-up

For many years industrial tribunals, when faced with an employer who had failed on some point of procedure (eg, a failure to consult the employee) applied what came to be known as the 'any difference test' *(British United Shoe Machinery Co Ltd v Clarke)*. They asked whether, if the employer had adopted the correct procedure, it would have affected the outcome: would it have made any difference? Often the answer arrived at was no and many tribunals concluded on this basis that the dismissal was therefore fair, despite the statutory test being one of reasonableness. The position was changed fundamentally in 1987 by a ruling of the House of Lords in *Polkey v AE Dayton (Services) Ltd*. Here it was held that the previous approach was wrong. The correct test was reasonableness, and the any difference test had no part to play in this. However, while the any difference test could not be applied to the question of whether or not the dismissal was fair, it could be applied perfectly properly to the issue of compensation. Therefore, the chances that a redundancy would have occurred even if proper procedure had been followed can be reflected in what has come to be known as a *Polkey* reduction in the compensation. If a redundancy would merely have been delayed (eg, because of consultation) the compensation may be restricted to the period of delay. *Polkey* requires a tribunal to ask whether, if proper procedure had been followed, there would have been an offer of continued employment. If so, what would that employment have been and what wage would have been payable *(Red Bank Manufacturing Co Ltd v Meadows)*? A percentage reduction should be applied to the compensation to reflect the chance that the applicant would have been dismissed even if the procedure had been correct, ie dismissed fairly and without compensation *(Rao v Civil Aviation Authority)*.

The House of Lords in *Polkey*, however, left room for what has become known as the *Polkey* exception. Thus, failing to take proper procedural steps will render a dismissal unfair unless the employer can reasonably conclude in the light of circumstances known to him at the time of dismissal that consultation or warning will be utterly futile. This has been taken to mean that the employer must make a conscious decision, at the time of dismissal, that consultation would be a useless exercise. However, the EAT now holds that the test is an objective one: could a reasonable employer on the facts known at the time of dismissal have dismissed without consultation *(Duffy v Yeomans & Partners)*? This test does not require a conscious decision at the time and appears to allow an employer to justify a procedural lapse. Moreover, it is difficult to reconcile with the EAT's decision on *Robertson v Magnet Ltd* in which it was held that the industrial tribunal had erred in law when applying *Polkey* by not giving sufficient weight to the fact that the employers had not applied their minds at all to the question of consultation. This decision seems to uphold the subjective test, ie how the employer viewed the matter at the time and whether the view was a reasonable one.

This chapter has sought to identify procedures in relation to the employee which will constitute good practice and should reduce the likelihood of unfair dismissal claims. In chapter 18 certain other procedural matters are highlighted, including the requirement to consult with independent, recognized trades unions.[20]

NOTES

1   ERA, s 139(1). The business of the employer and any associated employer(s) is to be treated as one unless (a) or (b) on page 338 above is satisfied without the need for doing so. The same principle is applied to the activities of local authorities and school governors in respect of schools maintained by the local

authority: ERA, s 139(3). For a fuller treatment of the subject of redundancy see Lewis, P., *The Successful Management of Redundancy* (Oxford, Blackwell,1993) and McMullen, J. (ed), *Redundancy: The Law and Practice* (London, FT Law & Tax,1997).

2 ERA, s 139(6).

3 However, surprisingly, in *Frame It v Brown*, the EAT held that a cost-saving exercise in which three people took on the work of four, and the fourth was dismissed, was not dismissal by reason of redundancy because the requirement for the work had not diminished.

4 The balance of convenience test is used to determine whether or not an injunction should be granted. See page 311.

5 Since there was a redundancy there was a breach of what is now TULR(C)A, s 188(1) because there had been no consultation with the recognized trades union.

6 TULR(C)A, ss 152–153 and ERA, s 105.

7 Deregulation and Contracting Out Act 1994.

8 ERA, s 105.

9 Under what is now TULR(C)A. The dismissal was on grounds of trades union activities as defined in s 152(1) and therefore was held to be automatically unfair under s 153.

10 ERA, s 98(4).

11 These cases were decided when the onus of proof of reasonableness lay upon the employer. The onus of proof is now neutral. As a matter of good practice, an employer should explain the selection process to his employees and ensure that managers and supervisors have been instructed and trained in the selection method. After all, they are the people applying it.

12 *Redundancy Arrangements* (ACAS Occasional Paper 37, London, Advisory, Conciliation and Arbitration Service, 1987), page 25. However, the need for employers to take care is underlined by the potential cost of employees taking unfair dismissal claims as a group. For example, it is reported that Hoover in South Wales settled 151 simultaneous individual claims which in aggregate cost £500,000 before any legal charges. An earlier case involving 36 port workers lasted over two years and cost in excess of £1 million (*Financial Times*, 6 January 1993).

13 There seems to be no reason why a serious defect in redundancy procedure (eg, in the application of the selection criteria), which could make a dismissal unfair, cannot be remedied by a proper application of the procedure on appeal. This follows the general unfair dismissal principle set out by the Court of Appeal in *Sartor v P&O European Ferries (Felixstowe) Ltd.*

14 See, eg, *Freud v Bentalls Ltd*; *Kelly v Upholstery and Cabinet Works (Amesbury) Ltd*; *Holden v Bradville Ltd*; and *Ferguson v Prestwick Circuits Ltd*. The last-mentioned raises the question of whether employees want to be consulted. In a redundancy some three years earlier, the employers went through a consultation exercise only to be informed by the workforce that they would have preferred to have been told about their redundancy on the day that they were being made redundant. Therefore, in a second redundancy, the firm dispensed with consultation. This was not sufficient reason for failing to consult and in

any case there was no evidence that the applicants had waived any right to consultation. 'Good industrial practice and the law require that, wherever possible, employees should be consulted before being dismissed on grounds of redundancy.' The Industrial Relations Code of Practice 1972, which required consultation save in exceptional circumstances (at para 44) was revoked in 1991. In its absence tribunals may still regard consultation as part of the concept of reasonableness.

15 ERA, s 96(4).

16 ERA. There is a dismissal by virtue of s 96 and it is automatically unfair as a result of the operation of s 99(1)(e).

17 ERA. This is because the definition of dismissal for redundancy payments purposes in s 137 is different from that in s 96 for unfair dismissal purposes (s 96(2) prevents there being a dismissal).

18 This stems from the case of *British Leyland UK Ltd v Swift*. See also: *Iceland Frozen Foods Ltd v Jones*. See chapter 16.

19 It will be rare for there to be an unfair dismissal for redundancy where redundancy has been voluntary *(Tocher v General Motors (Scotland) Ltd)*.

20 On the question of redundancy procedures generally, see ACAS, *Redundancy Handling* (Advisory Booklet No 12, London, Advisory, Conciliation and Arbitration Service, 1988).

Redundancy: Consultation with Employee or Union Representatives

In redundancies there are procedural requirements at the collective as well as at the individual level. Representatives of employees or – where an independent trades union is recognized – representatives of the trades union, will need to be consulted. A failure to meet the requirements can prove expensive, since remedies are expressed in terms of an employee's pay and substantial number of employees may be involved. Furthermore, the Secretary of State for Employment must be informed when 20 or more redundancies are proposed and a failure here is a criminal offence.

The provisions here were amended in 1995 following the ECJ rulings in *Commission of the EC v UK* (two cases) in which the UK was found to have failed to comply with EC directives on collective redundancies[1] and transfers of undertakings[2] by not providing for consultation with worker representatives where there was no recognized trades union. The amended requirements provide for consultation with either employee or union representatives: where there are both the choice lies with the employer.[3] Employee representatives are given statutory protection parallel to that already given to union representatives (see chapter 21). The threshold for triggering consultation right is increased from one to 20: that is, the duty to consult now arises only if the proposal is to dismiss as redundant at least 20 employees.[4]

The Regulations effecting the 1995 changes were challenged as not fully implementing the EU provisions *(R v Secretary of State for Trade and Industry ex parte Unison)* but unsuccessfully. The government is, however, now engaged in a consultation exercise to determine whether improvements are necessary, including the abolition of the 20 employees threshold and the setting of rules for conducting elections for employee representatives.

THE DUTY TO CONSULT

General points

Where an employer is proposing to dismiss 20 or more employees at one establishment within 90 days or less by reason of redundancy, he must consult either the representatives of employees or the representatives of any independent trades union that he recognizes.[5] The available defence is that special circumstances have made it not reasonably practicable to consult, but in such cases employers still must take all steps that are reasonably practicable. The employees covered by these provisions are not required to have any periods of qualifying employment, nor any continuous employment at all (so that the number of hours worked is not relevant). However, some employees are excluded: Crown employees, House of Commons staff, merchant seamen, share fishermen, employees ordinarily working outside Great Britain; employees working under contracts for three months or less or task contracts expected to last for three months or less, unless in both cases they have already worked for more than three months; and those employed in the police service.[6] There still will be a right to consultation in cases where the employee is not entitled to a statutory redundancy payment.

Consultation with trades unions

Where consultation is with union representatives, they must be consulted about the proposed redundancy of an employee even if he is not a union member, as long as he is of the description of employees for which the union is recognized (*National Association of Teachers in Further and Higher Education v Manchester City Council*).

A trades union is an organization of workers whose principal purposes include regulating the relations between those workers and employers or employers' associations. The definition includes federations of unions.[7] Independent means that a union is not under the domination or control of an employer and is not liable to interference by an employer tending towards such control. A union may apply to the Certification Officer for a certificate of independence.[8] Recognition[9] means that a trades union is accepted by an employer (or associated employers) for the purposes of collective bargaining, ie for the purposes of negotiations related to or connected with:

(a) terms and conditions of employment, or the physical conditions in which any workers are required to work,

(b) engagement or non-engagement, or termination or suspension of employment or the duties of employment, of one or more workers,

(c) allocation of work or the duties of employment as between workers or groups of workers,

(d) matters of discipline,

(e) the membership or non-membership of a trades union on the part of a worker,

(f) facilities for officials of trades unions, and

(g) machinery for negotiation or consultation, and other procedures, relating to any of the foregoing matters, including the recognition by employers or employers' associations of the right of a trades union to represent workers in any such negotiation or consultation or in the carrying out of such procedures.[10]

A collective agreement is an agreement between union(s) and employer(s) on one or more of these matters.[11] In this context, the term 'associated employers' does not refer to membership of an employers' association. Rather, it refers to employers where one is a company controlled by the other, or where both are companies controlled by some third person.[12]

The case law confirms that recognition means direct recognition by the employer. It is not sufficient that the employer is a member of an employers' association which recognises various unions on an industry-wide basis *(National Union of Gold, Silver and Allied Trades v Albury Bros*; see also *Cleveland County Council v Springett)*. Representation of an employee by a full-time union official in respect of a disciplinary matter is not recognition for bargaining purposes *(Transport and General Workers' Union v Courtenham Products)* nor is the granting of general representational (as opposed to bargaining) rights *(Union of Shop, Distributive and Allied Workers v Sketchley Ltd)*. Presumably the same is true where a union is afforded consultation rights. There must be an express or implied agreement to recognize, and, if implied, there must be clear and unequivocal conduct consistent with recognition *(National Union of Tailors and Garment Workers v Charles Ingram Co Ltd)*. Stating on an official form (such as that used for notifying proposed redundancies to the Secretary of State) that a union is recognized would be strong evidence. Recognition can be partial, ie granted in respect of some issues but not others; but if it is limited to certain grades of employees or locations, the consultation rights will be similarly limited. The onus of proof appears to lie with the trades union to demonstrate the existence of a recognition agreement *(Transport and General Workers' Union v Andrew Dyer)*. It is of no relevance that recognition was forced upon an employer by the employees taking industrial action.

The right to be consulted is given to the 'trades union representative', which means 'an official or other person authorized by the trades union to carry on collective bargaining with that employer'.[13] If the Act is to apply, the employer actually must be proposing redundancy rather than just considering it. Proposing means that an employer is at least somewhere near making a decision to dismiss. That is, the stage should have been reached where a specific proposal has been formulated *(Hough v Leyland DAF Ltd)*. This means that the employer should have a view as to numbers, timing and manner of execution *(Association of Patternmakers and Allied Craftsmen v Kirvin Ltd)*. There is a presumption that redundancy is the reason for the dismissal (or proposed dismissal) unless the contrary is shown.[14] Where redundancies are not proposed, but occur as a result of a court winding-up order, there will be no duty to consult *(Re Hartlebury Printers Ltd)*.

Consultation rights extend to non-unionists of the same description as the members represented by the union.

Consultation with employee representatives

As noted, 'appropriate representatives' are either union representatives or employee representatives. The latter are elected by the employees for the specific purpose of being consulted by their employer about the proposed dismissals, or have been elected other than for that specific purpose but it is appropriate to consult them about the dismissals. Such representatives must be employed by the employer at the time when they are elected.

Where the employer invites dismissed employees to elect representatives and the timing of the invitation is such to allow the employees to begin the election of representatives prior to consultation at the required time, the employer will have complied with the requirements if he consults as soon as is reasonably practicable after the election. The legislation lays down no rules about the manner in which representatives should be elected or how many there should be.

Meaning of redundancy

The meaning of redundancy in the provisions relating to consultation is different from that which applies in the case of unfair dismissal or redundancy payments. Here, redundancy means dismissal for a reason not related to the individual or for a number of reasons not so related.[15] This is clearly a much wider definition than that contained in ERA, s 139 and flows from the requirements of the EU Collective Redundancies Directive, as amended in 1992.

Access to employees

Employers must allow representatives access to the employees whom it is proposed to dismiss as redundant and must provide appropriate accommodation and other facilities.

THE CONSULTATION PROCESS

Where the employees do not elect any representatives and there is no recognized trades union, there will be no duty to consult. Where there is such a duty, however, the consultation must 'begin in good time'.[16] More specifically, where the proposal is to dismiss 100 or more employees within 90 days or less it must begin at least 90 days before the first dismissal. In other cases, it must begin at least 30 days before the first dismissal.

'Establishment' is not defined in the legislation and has to be determined on the facts of each case. In *Barratt Developments (Bradford) Ltd v Union of Construction, Allied Trades and Technicians*, the EAT held that 14 building sites administered from one head office were a single establishment. It seems that the degree of management control, the extent of geographical separation and perhaps the permanence or otherwise of the operation may be relevant factors. However, establishment relates to the employer proposing to dismiss. Where several employing companies operate on the same site, and are owned by a holding company, there is no question of treating them as one establishment because they are separate employers *(E Green and Son (Castings) Ltd v (1) Association of Scientific, Technical and Managerial Staffs (2) Amalgamated Union of Engineering Workers)*.

Proposing to dismiss means intending to give notice of termination or to dismiss without notice. Since an employer proposing to dismiss must consult, it follows that there must be some consultation before notice of dismissal is given *(National Union of Teachers v Avon County Council)*. Consultation must start before the proposed date of the first dismissal *(E Green and Son; Transport and General Workers' Union v Ledbury Preserves (1928) Ltd)*. As a matter of good practice, consultation should start before any public announcement of the redundancies. There must be 'sufficient meaningful consultation' before dismissal notices are sent out in order to give representatives time to consider properly the proposals being put to them *(Ledbury)*. In another case, an industrial tribunal held that there should be sufficient information to allow representatives to make constructive proposals *(General and Municipal Workers' Union (Managerial, Administrative and Technical Staffs Association) v British Uralite)*. Post-dismissal consultation is not consultation. Thus, a letter giving notice of dismissal but offering the opportunity of discussion did not meet the statutory requirements. The employer must consult pre-dismissal upon such matters as the selection criteria and their application, any special factors mitigating against dismissal, whether dismissal could be avoided and the possibilities for alternative work. Meaningful consultation means 'giving the body consulted a fair and proper opportunity to understand fully the matters about which it is being consulted, and to express its views on those subjects with the consultor, thereafter considering those views properly and genuinely' *(Rowell v Hubbard Group Services Ltd)*.

The consultation process itself comprises the employer disclosing in writing to representatives the whole of the following:

(a) the reason for his proposals;
(b) the numbers and descriptions of employees whom he proposes to dismiss;
(c) the total numbers of employees of such description(s) employed at that establishment;
(d) proposed method of selection;
(e) the proposed method of carrying out the dismissals, having regard to any agreed procedure, and the period over which they are to take effect; and
(f) information necessary to show how extra-statutory severance pay is calculated.[17]

Consultation does not require that the employees to be made redundant are named *(Spillers-French (Holdings) Ltd v Union of Shop, Distributive and Allied Workers)*, but an employer must provide more detail about the proposed method of selection than a statement indicating that it will be determined in consultation with representatives *(E Green and Son)*.

Consultation must include consultation about ways of avoiding the dismissals, reducing the number of employees to be dismissed and mitigating the consequences. It must be undertaken by the employer with a view to reaching agreement with the representatives.

Employers as a matter of good practice may consult, or negotiate, in respect of other matters, such as:

- earnings and other money issues (eg, relocation expenses) where there is redeployment;
- the basis of selection (eg, department or company);
- whether employees may leave before their notice expires, without losing entitlement to their redundancy payment;
- extension of the length of trial periods on redeployment;
- retention of company benefits after redundancy;
- provisions to avoid the redundancy of apprentices and other trainees; and
- time off in excess of that required by the legislation.

An employer may argue that there were 'special circumstances' for failing to comply with one or more of the statutory provisions, namely the time requirements (effectively an advance warning of redundancy), the written information requirements and the obligation to consider and reply to any representations. Tribunals will generally ask:

- what are the 'circumstances'?
- are they 'special'?
- did they make full consultation not 'reasonably practicable'? and
- did the employer do as much as was 'reasonably practicable'?

Special means 'exception or out of the ordinary' *(Bakers' Union v Clark's of Hove Ltd)*. Therefore, insolvency does not of itself constitute special circumstances *(Clark's of Hove)*. Nor does the dismissal of workers to make an insolvent company more attractive to buyers, and the subsequent closure of the company: these are common occurrences *(General, Municipal and Boilermakers' Union v Rankin and Harrison)*. Where a redundancy decision is made by someone who controls the employer (eg, a parent company in another EU Member State or outside the EU) and the employer is not provided with information about the redundancy, the employer will not be permitted to argue the special circumstances defence if there is a failure to consult or to notify the Secretary of State. In contrast, the sudden withdrawal of credit facilities and the appointment of a receiver by a bank were special circumstances *(Union of Shop, Distributive and Allied Workers v Leancut Bacon Ltd)*. Once the special circumstances defence is established, it will be unjust for a tribunal to make an adverse declaration *(Clark's of Hove)*.

COMPLAINTS

An employee representative, a recognized, independent trades union (but not a trades union representative) or an employee dismissed as redundant, may make a complaint to an industrial tribunal either before or no later than three months after the last dismissal takes effect that one or more of the statutory requirements has not been met. An employer arguing special circumstances will have the burden of proof upon him on this point. The tribunal, if it finds an infringement of the statute, must make a declaration to that effect, and may also make a 'protective award'. This is an award that the employer shall pay the employee remuneration for a protected period. The award does not name individual employees; rather, it specifies the description of employees to which it relates *(Spillers-French)*.

The period is at the discretion of the tribunal, but must not exceed 90 days in the 100 or more employees case or 30 days in any other case. The test is what is 'just and equitable ... having regard to the seriousness of the employer's default'.[18]

What is just and equitable is a matter for the industrial tribunal *(Sovereign Distribution Services Ltd v Transport and General Workers' Union)*. The protective award compensates for loss arising out of the lack of consultation but is also punitive because the tribunal must have regard to the seriousness of the employer's breach *(Spillers-French)*. Such a breach may not be considered very serious if it comprises nothing more than a failure to put in writing information which was given orally, as in *Association of Scientific, Technical and Managerial Staffs v Hawker Siddeley Aviation Ltd.* A failure to give reasons for the redundancies, or a failure to provide information on one of the other matters listed in (a) to (f) on page 359 might be viewed more seriously *(Transport and General Workers' Union v Nationwide Haulage Ltd)*. A failure to consult at all (as in *Clark's of Hove*) or consultation undertaken only at the last minute (as in *E Green and Son*) might be even more serious. The financial significance of these awards can be considerable because there are often substantial numbers of employees covered by them. As an example, an industrial tribunal in Edinburgh was reported as making a protective award of 48 days' pay against GEC Defence Systems. This was thought to amount to somewhere between £600,000 and £800,000. The award may be reduced by any contractual payments made in respect of the protected period, including damages for breach of contract. Conversely, the award can be set off against any contractual liabilities. The award runs from the date of the first dismissal; or the date of the award if that is earlier. The date of the first dismissal means when the first of the proposed dismissals was expected to take effect *(E Green and Son; Transport and General Workers' Union v Ledbury Preserves (1928) Ltd (No 2))*. The protective award does not extend the employee's employment for the purpose of calculating a statutory redundancy payment or for the purpose of the qualifying period for a statutory redundancy payment. Where the employer is insolvent, up to eight weeks' pay from any protective award (subject to the maximum weekly limit) is payable from the National Insurance Fund.[19]

An employee will lose the right to a protective award if while still employed he unreasonably terminates his contract of employment or is fairly dismissed for a reason other than redundancy. An unreasonable refusal of suitable alternative work will lose the employee the protective award for that part of the protected period during which he would otherwise have been employed. If the employee accepts the offer there is a trial period during which reasonable termination by the employee preserves entitlement to the protective award.[20]

An employee whose employer fails to pay him during the protected period may apply to a tribunal within three months of the last day of non-payment. A tribunal may order an employer to pay. In practice therefore those employers who fail to consult and pay a protective award are simply buying-out the union's right to consultation.

The statutory requirements may be adapted, modified or excluded if there is a collective agreement which is 'on the whole at least as favourable' as the legislation, but there must be provision for independent resolution of disputed matters.[21] The statutory requirements may be adapted, modified or excluded only upon the application of all the parties to the collective agreement to the Secretary of State and by order of the Secretary of State. However, employers are free to use the statutory provisions as a minimum. They may offer consultation beyond the requirements of the law, for example, by consulting over longer periods, by consulting with organizations other than recognized trades unions (eg, staff bodies which are not independent, recognized unions) and by consulting over a range of matters which is wider than that specified in the legislation.

Where there is a change of employer falling under the Transfer of Undertakings (Protection of Employment) Regulations there will be no redundancy as a result of the transfer itself but the consultation requirements of the regulations will apply (see chapter 20). The provisions described above will operate where the transferor or the transferee is proposing to make 20 or more employees redundant. Union recognition and any redundancy agreements are likely to be transferred to the transferee.

EMPLOYMENT RIGHTS OF EMPLOYEE REPRESENTATIVES

Trades union representatives have for some considerable length of time been protected against dismissal or action short of dismissal on the ground of their union membership or activity and had rights to time off with pay (see chapter 21). Those suffering a detriment or dismissal because of matters connected to their role as union representatives in the redundancy consultation process would be protected by the general provisions. The extension of consultation rights to employee representatives raises the issue of providing equivalent protection for those representatives.

Equivalent rights are conferred where an employee representative, or a candidate in an election for such a representative, suffers a detriment other than dismissal because he performed or proposed to perform any functions or activities as such a representative. These rights are couched in terms similar to those applying to employees who suffer a detriment in health and safety cases (see pages 304–5). Where there is a dismissal, it will be automatically unfair.

A right to time off is given to employee representatives, the rights being set out in terms similar to those relating to time off for ante-natal care (see pages 259–60).

NOTIFICATION OF PROPOSED REDUNDANCIES TO THE SECRETARY OF STATE FOR EMPLOYMENT

An employer must notify the Secretary of State of proposed redundancies involving 20 or more dismissals in accordance with certain time periods (see page 358).[22] The unit for consideration is the establishment rather than the organization. Where redundancies have already been notified they do not count again if there are further redundancies requiring notification. Thus, 40 redundancies within 30 days (requiring notification 30 days before dismissal) followed by another 80 within 30 days (requiring 30 days' notification) do not become 120 requiring 90 days' notification. Compliance with the notification process does not prevent an employer from altering his plans (eg, abandoning the implementation of redundancies or postponing them) if circumstances change. Failure to comply leaves the employer liable to a fine.[23] Copies of the notification must be sent by the employer to employee or union representatives but the duty to notify the Secretary of State arises even in the absence of representatives.[24]

The notice to the Secretary of State must 'be in such form and contain such particulars ... as the Secretary of State may direct'.[25] Where consultation with representatives is required the notice must identify the union or representatives concerned and specify the date when consultation started. The Secretary of State can by written notice require further information.[26] The Department for Education and Employment encourages use of a standard form for notification. A copy of this is included as Figure 18.1 An employer may plead 'special circumstances' as a defence if there has not been notification, but must do all that is reasonably practicable to comply with the requirement to notify.

TIME OFF TO LOOK FOR WORK OR TO ARRANGE TRAINING

An employee given notice of dismissal by reason of redundancy is entitled to a reasonable amount of paid time off before the expiry of his notice.[27] The time off is within working hours in order to look for new employment or make arrangements for training for future employment. There is a two-year qualifying period. The right to paid time off is not affected by the fact that an employee may not be eligible for a statutory redundancy payment (*Dutton v Hawker Siddeley Aviation Ltd*).[28] An employee refused time off or pay for time off may complain to an industrial tribunal within three months. The maximum compensation payable is two-fifths of a week's pay. The amount of paid time off can be extended beyond this in practice, for

Employment Department
Employment Protection Act 1975, Section 100

Advance notification of redundancies

What is this all about?
As an employer, you are required by law to notify proposed redundancies of ten or more employees.

When do I have to do that?
If 10 to 99 employees might be dismissed as redundant from one establishment over a period of 30 days or less – **you must give at least 30 days' notice.**

If 100 or more employees might be dismissed as redundant from one establishment over a period of 90 days or less – **you must give at least 90 days' notice.**

The date of notification is the date it is received by the Employment Department. For more details please see leaflet PL833 'Redundancy consultation and notification'. You can get one from any Jobcentre or Unemployment Benefit Office.

What information do I have to give?
It is the information requested in the form below. You can send a letter instead but you must give the information asked for in the form. Please send a separate notification for each establishment where it is proposed that ten or more employees will be made redundant.

Where do I send the form or letter?
You may have been given an addressed envelope for the return of the form. If so, please use it, if not, please return the form to the Employment Department, Redundancy Payments Office, Hagley House, 83–85 Hagley Road, Birmingham B16 8QG, or to the nearest Employment Department office.

What if I notify you about redundancies and the circumstances change?
The fact that yo hve notifice us about redundancies does not commit you to them. But if the circumstances change, please let us know.

Anything else?
Yes. One or more groups of workers to be made redundant may belong to a recognised independent trade union. If so, you must send a copy of your notification to the representatives of each such trade union.

Data Protection Act 1984
We will put the information you give us on to a computer. We will pass it to selected government agencies who may offer to help you deal with the proposed redundancy. Information will not be given to any non government agencies without your consent.

These notes are for guidance only. They are not a full and authoritative statement of the law.

- *Where there are boxes offering a choice of answer, please tick those that apply.*
- *If there is not enough space for your reply, please continue on a separate sheet of paper and attach it to this form.*
- *Use a separate form for each establishment where redundancies will occur.*

1 Name of employer (CAPITALS please)

2 Address

    Postcode

3 Telephone number

4 Who should we contact if we have any queries about this form?
Name (CAPITALS please)

5 Please give this person's business address and telephone number if either is not the same as given above:
Address

    Postcode

6 Telephone number

7 What is the address of the establishment at which the employees are employed?

- as given at 2 ☐
- as given at 5 ☐

or give details below:

8 What is the nature of the main business at that establishment?

9 Plase tick one or more boxes to show the main reason(s) for the redundancies:

- lower demand for products or services ☐ A
- completion of all or part of contract ☐ B
- transfer of activities to another workplace following a merger ☐ C
- introduction of new technology ☐ D
- introduction of new plant or machinery ☐ E
- changes in work methods or organisation ☐ F*
- transfer of activiites to another workplace for other reasons ☐ G*
- something else ☐ H*

*please give details below

Figure 18.1 Advance notification of redundancies

10 How many people do you currently employ at this establishment?

employees

11 How may employees at this establishment do you think **might** be made redundant?

employees

12 If you have the information available, please give figures below to show the numbers employed/to be made redundant:

Occupational group	Number employed now	Number to be made redundant
Manual		
• skilled		
• semi-skilled		
• unskilled		
Clerical		
Managerial/ technical		

13 How many apprentices and long term trainees may be made redundant?

apprentices/trainees

14 How many employees under 20 years old (including apprentices and trainees) may be made redundant?

employees

15 Do you propose to close down the establishment?

Yes ☐   No ☐

16 When will the first proposed redundancy take effect?

Day	Month	Year

17 When will the last proposed redundancy take effect?

Day	Month	Year

18 Briefly, how do you propose to choose which employees should be made redundant?

Trade union involvement

19 Are any of the groups of employees who may be made redundant represented by a recognised trade union?

Yes ☐

No ☐ ▶ go to 'Declaration' below

20 Please give below the name and address of each such trade union:

21 When did consultation with the trade union(s) start?

Day	Month	Year

22 Has full agreement with the trade union(s) been reached?

Yes ☐ ▶ *please enclose a copy of the agreement or give brief details below:*

No ☐

Declaration

I certify that the information given on this form is, so far as I know, correct and complete.

Signed

Date

Position held

For our use

Figure 18.1 (contd)

example, to one week.[29] It should be noted that the two-fifths of a week's pay is not subject to the statutory limit.

NOTES

1 75/129/EC, OJ 1975, L48/29.
2 77/187/EC, OJ 1977, L61/26.
3 The Collective Redundancies and Transfer of Undertakings (Protection of Employment) (Amendment) Regulations (SI 1995/2587) (issued under the European Communities Act 1972).
4 Ibid, reg 3.
5 TULR(C)A, s 188(1).
6 TULR(C)A, ss 273, 278, 280, 282–285 and 295–296.
7 TULR(C)A, s 1.
8 TULR(C)A, ss 5–6; providing that it is listed. The Certification Officer is part of the Department of Employment, and is an independent statutory authority. The Certification Officer exercises functions specified in various statutes including the listing of trades unions. Being listed is evidence that an organization is a trades union. The process of listing is voluntary, but being listed is a prerequisite for obtaining a certificate of independence and tax relief for provident funds. See pages 409–10.
9 TULR(C)A, s 178(3).
10 TULR(C)A, s 178(2).
11 TULR(C)A, s 178(1).
12 TULR(C)A, s 297.
13 TULR(C)A, s 196.
14 TULR(C)A, s 195(3). This presumption applies also to the provisions requiring notification of proposed dismissals for redundancy to the Secretary of State.
15 TULR(C)A, s 295.
16 TULR(C)A, s 188(1A).
17 These requirements are laid down in TULR(C)A, s 188(4). The information, in writing, may be conveyed by personal delivery or by letter to a union-nominated address or the union's head office (s 188(5)). A public body's failure to consult as required by its own procedure may be subject to judicial review. British Coal's 1992 decision to avoid using the industry's colliery closure consultative procedure was held to be unlawful because it was in breach of the industry procedure and was irrational. It was also in breach of the TULR(C)A requirements *(R v President of the Board of Trade ex parte NUM)*.
18 TULR(C)A, s 189(4)(b).
19 ERA, s 184.
20 TULRC(C)A, s 191.
21 TULR(C)A, s 198
22 TULR(C)A, s 193. There is no requirement to notify where it is proposed to make redundant fewer than 20 employees. The following are not subject to the

notification requirement: Crown employees, House of Commons staff, merchant seamen, share fishermen, employees ordinarily working outside Great Britain, and employees on contracts for terms of three months or less, or on task contracts lasting for less than three months, unless, in both cases, there is already more than three months' continuous employment (TULR(C)A, ss 278, 282–285 and 295–296). Those employed in the police service are not subject to the notification requirement because they are expressly excluded from the definition of employee (TULR(C)A, s 280).

23 The employer is liable on summary conviction to a fine not exceeding level five on the standard scale, currently £5,000 (TULR(C)A, s 194(1) and Criminal Justice Act 1991, s 17).

24 TULR(C)A, s 193(6), but there appears to be no penalty if this is not done.

25 TULR(C)A, s 193(4)(c).

26 TULR(C)A, s 193(5).

27 ERA, s 52. The following are excluded: employees normally working outside Great Britain, merchant seamen, share fishermen and members of the police service.

28 An employee might be ineligible for a redundancy payment but eligible for time off where an offer of suitable alternative employment is unreasonably refused. The right to paid time off is not qualified in this way.

29 *Redundancy Terms* (IDS Study 464, London, Incomes Data Services, 1990), page 6.

N I N E T E E N

Redundancy Payments

This chapter deals with payments arising out of redundancy, lay-off and insolvency. Its principal focus is the statutory redundancy payments scheme.

THE STATUTORY REDUNDANCY PAYMENTS SCHEME

Eligibility

An employee dismissed by reason of redundancy may be entitled to a statutory redundancy payment (RP). To qualify, the employee must have been continuously employed by the employer or an associated employer for two years or more,[1] be dismissed by reason of redundancy and be below the upper age limit. However, it should be noted that in *R v Secretary of State for Employment ex parte Seymour-Smith*, the Court of Appeal held the two-year qualifying period to be indirect sex discrimination which was not objectively justified (see chapter 6) (this case has been referred to the ECJ). Where normal retiring age (NRA) does not discriminate on grounds of sex and is 65 years or lower, the NRA will be the limit. In any other circumstances 65 applies (see Table 19.1)[2] (the concept of NRA is explained on page 315).

Since employment before the age of 18 years does not count towards computation of continuous employment, a person has to be at least 20 to obtain a payment.[3]

Some employees are excluded from the legislation, namely:

- share fishermen;[4]

Table 19.1   *Maximum age limit for entitlement to statutory redundancy payments*

	eligibility limit (must be under)
Non-discriminatory NRA of 65 or below	NRA
Non-discriminatory NRA above 65	65
No NRA at all	65
Discriminatory NRAs	65

- Crown servants – these are covered by their own separate agreements;[5]
- employees whose contract requires them to ordinarily work outside Great Britain, unless they are working in Great Britain on the instructions of their employer[6] at the time of the redundancy;
- an employee who is outside Great Britain at the time of redundancy will be entitled to an RP only if he ordinarily works in Great Britain;[7]
- employees of foreign governments;[8]
- domestic servants who are close relatives of the employer;[9]
- members of the armed forces;[10] and
- staff of the Houses of Parliament.[11]

There are special provisions for former registered dock workers.[12] National Health Service employees and merchant seamen are no longer excluded[13] and, following the House of Lords ruling in *R v Secretary of State for Employment ex parte EOC* and the Employment Protection (Part-Time Employees) Regulations 1995, part-time employees are also covered. The Secretary of State may make regulations to extend the statutory RP scheme to holders of public office who are not employed under a contract of employment.[14] There are also provisions bringing offshore workers within the statutory scheme.[15]

The scheme includes those on fixed-term contracts, excluding apprenticeships. Where the contract is for a term of two years or more there will be a right to claim a payment on expiry of the contract unless there has earlier been a written agreement to waive that right. It would then have to be decided whether the non-renewal was for reason of redundancy (see *Nottinghamshire County Council v Lee*; *North Yorkshire County Council v Fay*). The waiver applies only to the time of expiry and not to redundancy within the term of the contract, although there would be no entitlement to an RP unless the two-year qualifying period had already been met. The waiver may be made at any time before the fixed term expires, but lapses on expiry, although it can be renewed.[16]

Meaning of dismissal and onus of proof

The onus is upon the employee to establish that there was a dismissal. Dismissal was defined in chapter 16.[17] Any notice must specify a date of termination or contain material from which a date is ascertainable. Otherwise, there will be no dismissal. Thus, an application for voluntary redundancy and the employer's agreement to release, but with the date to be decided, did not constitute dismissal *(Burton Group Ltd v Smith)*.

A fixed-term contract must have a date of expiry, and the expiry of such a contract is a dismissal. A contract which is to last as long as it takes to perform a particular task, without any fixed date of expiry, is not a fixed-term contract and the end of the contract does not constitute a dismissal *(Wiltshire County Council v NATFHE and Guy)*. The same is true of a contract, again not for a fixed period, which is determined by something other than performance. In the case of *Brown v Knowsley Borough Council* the contract was to last as long as outside finance remained available. When outside finance ceased, the contract ended, but it was not a dismissal.

There are also provisions to ensure that certain events which normally would not be treated as dismissal are so treated.[18] These are the death of a personal employer, the dissolution of a partnership, the receivership and liquidation of a company and the frustration of the employment contract by any event affecting the employer. The dismissal will be taken to be by reason of redundancy if there is no renewal of contract or re-engagement under a new contract by the employer, any person to whom the power to dispose of the business has passed or any new owner of the business, providing that the reason for such non-renewal or non-re-engagement is redundancy.

Once the fact of dismissal is established the dismissal is to be taken as for reason of redundancy if not proved otherwise. This means the employer has to show that the reason was not redundancy. Where unfair dismissal is also alleged, the onus is upon the employer to show the reason for dismissal.

The concept of redundancy was analysed in chapter 17. It was noted that it involved a dismissal wholly or mainly due to:

- a cessation of the entire business;
- a cessation in the particular place where the employee was employed; or
- a diminution in the requirement for employees to perform work of a particular kind (either generally or in the place where the employee was employed).

The Court of Appeal has applied a contractual test to work of a particular kind so that it refers to work that the employee can be required to do under his contract of employment *(Nelson v British Broadcasting Corporation; Haden Ltd v Cowen;* applied by the EAT in *Pink v (1) White (2) White & Co (Earls (Barton) Ltd)*. Similarly, place of work means the contractual place –

wherever the employee can be required to work *(United Kingdom Atomic Energy Authority v Claydon; Hawker Siddeley Aviation Ltd; Rank Xerox Ltd v Churchill)*. However, a distinction may be drawn between a mobility clause and a broadly defined place of work: see *Bass Leisure* (on page 340). Terms relating to place of work may be express or implied. They may be implied from collective agreements, custom in the firm or from the nature and practice of the work. In *O'Brien v Associated Fire Alarms Ltd* the court implied a mobility term from the nature and practice of the work but held that it limited mobility to daily travelling distance from home or to within a reasonable distance from home.

Industrial action or misconduct by the employee[19]

If before giving notice of redundancy the employer is entitled to dismiss for misconduct, a redundancy payment will not be payable even if the reason for dismissal is redundancy *(Simmons v Hoover Ltd)*. The test is a contractual one – whether the employee is in breach of contract such that dismissal is justified – rather than that of reasonableness, as found in unfair dismissal law *(Bonner v H Gilbert Ltd)*. An employee will thus lose entitlement to an RP if dismissed for striking prior to his employer giving him the 'obligatory' notice, ie that required by contract or statute (whichever is greater). Where misconduct, other than taking part in a strike, occurs (or is discovered) during the 'obligatory' notice period, and the employer dismisses for that misconduct, the tribunal has discretion to award the whole of the RP or such part as it thinks fit. An employee will retain his right to an RP if dismissed for striking during the 'obligatory' notice period. An employee also will retain his right to an RP even if the redundancy was caused to some extent by earlier industrial action in which he took part. This might be the case, eg where the action caused permanent loss of customers. Equity is not the principle to be applied, however *(Sanders v Ernest A Neale Ltd)*.

Lay-offs and short-time working

A redundancy payment may be paid when an employee is laid-off or put on short-time working.[20] A person is laid-off for the purposes of the legislation where in any week the employer provides no work of the kind that the employee is employed to do, and under the contract of employment there is no entitlement to be paid. Short-time is where there is a diminution in the work provided which leads to at least a 50 per cent reduction in pay. Where the employer offers alternative work which is within the terms of the employee's contract and which would prevent the occurrence of short-time working, he shall be taken to have 'provided' the work even if it is refused by the employee *(Spinpress Ltd v Turner)*. In the case of both short-time working and lay-off there must be four consecutive weeks or six weeks in 13 (no more than three being consecutive). Weeks of lay-off or short-time caused by strikes or lock-outs anywhere cannot be counted. To claim an RP, the employee has to give notice of termination of employment and follow a rather complicated procedure.[21]

This involves the employee giving written notice to the employer of intention to claim an RP. Such notice must be given within four weeks of the last of the weeks of lay-off or short-time on which the claim is based, but must occur after the period of lay-off or short-time working relied on is complete (*Allinson v Drew Simmons Engineering Ltd*). The employer then has seven days to serve a counter-notice stating that he will contest liability. An offer of alternative work will not constitute a valid counter-notice (*Reid v Arthur Young and Son*). Where such a counter-notice is served, and not withdrawn, an employee will not be entitled to an RP unless he or she applies to an industrial tribunal and is successful. An employer's defence is that normal working is reasonably to be expected no later than four weeks after the date on which the employee serves notice of intention to claim, and that such working can reasonably be expected to last for at least 13 continuous weeks without there being a lay-off or short-time in any week. Normal working involves the employee being employed under the same contract as before (*Neepsend Steel and Tool Corporation v Vaughan*). The defence is available only if a valid counter-notice has been served by the employer.

The employee must give whatever length of notice of termination of contract is required by the contract. Where the employer has not served a counter-notice, the employee's notice of termination must be within four weeks of his notice of intention to claim. Where there has been a counter-notice which has been withdrawn, notice of termination must be within three weeks of the withdrawal. Where the employer has not withdrawn his counter-notice and an RP has been awarded by an industrial tribunal, notice of termination must occur within three weeks of the employee being notified of the tribunal's decision.

The time limits in the above scheme cannot be extended. Therefore an employer may be able to defend a claim on the basis that the employee has failed to give one or both of the required notices within the allowed time. On the other hand, an employer may lose a case by not serving a counter-notice in time.

The lay-off or short-time must be lawful. Otherwise, if the employee is ready and willing to work, he is entitled to be paid and these provisions will not apply. Where lay-offs or short-time working is in breach of contract, employees may succeed in claiming constructive dismissal by reason of redundancy and obtaining an RP by this route (*Powell Duffryn Wagon Co Ltd v House*; *Miller v Hamworthy Engineering Ltd*). An employer will not be able to argue that the lay-off was caused by a strike if the case is pursued as a constructive dismissal. That argument relates only to the separate lay-off and short-time provisions *(RH and DT Edwards Ltd v (1) Evans (2) Walters)*. Contractual guarantee pay of at least half a week's pay will remove entitlement to an RP under the lay-off and short-time provisions but statutory guarantee pay (see page 384) may not, since it is not remuneration under the contract.

Alternative employment

An employee will not be entitled to a redundancy payment where the employer, an associated employer or, where a business changes hands, the new owner, offers 'suitable' alternative employment and the employee 'unreasonably' refuses it. An offer must be made before the expiry of the old contract and must take effect immediately on the ending of that contract or no later than four weeks afterwards. It would not be a valid offer under the legislation if it took effect before the ending of the old contract *(McHugh v Hempsall Bulk Transport Ltd)*. It need not be in writing.

Whether the employee will retain the right to a redundancy payment after refusing an employer's offer of alternative work (or terminating the contract during the trial period: see below) will depend on it being established that either the new employment was unsuitable, or that it was suitable but the employee was reasonable in refusing it. In the statute these two questions are to be decided separately, but in practice they become fused. Indeed, in *Spencer and Griffin v Gloucestershire County Council* the Court of Appeal warned against too rigid a distinction between the two because some factors might be common to both. The onus is upon the employer to prove both suitability and unreasonableness *(Jones v Aston Cabinet Co Ltd)* and these are matters of fact for a tribunal to decide *(Standard Telephones and Cables Ltd v Yates*, in respect of suitability).

'Suitable' means suitable 'in relation to him' (the employee).[22] In general it means 'substantially equivalent' *(Taylor v Kent County Council)*. Skills, earnings, nature of previous work, what is traditionally acceptable and geographical location have all been important.[23] In *Smith v R Briggs and Co Ltd* a big drop in earnings potential made the work unsuitable. In the *Yates* case, alternative work as an assembly line operator was not sufficiently skilled and therefore was not suitable for someone who was a skilled craft worker. Lower status can also make alternative work unsuitable, as in *Harris v E Turner and Sons (Joinery) Ltd* in which an instructor was offered alternative work back on the shop floor. In *Taylor v Kent County Council* a headmaster was offered alternative work in a mobile pool of teachers. This was unsuitable despite the fact that the previous level of pay was safeguarded. Sometimes a number of factors operate together: in *Jackson v Harris Queensway plc* there was no proposal to compensate the employee for extra travelling time, his guarantee wage was going to be reduced by a fifth and the job involved more responsibility. The EAT held that such alternative employment was not suitable.

Whether it is reasonable for the employee to refuse suitable alternative employment has often been a matter of the employee's personal or domestic circumstances, although job-related factors also can be relevant. Thus, in *Tocher v General Motors (Scotland) Ltd* it was reasonable to refuse alternative employment which involved a drop in both pay and status. In *Morganite Crucible Ltd v Street* it was unreasonable to refuse a temporary job which would last 12–18 months, but it might be reasonable to refuse something likely to last for a very short period. In *Spencer and Griffin*, alternative cleaning work at a lower standard of cleanliness was suitable, since it is for the employer to determine standards, but the employees' refusal to accept the work on the ground that they did not wish to work at the lower standard, was reasonable. Significant extra travel time and/or cost is another factor which may make a refusal reasonable.[24]

Where an employee accepts renewal of contract or re-engagement under a new contract, there will have been no dismissal.[25] An offer of re-engagement will need to have been made before the expiry of the old contract but this is not the case where the contract is renewed (confirmed by the EAT in *SI (Systems and Instruments) Ltd v Grist and Riley*). An offer must take effect immediately on the ending of the old contract or no later than four weeks afterwards. Again, the offer need not be in writing, but it will need to conform to the general requirements of the law of contract, namely the offer must be sufficiently certain and unconditional, and it must be communicated to the employee. If there is to be renewal or re-engagement, the employee must accept it without qualification. Continuity is preserved for statutory purposes.[26] Where the terms of the new employment differ from those of the old there is a requirement for a 'trial period' of four weeks to establish whether the employment is suitable, without loss of entitlement to claim the RP. 'Four weeks' means four calendar weeks, so that if the period includes a shut-down of work the employee will have less than four weeks to try out the new employment *(Benton v Sanderson Kayser Ltd)*. The statutory trial period can be extended by agreement but only for the purpose of retraining (confirmed by the EAT in *Meek v (1) J Allen Rubber Ltd (2) Secretary of State for Employment*). Any such agreement must be in writing, must specify the end of the trial period and the terms and conditions which will apply afterwards, and be made before the employee starts work under the new contract. There can be more than one statutory trial period where an employer makes a further offer of alternative employment.

A common law trial period occurs where new terms are imposed by an employer in the context of a redundancy and in breach of contract, but the employer does not dismiss and the employee neither resigns (claiming constructive dismissal) nor accepts the new terms *(Air Canada Ltd v Lee)*.

The trial period will be of a reasonable length, but can be a specific period by agreement. The common law trial period stems from the general contractual rule that a party to whom an offer is made should have the opportunity to appraise the terms of the offer. Once the employee has had a reasonable length of time to appraise the new terms, the old contract ends, the new one begins and the statutory trial period commences *(Turvey v CW Cheyney & Son Ltd)*. Therefore, the statutory trial period follows any contractual trial period. None of the above prevents contractual trial periods of a longer duration (eg, six weeks, 13 weeks etc) but these would not preserve the statutory right to an RP unless the statutory requirements were met (ie, the purpose would have to be retraining, the agreement would have to be in writing etc). However, they would preserve the contractual right to an RP if this had been agreed.

Where there is a change in the ownership of a business, and a new owner agrees to continue the employment of the employee on the same or mutually agreed new terms, the provision for suitable alternative employment and a trial period apply as if it was still the original employer. The Transfer of Undertakings (Protection of Employment) Regulations 1981 may also apply[27] (see chapter 20).

Continuity of employment

Continuous employment was defined on pages 88–9. Employment is assumed to be continuous unless proved to the contrary. Thus the onus here is on the employer. Continuous employment ends on the 'relevant date'. Where there is notice it is the date of expiry of notice. Where there is no notice it is the date of termination. Where it is the expiry of a fixed-term contract, it is the date of expiry of the contract. The trial period delays the relevant date only for the purposes of calculating the time available for making a claim. For RP purposes, employment before the age of 18 years does not count when computing the length of continous employment.

Continuous employment for statutory RP calculation purposes excludes any service which has counted for a previous statutory RP[28] (confirmed by the EAT in *Rowan v Machinery Installations (South Wales) Ltd*). However, the previous service will be included if the employer was not liable to make that earlier payment (for example, because the operation of the Transfer of Undertakings (Protection of Employment) Regulation meant that there was no dismissal) *(Gardener v (1) Haydn Davies Catering Equipment (1988) Ltd (in liquidation) (2) ABE Catering Equipment Ltd)*. This is because the earlier payment was not a statutory RP. Continuous employment will be reduced by the payment of a statutory RP only for statutory RP purposes. This was confirmed by the EAT in *Hempell v WH Smith & Sons Ltd* where an employee was re-engaged by her former employer in a new job after being dismissed for redundancy and receiving an RP. She was dismissed a second time, shortly afterwards, on the ground that she was unsuitable. Her continuity for the purposes of an unfair dismissal claim included the period prior to the first dismissal.

Once an employee has become qualified for an RP he or she will remain so until they cease to be employed under a contract of employment.[29]

A strike does not interrupt continuity of employment, but the week in which a strike takes place does not count for the purpose of reckoning service.[30] During periods in which there is no contract of employment there is no break in continuity if there is sickness or injury lasting up to 26 weeks and these weeks also count. There is no break if there is a temporary cessation of work, absence by arrangement or custom, or because of pregnancy or confinement, and, again, the weeks count.

For RP purposes, movement between local government employers does not break continuity of employment.[31] Similar provisions apply to the national health service.[32]

Computation of payment

The payment is calculated on the basis of age, length of employment and earnings according to the formula in the table below.[33] The Department of Employment produces a ready-reckoner for RPs which is included below. There are no current proposals to standardize RPs throughout the EU or to lay down a minimum level.

Table 19.2 *Government ready reckoner for statutory redundancy payments*

Service (years) Age (years)	2	3	4	5	6	7	8	9	10	11	12	13	14	15	16	17	18	19	20
20	1	1	1	1	–														
21	1	1½	1½	1½	1½	–													
22	1	1½	2	2	2	2	–												
23	1½	2	2½	3	3	3	3	–											
24	2	2½	3	3½	4	4	4	4	–										
25	2	3	3½	4	4½	5	5	5	5	–									
26	2	3	4	4½	5	5½	6	6	6	6	–								
27	2	3	4	5	5½	6	6½	7	7	7	7	–							
28	2	3	4	5	6	6½	7	7½	8	8	8	8	–						
29	2	3	4	5	6	7	7½	8	8½	9	9	9	9	–					
30	2	3	4	5	6	7	8	8½	9	9½	10	10	10	10	–				
31	2	3	4	5	6	7	8	9	9½	10	10½	11	11	11	11	–			
32	2	3	4	5	6	7	8	9	10	10½	11	11½	12	12	12	12	–		
33	2	3	4	5	6	7	8	9	10	11	11½	12	12½	13	13	13	13	–	
34	2	3	4	5	6	7	8	9	10	11	12	12½	13	13½	14	14	14	14	–

Service (years) Age (years)	2	3	4	5	6	7	8	9	10	11	12	13	14	15	16	17	18	19	20
35	2	3	4	5	6	7	8	9	10	11	12	13	13½	14	14½	15	15	15	15
36	2	3	4	5	6	7	8	9	10	11	12	13	14	14½	15	15½	16	16	16
37	2	3	4	5	6	7	8	9	10	11	12	13	14	15	15½	16	16½	17	17
38	2	3	4	5	6	7	8	9	10	11	12	13	14	15	16	16½	17	17½	18
39	2	3	4	5	6	7	8	9	10	11	12	13	14	15	16	17	17½	18	18½
40	2	3	4	5	6	7	8	9	10	11	12	13	14	15	16	17	18	18½	19
41	2	3	4	5	6	7	8	9	10	11	12	13	14	15	16	17	18	19	19½
42	2½	3½	4½	5½	6½	7½	8½	9½	10½	11½	12½	13½	14½	15½	16½	17½	18½	19½	20½
43	3	4	5	6	7	8	9	10	11	12	13	14	15	16	17	18	19	20	21
44	3	4½	5½	6½	7½	8½	9½	10½	11½	12½	13½	14½	15½	16½	17½	18½	19½	20½	21½
45	3	4½	6	7	8	9	10	11	12	13	14	15	16	17	18	19	20	21	22
46	3	4½	6	7½	8½	9½	10½	11½	12½	13½	14½	15½	16½	17½	18½	19½	20½	21½	22½
47	3	4½	6	7½	9	10	11	12	13	14	15	16	17	18	19	20	21	22	23
48	3	4½	6	7½	9	10½	11½	12½	13½	14½	15½	16½	17½	18½	19½	20½	21½	22½	23½
49	3	4½	6	7½	9	10½	12	13	14	15	16	17	18	19	20	21	22	23	24
50	3	4½	6	7½	9	10½	12	13½	14½	15½	16½	17½	18½	19½	20½	21½	22½	23½	24½
51	3	4½	6	7½	9	10½	12	13½	15	16	17	18	19	20	21	22	23	24	25
52	3	4½	6	7½	9	10½	12	13½	15	16½	17½	18½	19½	20½	21½	22½	23½	24½	25½
53	3	4½	6	7½	9	10½	12	13½	15	16½	18	19	20	21	22	23	24	25	26
54	3	4½	6	7½	9	10½	12	13½	15	16½	18	19½	20½	21½	22½	23½	24½	25½	26½
55	3	4½	6	7½	9	10½	12	13½	15	16½	18	19½	21	22	23	24	25	26	27
56	3	4½	6	7½	9	10½	12	13½	15	16½	18	19½	21	22½	23½	24½	25½	26½	27½
57	3	4½	6	7½	9	10½	12	13½	15	16½	18	19½	21	22½	24	25	26	27	28
58	3	4½	6	7½	9	10½	12	13½	15	16½	18	19½	21	22½	24	25½	26½	27½	28½
59	3	4½	6	7½	9	10½	12	13½	15	16½	18	19½	21	22½	24	25½	27	28	29
60	3	4½	6	7½	9	10½	12	13½	15	16½	18	19½	21	22½	24	25½	27	28½	29½
61	3	4½	6	7½	9	10½	12	13½	15	16½	18	19½	21	22½	24	25½	27	28½	30
62	3	4½	6	7½	9	10½	12	13½	15	16½	18	19½	21	22½	24	25½	27	28½	30
63	3	4½	6	7½	9	10½	12	13½	15	16½	18	19½	21	22½	24	25½	27	28½	30
64	3	4½	6	7½	9	10½	12	13½	15	16½	18	19½	21	22½	24	25½	27	28½	30

Read off employee's age and number of complete years' service. Service before the employee reached the age of 18 does not count. The table will then show how many weeks' pay the employee is entitled to. For the definition of a week's pay, see pages 378–80. The redundancy payment due is to be reduced by one-twelfth for every complete month by which the age exceeds 64 years. Entitlement ceases entirely at 65 or at normal retiring age if below 65 and non-discriminatory.

Table 19.3 *Formula for computation of statutory redundancy payments*

Age	No of weeks' pay per year of employment in the particular age category
under 22 years	½
22–40	1
41 and over	1½

No employment beyond 20 years is counted, so the maximum payment is $20 \times 1½ = 30$ weeks' pay. There is a maximum level of weekly pay which is counted, currently £220 (from 1 April 1998).[34] The maximum statutory RP is therefore £6,600. The earnings limit is reviewed annually as required by the ERA,[35] although this does not require there to be an increase. As the age of 65 is approached, payments are reduced by one-twelfth for each complete month over 64.[36]

The statutory scheme lays down minimum RPs. Payments must not be below the level provided by the scheme, but may be added to voluntarily. However, the right to make enhanced RPs sometimes may be circumscribed. A district auditor has successfully challenged the authority of local government to make RPs in excess of the amount provided for by statute, although the relevant statute – regulations under the Superannuation Act 1972 – allows payments in excess of those under the ERA by removing the limit on weekly earnings.[37] It also places an upper limit on payments and the employers exceeded this *(R v North Tyneside Metropolitan Borough Council ex parte Allsop)*.

Rules for calculating a week's pay are laid down in ss 220–229 of ERA. The date on which pay is ascertained – the calculation date – is when the minimum statutory notice was due, or where there was notice less than the statutory minimum, or no notice, when the contract of employment ended.[38] A week's pay for those whose pay does not vary with the amount of work done will be the pay received for working normal weekly hours. The concept of normal weekly hours is not defined but where there is entitlement to overtime pay it will be the number of hours beyond which overtime becomes payable.[39] Where there is contractual overtime normal weekly hours will include it. Otherwise, overtime pay will not count for RP purposes *(Tarmac Roadstone Holdings Ltd v Peacock)*. Where pay does vary with the amount of work done, hourly pay is averaged over 12 weeks and the result multiplied by normal weekly hours. If there is shift working so that pay varies from week to week according to shift pattern, the total number of hours over 12 weeks is divided by 12 and the result multiplied by average hourly pay. If there are no normal weekly hours a week's pay will be weekly remuneration averaged over 12 weeks.

The treatment of overtime will depend upon the type of case. As noted, where pay does not vary with the amount of work done, overtime is to be excluded unless it is contractual. Where pay varies with the amount of work done or from week to week because of shift patterns, overtime hours are to be included in the calculation of average hourly pay but stripped of the overtime premium. This can give rise to anomalies where an incentive bonus does not increase with overtime working because the effect of working overtime is to reduce hourly pay *(British Coal Corporation v Cheesbrough)*. The example in Table 19.4 illustrates the point.

Table 19.4   *Inclusion of overtime in the calculation of average hourly pay for statutory redundancy payments purposes*

	Bonus (£)	Pay at £4 per hr (£)	Total pay (£)	Total hours	Average hourly pay (£)
Normal weekly hours (40)	40	160	200	40	5.00
Normal weekly hours plus 10 hours' overtime	40	200	240	50	4.80

Remuneration means money paid by the employer under the contract of employment for work done by the employee.[40] It includes all contractual payments by an employer and is gross *(Secretary of State for Employment v John Woodrow and Sons (Builders) Ltd)*, but does not extend to payments in kind. Thus, company cars, free meals and free accommodation will not form part of 'a week's pay', although a deduction from pay in respect of such an item might be a basis on which it could be included. Expenses will not form part of pay (because they are not a payment for work done) unless there is an element of profit for the employee (eg, mileage expenses paid at something in excess of the expense actually incurred). In tax law, anything beyond the true expense is taxable income *(Perrons v Spackman (HM Inspector of Taxes))* and if the employer and employee have agreed to treat taxable income as untaxed expenses in order to reduce the amount of tax paid, the contract of employment will be void for illegality and no RP will be payable. Courts and tribunals will investigate this issue where the evidence points to it even if it is not part of the pleadings. Tips and gratuities will not form part of pay since these are not a payment by the employer. However, the proceeds from a service charge upon customers, which were paid by an employer to his employees, were held to form part of pay *(Tsoukka v Potomac Restaurants Ltd)*. According to the decision in *Nerva v Paradise Inferno*, so will gratuities added to bills by cheque or credit card payments, since these are monies dispensed by the employer as remuneration. Discounts on the company's products and cheap loans etc are excluded because they do not represent a payment for work done. Pay will not include an *ex gratia* Christmas bonus. By the same token, production bonuses and commission will form part of pay if they are contractual. Contractual guarantee pay will not be remuneration because it is not a payment for work done by the employee, but a payment for being on call probably will be. Allowances for working in abnormal conditions may be included. Such an allowance – for working in excessive heat – was included when a tribunal calculated the average remuneration of shiftworkers in *Randell v Vosper Shiprepairers Ltd.*

An employer must give an employee a written statement indicating how the amount of any statutory RP has been calculated.[41] If an employer fails to comply 'without reasonable excuse' he will be guilty of an offence and liable on summary conviction to a fine not exceeding level one on the standard scale (currently £200). In such circumstances the employee may by notice in writing require the statement from the employer within a period specified in the notice. The period must be no less than one week. If the employer fails to comply with the notice (again, 'without reasonable excuse') there will be a further offence and liability on summary conviction to pay a fine not exceeding level three on the standard scale (currently £1,000). If an offence is committed by a corporate body with the 'consent or connivance of', or is 'attributable to any neglect on the part of, any director, manager, secretary or similar officer', he as well as the corporate body shall be guilty and liable to prosecution.[42]

Applications to industrial tribunals

If the payment is not agreed and made, the employee who wishes to claim must make a complaint to an industrial tribunal or an application in writing to the employer. If neither of these is done within six months the application is time-barred unless an unfair dismissal application has been made to a tribunal. However, a tribunal can still award a payment if a claim is made within the following six months if it is 'just and equitable' to do so. An application is made to a tribunal when it is received at the tribunal office rather than when it is posted *(Secretary of State for Employment v Banks)* but if the applicant has already written to the employer making a claim, and this was done within the time limit, he may apply to a tribunal at any time thereafter. Where a tribunal hears a claim from a Crown servant under a contractual scheme, the time limit will be as laid down in the contractual scheme, or if no limit is stated, six years[43] *(Greenwich Health Authority v Skinner).* Where an employee wishes to claim unfair dismissal for redundancy as well as for payment of an RP, the tribunal application in respect of unfair dismissal will need to be made within three months. A woman who received a lower RP than a man under discriminatory arrangements later found to be in breach of EU law can claim retrospectively. The time limit runs from the date when the Member State fully implements the EU directive. As regards discriminatory maximum ages for entitlement to RP, this was 16 January 1990. A claim one month and 12 days after this date was not out of time. The redundancy had occurred in August 1985 *(Cannon v Barnsley Metropolitan District Council)*. Prior to this it had been held by the EAT that there was no time limit on cases pursued under article 119 of the Treaty of Rome *(Stevens v Bexley Heath Authority*; followed by an industrial tribunal in *Hughes v Strathclyde Regional Council)*. More recently, the EAT has applied the statutory time limits from the time of dismissal *(Biggs v Somerset County Council)*. An industrial tribunal has jurisdiction to hear a case brought directly under EU law where the applicant has no remedy under domestic legislation, eg exclusion from the right to a contractual RP because of being a part-time employee *(Secretary of State for Scotland and Greater Glasgow Health Board v Wright and Hannah)*. Similarly, a direct application under article 119 was possible for a woman over 60 who was not entitled to claim under British law *(McKechnie v UBM Building Suppliers (Southern) Ltd)*.

Where a claim is made in respect of unfair dismissal for redundancy, but there is no claim for an RP, the tribunal must give the parties the opportunity to call evidence and make representations if it is contemplating the award of a RP *(Ransomes Sims and Jeffries Ltd v Tatterton)*.

Where there is no dispute about entitlement and amount the matter is settled, providing the payment is calculated in accordance with the statutory rules. An employee may claim a payment, or any unpaid part of it, direct from the NI Fund after taking all reasonable steps (other than legal proceedings) to recover the payment from the employer, or when the employer is insolvent.[44] The Secretary of State then tries to pursue a claim against the employer. An employee refused a direct payment by the Secretary of State can contest the decision by applying to an industrial tribunal. There is also provision for the Secretary of State to challenge liability, or the amount of RP, by referring a claim to the tribunal.

Rebates to employers

Originally rebates were paid to all employers making statutory RPs but the proportion of the RP refunded was reduced over the years. More latterly, rebates were restricted to small firms. The system of rebates was abolished completely in January 1990.[45]

Early and late leaving and notice

There can be mutual agreement to bring forward the termination date. A second possibility is that the employee, under notice of redundancy, and during the 'obligatory' notice period, gives notice in writing to the employer to leave early. This notice does not have to be of the length needed for termination – simply some notice *(Ready Case Ltd v Jackson)*. The termination will still be held to be a dismissal for redundancy. The 'obligatory' notice period is that required by statute or contract, whichever is the longer. Where the employer gives notice in excess of the obligatory amount, the obligatory period is the later rather than the earlier part of the notice. Some examples are given in Table 19.5. Notice from the employee earlier than the obligatory period will be treated as a resignation and will result in a loss of entitlement to RP.

Table 19.5 *Obligatory notice period: examples*

Employee with five years' continuous employment

Example	Minimum statutory notice (weeks)	Contractual notice (weeks)	Actual notice (weeks)	Obligatory notice
1	5	5	5	5
2	5	4	5	5
3	5	8	8	8
4	5	8	13	weeks 6–13 of the 13-week period

An employer can give a further notice, which must be in writing and be served before the employee's counter-notice expires, to tell the employee to withdraw his counter-notice and work until the full notice period expires. This notice must also state that unless the employee complies, the employer will contest liability to pay RP. Where such a case is pursued to an industrial tribunal, the tribunal will determine how much of the RP, if any, is payable.[46]

There can be mutual agreement to defer notice of termination. In *Mowlem (Northern) Ltd v Watson*, the notice was suspended by mutual agreement and although there was no new leaving date, the right to a statutory RP was preserved. This was because the original notice of dismissal stood. Where there has been a strike during the notice period, an employer can require that the notice period be extended.[47]

The two-year period of qualifying employment must be measured to the 'relevant date' (see page 375). A failure to give the statutory minimum notice required causes the relevant date to be postponed until the date on which the proper amount of notice would have expired, but this is true only for the purposes of determining the two-year qualifying period and length of employment for the RP calculation. The relevant date may be postponed even where an employee has accepted pay in lieu of notice because neither the acceptance of pay in lieu nor the waiving of notice rights can prevent the operation of the statutory provisions as regards the qualifying period for the right to an RP *(Staffordshire County Council v Secretary of State for Employment)*.

Statutory exemption orders

Where an employer and one or more trades unions have a redundancy agreement, they may jointly apply to the Secretary of State for Employment to exempt certain employees from the statutory provisions. However, issues in dispute will still have to be dealt with by industrial tribunals.[48]

Exclusion or reduction of RP on account of pension rights

Entitlement to a statutory RP may be excluded because of pension rights. ERA, s 158 allows the Secretary of State to make regulations for excluding the right to a statutory RP, or reducing the entitlement, where an employee is entitled to an occupational pension at the time of redundancy. The regulations, issued in 1965, specify that an employer may reduce or exclude an RP, should he so choose, where a pension is payable within 90 weeks of the termination of employment.[49] The pension scheme must be satisfactory as far as the Secretary of State for Employment is concerned and the pension must be payable for life (or commutable into a lump sum). The RP can be excluded altogether where the employee is entitled to a pension which is equal to at least a third of his annual pay and where he has a right to payment of the pension immediately upon termination of employment. Annual pay is determined by multiplying weekly pay by 52. Weekly pay is subject to the statutory limit, currently £220. Where the pension is less than a third of the employee's annual pay, the RP may be reduced by the formula

$$\frac{\text{annual pension}}{\frac{1}{3} \times \text{annual pay}} \times 100$$

Thus, if annual pay is £9,000 and the annual pension is £2,000, the RP may be reduced by 67 per cent. Where pension is not payable immediately, but is payable in no more than 90 weeks' time, the same calculation is done but the weekly pension is multiplied by the appropriate number of weeks and the result added on. Where an RP is to be reduced or excluded, an employer must give the employee notice in writing of the intention to reduce or exclude, explain how it is to be done and state the amount which will be payable. The notice must be served within a reasonable time of the employer coming to know of the employee's claim for RP *(Stowe-Woodward BTR Ltd v Beynon)*. Three months was not reasonable.

In *British Telecommunications plc v Burwell* the EAT decided that the regulations applied to a situation where a person was, at termination of employment, already in receipt of a pension (arising out of a previous termination). However, the Court of Appeal has held that this is not so (*Royal Ordnance plc v Pilkington*).

Extra-statutory additions to the lump sum

An employer must not make a payment which is less than the statutory amount but is at liberty to make a payment which is greater. Part of such a payment would be to meet statutory obligations and the remainder would be a voluntary payment (unless contractually required).

GUARANTEE PAY

ERA requires that there shall be a daily guarantee payment where the employer is unable to provide any work at all during a day when the employee would normally be required to work.[50] Crown employment is included but the armed forces and police services are excluded, as are share fishermen and employees ordinarily working outside Great Britain. One month's qualifying employment is needed and any employee of a fixed-term contract of three months or less, or on a specific task contract expected to last for three months or less is excluded, unless there is already more than three months' continuous employment.

If the failure to provide work stems from industrial action in the employer's firm or any associated employer's firm, no payment will be due. Nor will it be due if suitable alternative employment (even if not permitted by the contract) is unreasonably refused, or if the employee does not conform to the employer's requirements relating to availability for work. The amount of daily payment is the number of normal hours multiplied by the hourly rate, subject to a statutory maximum, currently £15.35 but reviewed annually. No payment is due where there are 'no normal working hours on the day in question'.[51] The maximum number of days' guarantee pay is five in any three-month period. An employee may complain to an industrial tribunal that his employer has not paid part or all of the guarantee payment. This complaint must be made within three months of the day to which the application relates. Any remuneration for the day may be offset against the liability to pay statutory guarantee pay and *vice versa*. Where there is a collective agreement on guarantee pay, and at the request of the parties, the Minister may issue an Order exempting from the statutory provisions the employees covered by that agreement, but the agreement must provide for disputes to be resolved by independent arbitration or by industrial tribunals.[52] Guarantee pay has no bearing on the issue of whether the employer has a right under the contract to dispense with some or all of the employee's pay during a lay-off or short-time working when there is insufficient work. This will depend on the terms of the contract.

INSOLVENCY[53]

Rights of employees

Insolvency rights fall into two categories:

- some debts are given priority (up to a statutory maximum which may be changed from time to time by the Secretary of State); and
- some debts can be paid out of the NI Fund.

Priority debts
These include:

(a) statutory guarantee payments;
(b) remuneration payable on suspension on medical grounds;
(c) payment for time off for union duties or to look for work or arrange training on being made redundant;
(d) remuneration payable under a protective award;
(e) payment for time off for ante-natal care;
(f) statutory sick pay;
(g) up to four months' wages or salary;
(h) accrued holiday pay; and
(i) contractual sick pay and holiday pay.

Debts which may be claimed from the NI Fund
These are:

(a) arrears of pay for up to and including eight weeks; pay includes wages, salaries, bonuses, commission, overtime pay and the statutory items (a) to (e) in the priority debts above; the maximum earnings limit, currently £220 per week, applies;
(b) holiday pay for up to and including six weeks – again the maximum earnings limit applies; the entitlement must have occurred within the previous 12 months;
(c) pay for the statutory notice period or compensation for the employer's failure to give proper statutory notice (again the earnings limit applies);
(d) unpaid basic award of unfair dismissal compensation;
(e) reasonable reimbursement of apprentices' or articled clerks' fees; and
(f) statutory maternity pay, statutory sick pay and statutory redundancy pay (these may also be met from the NI Fund in certain cases where there is no insolvency).[54]

Claims
Claims in the first instance should go to the employer's representative on

prescribed forms. Debts in addition to those above will be considered by that representative, but will not be paid from public funds. The legislation, however, does safeguard pension contributions left unpaid by an insolvent employer. The pension scheme administrator applies to the employer's representative in the first instance, but ultimately the NI Fund may pay. As regards any of the debts claimed from the NI Fund, a complaint may be made to a tribunal that the Secretary of State has failed to make a payment, or that the payment is less than the amount it should be. Prior to the EA 1989, the legislation provided that the Secretary of State must await a statement from the receiver or liquidator of the amount payable before making such a payment, unless there was likely to be unreasonable delay. The position now is that the Secretary of State is allowed to make payments without a statement if he feels that a statement is not necessary. Moreover, the legislation now makes it clear that where payments are made to employees out of the NI Fund the right to a priority claim on the assets of the employer is transferred to the Secretary of State. In the case of unpaid pension contributions an application will be made by an officer of the pension scheme, while in respect of other debts the application is made by the ex-employee. The time limit for claims is three months from the Secretary of State's decision. There is no hours qualification for the insolvency rights, nor any qualifying period of employment.

Insolvency and business transfers[55]

The fact that a company is insolvent, in receivership or about to cease trading does not preclude the operation of legislation relating to business transfers (Teesside Times Ltd v Drury). Where an insolvency practitioner manages the company and succeeds in selling all or part of it as a going concern there is likely to be the transfer of an undertaking. By contrast, the legislation may not apply where a business is broken up and the assets sold, since there would be no transfer of a going concern.

A receiver who is also a manager is called an administrative receiver.[56] Where appointed voluntarily he is an agent of the company and has authority to continue its business and to sell it. His appointment is not a transfer under the Transfer of Undertakings (Protection of Employment) Regulations, nor does it terminate the contracts of employment of employees. The above also is true of an administrator under the Insolvency Act 1986 (appointed under a court administration order as an expert to manage the affairs, business and property of the company) and of a liquidator appointed following a voluntary liquidation.

The position in relation to compulsory liquidation is different. The liquidator is appointed by the court and is an agent of the court. His appointment automatically terminates contracts of employment. If he wishes to continue the employment of employees he must employ them. Moreover, the Acquired Rights Directive apparently does not apply to insolvency proceedings supervised by a judicial authority *(Abels v Administrative Board of the Bedrijfsvereniging voor de Metaal Industrie en de Electrotechnische Industrie; D'Urso v Ercole Marelli Elletromeccanica Generale SpA)*. In the UK, this would mean a compulsory liquidation (or, in the case of an individual, personal bankruptcy) but the position is uncertain and generally it is assumed that the Transfer of Undertakings (Protection of Employment) Regulations would apply.[57] In practice, there is often no actual business to transfer, merely a collection of assets.

Finally, there is the question of the hiving down of a business by a receiver, administrator or liquidator, ie the separation of the employees from the business in order to make the latter more attractive to potential buyers. This involves:

- creating a wholly-owned subsidiary;
- transferring the business to it;
- retaining the employees in the original company but lending them to the subsidiary;
- disposing of the subsidiary business by transfer or by sale of shares; and
- dismissing the employees from the original company before disposal of the subsidiary.

Although no provision for this is made in the Acquired Rights Directive, the Transfer of Undertakings (Protection of Employment) Regulations have the effect of postponing the transfer on hiving down until either disposal of the share capital of the subsidiary to a buyer or disposal of the subsidiary business to a buyer.[58] The initial transfer to the subsidiary therefore is not covered by the regulations so that contracts of employment do not transfer. However, one view has it that the rule in *Litster* (see chapter 20) applies even in the context of a dismissal following a postponed transfer after hiving down, so causing a transfer of liability to the transferees if there is no economic, technical or organizational reason; but this remains untested.[59]

TERMINATION PAYMENTS AND TAXATION

Contractual termination payments normally will be taxable as income under Schedule E, but non-contractual payments are treated separately, attracting a measure of tax relief.[60] Under the current provisions the first £30,000 is tax-free.[61] Statutory and genuine extra-statutory RPs fall to be treated in the same way.[62] Where something less than contractual notice is given, and there is no contractual right to make a payment in lieu of notice, any payment is likely to attract tax relief. However, it will be included as a compensation payment to be aggregated with the RP for purposes of the £30,000 limit on compensation which is subject to tax relief. To the extent that wages in lieu of notice are technically damages for breach of contract they should be paid net, although in practice they are usually paid gross. Since wages in lieu will vary from individual to individual according to notice requirements, a standard wages in lieu payment (eg, 12 weeks' pay) may be regarded as an RP, thus leaving unfulfilled the duty to pay wages in lieu.

Ex gratia payments which are compensation for loss of office or employment should also be subject to tax relief, but again they will need to be aggregated along with the RP and any other termination payments not charged under Schedule E in applying the £30,000 ceiling to the amount of tax-free compensation. The early payment of retirement benefits should not affect the tax treatment of compensation for loss of office or employment.[63]

In contrast to compensation for loss of employment, *ex gratia* payments on retirement or death will be subject to the tax rules governing pension schemes, since they are a 'relevant benefit' under s 612 of ICTA. Thus, a lump sum retirement benefit will be taxable unless it qualifies for exemption under the rules: these allow tax-free payments of up to 150 per cent of final salary.

NOTES

ERA, ss 135 and 155.

1   1 ERA, ss 135 and 155. Continuous employment is defined in on pages 88–9. Overseas employment will count for RP qualifying period and calculation purposes if the employee remains an employed earner as defined in the NI scheme.

2   ERA, s 156.

3   ERA, s 211.

4   ERA, s 199.

5   Crown servants are excluded by the absence of express inclusion (unlike in respect of unfair dismissal legislation: ERA, s 191(2)(e)).

6   ERA, s 196(6). The employee's base is to be ascertained by looking at the terms of the contract and over the whole period contemplated by the contract (*Wilson v Maynard Shipping Consultants AB*).

7   ERA, s 196(6).

8   ERA, s 160.

9   ERA s 161.

10 ERA, s 192.

11 ERA, ss 194–195.

12 Dock Work Act 1989; Dock Work (Compensation Payments Scheme) Regulations (SI 1989/1111), under s 5(1) of the 1989 Act.

13 National Health Service and Community Care Act 1990, s 66(2) and Sched 10. Merchant seamen were excluded by the Secretary of State by an order under what is now ERA, s 209(1) but are now included by virtue of SI 1990/1583, which revoked the Redundancy Payments (Exclusion of Merchant Seamen) Order (SI 1968/1201).

14 Under ERA, s 171, eg Redundancy Payments Office Holders Regulations (SI 1965/2007) including, eg registrars of births and deaths; and the Redundancy Payments Termination of Employment Regulations (SI 1965/2022), including, eg chief constables.

15 Employment Protection (Offshore Employment) Order (SI 1976/766) as amended. This extends RP and unfair dismissal rights to employees on oil or natural gas rigs within British territorial waters or in designated areas of the continental shelf, with the exception of areas adjacent to Northern Ireland. The Employment (Continental Shelf) Act 1978 makes provision for those employed further afield to be covered by British employment legislation if they are employed by British-based firms.

16 ERA, s 197(3).

17 In respect of RPs: ERA, ss 136–137; in respect of unfair dismissal: ERA, s 95; and in respect of redundancy consultation: TULR(C)A, s 298.

18 ERA, ss 136(5) and 174. See also ss 206–207.

19 ERA, s 140.

20 ERA, s 148.

21 ERA, s 150.

22 ERA, s 141(4).

23 286 *IDS Brief* 3–5.

24 281 *IDS Brief* 8.

25 ERA, s 138(1).

26 ERA, s 213(2).

27 Transfer of Undertakings (Protection of Employment) Regulations (SI 1981/1794).

28 ERA, s 214(2).

29 ERA, s 212(1).

30 'Strike' is defined, for this purpose in ERA, s. 235(5).

31 Redundancy Payments (Local Government) (Modification) Order (SI 1983/1160), as amended under EP(C)A, s 149. A number of bodies, apart from local authorities, are to be treated as local authorities, and like local authorities, all are deemed to be associated employers for RP purposes. Organizations not specified can be similarly regarded but only if they perform current local authority functions as contractors or agents *(West Midlands Residuary Body v Deebank)*.

32 The RP (NHS) (Modification) Order (SI 1993/3167).

33 ERA, s 162. It is a payment for loss of security. It is not intended to be unemployment pay *(Lloyd v Brassey)*.

34 ERA, ss 162(3) and 227.

35 ERA, s 208.

36 ERA, s 162(4) and (5).

37 Local authorities may make enhanced RPs under s 111 of the Local Government Act 1972 but the enhancement is limited by regulations made under the Superannuation Act 1972.

38 ERA, s 226(5) and (6).

39 See ERA, s 234. For overtime to be contractual, the employer must be obliged to provide it and the employee be required to work it.

40 See Grunfeld, C., *Law of Redundancy* (3rd edition, 1989), pages 268ff for a fuller discussion.

41 ERA, s 165.

42 ERA, s 180.

43 These are claims under ERA, s 177. The more general limit of six years is laid down in s 5 of the Limitation Act 1980.

44 The Redundancy Fund was merged with the National Insurance Fund by the Employment Act 1990. Insolvency for this purpose is defined in ERA, s 183.

45 Employment Act 1989, s 17.

46 ERA, s 142.

47 ERA, s 143.

48 ERA, s 157. See *Southern Electricity Board v Collins* and Redundancy Payments (Exemption) (No 1) Order (SI 1970/354) and Redundancy Payments (Centrax Group) (Exemption) Order (SI 1969/207).

49 Redundancy Payments (Pensions) Regulations (SI 1965/1932).

50 ERA, s 28.

51 ERA, s 30(1).

52 ERA, s 35.

53 Insolvency Act 1986.

54 On statutory maternity pay see the Social Security Contributions and Benefits Act 1992, ss 164-171 and Sched 13 and the Statutory Maternity Pay (General) Regulations (SI 1986/1960) as amended. On statutory sick pay see the SSCBA 1992 ss 151–163 and Scheds 11 and 12 and the Statutory Sick Pay (General) Regulations (SI 1982/894) as amended. See also the Social Security Administration Act 1992. On statutory redundancy pay see ERA, s 166(1).

55 For a fuller discussion of this subject see McMullen (1992), pages 218–231.

56 Insolvency Act 1986, s 29(2). Where voluntarily appointed, an administrative receiver will be personally liable for the contracts of employment of employees adopted by him or entered into by him, but will be entitled to an indemnity out of the company's assets (Insolvency Act 1986, s 44).

57 McMullen (1992), page 221.

58 Regulation 4.

59 McMullen (1992), pages 226–227.

60 They fall to be dealt with under s 148 of the Income and Corporation Taxes Act (ICTA) 1988 instead of the normal charging provision in s 19.

61 ICTA, s 188(4) as amended by Finance Act 1988, s 74. It should be noted that the Inland Revenue is proposing to introduce greater flexibility into the treatment of those payments which continue in years after the termination of employment.

62 *Ex Gratia Awards Made on Termination of an Office or Employment by Retirement or Death* (Statement of Practice SP13/91, London, Inland Revenue, 1991). Statutory RPs are exempt from Schedule E charging by virtue of ICTA, s 579. They are charged under s 148 (with relief under s 188) by virtue of s 580.

63 *Loc cit.*

Transfers of Undertakings

THE LEGAL CONTEXT

Common law and statute

The common law position is that a change of employer automatically terminates the contract of employment because the contract is viewed as involving personal service. The employee would not be transferred between employers unless there was express agreement by the parties *(Nokes v Doncaster Amalgamated Collieries Ltd)*. The terms, and any continuity, would be a matter for agreement between the parties. If the employee joined the new employer on the condition that continuous employment with his previous employer was to count with the new employer, this could amount to a contractual promise, since the employee was not obliged to work for the new employer. An employer's subsequent refusal to abide by what was agreed would leave the door open for the employee to claim in respect of breach of contract.

In practice, changes of employer may be covered by one or more of the statutory provisions.[1] These form a complex area of law which contains a mixture of legislation, some pre-dating the UK's membership of the European Community and some deriving from it. The first issue which needs to be established is whether the change of employer is within the legislation's coverage, and in this respect it is important to note that there is no change of employer when there is a company takeover by means of share acquisition. The company, albeit owned by (and more importantly, controlled by) different people, is still the employer. This is because of the principle of corporate personality, whereby the company has a separate identity from that of its shareholders *(Salomon v A Salomon & Co Ltd)*. Since in law there is no change of employer, there is no interruption to continuity of employment for contractual or statutory purposes. If there is a reorganization or a redundancy, actions constituting unfair dismissal and/or breach of contract will need to be avoided as in any normal case, but legislation relating to changes of employer will not apply.

Some of the legislation is found in ERA and applies to a number of specific types of change of employer.[2] The effect of these provisions is to protect continuity of employment for the purpose of entitlement to statutory rights (for example, the right to receive a statutory redundancy payment). ERA provisions also create a presumption in favour of continuity, but not apparently where there is a change of employer *(Secretary of State for Employment v Cohen & Beaupress Ltd)*.[3] The provisions do not transfer contractual rights.

More significant provisions are to be found in the Transfer of Undertakings (Protection of Employment) Regulations 1981 (TUPE), enacted to give effect to the EU Acquired Rights Directive 1977.[4] The regulations aim to protect employees in the context of the transfer of an undertaking and specifically provide for contracts of employment to transfer to the transferee, for safeguards against dismissal and for certain collective employment rights such as consultation with trades union or employee representatives. The EU directive upon which TUPE is based was perhaps envisaged as applying to conventional takeovers and mergers (such as the sale of a business) but in practice has been applied, amid some controversy, to the process of contracting-out parts of an organization's operations and to transfers arising out of privatization and other forms of reorganization.[5] The policy aspects of this are highlighted in chapter 28.

Employment Rights Act provisions

Changes of employer other than business transfers

One of the types of situation covered by ERA is where there is a change of employer brought about by Act of Parliament.[6] This might happen, for example, where there was restructuring of a public service such as local government. Another type of situation is where the employer dies.[7] Under common law the contract of employment would be ended by the death because the contract is held to be of a personal nature. ERA extends the contract for statutory purposes to cover employment by the personal representatives or trustees of the deceased. Moreover, continuity can be preserved – that is, there will be no dismissal – if there is renewal or re-engagement by the personal representatives which takes effect within eight weeks of the death.[8] In the absence of renewal of contract or re-engagement the employee will be treated as having been dismissed by reason of redundancy.[9]

A further type of situation covered by ERA provisions is where there is a change in the composition of a partnership, personal representatives or trustees. Again, common law would say that the contract terminates upon such changes (see *Briggs v Oates*) but ERA maintains continuity.[10] There is some uncertainty about whether a change from a partnership to a sole trader would be covered, but in any case this might be a business transfer (see below). ERA provisions also deal with changes of employer where the employers are associated companies.[11] Association is defined in terms of control[12] rather than in terms of membership of an employers' association. Control means voting power in the general meeting and company means a limited company. Therefore, organizations such as unincorporated associations, partnerships and local authorities cannot be associated companies *(Merton London Borough Council v Gardiner)*,[13] although the Employment Appeal Tribunal (EAT) took a more liberal line in *Pinkney v Sandpiper Drilling Ltd.* ERA provisions also cover transfers of employees between a local education authority and the governors of schools maintained by that authority, and *vice versa.*[14]

If there are gaps between the employment of the employee by the first and second employer in any of the situations already mentioned, the test of whether there is continuity – apart from any specific provision – is the general one. That is, are the employee's relations with the employer governed by a contract of employment? In the absence of a contract, continuity can be achieved only if one of the specific statutory circumstances applies (for example, the occurrence of a temporary cessation of work) (see pages 90–92).[15]

Business transfers

The ERA provisions also apply to business transfers.[16] As with the other types of change, the ERA provisions relate only to continuity for statutory purposes. The Act states that where 'a trade or business or an undertaking ... is transferred from one person to another'[17] the period of employment of an employee employed 'at the time of the transfer' will count as employment with the transferee. The transfer does not break the continuity. 'Person' includes a body of persons, whether corporate or unincorporated.[18] ERA does not define trade or undertaking but states that business includes 'a trade or profession ... and any activity carried on by a body of persons (whether corporate or unincorporated)'.[19]

MEANING OF A TRANSFER

Whether there is a transfer will be a matter of fact for an industrial tribunal to determine *(Melon v Hector Powe Ltd)* but in applying TUPE there will remain the possibility that the directive is not being properly interpreted, so giving rise to points of law and potential appeals. The label attached to the transfer by the parties will not necessarily determine the issue: the matter has to be judged on its facts *(Kenmir Ltd v Frizzell)*.

TUPE applies to a relevant transfer, ie to 'a transfer from one person to another of an undertaking'.[20] The regulations apply where there is a transfer 'effected by sale or as a result of a sale, by some other disposition, or by operation of law',[21] but this does not include changes in control which arise simply from changes in share ownership. They apply to undertakings. An undertaking includes 'any trade or business'.[22] From the above it is clear that a transfer can be effected by means other than a sale, for example, by the law of succession under a will or trust. In *Dr Sophie Redmond Stichting v Bartol* the transfer was effected by a local authority withdrawing a subsidy from one organization and giving it to another.

It is also clear that something more than a mere transfer of assets must be involved *(Woodhouse v Peter Brotherhood Ltd)*. The ECJ confirmed this as regards TUPE in *Spijkers v Gebroeders Benedik Abattoir CV*. The transfer of goodwill often can be an important factor in distinguishing a transfer from an asset sale, but not conclusively so, especially in the case of the transfer of franchises where the franchiser may retain the goodwill. Another indication of a transfer is the transferee taking over the transferor's customers, especially if the transferor assists by providing a client and/or customer list. Other indicators are the transfer of work in progress, an agreement by the transferor not to compete with the transferee (without which there might not be goodwill) and use of the transferor's name, trademark and so on by the transferee.

A further issue is whether a transfer requires a change of ownership. It is clear from the case law that no transfer of absolute ownership is required. The transfer of leases, involving a double transfer (back to the lessor and then from lessor to new lessee) can count as a transfer *(Foreningen af Arbejdsledere i Danmark v Daddy's Dance Hall A/S)*. So too can the transfer of a lease back to the lessor followed by the owner taking over the running of the business *(P Bork International A/S (in liquidation) v Foreningen af Arbejdsledere i Danmark; Landsorganisationen i Danmark v Ny Molle Kro)*. The general principle appears to be that the application of the EU directive is not precluded provided that the undertaking retains its identity as an economic unit. The EAT later upheld this principle in relation to franchises in *LMC Drains Ltd and Metro Rod Services Ltd v Waugh*. As a result of TURERA, the regulations now make clear that a transfer does not need to involve a transfer of property.[23] They also make clear that the transfer can be effected by means of two or more transactions.

The correct test for a transfer appears to be whether there is a change of management – a change in the person operating the undertaking and accepting responsibility for the employees. This is the drift of the major cases including *Daddy's Dance Hall*, *Ny Molle Kro*, *P Bork* and *Berg and Busschers v IM Besselsen*. As it was put in *Daddy's Dance Hall*:

> The Directive ... applies as soon as there is a change resulting from a conventional sale or from a merger of the natural or legal person responsible for operating the undertaking who consequently enters into obligations as an employer towards the employees working in the undertaking.

The test was usefully divided into two constituent parts by the EAT in *Council of the Isles of Scilly v (1) Brintel Helicopters Ltd (2) Ellis*. The first question is whether there is an undertaking, the second is whether there has been a transfer. The emergent ECJ concept of an undertaking is that of an economic entity, although this should not be equated with commercial (ie, profit-making) activity. The overall test becomes whether an identifiable economic entity performs essentially the same functions after a transfer as before.

Where only part of an undertaking is transferred, the test is whether the employee was assigned to the part transferred *(Botzen)*. For UK cases in which this test has been applied see *Sunley Turriff Holdings Ltd* and *Michael Peters*.

An important question has been whether the transfer of a particular organizational function (eg, cleaning or catering) can amount to a transfer. The contracting-out of various functions to specialist firms has become widespread, but can that contracting-out process (or the subsequent process of changing contractors) be a transfer? Similarly, what of reorganization such as the transfer of further education from local authorities to college corporations or of health services from health authorities to NHS trusts?

The drift of domestic case law was firmly against seeing such changes as transfers within the scope of TUPE (see, eg, *Expro Services v Smith* and *Stirling v Dietmann Management Systems Ltd*, both EAT). However, the ECJ held in *Watson Rask and Christiensen v ISS Kantineservice A/S* that they can fall within the scope of the directive and the domestic courts have now followed that approach. The EAT has held that a relevant transfer *can* take place between successive contractors, even if the transfer takes effect *via* a third party, providing that it amounts to the transfer of a going concern. Deciding whether there is a going concern is a matter of fact for the industrial tribunal *(Curling v Securicor Ltd)*. Subsequent cases, including the Court of Appeal's decision in *Dines v Initial Health Care Services Ltd*, made the position clear.[24] However, a doubt is raised by the ECJ decision in *Ledernes*. Here there was no transfer involved in the contracting-out of the completion of some building work because the economic entity transferred was not a stable one.

Subsequently, the ECJ in *Suzen* signalled a substantially more rigorous test for deciding a transfer. Establishing that there was an identifiable economic entity which retained its identity post-transfer remained central but was not sufficient. There had to be something else if a change of contractor was to be a transfer under the Directive. There either had to be the transfer of significant tangible or intangible assets or the transfer of the major part of the staff. This new approach was immediately applied by the Court of Appeal in *Betts v Brintel Helicopters*, where there was found to be no transfer because there was no sufficient transfer of assets.

The government is currently consulting on a range of possible amendments to both the Acquired Rights Directive and the TUPE Regulations.

THE TRANSFER OF RIGHTS AND OBLIGATIONS

ERA's statutory continuity provisions apply where the employee is employed 'at the time of the transfer' and TUPE applies where the employee is employed 'immediately before the transfer'.[25] The drift of the case law is that the transfer occurs on completion *(Brook Lane Finance Co v Bradley)*. In *Macer v Abafast Ltd* the EAT held that the gap between employers could be of any length as long as it 'related to the machinery of transfer'. The *Macer* test was strictly applied in *Justfern Ltd*. A full week would otherwise defeat the normal continuous employment computation (see page 89). Where there is a pre-transfer dismissal, various factors may cause the employment to continue up to the transfer. A notice period will continue the employment contract even if the employee is not required to work. It may be prudent for employers to have a term in the employment contract to allow wages in lieu of notice. Where the notice given is less than the minimum required by statute, there is a possibility that it could be extended by statute.[26] Moreover, where a dismissal is in breach of contract, the employee can at common law keep the contract alive at least as long as the notice period by not accepting the repudiation. All of these factors may result in the employee's employment being prolonged up to the point of transfer such that liabilities pass to the transferee. Another, particularly important factor is the *Litster* principle (see below).

Under TUPE, all contractual rights transfer automatically to the transferee on completion of the transfer.[27] That is, all the transferor's rights, powers, duties and liabilities under or in connection with the contract so transfer. Similarly, liability for things done by or in relation to employees by the transferor also transfer automatically. It seems likely that this discharges the transferor from liability *(Berg and Busschers v IM Besselsen)*. Liability for tortious acts (such as negligence) committed in relation to an employee also appear to transfer (see *Secretary of State for Employment v Spence* on this general question; and *Taylor v Serviceteam Ltd*).

However, terms from collateral contracts may not transfer (for example, a share option scheme in *Chapman and Elkin v CPS Computer Group plc*). Nor, it seems, do those contract terms where there is an exclusion of liability clause which is not in breach of s 3 of the Unfair Contract Terms Act (UCTA), 1977. In *Micklefield v SAC Technology Ltd* liability was excluded even in the context of a wrongful dismissal. Criminal liabilities do not transfer, and occupational pension schemes are expressly excluded, confirmed in *Walden Engineering Ltd v Warrener*.[28] However, TURERA amended TUPE to provide for the transfer of occupational pension scheme provisions which do not relate to old age, invalidity or survivors. Protective awards do not transfer according to the EAT in *Angus Jowett & Co v National Union of Tailors and Garment Workers*, although the failure to pay, being a matter of contract, might.

Nothing in the regulations removes the individual's right to resign and claim a fundamental breach of contract, either for unfair dismissal or common law damages purposes. However this right is circumscribed to a degree by the wording of the regulations which says that either:

- 'a substantial change is made in his working conditions to his detriment'; or
- the change in identity of the employer itself is 'significant' and 'to his detriment'.[29]

The transfer itself will not be a repudiatory breach of contract *(Newns v British Airways plc)*. However, in *Katsikas v Constantinidis*, the ECJ held that an employee had a right to object to being transferred. TUPE was subsequently amended to make this clear but while under these circumstances the transfer terminates the employment, that termination does not constitute a dismissal.[30]

A further question is whether the employee has to know of the transfer for it to take place. *Berg and Busschers v IM Besselsen* is authority for the proposition that the employee's consent is not needed but in *Photostatic Copies (Southern) Ltd* the EAT refused to extend this to knowledge. Instead it observed the contract law principle that novation of a contract requires the knowledge of all the parties affected by it.[31] Here, this means that the employee must be given notice of the transfer and of the identity of the transferee. More recently, the EAT has followed the EU approach and, in *Secretary of State for Trade and Industry v Cook*, held that a transfer occurred automatically even though the employees did not know about the identity of the transferee.

Finally, does TUPE transfer statutory continuity or just contractual rights, duties and liabilities?[32] There is no definitive ruling on this but if the answer were no, continuity would be preserved by the ERA provisions. If the answer were yes, the ERA provisions might be otiose.

TRANSFERS AND DISMISSAL

A dismissal before or after a transfer will be automatically unfair if the reason or principal reason is the transfer itself or something 'connected with' it,[33] but subject to whether there is 'an economic, technical or organizational reason entailing changes in the workforce' (ETO),[34] in which case the dismissal will be deemed to be for some other substantial reason under dismissal law.[35] In *Trafford v Sharpe and Fisher* the EAT rejected the argument that an ETO dismissal must be one that would have occurred even in the absence of a transfer. In ETO cases liability is determined according to the principle in *Secretary of State for Employment v Spence*. This makes it clear that responsibility would lie with the transferor where the 'effective date of termination' (EDT) or 'relevant date' preceded the transfer and with the transferee if it succeeded it (these terms are defined on pages 317 and 375). The *Spence* principle would also apply to dismissals which were not connected with the transfer. By contrast, where the dismissal is connected with the transfer, but where there is no ETO reason, the rule is as stated by the House of Lords in *Litster v Forth Dry Dock and Engineering Co Ltd*. This holds that where the employee has been dismissed prior to the transfer, he is to be treated as if he had not been dismissed. Any liability thus passes to the transferee.

In the absence of an ETO reason, any dismissal connected with the transfer will be automatically unfair. Automatic means that the unfair dismissal test of reasonableness (described in chapter 16) does not apply. For there to be an ETO reason, there will have to be changes in the workforce. The Court of Appeal has ruled, in *Berriman v Delabole Slate Ltd*, that changes in the workforce mean a deliberate change in the numbers and functions of employees. Straightforward changes in terms and conditions, it seems, will not constitute ETO. In *Wheeler v Patel and J Golding Group of Companies* the EAT held that an ETO must relate to the conduct of the business.

There can be an ETO reason where the same employees are kept on but asked to do entirely different jobs *(Crawford v Swinton Insurance Brokers Ltd)*. This situation might give rise a to a constructive dismissal (defined on page 316), but the correct approach is for a tribunal first to identify the employer's conduct and then, if it does amount to a constructive dismissal, decide whether or not the dismissal is fair. In general, ETO reasons must be sufficiently specified by employers *(Gateway Hotels Ltd v Stewart)* and the existence of a redundancy situation does not necessarily mean that redundancy is the reason for dismissal. Thus a dismissal by administrators in order to make the business more attractive to potential buyers was not dismissal for an ETO reason despite the fact that it was carried out in the context of redundancy *(UK Security Services (Midlands) Ltd v Gibbons)*.

An ETO constitutes 'some other substantial reason' under dismissal law, and requires the normal second stage (that is, the test of reasonableness) to be entered. The onus of proof of an ETO reason lies with the employer *(Litster)*. *Gorictree Ltd v Jenkinson* showed that dismissal for an ETO reason prior to a transfer can simultaneously be dismissal for redundancy giving rise to entitlement to a redundancy payment. This would be true even if the applicant was re-engaged subsequently, including immediately after the transfer, by the transferee. Where the dismissal is post-transfer because the transferee requires fewer employees this can also be due to an ETO reason *(Meikle v McPhail (Charleston Arms))*.

Where there is a redundancy in the context of a change of employer it is necessary to distinguish between situations where there is a redundancy in law (and a requirement to make a redundancy payment) and those where continuity is preserved and there is no redundancy in law (nor, therefore, any requirement to make a redundancy payment). As noted, the legislation reverses the normal common law position that a change of employer automatically terminates the contract of employment. TUPE states expressly that the contract of employment will continue as will rights and duties under it, including continuity of employment.[36] Thus, the mere change of identity of the employer does not give an employee the right to claim a redundancy payment. As already noted, the employee's statutory rights are transferred by virtue of ERA.

The relationship between business transfers and redundancy therefore is this. The transfer itself does not constitute a redundancy, but a dismissal by the transferor or transferee, connected with the transfer and because fewer employees are required, will be a redundancy. It will be a fair dismissal by constituting an ETO reason, which in turn is deemed under the regulations to be 'some other substantial reason' for dismissal under ERA. All this will be subject to meeting the general unfair dismissal test of reasonableness and the specific legal requirements relating to unfair selection for redundancy (see chapters 16 and 17).

In the absence of a dismissal (constructive or direct), there will be continuity of employment and the employee will be able to count his employment with his previous employer should he ever make a statutory claim against his new employer. Any dismissal, whether or not it is connected with a transfer, where the reason is other than a requirement for fewer employees, will not be dismissal by reason of redundancy.

The final part as regards dismissal is whether the two-year qualifying period required under unfair dismissal law applies to unfair dismissal complaints where the dismissal occurs in the context of a transfer covered by TUPE. It was held in *Milligan v Securicor Cleaning Ltd* that it did not apply since no qualifying period was laid down in the regulations themselves. The conventional wisdom was that the TUPE provisions were integrated with unfair dismissal law and that the qualifying period did apply in the transfer context. An amendment to TUPE now makes it clear that the qualifying period does apply.[37]

VARIATION OF TERMS POST-TRANSFER

It is in the context of the contracting-out of services that that the Acquired Rights Directive and TUPE have been particularly problematic in the UK. The logic of contracting-out is to get the work done more cheaply, with either fewer workers or lower per capita labour costs or both. By automatically preserving the terms of the contract on transfer, the legislation threatens part of the basis of contracting-out. It is against this background that the cases relating to the post-transfer variation of terms should be viewed.

In *Wilson v St Helen's Borough Council* and *Meade v British Fuels Ltd*, the EAT held any variation to be inoperative if due to a transfer. The Court of Appeal affirmed this approach. Where the dismissal was due to an ETO reason, however, it would be effective and the pre-transfer terms did not have to be maintained. Where terms are incorporated from a collective agreement, they continue in force post-transfer, and are subject to increases, even though the transferee is not party to the agreement *(Whent v T Cartlidge Ltd)*.

TRANSFERS AND INSOLVENCY

The principal questions to be addressed here are whether TUPE applies to insolvencies and whether dismissals by insolvency practitioners are 'connected with' the transfer. The general position is that insolvencies are not specifically excluded from TUPE but that, transfers involved in the 'hiving-down' process (see below) are exempted. Where an insolvency practitioner manages the company and succeeds in selling all or part of it as a going concern there is likely to be the transfer of an undertaking. By contrast, the legislation is not likely to apply where a business is broken up and the assets sold, since there would be no transfer of a business.[38]

A receiver is appointed voluntarily or by court order to realize the assets of a company and wind it up (ie, to achieve the liquidation of the company).

Where that receiver also manages the company he is an administrative receiver.[39] A receiver appointed voluntarily is an agent of the company and has authority to continue its business and to sell it. His appointment is not a transfer under TUPE nor does it terminate the contracts of employment of employees. The above is also true of an administrator under the Insolvency Act 1986 (appointed under a court administration order as an expert to manage the affairs, business and property of the company) and of a liquidator appointed in a voluntary liquidation. The position in relation to compulsory liquidation is quite different. The liquidator is appointed by the court and is an agent of the court. His appointment automatically terminates contracts of employment. If he wishes to continue the employment of employees he must employ them.

The ECJ has held only certain types of insolvency to be covered by the directive. The principal distinction is between insolvency proceedings where the aim is to keep the business going and those intended to realize the assets (ie, liquidation). Only the former are covered. Member States can apply the directive to the latter but on public policy grounds are not required to do so.[40] In *Abels and D'Urso* the ECJ held that the directive did not apply in situations equivalent to a compulsory liquidation.[41] The critical issue appears to be the fact that the procedures were judicial but the public policy grounds would seem relevant even in voluntary situations.

Next there is the question of hiving down a business, that is, the separation of the employees from the business in order to make the latter more attractive to potential buyers.[42] This process involves:

- creating a wholly owned subsidiary;
- transferring the business to it;
- retaining the employees in the parent company but lending them to the subsidiary;
- disposing of the subsidiary business by transfer or by sale of shares; and
- dismissing the employees from the parent company before disposal of the subsidiary.

No provision is made for this in the directive but TUPE makes express provision.[43] The method is to postpone the transfer on hiving down until either disposal of the share capital of the subsidiary or the sale of the subsidiary. The initial transfer to the subsidiary, therefore, is not covered by TUPE so contracts of employment do not transfer. Since the receiver then dismisses the employees pre-transfer, at the time the subsidiary is transferred it will have no employees to be transferred to the transferee.

A major issue here, however, is whether such behaviour is caught by the purposive construction of the directive embodied in the *Litster* principle. It seems possible that this might be so. Thus, in the absence of an ETO reason *Litster* might apply.

In situations where TUPE does apply to insolvency, an important concern is whether any dismissal is 'connected with' the transfer. In the absence of an ETO reason, dismissals by an insolvency practitioner immediately prior to selling viable parts of an insolvent business (ie, prior to one or more specific transfers) are likely to be caught by Litster because they are connected with the transfer. The contracts of the employees would thus transfer to the transferee. However, where an insolvency practitioner dismisses employees immediately upon his appointment, without any specific transfer in sight, in order to increase the company's chances of survival or sale, this may be a redundancy rather than a dismissal connected with the transfer *(Longden & Paisley v Ferrari Ltd and Kennedy International Ltd)*, although redundancy could be connected with a transfer, forming an ETO reason.

The position is less certain where there are dismissals in the context of tentative plans for a transfer. In *Harrison Bowden*, however, it was held that the *Litster* principle applied even in the absence of an actual or prospective transferee. A similar approach was taken in *Michael Peters*, but in *Ibex Trading* the EAT stressed that dismissal must be connected with the transfer. Thus if no offer has been made by the time of the dismissal, the dismissal may not be connected with the transfer. The test set out by the ECJ in *P Bork* is to look back in time and consider what happened. The absence of a transferee at the time of dismissal would not necessarily be fatal to an argument based on this test.

COLLECTIVE EMPLOYMENT RIGHTS

Collective agreements and union recognition

Like contracts of employment, collective agreements also transfer automatically, but unless specifically provided otherwise in the agreement these will not be legally enforceable. However the collective agreement terms may be incorporated into individual contracts, which can be enforced *(Marley v Forward Trust Group Ltd)*. Occupational pension schemes are again excluded from automatic transfer. Trades union recognition transfers automatically if the union is independent and the business preserves its autonomy. Any redundancy agreement will have been transferred automatically so in the event of a redundancy this may be relevant if the question of unfair dismissal arises.

Consultation with appropriate representatives[44]

An employer has a duty to inform and consult the 'appropriate representatives' of any employees who may be affected by the proposed transfer of the undertaking or measures taken in connection with it. Affected employees may be in the employment of the transferor of transferee, so the duty may arise in both cases. The purpose of the consultation is to seek agreement about the measures to be taken.

'Appropriate representatives' are employee representatives elected by the employees or representatives of an independent trades union recognized by the employer in respect of these employees. Appropriate representatives must be afforded access to employees who may be affected by the transfer and provided with accommodation and other facilities as may be appropriate.

The information to be divulged, in writing, comprises:

- the fact of the transfer, the date and the reasons;
- the legal, economic and social implications; and
- measures the transferor and the transferee propose to take *vis-à-vis* the employees; if there are no measures this must be stated.

Consultation involves considering representations and replying to them, giving reasons for the rejection of any of them. As with redundancy consultation the employer may argue 'special circumstances' (see pages 359–60).

Where a failure to inform or consult relates to a union representative, the union may make a complaint to an industrial tribunal. Where the complaint relates to an employee representative, that representative may make a complaint. In other cases, any affected employee may complain. Compensation of up to four weeks' pay may be awarded to each affected employee on the basis of what is 'just and equitable' taking into account the seriousness of the employer's breach of duty. Payments made for failure to consult over redundancy or for breach of contract during the protected period (see pages 360–61) cannot be deducted from this sum.

There is no timescale for consultation under TUPE but information should be provided 'long enough before' the transfer to allow consultations to take place. There is no requirement to consult if an employer does not envisage taking measures in relation to his employees in connection with the transfer.

NOTES

1 In addition to the general statutory provisions there are specific arrangements covering particular changes, such as those involving employees being transferred from district health authorities to NHS trusts. The National Health Service and Community Care Act 1990, s 6 establishes continuity of employment across such changes and transfers to the new employer the original

employer's rights, powers, duties and liabilities under or in connection with the contract of employment. See also ERA, s 218(8)–(10) which deals with multi-employer professional training in the NHS. ERA, s 172 allows the termination of certain employments by statute to be treated as dismissal by reason of redundancy. The Secretary of State exercises his power through regulations and has used this section where police forces are amalgamated and an officer will not agree to transfer.

2 ERA, s 218.

3 The presumption is found in ERA, s 210(5).

4 SI 1981/1794. The Regulations were issued under the European Communities Act 1972. The source is EC Council Directive 77/187 (of 14 February 1977) on the approximation of the laws of the Member States relating to the safeguarding of employees' rights in the event of transfer of undertakings, businesses or parts of businesses (OJ 1977, L61).

5 For a detailed and authoritative account of TUPE see McMullen, J, *Business Transfers and Employee Rights* (3rd edition, Butterworth's, 1998).

6 ERA, s 218(3).

7 ERA, s 218(4).

8 ERA, s 174.

9 ERA, s 136(5).

10 ERA, s 218(5). A partnership is an unincorporated association without a legal identity. Employees are employed by the association's members jointly. A change in partners is likely to be a change of employer unless there is express provision to the effect that, or it can be inferred that, the employment is with the partners as from time to time constituted (see *Briggs v Oates*).

11 ERA, s 218(6).

12 ERA, s 231.

13 See also *Southern Electricity Board v Collins* where it was held that a collective agreement which gave continuity on movement from one electricity board to another could not override the statute under which continuity depended upon employers being associated. The boards were not associated employers and so the employee did not have continuity for statutory redundancy payment purposes. As a result, two exemptions were sought and obtained under what is now ERA, s 157 (see page 390). Local authorities are not associated companies but continuity for redundancy payment purposes is preserved on transfer by the Redundancy Payments (Local Government) (Modification) Order (SI 1983/1160).

14 ERA, s 218(7).

15 ERA, s 212.

16 ERA, s 218(2).

17 ERA, s 218(2).

18 Interpretation Act 1978, Sched 1.

19 ERA, s 235(1).

20 TUPE, reg 3(1).

21 TUPE, reg 3(2).

22 TUPE, reg 2(2). Prior to the operation of TURERA, s 33 and Sched 10, the undertaking had to be 'in the nature of a commercial venture'. Deciding what

was a commercial venture was held to be a matter of first impression for an industrial tribunal *(Woodcock v The Committee for the Time Being of the Friends' School, Wigton)*. In response to an application for judicial review of the Further and Higher Education Act 1992 by the National Association of Teachers in Further and Higher Education, the government conceded that because TUPE was limited to commercial ventures it did not fully implement the EC Acquired Rights Directive. The European Commission was in any case taking infringement proceedings *(Commission of the EC v UK,* 1994) and the ECJ had made the position clear in *Dr Sophie Redmond Stichting v Bartol.* In *Sophie Redmond* the ECJ held that a local authority's termination of a subsidy to a charitable foundation, causing the foundation to cease operating, and the giving of the subsidy to another charitable foundation, was a transfer falling within the scope of the directive. There had been a change in the person carrying on the business, who was responsible for the employees. The deciding criterion is whether the unit retains its identity, that is, by continuing or resuming as before.

23 TUPE, reg 3(4).

24 The *Christel Schmidt* case, where the transfer involved one person, emphasized the scope of the directive. In the UK, the ECJ concept of a transfer has been applied in a number of cases including *Porter v Queens Medical Centre* and *Kenny v South Manchester College.* The response of the European Commission, under pressure from governments, including that of the UK, has been to attempt to exclude the transfer of organizational parts or functions from the definition of a transfer, as yet without effect.

25 ERA, s 218(2) and TUPE, reg 5(3). The directive refers to 'the date of a transfer' (article 3). The *Spence* case (see page 399) referred to moment or time.

26 ERA, s 97(2).

27 TUPE, reg 5 If a transferor wishes to retain some of the employees there may have to be a consensual variation or novation of contract agreed prior to the transfer *(Sunley Turriff,* but see also *A&G Tuck Ltd*).

28 TUPE, reg 7. In *Adams v Lancashire County Council,* the Court of Appeal held that the transferee was not obliged to give employees rights under an occupational pension scheme comparable with those provided by the transferor. Such rights were excluded from the transfer.

29 TUPE, reg 5(5).

30 TUPE, reg 5(4A) and (4B).

31 Novation of contract is the substitution of a third party for one of the original, contracting parties.

32 TUPE, reg 5(2).

33 TUPE, reg 8(1).

34 TUPE, reg 8(2).

35 ERA, s 98(1)(b).

36 The effect of the regulations is to transfer contracts of employment automatically. Therefore, a collective agreement purporting to prevent some of the employees being transferred was void *(D'Urso v Ercole Marelli Elletromeccanica Generale SpA).*

37 TUPE, reg 8(5) was amended by the Collective Redundancies and Transfer of

Undertakings (Protection of Employment) (Amendment) Regulations (SI 1995/2587).

38 On the application of what are now the ERA provisions prior to the introduction of TUPE, see *Teesside Times Ltd v Drury*.

39 Insolvency Act 1986, s 29(2). Where voluntarily appointed, an administrative receiver will be personally liable for the contracts of employment of employees adopted by him or entered into by him, but will be entitled to an indemnity from the company's assets (Insolvency Act 1986, s 44). In *Powdrill v Watson* the House of Lords made it clear that once the 14-day period specified in the Insolvency Act had elapsed, employees were adopted within the meaning of s 19 of the Insolvency Act 1986. The Insolvency Act 1994 was introduced to soften the effects of this judgment.

40 Acquired Right Directive, article 7. Otherwise, employees would be placed at an advantage *vis-à-vis* other creditors and detailed, well-established insolvency rules would be undermined.

41 Presumably the same would apply in cases where the business was unincorporated and there was personal bankruptcy.

42 TUPE, reg 4.

43 *Loc cit.*

44 TUPE, reg 10.

Trades Unions

TRADES UNION STATUS AND ADMINISTRATION

Meaning of trades union

A trades union is an organization of workers, one of the principal purposes of which is to regulate the relations between workers and employers.[1] A federation of trades unions, such as the TUC, is included in this definition.

Legal status

Trades unions have a quasi-corporate status.[2] They are not bodies corporate but:

- they are capable of entering into contracts;
- they are capable of suing and being sued in their own name; and
- criminal proceedings can be taken against them in their own name.

They are not to be treated as bodies corporate except in the ways the legislation specifies.[3] A trades union cannot register as a company except that some trades unions are 'special register bodies', a designation which derives from the long-repealed Industrial Relations Act 1971.[4] These unions are either registered companies or otherwise incorporated (for example by charter, as in the case of the Royal College of Nursing).

The legal status of a trades union therefore is as follows:

- a trades union is an unincorporated association (of individuals, ie natural persons); and

- it has no legal personality of its own, merely some corporate characteristics conferred on it by statute.

Therefore, it cannot sue for libel because the tort of libel must be founded on possession of a legal personality which can be libelled *(EETPU v The Times Newspapers)*. Corporate characteristics are given to trades unions on public policy grounds: trades unions can exercise considerable power so must be accountable. The origins of their quasi-corporate status are to be found in *Taff Vale Railway Company v ASRS*.

Property of trades unions

A trades union has the capacity to own property but only by vesting it in trustees in trust for it.[5] Depending on the true construction of the union's rules (and the rules of a branch of the union), property may be owned by a branch of the union rather than by the union as a whole *(News Group Newspapers v SOGAT)*. Judgments against a union can be enforced against any property held in trust as if it were a body corporate.

Listing

Listing is a process of registration with the Certification Officer.[6] The process involves submitting the following to the CO:

- the rules of the union;
- a list of officers;
- the address of the head office;
- the name of the union; and
- the appropriate fee.

The Certification Officer (and the Certification Office) are within the Department for Trade and Industry, the Certification Office being appointed by the Secretary of State for Trade and Industry after consulting ACAS.[7] The concern here is with the administrative role of the Certification Office: as will be noted later, there is also a judicial role.

It is mandatory for the Certification Office to keep a list of trades unions (which is open to public inspection) but it is not mandatory for unions to apply to be listed.[8] A trades union, if the Certification Office is satisfied it is a trades union and it applies using the correct procedure, will be listed. A union refused listing may appeal to the EAT on a point of fact or law. A union may want to be listed in order to obtain evidence that it is a trades union. This is significant for two reasons:

- There are tax advantages for friendly benefits provided by the union (eg, unemployment or death benefits provided by the union to its members). Historically such benefits were of considerable importance: these days relatively few unions provide these benefits and those that do tend to provide only small amounts. These benefits will not be liable to tax if the union is listed since listing confirms that the organization is a trades union.
- Unions are interested in being certificated as independent, for which listing is a prerequisite. Various rights, such as time off for union officials and union representatives' rights to be consulted in a redundancy, are given to independent unions recognized by employers.

Independence

An independent trades union is one not under the domination or control of an employer and not liable to interference tending towards such control.[9] The purpose here is to guard against employer-sponsored unions which may be a device to prevent *bona fide* trades unions from establishing a presence within a company.

The CO's criteria for determining whether a union is independent are to be found in *Blue Circle Staff Association v Certification Office*:

- whether there is finance from the employer;
- whether there is other assistance from the employer;
- whether there is interference by the employer;
- the history of the union;
- the union's rules;
- whether the union organizes only in one company;
- the union's organization; and
- the union's attitude.

The term 'liable to interference' is important in the definition of independence. In *Squibb UK Staff Association v Certification Office* it was taken by the Court of Appeal to mean 'vulnerable to interference' (ie, exposed to the risk of interference) rather than that interference was likely. The *Government Communications Staff Association* case is a more recent example of a certificate of independence being refused because the union was liable to interference.

A union refused its certificate of independence may appeal to EAT on a point of fact or law.[10]

Administrative requirements[11]

Unions, whether listed or not, must keep proper accounting records and establish and maintain systems of financial control.[12] They must also send an annual return to the Certification Officer, which must include their audited accounts. Where unions run superannuation schemes for their members, these must be subject to actuarial examination.[13] It is a criminal offence to refuse to perform or wilfully neglect these duties, or to falsify documents. These offences are punishable by fine.

In *Taylor v NUM (Derbyshire) (No 2)* the union spent money supporting an unofficial strike. This was held to be *ultra vires* and therefore a mis-application of funds. Sometime later, the NUM commissioned its own enquiry – the Lightman enquiry – which revealed a number of improper dealings. The Certification Office subsequently attempted, without success, to bring proceedings against the union and ultimately the statutory provisions were strengthened by TURERA. A union's annual return to the Certification Office must now contain additional information:

- details of the salary paid to and other benefits provided to the executive members, the president and the general secretary; and
- the total number of names on the membership register and the number of names without an address.

More significantly, the Certification Office now has powers to investigate unions' financial affairs, including the power to obtain documents and carry out inspections. New offences have been created and penalties for existing offences increased. The right of a union member to have an annual statement of his or her union's financial affairs was also introduced (see page 424).

Union mergers

TULR(C)A lays down various rules for trades union mergers and changes of name.[14] The legislation also covers unincorporated employers' associations. Of prime importance is the fact that mergers are of two types: amalgamations and transfers of engagements. Under a transfer of engagements the transferor loses its legal identity and the transferee continues with its legal identity unchanged. An amalgamation produces a new organization replacing the amalgamating bodies, which then cease to exist. In the latter case, therefore, there has to be a new rule book and a new name for the union. Unions wishing to merge must prepare an instrument setting out the proposed terms and an explanatory notice to members. These documents have to be approved by the Certification Officer before balloting on the instrument can go ahead. In a transfer of engagement only the members of the transferring organization need to vote on whether to accept the instrument. In an amalgamation, each amalgamating organization must have a ballot.

Where a majority of those voting are in favour, the union(s) can apply to the Certification Officer to have the instrument registered. An interval of six weeks is allowed for any members of a transferor union or amalgamating union to make a complaint that one or more of the statutory requirements of the ballot has not been met. The Certification Officer will investigate and make a decision on any complaint, which may include laying down conditions to be met before registration will be allowed. There is a right of appeal to the EAT on a point of law. The Certification Officer also has a responsibility to deal with changes of name of listed unions and employers' associations, and to approve changes as long as the new name is not the same as, or very similar to, any other listed organization.

As a result of TURERA 1993, the ballot requirements are now substantially the same as for union elections (see pages 416–19).

Trades union status and administration: summary

- Trades unions are organizations of workers whose principal purposes include the regulation of relations with employers.
- They are unincorporated associations without their own legal personality.
- However statute confers upon them some corporate characteristics on the public policy ground that they should be accountable.
- A list of trades unions kept by the Certification Officer provides a union with evidence that it is a trades union.
- Listing is a prerequisite for obtaining a certificate of independence, which is important because various legal rights are given to independent trades unions if they are recognized by employers.

THE CONTRACT OF MEMBERSHIP

The legal basis of the union–member relationship is founded in contract. The rules contain the contract which is a contract between the members, and is a contract of membership *(Lee v The Showmen's Guild)*. The contract may have implied terms *(McVitae v Unison)*. The essence of the contract is a subscription in exchange for the benefits and services derived from membership.

The courts will intervene in the contractual relationship between the member and the union to interpret the rules (as in *Showmen's Guild*) or to enforce the principles of natural justice. Of particular relevance in this context is the right of the member to know the allegations made against him, to have a chance to rebut them and to be given a fair hearing (which was not the case in *Roebuck*).

The common law concept of a contract of membership is not something unique to trades unions. The concept is applied to voluntary organizations more generally, such as social and sports clubs and political parties. Much of the case law in this field relates to questions of procedure: for instance, an organization has made a decision but the procedure by which it has been arrived at was flawed. There has been either a breach of the organization's rules (including standing orders) or a breach of the principles of natural justice, or both.

The case of *Iwanuszezak v General Municipal Boilermakers and Allied Trades Union* was unusual in that the member claimed that the union was in breach of contract by not representing him properly. It thus rested upon the substantive issue of whether or not the union was providing the service it was contractually bound to provide. The claim failed because there was no term in the contract on which the action could be based, although it is submitted that representation in good faith might conceivably be an implied term. This would allow for the fact that even the most effective representation would probably not satisfy all the members. A duty of care might also be implied, opening up the possibility of a claim in tort for damages for negligence.

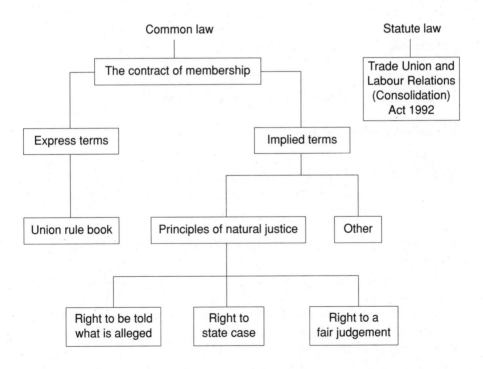

Figure 21.1 The legal framework for trades union governance

Common law claims would be taken through the normal courts, and following the extension of the role of the Commissioner for the Rights of Trade Union Members ('the Commissioner') as a result of the EA 1990 there is now assistance available to the member.

The common law contract of membership is statutorily recognized in TULR(C)A which says that the contract will have an implied term conferring a right on the member on giving reasonable notice, and complying with any reasonable conditions, to terminate their membership of the union.[15]

The rule book is the cornerstone of the contract of membership and for the most part a union is free to determine its own rules, although rules governing union mergers and political objectives require the approval of the Certification Officer. However, the rules will not reign supreme if they involve a breach of the principles of natural justice, nor if they conflict with statutory provision. There is now a substantial amount of statute law governing the internal functioning of trades unions. Ballots are necessary as laid down by statute if unions are to protect themselves from various adverse consequences in relation to industrial action, national executive committee elections, political objective and mergers. With the exception of mergers, already dealt with, these are discussed later in this chapter. Figure 21.1 summarizes the overall legal position.

EXCLUSION, EXPULSION AND DISCIPLINE

Exclusion and expulsion

An individual has a statutory right not to be excluded or expelled from a trades union.[16] Exclusion or expulsion is permitted only in accordance with the legislation: this admits four reasons where exclusion or expulsion is allowed. These are where:

- there is a failure to satisfy an enforceable membership requirement in the rules;
- there is a failure to qualify for membership because of geographical location (ie, the union operates only in part(s) of Great Britain);
- the union organizes one employer or a group of associated employers and the individual is not an employee of this or these employers; and
- it is justified by the conduct of the employee.

Enforceable membership requirements include factors such as occupational qualification.

Remedies are obtained by applying to an industrial tribunal within six months. The remedies are a declaration and compensation.

Discipline

Unjustifiable discipline[17]

Discipline is defined in terms of expulsion, fines, deprivation of benefits or services and any other detriment. It includes advising or encouraging another union not to accept the person as a member. The member has a statutory right not to be unjustifiably disciplined. Where the discipline is expulsion, unjustifiable discipline complaints must be heard under these provisions rather than those relating to unreasonable exclusion or expulsion.

The decision to discipline, for it to be covered by the legislation, has to be taken by a union in accordance with its rules, by an official, or by a group which includes an official. The legislation confers rights which are additional to any others that the member may have (for example, under union rules).

Discipline is unjustifiable if the reason for it is that the member's conduct includes one of the following or something which amounts to one of the following:

(1) Industrial action:
    (a) failing to participate;
    (b) indicating opposition or lack of support;
    (c) failing to refuse to perform certain contractual or other agreed duties; and
    (d) encouraging or assisting anyone else to perform such duties.
(2) Assertions:
    (a) asserting that the union, or its officials, representatives or trustees, have contravened or are proposing to contravene the union's rules, any agreement or law;
    (b) attempting to justify any such assertion; and
    (c) consulting or seeking advice or assistance from the Certification Office, the Commissioner or anyone else with respect to matters which form or might form the basis of such an assertion.
(3) Other:
    (a) refusing to comply with a penalty arising out of an act for which discipline has been ruled unjustifiable either in relation to that person or some other person;
    (b) proposing to do anything listed above (that is, (1), (2) and (3)(a)); and
    (c) preparing or doing anything incidental to engaging in anything listed above (that is, (1), (2) and (3)(a)).

Discipline against a member for working through a strike, crossing a picket line or working normally when partial sanctions are being applied (that is, partial performance of duties) will be unjustifiable under the terms of the

Act. So too will be discipline for speaking out against industrial action and refusing to pay a strike levy.

Asserting breaches of rule and so on will include the bringing of any proceedings. Making an assertion will not amount to unjustifiable discipline, however, if the individual making it, or helping another to make it, knows it is false or otherwise acts in bad faith. Nor will discipline be unjustifiable if it would have occurred irrespective of it being listed in the Act, for example discipline for disruptive behaviour in a meeting when alleging breach of a rule.

The procedure for a complainant in these cases is to apply to an industrial tribunal. Figure 21.2 summarizes the sequence. Cases can be transferred between EAT and tribunals (and *vice versa*) if they are in the wrong forum. Complainants must mitigate their losses, and compensation can be reduced it there is contributory fault. Other remedies are a declaration and the repayment of any fine. The procedure differs somewhat from the similar provisions on expulsions and exclusions:

- there are appeals on points of law only, from the declaration;
- the basis of compensation is different at an industrial tribunal; and
- the amounts of compensation are different at the EAT.

Unlawful discipline at common law

Apart from the statutory provisions, discipline may be unlawful at common law. In *Lee v Showmen's Guild* there was unlawful discipline because it was based on wrongful interpretation of the contract of membership (here, the rule book). In *Roebuck* discipline was unlawful because it arose out of a biased disciplinary hearing which was in breach of the principles of natural justice. In *McVitae v Unison* discipline was permitted by a term implied into the contract of membership.

UNION ELECTIONS

Members of a union's principal executive committee (but not members of other committees: *Paul v NALGO*), including non-voting members (ie, those who are members of the executive committee by virtue of some other position that they hold), and union general secretaries and presidents, must be subject to election at least every five years.[18] Special register bodies (see page 408) are subject to less strict requirements (that is, excluding non-voting members, presidents and general secretaries). Certain general secretaries and presidents who are largely ceremonial are excluded. Elected leaders nearing retirement age may have their period of office extended beyond five years as may some leaders involved in mergers. Ballots are not required for uncontested elections.

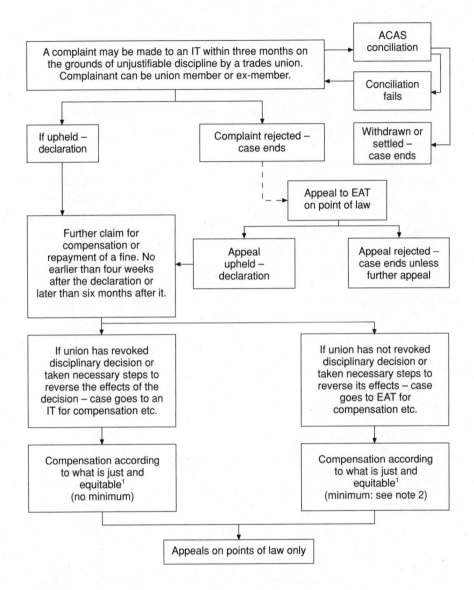

A complaint may be made to an IT within three months on the grounds of unjustifiable discipline by a trades union. Complainant can be union member or ex-member.

ACAS conciliation

Conciliation fails

If upheld – declaration

Complaint rejected – case ends

Withdrawn or settled – case ends

Appeal to EAT on point of law

Further claim for compensation or repayment of a fine. No earlier than four weeks after the declaration or later than six months after it.

Appeal upheld – declaration

Appeal rejected – case ends unless further appeal

If union has revoked disciplinary decision or taken necessary steps to reverse the effects of the decision – case goes to an IT for compensation etc.

If union has not revoked disciplinary decision or taken necessary steps to reverse its effects – case goes to EAT for compensation etc.

Compensation according to what is just and equitable[1] (no minimum)

Compensation according to what is just and equitable[1] (minimum: see note 2)

Appeals on points of law only

Notes:
[1] The sum of the basic and compensatory awards for unfair dismissal (see pages 330–31)
[2] The equivalent of the minimum basic award where dismissal is for reasons of trades union membership or activity or non-membership (see page 332)

Figure 21.2 Claims against trades unions for remedies for unjustifiable discipline

The elections must be fully postal, and must meet the following requirements. They must be secret, there must be no interference and there must be no direct cost to the voter. Everyone must have the opportunity to vote by marking a ballot paper which must specify the address to which, and date by which, it must be returned. Each paper must have a different serial number.[19] In *Veness v NUPE*, the union delegated the conduct of the election to the Electoral Reform Society. Some members did not receive ballot papers but the members' case against the union was struck out as disclosing no cause of action.

No member should be unreasonably excluded from being a candidate and all candidates have the right to prepare an election address and have it sent out with the voting papers at no cost to themselves.[20] They must have the opportunity to prepare the address in their own words. Facilities given to candidates and any restrictions put upon them must be applied equally to all candidates. The minimum length of the address is 100 words. Unions may set deadlines for submission of addresses. A candidate's address must not be changed without their consent except for production reasons. The same method of production must be used for all addresses. Civil or criminal liability for the contents of the address rest solely with the candidate.

There must be independent scrutiny of union elections.[21] The scrutineer has to be named in advance and on the ballot paper so that members can challenge the union's choice if they wish. The qualifications of scrutineers are laid down in a Ministerial Order.[22] They must be competent and independent of the union and must be one of the following:

- a solicitor with a practising certificate;
- a chartered or certified accountant who is accepted as an auditor;
- the Electoral Reform Society;
- the Industrial Society; or
- Unity Security Balloting Services Ltd.

These requirements also apply to political fund ballots. Independent scrutineers have the role of supervising the production and distribution of ballot papers, receiving voting papers returned by voters, reporting on the ballot to the union and retaining custody of the returned voting papers for one year.

The independent scrutineer's role was extended by the Trade Union Reform and Employment Rights Act 1993 (TURERA). The scrutineer must now inspect the union's membership register when he considers it appropriate to do so and in particular when requested to do so by a union member or election candidate who suspects that the register is not accurate or up to date. The scrutineer need not inspect the register if he considers the suspicion ill-founded or if the request is made outside the 'appropriate' period.[23]

The independent scrutineer's report[24] must state whether an inspection of the register was carried out and if so whether it was at the request of a member or election candidate, but without revealing that person's identity. The report must state whether anything was found which indicated that the register was not accurate and up to date. More generally, the independent scrutineer's report must say whether the ballot appeared to meet the legal requirements, whether the security arrangements were satisfactory and whether the scrutineer was able to carry out their functions without interference. The scrutineer must state the number of voting papers distributed, the number returned, the number of votes for each candidate and the number of spoiled or invalid papers. A union cannot publish the ballot result until it has received the scrutineer's report. Within three months of receiving the report it must provide a copy of the report to each member, as far as is reasonably practicable, or notify the members of the main details through normal channels. The union must also inform members that they can obtain a copy either free of charge or for a reasonable fee, and supply such copies.

A further change introduced by TURERA was the requirement for votes to be stored, distributed and counted by 'one or more independent persons'.[25] The independent person may be the scrutineer or any other person the union believes will carry out the functions competently and whose independence cannot reasonably be doubted.

Complaints by members about union elections being in breach of statute may be made to the Certification Officer or the High Court. The former, where possible, must give a decision within six months. The Certification Officer can make a declaration: only the courts can make enforcement orders (such as an order to rerun an election). The Commissioner may assist individuals wanting to pursue court actions. Applications to the courts or the Certification Officer relating to elections which have been held must be made within a year of the announcement of the election result. The applicant must have been a member at the time of their application and, if the election has been held, at the time of the election.

The Secretary of State may produce codes of practice in respect of trades union elections and ballots.[26]

TRADES UNION POLITICAL ACTIVITIES

The legal framework

Until it was decided in 1909 in *ASRS v Osborne* that political activities were *ultra vires* (beyond the powers of) the trades unions, it had been thought that trades unions could perfectly lawfully engage in such activities. The present position is that a union, regardless of whether it is listed (see pages

409–10), is permitted to have political objectives as defined by TULR(C)A.[27] Activities in furtherance of political objectives must be financed out of a separate fund and members not wishing to contribute to the fund have the right to be exempted (that is, to contract out). To have political objectives, a majority of the union's members voting in a ballot must be in favour.

The ballot rules have to be approved by the Certification Officer as do the political rules more generally and any changes in them. A member exempted from paying into the political fund must not be put at a disadvantage (except in relation to the control and management of the political fund) by being exempted. This means that they must not lose any benefits or be put at any disadvantage compared with other members who have not contracted out. Contribution to the political fund must not be a condition of admission to the union. Where a union is liable for damages for committing unlawful industrial action, political funds, like provident funds, are protected.[28]

The Certification Officer issues model political rules for trades unions to use and the actual rules of unions follow these closely if not exactly. The model rules contain an exemption form which members can use to serve notice that they seek exemption. Some other form, to like effect, may also be used. Exempted members must be relieved of payment of the political levy (if separate) or that part of the general subscription which is a contribution to the political fund. In the latter circumstances, the member must be told which part of the subscription is the political element. The exemption means that the member should not pay the political contribution at the time it is due to be levied, rather than having it deducted and later refunded.

Any member who feels that they are the subject of a breach of a union's political rules may complain to the Certification Officer or alternatively to the courts.[29] If, after a hearing, the Certification Officer believes that a breach has occurred, he may make a declaration. The Certification Officer's decision is subject to appeal to the Employment Appeal Tribunal on a point of law. Where an application is made to the court, the court will have the power to make an order as well as a declaration.

Membership ballots

The original legislation – the Trade Union Act 1913 – required a once-for-all ballot if a union was to have political objectives, but the Trade Union Act 1984 introduced a requirement that there be a ballot at intervals of no more than ten years. The principal ballot requirements are now as follows:

- voting must be by marking a voting paper;
- the ballot must be fully postal;
- there must be independent scrutiny (as described on pages 418–19) and

the name of the scrutineer must be communicated to members and must appear on the ballot paper;

- secrecy must be secured;
- there must be freedom from interference; and
- there must be no direct cost to the voter.

Complaints about ballots may be made to the Certification Office (whose decision should, if possible, be made within six months) or to the High Court, under the statutory provisions. The member complaining must be a member at the time of the complaint and, if the ballot has taken place, at the time of the ballot. The Commissioner may assist in court cases. The ballot is required if a union wishes to adopt political objectives. It then follows automatically from statutory requirements that there must be a separate fund from which these objectives are financed. Whether a union subsequently affiliates to a political party is not a matter of law but a matter of union policy.

Definition of political activities

The original definition was amended by the Trade Union Act 1984. Anything 'political' must be paid out of the political fund. Everything else can be paid out of general funds. 'Political' means:

the expenditure of money:

(a) on any contribution to the funds of, or on the payment of any expenses incurred directly or indirectly by, a political party;

(b) on the provision of any service or property for use by or on behalf of any political party;

(c) in connection with the registration of electors, the candidature of any person, the selection of any candidate or the holding of any ballot by the union in connection with any election to a political office;

(d) on the maintenance of any holder of a political office;

(e) on the holding of any conference or meeting by or on behalf of a political party or of any other meeting by or on behalf of a political party or of any other meeting the main purpose of which is the transaction of business in connection with a political party;

(f) on the production, publication or distribution of any literature, document, film, sound recording or advertisement the main purpose of which is to persuade people to vote for a political party or candidate or to persuade them not to vote for a political party or candidate.[30]

In (c), 'political office' means an MP, an MEP, a member of a local authority or any position within a political party.

Although decided prior to the operation of the 1984 Act, the following cases illustrate how the definition is applied in practice. In *Richards v NUM*, the Certification Officer held that a march and lobby organized by the Labour Party, and a contribution to the financing of a new headquarters for the Labour Party, were political within the meaning of the legislation. He thus declared that there should be a transfer of the relevant sums from the political to the general fund (from which they had originally been paid). In broad terms, the legislation refers to party political activities rather than political activities more generally. For example, in *Coleman v POEU* there was a complaint about the union's general fund being used to pay for affiliation to a campaign which was alleged to be party political. The complaint was rejected because, while the campaign was clearly political, it was not political within the meaning of the legislation.

In a more recent case, attempting to persuade people not to vote for the Conservative Party at election time was held to be political *(Paul v NALGO)*.

Other matters

The legislation makes it clear that political fund debts can be paid off only from the political fund and that no assets can be transferred into the political fund other than political fund contributions and property accruing from managing political fund assets.

There is a duty upon employers not to deduct political fund contributions from contracted-out members who have notified them in writing. An employer refusing to stop political fund deductions or cancelling the whole of the subscription deduction (when not done for others) may be subject to a complaint to a county court. Where a county court order is obtained a member may pursue a case at an industrial tribunal under ERA to seek repayment of an unlawful deduction.[31]

Unions must inform members of the right to contract out of the political levy and tell them that a standard form is available from the union or the Certification Officer.

THE RIGHTS OF TRADES UNION MEMBERS

Ballots prior to industrial action

While the Trade Union Act 1984 had removed trades union immunity in the absence of a successful ballot, the union member had no statutory right to insist that a ballot be held. The Employment Act 1988 remedied this matter.[32] It provided that there is a right to apply to court for an order to restrain a union from industrial action. The application can be made by any member induced or likely to be induced to take part regardless of whether they will be induced. If the court is satisfied that the union is responsible for the action it will make an order.[33] Assistance from the Commissioner may be available. The ballot must be conducted in accordance with the legal requirements (see pages 458–61). A ballot not so conducted would leave it open to members to seek restraining orders.

Access to the courts

Hitherto, courts could refuse to hear a case if a union member had not fully used the union's internal procedures in connection with any grievance. As a result of the Employment Act 1988 it became possible for courts to dismiss or adjourn cases for this reason provided a valid application has been made to a trades union and six months have elapsed since that application.[34] The kinds of cases to which this provision relates are those which the union's rules require or allow to be submitted to the union for resolution or conciliation, and for which the courts have jurisdiction. These are essentially issues arising under the common law contract of membership, but are restricted to points of law (such as interpretation or breach of rules) or breaches of natural justice (see pages 324–5).

Right not to suffer deduction of unauthorized or excessive union subscriptions[35]

An employer must ensure that no deduction of union subscription is made from a worker's wages unless it is authorized. A deduction will be authorized only if agreed to by the worker in writing within the previous three years. The authorization may be withdrawn at any time. An *employer* must notify the worker at least one month in advance of any increase in the amount to be deducted and such a notice must remind the worker of his or her right to withdraw their authorization. Deducting the amount of an unnotified increase or making a deduction without authorization will constitute a breach of the TULR(C)A provisions and a complaint may be made to an industrial tribunal within three months of the date of payment to which the unlawful deduction relates. Where it is not reasonably practicable for the complaint to be made within three months, it must be made within such further period as is reasonable. An application may also be made under other statutory provisions, eg the wages provisions of ERA.

The government is proposing to amend the rules which apply to the deduction of union subscriptions.

Right to terminate union membership

Historically, some unions would not allow members to terminate their membership. Because of this, TULR(C)A inserts into the contract of membership an implied term giving union members a right to terminate their membership on reasonable notice and on complying with any reasonable conditions.[36]

Union funds, property and accounts

Access to unions' accounting records

Trades unions are required to keep their accounting records open for inspection and to give members the right of inspection, including the right to be accompanied by an accountant if they wish.[37] Accounting records are a requirement of TULR(C)A and relate to a union or a branch or section of that union. They must be kept available for inspection for six years. The inspection right for any period is given to someone who was a member for at least part of that period.

A union must give a member access within 28 days of the request. Normally, access will be at the place where the records are kept and at a reasonable hour. Copies of accounts may be taken. If the union notifies the member in advance, a reasonable charge may be made for complying with the inspection request. The principles on which a charge is made must be indicated in advance and it must not exceed reasonable administrative expenses. Where an accountant accompanies a member, that accountant may be asked to protect the confidentiality of the records. A refusal to do so will allow the union to prevent the accountant accompanying the member.

A person who has a request refused may ask the court to order that:

- they be allowed to inspect the records;
- they are allowed to be accompanied by an accountant; and
- they are allowed to have copies of the accounts.

The Commissioner may give assistance with cases taken under these provisions. If a union refuses or wilfully neglects the duties under these provisions it commits an offence punishable by a fine. The same applies if a person falsifies documents.

Right to be provided with an annual statement of the union's financial affairs

This right was introduced by TURERA and requires a union to provide an individual copy of such a statement to a member if requested to do so. Otherwise, a union can use its normal means of disseminating information to members. A copy of the statement must be lodged with the Certification Office.

Indemnifying unlawful conduct

It is unlawful for a trades union to indemnify anyone in respect of a penalty imposed on them for contempt of court or for a criminal offence.[38] A union has power under TULR(C)A to recover such sums, and any member can apply to a court if the union fails to bring or continue proceedings for such recovery. Courts may make an order allowing the individual member to bring or continue proceedings on the union's behalf and at its expense. The assistance of the Commissioner might be available to the member under such circumstances.

Unlawful use of property by trustees

Union trustees cannot lawfully use union property, or allow it to be used, for unlawful purposes; nor can they lawfully comply with any unlawful direction given to them under the rules of the union.[39] A member may apply to the courts if the trustees have done any of these things or propose to do any of them. If the act has occurred, the member complaining must have been a union member at the time of the act. The Commissioner may provide assistance.

A court may require the trustees to take specified steps to protect or recover the union's property. It also has the power to appoint a receiver of the union's property who will stay in control of the union's funds until the court is satisfied that they can be returned to the trustees. It may remove one or more of the trustees. Where actions are proposed or taken in contempt of court all of the union's trustees will be removed except for any who can convince the court that they should remain. In contempt, trustees will be liable as individuals for any penalties for contempt and it would be unlawful for the union to indemnify them.

Inspection of a union's membership register

Unions are required to compile and keep up to date a register of the names and addresses of their members.[40] The legislation allows a member to check whether they are included in their union's register and to obtain a copy of their register entry which should be provided free of charge or for a reasonable fee, as soon as is reasonably practicable after the request is made. A member must give reasonable notice of wishing to check the register, which they can do so free of charge at a reasonable time. A complaint under these provisions may be made to the Certification Officer or to the High Court. Both may make declarations but only the latter can make an order for enforcement. Assistance from the Commissioner may be available.

426 / THE SUBSTANCE OF EMPLOYMENT LAW

Right not to be discriminated against on ground of race or sex

In their capacity as employers of staff, trades unions are governed by discrimination law in the same ways as other employers. However, trades unions are also subject to legislation covering the relationships they have with their members, that is, as providers of benefits and services. Trades unions must not discriminate as regards the terms of membership, or by refusing admission, or in access to any benefits, facilities or services. Nor must they deprive people of membership on any of the prohibited grounds, nor subject people to any other detriment. An exception is made here (as regards sex discrimination) for death or retirement provisions but not in relation to retirement provisions affecting promotion, demotion, dismissal, training and transfer. The decision of the ECJ in *Barber v Guardian Royal Exchange Assurance Group* seems to signal the end of discrimination of this sort being considered lawful. Unions may need to be careful if they are involved in an employer's recruitment process. Where a union provides all of the candidates for recruitment, there could be unlawful discrimination if the union membership is all male, for example, or all white. If a non-member was refused, this might be an unlawful refusal of employment under the access to employment provisions.

Unions may lawfully engage in a certain amount of positive discrimination. Seats on their national executive committees may be reserved for women. Election to such seats, however, must not be restricted to women members. Training can also be provided for those groups who are under-represented in respect of union positions. Thus, there may be women-only courses or courses for black people. Unions are advised by codes of practice to become involved with the introduction of equal opportunities policies and their monitoring.[41]

Facilities for ballots

Provisions relating to public funds for trades union ballots and rights to hold a ballot on the employer's premises have been repealed.[42] The right to time off for union activities remains, however, the relevant code of practice citing voting in union elections as an example of such activities.[43]

Rights of trades union members: summary

The relationship between member and union is governed by a contract of membership. However, there is a substantial amount of statute law governing the relationship. This covers ballots for industrial action, election ballots, political activities and many other areas, including membership discipline, exclusion and expulsion. The Commissioner exists to assist union members with legal action against their own unions (see pages 42–4).[44]

NOTES

1 TULR(C)A, s 1.
2 TULR(C)A, s 10(1).
3 TULR(C)A, s 10(2).
4 The general prohibition is in TULR(C)A, s 10(3). Special register bodies are provided for by TULR(C)A, s 117.
5 TULR(C)A, s 12.
6 TULR(C)A, ss 2–3.
7 TULR(C)A, s 254.
8 TULR(C)A, s 2.
9 TULR(C)A, s 5.
10 TULR(C)A, s 174.
11 TULR(C)A, ss 24–45C.
12 TULR(C)A, s 28.
13 TULR(C)A, s 39.
14 TULR(C)A, ss 97–107. See also the Trades Unions and Employers' Associations (Amalgamations etc) Regulations (SI 1975/536) as amended by SI 1978/1344, SI 1988/310 and SI 1994/546.
15 TULR(C)A, s 69.
16 TULR(C)A, s 174.
17 TULR(C)A, s 64.
18 TULR(C)A, s 46.
19 TULR(C)A, ss 50–51.
20 TULR(C)A, ss 47–48.
21 TULR(C)A, s 49.
22 Trade Union Ballots and Elections (Independent Scrutineer Qualifications) Order (SI 1993/1909).
23 This is defined in TULR(C)A, s 49(3B).
24 TULR(C)A, s 52.
25 TULR(C)A, s 51A.
26 TULR(C)A, s 203.
27 TULR(C)A, s 72.
28 TULR(C)A, s 23.
29 TULR(C)A, ss 80–81.
30 TULR(C)A, s 72.
31 TULR(C)A, s 88.
32 EA 1988, s l; now TULR(C)A, s 62.
33 The tests for this are laid down in TULR(C)A, ss 20–21.
34 TULR(C)A, s 63.
35 TULR(C)A, ss 68 and 68A.
36 TULR(C)A, s 69.
37 TULR(C)A, s 30.
38 TULR(C)A, s 15.
39 TULR(C)A, s 16.
40 TULR(C)A, s 24.

41 The CRE and the EOC codes of practice: see pages 121–2.
42 TULR(C)A, ss 115–116, repealed by TURERA, s 7. See also the Funds for Trade Union Ballots Regulations (Revocation) Regulations (SI 1993/233).
43 ACAS, *Time Off for Trade Union Duties and Activities* (Code of Practice 3, London, HMSO, 1998).
44 Administrative provisions relating to the Commissioner are to be found in TULR(C)A, ss 266–271.

Collective Bargaining

FREEDOM OF ASSOCIATION

Meaning

As noted in chapter 21, trades unions are unincorporated associations albeit with certain corporate characteristics. The term 'freedom of association' in this context, therefore, means the rights of workers to combine with each other, that is, to form an association (or union) to defend or advance their interests.

International standards

Various international standards apply in this area:

- the Universal Declaration of Human Rights 1948, article 20;
- the International Covenant on Civil and Political Rights 1966, article 22;
- the International Covenant on Economic, Social and Cultural Rights 1966, article 8;
- the European Convention on Human Rights, article 11;
- the European Social Charter 1961, article 5;
- the EC Social Charter, article 11; and
- ILO Conventions Nos 87 and 98.

Two examples are given below.

European Convention on Human Rights 1950, article 11

1. Everyone has the right to freedom of ... association with others, including the right to form trade unions ...

It should be noted that the European Convention on Human Rights has not been incorporated into UK law. However, the Human Rights Bill 1997, once enacted, will achieve this effect.

ILO Convention No 98 of 1949, article 1

Workers shall enjoy adequate protection against acts of anti-union discrimination in respect of their employment.

Freedom of association and national security

An important question is raised where the individual's freedom of association has to be balanced against the interests of national security. This was held to be the issue in *Council of Civil Service Unions v Minister for the Civil Service* where the government in its capacity as employer removed union membership rights from employees at its communications headquarters. It defended this action on the ground of national security because the employees had been engaged in strike activity. The unions challenged the decision by means of an application for judicial review on the basis that there had been no consultation. Ultimately there was an appeal to the House of Lords which held that the unions' appeal should be dismissed. The Minister's decision was based on considerations of national security which outweighed the requirement for consultation. Those employees who refused to give up their union membership were dismissed, in breach of ILO Convention No 87.[1]

UK statutory provisions

The statutory protection afforded to employees falls into three categories:

- protection against refusal of employment;
- protection against action short of dismissal; and
- protection against dismissal.

Protection against dismissal and action short of dismissal is discussed below: protection against refusal of employment on page 163.

Right not to be dismissed on trades union grounds[2]
It is unfair to dismiss an employee for:

- actual or proposed membership of an independent trades union;
- actual or proposed participation in the activities of an independent trades union at an 'appropriate time';

- actual or proposed non-membership of a trades union (whether independent or not); or
- to select for redundancy on any of the above grounds.

'Appropriate time' means outside working hours or at permitted times during working hours with the consent or agreement of the employer. 'Working hours' are defined as any time when, in accordance with the contract, the employee is required to be at work.

Once trade union grounds are established the dismissal is automatically unfair. That is, no test of reasonableness is to be applied. The protection applies without any requirement for qualifying employment. However, an employee with less than two years' qualifying employment will have the burden of proof in establishing that trade union grounds were the reason for the dismissal.

The statutory provisions have thrown up a number of interpretative problems, not least of which is whether trade union grounds are in fact the reason for the dismissal. In *City of Birmingham v Beyer*, the employee used a false name when applying for employment because they were a known union activist and thought that this would reduce their chances of obtaining employment. It was held that the dismissal was for deceit and that this constituted a dismissal for pre-employment activities not covered by the statutory provisions.

Another issue has been whether activities are in fact union activities. Here it has been held, in *Chant v Aqua Boats*, that the activities must be within the structure of the union. On the other hand, they must be the activity of the individual – since this is what is protected – rather than of the union as an organization *(Carrington v Therm-A-Stor)*.

Since protected activities must be carried out at an 'appropriate time', questions of working hours and consent have been raised. *Zucker v Astrid* appears to define working hours more narrowly than the statutory definition by requiring the employee not only to be engaged for paid work on the employer's premises but also to be actually performing the work. In *Marley v Shaw* the issue was whether the employer had consented to the activities. It was held that consent could be implied rather than express, although it was absent in this particular case.

One of the leading cases concerns the question of union activities with a former employer.

Fitzpatrick v British Railways Board

FACTS
The employee was dismissed after being employed by BRB for six months on discovery of her union activity with a former employer. BRB gave the reason for

> dismissal as failure to disclose her former employment. An industrial tribunal held that the reason for dismissal was union activity with a former employer. Since this is not covered by the statutory provisions, the industrial tribunal dismissed her application. On appeal, the EAT found no error of law or perversity and upheld the tribunal's decision.
>
> HELD (CA)
>
> The Court of Appeal reversed the decision of the EAT. Dismissal was for trades union reasons relating to the current employer. The employee had been dismissed because BRB feared that she would engage in trades union activity while in their employ, that is, that she proposed to take part in such activities. Her appeal was upheld.
>
> COMMENT:
>
> This decision appears to widen the scope of the protection, perhaps bringing it more in line with Parliamentary intention.

Where the dismissal is for reason of redundancy and it is alleged that selection is on trades union grounds, it has to be shown that at least one other employee holding a position similar to that of the complainant was not dismissed. In *O'Dea v ISC* the complainant was not able to show this because the rearrangement of his work in order to allow him to perform union duties meant that there was no other employee in a similar position.

Finally, the way in which union duties are performed may give rise to problems. In *Bass Taverns v Burgess*, a union official participated in a company induction course and in doing so criticized the company. This led to dismissal and the dismissal was held to be on trades union grounds.

Interim relief

Provision is made for an industrial tribunal to order the continuation of the contract of employment pending a full hearing of the case if the dismissal is alleged to be on trade union grounds. These provisions are considered on pages 332–3.

Right not to suffer action short of dismissal on trades union grounds

These are provisions parallel to those which apply to dismissal.[3] They apply to action short of dismissal where the 'purpose' of the employer is to prevent, deter or penalize independent trades union membership or activity or to compel membership of a union (whether independent or not). Moreover, the non-unionist must not have action short of dismissal taken against them if they refuse to make a payment (for example, to a charity) instead of a union subscription.

A complaint may be made to an industrial tribunal within three months. Once the employee has established the facts, the onus is upon the employer to show why the action was taken. Any industrial pressure upon the employer is to be ignored. Compensation will be what the tribunal considers 'just and equitable' given the infringement of rights and any loss sustained by the applicant and there does not appear to be a maximum. The applicant must mitigate their loss, and compensation will be reduced if there is contributory fault. The union may be joined in any proceedings involving a non-unionist, and may be required to pay some or all of the compensation. It appears that paying a wage increase to members of one union while not paying it to members of another union can constitute action short of dismissal because of union membership *(National Coal Board v Ridgway)*.

However, this decision may not be reliable given the House of Lords' subsequent ruling in *Associated Newspapers v Wilson*. The Court of Appeal had decided that paying employees extra if they agreed to have their terms settled by individual negotiation ('personal contracts') rather than collective bargaining was action short of dismissal on trades union grounds. Although, strictly, the employer was not preventing, deterring or penalizing union membership *per se*, union membership and the benefits thereof, specifically collective bargaining, could not realistically be separated. This approach, followed in *Harrison v Kent County Council*, is based on the earlier case of *Discount Tobacco and Confectionery Ltd v Armitage*. In *Wilson*, the House of Lords criticized this approach and reversed the Court of Appeal's decision although ultimately the case was decided on a different legal point. Since the employer's behaviour constituted an omission rather than the commission of an act, the case turned on whether an omission can be interpreted as an action. The House of Lords decided by a majority that in this context it could not be.[5] Parliament had, by the time of the House of Lords decision in *Wilson*, already amended the statutory provisions.[4] Where the purpose of the employer is to further a change in the relationship with employees (eg, by introducing 'personal contracts') as well as to deter or prevent trades unionism etc, then only the former purpose is to be taken into account. This leaves the employer clear of any breach of the statutory provisions relating to action short of dismissal on trades union grounds.

Another question which arises is the position when time spent on union duties or activities prevents an employee from obtaining the skills and experience necessary for promotion. In *Gallacher v Department of Transport*, a failure to promote in such circumstances was held not to be action short of dismissal on trades union grounds.

The 'closed shop'

'Closed shop' is an expression used by practitioners such as managers and union officials and when it had some support as public policy it had legal expression as 'union membership agreement'.[6] In practice a closed shop was either pre-entry or post-entry. The former required an individual to be a member of a trades union in order to obtain employment in a particular workplace. The latter permitted a non-unionist to obtain a post but required them to become a union member within a specified period of commencing their employment.[7]

There is nothing in the law which currently makes a closed shop agreement unlawful. However, as noted, the non-unionist has rights parallel to those of the union member, so action to enforce a closed shop is challengeable at law. Thus, refusal to employ a person on the ground of their non-unionism or dismissal or other action on the ground of their non-unionism is likely to constitute a breach of the individual's statutory rights.

RECOGNITION

Meaning of recognition

Recognition means that a trade union is accepted by an employer (or associated employers) for the purposes of collective bargaining, that is, for the purpose of negotiations related to or connected with various matters listed in TULR(C)A. These are, in essence, matters connected with employment:

(a) terms and conditions of employment, or the physical conditions in which any workers are required to work;

(b) engagement or non-engagement, or termination or suspension of employment or the duties of employment, of one or more workers;

(c) allocation of work or the duties of employment as between workers or groups of workers;

(d) matters of discipline;

(e) the membership or non-membership of a trades union on the part of a worker;

(f) facilities for officials of trades unions; and

(g) machinery for negotiation or consultation, and other procedures, relating to any of the foregoing matters, including the recognition by employers or employers' associations of the right of a trades union to represent workers in any such negotiation or consultation or in the carrying out of such procedures.[8]

A collective agreement is an agreement between union(s) and employer(s) on one or more of these matters. It should be noted that, in this context, the term 'associated employers' does not refer to membership of an employers' association. Rather, it refers to employers where one is a company controlled by the other, or where both are companies controlled by some third person.[9] Normally, non-unionists will obtain the benefits of collective bargaining along with union members. Indeed, if this were not the case an employer might be taking action short of dismissal against employees on grounds of their non-unionism (as in *NCB v Ridgway*).

Some employers are not prepared to go as far as recognizing trades unions for collective bargaining, but will accord them representational rights. That is, they will allow the union to represent individual members who have grievances or are subject to disciplinary action, through the appropriate procedures. There is no legal requirement for an employer to recognize or even give representational rights to a trades union. This is true regardless of the extent of union membership among the workforce and the view of the workforce on the question of union recognition. There has been legislation in this area which involved ACAS conducting enquiries among the workforce to establish the extent of union membership and the degree of support for union recognition. It gave rise to a number of difficult cases, among which *Grunwick Processing Laboratories Ltd v ACAS* was the *cause célèbre*. APEX sought recognition from Grunwick Ltd and a strike ensued. ACAS conducted its statutory enquiry but was unable to contact those employees who remained at work. It had no power to obtain the necessary details from the company, and the company would not divulge them voluntarily. The ACAS enquiry was inevitably lop-sided and was successfully challenged by the company in the courts. The company thus prevented ACAS from conducting a proper enquiry and then succeeded in getting ACAS' report set aside because the enquiry on which it was based was not properly conducted. The statutory procedure empowered ACAS to recommend recognition. In the event of an employer failing to comply, the Central Arbitration Committee (CAC) could make a legally enforceable award to the employees for whom recognition had been recommended. The legislation was repealed in 1989 and has not been replaced. The government, however, is committed to new legislation.

The case law confirms that recognition means direct recognition by the employer. It is not sufficient that the employer is a member of an employers' association which recognizes various unions on an industry-wide basis *(NUGSAT v Albury Bros)*. Representation of an employee by a full-time union official in respect of a disciplinary matter is not recognition for bargaining purposes *(TGWU v Courtenham Products)* nor is the granting of general representational (as opposed to bargaining) rights *(USDAW v Sketchley Ltd)*. There must be an express or implied agreement to recognize, and if implied, there must be clear and unequivocal conduct consistent with recognition *(NUTGW v Charles Ingram Co Ltd)*. Recognition can be partial, that is granted for some purposes but not for others. The issue of whether or not a union has been recognized is a mixed one of law and fact. The onus of proof appears to lie with the trades union to demonstrate the existence of a recognition agreement *(TGWU v Andrew Dyer)*.

Where an employer recognizes an independent trades union the officials of that union have various legal rights on behalf of the union. Official means an officer of the union (a member of the governing body or a trustee) or a person who is not an officer but is elected or appointed in accordance with the rules of the union to represent some or all of the members. This includes someone who is an employee of the employer rather than of the union (such as a shop steward or staff representative).[10] Subject to meeting any legal requirements, the rights of the official are as follows:

- paid time off for union duties, including training for such duties (see below);
- consultation in respect of redundancies (see chapter 18);
- consultation in respect of transfers of undertakings (see chapter 20);
- information for bargaining purposes (see below);
- to be appointed as a safety representative and have consequent legal rights[11] (see chapter 14); and
- information about pensions.[12]

The law does not require an employer to make available physical facilities such as office accommodation, telephone and filing cabinets but an ACAS Code of Practice does recommend that facilities be provided in the interests of good industrial relations (see below). The position in relation to safety representatives is different – they must be provided with the facilities necessary to enable them to carry out their statutory functions (see chapter 14).

The status of collective agreements

Other than those made during the brief life of the Industrial Relations Act 1971, a collective agreement is presumed in law to be intended by the parties as not being a legally enforceable contract unless the agreement is in writing and contains an express statement to the contrary.[13] Thus, unless the parties state in writing that they wish their collective agreement to be legally enforceable it will be binding in honour only *(Ford v AUEF)*.[14] During the life of the Industrial Relations Act 1971, employers and unions conspired to keep the law out of their relations – the British tradition of 'voluntarism' – by inserting TINALEA clauses into agreements. TINALEA signified that 'this is not a legally enforceable agreement'.

Nevertheless, as was noted in chapter 8 there is a process by which collectively bargained terms can become incorporated into individual contracts of employment. In the last resort, therefore, an action for breach of a collective agreement can sometimes be pursued indirectly through a breach of the contract of employment between the organization and the individual employee (for example, *Ferodo v Rigby*: see page 194). In such circumstances the parties might agree that one particular case be regarded as a test to determine the general position.

Regardless of whether or not a collective agreement is legally enforceable, no terms which restrict an individual's right to take industrial action will form part of the employee's contract of employment unless the collective agreement:

- is in writing;
- provides for express incorporation of the relevant term(s); and
- is reasonably accessible to the employee and may be consulted during working hours.

Moreover:

- the union (or each union) that is party to the agreement must be independent; and
- the individual employee's contract must expressly or impliedly provide for incorporation.[15]

It can be seen that while the recognition of trades unions is not required by law, and agreements with unions are not themselves legally enforceable, the act of recognition does have legal implications. This is primarily because union officials are given legal rights upon recognition and because the contract of employment can sometimes be used as a device for indirectly enforcing the terms of collective agreements.

Finally it should be pointed out that the legal status of collective agreements is not influenced by the level at which they are negotiated (industry-wide, company-wide or plant) or by their degree of sophistication or formality, except to the extent that legally enforceable agreements must be in writing. The law is less than clear about conflicts between the terms agreed at different levels and offers no consistent approach. In *Clift v West Riding County Council* the terms of a local agreement prevailed over those of a national one because the local agreement was made later. However, a national agreement made prior to a local one, and containing a provision that in cases of conflict the national agreement should prevail, was held by the Court of Appeal to take precedence in *Gascol Conversions Ltd v Mercer*.

Prohibition of union recognition requirements

Recognition requirements laid down as terms or conditions of contracts for the supply of goods and services are void by virtue of TULR(C)A, s 186. Thus a term requiring a supplier to recognize a union or to negotiate or consult with an official of a union will be void. Similarly, a duty is placed upon a person not to refuse to deal with a supplier or prospective supplier if one of the grounds is that the supplier does not or is not likely to recognize a union or negotiate or consult with an official of the union (s 187). A breach of this duty is actionable.

FACILITIES FOR TRADES UNION OFFICIALS AND MEMBERS

Time off for union duties and activities

These rights arise not simply out of being an employee, but out of being an employee *and* a union member or official. The burden of proof lies upon the employee to establish that a request for time off was made *(Ryford Ltd v Drinkwater)*. The rights give a 'reasonable' amount of time off during working hours and are of two types:

(1) paid time off for union officials for duties concerned with:
  - negotiations over one or more of the matters specified in TULR(C)A, s 178(2) (see page 434) for which the union is recognized; or
  - the performance of functions related to or connected with matters specified in s 178(2) with the agreement of the employer; or
  - training for such duties;[16] and
(2) time off, without obligation to pay, for union members for union activity.[17] Nothing in the legislation appears to restrict this activity (apart from that it must not amount to industrial action) but in *Luce v London Borough of Bexley* the EAT held that the activity must in some way be linked to the employment relationship. This will be a matter of fact and degree for the industrial tribunal.

The provisions relating to paid time off for union officials (but not unpaid time off for members) were altered by the EA 1989.[18] The effect of this has been to limit rights to paid time off so that they no longer cover duties:

- which neither concern negotiations with the employer nor have been agreed by the employer;
- which do not relate to or are not connected with any of the matters listed in TULR(C)A, s 178(2);
- which relate to any associated employer(s) but not to the employer themselves; or
- which concern negotiations with the employer over matters for which the union is not recognized, where the employer has not agreed to the duties being performed.

The term 'working hours' is defined to mean contractual hours, so excluding any non-contractual overtime. To attract paid time off, training must be relevant to the official's duties, and approved either by the TUC or the official's own union. The rights of both officials and members in relation to time off are subject to the union being independent, and recognized by the employer. The right to unpaid time off will be relevant to union officials who hold positions in geographically based branches, or who hold higher positions in unions where their duties may not (in the main) relate to their own employer. An ACAS code of practice, revised in 1991 following the changes made by EA 1989, provides detailed guidance.[19] A complaint may be made to an industrial tribunal within three months alleging refusal to give time off or refusal to pay for time off.

Many of the decisions made under the legislation prior to this amendment by the EA 1989 are no longer of relevance. However, the principle adopted in *British Bakeries (Northern) Ltd v Adlington* may well be applied to the amended provisions. The Court of Appeal decided that attendance at a course on the implications of the repeal of the Baking Industry (Hours of Work) Act 1954 was close enough to the duties defined in the legislation to warrant paid time off. The test – that of proximity – is a matter of fact for tribunals to decide.

For a union official to be carrying out a duty within the meaning of the legislation by attending a meeting, their attendance must be expressly or impliedly required by their union *(Ashley v Ministry of Defence)*. Whether it is reasonable to grant paid time off is a question of fact for an industrial tribunal to decide *(Thomas Scott and Sons (Bakers) Ltd v Allen)*. The facilities already existing under a collective agreement may be taken into account, and were adequate in *Depledge v Pye Telecommunications Ltd.*

Finally, as already noted, there is no legal requirement for an employer to provide physical facilities (except to safety representatives). However, the code of practice on time off for trade union duties and activities states that:

> Employers should consider making available to officials the facilities necessary for them to perform their duties efficiently and communicate effectively with their members, fellow lay officials and full-time officers. Where resources permit the facilities could include: accommodation for meetings, access to a telephone and other office equipment, the use of notice boards and, where the volume of the official's work justifies it, the use of dedicated office space.[20]

Figure 22.1 summarizes the position on time off for union duties and activities.[21]

Disclosure of information for bargaining purposes

This is another right given to the 'trade union representative', defined in the same way as in the redundancy consultation rights (see chapter 18). Again

---

**Time off for trades union officials
and members**

TULR(C)A, ss 168–169:

- officials
- union duties, and training for them
- with pay

TULR(C)A, s 170:

- members
- union activities
- no requirement to pay

Both:

- independent recognized trades union
- reasonable amount of time off
- ACAS Code No 3
- complaints to IT

Figure 22.1   Time off for trades union officials and members

the union must be independent and recognized. Union representatives have a right to information about the company which is both:

- information without which they would 'be to a material extent impeded' in their bargaining; and is
- information which it is good industrial relations practice to disclose.

An ACAS code of practice[22] sets out good practice as including disclosure of information on:

- pay and benefits, for example, principles and structure of payment systems and various distributions of earnings and hours;
- conditions of service, for example, recruitment policy and promotion policy;
- manpower, for example, manpower distributions and manpower plans;
- performance, for example, productivity data and return on capital;
- financial, for example, cost structures and allocation of profits.

The disclosure rights apply only to matters over which the employer already recognizes that union.

There are a number of restrictions upon the employer's general duty of disclosure. These mean that disclosure does not have to be made if:

- it is against the interests of national security;
- it would contravene a prohibition imposed by or under a statute;
- the information was communicated to the employer in confidence;
- the information relates to an individual (unless he or she consents to its disclosure);
- the information would cause 'substantial injury' to the employer (apart from through collective bargaining); or
- the information was obtained for the purpose of any legal proceedings.

The employer does not have to show original documents or their copies, nor be involved in an amount of work or expenditure 'out of reasonable proportion to the value of the information' in bargaining terms.[23]

If a union considers that an employer has failed to disclose the required information it may make a complaint to the Central Arbitration Committee (CAC). The Committee may ask ACAS to conciliate, but if that fails it will hear the complaint. If the complaint is upheld, the Committee will specify the information to be disclosed, and a period of time in which disclosure must take effect. A failure to disclose then gives the union a right to apply again to the Committee, this time for an award of improved terms and conditions. If the Committee makes such an award it has effect as part of the individual employees' contracts of employment, and is enforceable. The logic is that such an award:

- is in lieu of information which might have led the union to secure a better deal than it did secure;
- will deter employers from refusal to disclose information, since it removes the determination of labour costs from within an employer's control; and
- recognizes that employers cannot be directly forced actually to release information.

Unions have, perhaps surprisingly, not made great use of the disclosure provisions. Consequently, there is little case law. In an early case, however, the CAC decided that 'to a material extent impeded' meant that the information must be important and relevant (*Institute of Journalists v Daily Telegraph*). Later, the CAC decided that a company should disclose details of the distribution of percentage pay awards across certain categories of staff under a performance-related merit pay system. There was a genuine need for the unions to ensure that the system did not operate unfairly against particular categories (such as women and older workers) (*MSF and APEX Partnership v General Accident Fire and Life Assurance Corporation plc*).

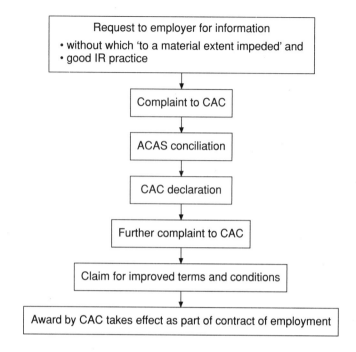

Figure 22.2   Disclosure of information for collective bargaining purposes (TULR(C)A, s 181 and ACAS Code No 2)

Claims can be made about the timing of disclosure. Thus in *MATSA and MSF v Smith's Meters Ltd* the CAC ordered the disclosure of gross and net profits as a percentage of sales prior to negotiations instead of subsequently. By contrast, the CAC made no such order about budgetary information in *NAPO v Merseyside Probation Committee* because there was no evidence that the union was to a material extent impeded by having it after the negotiations rather than prior to them.

The legal process relating to disclosure of information for collective bargaining purposes is set out diagramatically in Figure 22.2.

NOTES

1 See Brown and McColgan, 'UK Employment Law and the ILO', 21 *Industrial Law Journal* 265.
2 TULR(C)A, s 152.
3 TULR(C)A, s 146.
4 Particularly by means of TULR(C)A, s 148(3).
5 There was also some reluctance to accept that there had been an omission, since the employer was under no obligation to give an increase in pay.

6 See Trade Union and Labour Relations Act 1974, s 30 for the definition. This Act was repealed in its entirety by TULR(C)A, s 300(1) and Sched 1.

7 On the closed shop generally, see Gennard and Dunn, *The Closed Shop in British Industry.*

8 TULR(C)A, s 178.

9 TULR(C)A, s 297.

10 TULR(C)A, s 119.

11 Safety Representatives and Safety Committees Regulations (SI 1977/500), reg 3(1). These are regulations made under s 15 and in accordance with s 2(4) of the HSWA. The 1977 Regulations were amended by the Management of Health and Safety at Work Regulations (SI 1992/2051). There is now a specific duty to consult with such representatives and to provide facilities and assistance.

12 Occupational Pension Schemes (Disclosure of Information) Regulations (SI 1986/1046).

13 TULR(C)A, s 179. Where it is in writing and contains such an express statement it is to be conclusively presumed to be enforceable.

14 The 1991 Green Paper, *Industrial Relations in the 1990s*, proposed (at page 36) a presumption of legal enforceability but in January 1992 the government indicated that it would not proceed with the proposal.

15 TULR(C)A, s 180.

16 TULR(C)A, s 168.

17 TULR(C)A, s 170.

18 TULR(C)A, s 14.

19 ACAS, *Time Off for Trade Union Duties and Activities* (Code of Practice 3, London, HMSO, 1998).

20 *Loc cit.*

21 TULR(C)A, s 181.

22 ACAS, *Disclosure of Information to Trades Unions for Collective Bargaining Purposes* (Code of Practice 2, London, HMSO, 1998).

23 TULR(C)A, s 182(2).

Industrial Action

THE POSITION OF THE INDIVIDUAL EMPLOYEE

General remarks

It should be noted that the whole question of immunity in the context of industrial action (see page 450) applies only to the committing of torts; it does not apply to breaches of contract. Thus, a person who is in breach of contract will not be immune from actions in contract. The other relevant issue here will be whether they can benefit from the protection of unfair dismissal law.

The contract of employment

Whether a strike is a breach of contract

In 1968 in *Morgan v Fry*, Lord Denning looked at the intention of the parties and stated that the contract of employment was suspended rather than breached by a strike. By 1977, however, in *Simmons v Hoover*, the more traditional view was apparent: since, during a strike, the employee is not fulfilling his or her contractual duties, a strike must amount to a breach of contract. This was the view of the EAT, notwithstanding the Court of Appeal's decision in *Morgan v Fry*, and seems to be generally accepted. The likelihood, therefore, is that a strike will constitute a breach of the individual employee's contract of employment.

The effect of giving notice of a strike

In the light of the above and the common practice of giving notice of a strike, it has fallen to the courts to determine the legal effect of giving such notice. In *Boxfoldia v NGA*, the union gave notice of strike action but argued that it had given notice of termination of its members' employment contracts, acting as agent for those members.

On the status of the notice, the High Court found that the notice was a strike notice not a notice of termination of employment. The latter would be a lawful termination, if due notice were given, the former was merely notice of a breach of contract. The finding as to which type of notice applied in this particular case was a question of fact. On the agency issue, the court decided that a union could act as agent for its members in terminating their employment only if they had given the union specific authority. No such authority had been given here.

Whether action short of a strike constitutes a breach of contract

Prima facie, the question of whether action short of a strike constitutes a breach of contract seems less clear cut since the action could involve simply a withdrawal of goodwill or strict adherence to contractual or other rules. Such was the situation in *Secretary of State for Employment v ASLEF* which involved a work to rule on the railways. The rules in question were largely instructional, concerning the performance of the work. The effect of abiding strictly by the rules was to cause severe disruption to the railway system. The Court of Appeal held that an employee can withdraw goodwill but must not disrupt the employer's business. Such disruption would be a breach of the contractual term of fidelity (see chapter 10). There is an implied contractual term that rules will be construed and applied reasonably.

A similar approach was taken by the Court of Appeal in *British Telecommunications plc v Ticehurst*. This involved a go-slow, the employee being of managerial status. Here it was decided that where an employee has discretion and uses judgment, that discretion must be exercised faithfully on behalf of the employer. The courts had taken a different approach in the earlier case of *General Engineering v Kingston and St Andrew Corporation*. Here, the Privy Council found that a go-slow by firemen in Jamaica was a clear breach of contract but, more than this, the employer was not vicariously liable for the damage caused by his employees to the property of a third party. This was because the employees' actions were not conduct in the course of their employment. These were not authorized acts nor an unauthorized way of performing authorized acts.

In general, it is not possible to attempt to disrupt the employer's business in order to apply bargaining pressure *and*, at the same time, give loyal service. Any action which is concerted and aimed at bringing pressure is likely to be regarded as industrial action (see below). It should also be noted that industrial action is not defined only in relation to a trade dispute (see page 455): it may give rise to a trade dispute or some other form of dispute (for instance, a protest about government policy). In the circumstances of an employee's breach of contract, an employer may sue for damages (which would usually be limited to the employee's notice period) or for other remedies. In practice, the most likely outcome would be dismissal.

Action an employer may take in response to partial performance of the contract of employment

Several cases in recent years have helped clarify the position here.

Miles v Wakefield District Council

FACTS

Mr Miles was a Registrar who normally worked a 37-hour week including three hours on a Saturday morning. He refused to work on a Saturday morning as part of his union's campaign of industrial action. His employers deducted ³⁄₃₇ths of his pay.

HELD (HL)

The industrial action amounted to a breach of contract. The employers were entitled to make the deduction because the employee had failed to perform ³⁄₃₇ths of his duties.

COMMENT:

This seems to be a classical contract approach: the employee had not provided consideration for the pay so the employer was not obliged to pay (see chapter 8). It should be noted that deductions in response to industrial action are excluded from the wages provisions of ERA.[1] Miles may be contrasted with *Sim v Rotherham Borough Council* where it was held that the full amount of pay was due but that the employers could set-off an amount for partial non-performance.

Wiluszynski v London Borough of Tower Hamlets

FACTS

The employers made it clear that they would not accept partial performance of the contract of employment (here a refusal to operate new computerized methods of work). They informed the employee accordingly warning that there would be no pay whatsoever without full performance of duties.

HELD (CA)

An employer does not have to accept partial performance. He can refuse to accept it and require full performance, without which there is to be no pay, as long as this is made clear.

COMMENT:

The Court of Appeal later took the same approach in *British Telecommunications plc v Ticehurst*. In *Wiluszynski*, it was decided that as long as the employer made the position clear, he was not under any duty physically to debar the employee from the premises.

Dismissal

It should be noted that the government is committed to amending the statutory provisions relating to unfair dismissal in the context of industrial action.

Dismissal for cause

The general common law rule is that an employer may dismiss without notice where the employee has committed a fundamental breach of contract or indicated that they no longer intend to be bound by one or more of the contract's fundamental terms *(Laws v London Chronicle)*. Depending on the facts, it seems quite likely that industrial action would amount to a fundamental breach, so that the absence of notice would not make the dismissal wrongful.

Unofficial action and the law of unfair dismissal

Any litigation is more likely to be in the law of unfair dismissal and here the first issue to be determined will be whether or not the industrial action is unofficial. By TULR(C)A, s 237, an employee has no right to complain of unfair dismissal if at the time of dismissal he or she was taking part in unofficial industrial action.[2]

The term 'unofficial' is defined by what it excludes. It means, in relation to the particular employee, industrial action *except* the following situations:

- the employee is a member of the trades union and that union has authorized or endorsed the action;
- the employee is not a member of the union but amongst those taking the action are union members, and the action has been authorized or endorsed by the union; or
- none of those taking part in the action are members of a trades union.

In situations other than these, the action will be 'unofficial' and s 237 will apply.

The question of whether or not the action is unofficial has to be decided at the time of dismissal. This is defined differently from the EDT under unfair dismissal law. Although the time of dismissal without notice is on termination and in the case of a fixed-term contract is on expiry, in the case of dismissal with notice it occurs on the giving of notice rather than when the notice expires.[3] Whether the action is authorized or endorsed by the union is to be decided in accordance with the statutory test of liability (see pages 402–3).

Other industrial action and the law of unfair dismissal

Where the industrial action is not unofficial as defined above it falls into the category 'other'. These cases will be determined under TULR(C)A s 238 if the employee has a right to complain of unfair dismissal (ie, is qualified to complain) and at the time of dismissal there was a lock-out by the employer or the complainant was taking part in industrial action.[4]

In these cases, an industrial tribunal shall determine the fairness or otherwise of the dismissal only if:

- one or more 'relevant' employees have not been dismissed; or
- a 'relevant' employee has been offered re-engagement within three months of his dismissal but the complainant has not been offered re-engagement.

That is, there must be a degree of selectivity in the dismissal or re-engagement process which seems to imply a reason other than the industrial action itself. A 'relevant' employee is one at the same establishment who is taking part in the industrial action at the time of the complainant's dismissal. A wider definition applies in the case of a lockout *(Campey v Bellwood)*.[5]

It must be emphasized that the above provisions relate to the question of whether the industrial tribunal has jurisdiction. It can be seen that the dismissal of strikers is explicitly put outside the jurisdiction of industrial tribunals unless certain features apply. These features relate to selectivity of treatment of those taking the action. The unit within which comparisons are to be made is the establishment of the employer at or from which the complainant works. If everyone is treated the same, no complaint of unfair dismissal can be heard by a tribunal. If, however, some are dismissed and others are not, there is a possible unfair dismissal claim. The selectivity must apply, however, at the time of the complainant's dismissal, rather than from the beginning of the strike. Thus, if 100 people go on strike, and all are still on strike a month later, the dismissal of the six strike leaders will give rise to unfair dismissal claims. The dismissal of all 100 will not. Moreover, if 40 people had returned to work after a month, the dismissal of the remaining 60 would not give rise to claims, since there was no selectivity among those on strike at the time of the dismissal. Where strikers are dismissed, but only some are re-engaged, the critical factor will be the time interval between the dismissal of those re-engaged and their re-engagement. If this period is three months or more, none of the people who have not been re-engaged will have a claim.

Where a claim is made alleging that dismissal has been selective, it must be made within three months of the complainant's EDT. Where the claim is that there has been a selective re-engagement, it must be made within six months of the complainant's 'date of dismissal'. Date of dismissal is as defined earlier.

Interpretation

Meaning of industrial action and lock-out

Lock-out is not defined in TULR(C)A but it may be possible to draw upon the definition in ERA.[6] Here lock-out is defined as the closure of the workplace, the suspension of work or the refusal to employ employees in consequence of a dispute in order to compel those employees or another employer's employees to accept terms or conditions of or affecting employment. In deciding whether a situation is a lock-out or industrial action, a relevant consideration will be whether an employer has broken a contract term thus giving rise to action by employees *(Express and Star v Bunday)*. A strike is defined as 'any concerted stoppage of work'.[7]

Whether there exists a strike or other industrial action is a matter of fact for a tribunal to decide *(Express and Star Ltd v Bunday; Faust v Power Packing Casemakers)*. The key ingredients seem to be cessation of work (or some other sanction such as a work-to-rule or overtime ban), workers acting in combination or in concert, and an intention to exert pressure or make a protest in order to secure or prevent change (for example, to terms and conditions of employment).

The intention behind the acts done as well as their nature and effect should be taken into account *(Faust,* in which it was ruled that a refusal to work non-contractual overtime could be industrial action if it was used as a bargaining weapon).

Meaning of 'taking part' in industrial action

First, a distinction may need to be drawn between engaging in trades union activity, dismissal for which would be automatically unfair, and taking part in industrial action, where there is likely to be no right to make a claim. The dismissal must be one or the other, and this is a matter of fact for the tribunal to decide *(Drew v St Edmundsbury Borough Council)*. Secondly, what does taking part mean? *(Coats v Modern Methods and Materials Ltd; Naylor v Orton and Smith Ltd)*. Again this is a matter of fact for tribunals. They should judge the issue by what the employee is doing or omitting to do, rather than by what the employer knew, or should have known, at the time *(Manifold Industries Ltd v Sims)*. Thus in *Coates*, the Court of Appeal held that the complainant was taking part. They were absent from work due to illness during the strike but on the first day of the strike had come to work but refused to cross the picket line.

Another important issue is whether an individual acting alone can be taking part in industrial action. Despite the conventional wisdom that industrial action is by nature collective, an industrial tribunal held an individual to be taking part when acting alone in *Lewis v E Mason & Sons*. Moreover, the threat of industrial action by an individual also amounted to taking part in industrial action. The EAT dismissed the appeals holding that neither of the decisions was perverse.

Where action comprises a series of strikes, one day per week, taking part can be applied only to the actual days on strike. If dismissal is to be outside the jurisdiction of tribunals it will need to take place on a strike day *(Looker's of Bradford Ltd v Mavin)*. The same principle applied where there was an overtime ban in *Glenrose (Fish Merchants) Ltd v Chapman*.

Jurisdiction is the first issue for a tribunal to decide. The fact that a relevant employee had not been dismissed must be established at the end of the appropriate tribunal hearing. In *P&O European Ferries v Byrne* that employee was anonymous, but the name had to be disclosed in order to allow the employer to present his case. Where there is inadvertent re-engagement of dismissed strikers by another part of the company, the strikers so re-engaged will be relevant employees, so giving industrial tribunal jurisdiction *(Bigham v GKN Kwikform)*. If jurisdiction is established the normal two-stage unfair dismissal process is undergone. The fair reason for dismissal (or for non re-engagement) will have to be something other than going on strike in order to distinguish the case from those of strikers who were not dismissed (or were re-engaged). Picket line violence, damage to the employer's premises and unofficial continuation of a strike after a settlement are some of the reasons which have been put forward. A breach of contract by an employee will not automatically make any resultant dismissal fair. At the second stage, reasonableness will include proper procedure notwithstanding the tensions of an industrial dispute *(McLaren v National Coal Board)*.

In a redundancy, an employee will lose the right to a statutory redundancy payment if dismissed for industrial action prior to the obligatory notice period (see page 371).

TORTIOUS LIABILITY AT COMMON LAW AND STATUTORY IMMUNITY

Outline

There is no statutory or common law right to strike as such. A striker, unless due notice of termination of contract is given, will break his contract of employment *(Simmons v Hoover)*. The result is that an injured party has a right to seek a remedy – damages or an injunction. A strike will also often break a commercial contract between the employer and some other firm – a customer or supplier – again leaving an injured party with a right to sue. Anyone (such as a union official) inducing breaches of contract is likely to commit a tort.[8] Under such circumstances almost any industrial action would leave unions legally liable. For example, in *Falconer v NUR and ASLEF* the county court held that the two railworkers' unions were liable to pay damages to Mr Falconer, a passenger, for expenditure and inconvenience caused to him as a result of a one-day strike called by the unions, on the grounds that they had unlawfully induced interference with British Rail's obligations to its passengers.[9] To enable trades unions to function, Parliament has allowed them a degree of immunity from normal legal actions.[10] This immunity is granted, however, only in respect of certain types of legal action, namely claims in tort for:

- inducing breaching of contract;
- interference with contract;
- intimidation (here, threatening breaches of or interference with contract or threatening to induce such breaches or interference); and
- conspiracy, where the act if it was done by one person would be lawful.

Moreover, the union must meet certain legal requirements. First, the action must be 'in contemplation or furtherance of a trade dispute'.[11] A trade dispute is a dispute between workers and their employer which relates wholly or mainly to one or more of the matters listed on page 456 (these are the same matters which have to be considered in relation to paid time off for union officials).[12] It follows from this that there must be a dispute (see *NUS v Sealink* below); the dispute must be a trade dispute; and the trade dispute must be with the employer of the employees who are in dispute. In relation to the last point, a dispute between a union and an employers' association will not necessarily be a trade dispute unless there is a trade dispute with the individual company by which the employees are employed (see also *Kenny*, below).

Secondly, any act done by a trades union to induce a person to take part in industrial action must be supported by a ballot conducted in accordance with the legal requirements. A majority of those voting must be in favour of the action if immunity is to be obtained.[13] The detailed requirements are set out below.

Thirdly, the ballot result is live for four weeks. Action starting later than four weeks after the ballot will not be immune unless there is a second, 'successful' ballot. Next, regardless of the outcome of any ballot, secondary action is not immune except where workers involved in a trade dispute (that is, with their own employer) picket lawfully and in the process succeed in taking action which harms some other employer. An example would be pickets persuading the driver of a firm of suppliers to turn around and go away without delivering. Secondary action is where a person induces someone else to break a contract of employment (or threatens a breach of such a contract) with an employer who is not a party to the dispute.

Secondary action will be lawful only if the picketing satisfies the legal requirements, which include the need for it to be peaceful and at or near the picket's place of work.[14] Finally, there is no immunity for action which is in support of dismissed unofficial strikers,[15] which is in support of union membership (that is, to force membership upon an employee, or to force an employer to discriminate against a non-unionist),[16] or is pressure to impose a union recognition requirement.[17]

All of what has been described above refers to the immunity of trades unions as bodies. However, where industrial action is not endorsed by a union, or is repudiated by it, members will still be protected provided that they are acting 'in contemplation or furtherance of a trade dispute'. This protection applies only against certain actions in tort: members would not be protected from dismissal or from actions seeking remedies for breach of contract.

The following analytical framework has been adopted here in an attempt to provide a clear picture of a complex area of law. The framework comprises three stages of analysis each of which can be presented as a question:

(1) Is the industrial action tortious?
(2) If yes, is it protected by TULR(C)A, that is:[18]
   - is the tort one of the protected torts, ie those specified in TULR(C)A?
   - is the action 'in contemplation or furtherance of a trade dispute'?
(3) If yes, is immunity lost under any of the other provisions?

The protected torts

Inducing breach of contract

This is the first of the protected torts and takes two forms, direct and indirect (see Figure 23.1). The former is where a party directly induces one of the contracting parties to act in breach of contract (see *Lumley v Gye*). The inducement must be deliberate and be carried out with knowledge of the contract that is being broken. In contrast, indirect inducement occurs where the person induced is not one of the contracting parties but with the effect that one of the contracting parties cannot fulfil the terms of the contract (see *Thomson v Deakin*).

In *Thomson*, four conditions were laid down for tortious liability:

(1) the person charged with the tort knew of the existence of the contract and intended to procure its breach.
(2) the person so charged definitely persuaded the employees to break their contracts with that intent.
(3) the employees did in fact break their contracts.
(4) this led to the contract between the contracting parties being broken.

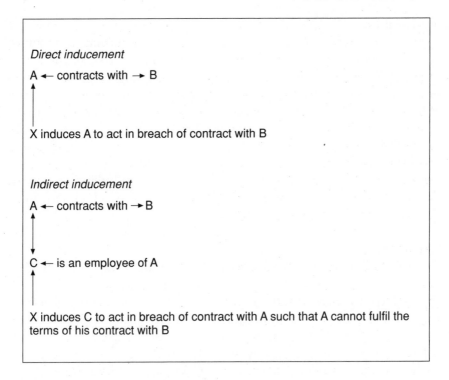

Direct inducement

A ◄— contracts with —► B

X induces A to act in breach of contract with B

Indirect inducement

A ◄— contracts with —► B

C ◄— is an employee of A

X induces C to act in breach of contract with A such that A cannot fulfil the terms of his contract with B

Figure 23.1   Direct and indirect inducement of breach of contract

However, the key ingredient is a fifth factor. There will not be tortious liability for indirect inducement of breach of contract unless *unlawful means* are used. In the context of Figure 23.1, the requirement is that X must be inducing C to do something unlawful, here, to act in breach of contract. In *Thomson* there was no breach of contract and therefore no unlawful means or tortious liability.

The statutory protection is provided by TULR(C)A which states that:

> An act done by a person in contemplation or furtherance of a trade dispute is not actionable in tort on the ground only (a) that it induces another person to break a contract ...[19]

Interference with contract

The principle of direct inducement of breach of contract as found in *Lumley v Gye* extends to hindering or preventing the performance of a contract. That is, interference with contract which does not amount to a breach but which prevents or hinders performance of the contract is tortious. This was put forward by Lord Denning MR in *Torquay Hotel Co Ltd v Cousins* and later confirmed by the House of Lords in *Merkur Island Shipping Corporation v Laughton*. Protection is offered by TULR(C)A.[20]

Intimidation

The third protected tort is intimidation, TULR(C)A providing immunity in situations where a person is 'threatening that a contract … will be broken or its performance interfered with … or that he will induce another person to break a contract or interfere with its performance'.[21] More generally the tort of intimidation involves threatening to do what there is no legal right to do, eg induce a breach of contract, commit some other tort or commit a crime. In *Rookes v Barnard* a union persuaded an employer to dismiss a non-unionist by using threats of unlawful industrial action. (Industrial action would involve breaches of contract). This was held to be intimidation and at that time (1964) it was not one of the protected torts, so liability arose. Protection is now afforded by TULR(C)A.[22]

Conspiracy

A combination wilfully to damage a man in his trade is unlawful at common law. Therefore, if the predominant purpose is to damage, and damage results, there is tortious conspiracy. However, if the defendants' predominant purpose is to protect or advance their own interests, and they believe action against the plaintiff is necessary for that purpose, the action will not be unlawful. The proviso is that lawful means are used. The 'predominant purpose' test is set out in *Crofter Hand Woven Harris Tweed v Veitch*. There is no defence that the predominant purpose was not to injure when unlawful means are used and injury is inflicted (see *Lonrho v Fayed*).

Statutory protection for conspiracy is found in TULR(C)A.[23] An agreement is not actionable if the act done without any agreement would not be actionable. That is, it is not actionable because it is done collectively rather than by an individual. There is no specific protection for conspiracy to use unlawful means. However, if the unlawful means themselves are protected (eg, inducing a breach of contract) conspiracy to use those means will also be protected.

Unprotected torts

Interference with trade or business by unlawful means

The principle was established in *Allen v Flood* that compelling a third party to injure the plaintiff by using lawful means gives rise to no liability even though there is an intention to injure. In *Merkur Island Shipping* the House of Lords confirmed the tort of interference with contract but was also of the opinion that a *prima facie* case had been made out for the common law tort of interference with trade or business by unlawful means. This can be seen as a general species of tort with inducing breach of contract, interference with contract and intimidation as sub-species.

There is no specific statutory protection for this tort. Therefore, if the tort is found to have been committed, in the absence of the sub-species which do have protection there would be tortious liability.

Inducing a breach of statutory duty

An example here would be action causing a local education authority to be unable to provide education *(Meade v Haringey)*. The Court of Appeal decision in *Associated British Ports v TGWU* confirms the tort of inducing a breach of statutory duty but limits it to where the breach is actionable as a separate tort.

Breach of an equitable obligation

In *Prudential Assurance v Lorenz* the High Court held in an interlocutory hearing, that there was such a tort, here a duty to account. However, in the later case of *Metall und Rohstoff AG*, the Court of Appeal denied the existence of a tort of inducing a breach of trust.

Economic duress

This can be a tort if the pressure takes an illegitimate form as in *Universe Tankships of Monrovia v ITWF*. The ship's owners were forced to pay money into the Union's welfare fund to secure the release of the ship from port, where it was held because the owners would not employ their employees on union terms and conditions. The House of Lords held that economic duress *per se* is not tortious; it depends upon the form it takes. In this case the pressure was illegitimate and the money had to be repaid. Strictly, the action is for restitution rather than for damages in tort.

THE GOLDEN FORMULA

Statutory protection limited to trade disputes

As noted, persons are protected from certain liabilities in tort by virtue of TULR(C)A. However, the protection applies only to acts done 'in contemplation or furtherance of a trade dispute' – the golden formula.[24] The next stage of the process of establishing whether or not a tortious act is protected by statute, therefore, is to determine whether it occurs in contemplation or furtherance of such a dispute.

Meaning of trade dispute

TULR(C)A defines a trade dispute as a dispute between workers and their employer which relates wholly or mainly to one of the following:[25]

(a)   terms and conditions of employment, or the physical conditions in which any workers are required to work;

(b)   engagement or non-engagement, or termination or suspension of employment or the duties of employment, of one or more workers;

(c)   allocation of work or the duties of employment as between workers or groups of workers;

(d)   matters of discipline;

(e)   the membership or non-membership of a trades union on the part of a worker;

(f)   facilities for officials of trades unions; and

(g)   machinery for negotiation or consultation, and other procedures, relating to any of the foregoing matters, including the recognition by employers or employers' associations of the right of a trades union to represent workers in any such negotiation or consultation or in the carrying out of such procedures.

Questions of interpretation

Whether or not there is a dispute

One of the issues which may arise is whether or not there is in fact a dispute. In *Bent's Brewery v Hogan* it was found that there was no dispute and therefore no protection.

Whether the dispute is between workers and their employer

In *Star Sea Transport v Slater* there was a dispute but it was between the *union* and the employer rather than between the *workers* and the employer, so again there was no protection.

In *Dimbleby v NUJ*, the workers were taking the action but because of the structure of ownership of companies the dispute was with someone other than their own employer, so that they were unprotected.

Whether the dispute relates 'wholly or mainly' to one or more of the items in TULR(C)A, s 244

There will not be a trade dispute if the dispute is essentially political. Cases where this has been held to be the situation include *NSU v Reed* (the General Strike), *BBC v Hearn* (refusal to transmit Cup Final pictures to South Africa) and *Mercury Communications v Scott-Garner* (protest against government privatization policy).[26]

These cases can involve the drawing of a fine line. For example, in *London Borough of Wandsworth v NAS/UWT*, the question which fell to be decided was whether the teachers' boycott of school tests arising out of the operation of the national curriculum was a principled objection to government policy or a protest at the workload caused by the tests. On the evidence it was held that the latter was the case. The action was in contemplation or furtherance of a trade dispute and was therefore protected.

A political dispute cannot be converted into a trade dispute simply by inserting some part of the definition of trade dispute into contracts of employment *(Universe Tankships of Monrovia v ITWF)*.

However, a dispute with the government in its capacity as employer can be a trade dispute *(Sherard v AUEW)*.

LOSS OF IMMUNITY

Introduction

It was noted that, in analysing the law of industrial action, the first stage is to establish whether or not a tort has been committed. The second stage is to determine whether, if a tort has been committed, it is protected under TULR(C)A. The final stage, now to be dealt with, is whether protection, where it applies, is lost by a failure to comply with any of the other statutory provisions. These are:

- restrictions on secondary industrial action;
- a requirement to give the employer a pre-ballot notice;
- a requirement to give the employer a pre-industrial action notice;
- a requirement to have the support of a ballot;
- restrictions on picketing; and
- the prohibition of certain reasons for industrial action.

Secondary action

Secondary action was first subject to specific legislation in 1980, the provisions being replaced in 1990 by a narrower definition of what is lawful.[27] The current position is that it is unlawful except for lawful picketing.[28] Secondary action is defined as industrial action where the employer suffering the action is not the employer involved in the dispute and the action constitutes one of the specified torts (inducing a breach of contract or inducing interference with contract, interference with contract, or threats to break or interfere or to so induce others).

An example of the sort of situation which might amount to lawful secondary action is as follows. Peaceful pickets, at their own place of work, acting in contemplation or furtherance of a trade dispute, dissuade a lorry driver from delivering supplies to their employer. That action as against the employer of the lorry driver is secondary action but it is lawful because it is lawful picketing. No other secondary action is lawful, so that, for example, it would not be lawful for university teachers to strike in support of nurses (or *vice versa*).

Failure to give an employer a pre-ballot or pre-industrial action notice

Pre-ballot notice

A union must give an employer at least seven days' written notice of an industrial action ballot.[29] The notice must describe the employees who the union reasonably believes will be entitled to vote in the ballot such that they can be identified. In *Blackpool and Fylde College v NATFHE*, the union described the employees reasonably believed to be entitled to vote as those union members employed by the college. This was held to be an insufficient description for the purposes of the statutory provisions because the college did not know who was or was not a union member.

An employer must also be given a sample voting paper at least three days before the ballot.

Pre-industrial action notice

An employer must be given a pre-industrial action notice at least seven days in advance of the commencement of the action.[30] This applies whether the action is continuous or discontinuous. In the former case the notice must indicate the start date; in the latter case the dates on which the action is to take place.

Action without the support of a ballot

As noted, a ballot is needed if there is to be immunity and detailed statutory requirements are laid down.[31] These are supplemented by a code of practice which was revised in 1995.[32] An employer may obtain an injunction preventing a ballot from taking place if any ensuing action would be unlawful. This was the case in *NUS v Sealink* where company assurances about the immediate future of NUS members' jobs in the ports meant that there was no trade dispute.

The balloting constituency

There are two issues here. First, if the members have different places of work, will separate ballots be required or can there be a single ballot? If those to be asked to vote comprise all the union's members or all of its members employed by one or more employers, aggregation is permitted. The same will be true if the members share a common, distinguishing factor relating to terms and conditions of employment or occupation. Otherwise, separate ballots will be required. The general rule is that there must be a separate ballot unless there is a common factor shared by everyone entitled to vote and no fellow union member sharing that factor and employed by the same employer as the members who do have a vote is excluded This prevents a union conducting a ballot at some plants of a company but not at others.

Secondly, within a workforce, who is entitled to vote? Any member who it is reasonable for the union to believe will be asked to take part in the action must have an opportunity to vote. No other person should have the opportunity. The union may choose whether to include or exclude overseas members. If included, they must be distinguished in the result. As a consequence of amendments made by the Employment Act 1989, members on contracts for services (such as freelance workers) will need to be balloted, as will Northern Ireland members if working in Great Britain, or if the industrial action will involve members in both Great Britain and Northern Ireland. Asking other members (for example, staff employees in a dispute involving manual grades) not to cross picket lines could amount to asking them to take part in the action and might require that they be entitled to vote. Otherwise, they might have to be allowed to cross picket lines. Depriving members of the right to vote makes a ballot invalid irrespective of whether the numbers deprived are greater or fewer than the difference in the ballot result *(British Rail v NUR)*. In the same case the Court of Appeal made clear that in a large balloting operation some margin of error was allowable as long as the union had done all that was reasonably practicable (there is a difference between denying an opportunity to vote (s 227(2)) and inadvertently failing to give such an opportunity).

Conduct of the ballot

Following changes introduced by TURERA, the method of balloting must now be postal. That is, ballot papers must be sent by post to the postal address of the person entitled to vote and there must be 'a convenient opportunity to vote by post'.[33] So far as is reasonably practicable voting must be in secret. Those voting must be allowed to do so without interference from or any constraints imposed by the union, its members, officials or employees ... A person should be able to vote without incurring any direct cost to themselves. The code of practice provides detailed guidance on the conduct of ballots.

TURERA introduced the requirement for independent scrutiny in industrial action ballots. There is, however, an exception where the number of persons entitled to vote does not exceed 50.[34]

Voting papers[35]

Voting must be by means of marking a voting paper. The following statement must appear on every voting paper and must not be qualified or commented upon by anything else on the paper:

If you take part in a strike or other industrial action, you may be in breach of your contract of employment.

The voting paper must also contain the name of the person who will be responsible for authorizing industrial action if the ballot result records a majority in favour, as well as the name of the independent scrutineer, an address and closing date for return and a unique number. It must contain at least one of two questions which ask if the person is prepared to take part in or continue to take part in:

- question 1: a strike; and/or
- question 2: action short of a strike;

such as to allow the answer yes or no. In *Post Office v Union of Communication Workers* it was ruled that a union wishing to pursue both a strike and action short of a strike, or at least to keep its options open, must obtain a yes majority in answer to each question. A yes to strike action cannot be taken as implying a yes to action short of a strike. A union will also have to make sure, if it is asking its members to cast one vote on several issues at the same time, that there is a trade dispute about each of the issues if subsequent industrial action is to be lawful *(London Underground v NUR).*

The result[36]

The votes must be fairly and accurately counted. Inaccuracies can be disregarded if accidental and too small to affect the result of the ballot. As soon as reasonably practicable after the holding of the ballot, the union should take reasonable steps to provide the following information to those entitled to vote:

- the number of votes cast;
- the numbers answering yes to the question, or to each question;
- the numbers answering no to the question, or to each question; and
- the number of spoiled voting papers.

The ballot result details should be provided to employers whose employees were entitled to vote.[37] The independent scrutineer must make a report to the trades union on the conduct of the ballot.[38]

A union must not call industrial action, nor authorize or endorse it before the last day of voting in the ballot, and for immunity to be preserved any action called must be called by the person specified on the voting paper. If the ballot result is in favour of action, immunity will be preserved providing the action commences before the expiry of a period of four weeks from the date of the ballot. However, if action during this period is prohibited by legal proceedings, the union may apply to have the period of immunity extended by the length of the prohibition. This will be possible only when the court's prohibition order lapses or is discharged, and is at the court's discretion. An extension will not be granted if the court thinks that the ballot result no longer represents the union members' views, or if there is an event likely to occur which would result in a vote against action if another ballot were to be held. In any event, the right to call industrial action on the basis of the ballot will lapse after a period of 12 weeks commencing with the date of the ballot.

In *Post Office* the employer complained that the discontinuity of industrial action meant that a new ballot was required to obtain immunity. The Court of Appeal thought that one ballot could support continuous industrial action over a long period, but might not support sporadic or irregular action. Moreover, considerable turnover of the workforce (so that a large proportion of current employees were not employees at the time of the ballot) may mean industrial action should be limited to those who were employed at that time and had a chance to vote in the ballot. These last two issues did not have to be decided to dispose of the case in *Post Office*, so were not ruled upon. The drift of opinion, however, is fairly clear.

The question arose, in *West Midlands Travel v TGWU*, as to whether the term 'majority of those voting in the ballot' (s 226) meant the majority of those voting for the particular question; or the majority of the total voting (ie, for the two questions aggregated). It was held that the former is the correct interpretation.

Unlawful picketing

There will be no protection against tortious liability for acts done in the course of picketing unless the picketing is lawful. The definition of lawful picketing is considered below.

Prohibited reasons for industrial action

Action is excluded from statutory protection if the reason or one of the reasons for it is:

- to enforce union membership;
- to secure the reinstatement of dismissed unofficial strikers; or
- to exert pressure in order to impose trade union recognition.[39]

Messenger Newspapers Group Ltd v NGA provides an example of industrial action for a prohibited reason and a good illustration of the working of the law of industrial action. The union sought to enforce the closed shop and in doing so committed unlawful primary and secondary action. Various torts were committed: unlawful interference with business, intimidation, public nuisance and private nuisance. The union was vicariously liable because it had authorized and endorsed the action. Since there was no immunity, damages were payable. Aggravated damages were awarded for recklessly or deliberately trying to close down the plaintiff's business and exemplary damages to show (as per *Rookes v Barnard*) that 'tort does not pay'.

VICARIOUS LIABILITY OF TRADES UNIONS

Unions may be vicariously liable for the acts of their officials.[40] Statutory provisions will determine this issue in respect of tortious acts covered by TULR(C)A. An act is taken to be authorized or endorsed by a trades union if it is done, authorized or endorsed by:

(1) anyone empowered by rule to do, authorize or endorse such acts;
(2) the principal executive committee, president or secretary;
(3) any other committee or official of the union. This includes officials not employed by the union, such as shop stewards. 'Committee' includes any group of persons constituted in accordance with the rules of the union.

An act will be taken as having been done, authorized or endorsed by an official if it is done, authorized or endorsed by a strike committee to which the official belongs, or by any member of that committee. Authorization etc in accordance with (2) or (3) above overrules anything in the union's rules or in any contracts or rule of law.

An act will not be taken as having being authorized or endorsed by virtue of item (3) only, however, if it is repudiated by persons mentioned in (2) 'as soon as reasonably practicable'. Repudiation involves written notice to the committee or official without delay, individual notices to members and notice to the employer(s). The notice to the members must contain the statutory wording:

> Your union has repudiated any call for industrial action to which this notice relates and will give no support to such action. If you are dismissed while taking official industrial action, you will have no right to complain of unfair dismissal.[41]

There is no repudiation if the union fails to comply with the above or fails to comply with the following. If a request is made within six months of repudiation by someone injured through interference with a commercial contract, and no written notice has already been given to that person, the union must provide confirmation of repudiation forthwith.

Where unions are liable for action which is not immune their funds will be at risk from claims for damages except where those funds are protected by statute. Protected property includes political and provident funds.[42] The maximum damages for each legal action (as opposed to each case of industrial action) vary according to the number of members of the union. Where a union has 100,000 or more members the figure is £250,000. This excludes interest *(Boxfoldia Ltd v NGA)*.

An employer may be more likely to seek an injunction than to press a claim for damages. Where an act is done in contemplation or furtherance of a trade dispute, all reasonable steps must be taken by the court to give the union an opportunity to be heard. In deciding whether or not to grant an injunction the court must assess the likelihood of the union's actions being immune.

The statutory test applies to contempt proceedings (although it did not at the time of *Express and Star v NGA*, in 1987) but does not apply outside the economic torts listed in TULR(C)A, s 219 and subsequent contempt proceedings *(Thomas v NUM)*.

Prior to the enactment of legislation in this area[43] case law had shown that unions might be vicariously liable under their own rules or by virtue of custom and practice *(Heaton's Transport v TGWU)*. Such liability again seemed likely in *Thomas v NUM* (interlocutory proceedings).

PICKETING

An act done in the course of picketing is protected by TULR(C)A only if it falls within the Act's definition of peaceful picketing and is done in contemplation or furtherance of a trade dispute.[44] Thus, when Kenny Services took over a British Rail contract with its own – ie, Kenny Services's – employees after British Rail had terminated a previous contract with another firm, the picketing by ex-employees of the former contractor at the British Rail site was unlawful because there was no trade dispute between these workers and their ex-employer. Rather, the picketing was directed at British Rail or possibly Kenny Services *(Kenny Services v TGWU)*. Picketing rights are limited to at or near a person's own place of work. A union official may picket at any workplace where members whom they represent work, providing they are accompanied by at least one of them. Where a person works or normally works at more than one place, or where the place of work makes picketing impracticable, they may picket at any of the employer's premises at which they work or from which the work is administered. In *(1) Rayware Ltd (2) Islington Pottery v TGWU*, the Court of Appeal ruled that since 0.7 miles away was the nearest public place for picketing, this was near the workplace. It observed that Parliament could not have intended to remove all picketing rights for any group of workers. Workplace means the principal place of work rather than places which may be visited during the course of work *(Union Traffic Ltd v TGWU)*. An employee dismissed from their last employment in connection with a trade dispute, or whose dismissal gave rise to a trade dispute, retains their picketing rights.

Picketing is defined as peacefully obtaining or communicating information, or peacefully persuading any person to work or abstain from working. There are no rights to stop people or vehicles. Thus in *Broome v DPP* the attempt to stop a vehicle was a breach of the Highways Act 1959. Peaceful picketing, as defined, carried out at or near a person's own workplace, is immune. Other picketing would not be. Moreover, there is no protection against actions in respect of interference with business by unlawful means or other torts not covered by s 219 of TULR(C)A. These would include private nuisance and trespass, for example, being on or inside an employer's premises without permission.

Nor is there any immunity for criminal acts such as obstructing a police officer in the course of their duty, obstructing the highway or creating a public nuisance *(Tynan v Balmer; News Group Newspapers Ltd v SOGAT (1982) (No 2))*. Criminal acts may result from breach of the common law or statute. Thus, in *Thomas v NUM (South Wales Area)* mass picketing was held to be a public nuisance at common law and an offence under the Conspiracy and Protection of Property Action 1875.[45] Among other things, TULR(C)A makes it a criminal offence to use violence or intimidation or watch or beset any place where a person happens to be.[46] Preventing other workers from entry to their workrooms through the medium of a sit-in has been held to be 'besetting' under the 1875 Act *(Galt v Philp)* and following non-strikers in cars was 'persistent following' *(Elsey v Smith)*. Various offences specified in the Public Order Act 1986 may be committed in the course of industrial action, and the Act also lays down rules for marches, processions and so on.

The statutory provisions on picketing are accompanied by a code of practice issued by the Department of Employment.[47] The code is probably best known for its pronouncements on the number of pickets. In general, the number should not exceed six at any entrance to a workplace; frequently a smaller number will be appropriate. It should be noted that this is a provision of the code – there is no limit laid down by statute. The police, however, have a great deal of discretion in the matter, and can limit numbers if they think a breach of public order is likely. Thus, in *Piddington v Bates*, the Divisional Court upheld a police constable's decision to limit the number of pickets to two. Mass picketing, the code suggests, may constitute a criminal offence in itself, through obstruction or possibly even intimidation.

The code suggests that a union should appoint a picket organizer who would have a letter of authority from the union. The organizer would consult with the police over issues such as numbers and locations. They would distribute badges and armbands to authorized pickets, and make sure arrangements to provide for essential supplies or maintenance were effective. They would ensure that outsiders were not allowed to join the picket. On this point it should be noted that it is not for the police to enforce the civil law. Such matters as identifying unlawful picketing are the responsibility of the employer or any other injured party.

Finally, in relation to picketing, it should be noted that the picketing provisions in TULR(C)A are to be read in conjunction with the statutory immunities.[48] That is, the picketing provisions are not free-standing, so if there is no tortious act to be protected by TULR(C)A, the picketing provisions will not come into play *(Middlebrook Mushrooms v TGWU)*.

OTHER MATTERS

Industrial action affecting the supply of goods or services to an individual

Where a person claims that an unlawful act by a union or other person induces anyone to take part in industrial action and the effect or likely effect is to prevent or delay the supply or reduce the quality of goods or services to the claimant, that individual may apply to the courts for an order to stop the act.[49] They may also apply to the Commissioner for Protection Against Unlawful Industrial Action for assistance.[50]

Remedies

Specific provisions are made as regards *ex parte* and interlocutory injunctions.[51] Where a union is liable for damages in tort, a financial limit is set for each action.[52] On contempt and sequestration proceedings, see *Kent Free Press v NGA*. Finally, TULR(C)A prevents a court from making an order or issuing an injunction to 'compel and employee to do any work or attend at any place for the doing of any work'.[53]

NOTES

1 By virtue of s 14(5).
2 This does not apply to dismissal on the ground of pregnancy or childbirth (ERA, s 99), in health and safety cases (ERA, s 100) or to the dismissal of employee representatives (ERA, s 103).
3 TULR(C)A, s 237(5); cf ERA, s 97.
4 The same exclusions apply: see note 25.

5 TULR(C)A, s 238(3)(a). This is because the narrowing amendments in EA 1982, s 9 applied only to industrial action. Relevant employee for the purposes of lock-out uses the constituency of the organization rather than the establishment and includes those involved from the outset of the dispute rather than just those still involved at the time of the complainant's dismissal.

6 TULR(C)A, s 235(4).

7 TULR(C)A, s 246. For the purposes of ERA there is a definition in ERA, s 235(5).

8 On the concept of a tort, see pages 7–8.

9 An individual now has a statutory right to seek and obtain an order restraining unlawful and industrial action (TULR(C)A, s 235A).

10 TULR(C)A, s 219.

11 TULR(C)A, s 219.

12 TULR(C)A, s 244.

13 TULR(C)A, s 226.

14 TULR(C)A, s 220.

15 TULR(C)A, s 223.

16 TULR(C)A, s 222.

17 TULR(C)A, s 225.

18 TULR(C)A, s 219.

19 TULR(C)A, s 219(1)(a).

20 TULR(C)A, s 219(1)(a).

21 TULR(C)A, s 219(1)(b).

22 TULR(C)A, s 219(1)(b).

23 TULR(C)A, s 219(2).

24 TULR(C)A, s 219(1).

25 TULR(C)A, s 244. This definition needs to be distinguished from the wider definition in s 218 which relates to the processes of dispute resolution (such as ACAS conciliation).

26 Some of these cases were decided under the old definition of trade dispute. The amendments were made by EA 1982, s 18. The *Reed* decision was criticized in Goodhart, 'The Legality of the General Strike', (1927) 36 *Yale Law Journal* 464.

27 EA 1980, s 17, repealed by EA 1990, s 4. The provisions are currently in TULR(C)A, s 224. On the interpretation of the pre-1980 provision see the 'Winter of Discontent' trilogy, *NWL v Woods; Express Newspapers v McShane; and Duport Steels v Sirs*. These cases gave rise to a certain amount of tension between the House of Lords and the Court of Appeal and provide a background to the enactment of EA 1980, s 17.

28 As defined in TULR(C)A, s 220.

29 TULR(C)A, s 226A.

30 TULR(C)A, s 234A.

31 TULR(C)A, ss 226–235. The ballot requirement is found in s 226(1). In *Shipping Company Uniform v ITWF*, the union was a federation of unions and did not have individuals in membership. Consequently, no ballot was conducted. Despite the absence of a balloting constituency, it was held that in the absence of a ballot there was no immunity.

32 *Code of Practice on Industrial Action Ballots and Notice to Employers* (London, Department of Employment, 1995).

33 TULR(C)A, s 230.

34 TULR(C)A, ss 226B and 226C.

35 TULR(C)A, s 229.

36 TULR(C)A, s 231.

37 TULR(C)A, s 231A.

38 TULR(C)A, ss 226B and 231B.

39 TULR(C)A, ss 222, 223 and 225.

40 TULR(C)A, ss 20–23.

41 TULR(C)A, s 21(3).

42 TULR(C)A, s 23.

43 By EA 1982, s 15.

44 TULR(C)A, s 220.

45 1875 Act, s 7 (now included in TULR(C)A, s 241).

46 TULR(C)A, s 241. Formerly these provisions were in s 7 of the 1875 Act.

47 *Picketing Code of Practice*, London, Department of Employment, 1992.

48 TULR(C)A, s 220 is to be read as accompanying s 219.

49 TULR(C)A, s 235A. On this see Morris, GS, 'Industrial Action: Public and Private Interests', (1993) 22 *Industrial Law Journal* 194.

50 TULR(C)A, ss 235B and 235C.

51 TULR(C)A, s 221.

52 TULR(C)A, s 22.

53 TULR(C)A, s 236.

Protection of Information and Property

DATA PROTECTION

Data Protection Act 1984

The Data Protection Act 1984 applies to the 'use of automatically processed information relating to individuals'. The personal data covered include options but not intentions. The Act introduces the concepts of data user and data subject. The former is a person who holds data, the latter a person who is the subject of personal data. A data user is within the scope of the Act if:

- the data is part of a collection to be processed by or on behalf of the user;
- he or she controls the content or use of the data; or
- data is in a form suitable for processing or reprocessing.

Data users must register under the Act, abide by the Act's principles and ensure that the data held are accurate.

Notwithstanding the above, there are some exemptions. Preparation of the text of documents (such as standard letters) is not within the definition of processing, so names and addresses held for this purpose are exempt. Payroll information need not be registered providing it is the minimum necessary for calculating pay and pensions. The exemption would not extend to personnel data (including absenteeism and disciplinary record). There is also an exemption for accounts or records of transactions providing the information is for payment or management forecasting purposes.

Information kept for domestic or personal uses (for example, on a home computer) is also exempt as is information held where there is an overriding question of national security.

Unincorporated members' clubs are exempt providing the members do not object to information being held. Mailing lists are exempt as long as the information does not exceed the minimum necessary and subject to some non-disclosure rules. Statutory information available to the public (for instance industrial tribunal decisions if computerized) are also exempt. Subject access is restricted where access might hamper crime prevention or tax collection. Some relaxation of the limits on disclosure is possible in certain cases, for example if urgently required for the health and safety of any person or in relation to health and social work activities. Finally, subject access to examination marks will be 40 days or five months from the date of request (whichever is earlier) where the request is made prior to the announcement of the results. Otherwise the normal 40 days applies. The definition of examinations may be wide enough to cover some of the tests used by employers in recruitment and promotion procedures.

Data protection principles

There is a set of data protection principles and the Act gives some guidance on their interpretation: The principles are:

(1) The information to be contained in personal data shall be obtained, and personal data shall be processed, fairly and lawfully.
(2) Personal data shall be held only for one or more specified and lawful purposes.
(3) Personal data held for any purpose or purposes shall not be used or disclosed in any manner incompatible with that purpose or those purposes.
(4) Personal data held for any purpose or purposes shall be adequate, relevant and not excessive in relation to that purpose or those purposes.
(5) Personal data shall be accurate and, where necessary, kept up to date.
(6) Personal data held for any purpose or purposes shall not be kept for longer than is necessary for those purposes.
(7) An individual shall be entitled:
    (a) at reasonable intervals and without undue delay or expense:
        (i) to be informed by any data use whether he holds personal data of which that individual is the subject; and
        (ii) to access to any such data held by a data user; and
    (b) where appropriate, to have such data corrected or erased.
(8) Appropriate security measures shall be taken against unauthorized access to, or alteration, disclosure or destruction of, personal data and against accidental loss or destruction of personal data.

The last principle applies to computer bureaux as well as to data users. In as much as computer bureaux are also data users, all the principles will apply to them. Principles (1) and (6) will not be breached just because data are held for historical, statistical or research purposes providing that they are not used in ways which cause (or are likely to cause) damage or distress to any data subject.

The Home Secretary may, by statutory instrument to be approved by Parliament, modify the principles to give additional safeguards in respect of the holding of sensitive information such as racial origin, political or religious beliefs, health or sexual life.

Operation of the Act

There is a Data Protection Registrar (DP Registrar), who is responsible for overseeing the legislation, and a Data Protection Tribunal (DP tribunal). DP tribunals comprise a legally qualified chairman, a representative of data users and a representative of data subjects. They hear appeals by data users from decisions of the DP Registrar.

Data users must register with the DP Registrar by providing the following details:

- their name and address;
- a description of the data;
- the purpose(s) for which data are to be held or used;
- a description of the sources of the data;
- a description of any person to whom they may wish to disclose the data;
- the names of any places outside the UK to which the data may be transferred, directly or indirectly; and
- one or more addresses for the receipt of requests from data subjects for access to the data.

It is a criminal offence to hold data without being registered or to hold or use data in ways which are not covered by the register entry. Entries may be altered upon application to the DP Registrar, and additional entires made. The register is available for inspection by members of the public free of charge. A copy may be obtained for a small charge.

The DP Registrar's role involves a general supervision of the legislation – that is, ensuring its terms are complied with – as well as the handling of specific complaints. He has substantial powers of entry, search and seizure, subject to judicial authorization. In pursuance of his supervisory role, he may issue enforcement, deregistration and transfer-prohibition notices as well as initiating criminal prosecutions.

Data users may appeal to a DP tribunal against the DP Registrar's decision to refuse registration or against any enforcement, deregistration or transfer-prohibition notice. An appeal will succeed if the DP Registar's decision is not in accordance with the law or, where the DP Registrar's discretion was exercised, if it should have been exercised differently.

The more serious offences such as holding data when unregistered, or knowing or reckless contravention of any of the particulars contained in a register entry, are subject to proceedings in either the magistrates' court or Crown Court. In the latter case, fines are unlimited. Other offences, for example failure of a registered person to notify a change of address, are to be heard only in the magistrates' court (current maximum fine, £2,000), but the maximum provided for by the Criminal Justice Act 1991 is £5,000. Liability may be individual as well as corporate. The former will apply if the offence was committed with the consent or connivance of any director, manager or secretary or was attributable to any neglect on their part.

The DP Registrar may consider any complaint involving a breach of the Act and must consider any complaint which raises a matter of substance and which is reported to him without undue delay by a person directly affected.

Once registration has been achieved the main effect of the legislation upon employers is likely to derive from requests for access to information by data users. The access rights are triggered by a request in writing to the data user, and payment of the appropriate fee, which has a statutory limit. Proof of identity needs to be given. Information must be supplied within 40 days of receipt of request, or within 40 days of proof of identity if later. The information must be accurate and up to date. Data subjects may only have access to data relating to themselves. The data should be intelligible and not identify any third parties without their consent.

A complaint can be made to the DP Registrar or to the civil courts – the county court or High Court – about any contravention of the Act. Such complaints may include:

- a refusal of a request for access;
- the holding of inaccurate information; or
- a loss of data or unauthorized disclosure.

Orders for access may be given, and compensation for damage suffered as a result of inaccurate information may have to be paid. Inaccuracy applies only to factual data (rather than opinion). Orders for rectification or erasure of data may be made.

EU Data Protection Directive 1995

New legislation will be required to implement the EU Data Protection Directive 1995[1] by 24 October 1998. The aim of the Directive is to harmonize data protection standards across the EU. In the UK, the 1984 Act will continue to operate, supplemented by the new legislation.

The new legislation will extend employees' rights so that there is access to manually held information. However,the government has indicated that it will take advantage of the 12-year transition period allowed by the Directive for employers to apply data protection principles to data currently held in manual form.

The new provisions will also prevent the collection of certain types of data about individuals (eg, ethnic or racial origins and political or religious beliefs) except for specific prescribed purposes. Individuals will also have to be told what information is being collected, why it is being collected and how to gain access to it.

CONFIDENTIAL INFORMATION

Competition and other work

Where an employee is in competition with their employer they are likely to be in breach of their contractual duty of fidelity and good faith. This duty requires faithful, loyal and honest service on the part of the employee. Being in competition is likely to be a failure to carry out such a duty as would be the making of secret profits out of the employment and the divulging of the employer's confidential information. In addition to the implied duty of fidelity there may be express terms which provide additional protection for the employer. However, if these terms are too widely drawn they may be unenforceable because they are in restraint of trade and therefore contrary to public policy.

Any work done other than for the employer during working hours is likely to be a breach of contract regardless of whether or not it is done in competition with the employer. This would be a breach of the implied term of fidelity. The situation is quite different, however, for jobs done outside working hours. In the absence of an express term to the contrary, an employee is free to do what they like with their spare time providing that the activities do not cause significant harm to the employer (*Hivac Ltd v Park Royal Scientific Instruments Ltd*). They might cause such harm if they materially aided a competitor or adversely affected the employee's own work. It is this question of harm caused to the employer which will determine (in the absence of express restrictions) whether there has been a breach of contract. Soliciting the employer's customers for their own or some third party's benefit is likely to be a breach of the term of fidelity by the employee and dismissal for such activity may be fair.

Express terms may be used to prevent an employee:

- from working for competitors during their employment;

- from conducting preparatory business activities during employment leading to them setting up in competition after termination of their employment; or
- from working elsewhere without permission;

although the last of these runs the risk of being unenforceable because it is so widely drawn. However, this would depend on the circumstances of the case. Adding a restrictive term after the commencement of employment without the employee's agreement will probably be a unilateral variation of terms and may amount to a breach of contract. A combination of express terms, of the type mentioned above, and what is known as 'garden leave', may prevent competition until the employment ends. Garden leave is the use of long notice periods where the employee is not required to be at work (an express term allowing lay-off with pay during the notice period may be of use here). The employment contract continues and therefore the restrictive express term operates throughout. A similar effect can be achieved by insisting on a fixed-term contract continuing until expiry. Courts may grant injunctions preventing the employee breaching the contract, as in *Evening Standard Co Ltd v Henderson,* but will award damages instead if they think that the intended restriction upon the employee is less important (see *Provident Financial Group plc v Hayward*). The courts may also refuse to grant injunctions where the employee needs to perform their duties in order to prevent their skills deteriorating.

The danger of employees being in competition may continue after employment. Employers may tackle this problem through restrictive covenants – contract clauses which govern behaviour after employment. In general, such clauses will be in restraint of trade and contrary to public policy unless they can be shown to be reasonable. This means demonstrating that they:

- offer adequate protection, but no more;
- serve the legitimate interests of the employer *(Nordenfelt v Maxim Nordenfelt Guns and Ammunition Co).*

Legitimate interests means trade secrets or trade connections.

Restrictive covenants may contain the following:

- non-competition clauses: restrictions on the ex-employee working for competing businesses including any business the ex-employee may set up themselves. These are designed to protect trade secrets and trade connections.
- non-solicitation or non-dealing clauses: these restrain the ex-employee from soliciting or dealing with the company's customers.

It may be possible to have a clause restricting the poaching of employees by a former employee. Such poaching may in any case be tortious if it induces employees to break their contracts of employment, for example, because they have non-competition clauses.

A reasonableness test will be applied to restrictive covenant. This involves judging:

- subject matter coverage;
- geographical area; and
- duration.

Non-competition clauses are clearly the most restrictive and employees might argue that a lesser restriction (such as a non-dealing clause) would suffice. Generally, the reasonableness test is to be applied to the facts at the time the clause was introduced. The burden of proof of reasonableness is upon the employer. In drafting such clauses, it should be remembered that contract terms must be certain and unambiguous if they are to be enforceable. However, where there is more than one restrictive clause, and only one clause is too wide to be enforced, the courts may sever the offending clause and enforce the others rather than refuse to enforce the whole. Much depends on whether it is possible in practice, that is, on whether each clause can stand on its own. A restrictive covenant can be part of the contract of employment or a separate, new contract to take effect when employment ends.

Sensitive information

The employee has an implied contractual duty not to disclose to third parties their employer's trade secrets and confidential information. This is part of the duty of fidelity and good faith *(Faccenda Chicken Ltd v Fowler)*. Much will depend upon the person's employment, the nature of the information, whether it has been made clear that the information is confidential and whether the information can be easily separated from more generally available information. Information which is part of the employee's know-how or stock-in-trade is unlikely to be regarded as confidential. Express confidentiality clauses are possible and are especially useful in showing what the employer regards as confidential. They may not add much in practice to the implied contractual terms, but may have a deterrent effect. Information which it is in the public interest to disclose will not be confidential even if it damages the employer (for example, tax fiddling) *(Initial Services Ltd v Putterill)*.

The implied duty of fidelity applies beyond the termination of employment in relation to trade secrets, but not generally to otherwise confidential information. Thus, ex-employees who retain trade secrets for ulterior purposes can be sued for breach of contract *(Robb v Green)*. Where confidential information other than trade secrets has been obtained as a result of a breach of the term of fidelity during employment this may also be subject to protection afterwards. There could be an express clause to deal with release of information after employment. To be enforceable this would need to be restricted to trade secrets and connections.

Company property: unauthorized access; removal; wilful damage

Unauthorized access to, removal of or wilful damage to company property will probably constitute a breach of disciplinary rules as well as a breach of the term of fidelity and good faith in the employment contract. Whether a dismissal for such acts will be fair will depend upon the decision passing the normal unfair dismissal tests of fair reason and reasonableness (see chapter 16). If a case is serious it may well amount to gross misconduct. Rules should state explicitly that access is restricted (for example, to computers or parts of the site) and that property must not be removed, and should indicate if such breaches might constitute gross misconduct or warrant dismissal. All this needs to be communicated clearly to employees. Actions of these sorts by employees may in any case be criminal, so that employers might need to decide whether the police should be notified.

Rules in this area will need to be reasonable as will any other security measures taken to prevent unauthorized access or removal of property. The rules may be strengthened by being laid down at the outset as a condition of employment, so securing consent by the employee. Searches of car boots or other receptacles raise no particular difficulty although they could amount to trespass to goods if damage is caused. Personal searches (for instance, by security staff) could constitute battery unless consented to by the employee. Where personal search is established as a condition of employment and a dismissal for non-compliance follows, a major question will be whether the rule was reasonable. A relevant issue will be whether such a requirement was a lawful and enforceable term of the contract. In apprehending someone who it is believed has committed or is committing an offence, a security (or any other) person must use force only if resisted and even then only an amount reasonable in the circumstances.

INVENTIONS AND INTELLECTUAL PROPERTY

Inventions

Prior to the Patents Act 1977 (which relates to employee inventions made on or after 1 June 1978) this area was covered only by common law.

The statutory patents system gives an exclusive right to exploit an invention for a period of up to 20 years. Patents are granted, however, only if the invention:

- is new;
- involves an inventive step;
- is capable of industrial application; and
- does not fall into one of the excluded categories (such as scientific theories and computer programmes) which are usually covered by copyright law: see below).

The Patents Act 1977 lays down that an invention will belong to the employer only if:

- it was made in the course of the employee's normal duties or some specially assigned duties; and either
- it might reasonably be expected to result from the carrying out of such duties; or
- the employee had a special obligation to further the employer's interests (this will be influenced strongly by the employee's status).

Compensation is payable to employees if the employer benefits from the invention in the ways indicated below. First, if the invention is owned by the *employer*, the employee will be entitled to compensation if they can show that:

- it has been patented;
- it is of outstanding benefit to the employer; and
- it is just that they should be compensated.

Where the invention is owned by the *employee*, compensation will be payable if they can show that:

- the invention has been patented;
- they have assigned or exclusively licensed the rights to their employer;
- the benefit to the employee is inadequate when compared with the benefit derived by the employer; and
- it is just that compensation be paid over and above the amount agreed for the licence or assignment.

The amount of compensation will be that which will secure a fair share of the benefits having regard to all the circumstances. Contractual arrangements cannot be used to overrule the employee's rights contained in the Act, but an employee is free to grant their employer rights subsequent to the making of the invention.

Intellectual property

This area is subject to the Copyright, Designs and Patents Act 1988 as well as to any contractual arrangements between the parties. The Act covers the following categories:

- literary work, that is, work which is written, spoken or sung; this includes tables and computer programs;
- artistic work, such as graphical work, photographs and sculpture;
- musical work; and
- dramatic work, such as mime and dance.

Sound recordings, films and broadcasts are included. The general rule is that ownership lies with the employer if the employee creates the work in the course of their employment, that is, it is part of the employee's job to create the work. This rule would not apply, however, where there was a contractual term to the contrary. Such a term might be expressed or implied, including through custom and practice.

SCREENING AND RECORDS

Employers in areas exempted from the Rehabilitation of Offenders Act 1974 may seek information about job applicants from the police, courts or government departments. Procedures for such checks are generally regulated by the Home Office or other departments of government. There should be no disclosure of information by any of these bodies (or indeed by private agencies) unless the employer is exempted and makes this clear.

Where employers require job applicants to make a subject access application to police computer records and present the results to them this is likely to be seen as an abuse of the subject access provisions of the Data Protection Act 1984. Moreover, police computer records do not, apparently, distinguish between spent and unspent convictions, so the information may be inaccurate or out of date, and so challengeable under the Data Protection Act. The information may also not be comprehensive so that its value to an employer might be in doubt.

Where a company is using a private vetting agency it would be as well to check that if the agency's information is computerized it has been registered with the DP Registrar. The individual subject will have access rights and all the other data protection principles will also apply. The individual may claim compensation from the agency for losses and distress if, for example, the information is inaccurate, and the DP Registrar may enforce criminal sanctions.

As far as a company's own records are concerned there is no justification for them to include spent convictions unless their employment is excepted from the 1974 Act. Unspent convictions should be regarded as confidential information and employer and employee should make clear who has access. The contractual term of mutual trust and confidence might be invoked where there are breaches.

The criminal law will have a stronger application where an employee has access to official records as part of their job. This would apply to certain people employed in the courts, police service, some government departments and local authorities. Disclosing information about spent convictions to another person except in the course of official duties is a criminal offence. Obtaining such information by means of fraud, dishonesty or bribe is also a criminal offence. In addition, an employee disclosing confidential information may be in breach of fidelity and/or discipline. An employer might be vicariously liable for the actions of the employee who has disclosed the information if the subject of the disclosed information pursues legal action. Important considerations would be the extent to which the employer has properly instructed the employee about confidentiality and generally done all that they can reasonably do to achieve security.

ACTIONS AND REMEDIES

As already indicated, restrictive covenants are a useful means of protecting the security of the company against competition, release of confidential information and so on. Ideally, these would be part of terms and conditions from the outset of employment. In some cases, however, it may be necessary to alter the terms of existing staff to include restrictions, and the question of refusal to accept the changed terms might arise. The various matters already considered in respect of changes in terms and conditions of employment (see chapter 10) would then be relevant. If there is a dismissal, it might be for some other substantial reason. A tribunal would want to know whether the restriction was for a reasonable period, territory and set of activities. Whether other employees had agreed to it might have a bearing on reasonableness as might the existence of past and/or present problems *(RS Components Ltd v Irwin)*.

Another possibility is to transfer the employee to a part of the organization where he or she does not have access to sensitive information. Again there is a risk of breach of contract through unilateral variation of terms if the transfer if not agreed, but again a fair dismissal might be possible if the transfer is reasonable.

Dismissal is also likely to be seen as a fair response if there is a clear breach of fidelity or of an express restrictive term. Indeed, the actions of the employee might amount to gross misconduct. Where the employee is moonlighting and his work performance deteriorates there may be a possibility of dismissing fairly on grounds of capability. In all cases of dismissal, however, there needs to be proper procedure and overall reasonableness on the part of the employer. Moreover, the employer must make sure that the dismissal itself is not wrongful, that is, in breach of contract. A failure to give due notice or to go through a contractual disciplinary procedure would be wrongful. The importance of this is that where an employer dismisses wrongfully they will not be able to rely on any restrictive covenant. This is because of the general rule of law which prevents a person who breaches a contract from subsequently relying on any of the terms to their own advantage. The payment of wages in lieu of notice may present a problem here since following the Court of Appeal's decision in *Delaney v Staples*, payment in lieu is confirmed as damages for wrongful dismissal. Thus it can be inferred from payment in lieu that dismissal has been wrongful, therefore any restrictive covenant might not apply. It may be possible to overcome this problem by drafting contracts to allow for termination by notice or payment in lieu of notice.

A major question arises where the ex-employee will not be bound by the term of a restrictive covenant. The ex-employer may seek an injunction or damages (or both if the injunction is an interlocutory (that is, interim) one). In deciding whether to grant an interim injunction the courts will apply the balance of convenience test except in extreme cases where the interlocutory hearing effectively disposes of the issue. In such instances the relative merits of the cases will be assessed. The courts will not, however, order specific performance if it involves compelling an employee to work for an employer, and this is in any case prevented by TULR(C)A.[2] If a restrictive covenant turns out to be unenforceable, there may be a claim on the basis of negligence against any solicitor who drafted it, provided that the six-year time limit for such cases has not expired.

Where the ex-employee is known to have important information and there is a real possibility that they will destroy it before any application for a hearing between the parties can be made, an *Anton Piller* order might be sought *(Anton Piller KG v Manufacturing Processes Ltd)*. This order is granted as a result of an *ex parte* application and confers a right to enter premises to search for and seize documents or property. To obtain an order it will be necessary to show that:

- there is a very strong *prima facie* case;
- the potential or actual damage must be very serious;
- the defendants are known to have the information or objects in their possession; and

- there is a real possibility that they will destroy them before any application *inter partes.*

There must be proportionality between the perceived threat to the plaintiff's rights and the remedy itself. Orders to allow copies of documents to be taken or to preserve or deliver-up documents are more likely to be granted than an *Anton Piller* order.

Finally there is the possibility of taking action against third parties. First, anyone inducing a breach of contract commits a tort, so there is the possibility of action in tort against anyone who induces existing employees to break their contracts. This includes the possibility of an injunction to stop the inducement. Secondly, anyone knowingly receiving information disclosed in breach of contract will be committing a tort and can be proceeded against.

NOTES

1 95/46/EC.
2 TULR(C)A, s 236.

PART III

PROBLEMS AND PERSPECTIVES

The Development and Impact of Employment Law

It is not feasible within the scope of a general text such as this to attempt a comprehensive and detailed account of the development and impact of employment law. Rather, the aim is to provide a brief summary of the development and a selective, broad-brush account of its impact. The latter focuses upon the key areas of discrimination, unfair dismissal, maternity, redundancy and collective rights (but not the union–member relationship). A comprehensive account would aim to assess the protection of wages and other contract terms, but that is not attempted here, while an assessment of the important area of health and safety at work is regarded as too ambitious a task for the present work. However, an attempt is made at putting forward a generalized assessment methodology.

EMPLOYMENT LAW AS A SUBJECT

In broad terms, employment law is concerned with the legal issues arising out of or connected with employment, and this concern operates at the micro-level of the individual or organization, as well as at the aggregated, societal or macro-level. At this latter level, employment law can be seen as being concerned with legal regulation of the labour market. The focus is the relationship between employer and employee but not exclusively so. First, employment relations may not be governed by a contract of employment, that is, the worker may not be an employee (see chapter 5). Secondly, employment law is also concerned with the collective relationship, between employers and trades unions. Indeed, in recent years, there has been a development of employment law governing the relationship between trades unions and their members.

While the broad content of employment law is quite easy to identify, the precise boundaries of the subject are more difficult to define. Clearly, employment law overlaps with other areas of law at certain points. For example, the law of taxation will sometimes be relevant, particularly perhaps upon termination of employment. Similarly with social security law including pensions. Historically, these areas tend to be excluded from the subject of employment law because they form separate, specialist bodies of law. The same applies, to some extent, to the law of health and safety at work. There is, therefore, a degree of tradition, and perhaps of arbitrariness, as to where the precise boundary of the subject is drawn.

One of the principal features of employment law as a subject is the centrality of the contract of employment.[1] Although there is a large volume of statutory provision in the employment field, it remains true that the focal point of the employment relationship in law, and therefore of the subject, is the contract of employment. This leads to a second, important consideration. Because the central relationship is a contract, employment law is inevitably linked to the wider, general body of contract law. As Lord Evershed MR put it in *Laws v London Chronicle*: 'A contract of service is but an example of contracts in general, so that the general law of contract will be applicable.'[2] A third feature of importance is that to a considerable extent employment law has its own legal institutions for resolving disputes (see chapter 3). In particular, it has the industrial tribunals (see chapters 4 and 25) but in addition an important conciliation role is played by ACAS and there are also other specialist bodies. However, notwithstanding these specialist institutions, employment law remains plugged into the mainstream legal system, so that appeals from the EAT are heard by the Court of Appeal (Court of Session in Scotland) and thereafter by the House of Lords.

This 'connectedness' leads to a further important feature of employment law. It has been subject to substantial influence by the UK's membership of the European Union (and formerly, the constituent European Economic Community) (see chapter 27). Employment is one of the areas where the EU has been particularly active in terms of policy-making and the logic is not hard to see. First, labour costs are an important factor in price competitiveness, so if EU Member States are to operate in an open European market on a 'level playing field', a degree of harmonization of legal requirements resulting in such costs is a prerequisite. Secondly, however, is the developing social policy of the EU, which increasingly is independent of the original economic motives of the EU and forms a *bona fide* objective in itself. Employment, inevitably, is seen as central to social policy because of its importance in determining individual welfare.

Next, it must be noted that employment law will always have a tendency towards controversy. There may be periods of calm and consensus, but because employment law has to balance the competing interests of employers and workers, and ultimately is capable of being one of the factors influencing the distribution of income between these interests, the subject will always have a potential for instability. Much will depend upon the balance of power in society and upon macro-economic performance.

Finally, in terms of the characteristics of the subject, it has to be stated that employment law contains a large amount of statutory provision, some of which is very detailed and complex, and generates a substantial volume of case law. It is perhaps these characteristics rather than any sophisticated concepts, arguments or principles which can sometimes make employment law difficult for those trying to understand it. An imperative, in dealing with employment law, therefore, is to have in mind a broad picture of the scheme of law in each of its main constituent areas. Otherwise, there is a risk of being lost in detail and complexity.

DEVELOPMENT OF EMPLOYMENT LAW

Historical development to 1979

The Statute of Artificers 1563, which included provisions derived from legislation in the fourteenth century, was the centrepiece of a system of regulation of wages, prices, labour mobility and training under which the combination of workers was a criminal conspiracy at common law. This system fell into disuse and was formally repealed early in the nineteenth century. However, while combination ceased to be illegal, criminal sanctions remained attached to industrial action until 1875.[3]

It can be seen that the regulation of trades union activity has been one of the key strands of employment law from early times. The more recent historical basis of that regulation has been the principle that a union should not be liable in tort if acting in contemplation or furtherance of a trade dispute (see chapter 23). The rationale here is that without such protection against liability, trades unions would not be able to function. Therefore, if public policy is that trades union activity is legitimate, it should also be public policy to have a legal regime which allows trades unions to function in practice.

The origins of employment law also indicate a concern with employment protection. Traces of this can be seen in the very early provisions. Thereafter, this strand is most visible in the attempt to correct the excesses of rapid industrialization. In particular, substantial amounts of nineteenth-century legislation were enacted in an attempt to protect health, safety and welfare and to require payment of wages in cash. The former development has continued to the present day to provide a comprehensive body of health and safety law. Legislation early in the twentieth century provided for statutory minimum wages in areas of employment where pay was low and union organization weak (these provisions have been repealed with the exception of those relating to agriculture).

A major factor shaping the relationship between law and employment in the UK was the development of trades unions and collective bargaining in advance of the granting of political rights to employees. Thus, a system evolved under which unions and employers jointly determined wages and other terms of employment without there being any specific employment law framework. The outputs of this system – collective agreements – were not legally enforceable and employees looked to unions rather than the law for protection. This system of industrial self-government shaped the relationship between law and employment for part of the nineteenth century and much of the twentieth. Kahn-Freund referred to it as 'collective laissez-faire'.[4] It was seen that the law was only peripheral and that the system was based on voluntarism rather than law. An 'auxiliary' function of employment law became the provision of support for this voluntary system.[5] This included government provision of fall-back facilities for the voluntary resolution of disputes and legislation to extend collectively bargained terms to workplaces where there was no collective bargaining.

The major challenge to the voluntary system as described above was the onset of full employment in the post-1945 period. The power of workers and unions during two world wars had been tempered by special wartime controls which were largely acceptable in the context of war but unlikely to be so in peacetime. Tight labour markets gave workers and unions considerable power which when exercised produced strikes, inflationary wage settlements and a constraint upon productivity improvement. The effects were recurring balance of payments deficits which were met with deflationary economic policy. In an attempt to break out of this disruptive 'stop–go' cycle, governments sought to intervene directly in the labour market. The objectives were to contain wages and prices, encourage productivity improvements and foster the development of new and growing industries. In legislative terms, this was reflected in the Industrial Training Act 1964, the Redundancy Payments Act 1965 and the Prices and Incomes Acts 1966–68.[6]

The longer-term response was a corporatist model of industrial relations based on reform of collective bargaining machinery and disputes procedures, but with a strong advisory and reforming role for a central standing commission (briefly the Commission on Industrial Relations). Strengthening the centralized authority of the trades unions to enable them to control lay officials and members and altering the *locus* of collective bargaining to a less devolved level were important parts of the scheme. In effect, this approach was resumed later (during 1974–79) within a less regulated framework than had been envisaged, but the immediate period saw a change in government and a wholly different approach. The period 1971–74 saw an attempt to put employment law on a completely different footing, with a comprehensive statutory framework and the operating principle that collective agreements were to be presumed enforceable at law. The failure of this 'grand scheme' approach is well-documented and is thought to have informed the step-by step approach to employment law change adopted by governments from 1979 onwards. From 1974, the corporatist approach was renewed in the form of a 'social contract' between government and unions. The unions were to deliver wage moderation and industrial peace, the government a range of employment protection legislation. Following a 'winter of discontent' during 1978–79, characterized by an outbreak of public sector strike activity, the government changed in 1979 to herald a new era.

From 1979: a revolution in employment law?[7]

Overview
The overall picture during 1979–97 is that the basic structure of employment law has remained unchanged. The collective, employer/union relationship is still binding only in honour: it is not legally enforceable. The legally enforceable individual relationship, the contract of employment, remains fundamental. The law surrounding the critical area of industrial action is still based upon immunity granted by statute to protect unions from actions at common law. The paradox is that within the above structure there has been qualitative change: perhaps a revolution.

Legal support for collective bargaining
In 1979, the Thatcher government inherited legislation which assisted the spread of collectively bargained terms. It provided:

- a statutory procedure for unions to obtain recognition from employers (or improved terms of employment in lieu of recognition);
- for extension to other employment in that industry of terms generally established or recognized in the particular industry; and
- for statutory minimum terms in certain industries.

Not surprisingly, given the government's free market philosophy, this area of law has been almost completely wiped out. All that is left is minimum wage-fixing in agriculture.

Individual rights

The picture here is less clear. In keeping with the notion of a free labour market and the idea of reducing the burdens on business, the government has sought to reduce individual employment rights. It has succeeded in doing so up to a point. Thus a number of areas of employee protection have been weakened including:

(1) Unfair dismissal:
- the qualifying period for claims has been increased from six months to two years;
- the minimum compensation level has been abolished;
- the burden of proof of 'reasonableness' has been lifted from employers and laid upon both parties; and
- there is now wider scope for deductions to be made from the compensation awarded.

(2) Maternity rights:
- a complex procedure has been instituted making it more difficult to exercise the right of return to work after childbirth; and
- rights to return have been weakened to allow employers to offer less favourable terms;
- however, there have also been improvements (see below).

(3) Payment of wages:
- the statutory right to payment in cash has been withdrawn.

(4) Tribunal procedure:
- a screening device has been instituted (the pre-hearing review) in order to deter applications which seem to lack substance.

However, the key areas of individual employment law nevertheless remain – unfair dismissal (albeit weakened), redundancy, equal pay, sex and race discrimination. The system of employment law institutions – industrial and appeal tribunals, the Central Arbitration Committee, ACAS, and the Certification Officer – is also still intact although parts of it have been adapted to carry out the new functions of employment law in the 1980s and 1990s.

More than this, some areas of individual employment law have been improved. A significant improvement in maternity rights has been achieved as a result of the implementation of the EU Pregnant Workers' Directive. This gives a woman a right to 14 weeks' maternity leave without any requirements about length of employment or hours of work (see chapter 13). Another improvement has been the extension of consultation rights in redundancies and transfers of undertakings, these being in the form of rights given to employee representatives (see chapter 18).

There have also been improvements in the statutory provisions governing health and safety at work and in the field of pensions. Equal pay and sex discrimination laws have been strengthened by additions required as a result of successful legal cases taken by the Commission of the EC against the UK, and by other decisions of the ECJ. Thus a woman can now take a case on equal value grounds, and discriminatory retirement ages are now unlawful. Wider protection against transfers of undertakings has been provided, the impetus again coming from Europe, and there is also a right to time off for ante-natal care. The wider coverage of the Wages Act 1986, compared with the legislation it replaced on questions of deductions from wages, may also be seen as an improvement, although the Act had the general effect of weakening employee protection (these provisions can now be found in ERA). Finally, statutory compensation levels have increased over the period, especially for those discriminated against on the grounds of union membership or non-membership, and the statutory limits on compensation for race and sex discrimination have been removed.

This is not to assume that these improvements have necessarily been of significance. Two potentially significant changes – equal value claims and the transfer of undertakings regulations – have in fact been fraught with problems.[8] The point is rather that, because of our membership of the European Union, a government wishing to reduce employee rights and deregulate the labour market has in fact been compelled, to some extent, to do the opposite. The former government's experience of European involvement in individual employment law thus provides some insight into the basis of the Conservatives' current hostility towards certain developments in Europe.

Union organization and democracy

This area of activity has been characterized by two philosophical approaches. First, leading Conservatives appear to have an almost pathological hatred of the closed shop. It appears to conjure up pictures of union bully boys and the infringement of personal liberty. As a result, the law of unfair dismissal has been amended to offer more generous remedies to the employee dismissed for being a non-unionist than it does to someone dismissed unfairly for some other reason (eg, alleged misconduct).[9] Dismissal for non-unionism is in any case automatically unfair. The legislation has, however, stopped short of making the closed shop unlawful. Entering into a closed shop agreement involves no breach of law, nor does the existence of the agreement itself. However, action against any non-unionist once employed would be unlawful. Similarly, a person now has a remedy if they are prevented from obtaining a job by virtue of their non-unionism (or unionism).

Secondly, the Conservatives painted a picture of trades unions as autocratic bodies with politically motivated, unrepresentative and militant national officials – 'bosses' – leading members into industrial action against the members' interests. The Conservative task, therefore, was to give the unions back their members. The main method was to impose a statutory requirement for ballots for various union decisions:

- to take industrial action;
- to continue having political objectives and funds; and
- to elect senior national officials and members of the principal executive committee.

A free market philosophy underpins some of the changes here. Thus, after a majority vote in favour of industrial action in a properly conducted ballot, an individual member is free to choose to opt out of the action. Discipline for doing so would probably be unjustified and a remedy would be available from an industrial tribunal. A further principle adopted in this area is the right of the individual to be a member of the union of his or her choice. Thus anyone expelled or excluded from a union can make a complaint to an industrial tribunal and the grounds of defence for a trades union are limited by statute.

In the area of member–union relations there are also remedies available through common law. A member may sue for breach of the contract of membership, in which the rulebook is paramount. The plaintiff will need to demonstrate which specific term of the contract has been broken. The principles of natural justice also play a part here. A member may also sue in tort, for example, if a union is negligent in its dealings with him. The effect of the post-1979 legislation is to add substantial statutory provision to the existing common law, some of it specifically overriding union rulebook provisions. If union members need help, the Commissioner for the Rights of Trade Union Members is available.

Industrial action

The legal framework has historically been one in which unions and their officials have had statutory protection against being sued under the common law in tort (ie, for civil wrongs) by employers and others for losses arising out of industrial action. This scheme – 'the system of immunities' – remains intact. The scope of the protection, however, has been drastically narrowed by:

- picketing being made lawful only if it is 'at or near' the person's workplace (with minor exceptions);
- most secondary action being made unlawful;
- the complete withdrawal of immunity from action in support of the closed shop and union membership or recognition in other firms;

- limiting immunity to disputes in which there has been a majority vote in favour of action in a ballot conducted according to the legal requirements;
- narrowing the definition of 'trade dispute'; immunity applies only where there is a trade dispute, ie a dispute between workers and their own employer wholly or mainly about terms and conditions of employment;
- making unions as organizations liable (subject to some legal rules) for the industrial action of their members; thus, union funds may be at risk during industrial action.

Strikers' protection against dismissal has also been weakened and has been completely removed where the industrial action is unofficial. Moreover, industrial action to support the reinstatement of dismissed unofficial strikers is no longer immune.

'New Labour': new employment law?

It is very early – only 12 months since the change of government – to draw any conclusions about whether employment law is entering a new phase and, if so, what might characterize that phase. However, there are certain indicators.

Employee rights

In general, the government appears to support the idea of increased protection for individual employees where this can be justified. Minimum wages, dismissal protection for strikers, information and consultation rights for workers, family-friendly policies such as childcare and parental leave, and human rights issues – these appear to be high on the agenda. The government seems generally supportive of EU social policy, although it may baulk at a further extension of EU legislation if it conflicts with the principle of subsidiarity (according to which only those matters best dealt with at the EU level are legislated at that level and everything else is determined by the individual Member States).

Trades unions

There is no evidence that the government will substantially alter the collective employment law framework. The changes here are likely to be the introduction of a legal right to recognition and a relaxing of the rules governing the authorization of check-off (ie, the deducting of union subscriptions direct from salaries). On 1970s experience, the former may not have a significant effect but the latter may result in a substantial increase in union membership (and therefore finance). The government will also channel money through the unions for community education purposes including union education.

Dispute resolution

The government's approach to the tribunal system does not appear to be substantially different from that of its predecessor. It wants to make the system cheaper, faster and more efficient. while not making it less accessible. The balance drawn may differ somewhat, but ultimately governments of any complexion have to deal with the public expenditure and operational effectiveness aspects of dispute resolution. The government may be more appreciative of ACAS than were some of its predecessors.

New employment law?

The signs are that there will be a steady increase in employment legislation in the UK, much of it emanating from the EU, but as yet there is no evidence of a radically different approach to the way employment law is organized. Rather, the government appears to be adopting a pragmatic approach. Therefore, the question of whether 'New Labour' means new employment law can tentatively be answered thus: certainly some new law, but not a new system.

ASSESSING EMPLOYMENT LAW: A METHODOLOGY

Before examining the impact of particular schemes or areas of employment law – dismissal, discrimination and so on – it is intended to consider the question of methodology. Can a generally applicable methodology be developed for assessing particular legislative schemes? Is it possible to establish a generalized set of criteria for judging the effectiveness of specific employment (and perhaps other) legislative schemes? An attempt is made here using a model which includes both extrinsic and intrinsic criteria. The former relate directly to the objectives of the particular legislative scheme, the latter to the characteristics of the scheme itself. The former can be seen as ends, the latter as means.

The objectives of legislation

The starting point here is the long title of a particular Act. For example, the long title of the Sex Discrimination Act 1975 is 'An Act to render unlawful certain kinds of sex discrimination and discrimination on the ground of marriage, and establish a Commission with the function of working towards the elimination of such discrimination and promoting equality of opportunity between men and women generally; and for related purposes.' The short title is the 'Sex Discrimination Act 1975'.

The objectives stated in the long title might be supplemented or elaborated upon by evidence from Parliamentary debates and other sources such as a (green) consultative paper or an ECJ decision which has given rise to the legislation. There may be other international obligations, eg conventions of the International Labour Organization. Objectives so derived may be regarded as the formal objectives of the scheme.

Such positive objectives can be supplemented by normative ones. It may be the case that a particular legislative scheme is regarded by some as not going far enough or going too far in a specific direction. Such a view may be based upon perceptions of what is fair to a particular party or upon perceived economic implications or upon what has been enacted in other countries. Thus the objectives themselves may be criticized.

There may be objective evidence against which to test the extent to which legislative purpose is being met. Thus, legislation aiming to reduce the number of strikes and days on strike can be tested against a historical series of published data. Similarly, legislation aiming to achieve or make progress towards equal pay could be tested against historical data on the relative pay of men and women.

There may be other objective data. Usage of the legislative scheme and any other impact (such as employers improving their procedures) can be considered. There may be data about the number of potential users. The success rate of complainants can be considered, although this is a difficult statistic to interpret. A low figure may reflect weak cases, poor presentation or deficiencies in the legislation or in procedure, or indeed, a combination of these. There may also be empirical evidence from researchers, who may have gathered data from users of the legislation and/or those involved in its operation.

A major consideration, however, will be to identify the non-law factors which have a bearing on the effectiveness of the legislation (ie, factors other than the law itself and the procedural and other 'system' factors connected with it). For example, the level and/or rate of growth of unemployment may have some bearing of the willingness of individuals in employment to pursue complaints against their employers. The same factor might also be important in any explanation of why there are fewer strikes and days on strike than, say, in the 1970s. Another non-law factor may be changes in the structure of employment, in particular the growth of employment in the private service sector and small firms, where there is less likelihood of unionization, and the increasing use of temporary contracts. Only when these non-law variables have been considered will a clearer view emerge of the extent to which legislation has been successful and of the relative importance of various law and non-law factors.

Finally, before considering the features which relate to legislation itself, there is the question of cost. Legislative schemes are a public cost and that cost needs to be considered in relation to the objectives of the scheme and any appropriate performance standards. As noted in chapter 26, this aspect of the functioning of the industrial tribunal system has attracted particular attention, albeit in relation to the system as a whole rather than any particular legislative scheme.

The legislative scheme

Turning from objectives to the particular legislative scheme itself, it is evident that certain factors will be influential in affecting the extent to which the scheme meets its objectives.

Scope

The scope of the legislation is the first consideration. Not everybody may be covered by the legislation. For example, in the general unfair dismissal case, there is a requirement for two years' continuous employment. Moreover, the legislation applies only to employees and not all workers are employees (see chapter 5). The scope of legislation may also be limited (or widened) by the way in which the courts have interpreted specific provisions. For example, the application of the Transfer of Undertakings (Protection of Employment) Regulations 1981 appears to be wider than some, perhaps most, people contemplated (see chapter 20).

Rights, duties and legal tests

Next there is the question of the nature of the rights conferred and/or duties imposed and the legal tests to be applied in operating the legislation. For example, in unfair dismissal law these are the establishing of one of the statutory reasons for dismissal and a test of reasonableness (see chapter 16). In race and sex discrimination law the tests are, first, that discrimination (as defined by the Acts) has occurred, and second that it is unlawful because it falls within a list of acts and omissions which the legislation declares unlawful. An important part of the assessment of any piece of legislation is likely to be an examination of how the legislation's tests are formulated and being applied (the unfair dismissal tests have attracted a considerable amount of criticism: see below).

Remedies and penalties

Another major criterion is the efficacy of the remedies. This may revolve around the question of whether financial compensation itself is an adequate remedy or whether the amounts of compensation awarded in practice appear adequate to compensate for the wrong suffered. Again taking unfair dismissal as an example, there has been criticism of the low incidence of reinstatement and re-engagement as remedies, and also of the level of compensation (particularly in relation to the position over a period of years and the effect of inflation). Where the law is in the form of a criminal regime, the nature and extent of the penalties will be an important factor in assessing the legislation.

Procedure and other aspects of the system

There may be procedural obstacles to people commencing complaints or succeeding with them, or both. Formality, complexity, cost and lack of knowledge are among the factors here. The *locus* of the burden of proof may be an important factor in the way any particular legislative scheme operates.

THE IMPACT OF UNFAIR DISMISSAL LAW

Nothing in the long title of ERA or of any of the earlier Acts containing the unfair dismissal scheme helps to explain its objectives. Thus it is not clear from the legislation whether the objective is employment protection, taken literally to mean that the unfairly dismissed employee should be kept in employment, or merely to provide financial compensation. However, the priority given to reinstatement and re-engagement in the legislation itself can be taken as supporting the former view.[10] Thus, a major measure of effectiveness would be the percentage of successful applicants obtaining reinstatement or re-engagement (see below). The success rate is about one-third and the number of applications about 30,000, arguably a small proportion of the total number of dismissals in a year.[11]

The Donovan Report 1968 gives further insights into the purposes of unfair dismissal law.[12] Not only does it reaffirm the employment protection function of unfair dismissal law but also it makes clear that an aim is to avoid disputes over dismissals. There was a widespread concern about strikes at that time: dismissals were a source and dismissals of union representatives particularly so since the action was regarded as being taken against the union rather than the individual. Proper procedures were felt to be a safeguard.

Issues relating to the scope of unfair dismissal law have been quite prominent as governments have first widened and then narrowed its scope. The principal exclusions are workers who are not employees and employees with less than two years' continuous employment. The latter category is thought to account for 25 per cent of full-time employees and 50 per cent of employees working part-time.[13] The former category is noted as increasing in size in recent years with the growth in atypical employment relationships (eg, use of agency staff, contractors etc). On the other hand, where dismissal is for one of a number of specified reasons, such as pregnancy, there is no qualifying period. However, it remains the position that a substantial number of workers are excluded from the protection of unfair dismissal law.

As with scope, the legal tests in the unfair dismissal scheme have also attracted a considerable amount of criticism.[14] It is noted that there is no great burden on the employer in establishing one of the statutory reasons (see *UCATT v Brain*) and that all that is required is for the employer to demonstrate the subjective beliefs which led him to dismiss *(Abernethy v Mott, Hay & Anderson)*. Moreover, apart from the reasons specified in the statute an employer may show 'some other substantial reason'.[15] This concept has been interpreted quite widely by the courts, in particular to include business reorganizations and unilateral contractual change by employers (see *Hollister v National Farmers' Union* and *RS Components Ltd v Irwin* respectively).

Similarly, the second stage of the unfair dismissal test is criticized.[16] Critics argue that the courts should set higher standards here rather than being constrained by having to relate the reasonableness test to current management practice. A dismissal can fail the reasonableness test only if no reasonable employer would have dismissed in those circumstances: this is held to be too low a standard.[17] On the other hand, it is quite clear that the ACAS code of practice on discipline and the operation of the reasonableness test have led to improvements in employer procedures and practice.

As regards remedies, it is clear that very few – approximately 2 per cent – of successful applicants obtain reinstatement or re-engagement.[18] Compensation levels have been quite modest throughout the legislation's history, there has been erosion due to inflation and there is a statutory limit.[19] The argument is that the sums do not fully reflect the cost of losing a job, particularly if the labour market is slack.

Strikes generally are not seen to be a problem so the objective of reducing strikes over dismissals is of no great relevance at the present time. The assessment of unfair dismissal law, therefore, has focused upon the balance between adequate safeguards for the employee on the one hand and sufficient management flexibility on the other. The view of the business interest is that the scheme is too burdensome for employers, particularly small employers. It increases costs, and so reduces employment, while maintaining inefficient workers in employment. The employee interest declares that the law does not prevent dismissal, encourages more careful recruitment and selection and leads to better procedures. Moreover, the scheme, by focusing on procedure rather than substance, and individual rather than collective, has strengthened rather than weakened managerial authority in this area.

Overall, the limitations of scope, legal tests and remedies have to be acknowledged. Nevertheless, there is clear benefit to employees through better procedures and the deterrent effect of the law. Finally, however, there are three points about the system. The cost argument in respect of the industrial tribunal system is noted in chapter 26. The next point relates to representation. There is an imbalance here in favour of employers: in a quarter of cases an applicant is representing himself or herself against an employer with a representative, and in half of these cases that representative is a lawyer.[20] Lastly, and against that, it should be noted that the burden of proof of reason for dismissal lies with the employer.

THE IMPACT OF DISCRIMINATION LAW

For the purpose of the analysis here the focus will be sex discrimination and equal pay. In many areas, however, the analysis will be equally relevant to race discrimination. Discrimination on the ground of disability is covered by a relatively new scheme: it is much too early to assess this but the old scheme based on the Disabled Persons (Employment) Act of 1944 was widely regarded as ineffective.

The objectives of sex discrimination law are to make certain types of discrimination on the ground of sex or marriage unlawful and to end discrimination as regards terms and conditions of employment. The long title of the SDA also confirms the objective of establishing a Commission to end discrimination and promote equality of opportunity.

As regards objective evidence, it seems that there is a higher female partic-ipation in the labour force and that the gap in male/female pay has narrowed.[21] However, although women's pay increased relative to men's pay in the early years of the legislation it has not continued to so increase. On participation, it is held that the additional involvement is mostly part-time work in traditionally female areas of employment, and that segregation still exists.[22]

In terms of the direct effect of the legislation itself, major criticisms surround the difficulties of use. There have been relatively few cases and a low success rate despite evidence of widespread discrimination, particularly in the form of sexual harassment. Because of the limited direct effect, it may be that the indirect, deterrent effect is also limited.

As regards the scope of the legislation there is little criticism. It applies to employment, which is defined more widely than employee.[23] No qualifying employment is required and there are very few exceptions.

However, the legal tests have been heavily criticized, to the extent that some would see the legislation's design as fundamentally flawed.[24] First, there is criticism because the legislation seeks to prevent discrimination rather than to encourage positive action. It focuses on fair procedures and equal treatment rather than equal outcomes. Secondly, it focuses upon the individual rather than tackling structural discrimination, which limits its impact. The concept of discrimination is criticized because it involves a comparison with male standards. This has posed problems in areas such as pregnancy and sexual harassment. It also means that female-dominated areas (such as part-time work generally) have been neglected until recently because comparisons with men are largely absent.

On the other hand, the concept of discrimination covers both direct and indirect discrimination, as well as victimization (see chapter 6). The range of acts and omissions made unlawful if they amount to discrimination is also wide, encompassing all aspects of the personnel management process. A difficulty, however, has been the interpretation of the legal tests by the courts, in particular the concept of indirect discrimination in the SDA and the material factor defence in the EqPA.[25]

The need for a 'requirement or condition' in the SDA has been interpreted to mean an absolute requirement, so that an employer expressing a preference will not be indirectly discriminating (*Perera v Civil Service Commission;* but note *Falkirk Council v Whyte* and the wider EU definition (see pages 109–10)). More significant, however, is the width allowed by the courts in their interpretation of the justification defence (see *Hampson v Department of Education and Science*). This allows economic grounds to be argued and ultimately for courts to weigh in the balance the discrimination and the business interest. Similarly under the EqPA, the 'material factor' defence has been interpreted to admit market forces as a factor justifying discriminatory pay (*Rainey v Greater Glasgow Health Board*; and *Enderby v Frenchay Health Authority*).[26] Overall, the courts have been criticized as unsympathetic to the legislation, at least partly because of a common law tradition of literal interpretation of law and an aversion to construing law in the light of social policy.[27]

As regards remedies, the legislation is criticized for the absence of powers of order or injunction in complaints made by individuals. Until recently, there was also a statutory cap on compensation and no compensation at all where indirect discrimination was unintentional. One commentator called the awards in discrimination cases 'derisory'.[28]

A major stream of criticism relates to usage. The legislation is seen as unnecessarily complex with a particularly slow and difficult procedure in equal value cases under the EqPA (although the expert report is no longer a requirement if a case proceeds). Moreover, the initial burden of proof lies upon the complainant but evidence of discrimination is difficult to obtain. Tribunals may draw inferences where discrimination is established *prima facie* and the employer provides no explanation *(King v Great Britain–China Centre)*.

Overall, there is so much and such varied criticism of discrimination law that it is easy to lose sight of any gains whatsoever. Clearly the objective facts support the view that some progress has been made, and decisions such as *Webb v EMO Air Cargo (UK) Ltd* and *King v Great Britain–China Centre* are without doubt helpful to complainants. European Union law generally has strengthened the legislative scheme for complainants (see chapter 27).

THE IMPACT OF INDIVIDUAL AND COLLECTIVE EMPLOYMENT RIGHTS

Individual rights

The key individual rights of protection against unfair dismissal and unlawful discrimination have already been discussed but in addition to these the law of employment contains a panoply of other individual rights. Some, such as those relating to maternity, are important in their day-to-day significance whereas others, such as the right to time off for public duties, are of relatively minor practical importance. The aim here is to focus on two important areas – maternity and redundancy – and to give a brief assessment of each.

Maternity

The principal maternity rights are maternity leave, maternity pay, protection against dismissal and protection against unlawful discrimination on the grounds of sex or marriage (see chapter 13).[29] There is no continuous employment qualification under sex discrimination law and neither is there the usual two-year qualification under the law of unfair dismissal if the dismissal is on maternity grounds.[30] Similarly, there is no continuous employment requirement for entitlement to basic maternity leave. However, extended maternity leave is not available to those with less than two years' continuous employment and SMP is not available to those with less than 26 weeks' continuous employment. In general, there are only limited exclusions although maternity leave rights are restricted to employees. SMP applies to a slightly wider category but excludes those earning less than the lower NI threshold. Protection against maternity dismissal applies to employees but protection against unlawful discrimination is covered by the wider definition of employment in the SDA (see chapter 6).[31]

In terms of scope, therefore, the maternity provisions have a wide application, but what of the rights conferred and the legal tests used to determine entitlement? As noted, the provisions relating to unfair dismissal and sex discrimination have been the subject of criticism (see above); so too have the rights to maternity leave and pay. The principal argument about maternity leave is whether basic leave of 14 weeks (the leave which has no continuous employment requirement) is sufficient. Unfavourable comparisons with other EU countries are sometimes drawn. Another major argument surrounds the complex information and notification provisions which have sometimes been the cause of women losing their right to maternity leave altogether. A further strand of criticism draws attention to the absence of statutory paternity and parental leave. As regards extended maternity leave, an important issue is the effect of such leave on terms and conditions of employment. The case law suggests that much depends on the contractual position.

Maternity pay is criticized particularly for its level – six weeks at 90 per cent of earnings and a further 12 weeks at a relatively low flat rate[32] – but also because of its duration. Critics would say it should be paid for a longer period. In any case, its 18-week duration sits uncomfortably with the 14-week maternity leave period to which many women will be limited.[33]

Overall, the maternity provisions can be seen as having widespread application and offering a range of important rights and protection. The major weakness is probably the level of SMP, although the complexity of the maternity leave and pay provisions is also an important consideration.

Redundancy

Individual redundancy rights comprise a right to a redundancy payment, a right to time off with pay to search for another job or arrange retraining for future employment and the right not to be unfairly dismissed.[34] There are also collective consultation rights (discussed under collective rights, below).[35] The three individual rights are all restricted to those with two years' qualifying employment except where the selection for redundancy was on a ground where the two-year rule does not apply (eg, maternity). Where selection is on the ground of sex or marriage, it will fall under the SDA, for which there is no qualifying period. With the exception of the SDA, the other protection is limited to employees. Considering this and the qualifying period, it is clear that there are significant exclusions from redundancy rights.

The test for redundancy (in the absence of a closure) is that the employer wants fewer employees to do 'work of a particular kind'.[36] The concept causes some difficulty in that the legislation does not make clear whether it relates to the work actually being performed or the work that could lawfully be required under the contract (see chapter 17). Either way, some might criticize the narrowness of the definition because it excludes reorganizations if they do not result in fewer employees being required. Similarly it excludes changes in terms and conditions where there is no diminution in numbers. The definition may be contrasted with the wider EU-determined definition in the provisions relating to consultation with union and employee representatives (see below). On the other hand, non-redundancy changes will still be caught by the law of unfair dismissal, subject to the employee's eligibility, if an actual or constructive dismissal occurs, and voluntary redundancy will still fall within the statutory definition providing that there is a dismissal.

The actual rights conferred, however, are rather limited when viewed from the employee's perspective. Paid time off is for a maximum of two days and the maximum statutory redundancy payment is quite modest. However, a small business might find such payments difficult to finance.[37]

The unfair dismissal protection relating to redundancy is subject to some of the more general criticism levelled at the law of unfair dismissal (see above) but also attracts the specific complaint that it legitimizes redundancy by making it a fair reason for dismissal.[38] Moreover, the case law (eg, *Moon v Homeworthy Furniture*) makes it clear that the courts are required to judge whether the reason is in fact redundancy but must not judge whether redundancy is an appropriate management decision in response to the situation facing the employer. This is a matter of managerial policy.

As with dismissals on other grounds, it may be that employers' procedures have improved as a result of the law of unfair dismissal.[39] Moreover, while the maximum redundancy payment is modest, the statutory payments system has provided a platform for widespread and substantial extra-statutory additions.[40] It is this feature and the legitimization of redundancy which prompt the criticism that the law in this area actually encourages redundancy, limiting the protective role to an insistence on proper procedure and a degree of financial compensation. The focus becomes the way redundancy is handled and/or compensated rather than whether the redundancy should occur at all. In addition, the individual emphasis of the law perhaps invites an individual rather than a collective response, again shifting the focus from any realistic opposition to the redundancy itself. Overall, however, this is a matter for public policy. Employers need to be able to respond to external change, so the issue becomes whether redundancy is or is not in the public interest. This issue is explored briefly in chapter 28.

Finally, it should be noted that there are special provisions in cases where there is a transfer of an undertaking (see chapter 20), so that redundancy does not occur simply by means of the transfer itself. These provisions are in the TUPE Regulations 1981 and have proved to have an application much wider than some, perhaps most, people expected. Although subject to some of the general criticism which may be levelled at unfair dismissal law, the most significant impact of the TUPE Regulations is probably the range of situations to which they have been found to apply, bearing in mind that any dismissal in connection with a transfer is automatically unfair unless it can be shown to be for an economic, technical or organizational reason.[41]

Collective rights

The principal collective rights can be seen as the right of association, the recognition of unions by employers, the rights of union officials and members to protection, facilities, information and consultation and the right to take industrial action.

There is protection against discrimination on union grounds at the recruitment and selection stage, during employment and in respect of dismissal, and in dismissal cases the dismissal will be automatically unfair and subject to enhanced compensation if union grounds are established. The two-year qualifying period does not apply. Employment law, therefore, does provide for freedom of association. Similar protection is given to the non-unionist.

It is in respect of recognition by employers that the collective rights of employees are weakest (see chapter 22). There is no requirement for an employer to recognize a trades union, not even in the extreme case of 100 per cent union membership and 100 per cent in favour of recognition. As noted earlier, the provisions in this area were repealed in 1980 (though the present government is committed to new legislation in this area).[42] However, where employers do decide to recognize trades unions, collectively bargained terms may become incorporated into individual contracts of employment notwithstanding that the collective agreement itself is not legally enforceable (see chapter 8). Collective bargaining is further supported by rights given to officials of recognized unions, for example in respect of bargaining information and redundancy consultation. Union officials, however, have no general right to information or consultation, nor is there a right to facilities.

A principal concern of employment law since 1979 has been to curb strike activity. As noted in chapter 23, there is no positive right to strike but rather a system under which there is immunity from liability in tort (see chapter 1) if unlawful industrial action is taken. The law has restricted what is lawful industrial action in terms of both its purpose and procedure. The position now is that it is much more difficult for trades unions to organize lawful industrial action and there can be financial consequences for them if action is not lawful. There is very little protection for employees dismissed while taking part in industrial action.

Overall, the focus of employment law has shifted from the collective to the individual. With unions losing membership and power, and with an individual rights emphasis apparent in EU-determined employment law, this is perhaps to be expected. With union membership declining throughout the whole period of 1979–96 and currently around 33 per cent, unions are less capable of being an effective channel for employment law rights. The collective rights picture, therefore, is that individuals are protected to a degree in terms of their trades union membership and activity. Moreover, recognized unions are given rights through their officials, eg the right to be consulted in a redundancy.[43] However, on the key issues of collective bargaining and industrial action, the law is either silent or restrictive. It will not force an employer to recognize a union and it will not allow unions to use industrial action except within defined limits. The public policy question (see chapter 28) is whether the balance between employers and unions is appropriate.

NOTES

1 On criticism of the concept of the contract of employment itself and on the tensions between contract and statute in employment law, see Davies, P and Freedland, M, *Kahn-Freund's Labour and the Law*, (3rd edition), Stevens, 1983, Chapter 1.

2 Although the terms 'contract of service' and 'contract of employment' are often used interchangeably, the definition of the latter in ERA is 'a contract of service or apprenticeship' (s 230(2)).

3 Employers and Workmen Act 1875 and Conspiracy and Protection of Property Act 1875.

4 Davies & Freedland, *op cit.*

5 *Loc cit.*

6 On the rationale here, influenced by the Swedish labour market model, see Lewis, P, *Twenty Years of Redundancy Payments in Great Britain.*

7 For more detail of the various changes, see Miller, K and Steele, M (IRJ) and Mackie, K in Towers, B (ed.), *Handbook of Industrial Relations Practice.*

8 Since the breadth of the ECJ's concept of a transfer of an undertaking became clear in 1993 this area of law has probably seen a significant improvement in individual employee rights (on the law itself, see chapter 20; on the policy issues, see chapter 28).

9 Although it should be noted that enhanced compensation is also payable where the dismissal is on the ground of union membership or activity.

10 ERA, s 112.

11 See Dickens *et al, Dismissed* (Blackwell, 1985), page 31, where the estimate is that only 12 per cent of dismissal cases result in industrial tribunal applications.

12 *Report of a Royal Commission on Trade Unions and Employers' Associations* (Chairman Lord Donovan, London, HMSO, Cmnd 3623, 1968), chapter X.

13 Hakim, C, 'Employment Rights: A Comparison of Part-Time and Full-Time Employees', (1989) 18 *Industrial Law Journal* 69–83 at 74.

14 ERA, s 98; see Collins, H, *Justice in Dismissal.*

15 ERA, s 98(1)(b).

16 See, for example, Hepple, BA, 'The Fall and Rise of Unfair Dismissal', in McCarthy (Lord) (ed), *Legal Intervention in Industrial Relations* (Blackwell, 1992), pages 79–102, particularly pages 84–85.

17 Collins (note 14 above). The band of reasonable responses test is set out in *British Leyland v Swift* and more fully in *Iceland Frozen Foods v Jones.*

18 See the figures published annually in the *Employment Gazette* (London, Department for Education and Employment).

19 Currently £6,600 for the basic award and £12,000 for the compensatory award, so £18,600 for the general unfair dismissal case. These awards are explained on pages 330–32. On this subject, see McMullen, J, 'Enforcing Contracts of Employment', (1995) 24 *Industrial Law Journal* 353–362.

20 See Hepple (note 16 above) at page 81.

21 See Dickens, in McCarthy (Lord) (ed), *Legal Intervention in Industrial Relations* (Blackwell, 1992), pages 103–146, particularly pages 106–108.

22 Ibid.

23 SDA, s 82(1).

24 Dickens (note 21 above) at page 125.

25 SDA, s 1(1)(b) and EqPA, s 1(3).

26 EqPA, s 1(3).

27 Dickens (note 21 above) at page 120.

28 Hepple, BA, 'Judging Equal Rights', (1983) 36 *Current Legal Problems* 71–90 at 73.

29 Other maternity rights are time off with pay for ante-natal purposes and specific health and safety provisions. For a detailed and up-to-date account of the employment law aspects of maternity, see Lewis, P, *Employment in Practice – Maternity* (London, Gee Publishing Ltd, 1996).

30 ERA, s 99.

31 SDA, s 82(1).

32 £57.70 from 6 April 1998.

33 This anomaly arises because the 18-week period originally applied in the context of what is now known as extended maternity leave. The basic maternity leave of 14 weeks was superimposed on the system in order to comply with the EU Pregnant Workers' Directive (see chapter 13).

34 ERA, ss 135, 52 and 94 respectively.

35 TULR(C)A, s 188. On the management of redundancy and the legal framework within which it takes place see Lewis, P, *The Successful Management of Redundancy* (Oxford, Blackwell, 1993).

36 ERA, s 139.

37 The maximum statutory redundancy payment is currently £6,600. On the background to and working of the statutory redundancy payment scheme, see Lewis, P, *Twenty Years of Statutory Redundancy Payments in Great Britain* (Nottingham, Leeds/Nottingham Occasional Papers in Industrial Relations, No 8, 1985).

38 ERA, s 98(1) and (2)(c).

39 Evidence can be found, eg in Daniel, WW and Stilgoe, E, *The Impact of Employment Protection Laws* (London, Policy Studies Institute, 1978), page 49.

40 See Lewis (note 35 above).

41 TUPE Regulations, reg 8(1) and (2).

42 Employment Act 1980, s 19.

43 This right may be given instead to an employee representative (see chapter 18).

The Functioning of the Industrial Tribunal System

The constitution and jurisdiction of industrial tribunals was dealt with in chapter 3 and their procedure in chapter 4. The present chapter considers how the industrial tribunal system functions in practice. Since most types of employment dispute are within the jurisdiction of industrial tribunals it is clear that such tribunals are central to the administration of employment law.

THE ORIGINS AND DEVELOPMENT OF INDUSTRIAL TRIBUNALS

Origins of the industrial tribunal

The original jurisdiction of industrial tribunals lay in the Industrial Training Act 1964.[1] This Act provided for a training board for each industry, with powers to levy firms within that industry in order to generate funds for training purposes. Firms had a right of appeal against the amount of the levy and against their industrial classification. The latter might be relevant where a firm lay at the boundary of two industries which had training boards with different rates of levy. Industrial tribunals were established as bodies to hear these appeals.

Industrial tribunals therefore started life as administrative tribunals. That is, they dealt with disputes arising out of public administration. They were not established to hear private, employer/employee disputes. Their earliest employer/employee jurisdictions were redundancy payments and statements of employment particulars, laying the foundations for their development as employment tribunals.[2]

Unfair dismissal and later jurisdictions

Since 1972, the major jurisdiction of industrial tribunals has been unfair dismissal.[3] Usually over half the case load, sometimes this has accounted for three-quarters of the tribunals' work.[4] The development of the tribunals' role continued in the 1970s with the addition of various other jurisdictions including sex and race discrimination, equal pay and a number of specific employment protection issues such as time off for public duties (see pages 37–40 for a full list of the jurisdictions). Other major developments have been the addition of disputes over wage deductions[5] and then, qualitatively different, disputes between individuals and their unions (eg, over expulsion), both in the 1980s. Finally in 1994, came the extension of jurisdiction to certain contractual matters[6] and in the Disability Discrimination Act 1995 a major role in respect of a new statutory scheme to outlaw disability discrimination.

The development of the system

It is clear that the industrial tribunals soon changed their character from administrative tribunals to bodies concerned with the resolution of private disputes. It is also clear that they have become part of the fabric of the employment law system and that they are the body on which any new employment jurisdiction is likely to be conferred. By 1994–95, industrial tribunals received approximately 88,000 applications and in recent years the number has been growing rapidly. By 1993–94, the cost of running the system was £25 million.[7]

Against the above background, it is not surprising that the government sought to review the functioning of the system. This it did by means of a consultative paper (the 1994 Green Paper) in December 1994.[8] The Green Paper indicated an unprecedented increase in the number of applications to the industrial tribunals from approximately 35,000 in 1989–90 to 72,000 in 1993–94. Consequently, the system was costing more to run. Although during this period there had been cost savings, total costs were increasing all the time and had risen by 60 per cent.[9] Reviewing likely future developments, the Green Paper expected a 15–30 per cent further increase in tribunal case load between 1993–94 and 1998–99.[10]

The Green Paper puts forward a number of reasons for the increase in applications to industrial tribunals.[11] New jurisdictions have already been mentioned, although the increasing availability of tribunals to part-time employees should also be considered. Unemployment is also seen as generating tribunal applications (eg, because of an increase in redundancy and a greater willingness to challenge job loss in a slack labour market). The growth in the number of small enterprises may also be a factor. This reflects small business creation and also the emphasis on privatization and contracting-out to small, specialist firms. Smaller firms tend to have a higher incidence of industrial tribunal applications. The size of the total employed workforce has in any case grown.

The effect of the above developments is that the system is not only increasingly expensive but also below its performance standards. Two have been set:

- 80 per cent of cases should come to a first hearing within 26 weeks of the application.
- 80 per cent of decisions should be promulgated (ie, published and sent to the parties) within five weeks of the hearing.

Actual performance in England and Wales in 1993–94 was substantially below this for the first hearing (54 per cent) and marginally below for promulgation (79 per cent). The figure for Scotland were 80 per cent and 52 per cent.[12] Moreover, the figures were worsening with the exception of promulgation time in England and Wales. However, as noted, cost savings have been achieved. Full-time chairmen now sit more (174.3 days in 1993–94) and the throughput of cases per member of support staff has increased.[13]

The role of the Council on Tribunals

It should be noted that industrial tribunals are but one type of statutory tribunal. There are a number of others, and, like these, industrial tribunals are under the general supervision of the Council on Tribunals by virtue of the Tribunals and Inquiries Act 1992.[14]

THE DISTINCTIVE FEATURES OF TRIBUNALS

Identifying what is distinctive about tribunals

A useful starting point is the Report of the Franks Committee on Administrative Tribunals of 1957.[15] Further evidence as to what is seen as distinctive about tribunals can be obtained from the Donovan Report on Trades Unions and Employers' Associations of 1968, which saw industrial tribunals as emerging labour tribunals.[16] These sources suggest that what is distinctive about tribunals is:

- accessibility;
- cheapness;
- speed;
- informality; and
- expertise.

The way these features have been built into the industrial tribunal system is considered below.

Accessibility

Accessibility in this context can perhaps be taken as meaning that an employee who genuinely believes that his or her rights have been infringed and has reasonable grounds for this belief should not face undue obstacles in pursuing an application. The most obvious obstacles would be cost, location and burden of administrative procedure, assuming that the person knew their rights had been infringed and knew where to seek a remedy. In order to make industrial tribunals accessible, the originating application form is kept brief and relatively simple and there is no requirement for legal representation at any stage of the procedure. The normal costs rule under which the loser pays the victor's cost is not applied so removing a possible deterrent for the applicant. Application forms are available in local job centres and hearings are held in most major cities. Publicity materials relating to employment rights are widely distributed locally in, for example, advice centres and libraries.

Cheapness

The principal factors at work here are the absence of any formal requirement for legal advice or representation and the absence of any fee for making the application. Expenses are paid to applicants attending a hearing in order to contribute to travel costs and any lost wages or salary. Again, the absence of the normal costs rules means that an unsuccessful applicant should not suffer financially as a result of making an application.

Another aspect of cheapness in the context of tribunals, however, is the cheapness of disposal of disputes when compared with the courts. The cost of the system will be less than that of the courts because the daily cost of a tribunal will be less than that of a court and because tribunal cases are of relatively short duration.

Speed

The intention is that tribunals offer a speedier resolution of disputes than a court. Hence for example, respondents are given only 14 days in which to reply to the originating application. Implicit in this idea is the notion that tribunals offer a more 'rule of thumb' type of justice when compared with the more thorough and consistent approach in the courts. The policy issue here is the trade-off between speed and economy on the one hand and consistency and fine tuning on the other. Finality is also a feature; the right to appeal is limited to questions of law to encourage final resolution of cases at the level of the tribunal. The Green Paper reveals that in 1993–94, 1.7 cases were completed at a hearing per session day.[17]

Informality

Franks specifically referred to freedom from technicality but the issue is perhaps wider than this. The physical setting of tribunals is designed to avoid the formality that characterizes the court. The rooms themselves do not carry the heavy atmosphere of courts, the tribunal members do not wear gowns or wigs and there is no requirement for advocacy to be carried out by lawyers. The tribunal regulations allow a tribunal to regulate its own procedure and mandate it 'so far as it appears appropriate, [to] seek to avoid formality in its proceedings'.[18]

Expertise

Expertise in the Franks sense means expert knowledge of a particular subject. The principal vehicles for achieving expertise in the matters within the jurisdiction of industrial tribunals are the use of lay members with industrial experience and the employment of full-time chairmen who therefore work exclusively in the employment law areas within the tribunal's jurisdiction. Lay members are appointed by the Secretary of State for Employment on the basis of their knowledge and experience of employment matters. Some, with particular experience of race relations issues, are deployed so that race discrimination cases have one lay member with such expertise. In sex discrimination cases, it is normal for one of the lay members to be a woman. Chairmen are appointed by the Lord Chancellor on the basis of their legal expertise and if not already specialists in employment law soon became so (because of a daily exposure to the subject in the case of full-time chairmen). However, it should be noted that the distinction between expertise in law does not fall clearly between lay members and chairmen. Many chairmen have been in practice and have some familiarity with employment matters while many lay members with experience as union officials or personnel managers have some legal expertise. Both lay members and chairmen receive expert materials to assist them in their roles and also undergo a certain amount of initial and continuing training.

Other distinctive features

The development of administrative tribunals accompanied the growth of legislation in the social welfare area. *Inter alia*, tribunals were thought to be better placed to take into account the social policy considerations on which legislation was based.[19] In contrast, the courts were constrained by rules of statutory interpretation which emphasized a literal approach to the construction of law. (In fact, since the decision in *Pepper v Hart* in 1993 extrinsic sources such as the record of Parliamentary debates may now be used in certain circumstances.) The use of lay members to perform a judicial role may be seen as part of the means of achieving this purposive approach. In industrial tribunals, however, the lay members also have other functions. First, the inclusion of people from both 'sides' of industry gives the tribunal a balance that helps secure a widespread acceptance of the system. Secondly, the fact that these people are appointed on the basis of their practical experience helps towards the objective of tempering legalism with industrial practice.

CRITICISM OF THE INDUSTRIAL TRIBUNALS

Overview

The Franks criteria provide an obvious basis upon which to assess the functioning of the industrial tribunals since these are the perceived advantages of tribunals over courts. It is probably true to say that the industrial tribunals have been criticized on all the criteria, but in particular their 'legalism', delays and cost. However, it should be noted that the assessment of industrial tribunals has been conducted on a more general basis than simply a comparison with the courts. The industrial tribunals would probably compare well with the courts on all the Franks criteria, but the assessment and consequent criticism now seems based on absolute (although not always well-defined) rather than relative standards. These include the standards of voluntary employment practice and standards set by the objectives of specific legislation (such as the re-employment of unfairly dismissed employees under the law of unfair dismissal). The criticism levelled at industrial tribunals is discussed below under the separate headings of Franks and some general conclusions are then drawn.[20] The perceived deficiencies of industrial tribunals have led some commentators to argue the superiority of arbitration over tribunals – this idea is explored later.

Informality and the question of legalism

This area is discussed prior to the others because it has a bearing on other criteria, notably accessibility, cost and speed. The starting point is the adversarial model of dispute resolution implicit in the industrial tribunal procedure regulations.[21] With this model disputants are required to organize and present their own cases in order to establish which of them is legally 'right'. This contrasts with the inquisitorial approach under which the initiative lies more with the court. An important effect of the adversarial approach is to emphasize the need for formal legal procedure in order to arrive at the facts. Without having parties on oath and subject to cross-examination, the facts are less likely to be obtained. This in turn emphasizes the need for a representative who is familiar with legal procedure and the relevant law. The adversarial approach thus encourages legal representation.[22]

So too does the law itself. Some areas are complex and in any case employment law is no less easy to interpret than law dealt with in the ordinary courts. It is not surprising that most parties are represented, that legal representation is the most common form and that industrial tribunals are more like courts than was intended. Furthermore, some of the key concepts in the statutes are quite imprecise, for example, the reasonableness test in the law of unfair dismissal, and in any case the fundamental employment relationship is a contract, subject to a complex body of principles in the wider law of contract. It is inevitable that interpretation will require legal knowledge and reasoning and that there is no simple, commonsense form of interpretation. It may be argued, therefore, that the issue is legal procedure rather than the pejorative 'legalism', which seems to imply excess.[23]

Figure 26.1 sets out the issue in a simplified, diagrammatic form.

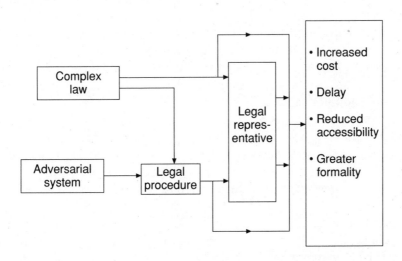

Figure 26.1   Industrial tribunals and legalism

What is clear is that much of what is presented above reflects the way industrial tribunals have been established and the nature of their jurisdictions. However, it is also clear that the effect is to reduce the possibilities of meeting the various Franks criteria. The need for legal representation has ensured that industrial tribunals behave like courts. Nevertheless, it should be noted that tribunal members do in practice ask questions of the parties (so that the inquisitorial role is not completely absent) and that chairmen often relax procedure in order to assist an applicant who is representing himself. Moreover, the atmosphere is usually quite informal. Ultimately, however, industrial tribunals are supposed to be institutions where the aggrieved employee can take his complaint and present it himself, but it is doubtful whether that could ever be a sound recommendation now.

Accessibility and cheapness

The issues of accessibility and cheapness need to be addressed in the context of what was said above about legal procedure and representation. In formal terms, representation is not required, but in practice it is highly desirable. It may be that an applicant will be represented without charge by a trades union or advice centre. However, where that is not possible or desirable and legal representation is sought, legal costs will be incurred. The Legal Advice and Assistance Scheme may be available to help an applicant complete the originating application form, but legal aid is not available. Only in certain race and sex discrimination cases will there be publicly funded legal representation. No financial recompense is available to respondents defending cases; hence the economics of the situation may encourage respondents to settle cases for relatively small sums rather than incur greater expense at an industrial tribunal hearing.

The criticism that there is insufficient advice and information for applicants, especially those who are representing themselves, is perhaps less justified than it was as both the system and the law itself become more widely known. In addition, a more user-friendly approach to publicity has made it easier to obtain information.

Against these arguments is the criticism from employers that the system is too accessible and that many meritless cases are pursued since there is no cost involved in pursuing them. Three devices exist to deal with this: the pre-hearing review, the costs rules and striking out. Under the first of these, a brief hearing is held to identify cases with no reasonable prospect of success. In such cases, a deposit of up to £150 can be required if the party is to continue. Secondly, the tribunal rules provide that costs can be awarded against a party in certain circumstances. Thirdly, an application can be struck out if it is not within the tribunal's jurisdiction. On all of the above, see chapter 4.

Overall, there has been an attempt to preserve the original ideal of an open system which could be freely used by applicants while protecting respondents from the cost and inconvenience of defending against meritless applications. Undoubtedly this has involved some shift in the balance between the competing interests of employers and employees but it would be difficult to argue that it has been a significant one.

Speed

As noted, the question of delays in the system is one of the issues taken up in the 1994 Green Paper.[24] In particular, attention has focused on the length of time between application and first hearing and the length of time between (final) hearing and promulgation. Undoubtedly the system has been groaning under the strain of rapidly increasing use but various measures have been proposed to alleviate the problem (see below).

It is perhaps surprising that the time between the initial application and promulgation has not been taken as a standard, since this is a measure of how long in total it takes to dispose of a case. Allowance would need to be made for delays caused by the parties, such as those caused by the unavailability of representatives or witnesses, but delays caused by the tribunal would be caught. In particular, this measure would show up delays caused by the need to adjourn cases part-heard because the length of time allotted to the case had been insufficient.

A final point about expedition of cases illustrates how the specific objectives of particular legislation may need to be considered in any assessment of the functioning of industrial tribunals. The primary remedy envisaged by the law of unfair dismissal is re-employment but in practice few successful unfair dismissal applicants seek this remedy. Some of the research suggests that this is because tribunals are reluctant to order re-employment; other research highlights the passage of time between dismissal and conclusion of the tribunal hearing and the adversarial nature of the relations between the parties during that period.[25] The tribunals' record in this area tends to invite a comparison with UK voluntary arbitration practice where the hearing is much sooner and the outcome is normally re-employment.[26]

Expertise

Criticisms under this head have focused on the seemingly small part played by the lay members in the proceedings. The chairman conducts the proceedings and the lay members ask questions at an appropriate point (normally after the cross-examination of the witness). However, each member of the tribunal has equal authority in arriving at the decision and there may be substantial discussion before a unanimous or majority decision is reached. Therefore, the dominant position of the chairman in the hearing may not be reflected when the tribunal retires to deliberate.

In the deliberations, the lay members are unlikely to be without some legal expertise just as the chairman is unlikely to be without some expertise in employment practice. All will be constrained, however, by the interpretative rules formulated in the higher courts. In this respect, the flexibility which may come from the practical experience of the lay members and their awareness of Parliament's purposes in enacting particular legislation may not easily be accommodated when reaching a decision. To some extent, therefore, the appeal mechanisms and the jurisprudence of the higher courts may stifle the expertise of the tribunal. A leading example put forward here is the reasonableness test of unfair dismissal where the tribunals are said to be norm-reflecting rather than norm-setting (see chapter 25).[27] This apart, it might be suggested that the lay members bring considerable practical experience to bear on tribunal proceedings.

General conclusions

It appears from the above analysis that the adversarial nature of industrial tribunal proceedings, the complexity of the law and the attendant need for legal representation are at the heart of the perceived deficiencies in the industrial tribunal system. They create cost, formality and delay and reduce accessibility. There are also, perhaps, concerns about whether the tribunals are to some extent less effective because they are inhibited by the rules laid down by the courts.

A further criticism of the industrial tribunals, however, relates to their orientation. This criticism can be seen as having two strands. First, it is said that, where tribunals have discretion, they generally exercise it to support managerial prerogative.[28] Secondly, it is argued that they embody the individualist approach of the common law and that this is unhelpful in certain types of case.[29] As regards the former, evidence is put forward concerning the formulation of the 'some other substantial reason' concept in the law of unfair dismissal. It is argued that tribunals have adopted an approach which leaves employers free to reorganize their business without any strong likelihood of being properly tested by unfair dismissal law.[30] As regards the latter strand, it is said that the individualist approach undermines legitimate collective rights in cases such as trades union dismissals and union discipline and is not appropriate where the individual complainant is bringing forward a grievance which relates to a group of people as perhaps under discrimination law.[31]

REFORM OF THE SYSTEM

The arbitral alternative

Critics of the industrial tribunal system have in some cases suggested that an arbitral alternative would be superior.[32] It has been argued that an arbitration-based system would offer a better prospect of meeting the Franks criteria discussed earlier. The evidence in support of the arbitration approach has been based primarily on the experience of voluntary arbitration in the UK and to a lesser extent on that of compulsory arbitration in the USA and the UK.

Among the perceived advantages of arbitration is the inquisitorial rather than adversarial approach which is accompanied by the objective of solving a problem rather than deciding who is 'right' in legal terms. The use of industrial relations specialists rather than lawyers is seen to be an advantage because such specialists can take into account the context in which the dispute has arisen when coming to their decision. Aside from questions of approach and constitution the practicalities of arbitration are also seen as advantageous: cheapness, informality and speed. The last-mentioned could be an important factor in making the use of re-employment more widespread in unfair dismissal cases.

Against all this there are some uncertainties. The evidence from the UK is based on the use of arbitration on a relatively small scale when compared with the scale necessary if it was to be used as the principal vehicle for resolving unfair dismissal complaints. Moreover, the UK experience is based upon the trades union organized sector where arbitration is a jointly agreed procedure. Such agreement is important in explaining both the willingness to use arbitration and the acceptability of its outcomes. The application of arbitration to the non-union sector, that is, employment covering the majority of UK employees, might be less straightforward. A further issue is the obvious lack of consistency when decisions are made in such an informal, context-related way. Furthermore, an attraction of arbitration is its finality, but this perhaps supposes no right of appeal.[33] A complicating factor here would be the existing body of interpretative case law. Nonetheless, according to a Parliamentary written answer in November 1995, the government intends to make binding, independent arbitration available as an alternative to a tribunal hearing (along with other changes) 'when a suitable legislative opportunity arises'.[34] The relative cheapness of an arbitration-based system seems likely to appeal to governments irrespective of their political complexion.

The 1994 Green Paper

Terms of reference, approach and principles

The aim of the government's enquiry was 'to review the operation of the industrial tribunals with a view to identifying any changes which would help them to cope with an increasing volume and complexity of cases with reduced delays, while containing demands on public expenditure'.[35] The government's approach was based upon the assumption that the system would continue to expand and that reform was needed in order to reduce delays. In financial terms, further efficiency savings were required in order to keep the total cost of the system under control.

The overriding non-financial principle of the review was a commitment to the original objectives of the system, namely informality, speed, cheapness, expertise and accessibility.[36] There was also a commitment to the tripartite nature of the system with lay members from both 'sides' of industry. However, some departure had been made from this with the introduction through TURERA of chairmen-only hearings in certain circumstances (see chapter 4) and the financial advantages of going further down this road as proposed in the Green Paper are fairly clear. However, the hostile reaction from both sides of industry seems to have led to the government abandoning this idea.

Possible areas of reform

The improvements proposed fall under four headings:

- greater in-house resolution of disputes;
- wider use of voluntary third-party conciliation and arbitration;
- improvements in industrial tribunal procedure; and
- better administrative support for industrial tribunals.

The purpose of resolving more complaints in-house is to reduce the case load of ACAS and the industrial tribunals. The approach is to encourage improvements in employment practice to reduce the number of disputes which arise and to strengthen in-house facilities for the resolution of disputes. The means by which the above may be achieved include the provision of better information and guidance to employers and the promotion of in-company procedures and compromise agreements.[37]

A number of changes to procedure were either put forward for consultation or proposed in the Green Paper. The government invited views on the idea of access to voluntary but binding arbitration as an alternative to a tribunal hearing. In addition, various detailed points were put forward about industrial tribunal procedure which were designed to increase speed and reduce delays. The suggestions included powers to determine or dismiss cases without a full hearing and a widening of the use of chairman-only hearings. Among the specific ideas were the requirement that employees pursue grievances with their employers before making applications to tribunals and the awarding of costs where an applicant has unreasonably refused a respondent's offer of compensation larger than the tribunal's award.

Finally, better administrative support for industrial tribunals was proposed. The possibility of more preparatory interlocutory work being done by administrative staff was raised. Possibly a legal officer, who would be cheaper than an industrial tribunal chairman, could be appointed to perform some of the work currently done by a chairman.

Employment Rights (Dispute Resolution) Act 1998

The government indicated in November 1995 that a large number of responses to the Green Paper had been received and that most of the proposals were widely supported. Where necessary there would be further consultation with interested parties. Legislation would be introduced. In fact, the Bill introduced was a private member's Bill

Independent binding arbitration will be available as an alternative to an industrial tribunal hearing and the rules for compromise agreements will be relaxed. The arbitration scheme will be limited to unfair dismissal with scope for later extension. The industrial tribunals are to be renamed 'employment tribunals' to reflect their modern role. Various procedural changes will be introduced to speed up the tribunal process. There will, however, be no statutory requirement for employees to attempt to resolve disputes in-house as a prerequisite of making a tribunal complaint although tribunals will have the power to reduce compensation where an appeal procedure was properly notified to an employee but not used, and conversely to increase compensation where the right to an appeal has been denied. Jurisdictions relating to the wrongful deduction of trades union political levies and subscriptions will be transferred to the tribunals.

NOTES

1   The jurisdiction is now in s 12 of the Industrial Training Act 1982 although there are now only two training boards in existence.
2   Currently found in ERA, Parts XI and I respectively. Other 'administrative' jurisdictions were also added, eg selective employment tax disputes (1967, under the Selective Employment Payments Act 1966) and appeals against health and safety notices (1974, under the HSWA).
3   Industrial Relations Act 1971, ss 22 and 106 (now ERA, ss 94 and 111).
4   Department of Employment statistics published annually in the *Employment Gazette* (various issues).
5   Wages Act 1986: the provisions are now in ERA, Part II.
6   The contract jurisdiction is found in s 3 of the Industrial Tribunals Act 1996 and the Industrial Tribunals Extension of Jurisdiction (England and Wales) Order (SI 1994/1623). There is a separate Order for Scotland.
7   There were approximately 72,000 applications in that year. See *Resolving Employment Rights Disputes: Options for Reform* (London, HMSO, Cm 2707, 1994), page 11.

8 Ibid.

9 The number of cases had risen by 150 per cent over the same period (Green Paper, page 11).

10 Green Paper, page 13. In fact, the predicted level of 88,000 applications in 1998–99 was reached in 1994–95.

11 Green Paper, pages 11–12 and 19.

12 Green Paper, page 14.

13 Green Paper, page 15.

14 Section 1 and Sched 1. The Council reports annually to Parliament. Every two years the Council holds a conference of tribunal presidents and chairman. The proceedings of the 1996 conference are described in 'Council on Tribunals Conference', (1996) 3 *Tribunals*, No 2, 16–17.

15 *Administrative Tribunals and Inquiries* (Report of a Committee, Chairman Lord Franks, London, HMSO, Cmnd 218, 1957); see particularly para 406. On access, see Lord Woolf, 'Tribunals – A Model for Access to Justice', (1995) 2 *Tribunals*, No 1, 1–2. On the role of lay members, see Vernon, S, 'The Role of Lay Members in the Tribunal System', (1995) 2 *Tribunals*, No 2, 5–8.

16 *Trades Unions and Employers' Associations* (Report of a Royal Commission, Chairman Lord Donovan, London, HMSO, Cmnd 3623, 1968), See chapter X. The Commission thought the jurisdiction of industrial tribunals should comprise 'all disputes arising between employers and employees' whether the source was the contract of employment or statute, providing in the latter case they arose out of the parties acting in their capacities as employer and employee (para 573).

17 Green Paper, page 15.

18 Industrial Tribunals (Constitution and Rules of Procedures) Regulations (SI 1993/2687), rules 13(1) (self-regulation) and 9(1) (formality).

19 Bell, K, *Tribunals in the Social Services* (London, Routledge & Kegan Paul, 1969).

20 There is now a considerable literature of criticism. See the Green Paper, page 4; *Industrial Tribunals* (Justice, 1987); Clark, J and Lewis, R, *Employment Rights, Industrial Tribunals and Arbitration: The Case for Alternative Dispute Resolution (Institute of Employment Rights*, 1993); Dickens and Cockburn, 'Dispute Settlement Institutions and the Courts', in Lewis, R (ed), *Labour Law in Great Britain* (Blackwell, 1986), chapter 19, pages 560–565; Dickens, Jones, Weekes and Hart, *Dismissed* (Blackwell, 1985), particularly chapter 7; Lewis, P, 'Industrial Tribunals and the Franks Criteria', (1982) 126 *Solicitors' Journal* 667–668; Munday, R, 'Tribunal Lore: Legalism and Industrial Tribunals', (1981) 10 *Industrial Law Journal* 146–159; McCarthy (Lord) (ed), *Legal Intervention in Industrial Relations* (Blackwell, 1992), chapter 7; and Lewis, P, 'Industrial Tribunals: Time to Reconsider?' (1982) 64 *Industrial Society* 36–37.

21 SI 1993/2687.

22 According to the research of Dickens, Jones, Weekes and Hart (note 20 above) at pages 88–93, representation conveys an advantage.

23 On the 'legalism' debate, see Munday (note 20 above).

24 Green Paper, pages 4, 14 and 15.

25 On the former, see Dickens, Jones, Weekes and Hart (note 20 above) at pages 111–122; on the latter see Lewis, P, 'An Analysis of Why Legislation Has Failed to Provide Employment Protection for Unfairly Dismissed Employees', (1981) 19 *British Journal of Industrial Relations* 316–326.

26 See pages 333–4; and Lewis, P, 'Industrial Tribunals: Time to Reconsider?' (1982) 64 *Industrial Society* 36–37.

27 Dickens and Cockburn (note 20 above) at page 565.

28 Ibid, page 560.

29 *Loc cit.*

30 Bowers, J and Clarke, A, 'Unfair Dismissal and Managerial Prerogative: A Study of "Other Substantial Reason" ', (1981) 10 *Industrial Law Journal* 34–44. See also Collins, *Justice in Dismissal*; Dickens, Jones, Weekes and Hart (note 20 above) at pages 97–103; and Anderman, in Lewis, R (ed), page 416.

31 Dickens and Cockburn (note 20 above) at page 560.

32 See Clarke and Lewis (note 20 above); Justice (note 20 above); Dickens, Jones, Weekes and Hart (note 20 above) at chapter 9; and Lewis, P, 'Industrial Tribunals: Time to Reconsider?' (1982) 64 *Industrial Society* 36–37.

33 The commercial arbitration system might perhaps be a model here. A right of appeal from arbitration to an industrial tribunal might be possible.

34 Written answer to a Parliamentary question from Paul Butler MP, 20 November 1995. See (1995) 534 *Industrial Relations Law Bulletin* 15. The new government seems similarly sympathetic to this idea.

35 Green Paper, page 4.

36 Ibid, pages 5 and 45.

37 Compromise agreements are defined in ERA, s 203 (see pages 55–6).

Employment Law and the European Union

The purpose of this chapter is to examine the relationship between UK employment law and that emanating from the EU. This relationship involves considering the EU not only as an originator of employment law but also as a major interpretative mechanism. In addition, there are important issues relating to the partial or non-implementation of EU law in Member States. The most fundamental issue of all, however, is that of the balance between domestic and EU employment law, but this is part of the wider debate about the sovereignty of Member States and the role of the EU itself.

The starting point is an examination of the developing concept of European employment law. The impact of EU law is then discussed under the headings of discrimination law, employment rights and health and safety at work. The chapter concludes with a brief analysis of the UK/EU employment law relationship.

THE CONCEPT OF EUROPEAN EMPLOYMENT LAW

Approaches to European employment law

Probably the most common approach among UK employment lawyers is to view EU law in terms of its effects on UK domestic law. The focus, therefore, tends to be upon what is necessary in order to comply with European law and what may happen if there is non-compliance or only partial compliance. The UK academic lawyer would go beyond this to analyze the mechanics of the relationship between EU and UK law, to assess the impact of the former upon the latter and to seek to explain various phenomena.

More recently, there has emerged the academic study of European employment law in its own right. This, perhaps, is a departure from the more traditional approaches to EU law which analyzed it within the context of international law more generally or alternatively within the framework of national employment law systems. Bercusson argues that European employment law is a distinct entity requiring its own unique framework of analysis.[1] He suggests a framework based on three specific qualities of EU employment law: its variety of legal strategies; its substance; and its structural pillars. Each of these is dealt with briefly below.

Legal strategies of EU employment law

The development of the EU has occurred against a background of differing economic and political situations. Consequently, the legal strategies adopted by the EU have varied. Bercusson identifies five types of strategies used by the European Union and its predecessors in relation to employment law:

- labour market intervention;
- labour market non-intervention;
- harmonization of laws;
- financial and constitutional strategies; and
- social dialogue.

Active labour market policy can be seen in the provisions of the Treaty of Paris 1951 (and its subsidiary legislation) which set up the European Coal and Steel Community. The aim here was to encourage and control adaptation to economic change. For example, provisions were made for special redundancy schemes in the steel, coal and shipbuilding industries with finance available from the Community. In contrast, a policy of non-intervention can be seen in the development of the common market from the Treaty of Rome 1957 until the adoption of social policy in the early 1970s. The aim was an economic one – to form a tariff-free union of States. Social policy was not an objective *per se*.

Once social objectives became accepted, harmonization became a major strategy. It had, however, already existed as a by-product of the economic objective of a common market, since there could not be a level playing field for competition if there were significant differences in labour costs among Member States by virtue of their employment law regimes. Another strategy developed by European policy-makers has been the use of financial and constitutional mechanisms in support of their objectives in the employment field. Thus, the European Social Fund has been used to finance training and related developments arising out of structural change or thought necessary to reduce disparities within the EU. A major constitutional strategy has been to transfer employment matters from a unanimous voting procedure in the Council of Ministers to a majority one (see chapter 2). This was at the root of the UK's (unsuccessful) objection to the Working Time Directive being based upon article 118A of the Treaty of Rome (permitting majority voting). Finally, the EU encourages dialogue between the 'social partners' (employers and unions) and EU legislation may be implemented, for example, by collective agreements between these parties.

The substance of EU employment law

It is clear that European employment law is not all-pervasive in terms of its subject matter. Neither in fact is domestic employment law: for example, it was noted in chapter 11 that it has very little to say about the level of pay of employees. However, the domestic law of employment is more varied than that of the EU – the latter has tended to focus upon particular areas. This, it is said, provides another distinctive feature.[2] Equality between men and women and health and safety at work have been foremost among the EU's concerns. There has also been a concern with the free movement of workers. Finally, a number of provisions may be aggregated under the heading employment standards: these relate to redundancy, transfers of undertakings and worker information and consultation rights.

The structural pillars of EU employment law

The third distinctive quality of European employment law is said to be its structural pillars.[3] These are first, that EU law is based upon a typology of individual employment relationships – temporary, part-time and so on – in contrast to the UK's concern with the issue of whether or not the worker is employed under a contract of employment. One argument here would be that the EU approach is related more closely to the type of relationships found in practice and is therefore less likely to exclude people from protection (as, for example, agency staff have sometimes been in the UK). The second structural pillar is the use of dialogue between the social partners and the role of collective agreements. Historically this had been a pillar of the UK employment situation – Kahn-Freund called it collective laissez faire (see chapter 25 on the development of employment law) – but such policies have not been pursued in the 1980s and 1990s because of a preference for unregulated labour markets.

THE EU AND HEALTH AND SAFETY AT WORK

The emphasis on health and safety in the EU's objectives

Because of changes introduced by the Single European Act 1986, health and safety has become an important area of European legislation. Two aspects of the SEA are of particular significance.

Article 118A

First, the introduction of article 118A into the Treaty of Rome gives health and safety a particular prominence in the objectives of the European Union. Article 118A states that particular attention shall be paid to encouraging improvements in the working environment as regards the health and safety of workers in order to harmonize conditions within the Union. To help achieve this, the qualified majority voting procedure introduced by the SEA can be used to adopt directives. This means that health and safety matters are less likely to get held up in the EU legislative machine since unanimity is no longer required. The vehicle of a 'framework' directive (see below) has been used to give effect to the objectives of article 118A.

Technical standards

The second aspect of the SEA that is particularly relevant to health and safety is article 100A. This allows the Council to adopt by a qualified majority, in co-operation with the European Parliament, measures to further the establishment and functioning of the internal market. While article 100A excludes matters of taxation, free movement of people and provisions relating to the rights and interests of employed people, it has been held to *include* technical standards and safety requirements for specific products.

In addition to developments arising out of the introduction of articles 100A and 118A which use the qualified majority voting procedure, there are health and safety provisions in the Charter of Fundamental Social Rights (the 'Social Charter': see chapter 2) and in the EU's environmental protection programme.

The EU's approach to health and safety at work

The EU has formulated separate action programmes for health and safety at work. The Commission's third action programme, agreed in 1988, focused upon safety and ergonomics (including the high-risk sectors of construction, agriculture and shipping) and health and hygiene (including carcinogens, biological agents and noise). Particular stress has been laid upon information and training, especially in relation to work with chemicals. Some initiatives were targeted at small and medium-sized enterprises and at developing a dialogue between employers' and workers' organizations.

The approach of the EU to health and safety at work contrasts with that of the HSWA. The latter adopted an approach based upon the idea of broad, generally applicable duties (see chapter 14) while the EU legislation tends to set out the various obligations in considerable detail. The result is that the HSWA now provides an umbrella for numerous sets of EU-inspired regulations. An important feature of the EU approach has been the emphasis on health and safety management, and in particular upon the risk assessment as a basic management tool. Risk assessments have now become a major requirement under the UK law (see chapter 14).

The EU's fourth action programme covers the years 1994–2000. The emphasis is somewhat different from that of the previous period, where there was a strong legislative impetus. The emphasis for 1994–2000 reflects the EU's increasing concern to create jobs and be competitive on the wider world stage. Thus, this period will see:

- consolidation of legislation and implementation by all Member States;
- an evaluation of legislation already implemented;
- attempts to achieve consistency of enforcement;
- an awareness of the impact on small firms; and
- a thrust towards investigation and guidance rather than legislation.[4]

The EU's impact on health and safety at work in the UK

Earlier EU initiatives

A large number of EU health and safety initiatives were connected with the formation of the Single European Market in 1992, but by the late 1980s there had already been a considerable amount of significant EU legislation. The results of this in the UK were important sets of regulations governing, among other things:

- the control of substances hazardous to health;
- electricity;
- noise; and
- pressure systems.

Developments associated with the formation of the Single Market

As noted earlier, the SEA provided an impetus for the development of health and safety legislation through the process of qualified majority voting. The result has been the adoption of a broad, framework directive and of numerous specific directives. The 'framework' directive adopted in 1989 can be seen as an EU equivalent of the HSWA.[5] It lays down broad duties akin to those contained in s 2 of the HSWA and embodies the principle (found in British law, in, for example, the COSHH and Noise Regulations) that the risks inherent in work activities should be assessed, and appropriate control (including preventive) measures introduced. The directive has been given effect in Great Britain through the Management of Health and Safety at Work Regulations 1992 and an approved code of practice (see chapter 14).

Some of the more important specific directives are mentioned below:

- workplace health and safety: this directive is given effect through the Workplace (Health, Safety and Welfare) Regulations 1992 and an approved code of practice.
- use of work equipment: this directive is given effect through the Provision and Use of Work Equipment Regulations 1992, which are accompanied by guidance.
- use of personal, protective equipment (PPE): this directive is given effect through the Personal Protective Equipment at Work Regulations 1992 and accompanying guidance.
- manual handling of loads: this directive is given effect through the Manual Handling Operations Regulations 1992 and accompanying guidance.
- display screen equipment: this directive is given effect through the Health and Safety (Display Screen Equipment) Regulations 1992 and accompanying guidance.
- temporary workers: this directive is given effect through the Management Regulations.
- protection of pregnant women at work: this directive deals with a number of employment issues, such as maternity leave, but also contains health and safety provisions. A duty is placed upon employers to assess the risks to the health and safety of pregnant women and to take health and safety measures in the light of the assessment. This requirement is given effect through amendments made to the Management Regulations.
- health and safety on temporary or mobile construction sites: this directive has given rise to an important set of new regulations, the Construction (Design and Management) Regulations.
- other directives cover safety signs at the workplace, the protection of young people at work and the organization of working time.

Assessing the impact

Historically the UK approach to health and safety was a piecemeal one because legislation was an *ad hoc* response to problems arising out of specific hazards in particular types of workplace. The Robens Report argued for a simpler, all-embracing approach which was given effect through the HSWA.[6] As noted earlier, the EU legislation has reintroduced a great amount of detail into UK legislation, in sharp contrast to the Robens approach.

It is difficult to assess the impact of the EU-derived law but the starting point is to recognize that EU law has to be implemented in the Member States. The UK has been one of the most active countries in implementing EU health and safety legislation[7] and the impact seems to have been as follows. First, much of the EU law makes explicit those duties which already existed in a general form. Thus, the general duties under the HSWA, s 2 could be said to imply that a risk assessment should be carried out. Secondly, some areas are completely new: eg, the new construction management regulations. The effects are difficult to separate from those caused by a general decline in the high-risk mining and manufacturing sectors, and from those caused by existing legislation, but progress appears to be being made, particularly on the safety front.[8] On the other hand, there is increasing awareness of the burden being placed on employers (felt disproportionately by small and medium-sized employers) by a very substantial increase in detailed regulation. The HSE thus conducted a review of the legislation in which individual sets of regulations were subjected to a cost/benefit analysis.[9] Another concern is the differential rate of implementation between Member States and the unevenness of enforcement regimes across the EU.[10] These concerns are visible in the framework of the EU's fourth health and safety action programme and will be matters which will be examined by the newly established EU European Institute for Occupational Health and Safety.

THE IMPACT ON UK SEX DISCRIMINATION LAW

The relevant law is set out in chapters 6 and 11. The basis of much of the impact on UK discrimination law has been article 119 of the Treaty of Rome and the Equal Treatment Directive relating to employment.[11] The impact is briefly discussed below in respect of the scope of UK discrimination law, the legal tests used and the remedies available.

Scope

The EU has significantly extended the scope of discrimination law in the UK. The first factor impinging upon the scope of discrimination law in the UK is that article 119 of the Treaty of Rome, establishing the principle of equal pay for work of equal value, is directly applicable in Member States. By this is meant that a complainant in a Member State may use article 119 to found an independent cause of action. This would be relevant, for example, where there was no domestic law governing their complaint or domestic law was restrictive when compared with article 119.

The next aspect of scope is the concept of pay as defined by the EU. As noted in chapter 11, the definition is very wide. Article 119 defines it in terms of consideration, a concept familiar to lawyers and meaning something of value (see chapter 8). The ECJ, in a succession of cases, has interpreted this to include, *inter alia*, pensions and redundancy pay. The significance is that, once something is included in the definition of pay, it has to be equalized between the sexes if the employer is not to be in breach of article 119. Thus, since pensions are pay *(Barber v Guardian Royal Exchange)*, various pension arrangements must be equalized, including pensionable age (the same is not true of state pensions because this is covered by an exclusion contained within the Equal Treatment Directive on social security).

Another major influence upon the scope of discrimination law is its extension to protect part-time employees. Part-time employees were not excluded from protection under discrimination law itself, but they were not protected from inferior treatment when compared with full-time employees, including inferior treatment in terms of legal protection. Ultimately the government equalized the legislative arrangements for part-time and full-time employees by means of regulations in 1995.[12] It is now fairly clear that any detrimental treatment of part-time employees will be unlawful sex discrimination if it can be shown that part-time employees are predominantly of one sex.

The indirect sex discrimination argument has also so far succeeded in respect of the two-year qualifying period for unfair dismissal applications *(R v Secretary of State for Employment ex parte Seymour-Smith)*, although an appeal is pending. The basis of the argument here is that a considerably smaller proportion of women have continuous employment of two years or more when compared with men.

Finally, both the Equal Pay Act and the Sex Discrimination Act as originally enacted were found to be deficient by the ECJ in infringement proceedings brought by the European Commission.[13] The former was significantly extended as a result by the addition of a new category of claim, based on work being of equal value. The latter was improved by the removal or limitation of exclusions. For example, the small employer exclusion was completely removed.

Legal tests

There have been several effects of the ECJ taking a more purposive approach to legislation than is normally the case in the UK. Thus, recognizing the difficulty of the complainant in discharging the burden of proof of discrimination, the ECJ has held that once discrimination is established *prima facie*, the burden shifts to the employer to explain the discriminatory treatment. Moreover, it appears that this would be permitted on a statistical basis (eg, a group of women obtaining less pay than a comparable group of men) rather than being restricted to individual comparators as under the Equal Pay Act

(Enderby v Frenchay). The ECJ has also taken a generally robust line on the defences to discrimination. The justification defence to indirect discrimination must be objective and the genuine material factor defence to pay differences must be justified. The ECJ has also refused to allow employers (and others) to use discriminatory state pension ages as a reason for discrimination. Differential compulsory retirement ages are therefore unlawful (originally decided in *Marshall v Southampton and South West Hampshire Area Health Authority*, but now part of legislation).

One of the biggest influences of the EU has been in the area of pregnancy. The UK courts struggled with pregnancy dismissals in the context of the SDA which required a comparison with how a man was or would have been treated in the same or not materially different circumstances.[14] Initially the courts thought that the Act must not apply to pregnancy; then they considered that a comparison ought to be made with a man absent through illness. Ultimately in *Webb v EMO Air Cargo UK Ltd* the ECJ made it plain that since only women could be pregnant, unfavourable action against a woman because of her pregnancy must be unlawful sex discrimination without any comparison being necessary. The Pregnant Workers Directive of 1993 added to pregnant workers' rights by strengthening the protection under unfair dismissal law, widening access to maternity leave and making other improvements.

Remedies

In *Marshall v Southampton and South West Hampshire Area Health Authority (No 2)* it was made clear that European law requires the complainant to be fully compensated for the wrong they have suffered. Thus there must be no artificial statutory limit on compensation and interest must be paid on sums due. Consequently the statutory provisions on interest payments were improved and the statutory limit on compensation was removed.[15] Later, the provision which prevented compensation where there was unintentional indirect discrimination was also challenged and a statutory amendment made.[16]

Overall, EU law has had a major impact in the sex discrimination area. Not only is the law applicable more widely, but its remedies are improved and its legal mechanisms are more effective. However, all this needs to be seen in the context of the various criticisms of the legislation cited in chapter 25: UK sex discrimination law remains problematic.

THE IMPACT ON EMPLOYMENT STANDARDS

In general, the impact here has not been as significant as in the area of sex discrimination. However, part of the EU influence in the sex discrimination area has had an important spill-over effect on employment standards. First, the equality of treatment given to part-time employees means that they are now able to use a wide range of employment legislation previously denied to them either completely or without a substantial period of qualifying employment. The qualifying period is now the same regardless of hours of work. Secondly, the qualifying period is itself under challenge in the case of *R v Secretary of State for Employment ex parte Seymour-Smith*. The outcome of the appeal in this case is of considerable importance. In addition to these sex discrimination influences, the Acquired Rights Directive (see chapter 20) has considerably widened the range of business transfers protected by UK employment law.

There has also been a development in EU-originated substantive employment law. The EU provisions giving information and consultation rights to workers' representatives have been strengthened. Moreover, infringement proceedings were taken against the UK by the European Commission. As a result, UK information and consultation rights have been extended to employee representatives (see chapter 18) and the definition of redundancy widened for information and consultation purposes (compared with unfair dismissal and redundancy payments legislation) so that it covers any dismissal for a reason not related to the individual.[17]

Finally, the TUPE Regulations which implement the Acquired Rights Directive, apart from their breadth of application, give stronger protection than previous UK legislation by protecting contract terms, union bargaining rights and agreements, making dismissal automatically unfair and providing for information and consultation rights. The last-mentioned have been extended to employee representatives following EU infringement proceedings.[18]

The effects of the Working Time Directive and the Works Councils Directive are yet to be felt.

THE RELATIONSHIP BETWEEN EU AND UK EMPLOYMENT LAW

The development of the EU/UK employment law relationship can be analyzed first of all in terms of a flow of substantive law from the EU. As noted, this has been particularly significant in the fields of sex equality and health and safety at work. This flow includes the direct effects of certain articles of treaties and directives where unconditional, clear and precise *(Becker Finanzamt Munster Innenstadt)*. Secondly, it has been held that national courts should interpret EU law in a purposive manner to give effect to the EU's intentions when legislating *(Marleasing v La Commercial)*. National courts are helped in this respect by being able to refer questions to the ECJ where they seek clarification on points of European law.[19]

Where directives are not implemented or not fully implemented, individuals may take legal action against their employers if their employer is the State or an emanation of the State *(Foster v British Gas Corporation)*. The most recent case of *Griffin v South West Water* raises the question of whether privatized utilities might be caught by this definition. Otherwise, the individual's action lies against the State under the Francovich principle (see chapter 2).

The major consideration, however, is the balance between EU and UK employment law. Judging by the detailed social policy work programme of the European Commission for the years 1996–98, the substantive law focus put forward as a distinctive feature of EU employment law is likely to widen considerably. Moreover, the possibility of extending the Social Charter to cover a wider range of rights and responsibilities is under discussion. The Social Affairs Committee of the European Parliament wants specific EU legislation on individual dismissals.[20] Moreover, the Working Time Directive has yet to be implemented in the UK and even if the UK government remains opted-out of the Maastricht Social Chapter, the Works Councils Directive is likely to have an indirect effect through multinational companies applying it voluntarily to their UK employees.

The evidence seems to point to a continuing expansion of European employment law. How is this development to be judged? One possible criterion to apply is a technical one. The EU principle of subsidiarity is perhaps a manifestation of this: laws should be enacted at the most appropriate level, EU or Member State. Unfortunately, what is *prima facie* a technical, objective matter in practice is often open to argument.[21] Another possible criterion is the appropriateness of different approaches to the regulation of the labour market. Here the generally interventionist stance of the EU is in marked contrast to the free market approach of the UK government and this has been a principal source of tension in the UK/EU employment law relationship for many years. Finally, there is the normative approach: how far should the UK go in ceding sovereignty to the EU? Clearly, it is the question of the UK's overall involvement in the EU which will finally determine the UK/EU employment law relationship.

NOTES

1 Bercusson, B, *European Labour Law* Butterworths, 1996, Chapter 1.
2 *Loc cit.*
3 *Loc cit.*
4 *HSC Newsletter*, No 93, February 1994, page 8.

5 Directive on the introduction of measures to encourage improvement in the safety and health of workers at work, 89/391/EC.

6 *Safety and Health at Work* (Report of a Committee, Chairman Lord Robens, London, HMSO, Cmnd 5034, 1972).

7 *European Parliament News* (UK edition), 13–17 December 1993, page 3.

8 *HSC Annual Report 1992–3*. See *HSC Newsletter*, No 92, December 1993.

9 *HSC Review of Health and Safety Regulation* (HSE Books, 1994).

10 Baldwin, R and Daintith, T (eds), *Harmonization and Hazard: Workplace Health and Safety in the European Community* (London, Graham & Trotman, 1992).

11 Other equal treatment directives deal with social security and there is a separate directive on equal pay.

12 Employment Protection (Part-Time Employees) Regulations (SI 1995/31). It should also be noted that the SDA 1975 (Application to Armed Forces etc) Regulations (SI 1994/3276) were introduced to bring the armed forces within the scope of the Act following decisions that the armed forces were covered by EU law. This resulted in the Ministry of Defence making substantial compensation payments to pregnant servicewomen it had unlawfully dismissed.

13 *European Commission v UK* [1982] IRLR 333 (equal pay) and [1984] IRLR 29 (SDA).

14 SDA, ss 1 and 5(3).

15 Sex Discrimination and Equal Pay (Remedies) Regulations (SI 1993/2798). Now revoked by SI 1996/2803, the Industrial Tribunals (Interest on Awards in Discrimination Cases) Regulations 1996.

16 Sex Discrimination and Equal Pay (Miscellaneous Amendments) Regulations 1996/438.

17 *Commission v UK* 1994. Some improvements were made *via* the Trade Union Reform and Employment Rights Act 1993 but the extension of rights to employee representatives was made by means of the Collective Redundancies and Transfer of Undertakings (Protection of Employment) (Amendment) Regulations (SI 1995/2587).

18 *Commission v UK* (1994). See SI 1995/2587.

19 Treaty of Rome, article 177.

20 *European Parliament Briefing*, 15–19 January 1996, pages 5–6.

21 There is also the question of the powers of the ECJ. The UK government has been seeking to influence the governments of other Member States to obtain agreement on some restrictions.

Policy Issues and the Employment Law System

THE CONCEPT OF AN EMPLOYMENT LAW SYSTEM

A systems approach

The idea of using a systems approach to analyse employment law at the macro-level is founded upon the belief that the body of employment law, its procedures and institutions can be seen as interrelated and intended to meet certain objectives. These objectives are set in response to an environment external to the system, comprising a range of economic, political, legal and social factors. A systems approach, being an analytical framework, is intended to make it easier to see the overall coherence and functions of employment law and to enable relationships between system components, and between such components and external variables, to be more clearly identified and more precisely measured.[1]

The objectives of employment law

In looking at the objectives of employment law there is the possibility of a normative or positive approach. The latter, taken here, examines the objectives of employment law historically. The former, adopted later in the discussion of policy issues, elaborates the objectives that are considered desirable on the basis of various principles or values.

As noted, employment law can be seen as being concerned with the legal regulation of the labour market.[2] Within this framework, three broad objectives can be determined historically:

- protection of employees;
- regulation of trades unions; and
- other forms of labour market intervention.

At this level of abstraction, the objectives of employment law are unlikely to be controversial except in the view of those who would argue for a completely free labour market or for an unconstrained role for trades unions. Within each of the above categories, however, lie the major policy questions about the degree of protection, control and regulation and the balance between competing interests. These questions of degree and balance are in turn informed by wider political and economic influences such as the need for the UK economy to be competitive in international markets.

Policy towards redundancy law provides a good example of the issues surrounding the framing of objectives in employment law. A case can be made out on social grounds for protecting employees against redundancy, but this begs the question of the degree of protection. One possibility is the current degree of protection which is in the form of financial compensation and some procedural safeguards. Another would be a requirement for employers to justify redundancies to a government department or industrial tribunal, without which dismissal would not be permitted. How are these different degrees of protection to be assessed in terms of a desirable balance between the competing interests of employers, employees and what is perceived to be wider national interest? Such an assessment can realistically only be made by relating the employment law system to the external environment.

If this is done, the macro-economic effects of the different degrees of protection need to be considered. On the one hand, redundancy can be seen as a sound economic response to market change, especially if the labour market works efficiently and displaced workers find jobs in expanding sectors. Thus, it could be said that employment law should not discourage employers from declaring redundancies, perhaps ought to encourage employees to accept redundancy and should seek to minimize the number of disputes over redundancy. On the other hand, employees need a reasonable degree of security, may be more willing to accept change if they have such security and will incur substantial personal and public costs if they remain unemployed after being made redundant. This analysis exemplifies the balance of competing interests in employment law and the relationship between the employment law system and its external environment.

Considering other forms of labour market regulation, it can be seen from historical analysis that these are principally incomes policy, labour market efficiency measures (eg, to encourage labour mobility or retraining) and dispute resolution. The role of employment law in supporting collective bargaining may be seen as part of the broad area concerned with regulating trades unions (eg, conferring rights on trade union representatives) or where the rights are extended to non-union situations (legislation now repealed), perhaps employment protection. The point here, however, is that regulation of trades unions does not imply only restriction: it also encompasses positive measures.

Measuring the system's effectiveness

Measuring the effectiveness of employment law is a difficult process for a number of reasons. First, the objectives of an employment law system are not always (or not always capable of being) formulated precisely. For example, protection against unfair dismissal would be difficult to quantify. Even an acceptable rate of wages inflation under statutory incomes policy may not be precisely stated. Similarly, what degree of worker mobility is expected from the redundancy payments scheme? What level of employment disputes is acceptable? Secondly, those objectives may in any case vary, or vary in degree of relative importance, over time and between countries.

Thirdly, it may be difficult to separate the effect of law from the effect of the legal system or the effect of employers' or others' response to law. Finally, there will be significant non-law variables which will have a considerable influence over the effectiveness of employment legislation. In particular, the effectiveness of employee rights is likely to be heavily influenced by the level and/or rate of growth of unemployment.

Explanatory variables and the significance of comparative methodology

It follows from the above that specification of a model in which the dependent variable is the effectiveness of the employment law system is a very difficult process. Yet it is one in which policy-makers, and particularly public policy-makers, are especially interested, since a model with predictive value could inform policy-making. Two main methodological approaches have been taken. The first may be seen as historical. This is based on an examination of the effectiveness or otherwise of employment law when used in any particular part of the labour market in the past. For example, any UK government seeking to introduce legislation giving statutory recognition rights to trades unions would no doubt be influenced by the meagre results of legislation in this area in the 1970s. More dramatically, it seems that

Conservative governments from 1979 onwards learned several lessons from the experience of the Industrial Relations Act 1971.[3] They determined that a gradualist approach was more likely to be effective than one in which dramatic change is sought overnight. Commentators comparing the 1971–74 experience with that of 1979 onwards may also point to differences in economic and industrial relations factors as well as differences in legislative design. Growing unemployment and declining trades union membership provided a sounder base for attempts to regulate trades unions more closely.

The other main method is comparison between systems, usually referred to as a comparative approach (although the historical analysis is also comparative). There are numerous examples of this approach being used in the UK. For example, a comparative approach was used in an attempt to determine how employment law could be used to reconcile full employment, economic growth, control of inflation and the avoidance of industrial disputes in the 1960s. The Swedish model of labour market intervention (eg, to encourage labour mobility and retraining) and centralized labour market institutions and procedures provided much of the evidence on which the corporatist employment law system of the 1970s was based. In 1971, cooling-off periods in the Industrial Relations Act were a device used in the USA.[4] In the 1980s, relatively uncontrolled employment relationships in the USA provided an impetus for the attempt to deregulate the labour market in the UK, although contractual flexibility in Japan may have been a further influence.

Such analysis may be undertaken in respect of the employment law system as a whole or in respect of one or more of its component parts. The aim would be identify the explanatory variables which might be related to the effective functioning of a particular part of the system, eg the law of unfair dismissal. The assessment methodology outlined in chapter 25 may be of use here by classifying the variables as follows:

- scope, design and interpretation of the legislation itself;
- factors relating to the legal system, eg accessibility; and
- external environment factors, such as the level of unemployment.

Analytical work of the sort described above is at a relatively early stage in the employment law field. Much of what is done within the subject is concerned with conceptualizing using judicial interpretation, and with policy analysis and prescription which tends to be informed more by normative approaches than positive ones. With increasing globalization and further advances in information technology, the scope for model building in employment law based on comparative methodologies seems to be much increased.

EMPLOYMENT LAW AND MANAGEMENT DECISION-MAKING

The micro-level analysis: management decision-making as an analytical framework

The discussion so far has been concerned with the macro-level – the operation of the employment law system. The focus now shifts to the micro-level, that of the organization. The analytical framework adopted here is a management decision-making model where law is seen as intervening in the management process in order to moderate the relations between the organization and other parties, for example, employees. Sometimes the intervention is direct (eg, the placing of obligations upon employers), sometimes indirect (eg, altering power relations in the labour market through restrictions on trades unions). The framework is based on three principles:

- the management process can be seen as a network of relationships governed by law: between the company and its shareholders, suppliers, agents, employees, customers/clients, competitors and the State. These relationships may take many legal forms including various types of contract and will be subject to the general law (eg, the law of negligence).
- all these relationships can be viewed as reflecting management decisions, although the decision-making power often will have to be shared with others through the process of negotiation.
- legal regulation can be seen as an involvement of the State in management decision-making, and different objectives of intervention can be identified. In particular, legal intervention can be seen as attempting to influence the substantive decision itself, the criteria or procedure by which the decision is made, or the form in which it is made.

Micro-level functions of employment law

Substantive decisions

The most direct evidence here would be where the State substitutes its own decision for that of management. In the employment field, a government-imposed pay policy (stating, for example, that all public employees will receive a pay increase of 2 per cent) would fit into this category. Less draconian would be law which restricted the range of the management decision, for example, by laying down a minimum wage.

Criteria by which substantive decisions are made

The concern here would be with law which determines the criteria by which management arrive at their decision. Such law may lay down criteria, as in the case of the law of unfair dismissal, or prohibit the use of certain criteria, as in discrimination law.

Procedure in arriving at decisions

Law may be less concerned with the substantive decision and the criteria used and more concerned with the procedure by which the decision is reached. Important examples of this in the employment field are disciplinary and redundancy procedures.

The form of the decision

The law may require the management decision to be in a particular form. For example, if a collective agreement is to be legally enforceable it has to be in writing. A possibility is that the decision, which may be oral, has to be evidenced in writing. For example, certain particulars of the employment contract have to be provided in writing to the employee although the contract itself may be wholly oral.

Institutional support for management decisions

The law may provide institutional support for management decisions. The aim here would be to encourage higher quality decision-making through the provision of advice and information, eg through ACAS and other services.

The juridification process

A major characteristic of employment law is its expansion to the point where it now forms a substantial specialist body of law. The concept of juridification has been applied to this development.[5]

Juridification is a process by which the State comes to take more and more of society's decisions. The legislature believes it is necessary and legitimate to intervene in order to direct society along certain lines, and in particular to limit conflict. The State gradually replaces contractual arrangements by legislation. In the employment field juridification means less freedom of action for employers and employees in shaping their work relations, and can involve a reduction in the regulatory powers of collective bargaining.

The initial stage of juridification may be reactive: the State intervenes to counter the specific and extreme consequences of industrialization. The form of such intervention will be unrelated statutory provisions designed to counter particular excesses and abuses where contractual relationships have failed. Examples are laws relating to child labour, hours of work and manner of payment. A pressing need for the protection of the vulnerable legitimizes the process of State intervention. A further phase has been described as integrative: the State integrates legislation into a longer-term policy for the avoidance of social conflict. In the employment field, an example can be found in labour market policy.

While the normal vehicle for juridification is legislation, there are other means. Administrative regulation and judicial decision-making are important as is what has been called indirect steering, where the State recognizes and guarantees autonomous and voluntary regulation (eg, collective bargaining) because it functions to uphold social order, although it also lays down the ground rules.

Juridification is put in the form of a thesis which has a wider applicability than the employment field which is the subject of concern here. Juridification is argued to be inevitable in all democratic societies as a consequence of industrialization.[6]

Three perspectives appear to have been taken against increasing legal regulation. The first, typified in what might be called the deregulation debate, takes an employer view. Here the focus is on the damage inflicted on business performance (see below). The second is an employee-centred view focusing upon the oppressive and bureaucratic characteristics of regulation. It is said that the State colonizes certain areas of work relations, such as health and safety and social security, and dictates what is done (eg, medical tests, personal health data etc). Finally, trades unions are restrained (and if necessary, penalized) by legislation to ensure that they follow State policy. This can be seen as the price they pay for being regarded as lawful and for having their operations protected. Unions may also be made more conformist because legislation, such as that relating to redundancy payments and procedures, causes them to focus upon secondary issues rather than the fundamental areas, such as challenging redundancy itself.

The deregulation debate

The imperative for deregulation can be seen as having a number of sources. The immediate, practical one is the view of business managers that regulation is hindering business innovation, competitiveness and profitability. First, it restricts employers so that they are unable to act quickly, flexibly and cost-effectively to changing market requirements. It is said that this is particularly important during a recession. Secondly, legislation may have the opposite effect to that intended, eg dismissal law may restrict employment, although there seems little concrete evidence of this. Thirdly, the costs of employment protection seem to suppose medium-to-large-scale organization in terms of resources. Small firms may be hampered or even put out of business.

The business performance arguments above contrast with other imperatives which are of a more ideological nature. Prime among these is the resurgence of classical economic opinion in favour of free markets on the grounds that such markets permit the optimum allocation of resources. The jurisprudence which underpins the economic theory is the doctrine of freedom of contract. This holds contractual freedom to be a fundamental characteristic of any free society.

The major criticism of the position of the ideological deregulators is the absence of the perfect competition model in practice. Thus, the seeming paradox of government legislating to keep markets free, typically through competition law to prevent monopoly, price fixing and other anti-competitive practices. In the legal arena, since contract law is concerned with enforcing what is agreed rather than pronouncing on its fairness, the doctrine of freedom of contract is criticized as providing no protection for the weaker contracting party against abuses and excesses by the party in the stronger contractual position. Often, that weaker party will be an employee, consumer or a small firm.

On a more pragmatic basis the deregulators in the business community are criticized for wanting to alter the legislation in their favour. The argument rages about whether the balance has already shifted too far towards employers, or not far enough (see below).

The challenge for management

The management response to employment law

The challenge for management is to be able to inform its decision-making in the light of the requirements of employment law. The adequacy or otherwise of management's response can influence an organization's ability to achieve its business goals. For example, an inadequate response can result in:

- increased costs through fines, damages, compensation and legal fees;
- necessary change being inhibited or delayed;
- damage to an organization's image, which may affect the quality of staff recruited, staff morale and commitment, or even sales; and
- consumption of a large amount of management time.

Moreover, individual managers may be the subject of litigation and prosecution.

It follows that managers need to be aware of:

- the areas and ways in which the law intervenes in the management process, focusing in particular upon legal change and problem areas; and
- the policy, strategy and practice issues connected with fulfilling management's legal obligations. These extend beyond substantive policies to questions of legal resourcing.

The starting point is to determine what problems exist for managers operating at the interface of the management process and employment law system. Three types of problem can be identified:

- those arising out of the law itself, ie substantive law;
- those arising out of the contact managers have with the legal system; and
- those relating to resources (ie, management's response to the law).

Each of these is briefly dealt with below.

Key problems of substantive law

Five particular problem areas are noted here with reasons. This is not to imply that other areas of employment law cannot give rise to problems but rather to suggest that problems in other areas tend to be less pervasive.

Discrimination law is the first area put forward. The scheme of the law is complex and there have been uncertainties arising out of the tension between domestic and EU law (see chapter 27). There is also a degree of uncertainty about whether the organization may unintentionally be discriminating indirectly (see chapter 6). Cases probably require more legal resourcing than most in the employment field and those in the equal pay area may be drawn out over a long period. However, only a relatively small number of cases reach industrial tribunals. Discrimination cases are perhaps more likely to cause embittered relationships between the parties. The nature of the complaint is by definition very serious and there may be the complicating factor of the relationship still continuing. In some cases, the problem will centre on the relationship between the complainant and his or her colleagues. An adequate response in this area of employment law is likely to require substantial legal resources and management training.

A second area is that of the law of unfair dismissal. Problems here are more surprising since the structure of the legislation is quite straightforward and well established. The problem area is that of procedure: many unfair dismissal cases reveal procedural flaws. However, there is a well-known code of practice and much guidance from ACAS and a competent manager should be able to obtain the necessary information in this area without too much difficulty. This, then, may be a case of inadequate training.

A third area is that of contractual change. Managers appear to have difficulties interpreting contracts and many of the reported cases contain an element of contractual change. The general position here has been aggravated by uncertainties over the application of the TUPE Regulations (see chapter 20), which protect contract terms on transfer, and which also affect the issue of whether or not there has been an unfair, or indeed any, dismissal. This area is a good example of where the nature of legal concepts is itself problematic for managers, and where managers will continue to need expert legal advice.

Health and safety law is a problem for different reasons. There are difficulties in translating legal duties into management practice, in part because, of necessity, the balance between the parties has to be related to the specific work environment. In addition, there are substantial compliance costs because of the need for specific hardware and safe working procedures. There is good provision of guidance from the HSE but the threefold technical nature of health and safety management (law, specialist management techniques and medical knowledge) makes compliance difficult in the absence of specialist expertise.

Finally, there is the maternity area.[7] Perhaps the most complex area of employment law, this is a mixture of complicated statutory provisions, underlying contractual relations and detailed administrative requirements. Personnel administration expertise is a prerequisite in matters of maternity leave and pay, but there is also a major need for specialist legal resourcing, particularly as regards areas of uncertainty such as the contractual position during extended maternity leave.

Managers and the legal system

The starting point here is to ask how managers are likely to come into contact with the employment law system. Such contact may be direct, that is, in the form of involvement in legal proceedings, or indirect in that management decisions have legal implications. The most likely direct contact will be as a witness in cases brought before industrial tribunals or courts. An example would be a manager who has dismissed an employee. Such a manager is likely to be the principal witness for the respondent employer in an unfair dismissal hearing. If the manager is to be a witness, legal procedure and oral communication skills need to be part of his training.

A second possible direct role for a manager is advocate – the person responsible for defending the organization in the hearing. This is more likely in smaller organizations, or where the manager is a personnel specialist, even in larger firms. Here the manager needs not only knowledge of legal procedure but also knowledge of the substantive law under which the case is being pursued and defended and the ability to apply that knowledge to the facts of the particular case. This implies a high level of legal knowledge compared with that typically found among managers.

Indirect contact with the legal system is conceptualized as that taking place during the management process itself. In the employment field, almost any management decision could have legal implications, but the recruitment, selection and appointment process is a good example because it is heavily circumscribed by law. First of all, there are the requirements of discrimination law. Secondly, the appointment process involves the creation of a legally enforceable relationship. In all this, non-lawyers will be producing documents (such as job advertisements, job descriptions, letters of offer and particulars of employment) which are of strong evidential value and may ultimately come before a court or tribunal for interpretation.

Indirect contact with law may also be made in relation to dismissal, remuneration policy, health and safety and other areas of people management. Indeed, the daily process of instructing employees has potential legal implications in terms of the contract of employment and perhaps health and safety at work.

The management response: legal resourcing

How the knowledge necessary for managers effectively to handle direct and indirect contact with the law is obtained raises the question of legal resourcing. This will be a major factor in management's response to its legal environment, and will require a number of strategic issues to be addressed. First, how far does the organization want to go in equipping its managers with legal knowledge as an alternative to the use of expensive and probably less accessible specialist legal expertise? The answers here will be important in determining the legal training needs of managers. Secondly, realistically there will need to be some specialist legal expertise. In larger organizations, the question will be whether it is best employed directly in-house or bought from outside, or a combination of the two. What rules will govern access to this resource? With increasing use of devolved management structures, a major question will be whether it is accessible to local managers. Thirdly, another important consideration is that of management procedure: how is this to cater for the non-lawyer making decisions which have legal implications? At what stage should a manager be required to seek in-house advice (eg, when contemplating a dismissal)? Fourthly, what is to be the position as regards documentary help for managers? That is, can standard documents be made available to reduce the risk that might come from a plethora of 'homemade' versions? Documents with implications for interpretation of employment contracts are an important example. Finally, can managers be provided with updating and other materials to keep their legal knowledge topped-up, either by an in-house system or by supplying them with externally produced material?

Business micro-legal systems

The need for the legal resourcing of business can be taken to imply that an organization must have something akin to its own internal legal system if it is to respond satisfactorily to its external legal environment. The concept developed here is that of a business micro-legal system. This is defined as a set of arrangements designed to equip a business with the capability for effective response to its legal environment. In particular, it is taken to include:

- contractual framework;
- legal decision-making structure;

- legal resourcing; and
- evidential arrangements.

The hypothesis would be that type of business micro-legal system is related to success in dealing with the organization's external legal environment.[8] The concern here would be with the system in so far as it relates to employment matters. The dependent variable could be overall employment law performance or some constituent part of it, eg employment law performance in relation to the management of employment change.

Contractual framework comprises a measure of contractual flexibility. In particular, it embraces the extent to which widely drawn terms and employer discretion are built into the contractual environment. The measure is based upon the full range of sources – express and implied terms, oral and written evidence, and includes incorporated terms (see chapter 8). Legal decision-making structure involves a measure of the extent to which legal expertise is available to those making decisions which may have legal implications. Included here are non-lawyers' access to legal expertise and the use of procedures where reference to those with legal expertise is a prerequisite of the decision being made.[9] Legal resourcing is a composite of the extent and accessibility of legal advisors, the legal education and training of managers and the provision of management legal information on a day-to-day basis. Evidential arrangements comprise the documentation for providing evidence. In the employment field, this includes letters of appointment, workplace rules, written particulars of employment and, where applicable, collective agreements with trades unions. Evidential arrangements measure the extent to which the contractual framework is actually underpinned by written evidence.

GENERAL POLICY CONSIDERATIONS

Policy considerations may be purely legal, for example, relating to legal interpretation or procedure, or may be contextual, relating to the broader aspects of public policy, such as economic competitiveness. In practice, many considerations are a mixture of legal and contextual. For example, there are legal policy issues relating to the determination of employment status (see chapter 5) but there are also wider issues because of tax and public expenditure implications. The concern here is with policy considerations at the macro-level but the question is also relevant at the level of the organization. A firm has to decide whether or not to adopt various policies, eg equal opportunities policy, and if so, in what form. It also has to equip itself with a legal infrastructure (or micro-legal system) in order to respond effectively to its legal environment.

A major theme running through the analysis of employment law in the 1980s and 1990s has been the balance between the competing interests of employees and trade unions on the one hand and employers on the other. Successive governments have sought to alter this balance in favour of employers. As the government put it in 1991, one of its objectives had been 'to establish a fair balance of bargaining power between employers and trade unions'.[10] The central debate has been about the growth of employee and union rights up to 1979 and the consequent constraints upon employers. Thus the need to reduce union and employee right to allow employers to be more competitive in their product or service markets. In essence, the debate has been about juridification and the need to deregulate.

There are two major problems with this debate. The first is that where the balance lies may be a matter of social or political policy which can be explained only in terms of the normative preferences of those in power. That is, there is no obvious objective explanation of why the balance should lie in any particular way. Secondly, the more objective relationship between the balance and economic performance (micro and macro) is difficult to resolve on the evidence. Successive governments frame the relationship between employment protection and business competitiveness as necessarily involving a trade-off, but is this a correct formulation of the relationship? The human relations theorists would argue that employee welfare and performance are positively correlated. Industrial relations academics would argue that a union presence and involvement has positive effects in terms of organization performance. On the other hand, is a worker with a job for life going to be flexible and committed? Was strong trades unionism in the 1950s and 1960s associated with micro- and macro-economic success? The *prima facie* answer to the latter seems to be negative but it should be noted that the relationship between unions and economic performance is the focus of major debate (which it is not appropriate to enter here).

Two other general considerations of employment law policy need to be mentioned. The first concerns the international dimension of employment law. The principal manifestation of this is in the relationship between domestic and EU employment law (see chapter 27). Suffice it to say that there is no more likelihood of a consensus on this than on the balance between employers and unions/employees, particularly as this is to some extent a microcosm of the debate about UK/EU relations more generally. Critics condemn the increasing dominance of EU law. This has been particularly noticeable in certain areas, and in the case of transfers of undertakings EU law has to some extent undermined government policy as regards flexibility of employment and the contracting-out of public services. A second international consideration is the increasing globalization of business and the growing incidence of employees working abroad. The main implication for employment law is the question of which law is applicable in the context of international contracting.[11] The other general consideration is the issue of the efficiency of the employment law system. How efficient is it in terms of meeting its objectives? The functioning of industrial tribunals was examined in chapter 26 and has been the subject of much attention, but what about the amount, complexity and uncertainty of employment law itself? And what about the inequalities between those using it, in particular the positions of the self-represented employee and the small business? Some attempts have been made to improve the information supply to these users but their resourcing remains problematic.

POLICY ISSUES: THE POSITION OF TRADES UNIONS AND EMPLOYEES

Trades unions

The central policy issue relating to the position of trades unions is whether employment law has gone too far in restricting their activities. The previous government's view was that it has not gone far enough – more was proposed in a Green Paper published towards the end of 1996.[12] Others might argue that basic freedoms such as the freedom to associate are at the risk of being infringed because workers are denied an effective, independent means of protecting and advancing their interests.[13] The principal weaknesses in the unions' legal position can be seen as:

- the lack of support for union recognition, ie the absence of any legal procedure for obtaining recognition from employers;
- the tight procedural and substantive constraints upon lawful industrial action; and
- the absence of protection from dismissal for those involved in industrial action.

A government concerned with altering the balance between unions and employers in favour of the former would probably legislate in all three of these areas. The new government is committed to the first and third of them.

There is also an issue about the suitability of detailed law and legal procedures for resolving disputes between employers and unions. The law can be seen as testing the conduct of disputes against legal rules rather than as trying to settle a dispute. The legal method is seen as being based on the view that one party or the other is right, the law determining which party is right. This contrasts with a traditional industrial relations approach based on the parties having a mutual interest in settlement.[14]

Finally, on trades unions, there is concern as to whether detailed legal intervention in trades unions' internal affairs is consistent with their right to independence. ILO Convention No 87 provides for trades unions to draw up their own constitutions, rules and administrative arrangements without State interference.[15] The former government, in response, pointed to the lack of unions' financial propriety as evidenced in the Lightman Report on the National Union of Mineworkers.[16]

Employees

Again, the central question is whether the rights of workers need to be improved, maintained or reduced. Assuming the first of these options, there are a number of areas of potential legal change.

One relates to employment status (see chapter 5). There is an increasing number of workers whose employment status is uncertain. The facts of their situation often contain elements typical of a contract of employment while also revealing elements typical of other relationships. The legal tests can be inconclusive. The law would be more certain in its scope and would offer more widespread protection if it applied to workers rather than merely employees.[17]

A second area concerns the strengthening of existing law which has been criticized as deficient. Discrimination law has been severely criticized (see chapter 25) and is an obvious candidate for reform should government wish to improve worker protection. The Equal Opportunities Commission has recently issued a consultation document containing proposals for a radical reform of discrimination law. Similarly, there has been criticism of unfair dismissal law on a number of fronts (again, see chapter 25). Certainly its scope could be widened by reducing the continuous employment qualification and its remedies enhanced. A more contentious issue relates to redundancy law: whether or not there should be any legal controls over the redundancy decision itself. Some of the arguments on this point were rehearsed earlier.

Finally, are there any areas into which the law needs to extend? Because of the UK's membership of the EU, it will be necessary to enact legislation to implement the EU Working Time Directive (see chapter 12). No proposals were in evidence at the time of writing even though the implementation date was in November 1996.[18] There is no similar pressure to enact legislation protecting whistleblowers but attempts have been made by means of private members' Bills in Parliament and there is not inconsiderable support because of the human rights implications and a well-publicized scheme in the USA. The government is committed to introducing minimum wage legislation (see page 225). The arguments here reflect the classical free market approach on the one side and the social intervention stance on the other: will minimum wage legislation lead to reduced employment prospects because labour is dearer or will this be of minimal effect or counterbalanced by other factors such as a positive effect on aggregate demand in the economy? Otherwise, much legislation is likely to flow from the government's positive stance on EU social initiatives. Various directives will need to be implemented in the UK including those relating to European works' councils, parental leave, part-time work and the burden of proof in sex discrimination cases.

NOTES

1 A systems approach need not imply any particular set of values or objectives; nor is it problematic that relationships between the parts are not capable of the precise quantification that is possible in, for example, an electrical or mechanical system.

2 The term regulation is used here in a broader way than by Kahn-Freund who regarded it as the setting of standards, rights and obligations. Law that made rules for the settlement of these things was categorized as auxiliary. See Davies, P and Freedland, M, *Kahn-Freund's Labour and the Law* (3rd edition, London, Stevens, 1983), pages 60–64.

3 On the 1971 Act see Weekes *et al, Industrial Relations and the Limits of the Law* (Blackwell, 1975). The government described its approach in the 1980s as 'a step-by-step reform of industrial relations law'. See *Industrial Relations in the 1990s* (London, HMSO, Cm 1602, 1991), page 4.

4 Industrial Relations Act 1971, ss 138–140.

5 See Clark, J, 'The Juridification of Industrial Relations', (1985) 14 *Industrial Law Journal* 69–90.

6 Ibid.

7 See Lewis, P, *Employment in Practice – Maternity* (London, Gee Publishing Ltd, 1996).

8 This would be a step towards a theory of employment law competence. Arguably, identifying and measuring the variables which are related to employment law competence should be a research priority.

9 The effect of law on the internal structures and procedures of organizations has not been the subject of a great deal of research. See, however, Sitkin, SB and Bies, RJ, *The Legalistic Organization* (Sage, 1994).

10 *Industrial Relations in the 1990s* (note 3 above) at page 4.

11 There are already provisions in this area, the Contracts (Applicable Law) Act.

12 Green Paper, December 1996.

13 Report of an ILO Committee of Experts, 1990.

14 See Wood, J in McCarthy (Lord) (ed), *Legal Intervention in Industrial Relations* (Blackwell, 1992), pages 267–269.

15 Article 3.

16 Lightman, G, *The Lightman Report on the NUM* (Penguin, 1990). The findings of the report are set out under the heading 'The case for further legislation' in the Green Paper, *Industrial Relations in the 1990s* (note 3 above) at pages 29–30. The proposals were effected through the Trade Union Reform and Employment Rights Act 1993.

17 The definition already used in the SDA could be adopted. See SDA, s 82(1).

18 The reason for the delay is attributable to the government challenging the Treaty basis of the directive, alleging that it was not properly a health and safety measure susceptible to majority voting under article 118A. The ECJ rejected this view. The government has indicated that new regulations will be in force from October 1998.

Bibliography

ACAS *Discipline at Work* ACAS,1987

ACAS *Disciplinary Practices and Procedures in Employment Code of Practice 1*, HMSO, revised edition 1998

ACAS *Disclosure of Information for Bargaining Purposes* Code of Practice 2, HMSO, revised edition 1998

ACAS *Time Off for Union Duties and Activities* Code of Practice 3, HMSO, revised edition 1998

ACAS *Redundancy Arrangements* Occasional Paper 37, ACAS 1987

ACAS *Redundancy Handling* Advisory Booklet 12, ACAS 1988

Baldwin R & Daintith T (Eds) *Harmonisation and Hazard: Workplace Health and Safety in the European Community* Graham and Trotman 1992

Bateman M, King B & Lewis P *The Handbook of Health and Safety at Work* Kogan Page 1996

Bercusson B *European Labour Law* Butterworth 1996

Bowers J & Clarke A 'Unfair Dismissal and Managerial Prerogative: A Study of Some Other Substantial Reason' (1981) *10 Industrial Law Journal 34–44*

Brown & McColgan 'UK Employment Law and the International Labour Organisation' (1992) *21 Industrial Law Journal 265*

Clark J 'The Juridification of Industrial Relations' (1985) *14 Industrial Law Journal 69–90*

Clark J & Lewis R *Employment Rights, Industrial Tribunals and Arbitration* Institute for Employment Rights 1993

Collins H *Justice in Dismissal* Clarendon Press 1993

CRE *Code of Practice for the Elimination of Racial Discrimination and the Promotion of Equal Opportunity in Employment* CRE 1984

Daniel WW & Stilgoe E *The Impact of Employment Protection Law* Policy Studies Institute 1978

Davies P & Freedland M *Kahn-Freund's Labour and the Law* 3rd edition, Stevens 1983

Department of Employment *Code of Practice on Picketing* DE 1992

Department of Trade & Industry *Positive Action* Race Relations Advisory Service DTI 1994

Department of Trade & Industry *Code of Practice on Industrial Action Ballots and Notice to Employers* DTI 1995

Dickens L Jones M Weekes B & Hart M *Dismissed* Blackwell 1985

Dunn S & Gennard J *The Closed Shop in British Industry* MacMillan 1984

EU *Recommendation on the Protection of the Dignity of Women and Men at Work* 1991 OJ 1992 L49/1

Goodhart W 'The Legality of the General Strike' (1927) *36 Yale Law Journal 464*

Grunfeld C *Law of Redundancy* 3rd edition Sweet & Maxwell 1989

Hakim C 'Employment Rights: A Comparison of Part-time and Full-time Employees' (1989) *18 Industrial Law Journal 69–83*

Hepple BA 'Judging Equal Rights' (1983) *36 Current Legal Problems 71–90*

HMSO *Administrative Tribunals and Inquiries* Report of the Franks Committee Cmnd 218, 1957

HMSO *Disability Discrimination Act Code of Practice* 1996

HMSO *Enforcing Health and Safety Legislation in the Workplace* National Audit Office 1994

HMSO *EOC Code of Practice for the Elimination of Discrimination on the Grounds of Sex and Marriage and the Promotion of Equal Opportunity in Employment 1985*

HMSO *EOC Equal Pay Code of Practice* 1997

HMSO *Industrial Relations Code of Practice* 1972

HMSO *Industrial Relations in the 1990s* Cm 1602, 1991

HMSO *Industrial Tribunals: Compensation for Loss of Pension Rights* 1990

HMSO *Report of the Robens Committee* 1972

HMSO *Resolving Employment Rights Disputes: Options for Reform* Cm 2707, 1994

HMSO *Trades Unions and Employers' Associations* Report of the Donovan Royal Commission Cmnd 3623, 1968

HSE *HSC Review of Health and Safety Legislation* HSE Books 1994

HSE *New and Expectant Mothers at Work: A Guide for Employers* HSE Books 1995

HSE *Publications in Series* HSE 1990

IDS *Redundancy Terms* Study 464, 1990

Inland Revenue *Ex Gratia Awards Made on Termination of an Office or Employment by Retirement or Death* Statement of Practice SP 13/91, 1991

Institute of Personnel Management (now IPD) *Recruitment Guide* 1990

International Labour Organisation *Report of a Committee of Experts* ILO 1990

Justice *Industrial Tribunals* Justice 1987

Law Commission *Aggravated, Exemplary and Restitutionary Damages* Report 247, 1997

Lewis P 'An Analysis of Why Legislation has Failed to Provide Employment Protection for Unfairly Dismissed Employees' (1981) *19 British Journal of Industrial Relations 316–26*

Lewis P *Employment in Practice Maternity* Gee Publishing Ltd 1996

Lewis P 'Industrial Tribunals and the Franks Criteria' (1982) *126 Solicitors' Journal 667–8*

Lewis P *The Successful Management of Redundancy* Blackwell 1993

Lewis P *Twenty Years of Statutory Redundancy Payments in Great Britain* Leeds/Nottingham Occasional Papers in Industrial Relations 8, 1985

Lewis R (Ed) *Labour Law in Great Britain* Blackwell 1986

Lightman G *The Lightman Report on the NUM* Penguin 1990

McCarthy (Lord) (Ed) *Legal Intervention in Industrial Relations* Blackwell 1992

McMullen J *Business Transfers and Employee Rights* 2nd edition Butterworth 1992

McMullen J 'Enforcing the Contract of Employment' (1995) *24 Industrial Law Journal 353–62*

McMullen J (Ed) *Redundancy: The Law and Practice* FT Law & Tax 1997

Morris G 'Industrial Action: Public and Private Interests' (1993) *22 Industrial Law Journal 194*

Munday 'Tribunal Lore: Legalism and Industrial Tribunals' (1981) *10 Industrial Law Journal 146–59*

Royal Society for the Prevention of Accidents *Development of Factory Legislation* undated

Sitkin SB & Bies RJ *The Legalistic Organisation* Sage 1994

Weekes B et al *Industrial Relations and the Limits of the Law* Blackwell 1975

Index